Contemporary Issues

in Higher Education Law

4th edition

Susan C. Bon

David H. K. Nguyen

Jennifer A. Rippner

Editors

EDUCATION LAW ASSOCIATION

Disclaimer

The Education Law Association (ELA) is a private, nonadvocacy, nonprofit member association. The opinions expressed in this publication are those of the authors and do not represent official views of the Association.

Editors

Susan C. Bon, Lead Editor

Susan C. Bon has authored and coauthored over fifty publications addressing the legal and ethical principles that inform administrative practice and impact leadership in education and special education. She has taken on a new role at the University of South Carolina, serving as a Presidential Faculty Fellow. Bon is an active leader in national organizations focusing on education and special education law. She spent one year as a part-time intern at the U.S. Education Department working on Title I, Part D (Neglected or Delinquent Youth), McKinney-Vento (EHCY), and Homeless Education Disaster Assistance (HEDA) Grant Programs. Her experience also includes serving as coordinator of the Education Policy Fellowship Program (EPFP) in Washington, D.C., an education policy and leadership program developed by the Institute for Leadership (IEL). She has served on several executive boards for nonprofit organizations including the Dream Project in Arlington, Virginia, and in 2020 is serving as president of the Education Law Association. Prior to her university faculty service, she worked as the ombudsman in the State Superintendent's Division of the Ohio Department of Education. Bon received her law degree and a doctorate in education policy and leadership from The Ohio State University.

David H. K. Nguyen

David Hòa Khoa Nguyễn is an Assistant Professor of Urban Education Leadership and Policy at the IUPUI School of Education and Adjunct Professor of Law at the IU Robert H. McKinney School of Law on the Indiana University - Purdue University Indianapolis (IUPUI) campus. Previously, he was assistant professor at The University of Texas at San Antonio and the University of North Dakota. David received both his undergraduate degree and joint MBA/JD degree from Indiana University, and practiced law in Indianapolis before returning to IU for doctoral studies in 2011. David also has a Master of Advanced Legal Studies (LL.M. adv.) in European & International Business Law from Leiden University in the Netherlands as a Rotary Foundation Ambassadorial Scholarship recipient. While completing his masters studies, David was named Visiting Professor of Business Ethics at Vietnam National University in Ho Chi Minh City, Vietnam, where he developed and taught graduate courses. Licensed to practice law in the state and federal courts of Indiana, North Dakota, and Texas, he was pro bono director of the American Bar Association's Disaster Legal Services program.

Jennifer A. Rippner

Jennifer Rippner is a Visiting Lecturer in the Educational Leadership and Policy Studies Department at Indiana University-Bloomington where she teaches a variety of graduate-level education law courses. She has taught K-12 law and higher education law for several research universities including George Washington University, Southern Methodist University, and the University of Georgia. Much of her academic research focuses on constitutional issues in education. Prior to joining the faculty at Indiana University, Jennifer served as a gubernatorial education advisor, state education agency director, legal and policy advisor for a national education law firm, and the director of an elementary public charter school. She has been named one of *Georgia Trend's* 40 under 40 to watch and was one of three Americans selected for an international higher education fellowship from the Institute of Higher Education Policy in D.C. In 2015, she published the *American Education Policy Landscape*, an overview of the U.S. P-20 education structure. She earned her B.A. in political science and her law degree from the University of Florida and her Ph.D. in higher education from the University of Georgia.

Chapter Authors

Delia B. Allen, Ph.D.: Research Associate, Center for Education Policy and Leadership, The Riley Institute at Furman University, Greenville, South Carolina

Scott R. Bauries, J.D., Ph.D.: Associate Dean of Faculty Research, Willburt D. Ham Professor of Law, University of Kentucky College of Law, Lexington, Kentucky

Joy Blanchard, Ph.D.: Associate Professor of Higher Education, Louisiana State University, Baton Rouge, Louisiana

Susan C. Bon, J.D., Ph.D.: Presidential Faculty Fellow; Faculty Civility Advocate; Professor, Department of Education Leadership & Policies; Affiliate Professor, College of Law; University of South Carolina, Columbia, South Carolina

Kevin P. Brady, Ph.D.: Associate Professor, Curriculum and Instruction, University of Arkansas, Fayetteville, Arkansas

Janet S. Bubert, J.D.: Underwood Law Firm, P.C., Fort Worth, Texas

Robert C. Cloud, Ed.D.: Professor of Higher Education, Baylor University, Waco, Texas

Luke M. Cornelius, Ph.D., J.D.: Associate Professor, Leadership, School Counseling & Sport Management, College of Education & Human Services, University of North Florida, Jacksonville, Florida

Philip T.K. Daniel, J.D., Ed.D.: William and Marie Flesher Professor of Educational Administration Emeritus, The Ohio State University, Columbus, Ohio

John Dayton, J.D., Ed.D.: Professor of Education Law and Adjunct Professor of Higher Education, The University of Georgia, Athens, Georgia

Suzanne E. Eckes, J.D., Ph.D.: Professor, Department of Educational Leadership & Policy Studies, Indiana University, Bloomington, Indiana

Frank J. Fernandez, Ph.D., Assistant Professor of Higher Education, University of Mississippi, University, Mississippi

Richard Fossey, J.D., Ed.D.: Paul Burdin Endowed Professor of Education, University of Louisiana at Lafayette, Louisiana

Neal H. Hutchens, J.D., Ph.D.: Professor, and Chair Department of Higher Education, University of Mississippi, University, Mississippi

Amelia L. King-Kostelac, M.A.: Doctoral Candidate, Department of Education Leadership & Policy Studies, University of Texas at San Antonio, Texas

Martha M. McCarthy, Ph.D.: Presidential Professor of Educational Leadership, Loyola Marymount University, Los Angeles, California and Chancellor's Professor Emeritus, Indiana University-Bloomington, Indiana

Kerry Brian Melear, Ph.D.: Professor of Higher Education and Affiliate Faculty, School of Law, University of Mississippi, University, Mississippi

David H. K. Nguyen, J.D., Ph.D.: Assistant Professor of Urban Education Leadership & Policy, Adjunct Professor of Law, Indiana University – Purdue University Indianapolis (IUPUI), Indiana

Mark Paige, J.D., Ph.D.: Associate Professor of Public Policy, University of Massachusetts-Dartmouth, Massachusetts

Patrick D. Pauken, J.D., Ph.D., Professor and School Director, Educational Foundations, Leadership, and Policy, Bowling Green State University, Bowling Green, Ohio

Jennifer A. Rippner, Ph.D., J.D.: Visiting Lecturer of Education Law, Indiana University School of Education, Bloomington, Indiana

Charles J. Russo, J.D., Ed.D.: Panzer Chair in Education, School of Education and Health Sciences, and Research Professor of Law, University of Dayton, Dayton, Ohio

Jeffrey C. Sun, J.D., Ph.D.: Professor of Higher Education, Affiliate Professor of Law, and Associate Dean for Innovation & Strategic Partnerships, University of Louisville, Louisville, Kentucky

Christopher C. Thomas, J.D., M.Ed.: Attorney at Law, Frost Brown Todd LLC, Columbus, Ohio

LaWanda W. M. Ward, J.D., Ph.D.: Assistant Professor of Higher Education, Research Associate, Center for the Study of Higher Education, Penn State University, University Park, Pennsylvania

R. Craig Wood, Ed.D.: Professor, Educational Administration and Policy, University of Florida, Gainesville, Florida

Table of Contents

Chapter 3 — Pages 35-62 — Charles J. Russo
Private and Religious Schools

Chapter 4 — Pages 63-100 — Kevin P. Brady
Faculty Employment and Tenure

Chapter 5 — Pages 101-128 — Jeffrey C. Sun & Neal H. Hutchens
Faculty Speech and Expression

Chapter 6 — Pages 129-148 — Luke M. Cornelius
Legal Rights of Non-Academic Personnel

Chapter 7 — Pages 149-186 — David H. K. Nguyen
Employment Discrimination and Title VII

Chapter 8 — Pages 187-208 — Suzanne E. Eckes & Martha M. McCarthy
Sexual Harassment

Chapter 9 — Pages 209-234 — Susan C. Bon & Janet S. Bubert
Federal Disability Laws

Chapter 10 — Pages 235-270 — Scott R. Bauries
Liability for Negligence

Chapter 16 — Pages 395-420 — Philip T.K. Daniel & Christopher C. Thomas
Equal Protection Clause

Chapter 17 — Pages 421-444 — R. Craig Wood & John Dayton
Legal Issues in Business Management

Chapter 18 — Pages 445-492 — Philip T.K. Daniel & Patrick D. Pauken
Intellectual Property

Chapter 19 — Pages 493-516 — Joy Blanchard
Intercollegiate Athletics

Pages 559-580

Constitutional, Legislation & Case Index by Chapter

Pages 581-582

U.S. Constitution Overview

1

Introduction to the American Legal System

Susan C. Bon, J.D., Ph.D.
University of South Carolina

Jennifer A. Rippner, J.D., Ph.D.
Indiana University

Higher education law generally refers to a wide range of laws and legal principles that directly affect the functions, processes, and fundamental activities of higher education institutions. The laws are established according to the hierarchy of federal and state constitutional authority. Pursuant to the constitutional authority, subsequent laws may then be enacted by the legislative or executive branch and interpreted by the courts. Given these multiple sources of law, the study of higher education law must be examined, not in isolation, but as part of an interactive and evolving network of federal and state sources of law.

Sources of Law

In order to understand higher education law, it is also helpful to identify and examine the primary and secondary sources of law. The primary sources of law include the courts, legislatures, and executive branches at federal and state levels. Secondary sources, on the other hand, include, for example, law review articles, legal encyclopedias, and treatises. The distinction between primary and secondary sources is necessary because of the fundamental authority that primary sources have over secondary sources. This chapter provides a review of these multiple sources of law and presents the authority of courts across the United States. In addition, this chapter describes the legislative and judicial processes generally at both the federal and state levels.

As revealed further in this text, the primary sources of law significantly influence and guide higher education institutions and the higher education field. These laws and the legal system are relied upon to secure individual rights and freedoms, as well as to provide a system for resolving conflicts, which in turn protects societal order.[1] Collectively, these laws are considered to be fundamental to the democratic system of governance in the United States.

The American democratic system is also established pursuant to the principle of rule of law. According to the rule of law, laws are publicly shared, equally enforced by independent courts, and solidly established upon a foundation of justice that protects individual freedoms. The rule of law is an essential principle of a democratic nation, because it establishes a system of law that can be accessed by individuals and groups whose rights may otherwise be infringed upon with no recourse to a higher and stable authority.

Constitutional Law

As a democratic nation, the United States is founded upon essential beliefs and principles ratified in the Constitution for the United States of America in 1787.[2] The Constitution was subsequently amended to include the first ten amendments, which are referred to as the Bill of Rights. Additional amendments have significantly enhanced individual freedoms and liberties. For example, the Thirteenth Amendment formally abolished slavery in the United States and was passed at the end of the Civil War. Another notable change, passage of the Fourteenth Amendment, reaffirmed the protections secured by the Bill of Rights and extended the freedoms to be protected by state and local governments as well the federal government.[3]

Constitutions are generally broad and designed to be overarching frameworks subject to interpretations by legislatures and judges. The United States Constitution has survived the test of time and remains the oldest democratic constitution in the world. A number of structural provisions were included to promote and protect the balance of authority and powers between the federal and state governments. Notably, the Supremacy Clause established the U.S. Constitution and laws as "the supreme Law of the Land."[4] Given the primacy of the federal laws, state constitutions and statutes must conform with federal law.

State constitutions typically reflect the key rights that were similarly enacted as part of the U.S. Constitution. Although there are many similarities across state constitutions, a number of factors distinguish these legal documents, particularly regarding education. Despite widespread misunderstanding, authority over education was and continues to be uniquely reserved for

---

[1] Jeremy Waldron, *The Rule of Law*, STANFORD ENCYCLOPEDIA OF PHIL.(Edward N. Zalta, ed., Fall 2016 ed.), *available at* https://plato.stanford.edu/archives/fall2016/entries/rule-of-law/.

[2] U.S. CONST. amend. X (The powers not delegated to the United States by the Constitution, nor prohibited by it to the States, are reserved to the States respectively, or to the people.).

[3] U.S. CONST. amend. XIV, § 1 (([No state shall make or enforced any law which shall abridge the privileges or immunities of citizens of the United States....).

[4] U.S. CONST. art. VI, § 2 ((The Constitution, and the Laws of the United States ...shall be the supreme Law of the Land; and the Judges in every State shall be bound thereby....).

the states.[5] In other words, education is not an enumerated power in the U.S. Constitution; thus, authority over education is reserved for the states.[6]

While state constitutions tend to mirror the U.S. Constitution, the U.S. Constitution establishes definitive law which overrides state laws that may conflict. Furthermore, if a state law is found to interfere with any right protected by the U.S. Constitution, the federal courts may be asked to determine whether or not the state law is unconstitutional.

The rule of law principle is also embodied in the U.S. Constitution, which established the fundamental laws protecting and defining core values of the United States. The Constitution empowers both courts and legislatures to serve as venues through which rights are examined and protected, and responsibilities are established. The Constitution establishes federal and state governmental authority and responsibility to enforce the rule of law. While constitutions establish fundamental principles of law, at both the federal and state levels, the provisions contained therein are purposely flexible and subject to change as necessary.

It is also important to recognize the hierarchy of federal and state legal sources. As indicated earlier, primary legal sources include constitutions, statutes, case law, administrative regulations, and procedural rules. When determining legal authority, the primary sources have greater authority and thus are distinguished from secondary sources, such as law review articles, legal encyclopedias, or treatises. Statutes are the codified laws enacted by official governmental entities, which have been empowered through constitutional provisions. Other types of codified law include case law, administrative regulations, and procedural rules. The following sections will provide an overview of these forms of codified law.

Statutory Law

Federal and state legislatures are empowered via constitutions to propose laws, which will become codified in legislation upon successful passage through both chambers of Congress. We commonly refer to these laws as statutes or codes. Statutes are subsequently interpreted and applied by judges when conflicts or controversies arise. Legislative authority, as well as intent, may be considered by the reviewing courts. In such circumstances, justices are expected to provide an impartial review. Nonetheless, critical onlookers have asserted that political agendas may influence judges' decisions, particularly the Supreme Court Justices, given their lifetime appointments by the U.S. President and confirmation by the Senate[7].

The U.S. Congress is responsible for enacting all federal statutes, which are entered in the United States Codes (U.S.C.) or the United States Code

---

[5] THE FEDERALIST No. 39 (James Madison).

[6] U.S. CONST. amend. X (The powers not delegated to the United States by the Constitution, nor prohibited by it to the States, are reserved to the States respectively, or to the people.).

[7] Note that a good number of political scientists exclusively research and study judicial politics.

Annotated (U.S.C.A.). Similar to the passage and chronological arrangement of federal statutes, state legislatures likewise pass state laws that are codified using numerical designations. Across the fifty states, however, the codification of laws and structures of legislation may vary. Higher education institutions and the institutional leaders should be aware that all state codes are available online and warrant thoughtful attention so as to avoid costly errors when moving from state to state.

Legislative histories, including committee hearings and legislative debates, are pertinent to the interpretation and application of statutes. In particular, courts will access and assess these legislative histories when seeking to ascertain the intent of legislation when the particular law was enacted. Occasionally, Congress or a state legislature may adopt a law in direct response to a court decision. When a legislative body passes a law to counteract a judicial decision, it is said to have engaged in statutory reversal of the decision. Of course, these new laws may also be overturned by the courts in subsequent cases.

It is not uncommon for federal or state legislative efforts to align closely with external political agendas. For example, in a number of states, political pressures have led legislators to propose "restore free speech on campus" initiatives. Armed with model legislation from groups such as the Goldwater Institute,[8] legislators have successfully introduced bills to ban perceived restrictions on speech through the use of free speech zones. These bills have also included restrictions on disrupting speakers or infringing on the rights of others to hear the speakers. Introduction of bills, however, will not guarantee passage because bills must earn passing votes from both the Senate and House of Representatives, and survive the governors' veto privileges. In Alabama, for example, a free speech bill was recently signed into law by the governor after both houses reached agreement,[9] whereas similar bills in the Minnesota House and Senate have stalled in committee.[10]

When conflict arises over the application or constitutionality of federal and state legislation, the courts, depending on jurisdiction authority, provide a venue to resolve the dispute. Court authority to hear disputes is explained in detail in the section that follows. In brief, court decisions or judge-made laws represent judicial interpretations of federal and state constitutions, statutes, administrative regulations, or even previously decided court cases.

---

[8] *Restoring Free Speech on Campus*, GOLDWATER INST., *available at* https://goldwaterinstitute. org/campus-free-speech/

[9] John Bowden, *Alabama governor signs campus free speech bill into law*, THE HILL (June 8, 2019), *available at* https://thehill.com/homenews/state-watch/447586-alabama-governor-signs-bill-banning-colleges-from-limiting-students

[10] *Free Expression Policy*, H.F. 1383 (Feb 18, 2019); S.F. 1595 (Minn., 2019), available at https://www.revisor.mn.gov/bills/bill.php?b=senate&f=SF2380&ssn=0&y=2019

Case Law

Case law can be best explained as an extensive body of legal decisions that emerge from the courts to resolve disputes and guide subsequent actions. In these decisions, judges interpret and apply legal principles, constitutions, statutes, administrative regulations, or prior court cases. Collectively, these decisions or judicial opinions establish precedent, also known as stare decisis, a Latin phrase that means "let the decision stand."

Once precedent is established, the controlling case law should be considered by judges when deciding outcomes for subsequent disputes before the courts. Judges establish this body of precedential law on a case-by-case basis through issuing opinions. Adherence to precedent is also determined according to geographic boundaries of the courts. As explained in greater detail later in this chapter, federal and state courts are bound both by jurisdictional and geographical authority. Thus, court decisions from the U.S. Fourth Circuit Court of Appeals, for example, may be considered by other U.S. Circuit Courts of Appeals, those decisions will not establish precedent for the Ninth Circuit Court of Appeals. To put an even finer point on this, institutions of higher education not located within the jurisdiction of the Fourth Circuit Court of Appeals are not bound by its decisions.

While precedential law is typically applied when courts are interpreting outcomes for similarly situated parties and circumstances, courts on occasion have overturned or distinguished previous rulings. One of the oft-cited examples of a reversal of judicial precedent occurred in the public school law field. The Supreme Court ruling in *Plessy v. Ferguson*,[11] stating that racially separate but equal public education is constitutional, was overturned by the Court's 1954 decision in *Brown v. Board of Education*.[12]

Administrative Regulations and Law

Despite its quasi-legislative nature, administrative law in the higher education setting is influential and frequently guides decisions of higher education professionals. These regulations and laws are influential because they are adopted by federal and state agencies with oversight authority. Federal agencies are granted authority to adopt federal regulations for the specific purpose of guiding the implementation of federal legislation. Additionally, federal regulations carry the full force of the law while also clarifying the legislation meaning and implementation standards.

When administrative rules and regulations are passed, the administrative agency must first publish the proposed rules for a designated time period. During this time period, individuals and groups are invited to comment on the proposed regulations. After this process of public comment, the final regula-

---

[11] 163 U.S. 537 (1896).
[12] 347 U.S. 483 (1954).

tion must be published in the Code of Federal Regulations. These processes are similar for state regulations as well.

Judicial Systems

The judicial branch of government is responsible for interpreting and applying the constitutions, statutes, administrative regulations, or previous court decisions. Often referred to as common law, the court-issued opinions are instrumental in resolving the dispute before the courts. As described further, the judicial system is bifurcated between the federal and state court structures.

The federal and state courts have basically parallel structures (see Figure 1 for an example of state courts compared to the U.S. Federal courts) and procedures, but distinctly separate jurisdictions. Specifically, federal courts have exclusive jurisdiction over issues controlled by federal laws and governance of certain subject matters, concurrent jurisdiction over key areas, and a right of direct appeal from the states' highest courts to the U.S. Supreme Court. Whereas the state courts are varied and include specialized areas of focus, such as traffic, bankruptcy, and family law courts.

At the trial court level, one judge typically presides over and decides cases. The trial court is typically the stage at which a party, referred to as the plaintiff, initiates litigation against the opposing party, known as the defendant. Depending on the nature of the plaintiff's claim, (the harm caused, the right violated, or the legal principle offended), the case may or may not involve a jury at the trial court level.

The resolution of a plaintiff's claim or claims may or may not be issued in a written opinion by the judge. Quite frequently, trial court decisions are made, but the judges choose not to issue formal written opinions. In such circumstances, there is no record of the decision and no formal published document of the trial court's proceedings.

Figure 1. State & Federal Dual Court Structure

	STATE COURTS	FEDERAL COURTS
Courts of Last Resort	State court of last resort (State supreme court)	U.S. Supreme Court
Intermediate Appellate Level	State intermediate courts of appeals	U.S. courts of appeals (Circuit Courts)
Trial Level (original jurisdiction)	Courts of general jurisdiction and special trial courts (e.g., Probate Court)	U.S. district courts and courts of limited jurisdiction (e.g., Tax Court)

Federal and state courts are hierarchical in nature and similar in function, such that the higher courts have authority to review the lower or trial court decisions. Trial courts mark the beginning or initial phase of a legal dispute. These lower courts have authority to determine questions of fact and issue opinions in favor of or against the parties involved in the litigation.

Plaintiffs or defendants may decide to appeal a trial court ruling. On appeal, their claim or claims may be reviewed by an intermediate federal or state appellate court; however, review is not guaranteed solely because one of the parties disagrees with the trial court outcome. In other words, the intermediate appellate court has the authority to review questions of law and may determine if the alleged errors by the trial court warrant a review and subsequent ruling. Additional appeals may follow, again by either party, with a request for a ruling by a court of last resort, typically the U.S. Supreme Court or a state supreme court, depending on which court has final authority over the case.

Federal Judicial System

Although education is primarily a function of the states as the U.S. Constitution makes no mention of education, federal courts, particularly the U.S. Supreme Court, have been especially influential in the resolution of significant disputes in higher education. In particular, the U.S. Supreme Court plays an instrumental role in protecting the civil rights of students, such as through seeking enforcement of Title IX of the federal statutory code. Public higher education institutions and employees may also be sued in the federal courts for an alleged violation of the U.S. Constitution. For example, the Court has addressed essential constitutional guarantees, such as Fourteenth Amendment due process rights, the Equal Protection Clause, and First Amendment freedom of expression guarantees.

Although the federal courts have general jurisdiction over a wide variety of legal claims, the judicial system includes specialized jurisdiction over a narrow range of legal issues that are unlikely to be relevant to higher education institutions and professionals. The federal courts of general jurisdiction include the U.S. District Courts (trial); the twelve U.S. Circuit Courts of Appeals (intermediate appellate courts for Circuits 1-11, plus the D.C. Circuit Court of Appeals) and the Court of Appeals for the Federal Circuit; and the U.S. Supreme Court, which is the nation's highest appellate court (see Figure 2 – Map of Federal Courts' Jurisdiction).

Figure 2 – Map of Federal Circuit Courts' Jurisdiction

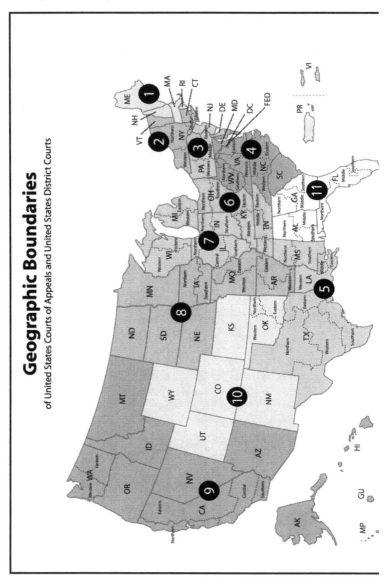

Federal District Courts

The U.S. district courts are established by Congress according to geographic boundaries and location (Northern, Southern, Eastern, Western, Central, or Middle). State boundary lines establish the structures for each district. A total of 94 federal trial courts have general subject-matter jurisdiction (89 across the 50 states, plus five in the federal and territorial jurisdictions of Washington, D.C., Puerto Rico, Guam, U.S. Virgin Islands, and Northern Mariana Islands).

Each state has at least one district court (trial court), and some states have up to four (*e.g.* California, New York, and Texas).

Circuit Courts of Appeal

Like the federal district courts, the intermediate courts of appeal are configured as courts of general jurisdiction based on geographical boundaries. The twelve intermediate courts of appeal include the eleven Federal Circuit Courts, plus the D.C. Circuit Court of Appeals. These courts have appellate jurisdiction, which means the federal circuit court judges hear cases concerning a range of diverse legal issues, which may also include cases on appeal from the federal administrative agencies, as specified by federal law. Circuit court cases may be heard by a panel of three judges or en banc, meaning all judges.

U.S. Supreme Court

The final arbiter of conflicts between federal and state courts is the U.S. Supreme Court, provided for explicitly under Article III of the U.S. Constitution, which outlines the Court's original and appellate jurisdiction authority. Although the U.S. Supreme Court hears only a small fraction of cases that are submitted for review each term, the Court's final rulings carry significant weight as their rulings are the only ones that apply to the entire nation. Further, justices have discretion over which appeals to hear. This is often referred to as the Rule of Four—at least four justices must vote in conference to hear an appeal. Although few specific education-related cases are heard each term (if any at all), seemingly unrelated cases should not be overlooked given that similar legal principles may transfer. For example, in 2015 the U.S. Supreme Court issued an opinion concerning the rights of same-sex couples to lawfully marry.[13] Although the case did not discuss education, the legal recognition of same-sex marriages had consequences for higher education, namely in the administration of employee benefits.

The number of justices on the U.S. Supreme Court is set by Congress, and individual Justices are nominated by sitting U.S. Presidents. Once nominated by the President, Justices must be confirmed by consent of the Senate after hearings in the Senate Judiciary Committee regarding the nominees' judicial qualifications. Supreme Court Justices are appointed for life, unless they are removed or resign. The nine Justices currently serving on the Court have been nominated by Presidents over a span of nearly thirty years. Given their lifetime appointments, a president's Supreme Court appointment is one of the most noteworthy opportunities that a President has to impact the future of our nation.

State Judicial Systems

Litigation impacting higher education institutions is still primarily pursued through the state and local court systems. This is the case because most of the

---

[13] Obergefell v. Hodges, 135 S.Ct. 2548 (2015).

issues and conflicts between individuals and higher education institutions are uniquely under the jurisdiction of state law. As indicated earlier, the structure of the state court systems is similar to federal court systems.

Structure

State court systems are similarly structured to federal courts with trial courts and appellate courts; however, there is a degree of variation across the states. Trial courts are still the entry point in the judicial system hierarchy at the state court level. In some states, these courts may be referred to as superior courts or district courts. The majority of litigation across the states is heard at the state trial court level.

These state trial court decisions are subject to review at the appellate court level, which includes the intermediate courts of appeal and the state supreme court. The state supreme court is a court of last resort, or the final stop before possible appeal to the U.S. Supreme Court. This final appeal has a relatively slim chance of being granted by the U.S. Supreme Court.

Legal Research

Conducting legal research—in other words, finding the law—is relatively straightforward, given the array of electronically based legal resources. These resources provide users with access to search engines and extensive databases. Although some of the resources may be accessible only with paid subscriptions, many are available free of cost through institutional and public libraries. An overview of some of the publicly available electronic resources follows. These resources include the most frequently utilized databases for legal research.

Congress.gov (formerly Thomas.loc.gov)
- About: "Congress.gov is the official website for U.S. federal legislative information. The site provides access to accurate, timely, and complete legislative information for Members of Congress, legislative agencies, and the public. It is presented by the Library of Congress (LOC) using data from the Office of the Clerk of the U.S. House of Representatives, the Office of the Secretary of the Senate, the Government Publishing Office, Congressional Budget Office, and the LOC's Congressional Research Service" (https://www.congress.gov/about). Users can search by Legislation (including Roll Call Vote), Congressional Record, Committee, Members of U.S. Congress, or Browse (Bills by Subject, Legislation, or Committee Report).
- Ease of Use: Novice researcher (browsing and searching only, tutorials not available)
- Access/Cost: Open/free
- Web Address: https://www.congress.gov/

Findlaw

- About: FindLaw is primarily a marketing tool for lawyers and is part of Thomson Reuters which owns West (see Westlaw entry below). FindLaw does provide several useful tools for public users including a legal dictionary (http://dictionary.findlaw.com/), basic "do it yourself" how to guides, legal forms, a legal blog for general guidance, and serves as a source for locating specialized legal professionals in the users home state (this site provides broad information only, hiring a professional lawyer is still advisable if users are looking for specific legal guidance). The legal professional side of the site provides an Opinion Summaries Archive (http://caselaw.findlaw.com/summary.html) going back to September 2000 by the U.S. Supreme Court, the U.S. Circuit Courts of Appeals and some state courts. Users can browse by court, company or topic. FindLaw is not an in depth legal research tool but is useful and reliable for quick searches and general legal information.
- Ease of Use: Novice researcher (browsing and searching only, tutorials not available)
- Access/Cost: Open/free
- Web Address: http://www.findlaw.com/

Nexis-Uni (formerly LexisNexis)

- About: Nexi-Uni is a research tool for case law, law review articles, and legal news. This tool is available for free to students, faculty, and university employees at most higher education libraries. Nexis-Uni enables a researcher to search by party (ether name), topic, or citation (must be exact), and provides full text searching in law review and journal articles. The advanced search option provides an array of fields for the user to narrow the search by federal or state courts, area of law, specific terms, and dates. Nexis-Uni also includes the option to Shepardize cases, which enables the researcher to locate related legal resources, including case law, legal encyclopedias, law review articles, and annotated codes. The Shepardizing tool is also necessary as it enables researchers to check for negative treatment of the case or possibly a reversal or subsequent court opinion.
- Ease of Use: Intermediate to expert researcher (help available via subscription, tutorials available on website through search box)
- Access/Cost: Subscription/$$$ costly, based on product purchased (Academic, Advanced, etc.)
- Web Address: https://advance.lexis.com

Conclusion

The study of law in higher education is a dynamic and critical field for those interested in higher education administration, faculty membership, student advocacy, college/university law practice, and many other roles. Many who benefit from the study of higher education law are not trained lawyers or law students; as such, the material may feel intimidating to some. From our years of teaching this material, we offer a few notes to those without a legal background:

- Know that the first few weeks of study may be the most difficult as you learn a new structure, language, and analytical way of thinking. Reading cases, locating statutes, and crafting a legal argument becomes easier over time.
- The law is not always the same as what one would find to be politically correct, moral, or "common sense." The system of law is in place to provide us with a common understanding of the rules for navigating society so that each institution (such as a public college) does not have to negotiate individual preferences to develop its own fundamental operating system.
- Understanding higher education legal issues does not take the place of working with institutional counsel. Most colleges and universities have dedicated lawyers at the institution or system level. Understanding the material in this text will make you a better issue-spotter and help you avoid legal pitfalls, but the practice of law remains the responsibility of licensed attorneys employed by the institution.

For those who have a legal background, but are new to the higher education arena, we urge you to take time to understand the culture and norms of your campus or system. Many practices and policies on campus stem from historic traditions that go back hundreds of years (such as faculty governance, academic freedom, pomp and circumstance). Partnerships between legal counsel and campus administrators provide the most solid footing for a legally productive relationship.

2

Higher Education Governance

Neal H. Hutchens, J.D., Ph.D.
University of Mississippi

Frank J. Fernandez, Ph.D.
University of Mississippi

Introduction

This chapter examines issues related to the legal control and oversight of colleges and universities—that is, who holds the legal authority to govern an institution. In the context of this chapter, the term "governance" is used to describe the legal structures and standards that determine which groups and individuals possess legal authority to direct and oversee the affairs of colleges and universities. Additionally, governance is meant to refer primarily to macro-level institutional authority and control rather than the day-to-day management and administration of colleges and universities.

As Michael McClendon has described, a "fundamental, even paradoxical tension" exists "between the dual demands of *institutional autonomy* and *public accountability*, or between the university's right to regulate its affairs from within and the state's authority (and responsibility) to regulate the university affairs from without."[1] Policy and legal debates over higher education governance often deal with striking the balance between institutional autonomy and public accountability, especially in the case of public colleges and universities. For instance, should the state legislature, or a system, or an institutional governing board have final authority to establish tuition rates for public institutions? Should a state law be able to prevent a public university from removing or relocating a monument on campus that commemorates the Confederacy? Or, to what extent should public institutions be able to prohibit firearms on campus? These are just three examples of governance-related issues that have arisen in recent years. At a surface level, issues related to the legal governance of colleges and universities may strike some as dealing with

---

[1] Michael McLendon, *State Governance Reform of Higher Education: Patterns, Trends, and Theories of the Public Policy Process, in* HIGHER EDUCATION: HANDBOOK OF THEORY AND RESEARCH: VOLUME XVIII 57, 57 (John C. Smart ed., 2003).

esoteric or abstract topics, but, as these examples illustrate, postsecondary governance structures and accompanying legal standards impact members of a campus community in multiple and significant ways.

When institutional leaders and state governmental leaders disagree about which actor has the authority over a specific college or university policy, they periodically turn to the courts to rule over disputes about law and governance. For example, Scott Gelber's legal history covers a century of governance disputes regarding who has the authority to set college admission and expulsion policies. Gelber charts the cyclical rise, decline, and re-emergence of academic deference. The data show periods when courts concede governing decisions to college or university leaders rather than state elected officials, followed by periods when courts side with states rather than defer to university boards.[2] Although Gelber's analysis stops in 1960, the process he describes—and also considered in McLendon's work—continues into the present.

Drawing on scholarship such as that of McClendon and Gelber, we posit that governance is a balancing act between university leaders, state elected officials, and courts; otherwise stated, governance exists in the relations between those three actors.[3] If governance is a continually negotiated process, then it is important to acknowledge that the outcome of those interactions can—and has—changed over time and will continue to do so. Higher education professionals may find that they start their careers in a period when courts or legislative bodies grant academic deference to colleges and universities, only to find that near the end of their careers, these same courts or legislative bodies are more likely to limit institutional autonomy in favor of public accountability or state authority.

Chapter Overview

A long-established facet of American higher education involves reliance on lay governing boards (primarily composed of individuals who are not academic professionals) to serve as the principal controlling bodies for both public and private colleges and universities.[4] Governing boards exercise final, or at least significant, decision-making authority or approval over fundamental

---

[2] SCOTT GELBER, COURTROOMS AND CLASSROOMS: A LEGAL HISTORY OF COLLEGE ACCESS, 1860-1960 (2016).

[3] Accrediting bodies are also often an important constituency in considerations of autonomy and accountability. As these bodies, however, draw their authority over higher education institutions or specific academic programs from voluntary participation by institutions and from authority delegated by the federal or state governments to various institutional and programmatic accrediting bodies—such as with professional licensure or certification or with eligibility for students to participate in financial aid programs—we do not categorize accreditors as a separate, primary actor in our consideration of governance.

[4] JOHN S. BRUBACHER & WILLIS RUDY, HIGHER EDUCATION IN TRANSITION: A HISTORY OF AMERICAN COLLEGES AND UNIVERSITIES 26 (4th ed. 1997); ARTHUR M. COHEN & CARRIE B. KISKER, THE SHAPING OF AMERICAN HIGHER EDUCATION: EMERGENCE AND GROWTH OF THE CONTEMPORARY SYSTEM 43 (2d ed. 2010); JOHN R. THELIN, A HISTORY OF AMERICAN HIGHER EDUCATION 7-12 (2d ed. 2011).

and important institutional decisions, such as the selection of an institution's or system's president, faculty hiring and the awarding of tenure, and the overall strategy or means a college or university should pursue in fulfilling its mission or purpose. Besides discussing the kinds of legal authority that governing boards possess over institutional functions and direction, this chapter considers how multiple legal standards help to shape, and at times constrain, the ways in which governing boards may act. To provide important context and background, the chapter begins with a brief historical overview of the development of governance structures and patterns in the United States.

Another significant aspect of governance involves how status as a public or private institution may have important implications for governance and the legal control of colleges and universities. The private/public division is not always as clear as one might initially assume, with some colleges and universities having both private and public attributes. Still, designation as public or private often holds legal significance, including in relation to governance issues. Private institutions, while far from immune to governmental regulation, generally possess greater legal latitude in governance matters than their public counterparts. With public colleges and universities, the degree of legally protected independence, or autonomy, an institution possesses depends on several factors. Besides consideration of the central role of the states in higher education matters, the chapter also considers the increasing role of federal legal standards in how colleges and universities operate, which has important implications for governance.

Historical Development of American Governance Patterns and Structures

In the United States, higher education evolved along decentralized lines, with activity occurring at the colonial and then state levels rather than any kind of centralized planning or oversight.[5] Early colleges, while influenced by the models and ideas found in Europe—Oxford and Cambridge in England, in particular—represented a response to the unique factors existing in the colonies.[6] Borrowing from Scottish institutions, and unlike the Oxford and Cambridge models, colonial and then U.S. colleges relied on an external (lay) governing board and a strong president to administer operations.[7] Lay governing boards often included seats for elected officials and clergy from the religious denomination that founded the college. Prominent citizens were also asked to help oversee colleges; for example, the prominent Boston merchant and future president of the Continental Congress, John Hancock, was elected as treasurer of Harvard College in 1773.[8] Another important aspect of higher

---

[5] COHEN & KISKER, *supra* note 4, at 19-26, 43-49.

[6] *Id.* at 19-26; THELIN, *supra* note 4, at 11-12.

[7] BRUBACHER & RUDY, *supra* note 4, at 24-25; COHEN & KISKER, *supra* note 4, at 19-26.

[8] SAMUEL ELIOT MORISON, THREE CENTURIES OF HARVARD, 1636-1936 145 (12TH PRTG. 1994).

education during the colonial period was that state legislators did not distinguish between public versus private higher education.[9] While a conception of public higher education as it is now understood did not exist, colonial legislatures gave important, if often inconsistent, support to schools.[10] This assistance included the granting of charters and also varying degrees of financial assistance, such as occasional donations or the granting of funds derived from taxes on items like tobacco or furs.[11]

The ambiguous status of governmental control over colleges in the colonial period resulted in tensions between institutions and legislatures.[12] Before the American Revolution, the issue of control over colleges also involved the English monarchy. Harvard and Yale did not seek royal charters, in part, out of concern over interference with institutional operations.[13] After the formation of the United States, just as during the colonial period, there was not a clear distinction between public and private colleges.[14]

The U.S. Supreme Court's decision in 1819 in a case involving Dartmouth College, while perhaps not having the dramatic and immediate impact on the development of private higher education as sometimes suggested,[15] did contribute to the establishment of legal standards that differentiate between institutions as public or private.

Trustees of Dartmouth College v. Woodward and Private Higher Education

The facts surrounding the case *Trustees of Dartmouth College v. Woodward*[16] illustrate the indeterminate legal relationships that existed between schools and state governments in the early American republic. Dartmouth, established in the colonial era, had gained a royal charter that permitted a self-perpetuating board of trustees and allowed the president to name his successor.[17] The founder of the college and its president, Eleazar Wheelock, designated his son, John Wheelock, to succeed him.[18] During his presidential tenure, John Wheelock came into conflict with the trustees, who eventually acted to remove him from office.[19] John Wheelock turned for assistance to the New Hampshire legislature, which amended the college's charter to create

---

[9] THELIN, *supra* note 4, at 71.

[10] BRUBACHER & RUDY, *supra* note 4, at 35-36; COHEN & KISKER, *supra* note 4, at 49-51; THELIN, *supra* note 4, at 12-13.

[11] BRUBACHER & RUDY, *supra* note 4, at 35-36.

[12] *Id.* at 30-32.

[13] *Id.* at 30-31.

[14] *Id.* at 32-33.

[15] THELIN, *supra* note 4, at 70-73 (discussing an exaggeration of the role of the Dartmouth decision in the formation of private higher education).

[16] 17 U.S. (4 Wheat) 518 (1819).

[17] BRUBACHER & RUDY, *supra* note 4, at 33.

[18] *Id.*

[19] *Id.*

Dartmouth University and enlarged the board of trustees to provide a majority supporting him as president.[20]

The dispute between the original board of trustees and John Wheelock festered and for a time two institutions—Dartmouth College and Dartmouth University—operated in opposition to one another.[21] As the conflict turned into a legal dispute, state courts in New Hampshire sided with the state legislature and John Wheelock. The case made its way to the U.S. Supreme Court, where famed politician and orator Daniel Webster, a Dartmouth alumnus, argued on behalf of the original trustees.[22] The Court, deciding against Wheelock, held that Dartmouth essentially constituted a private corporation, one created on the basis of a contract between the trustees and the government because of the charter granted to the institution.[23] According to the Court, the legislature's attempt to alter the charter violated the Contract Clause of the Federal Constitution.[24] Thus, the Supreme Court held that the state legislature could not interfere with the authority of the original trustees in their oversight of the institution.

The case is notable in the development of higher education in that the Supreme Court thwarted the legislative effort to alter the original charter and intervene in Dartmouth's internal governance struggle. The decision provided an important legal foundation for the long-term creation of clearly private higher education in the United States. But, as historian John Thelin cautions, one should not overemphasize the decision's influence in sparking the development of private colleges and universities in the United States.[25] Other trends and legal developments would contribute in significant ways to the formation of the public/private distinction in higher education.

For instance, the Fourteenth Amendment was ratified after the Civil War and created due process rights to protect citizens—particularly former slaves—from state (i.e., governmental) action. As higher education expanded in the late nineteenth century and into the twentieth century , including the creation of women's colleges and historically black colleges and universities (HBCUs),[26] the Fourteenth Amendment was used to selectively incorporate provisions from the U.S. Bill of Rights to apply to the states. When the Fourteenth Amendment was applied to the states, it helped spur development of legal distinctions between public and private entities, including in the educational realm. As discussed later in the chapter, the public/private divide becomes blurry at times in higher education. Accordingly, care should be taken not to overstate the Dartmouth case's immediate impact in the development of clearly private and public institutions. Still, the decision marked a noteworthy step in

---

[20] *Id.*

[21] *Id.*

[22] *Id.* at 34.

[23] *Dartmouth College*, 17 U.S. at 643-50.

[24] *Id.* at 654.

[25] THELIN, *supra* note 4, at 70-73.

[26] ROGER L. GEIGER (ED.). THE AMERICAN COLLEGE IN THE NINETEENTH CENTURY (2000).

the development of legal standards contributing to legal distinctions between public and private colleges and universities.

Emergence of More Clearly Public Higher Education Institutions

According to Cohen and Kisker, between 1790 and 1869, seventeen states engaged in efforts of varying quality to establish institutions that generally align with more contemporary notions of a public higher education institution.[27] However, the role of state governments in the development of public colleges and universities during the late eighteenth and early and middle decades of the nineteenth centuries was often characterized by narrow or unclear involvement and limited financial support.[28] Additionally, the authority of state governments in relation to institutions remained ambiguous.[29]

In the opening decades of the nineteenth century, states made some progress in developing more clearly or distinctly public colleges and universities. Thomas Jefferson helped found the University of Virginia, which served as an important example of creating an institution intended to function as a state university.[30] The University of Michigan provided another leading model.[31] Southern and more western states, which lacked the colonial-era religious colleges of the eastern states, proved more active in the establishment of state public universities in the opening and middle decades of the nineteenth century.[32] While the early state institutions faced difficult financial conditions, experienced animosity from schools with a more private orientation, and often initially failed to live up to lofty goals, they helped establish the foundation for publicly supported higher education.[33]

Other trends and initiatives helped foster the development of public colleges and universities and the drawing of clearer lines between public and private schools. Though the goals of providing technological and practical education were initially largely unrealized due to insufficient funding, passage of the first Morrill Act and establishment of state land-grant institutions contributed to the continued development of public higher education.[34] The original, but unfulfilled, promise of the first Morrill Act received a significant boost with the second Morrill Act in the 1890s, which provided annual federal appropriations to the land-grant institutions.[35] During the second part of the nineteenth century, states began to start normal schools for teacher education; a number of these developed into colleges and universities with their own

---

[27] COHEN AND KISKER, *supra* note 4, at 68.
[28] BRUBACHER & RUDY, *supra* note 4, at 145-146; COHEN AND KISKER, *supra* note 4, at 68-69.
[29] BRUBACHER & RUDY, *supra* note 4, at 145-146; COHEN AND KISKER, *supra* note 4, at 68-69.
[30] BRUBACHER & RUDY, *supra* note 4, at 147-53.
[31] *Id.* at 156.
[32] *Id.* at 145-158.
[33] BRUBACHER & RUDY, *supra* note 4, at 153-156; COHEN AND KISKER, *supra* note 4, at 94-97.
[34] BRUBACHER & RUDY, *supra* note 4, at; 62-63; COHEN AND KISKER, *supra* note 4, at 115.
[35] BRUBACHER & RUDY, *supra* note 4, at 62-64; THELIN, *supra* note 4, at 135-36.

governing boards in the twentieth century.[36] The emergence of public secondary education in the late nineteenth and, especially, in the early decades of the twentieth century provided a larger pool of students to attend the burgeoning public colleges and universities.[37]

Even as clearer conceptions of decidedly public higher education took hold during the nineteenth century, the institutions designated as "public" generally received wide latitude in their internal affairs from state governments, a pattern that continued into the twentieth century.[38] To insulate public institutions from political wrangling, some states (with Michigan the most prominent example) placed provisions in their constitutions establishing governing bodies with independent authority.[39] As the university structure emerged in the late nineteenth and early twentieth centuries, governors often appointed individuals to the governing boards of these emerging state institutions, but the board structure tended to provide schools with a degree of insulation from excessive governmental interference.[40]

Following World War II, states began to expand public systems of higher education, especially in regions like New England where strong systems of public schools previously did not exist.[41] The increase in size and types of public institutions reflected a large upswing in higher education enrollment that began after the war, with the Servicemen's Readjustment Act (the G.I. Bill) providing a significant boost to enrollment.[42] In 1900, only about 4% of the college-age population attended colleges, but this had risen to approximately 40% by 1964.[43] The decades after World War II marked the emergence of what Martin Trow has referred to as "mass higher education."[44] No longer thought of as an enterprise serving only an elite slice of society, higher education increasingly was viewed as an important means to achieving individual and national economic goals. Larger enrollment and state governmental interest marked a shift from the more limited state regulation of higher education that generally existed before World War II.[45]

---

[36] ROBERT O. BERDAHL, STATEWIDE COORDINATION OF HIGHER EDUCATION 27 (1971).

[37] COHEN AND KISKER, *supra* note 4, at 123.

[38] William Zumeta, *Public Policy and Accountability in Higher Education: Lessons from the Past and Present for the New Millenium, in* THE STATES AND PUBLIC HIGHER EDUCATION POLICY 155 (Donald E. Heller ed., 2001).

[39] Joseph Beckham, *Reasonable Independence for Public Higher Education: Legal Implications of Constitutionally Autonomous Status*, 7 J. L. & EDUC. 177-79 (1978).

[40] COHEN AND KISKER, *supra* note 4, at 161-62.

[41] *Id.* at 199.

[42] BRUBACHER & RUDY, *supra* note 4, at 257-58.

[43] *Id.* at 257.

[44] Martin Trow, *From Mass Higher Education to Universal Access: The American Advantage, in* IN DEFENSE OF AMERICAN HIGHER EDUCATION 123 (Philip G. Altbach, Patricia J. Gumport, & D. Bruce Johnstone eds., 2001).

[45] Zumeta, *supra* note 38, at 155-56.

Summary on Historical Development
of Governance Structures

Divisions between public and private higher education developed over a long period in American history, which helps to explain how the private/public line continues to create confusion in some legal contexts. This historical overview highlights that whether public or private, reliance on external governing boards has roots in practices established before the formation of the United States. Similarly, a tradition of state control over educational matters reflects well-established patterns and practices. The section also helps to highlight that tensions have always existed in American higher education regarding control of colleges and universities and the level of independence that institutions should possess to control their internal affairs. With these points in mind, the chapter shifts to a more contemporary consideration of issues related to the states and higher education governance.

State Oversight of Colleges and Universities

The concept of institutional autonomy refers to the authority possessed by a college or university to manage its internal affairs free of external controls or interference.[46] Berdahl, Altbach, and Gumport divide autonomy along its procedural and substantive dimensions.[47] Substantive autonomy entails "the power of the university or college in its corporate form to determine its own goals and programs (the *what* of academe)."[48] Procedural autonomy refers to the "power of the university or college in its corporate form to determine the means by which its goals and programs will be pursued (the *how* of academe)."[49] Among public colleges and universities procedural and substantive autonomy is a flexible concept with institutions across states (and sometimes even within states) subject to varying degrees of governmental control.[50]

The legal arrangements and structures developed by states to monitor and oversee higher education institutions comprise an important factor contributing to institutional autonomy, especially for public colleges and universities. But, a variety of elements, such as reliance on state funding and the authority to set tuition rates, shape the overall institutional autonomy possessed by a college or university. Even so, the concept of autonomy proves helpful in contemplating how state governmental regulation and oversight shapes and affects matters related to higher education governance and the legal control of colleges and universities.

---

[46] Robert O. Berdahl, Philip G. Altbach, & Patricia J. Gumport, *Introduction, in* IN DEFENSE OF AMERICAN HIGHER EDUCATION 5-6 (Philip G. Altbach, Patricia J. Gumport, & D. Bruce Johnstone eds., 2001).

[47] *Id.*

[48] *Id.*

[49] *Id.*

[50] *Id.*

As discussed at the beginning of the chapter, governance of public colleges and universities is marked by ongoing tension. How can states keep institutions sensitive to the public interest while also providing institutions with the requisite internal authority and flexibility to fulfill their academic, research, and service missions?[51] As noted, public colleges and universities generally enjoyed substantial latitude in the management of their internal affairs through World War II, but the decades that followed resulted in a consistent ratcheting-up of oversight by state governments.[52] After World War II, policy makers became more invested in the governance of higher education as public college and university enrollments increased and higher education came to be seen as essential to economic growth and national security during the Cold War. Additionally, the Federal Higher Education Act of 1965 required that each state have a coordinating agency for higher education.[53] Statewide coordinating or governing boards became the primary mechanism for increased regulation of public colleges and universities.[54] These boards were also envisioned as a means to help buffer the relationship between public institutions and state government by protecting schools from undue state control.[55]

This section outlines the multiple approaches taken by states in the regulation and oversight of higher education, particularly in relation to which agencies or boards possess responsibility for governing institutions. While much of this section deals with control over public colleges and universities, various state boards and agencies also exercise important oversight functions over private higher education, notably granting or denying permission to operate in a state. Discussion now turns to the different kinds of state-level higher education boards or agencies and their roles or legal authority over colleges and universities.

Types of State-Level Boards

State-level boards can be broken into three broad categories: (1) governing boards, (2) coordinating boards, and (3) planning or administrative/service agencies responsible for particular programs, such as ones involving financial aid, or for data services for the system.[56] Rather than rigid categories, they should instead be understood as providing a general means to distinguish different kinds of statewide boards and agencies. States have adopted and blended multiple approaches to governance structures for higher education,

---

[51] Michael K. McLendon, *Setting the Governmental Agenda for State Decentralization of Higher Education*, 74 J. HIGHER EDUC. 479, 479 (2003).

[52] *Id.*

[53] COHEN AND KISKER, *supra* note 4, at 254.

[54] BERDAHL, *supra* note 36, at 33.

[55] *See generally* BERDAHL, *supra* note 36.

[56] EDUCATION COMMISSION OF THE STATES, HIGH LEVEL ANALYSIS OF STATE POSTSECONDARY GOVERNANCE STRUCTURES, (MAY 2019), https://www.ecs.org/wp-content/uploads/PS-Gov-Structures-50_State-Analysis_Compacts_Other-States_May2019.pdf; *See also* Michael K. McLendon & Erick C. Ness, *The Politics of State Higher Education Governance Reform*, 78 PEABODY J. EDUC. 67 (2003).

resulting in considerable variation. As McLendon and Ness point out, "[n]o two states share precisely the same governance design."[57] Thus, the unique higher education governance arrangements existing in each state play a role in shaping legal implications for colleges and universities.

Governing Board

A state-level governing board exercises authority over all, or a portion, of the public colleges and universities in a state. North Carolina provides an example of this kind of arrangement, relying on two statewide boards, one for four-year universities and another for community colleges. The Board of Governors for the University of North Carolina possesses management authority over seventeen four-year public institutions in the state. Members of the board are appointed by the state's General Assembly.[58] Each campus also has a board of trustees with extensive control over academic matters and institutional functioning, but such authority is delegated by the statewide board of governors.

The State Board of Community Colleges is the governing body for the North Carolina Community College System and has responsibility for fifty-eight community colleges.[59] Other states lack a strong statewide board and instead have locally elected trustees.[60] The North Carolina example demonstrates how statewide governing authority over public higher education may be split among one or more state-level boards. Variations exist on this approach. For instance, a state might choose to exercise statewide governance authority over certain types of institutions, such as community colleges, but then leave other institutions under the authority of individual governing boards.

Coordinating Board

A coordinating board represents an agency that possesses some regulatory authority over public, and perhaps private, institutions in a state, but is not a governing body. Coordinating boards might have duties related to tuition, or budgeting, or approval of new academic programs. The authority over institutions may not be insignificant, but a coordinating board does not possess final governing or administrative authority in the same manner as a state-level or institutional governing board.

Kentucky represents a state with a coordinating agency, but where primary governance control for public higher education is dispersed among institutional-level boards for universities and a consolidated board for two-year institutions. The state's Council on Postsecondary Education has authority related to tuition-setting and approval of new academic programs, but it does

---

[57] McLendon & Ness, *supra* note 56, at 67.

[58] N.C. Gen. Stat. Ann. §§ 116-4, 116-6, 116-11.

[59] *Id.* at § 115D-2-1.

[60] Emily Miller, Janice Nahra Friedel, Jim Killacky, & Stephen G. Katsinas, Fifty State Systems of Community Colleges (2014).

not act as the legal governing authority for public institutions in the state.[61] Individual boards govern the eight public universities, and the sixteen colleges of the state's community and technical college system fall under the control of a single statewide governing board.[62] The council also serves as the licensing agency for many private postsecondary institutions in the state, including for-profit schools that grant baccalaureate degrees.[63] Thus, the council is meant to function as an intermediary agency for all public colleges and universities in the state, as well as private institutions, but it does not function as a governance authority over specific schools. Kentucky also provides a good example of how a state may mix and match approaches to governance and oversight of higher education.

Planning or Administrative/Service Agency

Finally, in some states, a state-level entity may possess a planning or policy role with no coordinating or governance authority over public or private higher education institutions. In these states, strong institutional or system governing boards have dominant legal authority over governance matters for public colleges and universities. Minnesota represents a state with this type of arrangement. The Minnesota Office of Higher Education is charged with helping to provide statewide data and information regarding higher education and to help facilitate collaboration among educational entities in the state, but it does not possess regulatory authority.[64] A constitutionally empowered board of regents governs the University of Minnesota's campuses.[65] Seven state universities and twenty-four two-year colleges fall under the authority of the Board of Trustees for the Minnesota State Colleges and University System.[66] Minnesota provides yet another example of how states follow unique approaches to issues of governance, coordination, and planning. A state-level planning agency exists alongside an institutional governing board for the state's flagship university and a consolidated board that has authority over both four- and two-year institutions.

Sources of Governance Authority

Public Colleges and Universities

Just as states have created various forms of governance structures, multiple sources of legal authority establish which entities or agencies possess legal control over colleges and universities. A select number of states include provisions in their constitutions that preserve the autonomy of institutions or systems

---

[61] Ky. Stat. Ann. §§ 164.011, 164.020.

[62] *Id.* at §§ 164.310, 164.5807.

[63] *Id.* at §§164.945-47.

[64] Minn. Stat. Ann. §§ 136A.01, 136A.05.

[65] Minn. Const. art. XIII, § 3.

[66] Minn. Stat. Ann. §§ 136F.06, 136F.11.

in the state from undue interference by other divisions of state government.[67] This type of constitutionally protected governance authority is often referred to as constitutional autonomy. California, Michigan, and Minnesota are typically identified as the states with the strongest grants of such constitutionally protected independence, with approximately seven other states having some degree of constitutional autonomy for one or more institutions.[68] One reason for referring to an approximate number is that while language may suggest that constitutional autonomy should exist for an institution, such a determination ultimately rests on judicial recognition of that independence. Thus, some states have constitutional provisions suggestive of constitutional autonomy, but courts have not issued decisions interpreting the constitutional language at issue.[69]

For California, Michigan, and Minnesota, courts have consistently determined that constitutional autonomy provides governing boards with legally protected authority.[70] In California, for example, a court stated in a 2000 decision that the Regents of the University of California were intended to "operate as independent of the state as possible."[71] In a 1975 Michigan case especially relevant for this chapter's discussion, the state's supreme court considered the constitutionality of several conditions placed on legislative appropriations to universities in the state, as well as a requirement that institutions had to submit new academic programs for approval to the state board of education.[72] The court held that while the legislature could impose certain conditions on appropriations, it could "not interfere with the management and control of those institutions."[73] In relation to review of new academic programs, the court discussed that it was acceptable for the legislature to require universities to submit new academic programs to the state board of education, but the board possessed no authority to prohibit any new programs.[74] The authority to approve or reject new programs remained with constitutionally empowered institutional governing boards in the state.

Even those institutions protected by judicially recognized constitutional autonomy have been subject to considerable pressure from state legislatures in recent years. In 2014, responding to concerns over rising tuition and the generous salaries of senior administrators, bipartisan lawmakers in California proposed a constitutional amendment that would put the University of Califor-

---

[67] Beckham, *supra* note 39, at 177-79; Neal H. Hutchens, *Preserving the Independence of Public Higher Education: An Examination of State Constitutional Autonomy Provisions for Public Colleges and Universities*, 35 J.C. & U.L. 271-72 (2009).

[68] Beckham, *supra* note 39, at 181; Hutchens, *supra* note 67, at 282

[69] Beckham, *supra* note 39, at 179.

[70] *Id.* at 34, at 181; Hutchens, *supra* note 67, at 282.

[71] Kim v. Regents of Univ. of Cal., 95 Cal. Rptr. 2d 10, 14 (Cal. Ct. App. 2000).

[72] Regents of the Univ. of Mich. v. State, 235 N.W.2d 1 (Mich. 1975).

[73] *Id.* at 6.

[74] *Id.* at 10-11.

nia system under the control of the legislature.[75] Minnesota's legislature has not attempted to challenge the University of Minnesota's autonomy directly, but it has sought to exert influence over the institution's decisions. In 2011, it attached conditions to some of the school's state funding; in order to receive the money, the university had to meet certain academic standards.[76]

In contrast to states with judicial recognition of constitutional autonomy, Utah provides an example of a state in which constitutional language would seem to grant some degree of constitutional autonomy to the University of Utah, but where state courts have rejected such a position. A 2006 decision from the state's supreme court squarely rejected any constitutional independence for the institution.[77] In *University of Utah v. Shurtleff*, the University of Utah sued the state's attorney general over a law that prohibited state and local entities from enacting or enforcing policies that interfered with the possession or use of firearms on public or private property. The university, which sought to prohibit guns from campus, argued that its firearms policy did not contravene the state law or, alternatively, that the university possessed the constitutional authority to enact and enforce a gun-ban policy.[78] During litigation over the law's applicability to the institution, the legislature amended the statute to explicitly include state universities. In upholding the law in relation to the University of Utah, the Utah Supreme Court held that the university was completely subject to full legislative oversight, even in matters related to the institution's "core academic functions."[79]

More common than a constitutional provision, public colleges and universities are often authorized by either a state-granted charter or statutory language, or a combination of these two approaches. For example, Wisconsin historically used state statutes to protect autonomy—through tenure—of University of Wisconsin faculty. State law prohibited dismissing tenured faculty except during financial crises. However, in 2015, the Wisconsin governor and legislature changed state law to change state statutes to give the state Board of Regents authority to lay off tenured faculty for a wider variety of reasons. The case of the University of Wisconsin shows how statutory language influences university governance and is more easily changed than constitutional provisions.[80]

Depending on the language in a charter and its treatment by courts, the governing board of a public college or university may possess a level of legally protected independence. For example, a board may have some protected

[75] Nanette Asimov, *UC's Rising Tuition Sparks Bill to End College's Autonomy,* S.F. Chronicle, Dec. 5, 2014, http://www.sfgate.com/education/article/State-senators-propose-wresting-control-of-UC-5936041.php

[76] James Nord, *The Untouchable U,* Minn. Daily, Sep. 19, 2011, https://www.tcdailyplanet.net/untouchable-u-older-state-university-minnesota-governs-itself/

[77] Univ. of Utah v. Shurtleff, 144 P.3d 1109, 1111 (Utah 2006).

[78] *Id.* at 1113.

[79] *Id.* at 1118.

[80] Kimberly Hefling, *Walker Erodes College Professor Tenure,* Politico (July 12, 2005), https://www.politico.com/story/2015/07/scott-walker-college-professor-tenure-120009.

legal authority to select a certain portion of the board's membership and have other legally independent governing authority. Representative of this approach is the governing board for The Pennsylvania State University, which was granted a charter by the state in 1855, and along with three other institutions is designated as a state-related university.[81] Except for The Pennsylvania State University, Pennsylvania's state-related schools (University of Pittsburgh, Temple University, and Lincoln University) were all historically private universities; they were granted state-related status in the 1960s and 1970s when they were near insolvency. As state-related schools they receive state funds but maintain their own boards of trustees (with some members appointed by the state).[82] In contrast, fourteen four-year schools in the state comprise the Pennsylvania State System of Higher Education, and these are considered public (state-owned) institutions under state law.[83] The "state-related" governance arrangement is a reminder that the public/private dichotomy in higher education is not always tidy.

A charter does not necessarily mean that a legislature does not ultimately hold legal authority over an institution, especially one considered primarily public in nature. In general, courts have recognized substantial authority for legislatures to regulate public corporate bodies.[84] But, a charter may provide a certain degree of legally protected autonomy for a public institution if a court views a governmental regulation as overly intrusive of a governing board's authority.

In general, the governing authority for most public higher education boards ultimately rests upon legislative power.[85] Language in a charter or constitution may provide for the creation of an institution's governing board but leave the defining of the powers and duties of the board to the legislature.[86] As a legal matter, then, the powers and duties of public governing boards typically rest on a legislative grant of authority. However, public colleges and universities traditionally have been afforded substantial autonomy over their internal operations by state governments, though states have shown increasing interest in oversight in recent years. Due to factors that include rising costs for students, concern over college completion rates, and interest in colleges and universities as economic drivers, state lawmakers have seemed more willing to scrutinize and question institutional practices and priorities.

---

[81] *See generally Corporate Charter of The Pennsylvania State University*, http://www.psu.edu/trustees/pdf/charter.pdf.

[82] Aims C. McGuinness Jr., *History and Evolution of Higher Education Systems* in Higher Education Systems 3.0: Harnessing Systemness, Delivering Performance 45 (Jason Lane D. & Bruce Johnstone eds., 2013).

[83] *Id.*

[84] *See, e.g.*, Henry N. Butler, *The Contract Clause and the Corporation*, 55 Brook. L. Rev. 780-81 (1989); Liam Seamus O'Melinn, *Neither Contract Nor Concession: The Public Personality of the Corporation*, 74 Geo. Wash. L. Rev. 242-43 (2006).

[85] Lyman A. Glenny & Frank A. Schmidtlein, *The Role of the State in the Governance of Higher Education*, 5 Educ. Evaluation and Pol'y Analysis 134 (1983).

[86] Beckham, *supra* note 39, at 179.

Beyond legislative or court mandates that directly implicate governance matters, other legal standards impact how institutions operate and coordinate their internal affairs. Notably, state open meetings and records laws mean that governing boards must conduct their affairs with a certain level of transparency.[87] Similarly, numerous state legal standards in such areas as civil rights protections, purchasing, regulation of collective bargaining for public employees, and health and safety influence how public colleges and universities must function, even those with substantial legally protected autonomy.[88] Beyond the issue of express legal authority of states over higher education institutions, the desire to receive funding operates as an important enticement for governing boards not to alienate elected officials, and represents a significant way for states to influences higher education policy and practice.[89]

In summary, while legal considerations are important in assessing governance-related matters, multiple variables influence the amount of control that institutions exercise over their internal affairs. Legislatures have traditionally shown considerable deference to public colleges and universities in relation to governance, though this state of affairs is potentially in a state of flux. Likewise, public institutions do not solely look to legal standards in determining how to respond to concerns voiced by public officials. The exercise of legal control is tempered by interest in receiving continued governmental and public support. While important, legal standards related to governance exist alongside numerous factors shaping and influencing the autonomy possessed by public higher education governing entities.

Private Colleges and Universities

Just as with many of their public counterparts, private colleges and universities often operate on the basis of a charter granted by the state or through a statutory process that establishes them as nonprofit, private corporations. As to the for-profit sector, these businesses may be treated in a legally distinct manner in certain respects from private, nonprofit higher education institutions for purposes of state regulation. One notable difference is that private, nonprofit higher education institutions often enjoy certain kinds of tax exemptions. At a minimum, both nonprofit and for-profit private schools must gain permission to operate in a state.

While private institutions may be subject to considerable state regulation, they generally operate with a degree of legal control over their internal affairs greater than that of many of their public counterparts. Private institutions, for instance, often have a self-perpetuating governing board, which often is not the

---

[87] Michael K. McLendon & James C. Hearn, *State Law, Policy, and Access to Information: The Case of Mandated Openness in Higher Education*, 112 Tchrs. C. Rec. 7-8 (2010), *available at* http://www.tcrecord.org.

[88] *See generally* William A. Kaplin, Barbara A. Lee, Neal H. Hutchens, & Jacob H. Rooksby, The Law of Higher Education: A Comprehensive Guide to Legal Implications of Administrative Decision Making (6th ed. 2019).

[89] Glenny & Schmidtlein, *supra* note 85, at 134.

case for public college and university boards. Private institutions also typically possess greater legal control over matters related to their internal academic and management operations. A private school would not be subjected to the same kinds of purchasing and open records rules, for instance, which often apply to public colleges and universities. Another important distinction, addressed in more depth in Chapter 3, concerns the fact that a private college or university would not be treated as a state (governmental) actor under the U.S. Constitution's Fourteenth Amendment, which limits the application of constitutional and statutory standards to the operations of private institutions. As a general matter, then, private institutions operate with more legal independence or autonomy in governance matters than their public counterparts.

In considering the private/public distinction, one should keep in mind that the division may blur at times. As previously mentioned, the legal relationship existing for several institutions in Pennsylvania illustrates how the private/public distinction is not always precise. Four institutions (The Pennsylvania State University, Temple University, the University of Pittsburgh, and Lincoln University) are designated as state-related institutions based on either the charters granted to the schools or through legislative enactment, indicating how these institutions contain both public and private features.[90] While factors such as economic or political forces may affect how institutions are actually treated by the state, the arrangement in Pennsylvania demonstrates that institutions may have both private and public aspects in terms of governance matters and in their legal relationship to state government.

Cornell University provides another example of an institution with both public and private components. The institution is primarily private, but it has four statutory colleges under its control that are supported in part with public funds.[91] For the public funds spent on these programs, the university is subject to certain oversight by the trustees of the State University of New York and other divisions of state government.[92] State courts have considered cases involving the applicability of state open records laws to operation of Cornell's statutory colleges. In one of the cases, *Stoll v. New York State College of Veterinary Medicine at Cornell University,* the court addressed a request for records by a professor who had sought copies of complaints against him after he had been disciplined for sexual harassment.[93] The court held that disciplinary matters at the four statutory colleges fell under the control of Cornell and were not subject to the state's open records law.[94] In contrast, in another case involv-

---

[90] Commonwealth of Pennsylvania State Board of Education, *Master Plan for Higher Education* 7 (2005), http://www.portal.state.pa.us/portal/server.pt/community/master_plan_for_higher_education/8855/master_plan_for_higher_education/529145.

[91] Alderson v. N.Y. State Coll. of Agric. and Life Sciences at Cornell Univ., 825 N.E.2d 585, 586 (N.Y. 2005).

[92] *Id.*

[93] Stoll v. N.Y. State Coll. of Veterinary Med. at Cornell Univ., 723 N.E.2d at 65, 66 (N.Y. 1999).

[94] *Id.* at 68-69.

ing an open records request, the opinion stated that certain records related to funding issues were subject to disclosure.[95]

Even for institutions that are clearly private in nature, states may impose legal standards with governance implications. States, for example, often require schools or particular institutional academic programs (e.g., a private university's law school) to receive accreditation from a state-approved agency as a condition of receiving state funds, or for graduates to be eligible for licensure required to practice particular professions.[96] As a threshold matter, a state must grant a private institution the permission to operate, often in the form of a certain type of licensure. State agencies may also exercise authority over program approval and the degrees that private institutions offer. Laws generally affecting private, not-for-profit organizations, such as health and safety laws or hiring practices, often apply as well to private colleges and universities. While generally possessing legal control over governance and management issues greater than public institutions, a private college or university and its governing board still must comply with numerous state legal standards.

Responsibilities and Fiduciary Duties of Governing Board Members

Alongside their legal authority over colleges and universities, members of a governing board, often designated as trustees or regents, also possess important legal obligations.[97] Members are said to exist in a fiduciary relationship with the institution or system they serve. This term refers to how board members are supposed to act in the best interests of the institution or system and should not seek to use status as a board member for personal gain. As noted, the typical responsibilities of board members include such activities as selecting institutional presidents, helping to shape major goals and initiatives related to mission fulfillment, approving tenure decisions, and providing oversight of finances and budgeting. Governing boards, however, do not generally engage in the control or management of the day-to-day operations of an institution or system. Boards delegate this authority to institutional or system leaders, namely the president or chancellor, depending on the term used.

A well-publicized scandal involving the University of Illinois reveals the damage that can happen to an institution when governing board members act for personal gain or seek an inappropriate advantage for others. Trustees of the university used their positions to help relatives and other individuals gain admission to the institution outside of the regular admissions process.[98] When this "'shadow'" admissions system became public, it was reported that all of

---

[95] *Alderson*, 825 N.E.2d at 589-90.

[96] Judith S. Eaton, *An Overview of U.S. Accreditation* 2-3 (2015), https://www.chea.org/sites/default/files/other-content/Overview%20of%20US%20Accreditation%202015.pdf.

[97] *See generally* Judith Areen, *Governing Board Accountability: Competition, Regulation, and Accreditation*, 36 J.C. & U.L. 691 (2010).

[98] *Id.* at 709-10.

the trustees—except the newest member who had only been serving a month—had sought to circumvent the normal admissions standards.[99] An investigative committee convened by the governor eventually called for the resignation of all board members.[100] The state and national fallout from the episode highlights the potentially negative consequences that may occur when governing board members fail to uphold their fiduciary responsibilities.

While the fiduciary duties of board members entail an important oversight role, governing boards delegate considerable authority over the carrying out of institutional functions. Besides institutional or system administrators such as the president or chancellor, the faculty often plays an important role in governance matters. A specific faculty position may be reserved for membership on a governing board. Often most significantly, the faculty at many institutions is designated as having primary responsibility over curricular matters and other academic decisions, with the term *shared governance* used to describe this substantial role for faculty participation in governance issues.[101]

Additionally, governing boards may permit varying degrees of participation by staff and students in governance matters. A student position, for example, is commonly designated as part of a board's membership, though student members may not possess voting privileges. Student government associations may also exercise certain kinds of authority and advisory responsibilities, such as distribution of mandatory student fees to various groups on campus. Staff senates also often serve in an advisory capacity to institutional leadership, and governing boards may also include a staff representative. Thus, responsibility for governance may be delegated to and diffused among various constituencies and stakeholders on campus. However, student and employee membership on governing boards is not always the case. For public institutions, statutes or constitutional provisions typically define the makeup of governing boards. No matter its ultimate composition, a governing board serves as the dominant point of legal control, and, in general, bears final legal discretion over institutional or system policies and practices.

Federal Legal Standards and Governance Considerations

Much of this chapter has focused on the dominant role that the states play in relation to higher education, reflective of historic patterns of state control over educational matters. Commentators often point to the Tenth Amendment to the Federal Constitution as assigning the states control over education, as it reserves all powers not explicitly delegated to the federal government by the Constitution for the states or the people. Against this backdrop of historic state dominance over higher education, however, the federal government's

---

[99] *Id.*
[100] *Id.*
[101] *Id.* at 698-704.

"influence on American colleges and universities has been enduring and pervasive."[102] Both public and private institutions must adhere to numerous federal laws in areas that include financial aid, hiring and employment practices, nondiscrimination standards, student privacy, and guidelines related to research.[103] Federal legal standards have come to exert substantial influence, directly and indirectly, over higher education. Taking into account this increasing federal role in higher education matters helps provide a fuller understanding of how legal standards may impact matters related to governance.

Governing boards at both public and private institutions must comply with multiple federal statutory and constitutional mandates. A noteworthy example of historic importance involves the desegregation of public education. In fact, much of the precedent leading to the *Brown v. Board of Education*[104] decision was built on cases involving public higher education institutions.[105] Constitutional standards create boundaries on governance authorities in other areas, especially for public institutions. As developed more in Chapter 12, a public college or university, for instance, must adhere to due process requirements in the disciplining of students and must follow First Amendment standards related to speech and religious rights in dealing with students and employees.

At the same time, the Supreme Court has interpreted constitutional requirements to recognize the importance of showing substantial deference to colleges and universities, especially in relation to matters involving academic decisions. Illustrative of this deference, in *Regents of University of Michigan v. Ewing*,[106] the Supreme Court considered a case involving the dismissal of a student, Ewing, from an academic program that would have resulted in his receiving an undergraduate and a medical degree.[107] Challenging the dismissal in federal court, the student, among his claims, argued that he possessed a property right related to continued enrollment in the program that was protected by the Due Process Clause of the Fourteenth Amendment.[108]

The trial court dismissed the case, but the Court of Appeals reversed, holding that the university had acted arbitrarily in the student's dismissal.[109] In reviewing the case, the U.S. Supreme Court accepted the assumption that the student could challenge an academic decision under the Due Process Clause of the Fourteenth Amendment.[110] However, according to the opinion,

---

[102] Lawrence E. Gladieux, Jacqueline E. King, & Melanie E. Corrigan, *The Federal Government and Higher Education, in* AMERICAN HIGHER EDUCATION IN THE TWENTY-FIRST CENTURY: SOCIAL, POLITICAL, AND ECONOMIC CHALLENGES 163 (Philp G. Altbach, Robert O. Berdahl, & Patricia J. Gumport eds., 2d ed. 2005).

[103] *Id.*

[104] 347 U.S. 483 (1954).

[105] See Leland Ware, *The Story of Brown v. Board of Education: The Long Road to Racial Equality, in* EDUCATION LAW STORIES 21-36 (Michael A. Olivas & Ronna Greff Schneider eds., 2008).

[106] 474 U.S. 214 (1985).

[107] *Id.* at 216.

[108] *Id.*

[109] *Id.* at 220-21.

[110] *Id.* at 223.

"[c]onsiderations of profound importance counsel restrained review of the substance of academic decisions."[111] The Court also discussed a reluctance to interfere with state and local control over educational matters and noted the "responsibility" to "safeguard" the academic freedom of institutions. Looking to a previous decision, *University of Missouri v. Horowitz*,[112] which also dealt with the dismissal of a student from a medical degree program, the Court held in favor of the university and reaffirmed the proposition that federal courts should not seek to interfere with good-faith academic decisions by colleges and universities.

Besides constitutional standards, colleges and universities must comply with numerous statutory requirements enacted pursuant to valid exercises of congressional power, such as the authority to regulate matters that affect interstate commerce and the national economy. Thus, colleges and universities, both public and private, must follow laws in such areas as nondiscrimination practices in hiring. While such federal laws do not directly usurp governance authority over higher education from the states, or from institutions or systems, governing boards bear a responsibility to ensure that institutional policies and practices conform to applicable legal requirements imposed by the federal government.

Rather than directly exercising its authority by expressly requiring colleges and universities, both public and private, to abide by certain conditions, the federal government predominately leverages institutional compliance by placing conditions on the receipt of federal funds. Accordingly, spending conditions entice states and institutions to follow federal directives pertaining to higher education. To provide one of the most notable examples, institutions obey various federal standards and maintain institutional accreditation[113] so that students are able to participate in federal financial aid programs.[114] One of the most important functions of accreditation involves eligibility for an institution's students to receive federal loans and grants to pay for their education. As another example, the Family Educational Rights and Privacy Act (FERPA)[115] places conditions on how colleges and universities use and protect student data, with receipt of federal funds used to ensure compliance. The allure of federal money has meant that colleges and universities, both public and private, have agreed to follow numerous federal standards.

The states continue to exert primary control over higher education institutions, but the federal role has become increasingly significant. Some legal requirements are imposed directly on colleges and universities while others are "voluntary" conditions accepted so that institutions or their students may be eligible to receive federal aid. Whether resulting from required or voluntary

---

[111] *Id.* at 226.

[112] 435 U.S. 78 (1978).

[113] See generally Judith Areen, *Accreditation Reconsidered*, 96 Iowa L. Rev. 1471 (2011).

[114] Eaton, *supra* note 96, at 3; Gladieux, King, & Corrigan, *supra* note 102, at 164.

[115] 20 U.S.C. § 1232g (2006).

legal standards, governing boards oversee institutions and systems that must conform to multiple and increasing federal legal requirements.

Conclusion

Consideration of legal aspects of higher education governance defies simple characterizations. Contemporary legal issues related to governance reflect deeply established patterns and practices, with the continuing role of lay governing boards being a principal example. The lack of centralized control over educational matters has resulted in notable variations in how states regulate higher education. With public institutions, some states operate with strong, centralized statewide governing boards, while others provide legally protected autonomy to select universities. Given the diversity of governance arrangements found in American higher education, even seemingly straightforward terms such as public and private may blur at times, depending on institutional and state context. Alongside state standards, the national government exercises an increasingly important role in higher education.

Higher education governance, from a legal perspective, requires recognition of the important variations that exist across colleges and universities, including their board structures and state contexts. In practice, governance depends on the same sets of actors (e.g., governments, boards) who periodically look to the courts to settle disagreements about which party holds the legal authority to determine how a college or university should operate. Rather than a static topic, the issue of higher education governance changes and evolves. At times, courts and legislatures have been more apt to defer to the autonomy of institutions. At other points, such as is often the case as we approach the third decade of the twenty-first century, legislatures and courts are often less likely to prioritize autonomy for colleges and universities, and, instead, place a greater emphasis on accountability and oversight.

3 Private and Religious Schools

Charles J. Russo, J.D., Ph.D.
University of Dayton

Introduction

During the seventeenth and early eighteenth centuries, some of the most prestigious colleges and universities in the United States were founded as religious institutions to prepare future ministers.[1] Throughout the nineteenth century, though, three phenomena occurred impacting the nature of these institutions. First, many of the religious schools departed from their religious roots and became secular.[2] Second, many private colleges and universities were opened without religious affiliations, often through the efforts of wealthy individuals who wished to demonstrate their social consciences through philanthropic activities.[3] Third, states created their own colleges and universities,[4] generally intended to meet vocational and agricultural needs not addressed in

---

This chapter consolidates and updates *Chapters 3, Private Colleges and Universities and 4, Religious Colleges and Universities*, authored by Ralph D. Mawdsley in previous editions of CONTEMPORARY ISSUES IN HIGHER EDUCATION.

[1] *See* JOHN S. BRUBACHER & WILLIS RUDY, HIGHER EDUCATION IN TRANSITION: A HISTORY OF AMERICAN COLLEGES AND UNIVERSITIES 10 (4th ed. 1997) (noting all pre-Revolutionary War colleges, except the College of Philadelphia, intended to educate students for the Christian ministry).

[2] For example, Antioch College opened in 1852 under the auspices of the Christian Church with Horace Mann as its first president, but was reorganized as an independent nonsectarian college. *See* www.antioch-college.edu/aboutantioch.html

[3] *See generally*, FREDERICK RUDOLPH, THE AMERICAN COLLEGE AND UNIVERSITY 244-247 (1962). Among the prominent colleges and universities founded with post-Civil War industrial money were Cornell, Vassar, MIT, Johns Hopkins, and Lehigh. Industrialist Andrew Carnegie founded Carnegie Mellon University in 1900 as a vocational training school for the sons and daughters of working-class Pittsburgh residents. Oberlin College was founded in 1833 with evangelical religious roots but became independent and was the first institution in the United States to grant baccalaureate degrees to women. By 1900, one-third of all African Americans who graduated from predominantly white colleges were from Oberlin, www.oberlin.edu/coladm.

[4] Thomas Jefferson founded the first public American university, the University of Virginia, in 1818. It included professorships in ancient and modern languages, mathematics, natural philosophy, anatomy and medicine, moral philosophy, and law, but not theology.

private institutions.[5] The creation of public colleges and universities received a significant boost when Congress enacted the Morrill Act, the first organized federal allocation of aid to public higher education.[6]

Private colleges and universities can be delineated as sectarian, religious, faith-based, or nonpublic—terms used interchangeably in this chapter—and nonsectarian, or private. Against this background, the purpose of this chapter is to review key legal issues relating to the operations of private and religious colleges and universities. Many of the statutes, regulations, and cases discussed in this chapter apply to both private and faith-based institutions; further, the chapter highlights issues with particular significance for religious colleges and universities.

In examining legal issues in private and faith-based colleges and universities, this chapter is divided into five main sections. The chapter opens with a discussion of the state-action doctrine before turning, in the second section, to the organization and management of private and faith-based colleges and universities. The third part, addressing colleges and universities doing business in other states, is subdivided into sections on distance learning, ownership of course materials, and regulatory issues concerning out-of-state institutions.

The fourth section, on faculty rights, begins with an overview before examining faculty conduct and published contract language, compliance with contract language, and good faith and fairness in contract enforcement, Title VII generally, and Title VII issues unique to faith-based institutions. The fifth part starts by reviewing student rights generally before examining student conduct and published contract language, compliance with contract language, and good faith and fairness in contract enforcement. The chapter ends with a brief conclusion

State-Action Doctrine

Private and faith-based colleges and universities are not subject to federal constitutional provisions unless it can be proven that their officials engaged

---

[5] Rensselaer Polytechnic, founded in 1824, as the first degree-granting technological university in the English-speaking world, offered classes in the applied sciences of husbandry, mechanics, and domestic science, www.Rensselaer.edu/About/Welcome/ history.html.

[6] The Morrill Act, enacted by Congress in 1862, 7 U.S.C.A. §§ 301 *et seq.*, donated land to states to create institutions of higher education based on their numbers of senators and representatives; the Act was amended in 1890, 7 U.S.C.A. §§ 321 *et seq.* to disallow payments of federal funds to states prohibiting admission of African Americans to state-funded institutions

in state action.[7] Because the Fourteenth Amendment is a limitation on states,[8] the guarantees in the Constitution extend only where state government can be viewed as having acted. Similarly, injured plaintiffs cannot use Section 1983 of the Civil Rights Act of 1871 to seek redress for alleged constitutional or statutory wrongs without satisfying the same state-action concept.[9]

Proving that officials in private or religious colleges or universities engaged in state action, thereby exposing themselves to liability for violations of constitutionally protected rights, is difficult.[10] Plaintiffs have alleged a variety of state-institutional contacts in order to meet the threshold test for state action, but courts have largely rejected claims premised on schools' receipt of funds,[11] establishing state-mandated policies,[12] and/or submission to state inspections[13] as insufficient to qualify as state action.

The leading case on state action is *Rendell-Baker v. Kohn (Rendall-Baker)*,[14] where the Supreme Court rejected alleged constitutional violations of the First, Fifth, and Fourteenth Amendments filed after four school counselors were discharged by their private, nonprofit school that relied on public funds to operate. The Court held that dismissals had no connection to the school's

---

[7] Almost needless to say, state officials have the right to regulate private and religious institutions within their jurisdictions. *See, e.g.*, Illinois Bible Colls. Ass'n v. Anderson, 870 F.3d 631 [347 Educ. L. Rep. 121] (7th Cir. 2017) (affirming that laws requiring private junior colleges and universities offering degrees to obtain certificates of approval did not violate the Establishment or Free Exercise Clauses because states have valid secular interests in maintaining standards for post-secondary institutions). In Pierce v. Society of the Sisters of the Holy Names of Jesus and Mary, 268 U.S. 510, 534 (1925), a K-12 case affirming the right of nonpublic schools to exist, the Supreme Court ruled that state officials could "reasonably [ ] regulate all schools, to inspect, supervise, and examine them, their teachers and pupils." States have followed this in regulating faith-based and private colleges and universities.

[8] Pursuant to Section 1 of the Fourteenth Amendment "[n]o State shall make or enforce any law which shall . . . deprive a person of life, liberty, or property without due process of law...."

[9] 42 U.S.C.A. § 1983 provides in part: "[e]very person who, under color of any statute, ordinance, regulation, custom or usage, of any State . . . subjects, or causes to be subjected, any citizen of the United States or other person within the jurisdiction thereof to the deprivation of any rights, privileges or immunities secured by the Constitution and laws, shall be liable to the party injured . . . ."

[10] For a relevant commentary, see Ralph D. Mawdsley, *State Action and Private Educational Institutions*, 117 EDUC. L. REP. 411 (1997).

[11] *See, e.g.*, Imperiale v. Hahnman Univ., 996 F. Supp.2d 125 [75 Educ. L. Rep. 1024] (3d Cir 1992) (affirming that a state-aided but not state-funded hospital was not a state actor operating under color of law, thereby rejecting the plaintiff's claim over the revocation of his degree).

[12] *See, e.g.*, Logan v. Bennington Coll., 72 F.3d 1017 [106 Educ. L. Rep. 51] (2d Cir. 1995) (involving the adoption of a sexual harassment policy required by state law); Missert v. Trs. of Boston Univ., 73 F. Supp.2d 68 [140 Educ. L. Rep. 554] (D. Mass. 1999) (over the creation of a human subjects research board necessary for federally funded research).

[13] *See, e.g.*, Tavolini v. Mt. Sinai Med. Ctr., 984 F. Supp.196 [123 Educ. L. Rep. 195] (S.D.N.Y. 1997); Mogimzadeh v. Coll. of St. Rose, 653 N.Y.S.2d 198 [115 Educ. L. Rep. 1012] (N.Y. App. Div. 1997); Gardiner v. Mercyhurst Coll., 942 F. Supp. 1055 [114 Educ. L. Rep. 162] (W.D. Pa. 1996).

[14] 457 U.S. 830 (1982).

receipt of public funds. *Rendell-Baker* applies both to faculty and students, with the same outcome in most cases.

Twenty years after *Rendall-Baker*, the First Circuit reinforced the notion that state action remains an elusive concept in private education.[15] The case involved a public school board that, lacking its own high school, entered into a renewable ten-year contract with a private school, Maine Central Institute (MCI), to educate its ninth- through twelfth-grade students. When school officials extended the ten-day suspension of one of MCI's students to seventeen days awaiting a psychological evaluation, his parents filed a Section 1983 action claiming that the suspension in excess of ten days without a hearing violated state law and the student's Due Process Clause rights.

In its judgment, the First Circuit recognized the dilemma for students suspended or expelled from MCI because they would have no school to attend. Even so, the First Circuit decided that creating new exceptions to the state action theory is the responsibility of the Supreme Court. Although the court observed that the private school's affording due process rights might be included in MCI's registration contract, it nonetheless reasoned that that even if school officials did not follow the contract, the responsibility under the state's constitution ultimately would fall on the public school district to provide education for the student.[16]

Other cases have reached the same results. For instance, students at a private college failed in alleging that officials violated their First Amendment right to form a student government. Dismissing the claim, the federal trial court in the District of Columbia determined that the students were unable to prove that college officials engaged in state action.[17]

Organization and Management of Private and Faith-Based Colleges and Universities

Faith-based and private colleges and universities receive their authority to operate from state statutes. All states have nonprofit incorporation laws covering colleges and universities, as well as other organizations. Although sectarian and nonsectarian colleges and universities may be immune from constitutional liability due to the absence of state action, they are not immune from state statutory requirements.

Like any corporation, nonprofits generally fall within the authority of secretaries of state who are responsible for such organizations within their jurisdictions. The authority of secretaries of state to act is set forth in state statutes

---

[15] Logiodice v. Trustees of Me. Cent. Instit., 296 F.3d 22 [167 Educ. L. Rep. 85] (1st Cir. 2002). For an earlier case reaching the same result in higher education, see Blackburn v. Fisk Univ., 443 F.2d 121 (6th Cir. 1971) (rejecting claims that students were expelled without receiving procedural due process). *See also* Powe v. Miles, 407 F.2d 73 (2d Cir. 1968).

[16] *See also* St. Johnsbury Acad. v. D.H., 240 F. 2d 163 (2d Cir. 2001) (suggesting that aggrieved parties have at best breach of contract actions, but not constitutional claims).

[17] Jackson v. Strayer Coll., 941 F. Supp. 192 [113 Educ. L. Rep. 1191] (D.D.C. 1996).

and requires colleges and universities organized in the state to file articles of incorporation,[18] usually with the stipulation that corporations are perpetual.[19] Some states laws are directed at educational nonprofit organizations,[20] giving their directors or trustees broad grants of authority to operate their institutions.[21]

State statutes regulate much of the manner in which religious and private colleges and universities are organized, but these requirements can be altered by the articles of incorporation. Among the areas covered by state statutes are voting rights of members,[22] elections of directors,[23] maximum term of office of directors or trustees,[24] and notice requirements for meetings.[25] Property of private institutions is tax-exempt when used for an educational purpose,[26] and specified functions of the colleges and universities may be exempt from state taxes.[27]

Along with their responsibilities to their institutions regarding board meetings, board members have fiduciary duties in their financial dealings with their institutions. Members who engage in business transactions with their own colleges or universities run the risk that their dealings may be voidable in a lawsuit by a corporation member or beneficiary.

In an illustrative case, the Supreme Court of South Carolina, setting aside as improper a board member's dealings with the organization he served because he purchased property from it, scrutinized his participation at the board meeting where his transaction was considered, the profit he made, the loss to the institution, the relationship of his transaction to fair market price, and his adherence to the organization's constitutional notice requirements. Even absent evidence of actual fraud, the court set the transaction aside, noting that the board member's conduct failed "to measure up to the high standard required by the law of one in his fiduciary relationship." [28]

Board members of private and religious colleges and universities also owe a fiduciary duty in all their actions as board members, although identifying the

---

[18] *See* 110 ILL. COMP. STAT. §§ 30/1-30/3 (stating that the issuance and filing of articles of incorporation deems educational institutions fully organized).

[19] *See* OHIO REV. CODE §§ 1702-59, 1702.60 (requiring non-profit corporations to file verified statements of continued existence).

[20] *See* 110 ILL. COMP. STAT. § 30/1.

[21] *See* TEX. EDUC. CODE § 1302-3.02.

[22] *See* OHIO REV. CODE § 1702.20 (entitling all members to vote subject to articles of incorporation).

[23] *See* OHIO REV. CODE § 1702.26 (specifying that unless changed by articles of incorporation, only nominated persons can be elected; also prohibiting voting by proxy).

[24] *See* ILL. COMP. STAT. 110 § 30/5 (setting the maximum term at three years).

[25] *See* OHIO REV. CODE § 1710.05 (requiring articles of incorporation to provide for meetings).

[26] *See* OHIO REV. CODE § 5709.121(A)(2).

[27] *See* OHIO REV. CODE § 5739.02(B)(3) (defining sales tax - sales of food sold to students only in a cafeteria, dormitory, fraternity, or sorority maintained in a private . . . college or university); TEX. TAX CODE § 171.061 (franchise tax); FLA. STAT. ANN. § 199.183 (applying tax exemptions to "non-profit private . . . colleges or universities conducting regular classes and courses of study required for accreditation by, or membership in, the Southern Association of Colleges and Schools, Department of Education, or the Florida Council of Independent Schools").

[28] Gilbert v. McLeod Infirmary, 64 S.E.2d 524, 531 (S.C. 1951).

person or persons to whom that duty is owed is not always easy. The Supreme Court of New Hampshire addressed whether the board owed a fiduciary duty to the college's alumni association. Three years after completing a $568 million fundraising campaign directed toward alumni, the college's board chose to eliminate all single-sex fraternities and sororities. The plaintiff-alumni alleged that the board's failure to announce this change at the start of the fundraising campaign was a breach of fiduciary duty to the alumni. The court refused to find a fiduciary duty owed to the alumni association because there was no evidence that "the alumni stood in such a submissive, inferior or dependent position with respect to the college in the capital campaign so as to support the existence of a fiduciary relationship."[29]

Acceptance of funds for specific purposes carries special responsibilities for a private college when governing officials later decide to make changes in the way the funds are utilized. For example, in 1930 the trustees of a charitable trust bearing the donor's name voted to donate funds for a quadrangle that would bear the name of the trust fund's donor. However, in 1996, university officials approved changes on the campus that included demolishing large parts of the quadrangle. Dismissing the suit by an heir of the settlor of the charitable trust, an appellate court in Connecticut indicated that the donor had neither placed restrictions on the grant nor reservations with regard to how university property constructed by trust funds would be used. [30]

The court in Connecticut also pointed out that the state attorney general had the primary, although not exclusive,[31] duty to sue to preserve the assets of charitable trusts.[32] Absent a state statute permitting a university board member to sue the rest of the board for acting *ultra vires*,[33] or a special interest by a person in the administration of the university, claims against boards for their financial decisions are left to attorneys general.[34]

Many of the day-to-day operating decisions of private and faith-based schools are made by administrative employees without the direct knowledge of board members. Even so, institutions may face liability as a result of these actions. Whether institutions are vicariously liable for the actions of their employees depends on the scope of the employees' responsibilities and the supervisory duty of higher officials. If those in leadership positions have cloaked employees with apparent authority to act, they may learn that persons relying

---

[29] Brizica v. Trs. of Dartmouth Coll., 791 A.2d 990, 995 [162 Educ. L. Rep. 853] (N.H. 2002).

[30] Russell v. Yale Univ., 737 A.2d 941 [138 Educ. L. Rep. 1999] (Conn. App. Ct. 1999).

[31] *See, e.g.,* Holt v. College of Osteopathic Physicians and Surgeons, 394 P.2d 932 (Cal. 1964) (allowing minority trustees of a charitable corporation to enjoin the improper use of corporate assets because of their fiduciary duty).

[32] *See* A. Scott, Trusts § 348.1 (4th ed. 1989).

[33] CONN. GEN. STAT. § 33-1038 (allowing a member or director to challenge a board action).

[34] *See, e.g.,* Steeneck v. Univ. of Bridgeport, 668 A.2d 688 [106 Educ. L. Rep. 203] (Conn. 1995) (affirming that life trustee lacked authority under state law to sue the board for the agreement in entered with a religious entity whereby it took over 60% of the board).

on such authority have triable claim against the institutions.[35] Similar to the manner in which board members may face liability for breach of a fiduciary duty to participate in board meetings, supervisory officials may be liable for failure to instruct or supervise adequately.

Colleges and Universities Doing Business in Other States

In light of the rapid growth of online or distance learning, many religious and private colleges and universities have expanded their offerings for enrolling students off campus without expending funds to build additional facilities. The earliest method was by mail, permitting students to take correspondence courses without attending classes at the campus,[36] but the results met with fragmented success because of student detachment from the instructor-student relationship.[37] A subsequent alternative to correspondence was learning centers located at strategic locations, often in other states, where students could gather for classes and have access to nearby libraries.

More recently, colleges and universities have turned to videos and web-based courses offering visual and real-time contact with instructors. Students who participate in such distance learning instruction may discover that courts in their states have only limited personal jurisdiction over the out-of-state institutions.[38]

Distance Learning

In contrast to correspondence courses involving relatively little preparation expense for institutions, production of videos and online web-based

---

[35] *See, e.g.*, Forum Financial Group v. President and Fellows of Harvard Coll., 173 F. Supp.2d 72 [159 Educ. L. Rep. 576] (D. Me. 2001) (denying the college's motions to dismiss as to whether an employee who made decisions about financial transactions with Russia was its responsibility).

[36] Under the Higher Education Act of 1965's regulations, 34 C.F.R. § 600.2 (2019), a correspondence course is

(1) A course provided by an institution under which the institution provides instructional materials, by mail or electronic transmission, including examinations on the materials, to students who are separated from the instructor. Interaction between the instructor and student is limited, is not regular and substantive, and is primarily initiated by the student. Correspondence courses are typically self-paced.

(2) If a course is part correspondence and part residential training, the Secretary considers the course to be a correspondence course.

(3) A correspondence course is not distance education.

[37] For a case on a related issue, see Bradford v. George Washington Univ., 249 F. Supp.3d 325 [347 Educ. L. Rep. 362] (D.C. 2017) (rejecting student claims for inadequate instruction in an online program as time-barred because the plaintiffs waited four years to file suit).

[38] *See, e.g.*, Khalil v. Chatham Coll., 391 F. Supp.2d 588 [203 Educ. L. Rep. 675] (S.D. Tex. 2005) (refusing to treat a university's passive website as sufficient contact with Texas as required for state courts to have jurisdiction over the school; adding that contacts between the applicant and university did not support exercise of specific personal jurisdiction over the latter).

courses require investments in technology, not only for institutions but also for students. Inhibiting the extensive use of various technological distance-learning academic courses and programs have been two federal requirements regarding financial aid. Regulations of the Higher Education Act[39] forbid the institutions of higher education offering more than fifty percent of their courses through correspondence or enroll more than fifty percent of their students in correspondence courses from offering student financial aid.[40]

Effective May 26, 2019, the Department of Education amended its regulations to distinguish "distance learning" classes from correspondence courses for purposes of eligibility for financial aid. The regulation now defines "distance learning" as education that uses one or more of the technologies listed in paragraphs (1) through (4) of this definition to deliver instruction to students who are separated from the instructor and to support regular and substantive interaction between the students and the instructor, either synchronously or asynchronously. The technologies may include—

(1) The internet;

(2) One-way and two-way transmissions through open broadcast, closed circuit, cable, microwave, broadband lines, fiber optics, satellite, or wireless communications devices;

(3) Audio conferencing; or

(4) Video cassettes, DVDs, and CD–ROMs, if the cassettes, DVDs, or CD–ROMs are used in a course in conjunction with any of the technologies listed in paragraphs (1) through (3) of this definition."[41]

Ownership of Course Materials

An attendant problem in the development of online courses is the ownership of class materials. Issues arise around the federal copyright law's "work-for-hire" doctrine that gives employers ownership of the works their employees create when something is "a work prepared by an employee within the scope of his or her employment [or] a work specially ordered or commissioned ... if the parties expressly agree in a written instrument signed by them that the work shall be considered a work made for hire."[42] Although not all agree,[43] an argument can be made that the original materials prepared by college and university faculty for online courses are "works for hire;" if this were the case,

---

[39] 20 U.S.C.A. §§ 1001 *et seq.*

[40] 34 C.F.R. § 600.7(a)(1)(i-ii) and (b) (2000). *See also* 20 U.S.C.A. § 1091(k)-(l)(1)(A)(2000). Subsection k provides: "Special rule for correspondence courses. A student shall not be eligible to receive grant, loan, or work assistance under this ... title for a correspondence course unless such course is part of a program leading to an associate, bachelor or graduate degree." According to subsection (l), a student will not be considered enrolled in correspondence "unless the total amount of telecommunications and correspondence courses at such institution equals or exceeds 50 percent of the total amount of all courses at the institution."

[41] 34 C.F.R. § 600.2.

[42] 17 U.S.C.A. § 101.

[43] *See* Rochelle Cooper Dreyfuss, *The Creative Employee and the Copyright Act of 1976*, 54 U. Chi. L. Rev. 590 (1987).

then their contents are the property of their employers, regardless of whether these classes prepared for for-profit or non-profit institutions.[44]

The Supreme Court devised guidelines for what fits within the scope of employment.[45] However, lower courts are slow in considering whether faculty course materials belong to institutions. In one case, the federal trial court in Colorado ruled that an online course at a teaching college belonged to the institution as a work for hire.[46] Yet, no court has addressed the stratus of online materials. A pre-1976 Copyright Act[47] exemption from having professors' materials treated as works for hire[48] has not yet been extended to later situations.

Ownership of course materials for online courses has become an important issue because such classes now have commercial value. While traditionally delivered classroom lectures always had intrinsic value in terms of their content, their commercial value was limited. Now that courses can be preserved and marketed for later presentations via a variety of technological means, the content of class lectures may have considerable commercial value to their owners. Until Congress clarifies ownership of online materials, and absent settled law in the field, ownership of course materials is left to the language of contracts between faculty members and their institutions.

Regulatory Issues Concerning Out-of-State Institutions

Most states have statutes regulating foreign corporations, including higher education institutions doing business within their boundaries.[49] These statutes present a variety of legal issues under federal and state law. At the very core of litigation, plaintiffs must bring their complaints before a court that has personal or subject matter jurisdiction. In such a dispute, an appellate court in California dismissed a case for lack of jurisdiction because the contacts the institution in Virginia had with the in-state plaintiff from California were insufficient.[50]

In a case over a state statute regulating career schools,[51] the Ninth Circuit upheld the regulation of an out-of-state career center offering paralegal courses

---

[44] *See* Jacob H. Rooksby, *Copyright in Higher Education: A Review of Modern Scholarship*, 54 Duq. L. Rev. 197 (2016).

[45] *See* Community for Creative Non-Violence v. Reid, 490 U.S. 730 (1989) (asserting that insofar as a sculptor was an independent contractor when he created a sculpture for an association for homelessness, rather than an employee, it was a work for hire; the Court did identify criteria for distinguishing employees from independent contractors).

[46] Vanderhurst v. Colorado Mountain Coll. Dist.,16 F. Supp.2d 1297, 1307 [129 Educ. L. Rep. 1073] (D. Colo. 1998).

[47] 17 U.S.C.A. §§ 101 *et seq.*

[48] *See, e.g.*, Williams v. Weisser, 273 Cal. App. 2d 726 (Cal. Ct. App. 1969) (forbidding a faculty member from selling notes taken from his oral in-class lectures under a common law privacy theory involving usage).

[49] *See, e.g.*, Ohio Rev. Code § 1703.27; Ill. Comp. Code 805 § 5/13.10.

[50] Roman v. Liberty Univ., 75 Cal. Rptr. 3d 828 [231 Educ. L. Rep. 416] (Cal. Ct. App. 2008).

[51] Center for Legal Studies v. Lindley, 1 F. App'x 662 [153 Educ. L. Rep. 495] (9th Cir. 2001).

in Oregon.[52] The court explained that the statute was facially nondiscriminatory in response to the claim that it violated the Interstate Commerce Clause.[53]
Absent evidence that Oregon failed to enforce its regulations against state
schools, the court was of the opinion that the statute effected a valid state interest in exerting state "authority over schools which confer only non-degree
certificates" in order to ensure that the certificate will not "mislead the student
or the public to think it is a degree."[54]

State efforts to regulate out-of-state higher education institutions can
encounter First Amendment objections. Two cases involving the same private
university in Florida illustrate the issues. In the first, institutional officials challenged a statute from the District of Columbia requiring private educational
institutions seeking to operate in the district first obtain licensure from the
Educational Institution Licensure Commission (commission).[55] The statute
at issue requires that degree-conferring institutions incorporated outside of
the District obtain licenses to operate in the District without regard to where
degrees are conferred.[56]

The university, which offers its programs at cluster sites with twenty to
twenty-five students, uses a combination of its own full-time faculty from
Florida and part-time faculty from other traditional higher education institutions to teach its courses. When the university applied to the commission to
offer course sequences in the District for its Doctor of Public Administration
degree, the commission denied the license on the grounds that the university
had not complied with District of Columbia regulations "with respect to adequate full-time faculty and adequate library resources."[57]

Rejecting the university's claim that the statute interfered with freedom
of speech, the District of Columbia Court of Appeals maintained that the
District regulated the operation of out-of-District institutions the same as it
did in-District colleges and universities. The court added that being engaged
in First Amendment activities of teaching does not immunize institutions
from regulation: "[s]chools are not shielded from governmental regulation of
business conduct deemed detrimental to the public merely because they are
engaged in First Amendment activities."[58] Although educational institutions

---

[52] Oregon has a separate statute regulating career schools, Or. Rev. Stat. § 345.030. The state
created an Office of Degree Authorization whose authority to regulate degree and certificate
granting programs is detailed at Or. Rev. Stat. § 348.603.

[53] According to Article I, section 8, clause 3, Congress shall have the power "[t]o regulate
Commerce . . . among the several States."

[54] *Center for Legal Studies,* 1 F. App'x at 663, quoting Or. Admin. Reg. 583-020-0021.

[55] Nova Univ. v. Educational Inst. Licensure Comm'n, 483 A.2d 1172 [21 Educ. L. Rep. 558]
(D.C. Cir. 1984).

[56] D.C. Code § 29-815, recodified as § 29-615. In addition to mandating proof that the members
of the governing board are persons "of good repute," the statute requires that "the faculty is
of reasonable number and properly qualified, and that the institution is possessed of suitable
classroom, laboratory, and library." *Id.* at 29-615(a)(4).

[57] *Nova,* 483 A.2d at 1176.

[58] *Id.* at 1181 (emphasis in original).

"have a First Amendment right to teach and to academic freedom,"[59] the court did not think that a statute that "ensure[s] that degree-conferring educational institutions incorporated or operating in the District [meet] minimal academic standards—*whatever* their message [is]"[60] infringed on this right.

As the first of the two cases involving the university from Florida suggests, the principle is well-established that the First Amendment does not prohibit states from protecting the interests of their constituents regarding the operation of educational institutions. Clearly, states have the power to regulate degree conferral by their own institutions.[61] While the District of Columbia has no authority to affect the university's granting of degrees in Florida, it may choose "to impose the same regulations on Nova as it imposes upon its own degree-conferring schools."[62]

At the same time, the power to regulate out-of-state colleges and universities must be consistent with state law. In a second case involving the university from Florida, the Supreme Court of North Carolina struck down a state effort to deny the Board of Governors of the state university to issue a license to the institution from Florida.[63] The court refused to apply a state statute vesting the board of governors with authority to license degree conferred by in-state colleges and universities to the school from Florida's teaching its clusters in the state. The court indicated that the power to license the conferring of degrees by state institutions did not extend to the control of teaching leading to the conferral of degrees. Although an intermediate appellate court treated state regulation as an abridgement of teaching and an infringement on protected free speech, the state's highest court limited its order to statutory construction.

State regulatory efforts involving colleges and universities can affect other areas common to both in-state and out-of-state institutions. In the second case from Florida, an appellate court posited that the state board exceeded its authority in forbidding a consulting firm from using the term "college."[64] Where state statute restricted the use of "college" or "university" to accredited degree-granting institutions, the court held that the statute was inapplicable to the firm because, as a management consulting firm offering seminars, it did not offer academic degrees or academic credit.[65]

---

[59] *Id.* at 1182.

[60] *Id.* at 1183 (emphasis in original).

[61] *See, e.g.*, N.J. State Bd. of Higher Educ. v. Bd. of Dirs. of Shelton Coll., 448 A.2d 988 [5 Educ. L. Rep. 1170] (N.J. 1982) (upholding the state's authority to deny an in-state college the right to confer degrees).

[62] *Nova*, 283 A.2d at 1181.

[63] Nova Univ. v. Bd. of Governors of Univ. of N.C., 287 S.E.2d 872 [2 Educ. L. Rep. 872] (N.C. 1982).

[64] Philip Crosby Assocs. v. State Bd. of Indep. Colls., 506 So. 2d 490 [40 Educ. L. Rep.563] (Fla. Dist. Ct. App. 1987).

[65] Since *Philip Crosby*, the Florida legislature amended the law to provide that "[a]n entity shall not use the term "college" or "university" in its name in-state without board approval, unless the board determines that its name is clearly and accurately descriptive of the services provided by the entity and is not one that may mislead the public." FLA. STAT. ANN. § 246.121(4).

Faculty Rights

Generally

Faculty rights in private and faith-based institutions depend almost solely on statutory and contractual authority. Absent state action, faculty in private institutions ordinarily lack constitutional rights associated with their employment. As discussed earlier,[66] the law is well-established that religious and private institutions can have numerous contacts with state governments without subjecting themselves to constitutional liability under the state-action theory. Consequently, there is no state action because a private or religious institution receives funding from the state,[67] is granted a state charter,[68] is tax-exempt,[69] engages in delivering education that is considered a state function,[70] establishes policies required by government,[71] is subject to state inspection and regulation,[72] or includes public officials on the governing board.[73]

Of course, leadership in faith-based and private institutions can choose to confer the same rights on their faculties that their colleagues have in public institutions under the federal Constitution. Although such a situation seems highly improbable, it can occur. For example, an appellate court in California reviewed a faculty member's dismissal using free speech analysis under *Pickering v. Board of Education*[74] and *Mt. Healthy City Board of Education v. Doyle*[75] because university officials gratuitously declared the result would have been the same whether the institution had been considered public or nonpublic.[76] Even absent concessions by university officials to due process in this case,

---

[66] *See supra* notes 7-17 and accompanying text.

[67] *See, e.g.*, Grafton v. Brooklyn Law Sch., 478 F.2d 1137 (2d Cir. 1973); Smith v. Duquesne Univ., 612 F. Supp. 72 [26 Educ. L. Rep. 604] (W.D. Pa. 1985); Murphy v. Villanova Univ., 547 F. Supp. 512 [6 Educ. L. Rep. 715] (E.D. Pa. 1982).

[68] *See, e.g.*, Blackburn v. Fisk Univ., 443 F.2d 121 (6th Cir. 1971).

[69] *See, e.g.*, Browns v. Mitchell, 409 F.2d 593 (10th Cir. 1969).

[70] *See, e.g.*, Berrios v. Inter-Am. Univ., 409 F. Supp. 769 (D.P.R. 1975); Grossner v. Columbia Univ., 287 F. Supp. 535 (S.D.N.Y. 1968).

[71] *See, e.g.*, Logan v. Bennington Coll., 72 F.3d 1017 [106 Educ. L. Rep. 51] (2d Cir. 1995) (establishing a sexual harassment policy required by state law); Missert v. Trs. of Boston Univ., 73 F. Supp.2d 68 [140 Educ. L. Rep. 554] (D. Mass. 1999) (creating human subjects research board required for federally funded research).

[72] *See, e.g.*, Tavolini v. Mt. Sinai Med. Ctr., 984 F .Supp. 196 [123 Educ. L. Rep. 195] (S.D.N.Y. 1997); Mogimzadeh v. Coll. of St. Rose, 653 N.Y.S.2d 198 [115 Educ. L. Rep. 1012] (N.Y. App. Div. 1997); Gardiner v. Mercyhurst Coll., 942 F. Supp. 1055 [114 Educ. L. Rep. 162] (W.D. Pa. 1996).

[73] *See, e.g.*, Hack v. President and Fellows of Yale Coll., 16 F. Supp.2d 183 [129 Educ. L. Rep. 1020] (D. Conn. 1998).

[74] 391 U.S. 563 (1968) (acknowledging that educators have a right to freedom of speech on matters of public concern).

[75] 429 U.S. 274 (1977) (conceding that even if an employee was disciplined for exercising a constitutional right, an employer can prevail if it show by a preponderance of the evidence "that it would have reached the same conclusion . . . even in the absence of the protected conduct.")

[76] Franklin v. Leland Stanford Junior Univ., 218 Cal.Rptr. 228 [27 Educ. L. Rep. 525] (Cal. Ct. App. 1985).

courts still expect faculty members in private and faith-based institutions to receive treatment demonstrating "color of due process."[77]

With limited situations where constitutional standards are relevant to private and religious colleges and universities, the rights and responsibilities of faculty are established by their contracts. To this end, courts scrutinize whether institutional officials complied with contractual language in fulfilling their obligations to faculty members. Religious colleges and universities, in particular, are immune from scrutiny under statutory[78] or constitutional[79] theories to the extent that faculty responsibilities involve religious functions. Conversely, because private nonsectarian institutions do not enjoy such immunity, they cannot seek to devise constitutional theories to prevent scrutiny of contractually provided academic decisions.

In a novel case from the District of Columbia,[80] institutional officials sought to block judicial review of a faculty promotion process, claiming that academic freedom,[81] a hybrid free speech right, protected it from such scrutiny. The court refused to provide this private university the measure of immunity it requested, citing its own precedent, for the principle that "we do not understand why university affairs are more deserving of judicial deference than the affairs of any other business or profession.... [E]ven if there are issues on which courts are ill equipped to rule, the interpretation of a contract is not one of them." [82]

In terms of contract issues, both sectarian and nonsectarian institutions are equally affected. Except where faculty contracts at religious institutions

---

[77] *See* Flint v. St. Augustine High Sch., 323 So. 2d 229, 235 (La. Ct. App. 1976) (although a student case, it states the well-founded principle that treatment of persons in nonpublic institutions must satisfy the minimum requirements of due process).

[78] *See, e.g.*, Hall v. Baptist Mem'l Health Care Corp., 215 F.3d 618 [145 Educ. L. Rep. 216] (6th Cir. 2000) (affirming that a faith-based affiliated college was entitled to religious exemption under Title VII when dismissing an employee who was ordained as a lay minister by a church with a large gay and lesbian membership).

[79] *See* Alicia v. New Brunswick Theological Seminary, 608 A.2d 218 [75 Educ. L. Rep. 834] (N.J. 1992) (affirming that because the tenured position the faculty member was denied involved ministerial functions, the First Amendment required judicial abstention). *But see* Welter v. Seton Hall Univ., 608 A.2d 206 [75 Educ. L. Rep. 822] (N.J. 1992) (assuming jurisdiction in the breach of contract claim filed by two nuns who did not teach religious classes or perform religious functions).

[80] Kyriakopoulos v. George Washington Univ., 866 F.2d 438 [51 Educ. L. Rep. 740] (D.C. Cir. 1989).

[81] Academic freedom eludes a clear definition. While the term involves faculty members' right to teach and conduct research pursuant to the AAUP's 1940 "Statement of Principles of Academic Freedom and Tenure," it also carries the idea of self-governance. See Piarowski v. Ill. Cmty. Coll. Dist. 515, 759 F.2d 625, 629 [24 Educ. L. Rep. 46] (7th Cir. 1985) (reflecting on the equivocal nature of academic freedom, observing that "[i]t is used to denote both the freedom of the academy to pursue its ends without interference from the government ... and the freedom of the individual teacher (or in some versions—indeed, in most cases—the student) to pursue his ends without interference from the academy; and these two freedoms are in conflict."

[82] McConnell v. Howard Univ., 818 F.2d 58, 69 [39 Educ. L. Rep. 502] (D.C. Cir. 1987) (declaring that a tenured faculty member who was dismissed after an ongoing, in-class dispute with a student was entitled to a trial pursuant to his handbook as to whether university officials followed its language).

involve religious functions or impose religious requirements,[83] faculty in all nonpublic higher education institutions are similarly situated.

Contract issues involving college and university faculty fall into three categories: whether allegedly improper faculty conduct is covered by published contract language; whether institutional officials complied with theirs own contractual requirements in dealing with faculty members; and whether the institutional interpretations or enforcements of contract terms exhibited good faith and fairness.

Faculty Conduct and Published Contract Language

Institutional officials can have a big impact on the lives of faculty and their work. Termination of a faculty member's employment is probably the most traumatizing for the employee and the most contentious for both the individual and institution. In any contract termination, a threshold question always concerns the nature of the employee's contract.

Faculty contract essentially fall into one of three categories: employment at will, fixed term, or continuing. Generally, absent contract language to the contrary, employment-at-will contracts can be terminated at any time by either the faculty member or the institution. Indeed, in some states, contracts for an indefinite period of time are considered to be employment at will.[84] Unless they state otherwise, employment-at-will contracts can usually be terminated without cause.[85] Employment-at-will contracts can even be withdrawn before prospective employees begin working.[86] Still, some states have modified the at-will doctrine to limit dismissal or discipline in situations involving public policy, implied contracts, and covenants of fair dealing.

Contracts for fixed terms expire at the end of the terms with no official action required; the terms of faculty contracts govern. The ultimate measure is whether a faculty member can entertain a successful breach of contract claim when a term contract is not renewed. Generally, nontenured, tenure track faculty are probationary employees who have contracts for fixed num-

---

[83] *See, e.g.,* Maguire v. Marquette Univ., 814 F.2d 1213 [38 Educ. L. Rep. 4333] (7th Cir. 1987) (affirming the dismissal of the claim of a female applicant whose theological views were antithetical to those of the Catholic Church because what is taught in the theology department which represents the core of Catholic beliefs in the university); McEnroy v. St. Meinrad Sch. of Theology, 713 N.E.2d 334 [136 Educ. L. Rep. 541] (Ind. Ct. App. 1999), *cert. denied,* 529 U.S. 1060 (2000) (affirming the denial of a claim where the court lacked jurisdiction to resolve an alleged breach of contract claim involving a statement of faculty opposing a position of the Pope where academic freedom at the seminary included religious doctrine and ecclesiastical law).

[84] *See* Roberts v. Wake Forest Univ., 286 S.E.2d 120 [2 Educ. L. Rep. 296] (N.C. Ct. App. 1982) (viewing an indefinite contract for a golf coach as employment-at-will under state law).

[85] *See* Tramontozzi v. St. Francis Coll., 649 N.Y.S.2d 43 [114 Educ. L. Rep. 252] (N.Y. App. Div. 1996) (treating an athletic director as an employee-at-will who could be dismissed without cause).

[86] *See, e.g.,* Heinritz v. Lawrence Univ., 535 N.W.2d 81 [101 Educ. L. Rep. 1120] (Wis. Ct. App. 1995) (affirming that a university could not be liable for the breach of at-will employment contract for withdrawing a job offer before the employee started working).

bers of years.[87] Apart from expectations of employment during the terms of probationary contracts, tenure track faculty members usually cannot expect employment beyond those terms.

In a case from Louisiana, an appellate court upheld the action of university officials who chose not to renew the contract of a tenure track faculty member after the fourth year of his probationary contract because he had not met the requirements set down by the faculty review committee.[88] Moreover, in dismissing a tenure track faculty member's action for negligent misrepresentation following nonrenewal of his contract after his first year, an appellate court in Oregon observed that university officials owed no duty "to further the economic interests of the employee in the negotiation of the employment contract."[89]

In a case from New York, a probationary faculty member with a contract stating it was for one year and nonrenewable lacked a cause of action for breach of contract even though he received notice of nonrenewal two days late, according to the faculty handbook.[90] However, faculty handbooks that create rights prior to termination of term contracts can present a triable issue for faculty members.[91]

Continuing contracts are generally associated with tenure, thereby creating property rights under the Fourteenth Amendment in public institutions, entitling faculty member to due process before their contracts can be terminated or modified.[92] Yet, because faculty members in private and religious institutions lack the protection of the Fourteenth Amendment due to the absence of state action, continuing contract rights are set by the terms of the contracts they entered into with their institutions.

Tenure track faculty, absent language to the contrary, whose contracts specify teaching and/or service can be reassigned to service responsibilities without violating the terms of their contract, as long as their agreed-to compensation is not changed.[93] While a continuing contract creates an expectation of employment from one year to the next, it does not assure that a faculty member's status cannot be changed for contractual violations. For instance,

---

[87] *See, e.g.*, Tuamala v. Regent Univ., 477 S.E.2d 501 [113 Educ. L. Rep. 1337] (Va. 1996) (affirming that all faculty members had fixed term, renewable five-year contracts).

[88] Stanton v. Tulane Univ., 777 So. 2d 1242 [151 Educ. L. Rep. 714] (La. Ct. App. 2001).

[89] Conway v. Pacific Univ., 879 P.2d 201, 203 [94 Educ. L. Rep. 531] (Or. Ct. App. 1994).

[90] DeSimone v. Sienna Coll., 663 N.Y.S.2d 701 [121 Educ. L. Rep. 1126] (N.Y. App. Div. 1997). *See also* Muhitch v. St. Gregory Church and Sch., 659 N.Y.S.2d 679 [119 Educ. L. Rep. 632] (N.Y. App. Div. 1997) (affirming that a former teacher with one-year contract could not sue for breach of contract when it was not renewed).

[91] *See* United States *ex rel.* Yesudian v. Howard Univ., 153 F.3d 731 [128 Educ. L. Rep. 1030] (D.C. Cir. 1996) (remanding on the basis that whether the university's handbook created a binding employment contract was a question of fact for a jury).

[92] *See* Bd. of Regents v. Roth, 408 U.S. 564, 577 (1972) (holding that tenured faculty members who are dismissed during their continuing contracts "have interests in continued employment that are safeguarded by due process.").

[93] *See, e.g.*, Johnson v. Coll. of Art and Design v. Nulph, 453 S.E.2d 80 [97 Educ. L. Rep. 521] (Ga. Ct. App. 1995).

an appellate court in New York[94] affirmed that a tenured faculty member could be demoted in rank and issued a one-year terminal contract because he plagiarized.[95]

Compliance with Contract Language

The threshold issue in deciding whether officials at private or religious institutions complied with employees' contracts is establishing the terms and conditions of their employment. Although most colleges and universities probably consider the faculty handbooks to be part of faculty contracts, by no means is there agreement among institutions.[96]

Colleges and universities faculty handbooks may contain language to the effect that their officials reserve the right to modify them at any time. Ordinarily, while this right of unilateral change does not impact the contractual nature of handbook provisions, not all courts agree.

In an unusual case, an at-will admissions officer who was dismissed sought to enforce a personnel policy provision that an involuntarily discharged administrator was entitled to one month's salary for every six months of service. In the ensuing litigation, the federal trial court in Massachusetts pointed out that according to the manual, "[a]dditional policies and practices or changes may evolve and the Personnel Policy Manual may be amended, modified, or superseded at any time. Written notice of such changes will be distributed as soon as possible."[97] Rejecting the claim, the court held that under state law, "the Manual does not create any contractual rights between [the university] and [plaintiff] . . . because an employee cannot rely on statements in a manual if the manual can be altered or revoked at any time and for any reason. . . ."[98]

---

[94] Klinge v. Ithaca Coll., 663 N.Y.S.2d 735 [121 Educ. L. Rep. 1132] (N.Y. App. Div. 1997).

[95] For a similar case from the public sector, *see* Mueller v. Univ. of Minn., 855 F.2d 555 [48 Educ. L. Rep. 1093] (8th Cir. 1988) (affirming the dismissal of a tenured faculty member for using university resources to promote his private business).

[96] For cases including handbooks as part of employment contracts, *see* Moffice v. Oglethorpe, 367 S.E.2d 112 [46 Educ. L. Rep. 837] (Ga. Ct. App. 1988) (incorporating a faculty handbook into a contract by incorporation by reference into contract); Fogel v. Trs. of Iowa Coll., 446 N.W.2d 451 [56 Educ. L. Rep. 590] (Ia. 1989) (while treating the handbook as part of the contract, emphasizing that it was too ambiguous to support cause of action for breach of unilateral contract of employment); Dahlman v. Oakland Univ., 432 N.W.2d 304 [50 Educ. L. Rep. 895] (Mich. Ct. App. 1988) (affirming that a faculty member's failure to exhaust grievance procedures in his handbook precluded his breach of contract action). For cases where handbooks were not part of employment contracts, see, e.g., Faur v. Jewish Theological Seminary of Am., 536 N.Y.S.2d 516 [51 Educ. L. Rep. 586] (N.Y. App. Div. 1989) (deciding that because an admission policies was not part of employment contract, a seminary could admit women); Hannon v. Bepko, 684 F. Supp. 1465 [47 Educ. L. Rep. 150] (S.D. Ind. 1988) (refusing to apply the faculty handbook to an hourly employee); Wall v. Tulane Univ., 499 S.E.2d 375 [36 Educ. L. Rep. 1041] (La. Ct. App. 1986) (refusing to treat a university's change in its tuition waiver benefit as a violation of a contract where the handbook was not part of the employment contract).

[97] Dunfey v. Roger Williams Univ., 824 F. Supp. 18 [84 Educ. L. Rep. 219] (D. Mass. 1993); the case was heard in Massachusetts but governed by the law of Rhode Island.

[98] *Id.* at 22.

Conversely, an appellate court in Louisiana determined that university officials were obligated to provide a tuition benefit that was in place when a faculty member died, before the handbook was changed and eliminated the benefit.[99] The case from Massachusetts seems to present an interesting anomaly because presumably the university would expect employees to adhere to handbook provisions relating to conduct even though those provisions, like the rest of the handbook, could be changed at will.

Employment standards are created by faculty handbooks, not by external provisions, unless the provisions are expressly incorporated into handbooks. For instance, in a case from New York, a federal trial court granted a university's motion for summary judgment, essentially dismissing the objections of a non-tenured faculty member to his institution's tenure quotas on the ground that such an allegation could not form the basis of a breach of contract claim. [100]

In another case, the Supreme Court of Alabama affirmed that a guideline from the American Association of University Professors that the tenure track probationary period "should not exceed seven years"[101] did not confer tenure on a faculty member who taught at the college for ten years. Moreover, an appellate court in Pennsylvania, rejecting a librarian's claim, explained that employment standards in her law school were established by the faculty handbook, not by the standards of the accrediting bodies, the American Bar Association or the American Association of Law Schools.[102]

Good Faith and Fairness in Contract Enforcement

Generally, a covenant of good faith and fair dealing is implied in every contract, although such a covenant cannot be used to obliterate express contract language. "Good faith is the faithfulness of an agreed purpose between two parties, a purpose which is consistent with justified expectations of the other party. The breach of good faith is bad faith characterized by some conduct which violates standards of decency, fairness or reasonableness."[103] As such, a faculty member cannot claim a lack of good faith or fair dealing in the nonrenewal of a contract if it explicitly contains a "no tenure" provision.[104] Similarly, the nonrenewal of a one-year contract does not require notification where the faculty handbook only suggests, but does not require, notification;[105] nor do courts impose the requirement of an objective and justifiable cause for

---

[99] Fairbanks v. Tulane Univ., 731 So.2d 983 [135 Educ. L. Rep. 284] (La. Ct. App. 1999).
[100] Waring v. Fordham Univ., 640 F. Supp. 42 [34 Educ. L. Rep. 467] (S.D.N.Y. 1986).
[101] Hill v. Talladega Coll., 502 So. 2d 735, 739 [37 Educ. L. Rep. 999] (Ala. 1987).
[102] Krasek v. Duquesne Univ. of the Holy Ghost, 437 A.2d 1257 [1 Educ. L. Rep. 867] (Pa. Super. Ct. 1981).
[103] Braidfoot v. William Carey Coll., 793 So.2d 642 [157 Educ. L. Rep. 432] (Miss. Ct. App. 2000) (finding no breach of good faith where the party received all that was bargained for).
[104] See, e.g., Talley v. Flathead Valley Cmty. Coll., 857 P.2d 701 [85 Educ. L. Rep. 295] (Mont. 1993).
[105] See, e.g., Willitts v. Roman Catholic Archbishop of Boston, 581 N.E.2d 475 [70 Educ. L. Rep. 1207] (Mass. 1991).

nonrenewal before year-by-year contracts are not renewed if such an obligation does not exist in the contract.[106]

In a case from Vermont, a tenured faculty member who was dismissed for sexual harassment lost his claim that his allegedly flawed hearing demonstrated lack of good faith and fair dealing.[107] Insofar as the burden of proof to demonstrate lack of good faith and fair dealing is on the faculty member, and the First Circuit was convinced that the faculty member failed to prove either how alleged bias against him by two of the hearing committee members or how knowledge among some of the committee members of his past reputation for similar conduct and his drinking, violated his handbook rights to a fair hearing.

At the same time, a lack of good faith and fair dealing can be demonstrated where institutional officials act capriciously or arbitrarily. For instance, where an institutional official refuses to permit a faculty member to continue teaching after a court determined that he acquired tenure by default, an appellate court in Michigan thought that the plaintiff was entitled to recover his salary until he retired, minus anticipated earnings through his good-faith efforts to find employment elsewhere.[108] Likewise, when university officials neglected to follow the procedures set forth in their institution's faculty handbook involving discipline, the federal trial court in New Hampshire was satisfied that this failure demonstrate a breach of the good faith and fair dealing implied in every employment contract.[109]

Title VII Generally

Title VII is the workhorse, but not the only[110] federal statute impacting employment nondiscrimination in its prohibition against discriminatory em-

---

[106] *See, e.g.*, Tollefson v. Roman Catholic Bishop of San Diego, 268 Cal.Rptr. 550 [59 Educ. L. Rep. 803] (Cal. Ct. App. 1990).

[107] Logan v. Bennington Coll., 72 F.3d 1017 [106 Educ. L. Rep. 51] (2d Cir. 1995).

[108] *See, e.g.*, Bruno v. Detroit Inst. of Technology, 215 N.W.2d 745 (Mich. Ct. App. 1974).

[109] *See* Silva v. Univ. of N.H., 888 F. Supp. 293 [101 Educ. L. Rep. 704] (D.N.H. 1994) (calling for the reinstatement of a faculty member in a public university who was disciplined for using terms in class that allegedly constituted sexual harassment).

[110] Other key federal employment statutes include the Fair Pay Act, 42 U.S.C.A. § 2000e-5(3)(A), which proscribes discrimination in compensation; the Age Discrimination in Employment Act of 1967, 29 U.S.C.A. §§ 621 *et seq.*, which bans discrimination against persons forty years of age or older; the Americans with Disabilities Act, 42 U.S.C.A. §§ 12101 *et seq.* which prohibits discrimination on the basis of disabilities in employment by state and local governments and in public accommodations; and the Family and Medical Leave Act, 29 U.S.C.A. §§ 2611 et *seq.* which affords employees the right to extended leave for personal and family medical needs and illnesses. Statutes preventing discrimination premised on the receipt of federal assistance, a board concept, include the Rehabilitation Act of 1973, 29 U.S.C.A. § 794, which prohibits discrimination due to disabilities; Title IV of the Civil Rights Act of 1964, which forbids discrimination in public institutions by reason of race, color, religion, sex or national origin, 42 U.S.C.A. § 2000c-6; Title IX of the Educational Amendments of 1972, 20 U.S.C.A. §§ 1681 *et seq.*, which prevents gender discrimination; the Equal Pay Act of 1963, 29 U.S.C.A. § 206(d)(1), which outlaws gender-based wage discrimination; Title VI of the Civil Rights Act of 1964, 42 U.S.C.A. § 2000d. When litigation arises under these statutes in faith-based institution, the outcomes usually rest on whether specific jobs involve religious duties.

ployment practices in hiring, discharging, or classifying persons based on race, color, religion, sex, or national origin.[111]

Aggrieved plaintiffs must file Title VII complaints with the Equal Employment Opportunities Commission (EEOC) within 180 days of alleged discriminatory acts unless they filed claims with state or local agencies, in which case they have 300 days, or thirty days after the state or local agency has terminated proceedings, to file a complaint with the EEOC.[112] If plaintiffs allege continuing discriminatory acts, complaints must be filed within 300 days of the last of "a number of discriminatory acts emanating from the same discriminatory animus, each act constituting a separate wrong."[113] Once plaintiffs receive right-to-sue letters, the have 90 days to file suit.[114]

Unlike Section 1983, Title VI, and Title IX, which normally require proof of discriminatory intent, Title VII permits proof of disproportionate or disparate impact that does not require discriminatory intent;[115] Disparate treatment does require proof of such intent.[116]

A prima facie case requires plaintiffs to allege that they are members of a Title VII protected class, applied for positions or employment benefits for which they are qualified, but were rejected under circumstances giving rise to inferences of unlawful discrimination.[117] The failure of plaintiff to meet all elements a prima facie case results in courts granting the summary judgment motions filed by defendants.[118]

Once defendant-employers proffer evidence of nondiscriminatory reasons for their employment decisions, plaintiffs must prove discriminatory intent or

---

[111] 42 U.S.C.A. § 2000e-2(a).

[112] 42 U.S.C.A. § 2000e-5(d).

[113] 42 U.S.C.A. § 2000e-5(f)(1). Kassaye v. Bryant Coll., 999 F.2d 603, 606 (1st Cir. 1993) (affirming the dismissal of the Title VII complaint a faculty member filed after being denied tenure because it was not filed within 300 days).

[114] See Cabrero Pizarro v. Christian Private Acad., 555 F. Supp.2d 316 (D. Puerto Rico 2008) (allowing a plaintiff to file a Title VII sexual harassment claim on eighty-ninth day after receiving a right-to-sue letter).

[115] See, e.g., Frazier v. Garrison Indep. Sch. Dist., 980 F.2d 1514, 1424 (5th Cir. 1993) (affirming that the neutral practice of requiring candidates to pass the state teacher test could violate Title VII, but the statistical data were inadequate to state a prima facie disparate impact where "there [was] no significant statistical discrepancy between minority and non-minority pass rates.")

[116] See, e.g., Sable v. Univ. of Md., 778 F.2d 164 (4th Cir. 1985) (dismissing a Title VII claim by a faculty member who was denied tenure where she failed to produce evidence of discriminatory intent by the president).

[117] Texas Dep't of Cmty. Affairs v. Burdine, 450 U.S. 248, 253 (1981).

[118] See Stepheny v. Brooklyn Hebrew Sch. for Special Children, 356 F. Supp.2d 248 (E.D.N.Y. 2005).

that the reason employers gave for acting were pretexts for discrimination.[119] Title VII offers a broad range of remedies such back pay up to two years, injunctive relief including reinstatement, and attorney fees.[120]

The 1991 amendments to Title VII now allow plaintiffs to recover monetary damages and have jury trials. Pursuant to another new provision added in 1991: "an unlawful employment practice is established when the complaining party demonstrates that race, color, religion, sex, or national origin was a motivating factor for any employment practice, even though other factors also motivated the practice."[121] In effect, once plaintiffs produce evidence of mixed motives in employment actions, the burden of proof shifts to employers to produce evidence that their actions would have been the same without the impermissible race, color, religion, sex, or national origin motive. If employers fail to satisfy this burden of proof, plaintiffs prevail.[122]

Title VII Issues Unique to Faith-Based Institutions

Title VII includes special rules for faith-based institutions in recognizing the tensions that may arise between the authority of ecclesiastical employers as they seek to control hiring and the rights of their employees to be free from workplace discrimination. In so doing, Title VII provides significant protection to religious employers because it permits them to set bona fide occupational qualifications (BFOQs),[123] including religion, and allows them to limit hiring in key areas to members of their faiths.

Title VII's four exemptions impact personnel in faith-based colleges and universities because they shield institutional officials from charges of religious discrimination. The first, and threshold exemption, under Title VII applies to institutions with fifteen or more employees.[124] Insofar as private and

---

[119] *See* Hatton v. Hunt, 780 F. Supp. 1157 (W.D. Tenn. 1991) (dismissing a Title VII gender-based wage disparity claim where an employer's statement that a male was paid more because of his greater education and lengthy work experience provided legitimate nondiscriminatory reason for salary disparity); Lewis v. Cent. Piedmont Cmty. Coll., 689 F.2d 1207 (4th Cir. 1982) (reversing a finding of a Title VII race discrimination claim where the person hired as an accounting lab instructor was much better qualified than the plaintiff, a African American black woman who worked as a cashier in the college's business office).

[120] 42 U.S.C.A. § 2000e-5(g). *See* Wangness v. Watertown Sch. Dist., 541 F. Supp. 332] (D.S.D. 1982) (discussing all three remedies).

[121] 42 U.S.C.A. § 2000e-2 (m).

[122] *See, e.g.*, Nigrelli v. Catholic Bishop of Chicago, 794 F. Supp. 246 (N.D. Ill. 1992) (discussing the 1991 amendment but refusing to apply it retroactively to a claim from 1984).

[123] For such a case, *see, e.g.*, Hernandez v. St. Thomas Univ., 793 F. Supp. 214 (D. Minn. 1992) (ruling that university officials had the burden of proving its BFOQ as to privacy considerations for hiring only female custodians). *See also* Maguire v. Marquette Univ., 814 F.2d 1213 [38 Educ. L. Rep. 433] (7th Cir. 1987) (dismissing the claim of a female applicant whose theological views were antithetical to those of the Catholic Church because what is taught in the theology department represents the core of Catholic beliefs); Pime v. Loyola Univ. of Chicago, 893 F.2d 351 (7th Cir. 1986) (affirming a university's hiring a Jesuit over a woman for the philosophy department as BFOQ as reasonably necessary to its normal operations).

[124] 42 U.S.C.A. § 2000e(b).

faith-based colleges typically have fairly large staff, they are clearly covered by this provision.

The second, and arguably most important exemption, concerns instances where "religion, sex, or national origin is a bona fide occupational qualification reasonably necessary to the operations of that particular business or enterprise."[125] A closely related third exemption applies to "a religious corporation, association, educational institution, or society with respect to the employment of individuals of a particular religion to perform work connected with the carrying on by such corporation, association, educational institution, or society of its activities."[126] This is sometimes referred to as the ministerial exception, with the burden of proof of the necessity of BFOQs resting on employers, even if individuals are not ordained. In order to apply this exception, officials in religious institutions must be able to prove that staff members' teaching or other activities are so integrally related to furthering their spiritual and pastoral missions that their duties may be treated as ministerial.

In *Corporation of Presiding Bishops v. Amos (Amos)*[127] the Supreme Court upheld the constitutionality of the ministerial exception. *Amos* involved a building engineer who filed a class action suit on behalf of himself and others who were similarly situated when he was dismissed after sixteen years of employment at a gymnasium operated by the Church of Latter Day Saints. Officials dismissed the plaintiff because he was unable to qualify for a certificate of eligibility to attend one of the Church's Temples. The Court ruled that although the plaintiff was fired even though he did not perform religious duties, Title VII did not violate the Establishment Clause because earlier language, referring to an institution's "religious activities," was no longer in the law. In so doing, the Court extended the reach of the exemption to non-religious employment-related activities.

The Supreme Court again upheld the constitutionality of the ministerial exception, albeit under the Americans with Disabilities Act (ADA) rather than Title VII. At issue was whether officials at a Lutheran elementary school in Michigan could dismiss a teacher who was also a commissioned minister in the church. Reversing the Sixth Circuit's order to the contrary, in *Hosanna-Tabor Evangelical Lutheran Church and School v. Equal Employment Opportunities Commission (Hosanna-Tabor)*,[128] the Justices unanimously found that despite the teacher's allegation that her primary duties were secular, the ministerial exception precluded her ADA claim. The teacher alleged that she was dismissed in retaliation for threatening to take legal action when she refused to resign in a dispute over whether she could return to work due to her health problems.

---

[125] 42 U.S.C.A. § 2000e–2(e)(1).

[126] 42 U.S.C.A. § 2000e–1.

[127] 483 U.S. 327 (1987).

[128] 565 U.S. 171 (2011). For a commentary on this case, see Ralph D. Mawdsley & Allan G. Osborne, *Shout Hosanna: The Supreme Court Affirms the Free Exercise Clause's Ministerial Exception*, 278 EDUC. L. REP. 693 (2012)

Emphasizing that the First Amendment forbids the government from overriding the actions of church officials as to who can serve as ministers, the *Hosanna-Tabor* Court found that the exception applied to bar the teacher's claim even though she spent more than six hours of her seven-hour day teaching secular subjects, using secular textbooks, and not incorporating religion into these materials. The Court also pointed out that teachers at the school were not required to be "called" or members of the Lutheran faith in order to conduct job-related religious activities and the duties of contract teachers were identical to those lacking the title of minister.

In adopting the ministerial exception, courts have long acknowledged that they cannot intrude into religious organizations' selection of their leaders. In such a case, Circuit Court for the District of Columbia upheld the dismissal of a nun's sex discrimination complaint after she was denied tenure in the Canon Law Department.[129] The court maintained that because Canon Law plays a significant role in the education of priests and is important to the spiritual mission of the Catholic Church, those teaching in it qualified for the ministerial exemption. The court added that the EEOC's attempt to investigate the plaintiff's sex discrimination claim not only burdened the university's right to Free Exercise, but intruded excessively into its religious beliefs and practices under the Establishment Clause.

The fourth exemption applies to institutions "in whole or in substantial part, owned, supported, controlled, or managed by a particular religious corporation, association or society, or if the curriculum of such school, college, university, or other educational institution . . . is directed toward the propagation of a particular religion."[130] This exemption permits policies allowing institutions to enact hiring preferences for members of their own faiths. For example, the Eleventh Circuit permitted officials at a Baptist university to limit a faculty member's assignments to undergraduate classes and prevent him from teaching in its divinity school due to his religious differences with his dean.[131] The court posited that even though the university was no longer under the direct control of a religious governing body, it was entitled to the exemption because the same church still substantially provided financial support.

---

[129] EEOC v. Catholic Univ. of Am., 83 F.3d 455 (D.C. Cir 1996). For a commentary on this case, see Charles J. Russo, *The Camel's Nose In the Tent: Judicial Intervention in Tenure Disputes at Catholic Universities*, 117 Educ. L. Rep. 813 (1997).

[130] 42 U.S.C.A. § 2000–(e)(2)(e).

[131] Killinger v. Samford Univ., 113 F.3d 196 [118 Educ. L. Rep. 48] (11th Cir. 1997). *See also* Hall v. Baptist Memorial Health Care Corp., 215 F.3d 618 [145 Educ. L. Rep. 216] (6th Cir. 2000) (affirming a college's motion for summary judgment, thereby permitting the dismissal of an employee who was ordained by a church with a large gay congregation).

Student Rights

Generally

Student rights in private and faith-based colleges and universities parallel those of faculty to the extent that due to the absence of state action, they do not enjoy constitutional rights. Like their faculty counterparts, students have contract rights framed by the student handbooks of their institutions and perhaps by other documents such as brochures and admission applications. While contractual handbook rights do not have to be the same as the constitutional rights that students likely enjoy in public institutions, courts can compare contract rights with the requirements of due process.[132]

At the heart of due process is the expectation that students are treated fairly in being subject to school rules. In the public sector, this expectation has the constitutional appellation of substantive or procedural due process rights; on the other hand, in the nonpublic sector the expectation is for clearly stated rules and a review process that is neither arbitrary nor capricious.

The influence of due process on religious and private colleges and universities is reflected in a case from Vermont. The federal trial court decided that where a campus tribunal judged a student guilty of "disrespect of persons," mirroring language in his handbook, and failing "to respect the dignity, freedom, and rights of others," he was entitled to another hearing because he was charged but found not guilty of rape; also, he was not charged with the disrespect of persons prior to his hearing. Decreeing that the college's contractual duty was "to state the nature of the charges with sufficient particularity to permit the student to defend himself,"[133] the court was of the view that the two charges, rape and disrespect of persons, were different enough that the student should have been notified he would be expected to defend himself against both conduct standards.

Courts continue to grant considerable discretion to officials in religious and private colleges and universities to define their codes of conduct and will permit discipline for violations of general language.[134] Generally, the only due process to which students are entitled is having institutional officials conform to their own disciplinary procedures.[135] Even omissions in procedures required

---

[132] *See, e.g.*, McConnell v. LeMoyne Coll., 808 N.Y.S.2d 860, 861 [206 Educ. L. Rep. 696] (N.Y. App. Div. 2006) (affirming that a student was entitled to "the due process procedures set forth in the College's rules and regulations"); Harvey v. Palmer Coll. of Chiropractic, 363 N.W.2d 443, 444 [23 Educ. L. Rep. 667] (Ia. Ct. App. 1984) ("requirements imposed by the common law on private universities parallel those imposed by the due process clause on public universities").

[133] Fellheimer v. Middlebury Coll., 869 F. Supp. 238, 246 [96 Educ. L. Rep. 419] (D. Vt. 1994).

[134] *See, e.g.*, Aronson v. North Park Coll., 418 N.E.2d 776, 782 (Ill. App. Ct. 1981) (reinstating the dismissal of a student pursuant to handbook language because his "continuation in the school is detrimental to himself or his fellow students.")

[135] *See, e.g.*, Galiani v. Hofstra Univ., 499 N.Y.S.2d 182 [30 Educ. L. Rep. 1247] (N.Y. App. Div. 1986).

in student handbooks may be overlooked as long as the overall conduct of student disciplinary proceedings is neither arbitrary nor capricious.[136]

Student contractual rights are similar to those of faculty and involve the same three issues: whether allegedly improper student conduct is covered by published contract language; whether institutional officials complied with their own contractual requirements in dealing with students; and (3) whether officials' interpretation or enforcement of contract terms exhibited good faith and fairness.

Student Conduct and Published Contract Language

As suggested above, private colleges and universities can discipline students pursuant to general language in student handbooks. For instance, an appellate court in Illinois upheld a student's expulsion under a college provision allowing officials "to dismiss any time a student who in its judgment is undesirable and whose continuation in the school is detrimental to himself or his fellow students."[137]

In a tragic case from Maryland, an appellate court upheld the actions of university officials who refused to award a diploma to a student even though he had finished his academic program.[138] During the spring semester, when the student was not enrolled in any courses, he killed another student on campus, pled guilty, and was sentenced to thirty-five years in prison. The student handbook provided that an individual would not receive a diploma solely on the basis of completing course work and that to receive a diploma one had to have resolve any and all charges of misconduct before being approved for graduation. In a case of first impression, the court thus concluded that under the circumstances, university officials could withhold the diploma and expel the student.

A similar result occurred in a case from Massachusetts where students were ordered to withdraw from their university for one year and not participate in commencement due to their past misconduct. Granting the university's motion for summary judgment, the federal trial court observed that the students were not entitled to the award of degrees, even if they had completed degree requirements prior to board's action, because their handbook expressly au-

---

[136] *See, e.g.,* Ahlum v. Administrators of Tulane Educ'l Fund, 617 So.2d 96 [82 Educ. L. Rep. 1021] (La. Ct. App. 1993) (refusing to intervene where the failure of university officials to make a tape recording of a disciplinary hearing as provided in student handbook, due to a tape recorder failure, was not fatal because the student had an opportunity to present his version of the facts and was informed of the charges he faced him); Life Chiropractic Coll. v. Fuchs, 337 S.E.2d 45, 48 [29 Educ. L. Rep. 416] (Ga. Ct. App. 1985) (remarking that officials satisfied the statement that "[d]ue process is followed in all [disciplinary] cases" even though the student was denied the opportunity to confront witnesses).

[137] Aronson v. North Park Coll., 418 N.E.2d 776, 781 (Ill. App. Ct. 1981).

[138] Harwood v. Johns Hopkins Univ., 747 A.2d 205 [142 Educ. L. Rep. 980] (Md. Ct. App. 2000).

thorized officials to withhold degrees from those on disciplinary probation.[139] The court added that insofar as the disciplinary sanction against the plaintiffs were even more severe, they could not reasonably have expected more favorable treatment.

On another issue, private and faith-based institutions of higher education can withhold diplomas and transcripts for outstanding financial obligations, pursuant to language in student handbooks.[140] However, federal law can override the student-university contracts such that officials cannot refuse to send a transcript if a student has filed for bankruptcy under the Bankruptcy Code and listed the university obligation as one of the debts.[141]

Compliance with Contract Language

Unlike faculty handbooks, most parties do not challenge the proposition that student handbooks are part of the contracts between religious and private colleges and universities and their students. What is contested is not only whether the parties complied with handbook provisions, but also the extent to which the contracts include other institutional publications.

Grade disputes are subjects of considerable higher education litigation with courts generally deferring to the judgment of college and university faculty as long as they follow handbook procedures.[142] An appellate court in Arkansas reversed a breach of contract award in favor of student adjudicated guilty of an honor code violation, suspended for the balance of the year, and given an "F" in a course. Declaring that the trial court should have granted a directed verdict for the college, an appellate panel wrote that "once it was shown that [college officials] followed [their] own procedural guidelines and based its disciplinary decision on substantial evidence, judicial review of [the college's] actions should have ceased."[143]

More troublesome are student breach of contract or misrepresentation suits involving college or university performances or statements about academic programs, courses, and/or financial obligations. At issue is a concept of an institutional contract that goes beyond student handbooks to include official publications describing programs, courses, and financial obligations. In the first of three cases on point, a federal trial court in New York ruled in favor of a prospective medical student who sued on the theory of fraudulent misrep-

[139] Dinu v. President and Fellows of Harvard Univ., 56 F. Supp.2d 129 [137 Educ. L. Rep. 619] (D. Mass. 1999) (where students were suspended for one year after being judged guilty of taking money from a student account and were not permitted to participate in their commencement).

[140] Martin v. Pratt Inst., 717 N.Y.S.2d 356 [149 Educ. L. Rep. 872] (N.Y. App. Div. 2000).

[141] *See, e.g.*. Parraway v. Andrews Univ., 50 B.R. 316 [26 Educ. L. Rep. 304] (W.D. Mich. 1984); *In re* Scroggins, 209 B.R. 727 [119 Educ. L. Rep. 170] (D. Ariz. 1997); *In re* Lanford, 10 B.R. 132 (D. Minn. 1981).

[142] *See, e.g.*, Little v. Yale Univ., 884 A.2d 427 [203 Educ. L. Rep. 267] (Conn. Ct. App. 2005).

[143] Lyon Coll. v. Gray, 999 S.W.2d 213, 217 [137 Educ. L. Rep. 1132] (Ark. Ct. App. 1999).

resentation based on a claim that a university brochure described equipment and facilities that were not available when he arrived for classes.[144]

Next, an appellate court in Pennsylvania rejected the request by university officials to deny a student's breach of contract claim when they revoked life experience credits they granted her on enrollment. According to the court, "[w]hen an individual is induced to enroll in a university or college based upon the award of certain life credits, the institution cannot then, after the student's enrollment, revoke those credits.[145] Later, the Supreme Court of Vermont entered a judgment in favor of a student on his breach of contract and consumer fraud claims when college officials refused to refund his money after he withdrew from the school.[146] The court noted that insofar as such a course of action was consistent with catalog language in effect when the student enrolled, he was entitled to the refund.

Good Faith and Fairness in Contract Enforcement

As with contracts between faculty and higher education institutions, covenants of good faith and fair dealing are implied in contracts between colleges or universities and their students.[147] Even so, officials in educational institutions typically have broad discretion when interpreting rules, policies, and/or handbooks. Moreover, when academic standards are concerned, courts do not intervene absent bad faith by campus administrators.

In the first of a pair of cases from New York, a state trial court rejected a student's claim that officials in her law school acted in bad faith by continuing to include a failing grade in calculating her GPA even after she retook, and passed, the class. Because school officials complied with the school's published policy of counting failing grades, the court rejected the claim, treating the dispute as being within the sound discretion of officials "unfettered by contract and unreviewable by courts."[148]

In the second case, an appellate court affirmed the denial of claims a law student filed when institutional officials were unwilling to change his failing grades from an F to a W (withdrawn) and providing him with a letter to the effect that his dismissal was due to illness rather than his failure.[149] The court was reluctant to intervene on academic matters other than to consider whether

---

[144] Idress v. American Univ. of the Caribbean, 546 F. Supp. 1342 [6 Educ. L. Rep. 653] (S.D.N.Y. 1982).

[145] Britt v. Chestnut Hill Coll., 632 A.2d 557, 560 [86 Educ. L. Rep. 905] (Pa. Super. Ct. 1993).

[146] Reynolds v. Sterling Coll., 750 A.2d 1020 [144 Educ. L. Rep. 314] (Vt. 2000).

[147] See, e.g., Chenari v. George Washington Univ., 847 F.3d 740 [340 Educ. L. Rep. 36] (D.C. Cir. 2017) (affirming that medical school officials did not breach either their contract with a student or their implied covenant of good faith by expelling him for violating the honor code during an examination).

[148] Shields v. School of Law, Hofstra Univ., 431 N.Y.S.2d 60, 61 (N.Y. Sup. Ct. 1980).

[149] Daniel v. Brooklyn Law Sch., 60 N.Y.S.3d308 (N.Y. App. Div. 2017).

they are arbitrary and capricious, irrational, made in bad faith, and/ or are contrary to law.[150]

Similarly, a state court in New Jersey upheld the action of university officials to postpone the awarding of a student's degree because she plagiarized a term paper. The court held that it was not its function "to second-guess academic decisions and judgments in colleges and universities" and, as long as the faculty judgment had a rational basis, the court would not treat it as arbitrary and/or capricious.[151] Absent evidence of bad faith, the reluctance of courts to intervene in grade disputes reflects not only their lack of expertise in the subject matter, but also their deference for academic decision-making and a concern about promoting litigation by countless dissatisfied students.

On the other hand, courts do not hesitate to declare claims justiciable where students appear to have proof of bad faith. In such a case, an appellate court in Florida decided that a student who could prove bad faith on receiving a failing grade in his final course in medical school, resulting in his not being awarded a degree, was entitled to damages over the loss of his earning capacity without the medical degree.[152]

In another case, the federal trial court in Maine partially granted a student's motion for summary judgment in his breach of contract suit when, following a fight with an Asian-American peer, he was expelled for violating the college's racial discrimination policy.[153] Ordering the case to trial, a federal judge found that officials breached the college's contract with the student by not providing "fundamental fairness" in campus procedures as mandated in his handbook.

Conclusion

Nonsectarian and religious colleges and universities and their educational communities have many of the same rights and responsibilities as public institutions. While the concept of state action is a recognized dividing line between religious and nonreligious colleges and universities, states can enact statutes and regulations minimizing the differences. The effect of such state changes is to provide a measure of protection for faculty members, students, and those doing business with private and religious colleges and universities. However, insofar as such changes are not necessarily uniform, those interacting with faith-based and private colleges and universities, whether as students,

---

[150] On a related issue, see Sarwar v. N.Y. Coll. of Osteopathic Med. of N.Y. Inst. of Tech., 54 N.Y.S. 3d 96 [343 Educ. L. Rep. 1038] (N.Y. App. Div. 2017) (affirming the denial of a medical student's breach of contract and unjust enrichment claims as time-barred because he should have filed suit within four months of his dismissal for failing two of three courses in his initial semester rather than wait six years).

[151] Napolitano v. Princeton Univ., 453 A.2d 263, 278 [8 Educ. L. Rep. 74] (N.J. Super. Ct. 1982).

[152] Sharick v. Southeastern Univ. of the Health Sci., 780 So.2d 136 [152 Educ. L. Rep. 448] (Fla. Dist. Ct. App. 2000).

[153] Goodman v. President and Trs. of Bowdoin Coll., 135 F. Supp.2d 40 [152 Educ. L. Rep. 660] (D. Me. 2000).

employees, or in business capacities, would be wise to acquaint themselves with the relevant state law in the jurisdictions where the institutions are located.

Discussion Questions

1. Can one argue that the elimination of state action in private and religious colleges and universities, pursuant to the Supreme Court decisions in *Rendall-Baker v. Kohn*, represents the elimination of constitutional rights for their faculty and students? Please identify the constitutional rights litigated in the wake of *Rendell-Baker* and consider how these rights would likely be translated into acceptable and unacceptable student and faculty conduct policies.

2. States are permitted to regulate out-of-state colleges and universities, although the effectiveness of the regulation depend on the amount of contact within the state. In light of the litigation reviewed in this chapter about whether states can assert jurisdiction over out-of-state colleges and universities, please develop arguments for greater and lesser amounts of out-of-state regulation.

3. College and university officials can refuse to award diplomas to students who met the academic requirements but engaged in unacceptable conduct prior to graduation. Consider what legal theory or theories could apply to determine officials in private or religious institutions have the legal authority to sanction students for misbehavior.

4. Private and faith-based colleges and universities are increasingly relying on distance learning courses that utilize a variety of technologies. Discuss legal issues that arise when colleges or universities use technology to present course material, particularly focusing on ownership of content in the material, permission to use the material, and any limitations applicable to higher education institutions about online course materials and course content developed by their faculty members.

5. Title VII allows the administration in faith-based colleges and universities to grant hiring preferences to members of their own religions. In some countries this is referred to as positive discrimination because it grants preferences to particular faith. What do you think of this, especially the ministerial exception? Can, or should, this exception be allowed to continue?

6. Faculty members at private and religious colleges and universities have legal rights that are akin to the constitutional rights of faculty members at public institutions only if such rights are conferred by the governing board. Do you think faculty members at faith-based and private institutions should have the same free speech rights, rights to due process, and other constitutional rights their colleagues at public institutions enjoy?

4

Faculty Employment and Tenure

Kevin P. Brady, Ph.D.*
University of Arkansas

Introduction

This chapter addresses myriad legal postsecondary employment issues involving higher education faculty members and the inherently complex employment relationships found in higher education. Further complicating faculty issues, higher education employment is often influenced by a combination of common law doctrines, statutes, and constitutional provisions. Litigation involving the relationship between higher educational institutions and faculty is often fact-intensive, unique to a particular context, and complicated by a range of legal issues. Despite a reluctance to intervene in the academic decision-making process, judges are regularly asked to resolve legal disputes between higher education institutions and aggrieved faculty. The range of legal issues presented in appellate decisions begins with interpreting the specific nature of the contract between the parties and extends to a host of legal challenges to institutional decisions that may include allegations of arbitrary and capricious action as well as potential violations of state and federal antidiscrimination law.

Public and private higher education institutions often face similar contractual challenges, with the notable exception that faculty employed in public higher education institutions may assert constitutional rights involving due process and equal protection guarantees relating to the scope of the contract between the faculty member and the higher education institution. In addition, a faculty member employed at a public higher education institution carries the legal entitlement to assert First Amendment constitutional rights to free speech and expression. Although contemporary private institutions are not typically legally burdened with protecting a faculty employee's First Amendment rights, it is conceivable that the private higher education institution may contractually obligate itself to extend rights to free speech or academic freedom. Faculty free speech and expression issues are addressed in another chapter and will not, therefore, be covered in this chapter.

Faculty Employment Contracts

Faculty employment contracts often serve as essential documents in setting the legal boundaries associated with a faculty member's rights and responsibilities while employed at a particular college or university. Traditionally, faculty contracts are based on an offer by the higher education institution and an acceptance by the prospective faculty employee. A valid contract includes express terms or conditions specifying the period of employment, the duties and status of the employee, and the amount of compensation. In addition to specifying a faculty member's legal rights and duties, faculty employment contracts, especially at private colleges and universities can require faculty to abide by certain codes of conduct, including accepting certain tenets of a specific religion. A faculty member's contract may incorporate the provisions of a collective bargaining agreement or institutional policies, including provisions that are contained in what are commonly referred to as faculty handbooks, or manuals.[1] While employment contracts serve as the primary legal source of faculty rights and responsibilities at private colleges and universities, today's public higher education institutions are also legally governed by individual state statutory mandates or agency regulations that are influential in determining the scope of their rights and legal obligations.

Express and Implied Faculty Employment Contracts

An express contract is a written document specifically containing the terms and conditions of the employment agreement. In the absence of an express contract, a judge may consider the actions of the parties, oral communications, and institutional documents in order to determine whether an employment agreement may be implied. Given disagreements over what constitutes an express contractual agreement, courts are often asked to interpret whether or not intent was expressed within a written faculty employment contract.

In an illustrative case, the plaintiff, a faculty member employed by the university's medical school maintained that several positive letters from the dean of the medical school, combined with an oral promise by the dean to recommend the faculty member for early tenure and promotion, constituted a valid contract. When the university failed to grant the faculty member tenure, he filed suit arguing that the contract was breached.[2] The dean failed to submit a letter of recommendation on the faculty member's behalf and shortly thereafter resigned as dean and returned to become a full-time faculty member. While

---

* In previous versions of this chapter, Monoka Venters was listed as an author, and her prior work provided a foundation for this chapter in its current form. She has elected not to continue in this role beginning with this edition. The author wishes to thank her and acknowledge her prior contributions to this chapter.

[1] *See* Zuelsdorf v. Univ. of Alaska, 794 P.2d 932 (Alaska 1990) for a case in which the university's personnel regulations were a required condition of employment, and failure to give timely notice of nonrenewal breached the probationary employee's contractual rights.

[2] Lewis v. Loyola Univ. of Chicago, 500 N.E.2d 47 (Ill. App. Ct. 1986).

the university argued that the faculty member's recommendation letter and the dean's oral promises cannot be considered part of the faculty member's employment contract, the court disagreed. Instead, the court indicated that the faculty member was successfully able to demonstrate "ample evidence" that he would be been tenured despite the dean's failure to deliver a timely letter of recommendation.

When a faculty employment contract incorporates specific reference to faculty handbooks, institutional policies, or collective bargaining agreements, judges often refer to these documents as part of the faculty member's employment contract and hold the particular higher education institution to substantial compliance with the terms expressed in those documents.[3] This rule has been particularly applicable to colleges and universities that fail to comply with institutional procedures when making faculty termination and tenure decisions.[4]

A contract may also be construed to be consistent with the university's customary practices. In a relevant case, a professor entered into a contract for a tenure-track associate professorship with a proviso that the contract would be suspended until she began as faculty because she would begin serving as an associate dean. The contract did not specify a salary for the faculty position. When the professor resigned as dean and requested her faculty position, the university reduced her salary to an amount in the middle of the faculty salary range. The professor filed a lawsuit alleging that the university breached her contract by reducing her salary. The court ruled that the contract did not prohibit the university from doing so if she became faculty and found that the university was only required to set the salary at a rate comparable to what the university customarily paid faculty in similar positions.[5]

Oral Representations of Faculty Employment Contracts

In some instances, judges prefer to adopt a literal interpretation of express employment contract terms and are reluctant to permit the introduction of oral testimony when a comprehensive written employment agreement is introduced into evidence. In a representative case, a former assistant professor was denied the opportunity to present proof of an oral tenure agreement when the court ruled that the parties had entered into a fully integrated written contract that contained no tenure provision.[6] The refusal to admit oral testimony qualifying the written terms of a contract is referred to as the parole evidence rule. The rule was developed to protect the integrity of written contracts and prohibits

---

[3]   Brady v. Bd. of Trs. of Neb. State Colls., 196 Neb. 226, 242 N.W.2d 616 (Neb. 1976).

[4]   *See* Bennett v. Wells Coll., 641 N.Y.S.2d 929 (App. Div. 1996) (tenure denial) and Savannah Coll. of Art & Design v. Nulph, 265 Ga. 662, 460 S.E.2d 792 (Ga. 1995) (termination). *But see* Jacobs v. Mundelein Coll., 256 Ill. App. 3d 476, 628 N.E.2d 201 (Ill. App. Ct. 1993) and De Simone v. Skidmore Coll., 159 A.D.2d 926, 553 N.Y.S.2d 240 (N. Y. App. Div. 1990) in which statements in faculty handbooks concerning criteria for evaluating annual contract employees or establishing procedures for evaluation were not regarded by courts as creating a contractual right protecting the faculty member from an adverse employment decision.

[5]   Marks v. Smith, 65 A.D.3d 911, 885 N.Y.S.2d 462 (N.Y. App. Div. 2009).

[6]   Ozerol v. Howard Univ., 545 A.2d 638 (D.C. 1988).

a party to a written contract from contradicting the terms of the agreement with evidence of alleged oral representations.[7] In an illustrative case, a court refused to consider the testimony of a former president about the formula used to calculate the salary of an administrator returning to a faculty position when the contract did not contain the formula and unambiguously stated that the salary would be calculated in the same manner as salaries for faculty with similar rank and experience.[8]

However, there are exceptions to the parole evidence rule that permit a judge to consider additional evidence going beyond the express terms and conditions of a written agreement. Ambiguous terms in the contract of employment may require additional evidence concerning the intent of the parties.[9] Judges may rely on the representations of the parties to determine the nature of an employment contract. In one case, the intent of the parties was determined by judicial reference to letters and oral statements by the dean, who assured a faculty member recruited for a post as professor and department chair that he would be recommended for tenure. The professor prevailed by showing that the letters and oral representations of the dean were part of the employment agreement that induced the faculty member to come to the institution.[10]

Oral representations by authorized agents of the institution may influence the interpretation of the contract, but this is more likely to occur in the absence of a written contract and under circumstances in which it was reasonable for the employee to rely on such representations.[11] For example, a professor's assertions that her academic dean promised her lifetime employment did not create de facto tenure in the opinion of a federal court of appeals. The court found the professor's reliance on such an assertion to be unreasonable, given that her employment contract incorporated by reference the university's written policies, which stipulated a formal policy and procedure for the award of tenure.[12] Another court declined to find that an institution made material misrepresentations about its endowment, enrollment, faculty salaries, and financial stability in response to an applicant's questions during her interview, after which the

---

[7] *See* Kashif v. Cent. State Univ., 133 Ohio App. 3d 678, 729 N.E. 2d 787 (Ohio Ct. App. 1999) in which the court rejected parole evidence that might alter the unambiguous written contract of the parties.

[8] Homer v. Bd. of Regents of the Univ. Sys. of Ga., 272 Ga. App. 683, 613 S.E.2d 205 (Ga. Ct. App. 2005).

[9] *See* Tuomala v. Regent Univ., 252 Va. 368; 477 S.E.2d 501 (Va. 1996), in which testimony of members of the institutional governing board was necessary in order to determine the policy-making body's intention with regard to the terms of the agreement.

[10] Lewis v. Loyola Univ. of Chicago, 149 Ill. App. 3d 88, 500 N.E.2d 47 (Ill. App. Ct. 1986).

[11] Yates v. Bd. of Regents of Lamar Univ., 654 F. Supp. 979 (E.D. Tex. 1987),

[12] Geddes v. Nw. Mo. State Univ., 49 F.3d 426 (8th Cir. 1995). *See also* Gottlied v. Tulane Univ., 529 So.2d 128 (La. Ct. App. 1988) (holding that the "apparent authority" of a university administrator to grant tenure did not create a right to tenure in light of the specific and limiting terms of the employment contract agreed to by the professor and the procedures for award of tenure stipulated in the faculty handbook).

position was eliminated because of unforeseen economic conditions. The court found that the college did not have to predict its future financial condition.[13]

Employment Contracts for Part-Time Faculty

Since an increasing number of today's colleges and universities are facing financial constraints and hardships, higher education administrators are hiring more part-time faculty members at significantly lower salaries compared to tenure-track or tenured faculty members. In 2016, data collected from the U.S. Department of Education reveals that approximately 47% of faculty across all types of higher education institutions are considered part-time.[14] Emerging caselaw involving legal suits brought forth by part-time faculty illustrate the different financial issues faced by higher education administrators faced with the task of significantly reducing faculty salaries at their college or university. In one lawsuit in the state of Washington, a group of part-time faculty members filed suit based on their university's denial of paid health care coverage during the summer.[15] While the group of part-time faculty did not teach summer courses, they argued language in state regulations indicated that they would be provided paid summer health care based on their status as seasonal employees at the university. The court ultimately rejected the argument of the part-time faculty members, indicating that the state regulations excluded employees who did not teach for two consecutive semesters. Thus, the court indicated that the part-time faculty members were not entitled to paid summer health care because they did not fulfill the prerequisite of teaching at the university for two consecutive semesters. A second case, also originating from Washington, addressed the issue of overtime wages for part-time faculty members.[16] In this case, the state supreme court held against the part-time faculty members indicating that the college's practice of paying part-time faculty members based on their in-class instructional hours did not render the part-time faculty members as nonexempt from the state's existing wage laws. Since the part-time faculty members were considered professionals, their compensation based on the number of instructional hours taught was considered a salary and not a wage.

As the number of part-time faculty in higher education institutions throughout the country continues to grow, it becomes increasingly important to more closely monitor the legal and policy issues surrounding the use of part-time higher education faculty as a means to reduce the long-term financial implications of retaining tenured faculty members. More specifically, the AAUP has developed guidelines involving the use of part-time higher education faculty members. The AAUP report, "Contingent Appointments and the Academic Profession," is directed at higher education administrators and contains useful

---

[13] Bellon v. Ripon Coll., 278 Wis. 2d 790, 693 N.W.2d 330 (Wis. Ct. App. 2005).

[14] U.S. Department of Education (2018), National Center for Education Statistics (NCES) *Condition of Education*, available at https://nces.ed.gov/programs/coe/indicator_csc.asp.

[15] Mader v. Health Care Authority, 37 P.3d 1244 (Wash. Super. Ct. 2002).

[16] Clawson v. Greys Harbor College Dist. No. 2, 61 P.3d 1130 (Wash. 2003).

discussions and recommendations regarding the use of part-time and non-tenure-track faculty.[17]

Agency

If the faculty member is to demonstrate that the institution should be bound by the acts of an agent acting beyond the scope of actual authority, the institution must have clothed the agent with apparent authority, and the agent's promise must have been one that the institution could make and perform lawfully.[18] The faculty member must also demonstrate that the institution accepted and retained the benefit it received in return for the agent's promise and that the faculty member's reliance on that promise was reasonable in light of his or her knowledge and experience with the academic enterprise.

A memorandum from an individual in apparent authority may be sufficient to bind an institution to an offer of employment. In one case, a community college instructor received a written notice of re-employment for the upcoming academic year. The president of the college had signed the memo and directed the instructor to accept or reject the re-appointment, date, sign, and return the document to the college. The instructor complied, but received a second letter sixteen days later informing him that he would not be tendered a formal contract of employment because of insufficient student enrollment. In ruling for the instructor, a state appeals court found that the president could have conditioned the offer of employment on whether enrollment was sufficient to justify hiring, but his failure to do so created an employment agreement that justified the court in providing equitable relief to the employee.[19]

In contrast, a faculty appointee who sought to enforce a four-year term of employment negotiated with the director of the university program failed to bind the university to the negotiated agreement. Although claiming that the director had the apparent authority to contract for the four-year period, the state appeals court rejected the claim.[20] The appeals court noted that state law granted the authority to extend contracts beyond a year solely to the university chancellor, and reasoned that with the appointee's interpretation, "any multi-year contract made by an agent on behalf of a state institution of higher education would be valid unless expressly countermanded."[21] Such an

---

[17] AAUP (2003), "Contingent Appointments and the Academic Profession, available at https://www.aaup.org/report/contingent-appointments-and-academic-profession

[18] This analysis does not address the possibility that an agent's representations may create a basis for that agent's individual liability. *See* Bicknese v. Satula, 660 N.W.2d 289 (Wis. 2003) (finding the chair, in making an employment offer to the applicant, was bound to act in accordance with the express terms and conditions of the institution's policies and procedures, and if representations were not consistent with university policies, individual liability could ensue); Hirsch v. Columbia Univ., 293 F. Supp. 2d 372 (S.D.N.Y. 2003) (holding the dean's statements to candidate, if false and knowingly made, may constitute fraudulent inducement if made in an effort to induce the applicant to accept the position).

[19] Ashcraft v. Dist. Bd. of Trs., 615 So.2d 271 (Fla. Dist. Ct. App. 1993).

[20] Yasnoff v. Hallick, 155 Ore. App. 474, 963 P.2d 747 (Or. Ct. App. 1998).

[21] *Id.* at 749.

interpretation and application of the law would turn the chancellor's power of prospective appointment into a retrospective veto power that would be inconsistent with the state law.

In a similar case, a prospective faculty member received an offer from a dean that included a salary bump, provided the prospective faculty member completed his doctorate by a certain date. The contract between the faculty member and the board did not mention a salary increase upon completion of the doctorate. When the faculty member did not complete his doctorate by that date, the dean acknowledged the promised salary increase and attempted unsuccessfully to negotiate the increase with the board. The court found that state law specified that only the board has the power to contract with faculty; therefore, an administrator at the university would not have authority to contract absent an express delegation by the board, and no evidence existed that the board delegated its authority.[22]

While the general rule is that an institution cannot be contractually bound by the promises of an agent absent express authority, judges have artfully interpreted this standard. In one case, state law granted the authority to university presidents to make appointments and provide for compensation and other conditions of employment, and state law also provided that the president's designee could give salary increases. Deans regularly performed these functions, making appointments to the faculty and granting discretionary increases to faculty during the budget year. When a dean received express authorization from the university provost in the form of a promise to support whatever measures the dean took to retain a professor, the state appeals court held that the dean was acting within the scope of his employment when he entered into a contract with the professor and was an authorized agent of the university. In the state appeals court's view, the dean possessed both the general authority (under state law) and the specific authority (delegated by the provost) to commit the institution to the terms of a salary increase.[23]

Faculty Employment Contract Types

Faculty employment contracts are typically distinguished as "at will," "term," or "continuing contracts." Employment at will is employment for an indefinite term and is terminable for any nondiscriminatory reason by either party. A term or probationary contract is one in which the faculty member has no entitlement to employment beyond the period specified in the contract. The award of tenure grants a property right in the form of an entitlement to continuing contract.

At-will status is often associated with administrative positions in colleges and universities. Judges reason that absent a specific contract agreement

---

[22] Lakshman v. Mason, 486 F. Supp. 2d 574 (S.D. Miss. 2006).

[23] Parker v. State of Fla. Bd. of Regents, 724 So. 2d 163 (Fla. Dist. Ct. App. 1998). The agreement developed in the dean's memo was a conditional contract to raise the professor's salary "as soon as the budget situation permits." A jury could reasonably find that there were sufficient funds to raise the professor's salary within the first year of the agreement.

establishing a fixed term of employment, an employer is free to dismiss an employee at any time and for any reason without liability.[24] Similarly, the employee may abandon the position without notice to the employer. Under the at-will doctrine, a plaintiff cannot state a claim for breach of the employment contract if the position was for no specified or guaranteed period of time.[25] In an illustrative case, a chancellor who failed to establish a tenure process at a new community college was an at-will employee and could be dismissed.[26] However, the at-will employee may be entitled to some limited protection in a dismissal. For example, in private sector institutions, an internal grievance procedure may apply to the institution's adverse employment decision. In a public sector institution, either a grievance procedure or the stigmatizing nature of allegations against the employee may be such that an opportunity for a name-clearing hearing may be available under state administrative procedures or federal law.[27]

Probationary faculty typically are appointed under a term contract. Courts generally uphold nonrenewal of probationary faculty if the institution follows its internal procedures. For example, a court upheld a dental school's decision not to renew a faculty member's term contract because the faculty member received the procedures required by the policies, the contract, and the handbook. The court found the dental school's failure to promulgate additional policies was not a basis to overturn a decision, because the handbook only recommended that the policies be added.[28]

In public institutions, term contracts may require timely notice of nonrenewal prior to the ending date of the contract, but no additional due process protection is available unless state law grants additional entitlements.[29] In one case, a federal appeals court ruled that even though the faculty handbook was not expressly incorporated in the contract of employment, a probationary faculty member could reasonably rely on timely notice, given handbook provisions and the custom and practice of the institution. Failure to provide timely notice of nonrenewal meant that the institution was required to show

---

[24] *See, e.g.,* McCallum v. Coop. Extension Serv., 142 N.C. App. 485, 42 S.E.2d 227 (N.C. Ct. App. 2001) (rejecting claim of an at will employee that a protected property interest existed under the due process clause); Dunfey v. Roger Williams Univ., 824 F. Supp. 18 (D. Mass.1993) (finding the termination of a university administrator was not governed by a covenant of "good faith and fair dealing"); Rutherford v. Presbyterian Univ. Hosp., 417 Pa. Super. 316, 612 A.2d 500 (Pa. Super. Ct. 1992) (finding the employee's reliance on the general terms of an employee handbook did not create a property entitlement to due process).

[25] Kish v. Iowa Cent. Cmty. Coll., 142 F. Supp. 2d 1084 (N.D. Iowa 2001); Murtagh v. Emory Univ., 152 F. Supp. 2d 1356 (N.D. Ga. 2001); and Galloway v. Roger Williams Univ., 777 A.2d 148 (R.I. 2001).

[26] Bonaparte v. Bd. of Supervisors of La. State Univ., 24 So. 3d 232 (La. 2009).

[27] Starishevsky v. Hofstra Univ., 161 Misc. 2d 137, 612 N.Y.S.2d 794 (N.Y. App. Div. 1994) (sexual harassment and unethical conduct); Spiegel v. Univ. of S. Fla., 555 So.2d 428 (Fla. Dist. Ct. App. 1989) (finding the right to a hearing for department chair subject to removal under state administrative procedure act).

[28] Perinpanayagam v. Univ. of Buffalo, 39 A.D.3d 1220, 833 N.Y.S.2d 809 (N.Y. App. Div. 2007).

[29] Bd. of Regents v. Roth, 408 U.S. 564; 92 S. Ct. 2701; 33 L. Ed. 2d 548 (1972).

cause for termination, since a legitimate expectancy of another annual contract was created.[30]

If a term or annual contract employee were subject to an adverse employment decision during the period of the contract, the employee could claim a breach of contract. In a public institution of higher education, Fourteenth Amendment due process protections (principally notice and a hearing) would be applicable to the employee's entitlement. Thus, annual contract faculty in public institutions have a protected property right to employment and a concomitant due process right to notice and a hearing if they are subject to dismissal during the period of employment.[31]

Faculty Appointments, Renewals, Promotions, and Tenure

An overwhelming majority of accredited public and private postsecondary institutions have established written and published standards and criteria regarding initial faculty appointments, renewals, promotions, as well as the granting and termination of tenure. Yet, today's courts are less likely to become involved in legal disputes governing the substance of existing college and university standards governing these matters;[32] instead, courts are more focused on legal disputes about procedures used for applying existing standards and criteria to faculty members at the institutions. While the existing caselaw indicates that the majority of contemporary courts will legally enforce a college or university's existing standards and criteria, considerable discretion is granted both to the content and specificity.

The traditional criteria for evaluating the employment quality of higher education faculty personnel have been scholarship, teaching, and service. More recently, however, additional criteria have been adopted to evaluate faculty employment decisions, including attempts to evaluate interpersonal relationships, or perceived "collegiality" of the faculty member seeking renewal, promotion, or tenure.

A Maryland appeals court, for example, ruled in agreement with the university that collegiality is a factor that may be considered in a faculty member's promotion and tenure review, even though it is not expressly included in a higher education institution's promotion and tenure policy.[33] The court reasoned that collegiality plays an essential role in the categories of both teaching and service and found error in the trial court's failure to hold, as a matter of law, that collegiality was an appropriate consideration in the context

---

[30] Greene v. Howard Univ., 412 F.2d 1128 (D.C. Cir. 1969).

[31] Calhoun v. Gaines, 982 F.3d 1470 (10th Cir. 1992).

[32] Dorsett v. Bd. of Trustees for State Coll.& Univ., 940 F.2d 121, 123 (5th Cir. 1991) ("[o]f all fields that the federal courts should hesitate to invade and take over, education and faculty appointments at the university level are probably the least suited for federal court supervision").

[33] Univ. of Baltimore v. Iz, 123 Md. App. 135, 716 A.2d 1107 (Md. 1998).

of an assistant professor's review for tenure and promotion.[34] In a variety of faculty tenure termination lawsuits, the faculty plaintiffs have argued that collegiality was not expressly mentioned in the college or university's tenure and promotion standards or criteria, and thus should not be used in the faculty tenure evaluation process. In response, a number of court decisions have held that collegiality does not need to be explicitly mentioned in higher education institutional tenure and promotion documents. Rather, as long as appropriate evidence can be supplied that collegiality is implicit in the college or university's standards and criteria, it is an appropriate consideration in faculty tenure and promotion decisions.[35]

At both public and private higher education institutions, tenure is defined as a form of continuous faculty contract designed to create a contractually enforceable institutional commitment to appointment for an indefinite term that can be terminated only for good cause in accordance with procedures specified as part of the contract of employment. The higher education institution's agents can specify tenure in the institution's governing documents, faculty handbooks, collective bargaining agreements, or individual contracts of employment. Evaluated excellence in teaching, research, and service forms the traditional basis for the successful award of tenure.

The American Association of University Professors (AAUP) has played a formidable role in defining tenure at U.S. colleges and universities. Many faculty handbooks have adopted the language of the AAUP's 1940 Statement of Principles[36] as part of institutional policy. Even in the absence of a specific reference, ambiguities in faculty employment contracts will often be resolved by reference to AAUP guidelines as representing custom and practice in the academic profession. For instance, the Colorado Court of Appeals ruled that tenured faculty members' right to priority over nontenured faculty and right to relocation within the institution in the event of a reduction-in-force were substantive rights, based on expert testimony that removing these rights did not comport with industry standards set out by the AAUP.[37]

Judges grant considerable discretion to institutions in the context of tenure decisions if the institution has the foresight to establish express and relevant criteria. In one example, despite a faculty recommendation to grant tenure, an institution's president and board denied tenure to an assistant professor on the basis of predicting shifts in student enrollment and declining interest in the program with which the assistant professor was associated. A New York

---

[34] *Id.* At 166-167, 716 A.2d at 1123-1124. *See* Mayberry v. Dees, 663 F.2d 502 (4th Cir. 1981); Stein v. Kent State Univ., 994 F. Supp. 898 (N.D. Ohio 1998), *aff'd without opinion*, 181 F.3d 103 (6th Cir. 1999).

[35] Bresnick v. Manhattanville College, 864 F.Supp. 327 (S.D.N.Y. 1994); McGill v. The Regents of the Univ. of California, 52 Cal. Rptr. 2d 466 (Cal. Ct. App. 1996); Ward v. Midwestern State Univ., 217 F.App'x 325 (5th Cir. 2007); Butler v. Emory University, 45 F. Supp. 3d 1374 (N.D. Ga. 2014).

[36] American Association of University Professors, *Academic Freedom and Tenure, 1940 Statement of Principles and Interpretative Comments*, AAUP REDBOOK (1977).

[37] Saxe v. Bd. of Trustees of Metro. State Coll. of Denver, 179 P.3d 67 (Colo. 2007).

appeals court affirmed the award of summary judgment to the institution and rejected the assistant professor's challenge to the denial of tenure on the basis that the faculty handbook made it inescapable that the institution could consider future institutional need in tenure decisions.[38] In a separate case, the New York appeals court ruled that neither the board nor the president were required to state in detail the reasons for disagreeing with a faculty committee's recommendation for tenure when the private university's policies only specified that the administration should defer to faculty judgment. The court reasoned that the word "should" outlined an advisory or suggested course rather than a mandatory action.[39]

For-Cause Terminations of Faculty Tenure

One of the most significant and impactful personnel decisions made by higher education officials is whether or not to dismiss a tenured faculty member. Since for-cause terminations of faculty tenure are often agonizing for both the individual faculty member and other faculty members involved in the decision-making, these cases often give rise to both complex legal and ethical issues, such as what types of evidence are necessary to support the termination of tenure. Some examples where the courts have upheld for-cause faculty terminations of tenure include incompetence,[40] "neglect of duty,"[41] dishonesty,[42] "moral delinquency,"[43] and "moral turpitude."[44] Interestingly, there are a limited number of cases where the court overturned a tenured faculty member's termination because the faculty member's alleged misconduct did not meet the institution's contractual standard for dismissal.[45] In this case, the private college's faculty handbook adopted the language "grave cause" in their faculty handbook as the proper standard for determining whether or not to terminate tenured faculty. As such, the court interpreted this standard as preventing the college from terminating the faculty member and the court upheld the faculty member's legal claim of wrongful discharge from the college. Some legal scholars argue that the increased use of for-cause tenured faculty terminations would result in reduced litigation involving faculty termination as well as a lower success rate of faculty challenging their dismissals.[46] A more balanced

[38] Roklina v. Skidmore Coll., 268 A.D.2d 765, 702 N.Y.S.2d 161 (N.Y. App. Div. 2000).

[39] Berkeley-Caines v. St. John Fisher Coll., 11 A.D.3d 895, 782 N.Y.S.2d 309 (N.Y. App. Div. 2004).

[40] Weist v. State of Kansas Bd. of Regents, Kan. Dist. Ct., 2002).

[41] In re Bigler v. Cornell Univ., 698 N.Y.S.2d 472 (N.Y.App.Div. 1999).

[42] Lamvermeyer v. Denison Univ., (Ohio Ct. Appt. Ct. 2000) (falsification of faculty expense vouchers).

[43] Davenport v. Bd. of Trustees of State Center Comm. College Dist., 654 F.Supp. 2d 1073 (E.D. Cal. 2009) (inappropriate treatment of other faculty, students, and staff).

[44] Tarasenko v. Univ. of Arkansas, 63 F.Supp. 3d 910 (E.D. Ark. 2014) (faculty member made threatening verbal statements to a graduate student).

[45] Ohio Dominican College v. Krone, 560 N.E. 2d 1340 (Ohio Ct. App. 1990).

[46] See, J. Royce Fichtner and Lou Ann Simpson, *Trimming the Deadwood: Removing Tenured Faculty for Cause*, 41 J. COLL. & U. LAW 25 (2015).

perspective encourages higher education administrators to rely on alternative to faculty dismissals for-cause, including faculty retirement incentives, visiting professorships, or the use of non-tenure track appointments.

A much more common basis upon which a college or university denies tenure is the failure of a faculty member to demonstrate research excellence through publications in peer-reviewed journals and/or other accepted publication venues for a faculty member's scholarly work. Courts typically grant institutional discretion in certain circumstances. For example, existing caselaw has held that academic departments can interpret faculty tenure and promotion standards and criteria in a more demanding way compared to faculty tenure and promotion decisions of previous years. In an illustrative case, an assistant professor in accounting was denied tenure based on her perceived weak scholarly publication record and she introduced evidence that departmental standards changed during the years she was pursuing tenure.[47] Despite introducing evidence that a male faculty colleague with a similar scholarly publishing record received tenure two years earlier, the court held that the faculty member's denial of tenure was upheld and her evidence was insufficient to establish a discriminatory motive based on gender for tenure denial. In another representative case, a medical school faculty member was denied tenure because her publication record was deemed deficient and insufficient. The faculty member alleged that the university's failure to support her research led to her inability to publish, because the university did not maintain a sterile and uncontaminated tissue culture facility, denied her sufficient funding for her research, and assigned her to administrative duties. The appellate court upheld summary judgment in the university's favor because these actions were at most negligent, rather than arbitrary and capricious. Moreover, the faculty handbook did not guarantee a faculty member automatic tenure but merely granted an opportunity to be eligible for tenure. Because the university followed the standards detailed in the faculty handbook, which included scholarly publication as an explicit part of the criteria necessary for tenure, the court ruled that the university did not breach the contract with the faculty member by denying her tenure.[48]

Although judicial deference to academic decision-making applies to the decision to grant or deny tenure, these employment issues are not beyond judicial scrutiny. While the management of a higher education institution is uniquely the province of faculty and administrators within the institution, university agents are required to follow internal rules and procedures, and a court may determine whether institutional representatives violated the terms of the institution's handbook or acted arbitrarily and capriciously. In a case in which the faculty handbook provided that classroom performance is the prime criterion for tenure at the institution, and required that institutional representatives make classroom visitations as part of a tenure evaluation, the department

[47] Lawrence v. Curators of the Univ. of Missouri, 204 F.3d 807 (8th Cir. 2000).
[48] Allworth v. Howard Univ., 890 A.2d 194 (D.C. 2006).

chair's failure to undertake the requisite classroom visits was regarded by the court as an insufficient evaluation in light of the direction of the handbook, requiring the court to grant a de novo tenure review to the faculty member.[49]

In a similar breach of a faculty contract claim related to the denial of tenure, the Supreme Court of Connecticut noted that despite the faculty handbook's directive for the evaluation committee to be as specific as possible about an employee's tenure prospects, the committee was positive about the faculty member's work, vague about her deficiencies, and negligent in clarifying the criteria that would apply to an award of tenure. Under these circumstances, it was reasonable for the assistant professor to rely on the assurance that she should continue along the course of scholarship she had established. The court, in ruling that the institution had breached the contract of employment, concluded that if the college had been more specific in its evaluation of the plaintiff's candidacy, she might have been able to more judiciously allocate her time and energies in a fashion that would more closely address the institution's tenure requirements.[50]

De Facto Faculty Tenure

Beginning with the United States Supreme Court decision in *Perry v. Sindermann,*[51] federal courts have recognized that a faculty member may plead and prove that the institution maintained a custom and practice of de facto tenure. In the *Perry* decision, the Court weighed the lengthy service of a community college faculty member, the institution's repeated assurances that satisfactory performance would result in continuous employment, and the institution's failure to develop a formal tenure policy in holding that the faculty member had established a claim of de facto tenure.

However, institutions that specifically provide formal policies and procedures for award of faculty tenure may avoid these specific claims.[52] For example, in a case in which a probationary faculty member asserted that she had obtained tenure through completing a seven-year period of service at the institution, the reviewing court evaluated the claim in relationship to a faculty handbook that expressly provided that it was the institution's prerogative to award tenure. Given the specific terms of the handbook, the court rejected the professor's assertion that university officials had assured her of automatic tenure once she completed seven years of probationary service.[53] In a similar case, an untenured assistant professor who was not renewed for a third proba-

---

[49] Sackman v. Alfred Univ., 186 Misc. 2d 227; 717 N.Y.S.2d 461 (N. Y. Sup. Ct. 2000).

[50] Craine v. Trinity Coll., 259 Conn. 625, 791 A.2d 518 (Conn. 2002).

[51] 408 U.S. 593 (1972).

[52] *See* Gray v. Bd. of Regents of the Univ. System of Ga., 150 F.3d 1347 (11th Cir. 1998) (rejecting award of tenure by default based on express institutional policies on the award of tenure).

[53] Paul v. Howard Univ., 754 A.2d 297 (D.C. 2000). *But see* Harris v. Ariz. Bd. of Regents, 528 F. Supp. 987 (D. Ariz. 1981) (upholding terminated faculty member's claim of de facto tenure despite the existence of a formal tenure policy based on an offer letter that stated the employee would receive tenure automatically in his third year of employment).

tionary year claimed an entitlement protected by due process and a requirement that good cause accompany the nonrenewal. The Seventh Circuit rejected the claim, emphasizing that the contract of employment reserved broad discretion relative to reappointment in the institution's representatives. According to the court, general statements in the faculty handbook that reappointment would be guided by criteria related to teaching, scholarship, and service did not establish a legal entitlement to continued employment at the higher education institution.[54]

It is critical that today's higher education administrators, at both public and private institutions, expressly detail the procedures to be used for the internal review of faculty employment decisions in writing and make these guidelines widely available to all faculty personnel. Additionally, public higher education institutions must also legally comply with existing federal constitutional due process requirements, especially the procedural due process considerations of notice and the opportunity for faculty to provide their version of events. While private postsecondary institutions are not mandated to follow these constitutional due process requirements, it might be advisable to use these constitutional due process consideration as guiding legal principles for their own internal review of faculty guidelines.

Collective Bargaining Agreements Involving Faculty Employment

The contract of employment may be significantly influenced by collective bargaining agreements, but the applicable laws governing faculty collective bargaining differ between public and private sector institutions. State law regulates public institutions of higher education, while private institutions are governed by the National Labor Relations Act of 1935 as amended by the Labor-Management Relations Act of 1947.[55]

State laws vary significantly in the extent to which faculty may bargain collectively. In some jurisdictions, bargaining may be nothing more than a right to meet and confer with institutional management, while other states may authorize bargaining over a range of subjects that include mandatory items such as wages, hours, and a potentially inclusive category consisting of "conditions of employment." Permissive subjects may be negotiated when both parties agree to a negotiation.

What constitutes mandatory or permissive subjects for negotiation will be subject to judicial interpretation of applicable state or federal law. Certain items may be beyond the scope of bargaining in a particular state because legislative pronouncement has preempted the topic, or because the topic is a nondelegable function of the governing board. For example, the Supreme Court of South Dakota has ruled that a state appropriations statute providing for faculty salary increases to be made exclusively by the institutional governing board was constitutional, and rejected a faculty union's claim that the board

---

[54] Omosegbon v. Wells, 335 F.3d 668 (7th Cir. 2003).

[55] 29 *U.S.C.* § 141 *et seq.*

could not exercise that discretion absent a negotiated agreement.[56] In another case, the Ohio Legislature was justified in imposing a faculty workload policy that was held by the United States Supreme Court to be an inappropriate subject for collective bargaining.[57]

While private sector institutions may elect to voluntarily recognize faculty representatives of a union and commence bargaining, the usual approach to faculty collective bargaining in both the private and public sector is to insist that faculty representatives seeking recognition petition for a certification election and establish, usually by majority vote, that they represent the interest of faculty for purposes of collective negotiations. As a part of this process, defining the community of interest among employees will result in determining the nature of the bargaining unit. For example, the Supreme Court of Vermont held that adjunct faculty did not share a community of interest with full-time faculty and could be excluded from the faculty bargaining unit at Vermont public institutions.[58]

Faculty in private sector institutions may be restricted from the application of federal collective bargaining law if language in institutional handbooks appears to grant broad managerial and supervisory responsibilities to faculty.[59] This "managerial exclusion" from bargaining would apply when faculty participate broadly in institutional governance, effectively determining "the product to be produced, the terms upon which it will be offered, and the customers who will be served."[60] However, the exclusion has not precluded collective bargaining in all private sector institutions, as judges weigh limits on faculty influence over institutional decision making in assessing managerial status.

Recognition as the official bargaining agent for a particular unit carries a presumption of exclusive status for purposes of bargaining.[61] Exclusive status permits the designated faculty union to charge nonmembers an agency fee to underwrite the costs of union services,[62] but nonunion faculty are not obligated to pay for the costs of union political activity with which the nonunion faculty disagree.[63] Although the determination of what constitutes "political activity" that is not germane to collective bargaining is often speculative, it would include subsidies for legislative lobbying outside the scope of contract ratification or implementation of the terms of the agreement.[64]

---

[56] S.D. Educ. Ass'n v. S.D. Bd. of Regents, 1998 SD 84, 582 N.W.2d 386 (S.D. 1998).

[57] Cent. State Univ. v. Am. Ass'n of Univ. Professors, 526 U.S. 124, 119 S. Ct. 1162, 143 L. Ed. 2d 227 (1999).

[58] Vt. State Coll. Faculty Fed'n v. Vt. State Colls., 152 Vt. 343, 566 A.2d 955 (Vt. 1989).

[59] NLRB v. Yeshiva Univ., 444 U.S. 672, 100 S. Ct. 856, 63 L. Ed. 2d 115 (1980).

[60] Id. at 686.

[61] See Knight v. Minn. Cmty. Coll. Faculty Ass'n., 466 U.S. 284, 104 S. Ct. 1799, 80 L. Ed. 2d 302 (1984) (rejecting a challenge to a faculty union's exclusive right to negotiate subjects of mandatory bargaining).

[62] Abood v. Detroit Bd. of Educ., 431 U.S. 209, 97 S. Ct. 1782, 52 L. Ed. 2d 261 (1977).

[63] Chicago Teachers' Union v. Hudson, 475 U.S. 292, 106 S. Ct. 1066, 89 L. Ed. 2d 232 (1988).

[64] Lehnert v. Ferris Faculty Ass'n, 500 U.S. 507, 111 S. Ct. 1950, 114 L. Ed. 2d 572 (1991).

The application of collective bargaining agreements to contract disputes has resulted in mixed legal precedent. Faculty may be foreclosed from asserting rights under an implied contract when the bargaining agreement contains language expressly providing that the agreement constitutes the complete agreement between the parties.[65] Similarly, a grievance and arbitration provision in the bargaining agreement may limit the options available to a faculty member for redress of a breach of contract claim. Negotiated agreements often provide for a grievance procedure to resolve disputes related to the administration of the agreement. Arbitration is typically a final step in resolving disputes, and the agreement will define the powers and duties of the arbitrator.

Adverse Faculty Employment Decisions

Just as institutional governing boards are vested with the authority to hire, as well as assign and award tenure, these governing bodies may undertake adverse employment decisions against faculty. It is also relevant to highlight that public higher education institutions are also potentially subject to state statutes or administrative regulations regarding procedures and policies concerning adverse faculty employment decisions. In the context of faculty employee discipline, an adverse employment decision may include reprimand, suspension with or without pay, demotion, nonrenewal, layoff, or dismissal for cause. Judicial review of an adverse employment decision involves a series of inquiries: Did the institution comply with the contractual obligation to the employee? Were procedures for undertaking an adverse employment decision followed? Was substantial evidence provided in proof of the alleged facts justifying the adverse employment decision? Did the facts establish good cause under the terms of the contract?

While adverse employment decisions involving faculty at public institutions of higher education are subject to review based on constitutional constraints, judicial review of disciplinary decisions involving faculty of private colleges or universities is limited to whether the institution failed to comply with its own internal procedures and whether a decision was made arbitrarily, capriciously, or in bad faith. Whether the institution is public or private, judges recognize that some discretion must be afforded to the institution in determining whether an adverse employment decision is warranted. Stress on overly detailed written criteria and unnecessarily literal interpretation of those criteria cannot be permitted to eliminate consideration of relevant, but subjective, factors in evaluating employees.

As a corollary, judges emphasize that a court may not substitute its judgment for the judgment and discretion properly exercised by college administrators. For example, a state appeals court affirmed a ruling that a president's reprimand of a tenured faculty member was consistent with the terms of the institution's faculty handbook and was made in good faith. Despite the fact

---

[65] White v. Winona State Univ., 474 N.W.2d 410 (Minn. Ct. App. 1991) and McGough v. Univ. of San Francisco, 214 Cal. App. 3d 1577, 263 Cal. Rptr. 404 (Cal. 1989).

that the president's decision contravened the recommendation of a review committee that proposed the reprimand be invalidated, the court held that the president's final determination sufficiently set forth job-related reasons for the adverse employment decision based on continued neglect of academic duties and was supported by the record. It found no basis for further judicial intervention with respect to the exercise of administrative discretion.[66]

Progressive Discipline of Faculty Members

Unless faculty employee misconduct is determined to be so egregious or extreme that a single instance would justify cause for dismissal, the range of adverse employment court decisions permits a system of progressive discipline.[67] Under such a system, a faculty employee's single instance of misconduct might result in a written reprimand. If the behavior continues, an escalation of penalties, to include suspension or demotion, could be implemented. A documented pattern of continuing misconduct would result in dismissal. One state court reasoned that a record of progressive discipline effectively documented a history of repeated correction, counseling, and training of the employee about job-related deficiencies. In view of the evidence that the employee had not adequately conformed her conduct to the requirements of the job, the court found that dismissal was justified.[68]

Just Cause Faculty Dismissal

The American Association of University Professors (AAUP) proposes "adequate cause" as the standard for dismissal of faculty,[69] but it is the institution's burden to define the concept and relate it to the performance of faculty. Under the AAUP definition, dismissal is possible only if the institution can show demonstrated incompetence or dishonesty in teaching or research, manifest neglect of duty, or conduct that substantially impairs the individual's job-related responsibilities.[70] Among the specific grounds that are often incorporated in institutional disciplinary policies, unprofessional conduct, insubordination, immorality, neglect of duty, and incompetence typically are identified.

If the institution's policy or the employment contract does not specify a particular ground or relies solely on a vague standard for adequate cause, then the faculty member may challenge an adverse employment decision on the basis that the standard is so vague that reasonable people might disagree on its meaning.[71] An assertion that the grounds for an adverse employment

---

[66] Dalmolen v. Elmira Coll., 279 A.D.2d 929, 720 N.Y.S.2d 573 (App. Div. 2001).

[67] Trimble v. W. Va. Bd. of Dirs., 209 W. Va. 420, 549 S.E.2d 294 (W. Va. 2001).

[68] Reece v. Bd. of Trs. of Marshall Univ., 202 W. Va. 89, 502 S.E.2d 186 (W. Va. 1998).

[69] American Association of University Professors, *Recommended Institutional Regulations on Academic Freedom and Tenure,* ACADEME, Jan.-Feb. 1983, at 15a-20a.

[70] *Id.* Regulation 5(a), at 26.

[71] *See, e.g.,* Ohio Dominican Coll. v. Krone, 54 Ohio App. 3d 29, 560 N.E.2d 1340 (Ohio Ct. App. 1990); Korf v. Ball State Univ., 726 F.2d 1222 (7th Cir. 1984); and Garrett v. Matthews, 625 F.2d 658 (5th Cir. 1980).

decision are vague will be subject to a test of reasonableness. For example, a tenured university professor was dismissed for failure to maintain "standards of sound scholarship and competent teaching" because of his inappropriate and abusive treatment of visiting Chinese scholars; his failure to comply with a superior's directive; and his dishonesty in dealing with payroll, federal grant funds, and applications for an academic position. The federal appeals court rejected a challenge based on vagueness, reasoning that a tenured professor should "be expected to behave decently towards students and coworkers, to comply with a superior's directive, and to be truthful and forthcoming in dealing with payroll, federal research funds, or applications for academic positions. Such behavior is required for the purpose of maintaining sound scholarship and competent teaching."[72]

Unprofessional Faculty Conduct

Unprofessional faculty conduct includes a range of inappropriate behaviors. It may be implicated when a faculty member's lack of collegiality, harassment of department personnel, refusal to heed prior warnings regarding his conduct, or excessive filing of grievances are documented.[73] Intellectual dishonesty, including charges of plagiarism, may serve as a basis for unprofessional conduct leading to dismissal.[74] In one instance, a tenured faculty member in a community college was properly dismissed for "capricious disregard of accepted standards of professional conduct" based on instances of arbitrary treatment of students, rude and discourteous behavior to peers and staff, and insubordination toward supervisors. In response to complaints from students, faculty and administrative personnel, the department chair initially substantiated the complaints, then met with the faculty member and identified problems that, if not corrected, would result in termination. When this approach failed, the chair recommended termination, and extensive due process procedures were set in motion. The faculty member received written notice of the charges against her, and a faculty committee began an inquiry that led to a finding of cause for dismissal. Following a formal hearing, a recommendation for dismissal was advanced to the governing board, which affirmed discharge. The state supreme court ruled that the charges were established by clear and convincing evidence and held that dismissal was justified, because the faculty member had received repeated counseling, specific warnings, and reprimands about the behavior that ultimately led to her dismissal.[75] Unprofessional conduct was addressed in a case involving a tenured professor who had concealed his dual employment as a member of the faculty at two separate institutions. In responding to inquiries from his dean at one of the institutions, the professor misled the administrator by suggesting that the ap-

---

[72] San Filippo v. Bongiovanni, 961 F.2d 1125, 1137 (3d Cir. 1992),

[73] *See* de Llano v. Berglund, 282 F.3d 1031 (8th Cir. 2002).

[74] *See* Agarwal v. Regents of the Univ. of Minn., 788 F.2d 504 (8th Cir. 1986) and Yu v. Peterson, 13 F.3d 1413 (10th Cir. 1993).

[75] Phillips v. State Bd. of Regents, 863 S.W.2d 45 (Tenn. 1993).

pointment at the other institution was temporary and part-time, when in fact it was a tenured appointment. After resigning the post at one institution, the professor was subject to termination proceedings at the other on the basis that he failed to maintain a relationship of trust with professional colleagues. The state appeals court rejected the professor's contention that the institution must prove impairment in his teaching, research, or service, concluding that what constituted "unprofessional conduct" was best left to the determination of the professional community of which the individual was a part.[76]

In a Minnesota case, a state appeals court affirmed dismissal of two university gymnastics coaches on the basis of clear and convincing evidence of unprofessional conduct. Testimony from students and staff confirmed that one of the coaches had, on more than one occasion, directed students to lie concerning her failure to conform to university policies on student transportation to athletic activities. Further testimony confirmed that the other coach had, either intentionally or negligently, allowed students to view sexually explicit videotape footage that had been included on tapes of students participating in gymnastic competition. In the latter case, the court found that even if the distribution of the videos to students had been unintentional, the coach's negligent conduct seriously compromised his effectiveness as a representative of the university and a guide and teacher of young people.[77]

Unprofessional conduct also applies to dismissal for harassing students.[78] A tenured faculty member's insulting and demeaning letters to a former student who sought to receive a grade change were deemed "unprofessional" by a faculty panel convened to hear evidence of the professor's conduct. The professor challenged the hearing recommendations and filed suit when he was subject to demotion and reduction in salary. On review, a federal appeals court viewed the professor's letters to the student as attempts to compel or coerce an apology from the student and concluded that in balancing the professor's right to comment, the university's interest in ensuring that its students receive a fair grade and are not subject to demeaning, insulting, and inappropriate comments would outweigh the professor's interests.[79]

In another instance of unprofessional conduct, dismissal was justified in a case considering allegations that a professor had sexually harassed a student while on an international studies program. The professor challenged the cause for dismissal from the private college, alleging that it breached the contract of employment in terminating him. The federal appeals court looked to the college's faculty handbook, noting that there was no mention of cause for dismissal in the document, but recognizing that under the board-approved

---

[76] Zahavy v. Univ. of Minn., 544 N.W.2d 32 (Minn. Ct. App. 1996) *See* Garner v. Mich. State Univ., 185 Mich. App. 750, 462 N.W.2d 832 (Mich. Ct. App. 1990) (finding that a tenured professor alleged to have lied during a preemployment interview was entitled to due process and a right to an adversarial hearing before discharge even though the university sought to rescind the contract).

[77] Deli v. Univ. of Minn., 511 N.W.2d 46, 52 (Minn. Ct. App. 1994).

[78] *See* Korf v. Ball State Univ., 726 F.1222 (7th Cir. 1984).

[79] Keen v. Penson, 970 F.3d 252 (7th Cir. 1992).

sexual harassment policy, a hearing committee could recommend termination if charges of sexual harassment were substantiated. The court held that the provisions of the sexual harassment policy stated grounds for dismissal in the instant case and ruled that the dismissal should stand.[80]

Failure to effectively document instances of misconduct at the time they occur may jeopardize an institution's effort to undertake dismissal for unprofessional conduct. Judges often apply a whole record test that spans the faculty member's employment and considers evidence that supports the adverse employment decision as well as contradictory evidence. In ruling that a decision to dismiss was arbitrary and capricious, one court reviewed a record of six incidents allegedly involving harassing and threatening behavior on the part of a tenured faculty member. These incidents spanned a fifteen-year period and, in most cases, had not been documented at the time they occurred and did not lead to administrative reprimand or other progressive discipline. The length of time between the alleged misconduct and the disciplinary action taken in connection with that misconduct was considered by the reviewing court to be an indication of bad faith on the part of the university in its attempt to dismiss the professor.[81]

Faculty Insubordination

Dismissal for insubordination involves evidence of a repeated, constant, or continuing refusal to obey reasonable orders. Evidence of insubordination may be regarded as insufficient to sustain dismissal absent documentation that the employee was given a reasonable directive regarding his or her conduct and that the alleged misconduct was constant or continuous. Institutional administrators must make directives concerning the conduct that is prohibited as clear and unequivocal as possible, in order to avoid a factual dispute in which the employee asserts that he or she effectively complied with a directive or that the directive failed to warn of the prohibited conduct.[82]

Progressive discipline in cases involving insubordination is recommended as a means of providing notice of prohibited conduct. Written directives and reprimands provide a documentary record of previous instances of inappropriate behavior and corroborate testimony that the employee has been advised

---

[80] Logan v. Bennington Coll., 72 F.3d 1017 (2d Cir. 1995). *See also* McDaniels v. Flick, 59 F.3d 446 (3d Cir. 1995) (finding minimal due process procedures in pre-termination based on allegations of sexual harassment were adequate to justify summary judgment for the public college). *But see* Chan v. Miami Univ., 73 Ohio St. 3d 52, 1995 Ohio 226, 652 N.E.2d 644 (Ohio 1995) (finding that a faculty member subject to dismissal under the procedures set forth for the resolution of sexual harassment complaints was denied due process).

[81] Dismissal Proceedings Against Huang, 110 N.C. App. 683, 688, 431 S.E.2d 541, 547 (N.C. Ct. App. 1995).

[82] *See* Howard Univ. v. Baten, 632 A.2d 389 (D.C. 1993) (finding evidence of insubordination created a jury question concerning whether the university employee received adequate warning about prohibited non-job related work).

of what conduct is acceptable and what conduct would result in termination if continued.[83]

Neglect of Duty

Neglect of duty involves the repeated failure to perform duties prescribed by law or failure to comply with reasonable directives or institutional policies relating to employee responsibilities. Instances of neglect of duty are often appropriate for a plan of progressive discipline. For example, a faculty member's persistent absenteeism would justify an initial warning, followed by a formal reprimand and heightened oversight to ensure compliance with directives. If the behavior continued, the documented evidence of excessive absenteeism would constitute "good and sufficient reason" to suspend without pay or demote, and future instances might justify termination.

Repeated warnings, coupled with a persistent failure to comply with reasonable directives, were illustrated in a case in which a tenured professor of nursing challenged discharge for "significant neglect of duty." The record established the professor had been relieved of her teaching assignment and directed to develop two new graduate courses. However, she did not develop syllabi and other materials for these courses, and she ignored requests for the submission of these materials. When the professor left the university for a stay in Florida, she was repeatedly contacted by university officials, advised that she was absent without permission, and directed to report immediately and complete her assignments. Upon her return, she submitted no written materials related to the task of developing the graduate courses. The state appeals court found that the record provided clear and convincing proof that the professor's discharge was warranted.[84]

In all cases involving good cause for dismissal, it is the institution's burden to establish evidence to justify the adverse employment decision. For example, the dismissal of a tenured faculty member for neglect of duty was accompanied by evidence that the professor had disclosed confidential student information to a classroom of students and neglected her teaching duties by ending a course one month prior to the conclusion of the academic term. A state court affirmed the decision of an administrative law judge that the institution met its burden to establish by clear and convincing evidence that there was adequate cause for dismissal.[85]

However, in a case in which an institution's decision to dismiss for "neglect of professional responsibilities" was not affirmed, the reviewing court ruled the institution failed to evaluate the faculty member's actions according to appropriate professional standards. The faculty member refused to teach a class until the institution disciplined a disruptive student, and the governing

---

[83] See Nelson v. Pima Cmty. Coll., 83 F.3d 1075 (9th Cir. 1996) and Hanton v. Gilbert, 36 F.3d 4 (4th Cir. 1994) (upholding adverse employment decision based on consistent documentation of misconduct and clear administrative directives to the university employee).

[84] Josberger v. Univ. of Tenn., 706 S.W.2d 300 (Tenn. Ct. App. 1985).

[85] Peterson v. N.D. Univ., 678 N.W.2d 163 (N.D. 2004).

board rejected a faculty grievance committee's recommendation and moved to terminate his employment. The reviewing court remanded the case with an admonition that the professor should be allowed to present evidence that his conduct was within the bounds of reasonable behavior for the profession. In essence, the court determined that the phrase "neglect of professional responsibilities" includes consideration of whether the faculty member's actions were reasonable in refusing to teach the class, given the institution's failure to take steps to resolve the incident with the disruptive student.[86]

Faculty Immorality

Allegations of immorality involve conduct sufficiently egregious and notorious to bring the individual concerned or the higher education institution into public disgrace or disrespect and impair the individual's performance. In many cases, the immoral conduct would be so extreme that a single instance is sufficient for dismissal. Factors to be weighed in assessing a basis for immorality as a cause for dismissal would include 1) the likelihood of recurrence of the questioned conduct; 2) the extenuating or aggravating circumstances, if any; 3) the effect of notoriety and publicity; 4) any impairment of teacher-student relationships; 5) any disruption of the educational process; 6) motive; and 7) the proximity or remoteness in time of the conduct.[87]

When the employee is a faculty member, documenting impairment will often require demonstrating a nexus between the behavior and the individual's fitness to continue his or her professional responsibilities. The requirement for nexus is intended to balance the faculty member's right to privacy against the interest of the institution in insuring efficiency and realizing its mission as an educational institution. In an illustrative case, a teacher's misdemeanor convictions for possession of marijuana and cocaine and her actions in allowing drug sales to take place in her home provided just cause for dismissal. As in most cases of this type, once the arrest became public, the college suspended the teacher with pay pending the outcome of the criminal trial. In the administrative hearing held by the college, it was determined by extensive testimony that the teacher's effectiveness was substantially impaired. The board's review of testimony from other faculty and its conclusion that the teacher's conduct directly contradicted her teaching role as a psychologist preparing students for careers in drug counseling were significant factors upon which the court relied in affirming dismissal.[88]

In a case in which a teacher in a California community college was arrested and charged with possession and intent to sell cocaine, errors by law enforcement resulted in an acquittal. However, on review in an administrative proceeding, dismissal was regarded as the appropriate sanction for the teacher who, on the standard of substantial evidence, was found to have participated

---

[86] McConnell v. Howard Univ., 818 F.2d 58 (D.C. Cir. 1987).

[87] Morrison v. State Bd. of Educ., 1 Cal. 3d 214, 461 P.2d 375; 82 Cal. Rptr. 175 (Cal. 1969).

[88] Bd. of Dirs. of Des Moines Area Cmty. Coll. v. Simons, 493 N.W.2d 879 (Iowa Ct. App. 1992).

in the sale of cocaine at a private residence being monitored by police. The California appeals court affirmed dismissal based on a record that included extensive testimony from faculty and administrators that the conduct of the teacher compromised his effectiveness as a teacher, colleague, and role model for students.[89]

Faculty Competency

Faculty competency is associated with effective classroom teaching, knowledge of subject matter, and skill in the conduct of research. When dismissal for incompetence is implicated, it involves a pattern of behavior, and the institution must provide the necessary documentation to support the cause.[90] An important dimension of documentation is observation and evaluation of performance, an activity that is increasingly mandated by requirements for accountability in both public and private institutions of higher education. In an illustrative case, low student evaluations, testimony concerning student complaints, high withdrawal rates and low student enrollments in the professor's classes, and repeated efforts by superiors to improve the professor's performance were documented to warrant the adverse employment decision.[91]

Incompetence involves job-related performance falling below an acceptable standard and typically includes a remedial opportunity to correct deficiencies, if those deficiencies do not pose a significant and immediate risk of harm to students or compromise close working relationships with colleagues. When teacher competence is at issue, progressive discipline is replaced by the identification of performance deficiencies, assistance to correct deficiencies, a reasonable opportunity for remediation, and assessment of whether performance has improved.

As a formative process, evaluation requires that reasonable, job-related performance criteria be set and that the institution, through a process of observation, evaluation, and conferencing, assist the employee to improve. When efforts to correct deficiencies and improve performance fail, the evaluation process becomes a system for documenting deficiencies and justifying an adverse employment decision based upon lack of competence. A recommendation to dismiss may be compelled when the system of assessment documents that significant deficiencies persist in spite of reasonable efforts to improve performance.

Evaluation systems must yield a documentary record that confirms the fairness and reasonableness of the process, complies with legal mandates, and meets the test of substantial evidence. Unsubstantiated claims of inadequate performance, conflicting appraisals of performance, or lack of uniform stan-

---

[89] West Valley-Mission Coll. v. Concepcion, 16 Cal. App. 4th 1766, 21 Cal. Rptr. 2d 5 (Cal. Ct. App. 1993).

[90] *See* Bevli v. Brisco, 211 Cal. App. 3d 986, 260 Cal. Rptr. 57 (Cal. Ct. App. 1989) (upholding dismissal for evident unfitness based on evaluation of a community college chemistry teacher's teaching competency).

[91] Cotter v. Trs. of Pensacola Jr. Coll., 548 So. 2d 731 (Fla. Dist. Ct. App. 1989).

dards in the evaluation process may contribute to the view that there is insufficient evidence to support an adverse employment decision. Competent and substantial evidence—which may include classroom observations, student evaluations or complaints, testimony of colleagues, anecdotal memoranda, or a combination of sources—will sustain the legitimacy of the process and justify such a decision.

Proper notice of deficiencies, and time in which to correct those deficiencies, conforms to essential requirements of due process and helps rebut claims that the evaluation system is arbitrary or capricious. In an illustrative case, a reviewing court noted that the institution provided formal and informal notification to the professor of specific deficiencies in his performance over a four-year period. Periodic evaluations established that the professor did not improve performance; letters, memoranda, and oral warnings to the professor described how his performance was deficient, using language congruent with that later used in the formal charges involving lack of competence. This documentation was persuasive in convincing the court that the professor had adequate notice of the standard of performance required, sustaining dismissal.[92]

In a similar case, a cumulative record of the employee's problems with three different supervisors confirmed instances of complaints about a librarian's failure to complete assigned tasks and lack of skills—particularly computer literacy skills—necessary to perform his job. The state supreme court found that the collective bargaining agreement governing the institution's relationship with its employees stipulated that "just cause" for dismissal included incompetency. The employee had been given notice of performance deficiencies and an opportunity for remediation, but in a two-month period of remediation, there was no evidence that he had improved performance relevant to job requirements. The state court ruled that the cumulative evidence in the record sustained the dismissal decision.[93]

In a post-tenure review case, a professor was discharged for professional incompetence based on lack of collegiality after receiving unsatisfactory reviews for three consecutive years. The professor asserted that lack of collegiality was an improper basis for discharge, as tenured professors have a substantive due process right to protection from discharge except for incompetence, misconduct, or neglect of duty. The court found that the university's post-tenure review process specified that a tenured professor may be discharged for incompetence after receiving two consecutive unsatisfactory reviews, and furthermore, college regulations require faculty to work in a collegial manner. The discharge specifically alleged that the faculty member's interactions with colleagues were disrupting the operation of the department. Because the faculty member was both aware of the expectation of collegiality and received

---

[92] Riggin v. Bd. of Trs. of Ball State Univ., 489 N.E.2d 616 (Ind. Ct. App. 1986).
[93] McCauley v. Sch. of Mines, 488 N.W.2d 53 (S.D. 1992). *See also* Trejo v. Shoben, 319 F.3d 878 (7th Cir. 2003) (finding professor's coarse commentary and ribald comments to graduate students while attending an academic conference were not protected by the First Amendment).

unsatisfactory reviews for the requisite number of years, the court found that the board had sufficient evidence of professional incompetence.[94]

Institutions must follow internal policies in cases involving dismissals for incompetence. For example, a court ruled that a university failed to follow its policy in dismissing a tenured faculty member in 1999, based on consecutive unsatisfactory reviews from 1990 and 1991, because university policy required a hearing to be held within six months of a complaint for dismissal. Although the university began dismissal proceedings in 1992, the institution did not hold a hearing, but agreed to allow the professor to resign as a tenured faculty member and remain at the institution as a nontenured faculty member. After an intervening lawsuit to determine the terms of that contract resulted in the reinstatement of the faculty member to a tenured position in 1999, the university attempted to terminate the faculty member based on the consecutive unsatisfactory reviews from 1991 and 1992. When the faculty member filed a second lawsuit, the court held that conducting a hearing in 1999 on a complaint filed in 1992 violated university policy.[95]

Closure, Merger, and Reduction-in-Force

While most adverse faculty employment decisions are related to employee performance involving misconduct, incapacity, or incompetence, faculty layoff decisions involving bona fide financial exigency may compel a higher education institution to justify the necessity for layoff and the process for selecting employees. Faculty contracts are the necessary documents that should detail a particular college or university's legal duties and responsibilities regarding issues related to reductions in faculty and/or staff. Declining student enrollments and loss of program funding are the two most frequently cited justifications for a reduction-in-force (RIF) of higher education faculty. In considering these justifications, courts attempt to grant reasonable discretionary authority to the institution while construing RIF policies narrowly in order to balance the protections of tenure. Expressly incorporating policies on RIF in faculty handbooks or negotiated agreements can help insure that fair and reasonable procedures are applied to the selection of employees subject to layoffs when conditions of economic stringency are imposed on the institution.[96]

Another important contractual consideration involving higher education faculty layoffs are the permissibility of differing contract provisions between tenured and nontenured faculty members. For example, nontenured faculty members may not have their contracts renewed at the end of their contractual terms. However, even if a faculty contract involving either nontenured or tenure-track faculty contains no layoff, or termination provision regarding financial exigency, a higher education institution may still have the legal

---

[94] Bernold v. Bd. of Gov. of the Univ. of N.C, 683 S.E.2d 428 (N.C. Ct. App. 2009).
[95] The State of Nevada Univ. & Cmty. Coll. v. Sutton, 103 P.3d 8 (Nev. 2004).
[96] Katz v. Georgetown Univ., 246 F.3d 685 (D.C. Cir. 2001).

authority to terminate either a nontenured or tenured faculty member.[97] The legal reasoning for this possibility is that higher education institutions may dissolve themselves from faculty contractual obligations if unforeseen events, including financial-based emergencies occur and make it impossible for them to fulfill their contractual obligations to faculty (i.e., paying faculty salaries).[98]

In *Krotkoff v. Goucher College*,[99] the Fourth Circuit Court of Appeals examined a decision by a private college to terminate a tenured professor due to the college's severe financial problems. Hertha Krotkoff, a tenured professor in the modern languages department, challenged her dismissal on a number of grounds, including the fact that the college had no formal policy addressing reductions-in-force due to financial exigency. She also argued that the college should have sold some of its real estate holdings or invaded its endowment to deal with financial problems rather than dismiss her from her tenured position.

The Fourth Circuit ruled that "tenure is not generally understood to preclude demonstrably bona fide dismissal for financial reasons."[100] In fact, the court observed, "[n]o case indicates that tenure creates a right to exemption from dismissal for financial reasons."[101] Moreover, the court noted, there was no evidence of a general understanding of tenure at Goucher College that gave Goucher faculty members more protection from dismissal for financial reasons than the faculty of other colleges. Thus, Goucher was not prohibited from dismissing Krotkoff for financial reasons simply because its policies did not address that contingency. In addition, the court rejected Krotkoff's argument that Goucher should have addressed its financial crisis by invading its endowment or selling some of its land rather than dismissing faculty members. In the court's view, "the existence of financial exigency should be determined by the adequacy of a college's operating funds rather than its capital assets."[102]

Finally, the Fourth Circuit reviewed the process by which Goucher decided to dismiss Krotkoff rather than another faculty member. The court acknowledged that the college had an obligation to deal fairly with its faculty when selecting tenured faculty members for dismissal but concluded that Krotkoff's evidence challenging the reasonableness of Goucher's reduction-in-force procedures was insufficient to submit the issue of fairness to a jury. Nor, in the court's view, had Goucher breached any contractual obligation to Krotkoff concerning an offer of alternate employment. Goucher had rejected Krotkoff's proposal to transfer her to a vacant position in the economic departments, but the college had not acted unreasonably when it determined that

---

[97] Bauer v. College of Santa Fe, 78 P. 3d 76 (N.M. Ct. App. 2003).

[98] In AAUP v. Bloomfield College, 322 A.2d 846 (N.J. Super Ct. 1974), *affirmed,* 346 A.2d 615 (N.J. Super Ct. App. Div. 1975), one of the first and leading legal cases analyzing financial exigency in colleges and universities.

[99] 585 F.2d 675 (4th Cir. 1978).

[100] *Id.* at 679.

[101] *Id.*

[102] *Id.* at 681.

the time and cost of training Krotkoff for the economics position made such a transfer unfeasible.[103]

In a case in which a college met its burden to justify layoffs based on a system-wide reduction, a federal appeals court found the RIF was related to declining enrollment. In response to a faculty member's claim that he was selected for layoff because of a disability, the court affirmed that there was no evidence presented that the college deviated from the announced plan for the RIF, or that anything other than objective criteria for the selection of employees to be laid off was applied. Although the instructor asserted that a subsequent job posting for an electronics instructor established the college's intent to discriminate against him, the court rejected this contention, noting that the later posting was undertaken to comply with an immigration regulation and that the position was already filled by an immigrant whose job description did not match the former instructor's.[104]

Academic Program Discontinuation

Unlike financial emergencies, different issues occur when higher education faculty terminations are due to the closure of academic programs. In instance of the closure of academic programs at higher education institutions, the courts have largely held that colleges and universities have an implied contractual right to terminate the employment of tenured faculty members when a faculty position is being eliminated directly due to a significant change or closure of an academic program.[105]

Constructive Discharge

Constructive discharge occurs when the employer makes the employee's work environment so intolerable that the employee ultimately resigns. Claims of constructive discharge are evaluated under a reasonable person standard by most state and federal courts. It is not sufficient to assert that working conditions are difficult or unpleasant. The former employee must seek to establish that working conditions were so intolerable that a reasonable person would feel compelled to resign.[106] In other words, given the conditions, a reasonable person in the same or similar circumstances as that of the employee would have no other choice than to quit.[107] Applying an objective standard, a federal appeals court found that an employee—placed on leave with pay in a temporary but unsatisfying assignment, pending investigation of a serious allegation of misconduct, who chooses to resign rather than wait for the conclusion of rea-

---

[103] *Id.* at 683.

[104] Cable v. Ivy Tech State Coll., 200 F.3d 467 (7th Cir. 1999).

[105] Jimenez v. Almodovar, 650 F.2d 363 (1st Cir. 1981).

[106] *See* Hart v. Univ. Sys. of N.H., 938 F. Supp. 104 (D.N.H. 1996) in which a federal district court ruled there was sufficient evidence to support a finding of constructive discharge when a former department chair presented circumstantial evidence of discriminatory treatment.

[107] Lighton v. Univ. of Utah, 209 F.3d 1213 (10th Cir. 2000).

sonable due process proceedings—had not been constructively discharged.[108] Moreover, treating a reasonable pre-termination suspension with pay as a constructive discharge would create tension with U.S. Supreme Court decisions on pre-termination due process procedures.[109]

One federal appeals court distinguished constructive discharge from constructive resignation. A tenured faculty member reassigned to research activities after student complaints about his teaching objected to reassignment and failed to report for work. The federal appeals court affirmed the university's determination to treat this refusal as a resignation, noting that constructive resignation refers to situations in which the employee abandons his or her position without formally resigning, and the employer treats the employee as if he had formally resigned.[110]

If the employee resigns, however, a court may find that the employee was constructively discharged. The Superior Court of Pennsylvania found that a faculty member at a dental school, who was transferred to a clinic where he earned less money, was constructively discharged. The university argued that the faculty member was not constructively discharged because he was still collecting a six-figure salary. The court disagreed, because nothing requires that the employee assert poverty to prove that he was forced to resign under the reasonable person standard for constructive discharge. Although the faculty member was receiving a substantial salary after his transfer, his salary was reduced by two-thirds, and he was not supplied an office, clerical staff, or a computer. The jury found that these circumstances would have compelled a reasonable person to submit a forced resignation, and the appellate court found no reason to overturn the decision.

Faculty Contract Rescission

An employee's fraudulent conduct in procuring a contract may result in rescission of the employment contract,[111] but an institution should be prepared to provide appropriate due process in the event rescission is rejected by a court of competent jurisdiction.[112] The Supreme Court of Vermont concluded that a faculty member's misrepresentation regarding his past work history and

---

[108] Levenstein v. Salafsky, 414 F.3d 767 (7th Cir. 2005). *See also* Baylor Univ. v. Coley, 221 S.W.3d 599, (Tex. 2007) (finding that a tenured librarian removed from supervisory duties but reassigned duties consistent with her rank as an assistant professor was not constructively discharged).

[109] Levenstein v. Salafsky, 414 F.3d 767 (7th Cir. 2005). *See generally* Cleveland Bd. of Educ. v. Loudermill, 470 U.S. 532, 84 L. Ed. 2d 494, 105 S. Ct. 1487 (1985) (finding nine-month delay in holding a pre-termination hearing was not a violation of due process given the thoroughness of the proceedings); Gilbert v. Homar, 520 U.S. 924, 138 L. Ed. 2d 120, 117 S. Ct. 1807 (1997) (finding temporary suspensions without pay do not constitute a violation of due process).

[110] Patterson v. Porch, 853 F.2d 1399 (7th Cir. 1988).

[111] Morgan v. Am. Univ., 534 A.2d 323 (D.C. 1987).

[112] Garner v. Mich. State Univ., 185 Mich. App. 750, 462 N.W.2d 832 (Mich. Ct. App. 1990) (ruling an institution was required to provide due process to professor consistent with university policies).

references warranted rescission of the employment contract and supported just-cause dismissal.[113] The faculty member had failed to report his criminal conviction and incarceration, and had misrepresented his work history in that time period. Because honesty is an implicit duty of every employee, the plaintiff had notice that his misrepresentation was grounds for dismissal.

Constitutional Due Process

Standards of fundamental fairness dictate that when the institution adopts a rule or guideline establishing a procedure for its employees, the institution must substantially observe that procedure, and any inquiry involving allegations of misconduct will proceed in good faith.[114] While private institutions are governed by the standard of good faith in adhering to the material elements of the employment contract relative to disciplinary procedures,[115] a public institution may be held to constitutional due process standards related to the Fourteenth Amendment.

Due process standards will apply to term employees if the higher education institution adopts such standards as part of its policies. For instance, the Supreme Court of Alabama ruled that the policies of the institution required that a community college instructor under a term contract receive an opportunity for a hearing when he was dismissed prior to the end of his contract.[116]

Minimal constitutional standards required of public institutions when dismissal of tenured faculty is contemplated involve notice of the cause for dismissal, notice of the names of witnesses and their testimony, meaningful opportunity to be heard, and an impartial panel with appropriate academic expertise.[117] Other protections extended to a faculty member may include allowing objections to any prospective hearing panel member, permitting cross-examination of witnesses, and providing opportunities for the presentation of testimony and evidence on the faculty member's behalf.[118] The right to have representation by an attorney in a termination decision will often depend on the law of the particular jurisdiction.

One federal appeals court approved an institution's policy allowing counsel to be present and to advise, but prohibited the attorney from conducting cross-examination of witnesses. The court's justification for this policy was

---

[113] Sarvis v. Vt. State Coll., 172 Vt. 76, 772 A.2d 494 (Vt. 2001).

[114] *See* Harrington v. Harris, 118 F.3d 359 (5th Cir. 1997) (reasoning that administrative manipulation of the evaluation system to arbitrarily favor black faculty violated plaintiff's substantive due process rights to a "rationale application" of the institution's merit pay policy).

[115] *See* Fox v. Parker, 98 S.W.3d 713 (Tex. App. 2003) (holding that the private university carefully followed the procedural steps in the faculty handbook in dismissing a tenured faculty member for inappropriate sexual conduct with students).

[116] House v. Jefferson State Cmty. Coll., 907 So. 2d 424 (Ala. 2005).

[117] McDaniels v. Flick, 59 F.3d 446 (3d Cir. 1995) and Levitt v. Univ. of Tex., 759 F.2d 1224 (5th Cir. 1985).

[118] Johnson v. Ala. Agricultural and Mechanical Univ., 481 So. 2d 336 (Ala. 1985).

that due process did not require a full-fledged remediation trial.[119] The question of whether a post-termination hearing can remedy the failure to provide an adequate pre-termination hearing for an employee who possesses an expectation of continued employment (e.g. tenure) has been resolved differently in different jurisdictions.[120] The best advice to college administrators is to ensure that a sound and minimally adequate pre-termination hearing is provided to employees who have protected property interests in continued employment in order to avoid future litigation of that due process issue. Note, however, that the United States Supreme Court has ruled that a public employee who is charged with a sufficiently serious crime need not receive a hearing before being suspended without pay. In that case, the university acted immediately to suspend a campus police officer who was arrested on drug-related charges, and the Court reasoned that the employee was provided with a timely post-termination hearing and that the institution's interest in acting to suspend an employee accused of a felony was significant.[121]

In applying this standard, a Louisiana court found that the board did not state a compelling reason for placing a tenured faculty member on leave without pay on the basis of student complaints of sexual harassment before affording the faculty member a hearing. The court found that the complaints did not allege conduct of such an egregious nature that they warranted an immediate, emergency suspension; it provided examples such as criminal conduct, quid pro quo sexual demands, physical contact, or blatant racial discrimination in grading which could serve as the basis of an immediate emergency suspension with no need for a hearing. The court further found that holding a hearing one day after the effective date of the suspension did not change the indefinite suspension into a one-day loss.[122]

A faculty member's failure to comply with institutional procedures for instituting due process protections may bar the employee from establishing a denial of due process. In reviewing one faculty member's claim, a federal appeals court found that although the professor filed complaints and letters of protest with the administration of the institution, he did not comply with the two-step grievance process established by the university. The court reasoned that in order to state a claim for failure to provide due process, the professor must have taken advantage of the processes made available. In other words, a procedural due process violation cannot have occurred when the state university provided apparently adequate procedural remedies, and the employee had

---

[119] Frumkin v. Bd. of Trs., Kent State Univ., 626 F.2d 19 (6th Cir. 1980).

[120] *See* Ross v. Medical Univ. of S.C., 328 S.C. 51, 492 S.E.2d 62 (S.C. 1997) (finding that deficiencies in a pre-termination hearing relative to the right to respond to charges was remedied in the extensive due process permitted in the post-termination hearing). *But see* Stallworth v. City of Evergreen, 680 So. 2d 229 (Ala. 1996), *cert. denied*, 519 U.S. 1007, 117 S. Ct. 509, 136 L. Ed. 2d 399 (1996) (holding that a post-termination hearing cannot remedy due process violations that occur in a pre-termination hearing).

[121] Gilbert v. Homar, 520 U.S. 924, 117 S. Ct. 1807, 138 L. Ed. 2d 120 (1997).

[122] Delahoussaye v. Bd. of Supervisors of Cmty. and Technical Colls., 906 So. 2d 646 (La. 2005).

not availed himself of those remedies.[123] In another case, a professor who was given a one-year contract rather than tenure after the board discovered that he had an affair with a student at a previous institution waited until the end of the contract to file a grievance. Because the policy required any grievance to be filed within two weeks of the incident, the court ruled that the professor should have filed his grievance within two weeks of the date on which the contract was executed, rather than within two weeks of the end of the contract.[124]

Property and Liberty Interests

To state a claim for violation of due process, a faculty member must show that he or she was deprived of a right protected by due process of law and then identify an official action that caused that denial. The faculty member may claim a right to due process, including a hearing prior to the implementation of discipline, when the effect of a public institution's administrative action would be to deny a property entitlement under the contract of employment.[125] Alternately, stigmatizing statements disseminated by the institution may so injure the faculty member's reputation as to implicate a liberty interest under due process of law. If such a stigma were to have the effect of foreclosing other employment opportunities, then the faculty member might successfully claim a right to a name-clearing hearing.[126]

Most allegations of a denial of an entitlement arise from adverse employment decisions related to the discipline of employees, but other deprivations of a property right may implicate due process. For example, minimal due process, including notice of the reasons for a proposed deprivation of property rights and some opportunity to respond to those reasons, was required when administrators determined to reduce a faculty member's compensation from a discretionary fund and advised him that he must generate the lost compensation through grant funds.[127] Another potentially protected property interest is graduate-faculty status when such status includes increased pay and benefits.[128] However, claims of a denial of committee appointments, or denial of certain research, lecturing, and publishing opportunities, would be unlikely to establish a constitutionally protected entitlement. A contention that denying these opportunities would influence "chances for tenure" was considered unsupportable as

---

[123] Alvin v. Suzuki, 227 F.3d 107 (3d Cir. 2001).

[124] Suddith v. Univ. of S. Miss., 977 So. 2d 1158 (Miss. 2007).

[125] Cleveland Bd. of Educ. v. Loudermill, 470 U.S. 532, 105 S. Ct. 1487, 84 L. Ed. 2d 494 (1985). *But see* Gilbert v. Homar, 520 U.S. 924, 117 S. Ct. 1807, 138 L. Ed. 2d 120 (1997) (finding a post-termination hearing was sufficient to protect the rights of a university employee charged with drug possession).

[126] Wells v. Doland, 711 F.2d 670 (5th Cir. 1983).

[127] Williams v. Tex. Tech Univ. Health Sciences Ctr., 6 F.3d 290 (5th Cir. 1993).

[128] *See* Gunasekera v. Irwin, 551 F.3d 461 (6th Cir. 2009) (holding that a faculty member had presented enough evidence to withstand a motion to dismiss by alleging that university custom gave him a protected property interest in his graduate faculty status and that he lost pay for a summer research stipend and the benefit of a reduced teaching load).

a basis for creating an entitlement by one federal court.[129] Other claims courts have ruled that constitutionally protected property interests do not include an uncompensated work assignment,[130] as well as a specific term of appointment as department chair established by university custom when the express terms of the contract provide a shorter term.[131]

A faculty member alleging violation of a liberty interest must establish that the institution or its agents disseminated a false statement of a stigmatizing nature that precipitated an adverse employment decision, without providing the employee a meaningful opportunity to clear his or her good name. A stigma might be found if the institution publicly accused a faculty member of dishonesty, immorality, criminality, or racism. For instance, an appellate court found that a faculty member who was singled out during a press conference concerning widespread allegations of graduate student plagiarism would be entitled to a public name-clearing hearing to alert the public that the faculty member challenged the allegations. However, the appellate court did not determine the exact nature of the public name-clearing hearing, but remanded the case to the trial court to balance the burden placed on the university given its obligation to protect the privacy of the students involved.[132] On the other hand, allegations that a faculty member was a poor performer and could not get along with colleagues have not been sufficient to raise a liberty interest,[133] nor was a provost's statement, quoted in the student newspaper, that the faculty member's removal was in the best interests of the department.[134] Denial of tenure, or nonrenewal of appointment, would not constitute so significant a stigma as to create a right to due process.[135] While judges reason that these decisions may reflect negatively on the employee, this negative effect is insufficient, absent evidence of charges that would seriously damage reputation or foreclose other employment, to warrant due process protections.[136]

To prevail on a claim of stigma, there must be evidence that the institution publicly disclosed accusations against the employee[137] and there was a

---

[129] Miller v. Bunce, 60 F. Supp. 2d 620 (S.D. Tex. 1999).

[130] Ashfaq v. Anderson, 603 F. Supp. 2d 936 (N.D. Tex. 2009).

[131] Amaran v. Va. State Univ., 476 F. Supp. 3d (E.D. Va. 2007).

[132] Gunasekera v. Irwin, 551 F.3d 461 (6th Cir. 2009).

[133] See Meyer v. Univ. of Wash., 105 Wash. 2d 847, 719 P.2d 98 (Wash. 1986); Harris v. Ariz. Bd. of Regents, 528 F. Supp. 987 (D. Ariz. 1981).

[134] Garvie v. Jackson, 845 F.2d 647 (6th Cir. 1983).

[135] See, e.g., Haimowitz v. Univ. of Nevada, 579 F.2d 526, 529 (9th Cir. 1978) (finding denial of tenure not sufficiently stigmatizing to implicate a liberty interest that would entitle professor to due process).

[136] Bunger v. Univ. of Okla. Bd. of Regents, 95 F.3d 987 (10th Cir. 1996).

[137] Simonson v. Iowa State Univ., 603 N.W.2d 557 (Iowa 1999) (finding no evidence that would establish the institution had publicly disclosed the reason (alleged sexual harassment of students—ongoing investigation) for an employee's paid administrative leave). See also Phillips v. State of Minnesota, 725 N.W.2d 778 (Minn. Ct. App. 2007) (finding that the institution did not publicly disclose the reason for not rehiring the employee (violation of sexual harassment policy) and that the employee who informed coworkers of the reasons could not assert compelled self-publication in a claim for protection of liberty interests).

deprivation of an employee interest.[138] In a representative case, a Florida court rejected a professor's claim that denial of promotion to full professor had a stigmatizing effect that would require due process protection. The state appellate court found the denial of the professor's promotion left his legal status unaltered in that he remained a tenured associate professor.[139]

Substantial Compliance

Substantial compliance with institutional due process procedures is the applicable standard in employee discipline.[140] "Substantial," however, does not mean that compliance must be so rigorous that any deviation will result in overturning an adverse employment decision. In a North Dakota case, a faculty member challenged a nonrenewal decision on the grounds that the department failed to adequately follow the evaluation format outlined by the department. The written policy stipulated that nontenured faculty were to be evaluated at the end of the first semester of their first year and again at the end of their first year. The faculty member asserted that her second evaluation, coming in February, occurred several months before the end of the second semester. The reviewing court held that there was substantial compliance with the department's written evaluation procedures and that the purpose of evaluation—to inform the faculty member of her job performance—was accomplished.[141]

Even in cases in which the institution adopts ad hoc policies and procedures to address an initial instance of misconduct, judges have shown deference to institutional practices if fundamental due process protections are applied. In a case in which a tenured university professor was publicly censured and barred from administrative positions as a sanction for "seriously negligent scholarship," a federal appeals court examined the institution's ad hoc procedures involving plagiarism. The found that the professor had adequate notice of charges against her; an opportunity to challenge for cause any of the panel members who heard her case; to present evidence, call witnesses, challenge witnesses, and bring a colleague to the hearings to assist her. At the conclusion of the hearings, the committee recommended censure and forwarded its report to the academic dean. The dean asked the professor to respond in writing to the report, and this response was incorporated, along with the panel's recom-

---

[138] Edwards v. Cal, Univ. of Pa., 156 F.3d 488 (3d Cir. 1998).

[139] Herold v. Univ. of S. Fla., 806 So. 2d 638 (Fla. Dist. Ct. App. 2002)

[140] *See* Tonkovich v. Kan. Bd. of Regents, 159 F.3d 504 (10th Cir. 1998) (holding that while the institution's representatives might have failed to adhere to certain evidentiary rules or institutional polices, they did nothing to change the fact that the professor received notice, an opportunity to be heard by an impartial tribunal, and a full-blown evidentiary hearing with post-termination protections such as the right to counsel, to cross examine witnesses, and to present witnesses on his behalf); Deli v. Univ. of Minn., 511 N.W.2d 46 (Minn. Ct. App. 1994) (holding that failure to conform to specified procedures in termination is reversible only where a party's substantial rights have been prejudiced).

[141] Smith v. State, 389 N.W.2d 808 (N.D. 1986).

mendations and findings, in a report to the provost. The court regarded the university's procedures as providing appropriate due process safeguards.[142]

The standard of substantial compliance has also been applied to annual performance evaluation in the context of tenure decisions. In a West Virginia case, tenure denial was challenged on the basis that the institution failed to afford the candidate the requisite annual evaluations and third-year review required by the university handbook. The reviewing court found that third-year reviews were wholly discretionary under the terms of the handbook, and that any failure to conduct annual evaluations in selected years was overshadowed by annual evaluations that provided the candidate with repeated notices of her deficiencies throughout the period of her university service. The court affirmed a judgment that the university had substantially complied with evaluation and tenure procedures and that any procedural irregularities were harmless.[143]

Higher education administrators sometimes find that there are alternative due process procedures under institutional policy for dealing with issues of employee discipline. In one case, a tenured professor subject to suspension, based on allegations of sexual harassment of students, challenged the notice and hearing provided on the basis that it failed to conform to the specific requirements of the sexual harassment policy. The reviewing court ruled that the institution's decision to follow the due process procedures set forth in the bargaining agreement, rather than those established under the sexual harassment policy, did not violate constitutional standards. It emphasized that there is no requirement under the Fourteenth Amendment that an employee receive due process procedures of his or her choice.[144]

Discrimination in Faculty Employment

Discrimination on the basis of race, religion, national origin, sex, age, disability, or genetic information is prohibited under federal law and the provisions of many state laws, most of which are applicable to both public and private institutions of higher education. Principal among the federal statutes that cover employment discrimination are Title VII of the Civil Rights Act of 1964,[145] Title IX of the Education Amendments of 1972,[146] Section 504 of the Rehabilitation Act of 1973,[147] the Americans With Disabilities Act,[148] the Age Discrimination in Employment Act,[149] and the Genetic Information Nondis-

---

[142] Newman v. Burgin, 930 F.2d 955 (1st Cir. 1991) *See also* Agarwal v. Regents of the Univ. of Minn., 788 F.2d 504 (8th Cir. 1986) (identifying four elements of due process in a plagiarism hearing: 1) notice of reasons for termination of tenure, 2) notice of names of accusers, 3) opportunity to present evidence in defense, and 4) impartial tribunal).

[143] Karle v. Bd. of Trs., 575 S.E.2d 267 (W. Va. 2002).

[144] Shub v. Hankin, 869 F. Supp. 213 (S.D.N.Y.1994).

[145] 42 U.S.C. § 2000e et seq.

[146] 20 U.S.C. § 1681 et seq.

[147] 29 U.S.C. § 794.

[148] 42 U.S.C. §12101 et seq.

[149] 29 U.S.C. § 621 et seq.

crimination Act of 2008.[150] Since the litigation of employment discrimination claims is highly fact-intensive, summary disposition of the charges will be more likely where employment practices include documentary records that support a strong antidiscrimination posture. The principles associated with nondiscrimination in employment are elaborated in the chapter discussing the application of Title VII, but some examination of the employer's burden in employment discrimination is treated below.

Legitimate, Nondiscriminatory Reasons

The employer's burden in cases involving allegations of discrimination based on disparate treatment is to articulate a legitimate, nondiscriminatory reason for the adverse employment decision.[151] The requirement to "articulate," rather than prove, requires the employer to produce some evidence in support of the stated reason for the adverse employment decision. In order to meet the burden of production, higher education institutions must institute and uniformly apply evaluation and documentation systems that establish reasonable, job-related rationales for adverse employment decisions. For example, conference memoranda and formal complaints that a professor was repeatedly absent and tardy, failed to make arrangements for his absences to be covered, and failed to complete and turn in student grades on time overcame a claim of disparate treatment.[152] One institution met its burden to articulate a legitimate, nondiscriminatory reason for discharging a clinical nurse supervisor by presenting evidence that it had lost two nursing home training sites and was threatened with the loss of two more because of the nurse's ineffective supervision of nursing students.[153] A disability discrimination claim was overcome with evidence of corroborating evaluations indicating valid performance deficiencies in teaching.[154] An institution's decision to terminate was properly based on testimony and memoranda confirming unsatisfactory job performance, disregarding university directives, and misusing university resources.[155]

Assessments of teaching performance may be sufficient to rebut a prima facie case of employment discrimination if they are effectively documented.[156] For example, the use of student evaluations and classroom observation to substantiate inadequate teaching skills has been relied on to rebut a profes-

---

[150] 42 U.S.C. §2000ff et seq.

[151] Tex. Dept. of Cmty. Affairs v. Burdine, 450 U.S. 248, 101 S. Ct. 1089, 67 L. Ed. 2d 207 (1981).

[152] Sinha v. State Univ. of N.Y. at Farmingdale, 764 F. Supp. 765 (E.D.N.Y. 1991) (failure to promote).

[153] Hayes v. Invesco, 907 F.2d 853 (8th Cir. 1990) (discharge).

[154] Mayer v. Univ. of Minn., 940 F. Supp. 1474 (D. Minn. 1994) (alleged disability discrimination).

[155] Randall v. Howard Univ., 941 F. Supp. 206 (D.C. 1996).

[156] See Soares v. Univ. of New Haven, 154 F. Supp. 2d 365 (D. Conn. 2001) (holding that the professor's substandard performance evaluations justified the adverse employment decision); Schneider v. Northwestern Univ., 925 F. Supp. 1347 (N.D. Ill. 1996) (upholding denial of tenure on the basis that the institution's proffered reason was related to subjective factors that were reasonably related to scholarship and teaching).

sor's discrimination claims.[157] In another case, a college's concerns about an ethnic minority professor's lack of organization in lecture and difficulty in communicating with students were factors reflected in the record of the college's committee on promotion and tenure. When the professor challenged the committee's recommendation not to offer him a tenure-track position, the federal appeals court acknowledged that the committee's minutes provided the documentation for the articulation of a legitimate, nondiscriminatory reason for the adverse employment decision.[158] Another institution prevailed against an allegation of religious discrimination by citing negative student comments, the faculty member's lack of service, and declining enrollment as legitimate, nondiscriminatory reasons for denying tenure.[159]

A faculty member's lack of research and scholarship has been cited as a nondiscriminatory reason for an adverse employment decision.[160] For example, an institution's showing that the reason for denial of tenure and nonrenewal was the professor's failure to obtain research funding has rebutted claims of discrimination.[161] In a case involving allegations of sex discrimination, a federal appeals court noted the faculty member's failure to publish in top-tier journals, a publication record of largely coauthored articles, and criticism of her publication record by outside reviewers, in holding the university's proffered reasons for denying promotion and tenure were not pretextual.[162] Another federal appeals court recognized that failure to earn the doctorate degree and lack of scholarly productivity were all relevant considerations contributing to legitimate, nondiscriminatory reasons for a faculty member's nonrenewal.[163]

The articulated reason for an adverse employment decision should include a clear and reasonably specific factual basis for the employment decision.[164] Standards of quality should not be so subjective that they cannot be effectively communicated and consistently assessed in the faculty evaluation process. For example, if the proffered reason for an adverse employment decision is ineffective teaching performance, then the institution must establish that it maintains a policy in which teaching competence is a performance criterion and that it uniformly relies on a reasonable measure of teaching performance, such as student evaluations.[165]

---

[157] Akeyo v. O'Hanlon, 75 F.3d 370 (8th Cir. 1996); Lutz v. Purdue Univ., 133 F. Supp. 2d 1101 (N.D. Ind. 2001); Favetz v. Bd. of Control, Grand Valley State Univ., 903 F. Supp. 1181 (W.D. Mich. 1995).

[158] Bina v. Providence Coll., 39 F.3d 21 (1st Cir. 1994).

[159] Adelman-Reyes v. Saint Xavier Univ., 500 F.3d 662 (7th Cir. 2007).

[160] Anderson v. Univ. of N. Iowa, 779 F.2d 441 (8th Cir. 1985) and Lynn v. Regents of the Univ. of Cal., 656 F.2d 1337 (9th Cir. 1981).

[161] Bernofsky v. Tulane Univ. Medical Sch., 962 F. Supp. 895 (E.D. La. 1997).

[162] Lawrence v. Curators of the Univ. of Mo, 204 F.2d 807 (8th Cir. 2000).

[163] Jiminez v. Mary Washington Coll., 57 F.3d 369 (4th Cir. 1995).

[164] Morris v. Wallace Cmty. Coll.-Selma, 125 F. Supp. 2d 1315 (S.D. Ala. 2001).

[165] Girma v. Skidmore Coll., 180 F. Supp. 2d 326 (N.D.N.Y. 2001).

Conclusion

While the level of judicial scrutiny applicable to a college or university's employment decisions will vary, today's court are unlikely to interfere when the adverse employment decision is based upon criteria reasonably related to a faculty member's job requirements, free of impermissible discrimination or the denial of a constitutional right to free speech or association, reached by proper procedures, and supported by substantial evidence. Judicial intervention would necessitate review of a host of factors used by the academy to make employment decisions, a role courts have neither the competency nor the resources to undertake.

Nevertheless, if responsible administrators do not have reasoned, ascertainable standards for making adverse employment decisions, or if they fail to apply those standards in a particular employment decision, the consequences may implicate legally protected rights and result in legal challenge. Judicial review of the employment decision-making process can be anticipated when employment decisions appear arbitrary or capricious, lack supporting evidence, or deny the faculty member's legally protected rights.

Sound employment practices provide a record of events, incidents, appraisals, discussions, interviews, admonitions, and directives that can be relied upon to support the evidentiary sufficiency and credibility of an employment decision. When efforts to correct or improve a faculty member's performance have failed and an adverse employment decision is compelled, that decision must be predicated upon standards reasonably related to job requirements and upon substantial adherence to the procedural requirements established by law, contract, collective agreement, and institutional policy.

It is recommended that faculty and professional staff be included in the process of establishing professional competencies and encouraged to participate in every phase of the employment decision-making process. From policy formulation to implementation, employee participation in employment decision making enhances employee relations, provides for more informed decision making, and contributes to a perception of fundamental fairness and reasonableness that can deter lawsuits and reduce judicial intervention.

Development and implementation of legally sound employment practices and procedures will not eliminate legal disputes, but should yield a documentary record that substantiates the fairness and reasonableness of the process, establishes the proper predicate for an adverse employment decision, and elaborates the procedural integrity of the process. Evaluative criteria must be developed that are sufficiently specific and reasonably job-related to enable faculty to guide their conduct and provide a standard by which the faculty member's conduct can be evaluated. Systematic and uniform application of those criteria must characterize the process that will ultimately be relied upon to support employment decisions. Finally, employment practices must be procedurally correct, whether that procedure is express in institutional policies or implicit in the provision of due process of law.

5 Faculty Speech and Expression

Jeffrey C. Sun, J.D., Ph.D.
University of Louisville

Neal H. Hutchens, J.D., Ph.D.
University of Mississippi

Speech and speech-related activities (e.g., expressions on social media or through symbolic images) constitute an integral aspect of faculty life. At the most fundamental level, speech and other expressive activities take place regularly through professors' teaching and research. Those activities might include a class lecture, course syllabus, or discussions with a research work group. In addition, professors engage in various other types of communication. For instance, faculty members are expected to participate in matters related to institutional governance and administration. Whether providing feedback on a faculty candidate, offering views on proposed curricular revisions, or critiquing the actions of senior administration officials, professors regularly provide expressions about their perspectives or opinions as a part of fulfilling their roles as members of the academic community.

Faculty members often engage with audiences outside of their own institutions, such as through journal articles or presentations at academic conferences. They also regularly participate in speech activities—both internal and external, in relation to the college or university in which they work—not explicitly tied to their scholarly, teaching, or institutional service endeavors. A professor, for instance, may choose to voice support for a certain political candidate or advocate for a particular social cause.

Assessing legal protections for faculty speech takes into consideration multiple types of speech, both in terms of the content and the context in which the speech occurs. Another factor of potential legal importance involves whether a faculty member is employed at a public or a private institution. This chapter addresses key issues and concepts that help define the legal standards governing faculty speech.

The Academic Profession's Development
of Academic Freedom

Referring to the utopian society of the academic community, Plato espoused the initial concept of intellectual inquiry and academic freedom.[1] The principle of academic freedom regained recognition during the Middle Ages to address secular thought and scientific discoveries, but lacked the force of the protective measures that exist today. During the 1700s and 1800s, the German universities—known for their research-based approach to learning—revived the academic freedom concept, otherwise known as *akademische freiheit*.[2] Academic freedom additionally served as the overarching term to include other more specific freedoms; the Germans declared *libertas philosophandi*, which is "freedom of philosophizing," along with two other fundamental freedoms, *lehrfreiheit* (freedom of teaching) and *lernfreiheit* (freedom of learning), as the founding principles of the German university research model.[3]

American research universities were modeled after the German university system.[4] Like the German academics, American university professors recognized the need for independence from influences that would obstruct open discussions, and they freely pursued intellectual curiosity and exploration. As historians Brubacher and Rudy recount, Thomas Jefferson sought to further these academic ideals of the unfettered search for truth through the adoption of a radical mission for "an illimitable freedom of the human mind" when he established the University of Virginia in 1825.[5] This academic ideal of searching for truth was particularly important during a time of growing secularization among higher education institutions, as faculty began to challenge religious tenets of the founding organization, as well as beliefs of many in the local communities.[6] Indeed, academic freedom became a necessity to protect the interests of professors and provide more autonomy from administrative authority, community backlash, and donor influences.[7]

Even as these ideas concerning the role of the faculty were beginning to take hold in American higher education during the late nineteenth century and the early twentieth century, institutions would dismiss professors who espoused unpopular or unorthodox views.[8] In one high-profile incident, a professor at Stanford University, Edward A. Ross, was dismissed for championing populist

---

[1] JOHN S. BRUBACHER & WILLIS RUDY, HIGHER EDUCATION IN TRANSITION: A HISTORY OF AMERICAN COLLEGES AND UNIVERSITIES 308 (4th ed. 1996).

[2] *Id.* at 316.

[3] *Id.* at 174; JOHN R. THELIN, A HISTORY OF AMERICAN HIGHER EDUCATION (2004); William Van Alstyne, *Academic Freedom and the First Amendment in the Supreme Court of The United States: An Unhurried Historical Review*, 53 LAW & CONTEMP. PROBS. 79 (1990).

[4] RICHARD HOFSTADTER & WALTER P. METZGER, THE DEVELOPMENT OF ACADEMIC FREEDOM IN THE UNITED STATES (1955).

[5] BRUBACHER & RUDY, *supra* note 1, at 312.

[6] *See* HOFSTADTER & METZGER, *supra* note 4.

[7] BRUBACHER & RUDY, *supra* note 1, at 310-18.

[8] BRUBACHER & RUDY, *supra* note 1, at 318.

economic views, as well as his opposition to Chinese immigration. Both were stances that offended Jane Lathrop Stanford. She was the widow of the institution's original benefactor and a university trustee who also had significant financial interests in the railroad industry, which relied on low-paid Asian laborers.[9] This conflict, along with other similar events, continued throughout the early twentieth century as faculty members faced dismissal if they offered views that rankled presidents and governing board members (with the latter group often representing more elite segments of society).

Responding to these external influences, Arthur Lovejoy, of Johns Hopkins, and John Dewey, of Columbia, organized a meeting in 1915 to further the goals of academic freedom. This meeting ultimately led to the establishment of the American Association of University Professors (AAUP) and the 1915 Declaration of the Committee on Academic Freedom and Tenure. The purpose of the group evolved into a representative organization for faculty interests to redress unfair treatment and practices at colleges and universities.

To advance the concept of academic freedom, members requested the codification of some guiding rules and proper practices at institutions of higher education. Eventually, the AAUP—along with what is now the Association of American Colleges and Universities—adopted the 1940 Statement of Principles on Academic Freedom and Tenure (1940 Statement) to offer clarity and guidance. That statement explained that "[a]cademic freedom ... applies to both teaching and research."[10] It outlined that professors "are entitled to full freedom in research and in the publication of the results" with caveats of meeting an adequate level of performance.[11] In addition, the statement indicated that professors are "entitled to freedom in the classroom in discussing their subject," with the qualifier that content should be related to their subject and that religious or other organizational mission justifications may circumscribe that right.[12] The statement further acknowledged that professors are individuals with multiple roles; that is, they are "citizens, members of a learned profession, and officers of an education institution," and these different roles reflect different professional expectations and rights for external utterances such as speeches, writings, and other forms of expression.[13] The principles established in this and later AAUP documents (such as the addition of an "Interpretive Comments" part to the 1970 adoption of the *Statement of Principles* and the *Recommended Institutional Regulations on Academic Freedom and Tenure*) have served a major role in creating standards that define academic freedom as a system of professional standards in American higher education. Indeed, the AAUP even emphasized that the foundational 1940 Statement was not "a

---

[9] *Id. at* 313; WILLIAM G. TIERNEY & ESTELA M. BENSIMON, PROMOTION AND TENURE: COMMUNITY AND SOCIALIZATION IN ACADEME 23-24 (1996).

[10] AMERICAN ASSOCIATION OF UNIVERSITY PROFESSORS, AAUP POLICY DOCUMENTS & REPORTS 14 (11th ed. 2015).

[11] *Id.*

[12] *Id.*

[13] *Id.*

static code but a fundamental document designed to set a framework of norms to guide adaptations to changing times and circumstances."[14]

In crafting professional standards to safeguard faculty speech and independence, the concept of tenure emerged concurrently with the profession's recognition of academic freedom.

Tenure: A Legal Source to Support the Right of Academic Freedom

At many colleges and universities, tenure has become an integral part of the employment arrangements for certain classes of professors (i.e., tenured professors). For these faculty, tenure represents a specific type of contractual relationship, one in which following a probationary (pre-tenure) period, a college or university agrees to a continuing employment relationship with a professor absent some extraordinary circumstance such as financial emergency, professional misconduct, or incompetence.

According to the 1940 Statement of Principles on Academic Freedom and Tenure, tenure was adopted as "a means to certain ends."[15] For the academic profession, the two outcomes of tenure are (1) to support professors' "freedom of teaching and research and of extramural activities" and (2) to provide "a sufficient degree of economic security" for individuals to enter and remain in the profession.[16] Viewed another way, tenure represented an additional protection toward the furtherance of academic freedom in that it added an expectation of continuous appointment through a contractual relationship.

This employment arrangement is essentially limited to the United States, where it is available at many public and private colleges and universities. Eligible professors who are on the tenure track must satisfy required institutional standards. During the probationary period, the tenure-track professor must demonstrate achievement of the requisite criteria, typically in the areas of teaching, research, and service. While many institutions have adopted tenure provisions and standards with considerable similarity, differences still exist among institutions that reflect specific institutional characteristics and orientations. Colleges or universities may vary in the emphasis they place on scholarship or teaching when awarding tenure. Religiously affiliated institutions may require faculty members to support various beliefs and comply with certain conduct standards as a condition of continuing employment. Thus, while considerable overlap exists in tenure standards, specific practices may differ.

As a contractual relationship, the provisions of tenure generally are governed by state contract law. Accordingly, courts examine the appointment letter and supporting materials, such as faculty handbooks and policies.

---

[14] *Id.* at n.1.
[15] *Id.* at 14.
[16] *Id.*

These documents typically encompass the terms and conditions upon which the contract is based.

For public institutions, tenure additionally creates a legal property interest; therefore, when a faculty member at a public institution presents a tenure challenge, the case typically triggers questions of constitutional due process protections. In other words, the government must satisfy sufficient procedural fairness before taking away an individual's property (i.e., tenure) or denying a tenure-track professor an opportunity to seek a property interest (i.e., denial of tenure). Simply put, the stakes are quite high for faculty challenges involving the denial or removal of tenure at public colleges and universities.

Not all faculty members are eligible for tenure. Indeed, discussion of tenure often elicits strong views, with supporters of tenure emphasizing its relationship to protecting academic freedom and faculty independence, and its detractors bemoaning a system that they contend protects intransigent and unproductive faculty members.

Whatever one's view of tenure, recent trends highlight that this employment arrangement faces an increasingly uncertain future. According to data compiled by the AAUP, faculty members employed on tenure lines comprised nearly half of all faculty positions in 1975, but dropped below 30% by 2016.[17] While percentages vary by institutional type, the consistent trend reveals an overall erosion of tenure in higher education.[18] Assessment of issues related to academic freedom and faculty speech must take into account that the overwhelming majority of the individuals teaching at colleges and universities are now employed off the tenure track and without the legal protections for employment that result from tenure.

A large percentage of faculty positions now are part time, with individuals often employed on a semester-to-semester basis.[19] Many of these individuals are employed in an at-will capacity and work without any kind of contractual employment agreement; concomitantly, employing institutions may assert the right to dismiss at-will faculty at any time and for any reason. While certain limits exist on institutional authority over the treatment of part-time faculty employees, such as federal and state civil rights laws prohibiting discrimination on such bases as race and age, colleges and universities possess considerable discretion in the treatment of their faculty employed on an at-will basis.

Other non-tenure-line faculty members are employed as full-time employees on contracts of varying duration and reappointment standards. For instance, some individuals are on yearly contracts with no expectation of reappointment, with renewal subject to the determination of a single supervisor. By contrast, some full-time, non-tenure-track faculty members are employed on multi-year

---

[17] AMERICAN ASSOCIATION OF UNIVERSITY PROFESSORS, *DATA SNAPSHOT: CONTINGENT FACULTY IN US HIGHER ED* (2018), available at https://www.aaup.org/sites/default/files/10112018%20Data%20Snapshot%20Tenure.pdf.

[18] It should be noted that the percentage is based on total faculty in terms of headcount, not full-time equivalency.

[19] *See* AAUP, TENURE AND TEACHING-INTENSIVE APPOINTMENTS, *supra* note 17.

contracts and have an expectation of reappointment, with renewal decisions based on a committee evaluation approach. Just as with part-time faculty and for those on tenure-line positions, the standards for legal protections related to continuing employment may also be influenced by collective bargaining agreements.

This shift toward a reduction of faculty who possess established rights for continuing employment presents very practical problems for the professorate. For example, faculty members employed without the protections of tenure may be less likely to challenge administrative decisions, or may alter their expectations of students in order to receive more favorable student evaluations, if such choices influence decisions to renew a non-tenure-track faculty member. Accordingly, the increasing presence of faculty employment arrangements outside of tenured and tenure-track lines prompts serious consideration of other sources of legal protection for faculty speech.

For professors at public colleges and universities, a commonly held view assumes that faculty speech also receives strong First Amendment protection against undue institutional encroachment, in addition to legal protections afforded by contractual arrangements such as tenure. However, considerable legal instability exists in this area, as well.

The chapter now turns to consideration of legal protections for faculty speech potentially available through the First Amendment.

Constitutional Protection for Faculty Speech: An Uncertain Future

The previous section presented legal protections for faculty speech grounded in contractual arrangements, a legal source that pertains to faculty members at both public and private institutions. This part of the chapter introduces another potential area of legal protection for faculty, but it is limited to public colleges and universities. Such a limitation to the public higher education context is due to the legal source being the First Amendment, which, in relevant part, prohibits government from infringing on people's protected speech. While the First Amendment generally protects the speech of an individual—such as a faculty member—from undue interference, recent case law has started to alter what is recognized as a professor's protected speech and what constitutes academic freedom. Viewed another way, the courts appear to have refined notions of what is "undue" interference.

Supreme Court's Academic Freedom Decisions

This subsection presents an overview of the authoritative case law that first recognized academic freedom as a protected professional right derived from the First Amendment. During the 1950s, U.S. Supreme Court discussions of academic freedom arose as a part of a response to governmental efforts to root out perceived communist efforts to infiltrate American society and government during the Cold War.[20] During what is often referred to as the "McCarthy Era," a number of individuals found themselves targeted as communists and often subjected to intimidation and even loss of employment. Within this highly charged environment, academic freedom first received attention from a Supreme Court decision as deserving First Amendment protection in 1952, in a dissenting opinion in *Adler v. Board of Education*.[21] The case dealt with a New York law that prohibited employment in public education by individuals belonging to organizations deemed subversive.[22] While a majority of the Court upheld the law, Justice William O. Douglas's dissenting opinion argued that academic freedom must be protected in schools. He contended that the law at issue threatened to turn "the school system into a spying project" and subverted the First Amendment purposes of promoting free inquiry and preventing censorship.[23]

In 1957, a well-known concurring opinion in *Sweezy v. New Hampshire*[24] provided an important addition to judicial recognition of academic freedom as a protected right under the First Amendment. The case dealt with a college professor, Paul Sweezy, refusing to answer questions, which the New Hampshire attorney general's office posed, about Sweezy's public activities, including his lectures at the University of New Hampshire and his scholarly works. In a concurring opinion, Justice Felix Frankfurter discussed the importance of protecting intellectual independence at the nation's colleges and universities. Turning to a statement by South African scholars, the opinion stated that a college or university must possess the freedom "to determine for itself on academic grounds who may teach, what may be taught, how it shall be taught, and who may be admitted to study."[25]

A decade later—in 1967, in *Keyishian v. Board of Regents*[26]—academic freedom for the first time found support in a majority opinion. Once again considering the same state law at issue in *Adler* but a different set of provisions, the Court had a different outcome and struck down provisions of the law pertaining to loyalty oaths. Significantly, the opinion discussed the importance of protecting free speech and inquiry in the nation, including educational contexts. As stated in an often-cited part of the opinion:

> Our nation is deeply committed to safeguarding academic freedom, which is of transcendent value to all of us and not merely to the teachers concerned. That freedom therefore is a special concern of

---

[20] Robert J. Tepper & Craig G. White, *Speak No Evil: Academic Freedom and the Application of Garcetti v. Ceballos to Public University Faculty*, 59 CATH. U.L. REV. 125, 132 (2009).

[21] 342 U.S. 485 (1952).

[22] *Id.* at 488-89.

[23] *Id.* at 509.

[24] 354 U.S. 234 (1957).

[25] *Id.* at 263.

[26] 385 U.S. 599 (1967).

the First Amendment, which does not tolerate laws that cast a pall of orthodoxy over the classroom.[27]

Since *Keyishian,* Supreme Court decisions have intermittently continued to offer support for academic freedom, but opinions have not offered clear constitutional standards regarding the contours of First Amendment protection for a professor's academic freedom. Additionally, decisions have also created confusion as to whether the institution (i.e., college or university) or the individual faculty member may assert this First Amendment protection of academic freedom, and what happens when they are in conflict.

In a footnote in *University of Michigan v. Ewing,*[28] which dealt with a student challenging his dismissal from a medical degree program and where faculty and institutional interests were aligned, the Supreme Court acknowledged the potential tension between individual and institutional academic freedom. Unfortunately, the *Ewing* case did not offer any clarifying principles or standards on this observation to provide guidance to lower courts. While *Grutter v. Bollinger,*[29] which involved use of race as a factor in higher education admissions, seemingly rested, at least in part, on recognition of some form of institutional academic freedom, uncertainty has only increased regarding the status of any First Amendment protection for the academic freedom of individual scholars.

Consequently, legal ambiguity currently abounds regarding the extent of any First Amendment protection for the individual academic freedom of faculty members in public higher education. Although Supreme Court cases contain language with seemingly strong endorsements of academic freedom, these decisions tend to be stronger on rhetoric than in actually providing specific standards to guide lower courts in evaluating faculty speech claims based on principles of constitutional academic freedom for the individual faculty member.[30] As a result, legal uncertainty and debate have arisen regarding the issue of constitutional protection for faculty speech at public colleges and universities. Adding to these questions about the state of academic freedom, one circuit court went as far as to question the existence of the individual protection and only recognized the right, at most, for the institution.[31]

Several other U.S. Supreme Court cases after *Keyishian* included language about academic freedom, and references to institutional autonomy became much more explicit, as these cases did not deal with connections of individual expressions of faculty speech *per se* and government interferences to those

---

[27] *Id.* at 603.

[28] 474 U.S. 214, 226 n.12 (1985).

[29] 539 U.S. 306 (2003).

[30] Lawrence White, *Fifty Years of Academic Freedom Jurisprudence,* 36 J.C. & U.L. 791, 792-93 (2010).

[31] Urofsky v. Gilmore, 216 F.3d 401, 411-15 (4th Cir. 2000).

expressions.[32] Consequently, the emergence of institutional autonomy as a desirable and functional element within higher education seemed appropriate; at that instance, the concept of institutional autonomy was not in conflict with individual academic freedom. Subsequent cases place greater doubt about college professors' rights to speak freely, and this right, if it exists at all, has been applied more as a professional normative practice than a constitutionally recognized right.[33]

Garcetti v. Ceballos and Ongoing Debate over Constitutional Protection for Faculty Speech

In the contested terrain of constitutional protection for individual academic freedom, several courts and legal commentators have asserted that faculty members at public colleges and universities possess no other First Amendment rights than those enjoyed by any other public employees. According to this position, any special First Amendment academic freedom rights, if existing at all, accrue to institutions and not to individual scholars.[34] Such an interpretation of faculty rights would have especially significant consequences due to a 2006 Supreme Court decision, *Garcetti v. Ceballos.*[35] The Supreme Court held in this decision that public employees possess no First Amendment protection when speaking pursuant to carrying out their official employment duties.[36] The majority opinion noted in *dicta* that the decision did not address the applicability of *Garcetti* to professorial speech,[37] further increasing debate and uncertainty over constitutional protection for faculty speech in public higher education. As described later in the chapter, lower federal and state courts have reached differing conclusions regarding whether the decision's standards cover faculty members.

The *Garcetti* case involved an assistant district attorney who claimed that his employer violated his First Amendment rights when his supervisor retaliated against him for his communications with his superiors regarding concerns with a pending case.[38] The Supreme Court, turning to its public employee speech cases, drew a categorical line regarding First Amendment protection for speech by public employees. According to the opinion, a public employee does not speak for First Amendment purposes when communicating pursuant to his or her official employment duties.[39]

---

[32] Regents of the Univ. of California v. Bakke, 438 U.S. 265 (1978) (plurality); Regents of the Univ. of Mich. v. Ewing, 474 U.S. 214 (1985); University of Pa. v. E.E.O.C., 493 U.S. 182 (1990); Grutter v. Bollinger, 539 U.S. 306 (2003).

[33] Neal H. Hutchens, & Jeffrey C. Sun, *The Tenuous Legal Status of First Amendment Protection for Individual Academic Freedom*, 7 JOURNAL OF THE PROFESSORIATE 1 (2013).

[34] *See, e.g.*, Urofsky v. Gilmore, 216 F.3d 401 (4th Cir. 2000).

[35] 547 U.S. 410 (2006).

[36] *Id.* at 421.

[37] *Id.* at 425.

[38] *Garcetti*, 547 U.S. at 696-97.

[39] *Id.* at 421.

In making a distinction between speaking in one's capacity as a private citizen versus speaking pursuant to carrying out one's employment duties, the Supreme Court in *Garcetti* added a new wrinkle to the standards governing public employee speech. In previous cases, the Supreme Court had determined that a public employee could potentially receive First Amendment protection if speaking on a matter of public concern rather than only commenting on an internal issue of private concern to the employee. If a court determined that an employee had addressed an issue of public concern, then it would engage in a balancing test to weigh the employee's interest in commenting on the matter versus that of the governmental employer to restrict the speech. The *Garcetti* decision, however, created what many considered as a bright-line test for courts to follow in public employee speech cases. In other words, if an employee engages in speech pursuant to performing official employment duties, then he or she may not seek First Amendment protection for such speech.

Figure 1-1: Professor v. University: Professor Claims Protected Speech[40]

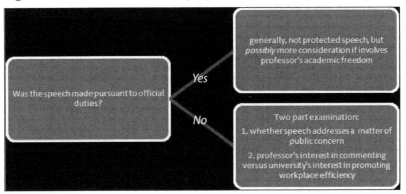

The *Garcetti* decision is of special significance in relation to First Amendment protection for faculty speech. Rather than turning directly to the academic freedom cases, courts have often looked to the public employee speech decisions in evaluating faculty speech claims. Thus, *Garcetti* raised the issue of whether the standards announced in the case should also apply to speech by faculty members at public colleges and universities. In a dissenting opinion, Justice David Souter wrote that he hoped the majority did not intend to include speech by faculty members under the *Garcetti* standards and undercut First Amendment protection for individual academic freedom.[41] In response, the majority stated that Justice Souter raised a potentially important question regarding limitations of *Garcetti* in relation to faculty speech and academic freedom, but replied in their opinion that the issue was not before the Court.[42]

---

[40] PHILIP T. K. DANIEL, E. GORDON GEE, JEFFREY C. SUN, & PATRICK PAUKEN, *LAW, POLICY, AND HIGHER EDUCATION: CASES AND MATERIALS,* 2012; WILLIAM A. KAPLIN, BARBARA A. LEE, NEAL H. HUTCHENS, & JACOB H. ROOKSBY, *THE LAW OF HIGHER EDUCATION* (6TH ED.), 2019.

[41] *Id.* at 438-39.

[42] *Id.* at 425.

Consequently, the decision explicitly left open the extent to which *Garcetti* pertains to faculty speech.

So far, lower courts have reached differing conclusions regarding *Garcetti*'s applicability to professors' speech in public higher education. Some courts have applied the decision's standards to faculty speech claims, while others have continued to follow the framework from pre-*Garcetti* cases and focused on whether the speech addressed a matter of public concern, which on balance may be protected if it outweighs the public employer's interest in promoting efficiency in the workplace. Another approach has been to continue looking for guidance to the Supreme Court's decision in *Hazelwood School District v. Kuhlmeier*.[43] In the *Kuhlmeier* case, a dispute arose between students and school leadership in which both groups claimed rights over speech. The students were enrolled in a journalism class and submitted two articles, one about teen pregnancy and another about family dynamics with divorced parents. The principal believed that the articles were inappropriate for the audience. The Supreme Court ruled in favor of the school as having an educator's authority over school-sponsored activities because the newspaper was a product of the journalism class. The Court determined that the classroom was not a public forum like a public park; and, the school could permissibly exercise its authority over matters that furthered legitimate pedagogical goals. Although this case involved a dispute between a school and students in a secondary school setting, some lower courts have applied the rules from this case to the higher education context.[44]

Questions over the appropriate legal framework to apply to faculty speech claims in public higher education seemingly will persist until the Supreme Court decides to resolve the issue, with the final resolution of the matter significant for higher education. If the First Amendment offers no special protection for individual academic freedom, then professors at public colleges and universities are entitled to only the same First Amendment rights as other public employees. But, *Garcetti* stands for the proposition that a public employee does not engage in speech for First Amendment purposes when carrying out official employment duties. The decision and questions over its applicability to faculty speech highlight current uncertainty over First Amendment protection for individual academic freedom.

---

[43] 484 U.S. 260 (1988).

[44] *See, e.g.,* Sheldon v. Dhillon, No. C-08-03438 RMW, 2009 WL 4282086 (N.D. Cal. Nov. 25, 2009) (discussing the U.S. Court of Appeals for the Ninth Circuit's reliance on *Hazelwood School District v. Kuhlmeier*, 484 U.S. 260 (1988), for cases involving teachers' instructional speech).

Figure 1-2: Professor v. University: Three Possible Legal Frameworks to Analyze the Case[45]

Public Employee Speech, Pre-*Garcetti*	Public Employee Speech, including-*Garcetti*

■ Is the speech a matter of public concern (i.e., does the speech involve an issue of social, political, or other interest to a community)?
  • If "no," not protected speech
  • If "yes," proceed below
■ Does the university's interest in promoting workplace efficiency outweigh the professor's interest in commenting?
  • If "yes," not protected speech
  • If "no," presumably protected speech
	■ Was the speech made pursuant to official duties?
	  • If "yes," not protected speech
	  • If "no," proceed below
	■ Is the speech a matter of public concern (i.e., does the speech involve an issue of social, political, or other interest to a community)?
	  • If "no," not protected speech
	  • If "yes," proceed below
	■ Does the university's interest in promoting workplace efficiency outweigh the professor's interest in commenting?
	  • If "yes," not protected speech
	  • If "no," presumably protected speech

Curricular Matters at Public Institutions

■ Has the university's justification for its actions over school-sponsored activities furthered legitimate pedagogical goals?
  • If "yes," within the school's authority and not violating speech rights
  • If "no," presumably protected speech

Since the *Garcetti* case, there has been some evidence that matters of public concern may override the *Garcetti* rule that public employees speaking on matters pursuant to official duties have no First Amendment protections. For instance, in *Lane v. Franks*,[46] the U.S. Supreme Court held in 2014 that a public employee, who worked at a community college, maintained First Amendment rights when he provided sworn testimony beyond the scope of his ordinary job duties. Thus, the Court has subtly modified the *Garcetti* rule to reference ordinary job duties as opposed to the broad concept of speaking about matters pursuant to official duties. Nonetheless, as the lower court cases have announced so far, the adoption of *Garcetti* within the professorial profession comes with mixed reviews. The discussion below highlights the tension between the *Garcetti* rule, which is a general application for the typical government employee, and the diminution of the professorial profession,

---

[45] DANIEL, GEE, SUN, & PAUKEN, *supra*, note 40.; KAPLIN, LEE, HUTCHENS, & ROOKSBY, *supra*, note 40.

[46] Lane v. Franks, 134 S. Ct. 2369 (2014).

which has prospered through reasoned debate and discussion to advance learning and knowledge.

Lower Courts and Faculty Speech Claims

Keeping in mind lingering questions about any kind of First Amendment rights for faculty speech, the chapter now turns to lower federal court decisions addressing faculty speech claims. Many cases involving faculty speech were decided before *Garcetti*. Still, depending on resolution of whether the *Garcetti* standards cover faculty, these decisions represent areas where First Amendment protection for professorial speech has been addressed. An examination of faculty speech cases shows that the context in which the speech occurs generally is of legal importance, with courts often willing to recognize institutional authority over issues related to the classroom and instruction. Faculty members have prevailed in some classroom-related cases, though, especially when the speech at issue touched on matters involving the faculty member's academic or teaching expertise.[47] Language from several decisions indicates that a professor stands a better chance of asserting a successful First Amendment claim outside of the classroom environment if scholarly speech is the issue. However, courts have not shown uniformity for speech occurring in this context, particularly in relation to the applicability of the *Garcetti* standards.

Faculty Speech Occurring in a Classroom or an Instructional Context

Non-instructional speech

While not demonstrating perfect consistency, courts have often determined that institutional authority generally trumps faculty speech claims when involving classroom-related speech indirectly related to instructional matters. One illustrative case, *Bishop v. Aronov*,[48] involved a faculty member challenging institutional authority to direct him not to interject his religious beliefs into classroom discussions or to hold optional classes that offered a Christian perspective on subjects covered in the course.[49] The professor alleged that the university encroached on his right to free speech and religion; the district court held in his favor, determining that the university had created a forum for the free exchange of ideas among students and faculty.[50] On appeal, the Eleventh Circuit overturned the lower court's decision,[51] determining that the university did not intend for its classes to be open forums.[52] The court held that the university could restrict the professor from injecting his religious views into the

---

[47] White, *supra* note 30, at 827-29.
[48] 926 F.2d 1066 (11th Cir. 1991).
[49] *Id.* at 1068-69.
[50] *Id.* at 1070.
[51] *Id.* at 1078.
[52] *Id.* at 1071.

courses he taught, stating that the school's "conclusions about course content must be allowed to hold sway over an individual professor's judgments."[53]

In a post-*Garcetti* case involving non-instructional speech in a classroom environment, *Piggee v. Carl Sandburg College*,[54] the U.S. Court of Appeals for the Seventh Circuit considered whether any First Amendment protection existed for an instructor to distribute materials to students on matters unrelated to a cosmetology course.[55] In *Piggee*, the faculty member distributed two pamphlets on the immorality of homosexuality during instructional time to a student who was gay, and invited the student to talk with her on the subject outside of class.[56] The opinion emphasized that the speech at issue did not take place outside of the classroom but, instead, happened within an instructional context.[57] As such, held the court, the school possessed a legitimate interest in regulating the instructor/student relationship in relation to the professor's professional demeanor and to the content covered in the class.[58] The court discussed that the principles announced in *Garcetti* supported recognition of institutional authority over classroom speech.[59]

Decisions such as *Piggee* and *Bishop* demonstrate how courts have recognized considerable institutional authority to limit faculty speech in a classroom on matters unrelated to instructional issues. The following section addresses how courts have dealt with cases involving instructional-related speech.

Instructional or Pedagogical-Related Speech

In classroom instructional matters, including issues related to grading, courts have also followed a general trend of recognizing considerable institutional authority.[60] This does not mean, however, that decisions always reflect consensus regarding the First Amendment rights of faculty members in instructional matters. Contrasting decisions dealing with student grading demonstrate how courts may reach different determinations about faculty members' First Amendment rights.

In *Brown v. Armenti*,[61] a professor alleged that he was disciplined for refusing to change a student's failing grade to an incomplete.[62] The faculty member also claimed he was impermissibly disciplined for writing a document critical of the treatment he received and presenting it to the institution's governing

---

[53] *Id.* at 1077.

[54] 464 F.3d 667 (7th Cir. 2006)

[55] *Id.* at 668.

[56] *Id.*

[57] *Id.* at 671-72.

[58] *Id.* at 672.

[59] *Id.* at 670-71; *see also,* Buchanan v. Alexander, 919 F. 3d 847 (5th Cir. 2019).

[60] *See generally* Richard Fossey & Joseph Beckham, *University Authority over Teaching Activities: Institutional Regulation May Override a Faculty Member's Academic Freedom*, 228 ED. LAW REP. 1 (2008); White, *supra* note 30.

[61] 247 F.3d 69 (3d Cir. 2001).

[62] *Id.* at 72.

board.[63] The district court determined that the faculty member's assignment of a grade and criticism of the incident constituted protected speech, but the U.S. Court of Appeals for the Third Circuit reversed.[64] Looking to an earlier Third Circuit decision, *Edwards v. California University of Pennsylvania*,[65] the court discussed that clear limits exist on a faculty member's speech rights in relation to institutional control over classroom instructional matters.[66]

The court in *Brown* adopted a similar stance as that followed in *Edwards*, stating that grading did not constitute protected speech: "Because grading is pedagogic, the assignment of the grade is subsumed under the university's freedom to determine how a course is to be taught. We therefore conclude that a public university professor does not have a First Amendment right to expression via the school's grade assignment procedures."[67] Looking to the public employee speech cases, the court also determined that the faculty member's criticism of the incident involved an internal issue that did not constitute a matter of public concern.[68] Just as in *Edwards*, the court was careful to note that different First Amendment issues were potentially at stake outside the classroom, where a faculty member was not acting as an institution's "proxy."[69]

Cases involving grading do not always yield the same analysis and result. In *Parate v. Isibor*, the U.S. Court of Appeals for the Sixth Circuit reached a very different conclusion than the opinion in the *Brown* case.[70] A faculty member claimed a violation of his First Amendment rights based on assertions that his dismissal stemmed in large part from a refusal to change several student grades at the direction of his dean.[71] In its analysis, the court noted the ambiguity in distinguishing between First Amendment protections for academic freedom that shielded higher education institutions from undue governmental interference, versus those protections that attach to individual scholars in relation to their employer colleges and universities.[72]

In the realm of institutional authority, the Sixth Circuit discussed how courts had recognized substantial authority for public colleges and universities to regulate the classroom activities of non-tenured professors.[73] Referring to other cases, the court discussed that this authority permitted a school to "choose not to renew the contract of a non-tenured professor whose pedagogical attitude and teaching methods do not conform to institutional standards."[74] At the same time, the Sixth Circuit noted that courts had recognized "substantial protection

---

[63] *Id.*
[64] *Id.* at 79.
[65] 156 F.3d 488 (3d Cir. 1998).
[66] *Brown*, 247 F.3d at 74-75.
[67] *Id.* at 75.
[68] *Id.* at 79.
[69] *Id.* at 75.
[70] 868 F.2d 821 (6th Cir. 1989).
[71] *Id.* at 825.
[72] *Id.* at 826-27.
[73] *Id.* at 827.
[74] *Id.*

to the First Amendment freedoms of individual university professors."[75] Along with outlining these general considerations concerning the parameters of First Amendment protection for faculty speech, the court determined that grading qualified as a form of symbolic speech, one "entitled to some measure of First Amendment protection."[76]

As to the interests of the professor in having certain independence in assigning grades, the court discussed how grading, as a reflection of a faculty member's assessment of student performance, represented a key part of the teaching process.[77] While noting that a faculty member "does not escape the reasonable review of university officials in the assignment of grades, she should remain free to decide, according to her own professional judgment, what grades to assign and what grades not to assign."[78] Thus, the university could not compel the professor to change the grade. The case made a distinction on the limits of institutional authority. An institution possessed the authority to administratively alter a student's grade, but it could not force the faculty member to do so.[79] Despite holding in favor of the professor, the court in *Parate* still acknowledged the institution as having considerable authority over classroom matters.

Lovelace v. Southeastern Massachusetts University[80] provides another example of a court recognizing significant institutional authority to control the learning environment, including standards related to the assessment of student work. In this case, an untenured professor claimed that his contract was not renewed because he refused to lower his academic expectations in relation to student work, both in grading and in the amount of homework assigned.[81] The court rejected the faculty member's First Amendment claims. Even if the professor ostensibly held a First Amendment right to advocate that a school should require students to meet certain performance criteria, the institution possessed the authority to establish overall academic standards.[82] According to the opinion, "[w]hether a school sets itself up to attract and serve only the best and brightest students or whether it instead gears its standards to a broader, more average population is a policy decision which we think universities must be allowed to set."[83] Issues such as "course content, homework load, and grading policy" represented "core university concerns" that should be subject to institutional control.[84]

---

[75] *Id.*
[76] *Id.*
[77] *Id.* at 828.
[78] *Id.*
[79] *Id.* at 829.
[80] 793 F.2d 419 (1st Cir. 1986).
[81] *Id.* at 425.
[82] *Id.*
[83] *Id.*
[84] *Id.* at 426.

In *Johnson-Kurek v. Abu-Absi*,[85] the U.S. Court of Appeals for the Sixth Circuit, in a case dealing with instructional speech that echoed the *Urofsky* and *Parate* decisions, held that a faculty member did not possess any additional First Amendment protections than those held by any other public employees.[86] The professor claimed that she was denied an additional teaching assignment because she refused to follow institutional directives to provide more detailed communication with students regarding steps needed to complete course requirements.[87] The Sixth Circuit stated that the professor was not required to profess any kind of endorsement for ideas or values she did not support.[88] Instead, supervisors directed the instructor to provide more detailed directions for students to enable them to complete the requirements of a course taught by the professor.[89] According to the court, these conditions placed on her teaching did not encroach on any of the professor's First Amendment rights.[90]

Other decisions have upheld college and university authority to regulate the classroom. Courts have determined that colleges and universities may require professors to adhere to institutionally established grade distributions,[91] decide not to renew a non-tenured faculty member because of concerns with pedagogical methods,[92] and require faculty members to distribute faculty evaluations to students.[93] With decisions involving use of profanity or lewd speech, or potentially sexually harassing speech, courts have also upheld institutional authority to regulate speech made without serving any kind of legitimate pedagogical purpose or related to some matter of public concern.[94] In *Silva v. University of New Hampshire*,[95] however, the court determined that a professor's use of sexual metaphors to make legitimate pedagogical points concerning writing should receive First Amendment protection.[96] *Silva* demonstrates that while courts generally favor institutional authority in classroom matters, the potential for a professor to initiate a successful claim in such a context is at a premium when involving the faculty member's academic expertise and a genuine pedagogical purpose. In fact, faculty members prevailed in several post-*Garcetti* cases involving such speech.

---

[85] 423 F.3d 590 (6th Cir. 2005).

[86] *Id*. at 591.

[87] *Id*. at 593.

[88] *Id*. at 595.

[89] *Id*. at 594-95.

[90] *Id.*

[91] Wozniak v. Conry, 236 F.3d 888 (7th Cir. 2001).

[92] Hetrick v. Martin, 480 F.2d 705 (6th Cir. 1973).

[93] Wirsing v. Bd. of Regents of Univ. of Colo., 739 F. Supp. 551 (D. Colo. 1990).

[94] *See, e.g.*, Martin v. Parrish, 805 F.2d 583 (5th Cir. 1986); Buchanan v. Alexander, 919 F. 3d 847 (5th Cir. 2019) (a teacher's "use of profanity and discussion of her sex life and the sex lives of her students was not related to the subject matter or purpose of training PreK–Third grade teachers" and not protected under the First Amendment. *Id.* at 853).

[95] 888 F. Supp. 293 (D. N.H. 1994).

[96] *Id*. at 316-17.

One of these cases, *Sheldon v. Dhillon* (2009),[97] involved an adjunct biology instructor. An offer for the instructor to teach a course was withdrawn after several students complained about comments she made in relation to the determinants of sexual orientation during a class on human heredity.[98] In considering the instructor's speech claims, the court rejected that the *Garcetti* standards should apply.[99] According to that federal district court, the Supreme Court in *Garcetti* did not address the issue of "teaching-related speech."[100] The court determined that a level of constitutional protection existed for teacher speech and required officials to act reasonably and with a legitimate pedagogical interest in regulating any such speech.[101]

Sheldon is important as it reflects a court's refusal to apply the *Garcetti* standards, but it also illustrates continuing ambiguity over the appropriate legal standards to assess faculty speech claims. Instead of looking to the academic freedom decisions or the public employee speech cases, the *Sheldon* court discussed that cases in the Ninth Circuit relied on the Supreme Court's decision in *Hazelwood School District v. Kuhlmeier*[102] when assessing speech claims involving instructional speech. Rather than an academic freedom case arising in higher education, *Hazelwood* involved a group of secondary students claiming First Amendment rights in relation to a student newspaper produced as part of a journalism class.[103] Thus, while not applying the *Garcetti* standards to the biology instructor's speech, the *Sheldon* case highlights how academic freedom cases have not resulted in legal criteria easily discernible or routinely applied by courts to speech claims involving faculty members, even among courts sympathetic to such claims. The standards applied in this case came from precedent involving secondary students, and also made no distinction between elementary and secondary teachers and faculty members in higher education.

Another post-*Garcetti* case involving classroom speech, *Kerr v. Hurd*,[104] further illustrates the confused state of affairs when it comes to the legal standards governing faculty speech claims in the classroom. In *Kerr*, a medical faculty member specializing in obstetrics and gynecology claimed that he was impermissibly retaliated against for advocating certain delivery procedures.[105] The court determined that *Garcetti* should not apply to such in-class instructional speech,[106] pointing out that the Supreme Court explicitly stated in *Garcetti* that the standards might not apply to faculty speech.[107] Also noted by the court was that decisions from the U.S. Court of Appeals for the Sixth

---

[97] Sheldon v. Dhillon, No. C-08-03438 RMW, 2009 WL 4282086 (N.D. Cal. Nov. 25, 2009).
[98] *Id*. at *2.
[99] *Id*. at *4.
[100] *Id*.
[101] *Id*.
[102] 484 U.S. 260 (1988).
[103] *Id*. at 262-64.
[104] 694 F. Supp. 2d 817 (S.D. Ohio 2010).
[105] *Id*. at 834-35.
[106] *Id*. at 843.
[107] *Id*.

Circuit, which provided controlling precedent for the district court deciding *Kerr*, had not made such a determination.[108] The opinion then discussed the need for recognizing an "academic freedom exception" to *Garcetti* in order to protect "the active trading floors in the marketplace of ideas."[109] According to the court, the views expressed by the faculty member fell "well within the range of accepted medical opinion" and were thus deserving of First Amendment protection.[110] The court, however, did not look to the academic freedom decisions but, instead, to the standards from the public employee speech cases.

As these decisions show, even when faculty speech in a classroom or instructional context addresses scholarly or pedagogical issues, courts have recognized substantial institutional authority over such speech. However, in certain instances faculty members have successfully asserted First Amendment claims. The cases also reveal a continuing struggle over uniform standards for courts to apply to faculty speech claims, including those dealing with scholarly or pedagogical matters involving the classroom and instructional issues. The chapter now turns to faculty speech arising outside the classroom.

Faculty Speech Outside the Classroom Context

It is rather well-settled that a professor at a public college, who acts independently of the work setting such as posting a personal tweet, holds the same constitutional rights of free speech as other citizens. For instance, when a Fresno State English professor tweeted about the death of former First Lady Barbara Bush calling her an "amazing racist" wishing her farewell stating an expletive "F-ck outta here with your nice words," the state university concluded that it could not take any disciplinary action against the professor.[111] In a public statement, the university president remarked that the English professor's "conduct was insensitive, inappropriate and an embarrassment to the university."[112] Nonetheless, the professor has protections because "she was acting in a private capacity and speaking about a public matter on her personal Twitter account. Her comments, although disgraceful, are protected free speech under the First Amendment of the U.S. Constitution."[113] Other incidents, which even demonstrated concerns about professors' inclusive and fair assessment of persons, have generally led to a public university's airing on free speech rights.[114] In one instance, a state university revoked an employment offer made

---

[108] *Id*.

[109] *Id*. at 843-44.

[110] *Id*. at 844.

[111] Cleve R. Wootson, Jr. & Susan Svrluga, *Fresno State Says It Can't Discipline the Professor Who Called Barbara Bush an Amazing Racist*, WASHINGTON POST, Apr. 25 2018, at https://www.washingtonpost.com/news/grade-point/wp/2018/04/25/fresno-state-says-it-cant-discipline-the-professor-who-called-barbara-bush-an-amazing-racist/?utm_term=.8bc037d494f1.

[112] *Id.*

[113] *Id.*

[114] *See, e.g.*, Steven Lubet, How Do We Curb Racism and Anti-Semitism – and Protect Free Speech?, Chicago Tribune, at https://www.chicagotribune.com/opinion/commentary/ct-perspec-chikindas-academia-political-correctness-offensive-0116-story.html

to an incoming tenured associate professor after the pending professor posted tweets, which a federal court "put it mildly" when describing the professor's tweets as "critical of Israel's actions and used harsh, often profanity-laden rhetoric."[115] The professor sued on multiple grounds including First Amendment free speech, and the federal trial court denied part of the university's motion to dismiss—notably the First Amendment retaliation claim. The case settled out of court in favor of the former professor for $600,000 plus legal fees.[116]

Although there are generally consistent holdings with public college faculty members' speech in one's personal content, these same professors' speech outside the classroom (but within the employment context) or instructional context also represents an arena of legal uncertainty and debate. As an initial matter, one should keep in mind that professors engage in multiple types of speech. A key aspect of faculty life often revolves around speech related to scholarship. However, as discussed earlier in the chapter, professors also regularly communicate in intramural settings (i.e., internal institutional contexts) regarding issues affecting campus life, such as in departmental meetings. Additionally, professors often engage in extramural communications to the general public, such as in providing interviews to news media, or authoring commentaries appearing in print or online. Such extramural communications may or may not involve a faculty member expressing views related to his or her scholarly expertise. Thus, in assessing faculty speech rights outside the classroom, an important factor to keep in mind involves the nature of the speech and the context in which it occurs.

Much of this section focuses on when a faculty member clashes with his or her institutional employer. Professors may look to the First Amendment to safeguard constitutional protection for academic freedom more broadly. Supreme Court cases such as *Keyishian*, discussed previously, dealt with professors seeking to challenge governmental regulations or authority not stemming directly from their colleges or universities. Other lower court decisions have dealt with efforts by parties external to the university to obtain through judicial means information from researchers, such as notes and data, and courts have been willing to rely on principles associated with academic freedom to shield academic work from such requests.[117] Greater uncertainty exists when a faculty member's speech interests are pitted against an employer institution. Despite a case like *Keyishian*, a faculty member at a public college or university may also face limitations in challenging the authority of state government on academic freedom grounds to regulate at least some aspects related to faculty speech. This potential difficulty is perhaps no more evident than in *Urofsky v. Gilmore*.[118]

---

[115] Emma Pettit, *'Ousted' From Academe, Steven Salaita Says He's Driving A School Bus to Make Ends Meet.* CHRONICLE OF HIGHER EDUCATION, Feb. 19, 2019, at https://www.chronicle.com/article/Ousted-From-Academe/245732

[116] *Id.*

[117] White, *supra* note 30, at 830-31.

[118] 216 F.3d 401 (4th Cir. 2000).

The *Urofsky* decision stands out as one of the most forceful instances of a court determining that faculty members at public colleges and universities possess no First Amendment rights beyond those held by any other public employees. The case involved a challenge by professors at public universities to a state law that prohibited access to or viewing of sexually explicit materials on state computers[119] The faculty members argued that applying the law to faculty members would curtail legitimate scholarly activities and infringe on First Amendment individual academic freedom.[120]

Sitting as a full court, the U.S. Court of Appeals for the Fourth Circuit held that faculty members at public colleges and universities possess no individual academic freedom rights protected by the First Amendment.[121] Faculty at public institutions enjoy only the general First Amendment rights of any other public employees, according to the court.[122] Any constitutional academic freedom rights, if they exist at all, vest in the institution and not the individual scholar.[123] While decided before *Garcetti*, under the rationale adopted in the *Urofsky* decision, the *Garcetti* standards would apply to faculty members at public colleges and universities. In both pre- and post-*Garcetti* cases, however, courts have reached differing conclusions regarding the extent of faculty speech rights in public higher education.

Other courts have reached differing conclusions than the *Urofsky* court regarding faculty members' First Amendment rights. One of these decisions, *Burnham v. Ianni*,[124] involved a display for a history department in which professors were pictured with items related to their areas of scholarship.[125] Following complaints about photographs showing several professors with weapons, the history department refused to remove the photographs.[126] Eventually, the school's chancellor ordered the department to remove them.[127] Several professors were among those who challenged the decision. While not determining that the university had permitted the creation of some type of public forum to justify the open display, the court concluded that the removal of the photographs violated First Amendment standards and infringed on the professors' speech rights.[128]

In another case dealing with an art exhibit, *Piarowski v. Illinois Community College District 515*,[129] the U.S. Court of Appeals for the Seventh Circuit considered an institution's authority to remove a campus art exhibit containing

---

[119] *Id.* at 404.
[120] *Id.* at 405-06.
[121] *Id.* at 410.
[122] *Id.* at 415.
[123] *Id.* at 412.
[124] 119 F.3d 668 (8th Cir. 1997).
[125] *Id.* at 670-71.
[126] *Id.* at 672.
[127] *Id.*
[128] *Id.* at 675-76.
[129] 759 F.2d 625 (7th Cir. 1985).

faculty work that sparked complaints.[130] The opinion stated that the college had not created an open forum generally available to the public with the art gallery, which gave the school greater control over the space.[131] Institutional authority, however, was not absolute, with the court stating that "public colleges do not have carte blanche to regulate the expression of ideas by faculty members in the parts of the college that are not public forums."[132] The court qualified this stance by pointing out the unsettled nature of legal standards governing First Amendment protection for professors' academic freedom.[133] According to the opinion, the concept of academic freedom represented an "equivocal" term, one "used to denote both the freedom of the academy to pursue its ends without interference from the government . . . and the freedom of the individual teacher . . . to pursue his ends without interference from the academy."[134] While the college may not have had the authority to forbid any display of the art exhibit, the court determined that it did not run afoul of the First Amendment in moving the art to a less heavily trafficked part of campus.[135]

The *Piarowski* decision captured the uncertainty that has persisted over First Amendment protection for individual academic freedom in relation to institutional authority, a tension that existed well before the *Garcetti* decision. Post-*Garcetti* cases reveal that courts continue to reach conflicting determinations regarding the existence of First Amendment protection for faculty speech. In several decisions, courts have determined that the *Garcetti* standards apply to such speech. One such case, *Renken v. Gregory*,[136] dealt with a tenured professor's claims that the university violated his First Amendment rights by reducing his pay through ending the institution's participation in a National Science Foundation (NSF) grant for which the faculty member was the principal investigator.[137] The professor and a colleague asserted that university conditions imposed on the grant violated NSF standards.[138] The faculty member argued that the *Garcetti* standards did not apply because any activities related to the grant dealt with discretionary activities on his part and did not constitute required employment duties.[139]

The U.S. Court of Appeals for the Seventh Circuit disagreed, holding that since the professor was expected to engage in research activities as a part of his employment responsibilities, the *Garcetti* standards applied.[140] As such, the professors could not look to the First Amendment to challenge the

---

[130] *Id.* at 627.
[131] *Id.* at 629.
[132] *Id.*
[133] *Id.*
[134] *Id.*
[135] *Id.* at 632.
[136] 541 F.3d 769 (7th Cir. 2008).
[137] *Id.* at 770.
[138] *Id.* at 771-72.
[139] *Id.* at 773.
[140] *Id.* at 773-74.

university's actions.[141] Courts have reached similar decisions in several other cases where faculty members have sought to rely on the First Amendment to challenge institutional decisions. These cases have dealt with comments made in faculty meetings[142] and, in one case, dealt with institutional hiring and teaching practices.[143]

In contrast to a case like *Renken*, the U.S. Court of Appeals for the Ninth Circuit has declared that an exception exists under the *Garcetti* standards for faculty speech, at least in the context of teaching and scholarship.[144] The case involved a journalism professor at Washington State University, Demers, who claimed that he was subjected to retaliation on the basis of two forms of communication. One dealt with a plan proposed by Demers that called for the reorganization of journalism education at the university. The other involved an in-progress book, which Demers worked on during a sabbatical. A federal district court, relying on legal analysis that included *Garcetti* and its official duties standard, initially denied First Amendment protection for either the reorganization plan or the book project.[145]

In reversing the district court, the U.S. Court of Appeals for the Ninth Circuit discussed that the *Demers* case presented exactly the kind of situation that "worried" former Justice Souter in *Garcetti*, as it dealt with faculty speech related to teaching and scholarship.[146] While "teaching and academic writing" constitute the core duties of professors, the Ninth Circuit held that *Garcetti* should not apply to such faculty speech.[147] To do so, stated the court, would "directly conflict with the important First Amendment values previously articulated by the Supreme Court" in its academic freedom cases such as *Keyishian*.[148]

Though looking to *Keyishian* as grounding for its decision, the Ninth Circuit turned to the public employee speech cases for the specific legal rules to evaluate the professor's speech claims.[149] Under these standards, the speech at issue must address a matter of public concern and the governmental employer— a college or university in the case of faculty—is able to assert a justification to restrict the speech under consideration. While turning to the public employee speech standards, the court discussed that this "balancing process in cases

---

[141] *Id*. at 775.

[142] Miller v. Univ. of S. Ala., No. 09-0146-KD-B, 2010 WL 1994910 (S.D. Ala. May 17, 2010); Plouffe v. Cevallos, Civ. Nos. 16-3187, 16-3188, 17-1548, 2019 WL 2451063 *1 (3d Cir. 2019) (professor's expression opposing the hire of a new faculty member was not protected under the First Amendment because such speech was based on information obtained through his service on the search committee, which is "part of the [professor's] employment" (*Id.* at *5).

[143] Hong v. Grant, 516 F. Supp. 2d 1158 (C.D. Cal. 2007), *aff'd*, No. 07-56705, 2010 WL 4561419 (9th Cir. Nov. 12, 2010).

[144] Demers v. Austin, 746 F.3d 402, 412 (9th Cir. 2014).

[145] *Id*. at 406.

[146] *Id*. at 411.

[147] *Id*.

[148] *Id*.

[149] *Id*. at 412.

involving academic speech is likely to be particularly subtle and 'difficult.'"[150] In essence, while applying the public employee speech standards, the Ninth Circuit in *Demers* cautioned that the concept of public concern possesses a particularized meaning in a higher education environment. The stance taken by the Ninth Circuit in this case in relation to faculty speech and academic freedom differs markedly from decisions such as *Renken*, in which courts have applied the *Garcetti* standards to faculty speech in a straightforward manner.

Nonetheless, when *Garcetti* is not applicable and the expression pertains to a matter of public concern, the courts gravitate to the prior rules and conclude free speech protections exist as with other citizens. For instance, in *Wetherbe v. Texas Tech University System*, the U.S. Court of Appeals for the Fifth Circuit ruled that a business school professor, who had been an outspoken critic of tenure, not necessarily just the tenure system and approach at Texas Tech, held First Amendment protections.[151] The professor had written about tenure in academic and public media outlets including editorials. The professor's expressions were about tenure, not his employment status, which removed the personal employment griping factor as the core concern.

While *Wetherbe* extends beyond the employee griping, contests around faculty free speech cases that do impute some forms of griping have restructured our notions of institutional governance and reshaped our expectations for the academic setting. For instance, in *Sadid v. Idaho State University* parts 1 and 2, the Idaho Supreme Court held that a professor's behavior reflected unprofessionalism falling below expectations or academic community standards when the professor asserted free speech rights on matters of the academic college's operations and decisions.[152] The professor also expressed his discontent with the university and college leadership's decisions in media editorials. On numerous occasions, he had been reprimanded for using university communications to express negative comments and that he was asked to "observe collegiality in the workplace" following the university's protocols to express concerns.[153] Similarly, when a professor vocalized his dissent of a dean's appointment, a federal appellate court described the exchange as "an embarrassing, vulgar, vituperative, ad hominem attack that was perceived in the workplace as disrespectful, demeaning, insulting, and rude."[154] The faculty member's gripe was comparing the administrator to the Egyptian President Hosni Mubarak and depicted him as a "'dictatorial leader' who went against 'democracy'."[155] These cases and others have set the stage that higher education has an unstated but court recognized set of behaviors in the workplace, and such behaviors must be attended to as a condition to First Amendment protections. That is,

---

[150] *Id.* at 413.

[151] Wetherbe v. Texas Tech Univ. Sys., 699 Fed. App'x. 297 (5th Cir. 2017).

[152] Sadid v. Idaho State Univ., 265 P.3d 1144 (Idaho 2011); Sadid v. Idaho State Univ., 294 P.3d 1100 (Idaho 2013).

[153] *Sadid,* 294 P.3d at 1104 (2013).

[154] Shi v. Montgomery, 679 Fed. App'x. 828, 835 (11th Cir. 2017).

[155] *Id.*

when expressions are categorized or depicted as contentious confrontations, they may be painted as behaviors that violate normative expectations. When those behaviors are associated with the public employment setting, they may well be casted away as unprotected.

Just as with faculty speech arising in the context of instruction, the future of faculty speech rights outside the classroom rests at a legal crossroads, including speech related to scholarship and curricular matters. If the *Garcetti* standards apply to faculty members at public colleges and universities in nonclassroom contexts, then these professors do not possess any First Amendment rights for speech made in the course of carrying out their official employment duties. This would likely encompass speech related to scholarship, as well as that involved in faculty participation in institutional governance. A faculty member would be able to rely on First Amendment protection only when speaking as a private citizen and not fulfilling some kind of official employment duty.

Of course, given the scope of work and activities undertaken by faculty members, courts might often face difficulty regarding whether a professor is speaking pursuant to carrying out his or her official employment duties, or as a private citizen.[156] Would all research activities, such as presenting at a professional conference, fall under a faculty member's employment duties? What about a professor communicating to the public in a newspaper article or an online blog posting about issues related to a faculty member's area of academic expertise? Even if the *Garcetti* standards are not held to apply to professors in public higher education, questions exist regarding the legal standards most appropriate to evaluate faculty speech claims. Courts would be left to wrestle with continued reliance upon the public employee speech cases, or developing standards derived from the academic freedom cases. Just as with speech involving classroom and instructional matters, ambiguity and debate surround legal protections for faculty speech taking place outside the classroom, including speech related to scholarship.

Conclusion

Legal protections for faculty speech are in a period of change and uncertainty. In this transitional period, the composition of the faculty is dramatically shifting as well, with the erosion of tenure as a contractual arrangement in higher education. Disagreement abounds regarding the continued usefulness of tenure and over the effectiveness of other faculty employment arrange-

---

[156] As noted, the faculty speech cases have often categorized a public college professor's complaints about the institution under the auspices of pursuant to official duties. However, in *Meade v. Moraine Valley Community College*, 770 F.3d 680 (7th Cir. 2014), the college conceded that an adjunct professor's letter to League for Innovation in the Community College in which she complained about the poor treatment of adjuncts and the negative impacts on student learning did not arise from the adjunct's official duties. Nevertheless, the college still terminated her for her letter and even stated that the letter was the basis for the termination. In a federal appellate decision, the adjunct faculty member prevailed over the college in the First Amendment retaliation lawsuit.

ments, such as multi-year contracts, to protect academic freedom and other forms of professionally based faculty speech. Alongside questions regarding tenure's future, uncertainty also surrounds the extent of any First Amendment protection for faculty members in public higher education. While the *Garcetti* decision added a new layer of legal haziness, constitutional protection for faculty speech and individual academic freedom at public colleges and universities has long been subject to uncertainty. Accordingly, both in terms of employment arrangements for professors at public and private institutions and First Amendment protection for faculty in public higher education, legal protections related to faculty speech face a precarious future. Compounding this effect of decremented rights for college faculty as outgrowths of the case law, state and federal legislators have questioned the campus practices respecting student free speech rights, which have forced discussions about faculty free speech too. For instance, Professors Sun and McClellan through one chapter of their book trace instances in which lawmakers have signaled displeasure with collective faculty decisions to exercise academic authority.[157] They illustrate how lawmakers have proposed bills intending to weaken faculty authority such as stripping control over selected areas of academic standards. Notably, in one section, they describe how lawmakers in Michigan proposed legislation that could restrict academic policies in selected graduate professional fields, including counselor education, so the faculty may not require students in these programs to counsel clients of diverse backgrounds (e.g., lesbian, gay, bisexual, transgender, and queer) when students assert conflicts with religious beliefs.[158] Most of the recently adopted state laws governing free speech on college campuses have been enacted to protect students' rights.[159] Also, the federal hearings, which have largely advocated for campus changes, not legislative mandates, have forwarded suggestions of ensuring greater student rights and weakening academic and campus controls. Despite the recommendations, in March 2019, U.S. President Donald Trump issued an executive order directing 12 federal agencies to ensure that colleges comply with standards of free academic inquiry as required by First Amendment law and stated institutional policies.[160] Campuses are required to take appropriate steps to ensure that it promotes free inquiry. While it is unknown what effect the Executive Order will have, constitutional law experts raise question of the

---

[157] JEFFREY C. SUN & GEORGE S. MCCLELLAN, STUDENT CLASHES ON CAMPUS: A LEADERSHIP GUIDE TO FREE SPEECH (in press, expected 2019).

[158] *Id.* (discussing Michigan's Julea Ward Freedom of Conscience Act, which is a dedicated portion of the state's proposed Religious Liberty and Conscience Protection Act).

[159] BRANDI HEPHNER LABANC, FRANK FERNANDEZ, NEAL H. HUTCHENS, & KERRY BRIAN MELEAR. FREE SPEECH IN HIGHER EDUCATION: EFFECTIVE PROFESSIONAL PRACTICE (forthcoming); SUN & MCCLELLAN, *supra*, note 157.

[160] Improving Free Inquiry, Transparency, and Accountability at Colleges and Universities, Exec. Order 13864 (Mar. 21, 2019).

validity of the order given its vague understanding and overbroad reach.[161] Still, this Executive Order along with various state laws send a message that academic authority, through its voice on determining academic policies and practices, is at a tenuous state, and possibly, encountering a debilitating effect on academic freedom through an increasing series of court decisions and legislative policies. Accordingly, scholars and students of higher education law continue to monitor activities pertaining to faculty speech and academic freedom to examine significant events and their patterns, which collectively shape the future state of this area of law.

---

[161] Erwin Chemerinsky and Howard Gillman, *Trump's Executive Order on College Free Speech Is Unconstitutional,* LOS ANGELES TIMES, Mar. 22, 2019, at https://www.latimes.com/opinion/op-ed/la-oe-chemerinsky-gillman-trump-free-speech-college-201903222-story.html

6

Legal Rights of Non-Academic Personnel

Luke M. Cornelius, Ph.D., J.D.
University of North Florida

Introduction

Although professors and instructors are the most visible employees on a college or university campus, they represent only a portion of the campus employees necessary for an institution to function. Even the smallest of colleges requires a range of non-academic employees, from secretaries and groundskeepers to presidents and senior administrators. Many schools operate their own hospitals, business enterprises, police departments, and even nuclear power plants. A large university can, in many regards, resemble a small city government in terms of the complexity of its operations and the range of its employees. While the legal rights and administrative requirements of such employees may closely mirror those of the instructional staff, there are some significant differences that merit consideration.

This chapter will attempt to generally detail the legal status and treatment of these non-academic employees. Although the best legal analogy for such employment may be to compare a college or university to a municipal government, a private company, or a religious denomination, depending on the type of institution, there are additional considerations that place unique challenges on the administration of such personnel. A distinctive consideration in college and university employment is the large number of personnel whose status as non-academic employees is complicated by their status as students, especially graduate students, or as faculty members. Another consideration, which cannot be fully addressed in an overview such as this, is the diversity of higher education organizations and their individual terms and conditions of employment. At some institutions, particularly small private colleges, nearly all non-academic employees may essentially have the status of "at-will" employees. On the other hand, in certain public universities, depending on state law, the majority of these employees will be covered by the state civil service system, requiring competitive examinations and objective hiring procedures and affording employees the rights of job tenure and due process that rival, or even exceed, the protections afforded to the academic faculty.

Organization

As indicated above, the nature of a particular employment relationship can vary depending on the type and location of an institution of higher learning. However, there are certain standard methods of classifying non-academic staff that, with variations in terminology and application, are generally utilized by many educational organizations.

"Classified Personnel" refers to that large body of workers hired to carry out specific support functions of the college or university. In a public institution, these employees may also be part of a state or local civil service system. Classified personnel are typically hired to perform specific non-academic duties on campus and are selected on the basis of possessing and demonstrating job-specific knowledge, skills, and abilities. Examples of classified personnel, typically the largest group of employees on campus, include clerks and secretaries, groundskeepers and maintenance persons, police or security officers, lab technicians, bus drivers and vehicle operators, warehouse personnel, nurses and medical assistants, and computer technicians. In most cases, such employees must demonstrate specific competencies in performing various duties through either work experience or entrance examinations. For some highly skilled or sensitive positions, the possession of external certifications, such as in law enforcement or nursing, may also be necessary.

Another large group of employees are those known as Administrative and Professional Personnel, or A&P employees. In a civil service system, these employees are often classified as Exempt Employees. These members of the college or university staff are those who, as a requirement of their employment, usually must possess high levels of formal education and experience. They are also employed based upon more subjective considerations, such as their potential to make a positive impact on the institution's operations and their ability to successfully work with other senior A&P staff. Examples of A&P personnel would include presidents, provosts, vice presidents, deans, and directors, as well as medical doctors, engineers, and curators. One characteristic of these employees is their relative lack of job security.[1] While A&P employees may enjoy high pay and prestige in their positions, they are usually referred to as "at-will" employees. Should their supervisor or the institution's governing board decide that such an employee is no longer effective, or simply decide that a change of personnel is desirable, an A&P employee can usually be terminated in accordance with whatever contractual guarantees the employee may have had.

There is, however, one exceptional circumstance of A&P, and other exempt, employees: those who also hold a tenured faculty position. Faculty administrators are fairly common and have been throughout the history of higher education. Colleges and universities have a large talent pool of highly educated

---

[1] *See generally* Idoux v. Lamar Univ. Sys., 37 F.3d 632 (5th Cir. 1994); Regents of the Univ. Sys. of Ga. v. Hogan, 298 Ga.App. 454, 680 S.E.2d 518 (Ga.Ct. App. 2009).

faculty whose training may make them gifted administrators in areas such as finance, student counseling, or marketing, for example. Additionally, through the process of rising through the ranks from department chair to president, nutritionists and philosophers may demonstrate innate talents of leadership and management that transcend their particular academic specialty. Furthermore, by both tradition and common sense on the part of faculty administrators, administrative assignments for tenured faculty, including those that are full-time administration, almost always contain a guarantee of maintaining tenure as a professor and a right to return to that status if they resign or are removed from their administrative role. Likewise, senior administrators (e.g., deans, provosts, presidents, et al.) who are hired externally but have previously been tenured at their former institutions will insist on a grant of tenured faculty status within their discipline at the new institution they are to lead, even if they are initially hired with no teaching or research expectations.

Such faculty-administrators can be problematic. When a pure A&P administrator demonstrates sufficient reasons why they should no longer be employed in their position, they can simply be dismissed not only from their position, but also from the campus. (For such employees, no cause is generally needed.) By contrast, while an administrator who also holds a tenured faculty line can be as easily dismissed from their administrative role, they generally cannot be terminated from their faculty position unless their behavior was so egregious it would warrant removal of a professor. Even then, they will generally be entitled to extensive due process before they can be fully removed from employment, as discussed previously in Chapter 4. Often the cause that justifies their demotion will not suffice for terminating their tenure. The classic example is when a faculty-administrator engages in notorious speech that disrupts or impairs the institution's reputation and ability to function. Under well-established precedents, if the disruption caused by such speech to the organization, on balance, outweighs its value as a matter of public concern, then they can be dismissed without violating the First Amendment.[2] However, faculty protections of academic freedom, as discussed in previously in Chapter 5, tend to be much stronger. Therefore, speech that is intolerable by an administrator, but not a professor, could result in a situation where the individual remains on campus, possibly for the rest of their professional career, even if they are terminated from their position of leadership for particularly notorious speech.[3]

Although classified and A&P staff may make up the majority of a school's non-academic employees, there are still several other categories that must be considered. Colleges and universities commonly make use of contract employees. Often such employees are hired to complete specific recurring or non-recurring tasks. They may also be hired to work with related campus organizations and enterprises such as student government or school-related businesses. Additionally, colleges and universities make use of considerable numbers of temporary employees. Grant-funded employees, for example, are

[2] Garcetti v. Ceballos, 547 U.S. 410 (2006), etc.
[3] See Jeffries v. Harelston, 52 F.3d 9 (2nd Cir. 1995), *et seq.*

hired to help an institution, some sub-agency, or even an individual professor of that institution fulfill the obligations of a grant provided by some outside agency or organization. Frequently, these grants involve research activities that require the facilities and expertise of a university and its faculty. Grant employment is very similar to contract employment in the sense that the expectation of employment cannot be considered to exceed the expiration or exhaustion of the grant funding.

Those workers who are also enrolled as students in an institution constitute a particularly nebulous class of employees. Colleges and universities traditionally hire large numbers of their own students as workers in a variety of temporary and part-time roles. Some of these are fairly unrestricted workers, hired under a grant or contract to fulfill some general duty. Others are employed as a condition of receiving financial aid, such as students hired under college work-study programs. Graduate assistants are a particularly unique type of student employee. They are typically hired in a variety of subcategories, such as teaching assistants and research assistants, which delineate the type of work they perform for the college or university. As with work-study students, graduate assistants usually receive tuition assistance in addition to their salary or hourly pay. However, many graduate assistants are employed for reasons other than their need for financial aid; for example, as part of their educational programs. Thus, while they receive payment as employees for performing a useful, or even vital, service to the institution, they are also receiving valuable training and instruction. Many professors and professional researchers consider the graduate student's assistantship to be a vital apprenticeship for his or her career development. This dual role of the assistantship is highlighted by the policies of many graduate degree programs that require students to serve as teaching or research assistants as a graduation requirement.

Hiring and Promotion

Both public and private institutions of higher education must conform to a series of federal laws related to employment. Of particular significance to the hiring and promotion process is Title VII of the Civil Rights Act of 1964.[4] Title VII operationalizes the protections not only of the Civil Rights Act regarding discrimination based on race, color, gender, and national origin, but also those of subsequent legal enactments, such as the Age Discrimination in Employment Act,[5] the Equal Pay Act,[6] Section 504 of the Rehabilitation Act of 1973,[7] and the Americans with Disabilities Act.[8] Title VII applies to all employers of

---

[4]   42 U.S.C. §§ 2000e *et seq.*

[5]   29 U.S.C. § 621 *et seq.*

[6]   Pub. L. 88-38, June 10, 1963, 77 Stat. 56

[7]   29 U.S.C. § 793.

[8]   42 U.S.C. § 12101 *et seq.*

more than fifteen employees, including all state and local public institutions.[9] The intended reach of Title VII, the number of employees required by even a small college to operate, and the prevalence of federal funding in colleges and universities, ensures that these federal antidiscrimination acts cover virtually all institutions of higher education.

State and local statutes and regulations, as well as the provisions of collective bargaining agreements, provide additional legal protections for non-academic personnel. For example, while not explicitly protected in federal statutes, many states bar both public and private employers from discrimination based upon sexual orientation and/or gender identity.[10] Specific state protections can cover a variety of potential employment issues. A case in point is Wisconsin, which bars discrimination based on marital status, arrest and conviction records, or the use or non-use of "lawful products" when not at the work site or performing work-related tasks.[11] New York[12] and New Jersey[13] go so far as to ban any employment decisions based upon the individual's genetic history and information.

It should be noted that these restrictions apply to all aspects of the employment relationship, from initial recruiting to termination. Particular care must be exercised at two specific junctures: recruitment and the application and interview process. Under Executive Order 11246,[14] issued in 1965, all employers in federally assisted or contracted programs, including higher education, must not only avoid invidious discrimination, but they must also state in all recruiting materials that they do not discriminate with regard to race, color, religion, sex, or national origin.[15] Care must be taken to engage in recruitment practices that will address a diverse population and not utilize recruitment media that excessively targets only specific applicant pools. For example, a college using radio advertisements to seek employees should ensure that its advertisements are not disproportionately played on music stations that appeal to persons of specific ages, races, genders, religions, or national origins. Employers should also be sensitive to the availability of specific media, such as trade publications or the Internet, among various populations, especially with regard to race and national origin.

---

[9] Under the Equal Employment Opportunity Act of 1972 (Pub. L. 92-261, Mar. 24, 1972, 86 Stat. 103). *See* JAMES A. BUFORD, PERSONNEL MANAGEMENT AND HUMAN RESOURCES IN LOCAL GOV'T 25-26 (1991).

[10] Most notably Colorado, Delaware, Illinois, Iowa, Maine, New Mexico, Washington, Utah, Connecticut, Maryland, Nevada, Massachusetts, New Jersey, New York, Minnesota, Wisconsin, California, Oregon, Rhode Island, Vermont, Hawaii, New Hampshire, and the District of Columbia. See Non-Discrimination Laws: State-by-State Information. *American Civil Liberties Union* website, *available at* https://www.aclu.org/map/non-discrimination-laws-state-state-information-map.

[11] WIS. STAT. ANN. § 111.31.

[12] N.Y. EXEC. LAW § 296 (McKinney 2010).

[13] N.J. STAT. 10:5-12.

[14] 41 C.F.R. § 60.

[15] *See* BUFORD, *supra* note 7, at 39-40; WILLIAM J. ROSENTHAL & STEPHEN D. SHAWE, EMPLOYMENT LAW DESK BOOK § 2.03[1].

These restrictions apply even more significantly in the application and interview process. Except when related to a bona fide occupational qualification or to achieve affirmative action goals, employment applications and interviewers should avoid questions related to an employee's status as a member of a protected class. If a requirement of a position might cause conflict with an applicant's potentially protected status, then the employment process should focus on that requirement as opposed to the individual's personal attributes or beliefs. For example, if a position requires working on weekends, which may cause conflicts with certain religious beliefs, an application or interviewer should ask the applicants if they are available to work weekends, as opposed to asking applicants directly about their beliefs. Also, it is important to remember that it is permissible to deny employment based on membership in a protected class when no reasonable employment accommodations can be made. For example, if an applicant for a position as a football coach indicates that he or she cannot work on Saturdays due to his or her religious beliefs, that person can be excluded, as it is axiomatic that working on Saturday is an essential duty of a college football coach. By contrast, if the applicant is seeking employment as a librarian, the willingness to work on Saturday might not be an essential characteristic of the job. Unless the librarian position is so specialized as to preclude scheduling another employee in the applicant's place, it would not seem essential that every librarian be available for Saturday work. Unless it relates to an essential requirement of a position, for which accommodations might be sought, questions should not be asked on applications or in interviews that compel applicants to declare their membership in a protected class. This issue has actually arisen recently in *Crider v. University of Tennessee, Knoxville*, where the courts were confronted with the dilemma of a Study Abroad Coordinator who was terminated for an unwillingness to carry an emergency phone on Saturdays, as required by her position.[16]

Federal Protections

To operationalize the above discussion, it is appropriate to review the various federal protections that apply to college or university employment. In addition to complying with all applicable federal statutes, college and university administrators should remember that collective bargaining agreements and institutional policies, such as antidiscrimination declarations, may also protect potential employees. What follows are brief summaries of the appropriate federal statutes that are universally applicable under Title VII to both public and private employers.

Title VII

Title VII is one of the most powerful and sweeping federal laws affecting employment in both the public and private sector. Applying to any organiza-

---

[16] 492 Fed. Appx. 609 (6th Cir. 2009).

tion with more than fifteen employees, it provides a sweeping mandate against discrimination on the basis of race, color, gender, national origin, or religion. This statute pertains to all personnel actions from the initial advertisement of vacancies through disciplinary and termination decisions. One significant aspect of Title VII is that it can be invoked using two different legal doctrines: disparate treatment and disparate impact.[17] Disparate treatment is normally applied when applicants or employee can show they are members of a protected class under Title VII and were treated differently than non-class members in employment decisions. Disparate treatment implies clear discrimination against an individual or specific group of protected persons. By contrast, disparate impact requires that a plaintiff show that an employer's personnel policies have an undue impact on persons of one or more protected classes. Rather than alleging a specific incident of discrimination, disparate impact requires plaintiffs to demonstrate a pattern of discriminatory hiring overall, regardless of intent.

A good example of the reach of Title VII in the employment of non-academic employees can be found in the ongoing litigation and consent decrees in *Shuford v. Alabama State Board of Education*.[18] Here, allegations were made that colleges and universities in the statewide system of higher education had consistently failed to hire and promote African Americans in general, and African American females in particular, for administrative and support staff positions. When these protected individuals were hired, they were often given lower job titles and pay than previous incumbents in the same positions. Although the courts accepted that in many of the specific cases listed, the reasons for these decisions were legitimate and nondiscriminatory, overall, the courts found a general pattern of discrimination sufficient to support a decree requiring affirmative action in the recruiting of minorities, especially minority women, across the state's higher education system. In addition, widespread reclassification of current employees was also deemed necessary. *Shuford* illustrates Title VII's application to two protected categories, race and gender.

The Age Discrimination in Employment Act (ADEA) of 1967[19]

The ADEA effectively expanded the protected classes defined in Title VII to include employees and job seekers over the age of forty. As with other Title VII actions, age discrimination can be proven through either disparate treatment or disparate impact. Not only does the ADEA prohibit discrimination in hiring decisions, but it also protects the jobs of older workers from arbitrary termination to eliminate the salary or benefits burden of employing senior staff. For example, in *Burger v. New York Institute of Technology*,[20] a reduction in force led to the layoff of the oldest and most senior employee in an accounting department. Although the college claimed that its decision was based on the fact that several of the employee's responsibilities were being eliminated, a

---

[17] L. DEAN WEBB & SCOTT NORTON, HUMAN RESOURCES ADMIN. 255-256.
[18] 968 F. Supp. 1486 (M.D. Ala. 1997).
[19] 29 U.S.C. §§ 621 *et seq.*
[20] 94 F.3d 830 (2d Cir. 1996).

federal appeals court affirmed a lower federal court's determination that the older employee met her initial burden to show that the layoff occurred under circumstances giving rise to an inference of age discrimination. The appeals court noted that many of her duties were not eliminated but were simply transferred to younger employees, and the institution had failed to establish that the job duties of these employees were so different from hers as to justify retaining a younger and less senior employee instead.

Employers need to be especially conscious of the protections of the ADEA when making reduction-in-force decisions or dealing with older employees who have above-average absences for illness and disability. The Act can also apply to older job seekers who apply for positions, such as student affairs and residence hall services, which are traditionally filled by younger employees. As a general policy, it is preferable to avoid the appearance of discrimination by asking potential employees if they meet a minimum age to work, usually 18, rather than to ask them to disclose their age or provide a specific date of birth.[21]

The Equal Pay Act of 1963[22]

The Equal Pay Act (EPA) sought to eliminate traditional pay disparities that existed between men and women by requiring that employees receive equal pay when performing jobs of substantially equal skill, effort, and responsibility.[23] The EPA does not, however, require that the jobs compared be identical. The legal comparison, therefore, focuses more on the relative difficulty and performance of two positions, as opposed to specific job duties and functions. To be enforceable, the EPA requires that jobs be "equal," which in practice means virtually identical; any difference allows different, less-favorable treatment, which is not considered to be discriminatory. Since few jobs are virtually identical, the judicial tendency to conflate equality with sameness has bedeviled plaintiffs who seek a remedy under this law. Although this act has been difficult to implement, it has proven successful in several challenges. For example, a Tennessee university was required to raise the salary of its female administrative managers in several departments when a male administrative manager was hired at a higher salary in one department of the same college.[24] It should be noted that on January 29, 2009, the Civil Rights and Equal Pay Acts were amended by the passage of the Lilly Ledbetter Equal Pay Act.[25] This act, which effectively overruled the Supreme Court's decision in *Ledbetter v. Goodyear Tire & Rubber*,[26] effectively resets the 180-day limitation period for fair pay claims with the date of each unequal paycheck, as opposed to the

---

[21] *See also* Wichmann v. Bd. of Trs. of S. Ill. Univ., 180 F.3d 791 (7th Cir. 1999); Hurd v. Pittsburg State Univ., 109 F.3d 1540 (10th Cir. 1997); Kalvinskas v. Cal. Inst. of Tech., 96 F.3d 1305 (9th Cir. 1996); Cella v. Fordham Univ., 644 N.Y.S.2d 53 (N.Y. App. Div. 1996).

[22] 29 U.S.C. § 206(d).

[23] BUFORD, *supra* note 7, at 37.

[24] Hatton v. Hunt, 780 F. Supp. 1157 (W.D. Tenn. 1991).

[25] P.L. 111-2 (2009).

[26] 550 U.S. 618 (2007).

commencement of employment at an unequal rate of pay. This amendment may pose particular risks to colleges and universities that employ long-term and loyal employees who may be victims of pay discrimination as the result of policies set by previous administrations decades in the past. Reviewing and correcting gender-based pay inequities is an effective method to remove the recurring threat of liability caused by perpetuating such inequities in each pay period. Absent corrective action, many institutions with numerous long-term employees may be at risk of significant litigation as this newer act is increasingly enforced.

Section 504 and the Americans with Disabilities Act

These two laws, Section 504 of the Rehabilitation Act of 1973[27] and the Americans with Disabilities Act (ADA),[28] provide similar protections to college employees depending on the nature of their employment. In its 1987 precedent, *School Board of Nassau County, Florida v. Arline*,[29] the Supreme Court held that Section 504 protected educational employees in federally funded institutions. Section 504 essentially requires nondiscrimination in employment decisions, including hiring, promotion, evaluation, and discipline, based upon an individual's disabilities.[30] In particular, Section 504 and the subsequently enacted ADA require an employer to make "reasonable accommodations" for disabled employees. The definition of reasonable is based on whether a particular accommodation would create an unreasonable burden on the institution or risk to others. In order to be protected under Section 504, an individual must be regarded as having a disability that impairs a "major life function." If an employee is qualified, reasonable accommodations may include changes in scheduling, the assignment of duties among similar employees, and the physical modification of the workplace and job-related equipment.

In 2001, the Supreme Court limited the application of the ADA in cases involving public institutions of higher education that may be considered "arms of the state" and protected by the U.S. Constitution's Eleventh Amendment. In *Board of Trustees of University of Alabama v. Garrett*,[31] the Court concluded that Congress, in passing the ADA, had not properly abrogated the rights of states and their agencies to immunity from federal laws under the Eleventh Amendment. Consequently, although Section 504 remains applicable to public higher education institutions and private institutions receiving over $10,000 in federal aid,[32] the ADA does not extend to those public institutions clothed with "arm of the state" status under the immunity provided by the Eleventh Amendment. However, as the ADA makes similar requirements in terms of both eligibility and accommodations, the requirements for private institutions

---

27 29 U.S.C. § 793.
28 42 U.S.C. §§ 12101 *et seq.*
29 480 U.S. 273, 107 S. Ct. 1123, 94 L. Ed. 2d 307 (1987).
30 Rosenthal & Shawe, *supra* note 13, at §18.02(7).
31 531 U.S. 356, 121 S. Ct. 955, 148 L. Ed. 2d 866 (2001).
32 29 U.S.C. § 793 (Section 503).

under the ADA are essentially the same as those for employers covered by Section 504.

While Section 504 and the ADA both protect employees with a range of disabilities, both physical and mental, there is one area of protected disability that merits particular mention. In the *Arline* ruling, the Supreme Court held that an individual infected with a serious disease, even if asymptomatic, was considered disabled within the meaning of Section 504. The case of *Bragdon v. Abbott*[33] expanded this definition by also applying the ADA to individuals infected by the HIV/AIDS virus. In employment cases involving infected employees, employers must demonstrate an unreasonable risk of disease transmission to justify excluding persons from employment or restricting their employment duties.[34] It must be noted that the Supreme Court standard requires the establishment of a significant risk of transmission, not merely some possibility, a standard that would typically require the expert testimony of competent medical personnel in order to substantiate the risk.

Bona Fide Occupational Qualifications

As previously stated, under ordinary circumstances, college employers should avoid asking questions on applications and during pre-employment interviews that would implicate a protected status. The exception is when such a question concerns a bona fide occupational qualification. In general, bona fide occupational qualifications, or BFOQs, must relate to a legitimate job requirement. BFOQs can include the possession of specific certification or licenses, possession of specific job-related skills, or the ability to perform particular tasks, such as lifting a particular weight or working irregular hours. Some BFOQs may also require inquiry into protected characteristics and may allow discrimination based on those characteristics, but courts narrowly treat an employer's claim of a BFOQ to restrict the application of this exception to employment discrimination. BFOQs may sometimes apply to sex, religion, national origin, and age, but not to race.

The classic example of this is the provision within Title VII that provides that the law "shall not apply ... to a religious corporation, association, educational institution, or society with respect to the employment of individuals of a particular religion to perform work connected with the carrying on by such corporation, association, educational institution, or society of its activities."[35] This provision allows religious institutions to advertise and fill positions with persons who are members of a specific faith and to inquire about the religious beliefs of potential employees. It can also permit the termination of employees who subsequently perform their duties or behave in a manner inconsistent with the doctrines of the employer.[36] Care should be exercised with

---

[33] 524 U.S. 624, 118 S. Ct. 2196, 141 L. Ed. 2d 540 (1998).

[34] Rosenthal & Shawe, *supra* note 13, § 18.02[7].

[35] 42 U.S.C. § 2000e-1(a).

[36] *See, e.g.*, Pime v. Loyola Univ. of Chi., 803 F.2d 351 (7th Cir. 1987).

this exception, as it applies specifically to those employees whose duties are directly connected with the college's religious purpose, such as administrators, chaplains, and counselors. At the same time, however, institutions have broad discretion in making these doctrinal decisions. In *Serbian Eastern Orthodox v. Milivojevich,*[37] the Supreme Court held that the First Amendment's requirement of separation of church and state forbids the courts from inquiring into the legitimacy and sincerity of doctrines asserted by religious organizations in making employment decisions.

The concept of BFOQs offers employers a great deal of guidance in making hiring and promotion decisions. For this reason, many organizations follow a detailed system of classification for their non-academic positions that includes a job analysis intended to detail the knowledge, experience, and competencies required for each job. By defining the essential functions and BFOQs for a given job and then designing application materials and processes around them, it is possible to not only avoid improper inquiries, but irrelevant ones as well. BFOQs also offer legal protection for employment decisions by basing those decisions on well-developed, objective criteria. Finally, under certain conditions, BFOQs may allow an employer to make inquiries and adverse decisions based upon otherwise protected status.

Evaluation, Discipline, and Termination

Given the myriad employment conditions experienced by employees in institutions of higher education, it is difficult to generalize the procedures used in employee evaluation, discipline, and termination. The obligations of state employment laws, collective bargaining agreements, and contract provisions all serve to dictate the procedures and protections available to college employees. Furthermore, there is again a clear distinction between public and private institutions.

Public employment precedents such as *Perry v. Sindermann*[38] and *Branti v. Finkel*[39] clearly establish a right to due process before terminating an employee who has some legitimate expectation of continuing employment. In general, long-term public employees and those within contracted periods of employment cannot be terminated or disciplined in an arbitrary fashion. Typically, they enjoy a right to receive notice of their alleged deficiencies or violations and a right to some impartial process of review in which they can contest specific allegations. Public employees are also protected from arbitrary discipline based upon the exercise of their constitutional rights or rights protected under federal and state laws. Such employees may also enjoy special statutory protection in the form of "whistleblower" laws. In many states, statutes specifically protect

---

[37] 426 U.S. 696, 96 S. Ct. 2372, 49 L. Ed. 2d 151 (1976).
[38] 408 U.S. 593, 92 S. Ct. 2694 (1972).
[39] 445 U.S. 507, 100 S. Ct. 1287, 63 L. Ed. 2d 574 (1980).

employees who bring to light allegations of malfeasance by their employers.[40] However, these protections are general in nature. With public employees hired in a clearly at-will position, typically high-profile persons such as university presidents, these protections may not apply. For example, in *Idoux v. Lamar University System,*[41] a federal district court upheld the termination of a university president for speaking out on unethical practices.

Private university employees do not enjoy the constitutional protections afforded to public employees. Absent protective state laws, collective bargaining agreements, or contract provisions, all such employees must be considered at-will. As previously mentioned, this holds especially true in sectarian institutions where courts are hesitant to intervene in matters of internal governance and faith, even when contract protections are present.[42] Otherwise, private colleges and universities are bound to follow their own internal procedures for discipline and evaluation. Furthermore, although a private college may enjoy relative legal freedom in making these employment decisions, care must still be exercised to ensure that these actions do not violate the federal employment laws cited previously, including Title VII, ADA, ADEA, and the Equal Pay Act. Due to the fact that private institutions operate primarily under contract law rather than constitutional law, an institution's obligations under contract law require good faith in performance, thus binding the private institution to principles of fairness that may mirror some of the elements of constitutional due process in the public institution.

Unions and Collective Bargaining

The rights of non-academic personnel to collective bargaining generally follow those of faculty.[43] As such, the law regarding employee organization and collective bargaining essentially creates three identifiable classes of colleges and universities. Public colleges and universities, as arms of the state, are explicitly excluded from coverage under federal labor laws and the National Labor Relations Act.[44] As a result, public colleges and universities are governed exclusively by state laws regarding rights to organize employees, collectively bargain, and strike. Predictably, while such rights have been extended in states with strong traditions of public labor unions, such as those in the Upper Midwest and the Northeast, the rights to unionize of all public employees, including those in higher education, are considerably weaker in other parts of the country, especially the South.[45] As a result, some states such as Minnesota

---

[40] *See, e.g.,* Swain v. Elfland, 550 S.E.2d 530 (N.C. Ct. App. 2001), interpreting N.C. GEN. STAT. § 126-85 (1999).

[41] 828 F. Supp. 1252 (E.D. Tex. 1993).

[42] *See, e.g.,* Killinger v. Samford Univ., 113 F.3d 196 (11th Cir. 1997).

[43] *See, e.g.,* 183 NLRB 329 (1970); Abood v. Detroit Bd. of Ed., 97 S. Ct. 1782 (1977); Minnesota State Bd. for Cmty. Colleges v. Knight, 104 S. Ct. 1058 (1984).

[44] 197 NLRB 291 (1989); National Labor Relations of 1935 (also known as the Wagner Act, Section 2(2)).

[45] BUFORD, *supra* note 7, at 380-1.

and Michigan permit the establishment of exclusive bargaining units and even closed-shop provisions for public employee representation. By contrast, many states, especially those in the South, have statutes that guarantee public employees the "right to work," thus preventing the mandatory membership of state employees in unions or associations. These states also maintain their statutory exemption from mandatory collective bargaining and make strikes and work stoppages by public employees illegal, further weakening both the effectiveness and appeal of unions in these states.

Private colleges and universities must be subdivided into two subcategories: secular and sectarian. In 1970, the National Labor Relations Board (NLRB) extended the reach of the National Labor Relations Act (NLRA) to private colleges and universities when it intervened to insure the recognition of employee bargaining units at Cornell University and Syracuse University.[46] As such, private colleges and universities, regardless of any nonprofit status, must accept the provisions of the NLRA and the jurisdiction of the NLRB. This act, which represents a series of federal laws dating back to the original Wagner Act of 1935, provides federal oversight to insure private employees the right to organize, collectively bargain, pursue grievances against their employer, and conduct legal strikes and work stoppages under certain conditions.[47]

Specifically, the NLRA guarantees the rights of private secular university employees to organize into collective bargaining units. Although subject to specific circumstances, the NLRB has generally upheld the right of these employees to organize in the workplace and to use university property for these purposes, as long as they are not impeding the business of the employer.[48] The law also requires employers to bargain in good faith with the identified representative units, permits election to organize and govern these units, and prohibits any interference with union organization or retaliation or discrimination against employees based upon union membership or activities.[49] The NLRB also exercises control over any grievances or disputes concerning union organization and activities and can protect the employment of workers who strike under certain circumstances.

However, the Supreme Court has limited the application of the NLRA to private colleges and universities that are operated by religious organizations. In the landmark ruling of *NLRB v. Catholic Bishop of Chicago*,[50] the Court ruled that the application of the NLRA to religious institutions would implicate a serious potential for conflicts between church and state. In that case, the Court decided that the NLRB was barred from exercising its authority over lay employees of religious colleges and schools based on the Court's conclu-

---

[46] Cornell University, 183 NLRB No. 41, 183 NLRB 329 (1970); Syracuse Univ., 204 NLRB No. 85 (1973).

[47] The National Labor Relations Act, the NLRA, is a combination of the Wagner Act of 1935, the Taft-Hartley Act of 1947, and the Landrum-Griffin Act of 1959.

[48] NLRA Section 7.

[49] ROSENTHAL, *supra* note 13, at §17.06.

[50] 440 U.S. 490, 99 S. Ct. 1313 (1979).

sion that Congress had shown a clear intent to extend the NLRA to religious institutions. Consequently, collective bargaining is not legally protected in sectarian institutions and remains a purely internal issue to be resolved by these institutions without the interference of federal or state authorities.

It is especially important, given the diversity of the college employment spectrum, that colleges and universities understand the concept of the representative bargaining unit. Although the NLRA only requires the employer to negotiate with the unit that represents the majority of its employees, it must respect certain precedents and procedures in this regard. The determination of the representative collective bargaining unit is a matter for the employees alone to determine, not the employer. Additionally, disputes regarding which organization represents certain employees must be referred to the NLRB regional offices for resolution and cannot be resolved by the administration. Furthermore, although the law recognizes exclusive bargaining units, the Supreme Court has ruled that employers may have to recognize multiple representative units that represent distinct groups or classifications of employees, especially in medical centers.[51] Therefore, it is possible that a university would have to separately recognize and collectively bargain with different unions or associations representing different types of employees such as nurses, maintenance workers, and police or security officers.

Colleges and universities must also be careful to respect the rights of non-union employees covered by their collective bargaining agreements. In *Abood v. Detroit Board of Education*,[52] the United States Supreme Court required employers to refund to non-union employees any dues collected under the collective bargaining agreement to support union political activities that they do not support. Although closed-shop agreements may require nonunion members to pay dues to support the collective bargaining process, they cannot require nonmembers to support other union activities that implicate their First Amendment rights. Recent case law supports the proposition that colleges and universities that help collect union fees under an agreement by means such as automatic payroll deductions must provide clear and well-publicized procedures for employees to exempt themselves from these additional dues for unsupported political or other union speech activities.[53] This requirement is best met either by an up-front exemption from these deductions or a prompt refund of any deductions at an employee's request.

Students as Employees

Traditionally, colleges and universities have employed large numbers of their own students to perform myriad tasks. Most of these student employees are hired as part-time temporary workers receiving an hourly wage to serve

---

[51] American Hosp. Ass'n v. NLRB, 499 U.S. 606, 111 S. Ct. 1539, 113 L. Ed. 2d 675 (1991).

[52] 431 U.S. 209, 97 S. Ct. 1782, 52 L. Ed. 2d 261 (1977); *See also* Lehnert v. Ferris Faculty Ass'n, 500 U.S. 507, 111 S. Ct. 1950 114 L. Ed. 2d 572 (1991).

[53] *See* Swanson v. Univ. of Hawaii Prof'l Assembly, 269 F. Supp. 2d 1252 (D. Haw. 2003).

as intramural sports officials, food service workers, ushers, bus drivers, and cashiers. Students are hired through normal procedures and paid an hourly wage, often derived from the revenues generated by activity fees or university enterprises. These employees are also appropriately classified simply as hourly employees and treated in the same way as non-student hourly employees in terms of hiring, benefits, and other employee rights.

However, colleges and universities also employ two general classes of students under a hybrid system that combines employment and financial aid: graduate assistants and work-study students. Work-study students are recipients of funds provided by the federal College Work Study Program funded under the Economic Opportunity Act of 1964.[54] Generally, these are undergraduates who perform various clerical or service tasks in return for a stipend and assistance in paying tuition and other expenses. Graduate assistants are a more diverse group. They can perform a variety of highly technical and skilled duties, ranging from conducting scientific research to teaching large sections of undergraduate courses. They also are paid from numerous sources, including institutional funds and outside research grants. Their pay and benefits can also vary widely. Some receive a modest stipend and remission of a portion of their tuition payments. Others can receive payment comparable to that of some full-time employees, allowances for room and board, full tuition, and even health and retirement benefits. All of these workers present several unique legal complexities to colleges and universities.

Traditionally, the courts have treated such workers as recipients of financial aid and as students, not employees. In the case of federal work-study students, the statute authorizing the program specifies that such workers are not employees in the traditional sense, but recipients of financial aid. However, the case law regarding federally funded work-study students has not always been consistent in this regard.

In many cases, the courts have cited the Economic Opportunity Act in establishing that funds paid to student workers under the College Work Study Program constitute federal aid and not wages, regardless of the duties performed, and therefore work-study students should be excluded from all other benefits and legal protections extended to other classes of employees. In *Murphy v. Villanova University*,[55] a district court twice held that students employed under the College Work Study Program were not eligible for any benefits or wages from any source outside the financial aid program. As such, work-study employees whose funding was terminated could not vindicate preferential employment claims for regular university employment and could not sue for wrongful termination. In Arizona and Hawaii unemployment compensation disputes, state courts have extended this limitation to bar the receipt of unemployment compensation by terminated work-study students.[56]

---

[54] 42 U.S.C. §§ 2251-2256.

[55] 520 F. Supp. 560 (D. Pa. 1981); 547 F. Supp. 512 (D. Pa. 1982).

[56] Pima Cmty. Coll. v. Ariz. Dep't of Econ. Sec., 714 P.2d 472 (Ariz. Ct. App. 1986); Univ. of Hawaii v. Befitel, 100 P.3d 56 (Haw. 2004).

Even parallel case law, in areas such as welfare eligibility, has accepted that monies earned under the work-study program cannot be construed as wages from employment.[57] Likewise, in *NLRB v. Certified Testing Laboratories*,[58] a federal appeals court upheld a determination that work-study students employed in off-campus training programs could not participate in certification votes to determine collective bargaining units, even when they performed the identical work of other eligible employees. Work-study students have also been denied eligibility for workers' compensation benefits.[59]

However, support for this proposition has not been universal. In *Richman v. Ross*,[60] a New York appellate court found that a student's receipt of federal work-study funds did constitute employment so as to limit eligibility for unemployment compensation from a previous employer. Another New York ruling found work-study students were, in fact, eligible under state law as employees for purposes of receiving workers' compensation.[61] And, in one of the most fully developed cases involving work-study students, the Eighth Circuit held that a student injured while working in a federal facility under the Vocational Education Act was to be considered a federal employee and eligible for compensation under the Federal Employees Compensation Act.[62]

The Eighth Circuit decision also raises a cautionary point about the treatment of work-study recipients as students instead of employees. In the unique circumstances of that case, based upon work location, the student was treated as an employee. However, in *Grant v. Tulane University*,[63] a former work-study student filed a tort claim against the university and a private oil company regarding her work as a lab assistant in a jointly sponsored project. The company moved to dismiss her claims, arguing that compensation for her illnesses, allegedly the result of being poisoned in the lab, was limited to the state workers' compensation system. In rejecting this contention, and therefore allowing the student to proceed on her claims for damages, the court noted that the traditional interpretation of the College Work Study Program as a form of financial aid meant that the plaintiff was not an employee under the law and, therefore, her claims could not be limited by workers' compensation. Colleges and universities should be aware that while the usual legal interpretation of the Economic Opportunity Act limits their responsibility under a host of employee's rights laws, this same interpretation may open them to more general torts for workplace injuries, especially in private universities and public institutions not protected by strong state sovereign immunity provisions.

The legal situation regarding graduate assistants of all types used to be very similar to that of college work-study students. In *Washington v. Jackson*

---

[57] Brown v. Bates, 363 F. Supp. 897 (D. Ohio 1973).

[58] 387 F.2d 275 (3d Cir. 1967).

[59] Grant v. Tulane Univ., 2001 WL 245785 (E.D. La. 2001).

[60] 412 N.Y.S.2d 222 (N.Y.A.D. 1979).

[61] Lopez v. CUNY, 750 N.Y.S.2d 194 (N.Y. A.D. 3 Dept. 2002).

[62] Waters v. U.S., 328 F. Supp 812 (D. Ark. 1971), *aff'd*. 458 F.2d 20 (8th Cir. 1972).

[63] 2001 U.S. Dist. LEXIS 3041 (E.D. La. 2001).

State University, a federal court ruled that the receipt of a graduate stipend did not constitute employment for purposes of claiming gender discrimination under Title VII.[64] A similar result was found in a case involving the University of South Florida.[65] Similarly, in *Becker v. Washington State University*, a state appellate court upheld the dismissal of age discrimination claims by a former teaching assistant who was terminated from her position after failing to make adequate academic progress in her degree.[66] The court determined that her position, which was predicated on her enrollment in a doctoral program, did not constitute employment under state law.

Another issue has been the question of whether or not graduate assistants can unionize and collectively bargain as employees in private universities subject to the jurisdiction of the NRLA. The classic example occurred at Yale University in the mid-1990s.[67] After years of agitation and attempts to organize and gain university recognition, teaching assistants at Yale held a dramatic "grade strike." Late in the fall semester, they voted to withhold all term grades until the university recognized the Graduate Employees and Students Association (GESO) as a collective bargaining unit. The university refused to bargain, instead firing all of the striking teaching assistants and proceeding to expel several. Eventually the strike fell apart and most of the graduate students were rehired. Although the strike failed, the GESO filed a complaint with the NLRB claiming unfair practices. The NLRB eventually settled the claim by finding that the strike, regardless of the legal status of the GESO, constituted an illegal strike under the NLRA.

A larger issue confronted the NLRB regarding the Yale strike. Although its tactics may have violated the NLRA, the Yale GESO was attempting to gain the same recognition as a legitimate employee bargaining unit that faculty and staff at private universities had enjoyed since the 1970s. By virtue of its ruling on the strike tactics the NLRB was able to sidestep this issue briefly. Prior to the incident at Yale, the NLRB had employed what was referred to as a "primary purpose test" in classifying graduate assistants.[68] Under this test, the question the NLRB posed was what was the primary purpose of graduate students' employment? In every instance, it was found that the main goal of such employment, as asserted by the universities, was to facilitate graduate education by providing students with financial aid and giving them experiences in teaching, research, or service that would serve to better prepare them for their professional and academic careers.

---

[64] 532 F. Supp. 2d 804 (S.D.Miss. 2006).

[65] Cuddeback v. Florida Bd. of Educ., 381 F.3d 1230 (11th Cir. 2004)

[66] 235, 266 P.3d 893 (Wash. Ct. App. 2011).

[67] Joshua Rowland, *'Forecasts of Doom': The Dubious Threat of Graduate Teaching Assistant Collective Bargaining to Academic Freedom*, 42 B.C. L. REV. 941 (July 2001).

[68] Grant M. Hayden, *'The University Works Because We Do': Collective Bargaining Rights for Graduate Assistants*, 69 FORDHAM L. REV. 1233 (March 2001); Gregory Gartland, *Of Ducks and Drakes: A Call for a Return to the National Labor Relations Board's 'Primary Purpose Test' in Determining the Status of Graduate Students Under the National Labor Relations Act*, 4 U. PA. J. LAB. & EMP. L. 623 (Spring 2002).

However, this test has since been abandoned by the NLRB. In *Boston Medical Center,*[69] the NLRB replaced the "primary purpose test" with a "compensated services test." In this test, the simple question is whether or not a person provides services or work for someone else in return for compensation.[70] Based upon this definition, the NLRB found that medical residents and interns, while undoubtedly fulfilling educational requirements, were being compensated for providing medical services to the university hospital. Applying this definition, it was not difficult for the NLRB to then extend its ruling to university graduate assistants. In *New York University,*[71] the NLRB rejected the university's attempt to draw distinctions between medical residents and academic graduate assistants. Although the latter did not yet possess terminal degrees, the NLRB found that under its simple definition, graduate students performed work under the supervision of other university employees and, in return, received wages and other compensation. As such, the NLRB found that graduate assistants, fellows, proctors, and other paid categories of graduate student workers were employees and were, therefore, eligible to organize and collectively bargain under the NLRA.

The determination in *New York University* may have been superseded by the Treasury Department and the U.S. Supreme Court. In *Mayo Foundation v. U.S.,* the Court held that medical residents, who already possessed a terminal degree, were distinct from other students for purposes of paying FICA taxes and therefore receiving Social Security benefits related to their residency.[72] Although it did not directly address the status of graduate assistants, the Court upheld a distinction between medical residents, who are considered full-time employees of hospitals, and student workers who are exempt from FICA under Treasury regulations.[73] Since the NLRB's authority is limited to private, non-sectarian institutions, these decisions will have no impact on sectarian colleges and universities. Nonetheless, the effects are already apparent. According to the Coalition of Graduate Employee Unions, a network of U.S. and Canadian graduate student organizations, some two dozen U.S. universities recognize collective bargaining units for graduate students.[74] What is interesting is that many of these are located at public universities outside the purview of the NLRB. Although the NLRB ruling in *New York University* does not apply to these institutions, the logic of this ruling has been adopted by state labor-relation boards and state courts in many locations. For example, in Illinois, the state courts have required the Illinois Educational Labor Relations Board to hold elections to certify a collective bargaining unit for graduate

---

[69] 330 NLRB 152 (1999).

[70] GARTLAND, *supra* note 66, at 635.

[71] 332 NLRB 111 (2000).

[72] Mayo Found. for Med. Educ. & Res. v. U.S., 562 U.S. 44. 131 S.Ct. 704 (2011).

[73] 26 U.S.C. § 3121(b)(10).

[74] The Coalition of Graduate Employee Unions, http://cgeu.org (2004).

student employees at the University of Illinois at Urbana-Champaign.[75] Two of the nation's largest multi-unit university systems, the State University of New York and the City University of New York, have also recognized collective bargaining units for graduate students.

The long-term implications of this movement remain uncertain. Some argue that extending collective bargaining protections to graduate students recognizes the vital labor they provide in return for little compensation. Alternate arguments contend that this trend, if not blocked by the federal courts, will lead to financial crisis, damage to academic freedom, and an end to the traditional mentoring relationship between faculty and graduate students.[76] Recognition of graduate assistants as employees may extend to them other employee rights and protections. For example, courts have not traditionally treated this form of employment as a property interest that bestows due process rights to graduate assistants.[77] While the temporary nature of such employment is generally recognized, it is possible that either the courts or collective bargaining agreements may extend additional due process protections to graduate assistants for the duration of a degree program.

Conclusion

The legal treatment of non-faculty and non-academic employees is at least as variable as the diversity of institutional types and organizational missions in American higher education. Factors such as public or private governance, religious or secular control, and the applicability of federal and state collective bargaining laws all affect the status of these employees and serve to make legal generalizations all but impossible, save in the area of federal antidiscrimination law. Religiously operated institutions would appear to have the fewest legal restrictions regarding their employee relations. Exemption from mandatory collective bargaining under federal and state law, combined with specific doctrine-based exemptions under the Civil Rights Act, leaves these institutions relatively free to operate within the sphere of contract law. By contrast, secular private institutions fall under the jurisdiction of nearly all federal and state employment and civil rights acts, as well as compulsory collective bargaining under the NLRA. Additionally, while public institutions may be beyond the reach of the NLRA, they are fully bound by the federal statutes and constitutional protections that apply to all public employees and possibly extensive state legal regulation, as well.

Colleges and universities must also be extremely cautious regarding the employment of students on campus. While many may fall into the category of temporary and part-time employees, others present special challenges. Jurisdictions across the country continue to grapple with the question of the

---

[75] Graduate Employees Org., IFT/AFT, AFL-CIO v. Ill. Educ. Labor Relations Bd., 315 Ill. App. 3d 278, 733 N.E.2d 759, 248 Ill. Dec. 84 (Ill. App. Ct. 2000).

[76] GARTLAND, *supra note 66*; HAYDEN, *supra*; ROWLAND, *supra* note 65.

[77] *See* Hupp v. Sasser, 490 S.E.2d 880 (W. Va. 1997).

nature of the employment of college work-study students. While most have not viewed them as employees, this legal perspective has not been universal. Furthermore, even if the language of the Economic Opportunity Act is ultimately upheld, the interpretation that work-study students are not employees may actually increase the tort liability risks for colleges and universities when these students are injured while on the job.

Finally, special attention must be paid to ongoing litigation and legislation regarding the employment status of graduate students. Although traditionally viewed legally in the same way as college work-study recipients, recent decisions of the NLRB and various state courts and agencies, accompanied by the rising militancy of graduate students on some campuses, may culminate in increased legal recognition for these students and greater challenges for the institutions that employ them. In addition to growing legal protections, these changes may also force institutions to reexamine the traditional academic relationships between graduate students, faculty, and other staff in their advanced degree programs.

Discussion Questions

1. When hiring non-academic employees, what sort of care and concerns should go into employing personnel of different classifications? How should new positions be classified and hired?

2. Discuss the various laws affecting employment discrimination as they apply to hiring, promotion, discipline, and termination of college and university employees.

3. What are BFOQs and how should they be applied. Can you think of legitimate BFOQs for particular positions that might otherwise generally violate employment discrimination laws?

4. Discuss collective bargaining. What types of institutions and employees may be unionized or preventing from unionizing? What is the legal effect of collective bargaining agreements?

5. Discuss the legal status and particular challenges inherent in employing students on campus. What procedures and safeguards should institutions apply to protect themselves legally when employing students in various roles?

7

Employment Discrimination and Title VII

David Hòa Khoa Nguyễn, J.D., Ph.D.
Indiana University – Purdue University Indianapolis (IUPUI)

Introduction

Discrimination on the basis of race, color, religion, national origin, sex, age, or disability is prohibited under federal law and the provisions of many state laws, most of which are applicable to both public and private institutions of higher education. Courts have also ruled that discrimination of transgender individuals qualifies as sex discrimination under Title VII.[1] Principal among the federal statutes that cover employment discrimination are Title VII of the Civil Rights Act of 1964,[2] Title IX of the Education Amendments of 1972,[3] Section 504 of the Rehabilitation Act of 1973,[4] the Americans With Disabilities Act,[5] the Equal Pay Act,[6] the Age Discrimination in Employment Act,[7] Immigration Reform and Control Act of 1986,[8] and the Genetic Information Nondiscrimination Act of 2008.[9] While sexual harassment and claims under Section 504 and the ADA are addressed elsewhere in this text, employment discrimination continues to be guided by the burden of proof developed in litigation under Title VII of the Civil Rights Act. This chapter addresses the burden of proof applicable to cases of employment discrimination, as developed in litigation involving Title VII and applicable to other federal laws prohibiting discrimination in employment.

---

[1] *See* Smith v. City of Salem, 378 F.3d. 566 (6th Cir. 2004).

[2] 42 U.S.C. § 2000e *et seq.*

[3] 20 U.S.C. § 1681 *et seq.*

[4] 29 U.S.C. § 794.

[5] 42 U.S.C. § 12101 *et seq.*

[6] 29 U.S.C. 206(d) (2004).

[7] 29 U.S.C. § 621 et seq. The Age Discrimination in Employment Act of 1967 (ADEA) prohibits age-based discrimination in employment for persons 40 years of age or older. The law prohibits age discrimination in hiring, discharge, pay, promotions and other terms and conditions of employment. As part of the Fair Labor Standards Act, its application is to institutions with twenty or more employees and which affect interstate commerce. The standards for coverage parallel those of Title VII.

[8] 8 U.S.C. § 1101 *et seq.* Along with Title VII, the Immigration Reform and Control Act of 1986 prohibits discrimination against aliens.

[9] 42 U.S.C. Section 2000ff *et seq.*

While the U.S. Constitution does not explicitly address employment discrimination, the Fifth and Fourteenth amendments limit the power of federal and state governments to discriminate. While the Fifth Amendment explicitly requires that the federal government not deprive individuals of "life, liberty, and property"[10] without due process of law, section five of the Fourteenth Amendment[11] grants Congress the authority to enforce the Equal Protection Clause and enact federal antidiscrimination law. The theme of federal employment discrimination law is that similarly situated employees or prospective employees should receive equal treatment by employers. These laws are intended to ensure equality in the employment relationship for groups or individuals who are different in some respect, such as race or sex.

Because these laws have broad application to institutions of higher education (exceptions for private religious institutions are discussed in earlier chapters) and considering that many of these laws are mirrored in corresponding state statutes, this chapter will focus on the principal federal statute forbidding employment discrimination in colleges and universities, Title VII.

Job Fit and Employment Discrimination in Higher Education[12]

In the higher education setting, many professionals, both faculty and student affairs professionals alike, may be challenged by their "fit" during the interview, hiring, and job performance stages. The understanding of "fit" is a result of a persistent invisibility of intersectionality that includes gender, race, and sexual orientation due to society and the courts using lenses that are colorblind and gender- and hetero-normative.[13] The dominant culture's expectations of appearance and behavior of applicants can outweigh as well as conflict with institutions' promotion of diversity and inclusion.

These expectations can be seen widely in the various cases that arise in courts. One example of this intersection follows when a public state college president commented on how well a new administrator was performing in their role, but expressed concern that they were not "fitting in" within their department.[14] The president did not give substantive feedback with their comment, leaving the administrator to ponder what it meant to not "fit in."

How do faculty and higher education and student affairs practitioners determine if they will "fit in" with a department and campus culture, especially

---

[10] UNITED STATES CONST., Fifth Amendment.

[11] UNITED STATES CONST., Fourteenth Amendment, section five.

[12] *See generally* David Hòa Khoa Nguyễn and LaWanda W.M. Ward, *Innocent Until Proven Guilty: A Critical Interrogation of the Legal Aspects of Job Fit in Higher Education* (pp. 27 – 48), In Brian J, Reece, Vu T. Tran, Elliott N. DeVore, and Gabby Porcaro (Eds.), DEBUNKING THE MYTH OF JOB FIT IN HIGHER EDUCATION AND STUDENT AFFAIRS (2019).

[13] *See generally* Devon W. Carbado, *Colorblind Intersectionality,* 38 SIGNS: J. OF WOMEN IN CULTURE AND SOCIETY 811 (2013).

[14] *See generally* William G. Tierney, *Organizational Culture in Higher Education: Defining the Essentials,* 59 J. HIGHER EDUC. 2 (1988).

if their skills, knowledge, and disposition match a job description? Applicants may possess the educational background, relevant experiences, and proven skills for a position, but their personality or "fit" is not always easily determined from their resumes or curriculum vitae. Title VII, applied rigidly to a perceived wrongful employment action such as hiring, firing, or demotion, makes it difficult to prove "fit" is a cloaked method for discrimination because courts are reluctant to allow the effects of historic and current systemic exclusionary behavior toward marginalized populations to serve as evidence.

Fit has been a central focus in organizational theory since the 1960s, and it is relevant because prior studies have revealed that "individuals were most successful and satisfied when their skills, aptitude, values, and beliefs matched the organizations."[15] Evaluating in what ways "fit" becomes a proxy for discrimination in higher education and student affairs is necessary to ensure inclusive-centered approaches are utilized and not ones that "collude to maintain disparities and reinforce social inequity."[16]

As a result, Kezar identified two key criticisms regarding the concept of organizational fit. First, historically marginalized people are challenged with how to best present themselves among dominant environments to be viewed as the right fit for positions.[17] Second, the likelihood of assimilation to dominant cultures increases because of the expectation to meet unspoken norms that may not align with one's own unique expression and values.[18] This assessment of "fit" is needed because it may be difficult for marginalized people in society to present themselves in an authentic way that will be considered the right "fit" for an organization.

Title VII Overview

Title VII is the most comprehensive of the federal antidiscrimination statutes and prohibits discrimination in employment on the basis of race, sex, religion, and national origin.[19] As the United States Supreme Court has pointed out, "(I)n enacting Title VII of the Civil Rights Act of 1964, Congress intended to prohibit all practices in whatever form which create inequality in employment opportunity due to discrimination on the basis of race, religion, sex, or national origin."[20] The law prohibits discrimination in individual employment decisions, as well as employer policies or patterns of conduct that discriminate broadly against members of protected groups.

---

[15] Adriana Kezar, *Investigating Organizational Fit in a Participatory Leadership Environment,* 23 J. Higher Educ. Pol'y and Management 85, 87 (2001).

[16] Renee Crystal Chambers, Law and Social Justice in Higher Education, 10 (2017).

[17] *See generally* Devon W. Carbado and Mitu Gulati, *Working Identity,* 85 Cornell L.Rev. 1259 (2000).

[18] *See generally* Kezar, *supra* note 15.

[19] Civil Rights Act of 1964, 701-716, 78 Stat. 241, 253-66 (1964) (current version at 42 U.S.C. 2000e-5 (2000)).

[20] Franks v. Bowman Transp. Co., 424 U.S. 747, 763 (1976).

Within the protected classifications of Title VII, it is unlawful to discriminate against any employee or applicant for employment with regard to hiring, termination, promotion, compensation, job training, or any other term, condition, or privilege of employment. The law extends to employment decisions based on stereotypes and assumptions about abilities, traits, or the performance of individuals. Discrimination on the basis of an immutable characteristic associated with race—such as skin color, hair texture, or certain facial features—violates Title VII, even though not all members of the race share the same characteristic.

Title VII prohibits both intentional discrimination and neutral job policies that disproportionately exclude marginalized populations and that are not job-related.[21] Equal employment opportunity cannot be denied because of marriage to or association with an individual of a different race; membership in or association with ethnic-based organizations or groups; or attendance or participation in school or places of worship generally associated with certain minority groups. The statute's standard of nondiscrimination is found in Section 703(a) and makes it unlawful for an employer to:

1. fail or refuse to hire or to discharge any individual, or otherwise to discriminate against any individual with respect to his compensation terms, conditions, or privileges or employment, because of such individual's race, color, religion, sex, or national origin; or

2. limit, segregate, or classify his employees or applicants for employment in any way which would deprive or tend to deprive an individual of employment opportunities or otherwise adversely affect his status as an employee, because of such individual's race, color, religion, sex, or national origin.[22]

Title VII has been amended to include pregnancy-based discrimination in its prohibition of gender-based employment discrimination. The Pregnancy Discrimination Act provides that "women affected by pregnancy, childbirth, or related medical conditions shall be treated the same for all employment-related purposes, as other persons not so affected but similar in their ability or inability to work, and nothing in section 2000e-2(h) of this title shall be interpreted to permit otherwise."[23] Similarly, the Family and Medical Leave Act[24] outlines similar requirements for pregnancy leave and pregnancy-related conditions to ensure that women are not unfairly discriminated against for their leave.

In 2009, the language of Title VII was expanded with a narrow focus to counteract damage created by a 2007 U.S. Supreme Court decision[25] in which

---

[21] *See, e.g.,* Hazelwood Sch. Dist. v. United States, 433 U.S. 299 (1977) (examining intentional discrimination); Dothard v. Rawlinson, 433 U.S. 321 (1977) (examining unintentional discrimination).

[22] 42 U.S.C. § 2000e-2(a) (2003).

[23] *Id.* at § 2000e(k).

[24] 29 U.S.C. § 2601-2654 (2006).

[25] Ledbetter v. Goodyear Tire & Rubber Co., 550 U.S. 618 (2007).

the Court determined that the statute of limitations runs from the date of a pay decision setting a discriminatory wage, rather than from the date of any paycheck affected by the prior discriminatory pay decision. That decision severely limited the ability of employees to successfully challenge discriminatory actions, given the extremely short timeline to not only learn of the discriminatory action, but also challenge it. While considering new legislation[26] to offset the effect of that ruling, Congress found that the outcome of the case "significantly impairs statutory protections against discrimination in compensation that Congress established and that have been bedrock principles of American law for decades."[27] In ultimately adopting the Lilly Ledbetter Fair Pay Act of 2009, Congress added language to Title VII that provides:

> [U]nlawful employment practice occurs, with respect to discrimination in compensation in violation of this title, when a discriminatory compensation decision or other practice is adopted, when an individual becomes subject to a discriminatory compensation decision or other practice, or when an individual is affected by application of a discriminatory compensation decision or other practice, including each time wages, benefits, or other compensation is paid, resulting in whole or in part from such a decision or other practice.[28]

Title VII also prohibits discrimination on the basis of a condition that predominately affects a protected group, unless the practice is job-related and consistent with business necessity, termed a Bona Fide Occupational Qualification, or BFOQ. BFOQ's may apply to situations involving religion or sex.[29] The protected characteristics of race and national origin are excluded as a BFOQ for college and university positions.[30]

Harassment is another form of employment discrimination that is in violation of Title VII of the Civil Rights Act. It is defined as unwelcome conduct that is based on race, color, religion, sex (including pregnancy), national origin, age, disability, or genetic information. Harassment is unlawful when 1) one endures offensive conduct as a condition of continued employment, or 2) the conduct is severe or pervasive enough to create a work environment that a reasonable person would consider intimidating, hostile, or abusive. The U.S. Supreme Court has recently made it more challenging for an employer to be liable for a hostile work environment by broadening employer latitude. In *Vance v. Ball State University,* the Supreme Court addressed who would be considered a supervisor for the purposes of Title VII hostile work environment harassment.[31] Since a supervisor can trigger hostile work environment liability more easily than a coworker, the interpretation of who is a "supervisor" is important.[32] The

---

[26] Lilly Ledbetter Fair Pay Act of 2009, Pub. L. No. 111-2, 123 Stat. 5 (2009).

[27] *Id* at 5.

[28] 42 U.S.C. § 2000e-5(e)(3)(A).

[29] *Id* at § 2000e-2(e)(1).

[30] William A. Kaplin and Barbara A. Lee, The Law of Higher Education 200 (3d. ed. 1995).

[31] 133 S. Ct. 2434 (2013).

[32] *See* Burlington Indus., Inc. v. Ellerth, 524 U.S. 742, 764-65 (1998).

Court defined "supervisor" narrowly, finding that for the purposes of hostile work environment harassment, a supervisor is an employee who can affect significant change in employment status, such as hiring, firing, promotion, reassignment, etc.[33] Based on this limited definition, Ball State University was not found to be liable for a hostile work environment because the harasser was found to be a coworker and not a supervisor.[34]

Title VII is enforced by the Equal Employment Opportunity Commission, which has issued a series of regulations and guidelines.[35] As a regulatory enforcement body, it may receive, investigate, and resolve complaints of unlawful employment discrimination. In addition, it may initiate lawsuits against violators or issue right-to-sue letters to complainants.[36] In order for an individual to succeed, Title VII gives employees two possible causes of action. Under a theory of disparate impact, plaintiffs allege that an employer's facially neutral policies have a discriminatory effect on a protected group, and the employer cannot justify the policies by business necessity. Under a theory of disparate treatment, plaintiffs allege that an employer intentionally discriminated against a member or members of a protected group and a shifting burden of proof applies to the determination of liability. Disparate treatment is more common in postsecondary education and can manifest when an individual is denied a job, promotion, tenure, or claims to be treated less favorably than his/her colleagues because of his/her race, sex, national origin, or religion and is subjected to a detrimental working condition.[37] Below, we examine how these two claims apply.

Disparate Impact

A plaintiff proves disparate impact by establishing that a particular employment practice has an adverse effect on employees of the plaintiff's race or sex, regardless of the employer's intent. In *Griggs v. Duke Power Company*,[38] for example, the employer required workers seeking promotion to achieve a particular score on aptitude tests.[39] The plaintiffs established that the test had an adverse effect on African American workers because they passed at a significantly lower rate than did other workers. The test was not shown to bear a reasonable relationship to the requirements of the job, as a passing score on the test was not predictive of success on the job. In *Griggs*, the test led to the employer's selection of a significantly greater proportion of white employees than of African Americans for promotional opportunities within the company. The test was said to have a disproportionately adverse effect on African Ameri-

---

[33] Vance, 133 S. Ct. at 2443.

[34] *Id.* at 2453.

[35] 29 C.F.R. Parts 1600 – 1610.

[36] 29 C.F.R. Part 1601.

[37] *See* Lynn v. Regents of the Univ. of California, 656 F.2d. 1337 (9th Cir. 1981) (plaintiff alleged sex discrimination after being denied of tenure).

[38] 401 U.S. 424 (1971).

[39] *Id.* at 427.

cans and, by using the test as the basis for selection, the employer effectively discriminated against the plaintiffs because of their race.

What distinguishes disparate impact claims based on the reasoning established in *Griggs* is that the plaintiffs were successful without proving that the employer intended to discriminate on the basis of race. The test was neither job-related, nor did it select employees for promotion opportunities at random. If the test had selected at random, the success rates of African Americans and other employees would have been representative of the proportions of these employees taking the test. The test would have had no adverse effect and would have been legal. Since the test was shown to have a disparate impact on a minority, the employer's use of the test to decide whom to promote meant the employer effectively made decisions based on race, whether it was the employer's intention to do so or not.[40]

The *Griggs* Court unanimously concluded that a facially neutral employment practice that has a disproportionately adverse effect on a minority cannot be used unless it is justified by a standard known as "business necessity."[41] Section 703(k)(1)(A) of Title VII, as amended by the Civil Rights Act of 1991, provides:

> An unlawful employment practice based on disparate impact is established under this subchapter only if (i) a complaining party demonstrates that a respondent uses a particular employment practice that causes a disparate impact on the basis of race, color, religion, sex, or national origin and the respondent fails to demonstrate that the challenged practice is job related for the position and consistent with business necessity.[42]

Disparate impact analysis has not been extensively litigated in higher education, and courts have provided little guidance on the nature of a plaintiff's proof and the requirements of an employer's business necessity defense.[43] Several factors may account for the lack of reliance on disparate impact theories. The Civil Rights Act of 1991 mandated that no compensatory or punitive damages are available under this theory, and this limitation on damages may discourage plaintiffs who seek more than equitable relief.[44] In addition, disparate impact claims involve compliance with the rigorous requirements of

---

[40] This reasoning begs the question of whether claims of disparate impact are constitutional under the Section Five enforcement provision of the Fourteenth Amendment. Violations of equal protection require deliberate intention to engage in invidious discrimination. Does a federal law aimed at prohibiting subconscious discrimination qualify as legislation enforcing equal protection?

[41] 401 U.S. at 432.

[42] 42 U.S.C.A. § 2000e-2(k)(1)(A).

[43] For a discussion of the potential application of disparate impact in employment settings, *see* E.W. Shoben, *"Disparate Impact Theory in Employment Discrimination: What's Griggs Still Good For? What Not?,"* 42 BRANDEIS L.J. 597 (Spring 2004).

[44] *See* M. Rothstein et al., EMPLOYMENT LAW, Vol. 1 § 2.31 (3rd ed. 2004).

class-action lawsuits under federal law, which may tend to restrict the number of individual plaintiffs who seek relief under this theory.

Perhaps most significant for higher education institutions, however, is the fact that selection devices such as aptitude tests and diploma requirements are seldom used as a basis for employment decisions. For example, faculty selection decisions are more often characterized by subjective, though job-related, criteria related to research, service, and teaching. Even for non-academic personnel, employment decisions are typically based on selection devices that have been validated as job-related and screened to reduce the possibility of invidious bias in test items.

Disparate Treatment

With respect to disparate treatment, the principal United States Supreme Court decisions interpreting Title VII have involved how to prove discriminatory intent. Under the standard most invoked in litigation, *McDonnell Douglas Corp. v. Green,*[45] a test of circumstantial evidence has evolved. However, in *Price Waterhouse v. Hopkins,*[46] a standard of "direct evidence" has received judicial recognition. With guidance from these two cases, lower federal courts have applied a standard in which a plaintiff may establish a claim of Title VII discrimination either by introducing direct evidence of discrimination or by proving circumstantial evidence that would support an inference of discrimination. A plaintiff need only prove direct evidence or circumstantial evidence because the two claims were mutually exclusive. Under the direct-evidence approach, once the plaintiff introduced evidence that the employer terminated him or her because of his or her race or other protected status, the burden of persuasion shifts to the employer to prove that it would have terminated the plaintiff even if it had not been motivated by discrimination.[47]

Direct evidence is "evidence, which if believed, proves [the] existence of [the] fact in issue without inference or presumption."[48] When a plaintiff offers direct evidence and the trier of fact accepts that evidence, the plaintiff has proven discrimination.[49] However, a proof based on direct evidence of discrimination is often difficult to establish in a higher education context be-

---

[45] 411 U.S. 792 (1973).

[46] 490 U.S. 228 (1989). What suffices as "direct evidence," and whether "direct vs. circumstantial" evidence remains an important issue may have been undercut by the Supreme Court's decision in Desert Palace, Inc. v. Costa, 539 U.S. 90 (2003). *See* Clark v. Claremont University, 6 Cal. App. 4th 639 (Cal. Ct. App. 1992) for an example of direct evidence of discrimination where an assistant professor who was denied tenure introduced evidence of numerous racial remarks that the court found to provide substantial evidence of race discrimination.

[47] *See* Kline v. Tennessee Valley Auth., 128 F.3d 337, 348 (6th Cir. 1997).

[48] Merritt v. Dillard Paper Co., 120 F.3d 1181, 1189 (11th Cir. 1987).

[49] McCarthney v. Griffin-Spalding Cnty Bd. of Educ., 791 F.2d 1549, 1553 (11th Cir. 1986).

cause vague and subjective judgments related to employee qualifications and performance are prevalent, particularly when faculty issues are involved.[50]

The influence of the *McDonnell Douglas* "circumstantial evidence" standard in application to federal antidiscrimination law has been pervasive. The first step of the standard requires a plaintiff to meet a modest proof in support of a prima facie case and seems to favor the plaintiff. After the employee establishes a prima facie case, the employer must articulate a legitimate, nondiscriminatory reason for the adverse employment decision. Once the employer does so, the plaintiff must demonstrate that the proffered reason was pretextual, a subterfuge masking intent to discriminate.[51] Applications of the test in higher education settings abound.

Racial and National Origin Discrimination

Historically, racial discrimination has been a primary issue in Title VII cases. Under the shifting burden of proof, also known as the "tripartite test" first articulated in *McDonnell Douglas,* a plaintiff challenging an employer's hiring practices must first carry an initial burden of proof. This may be done by showing that he belongs to a racial minority group; that he applied and was qualified for a job for which the employer was seeking applicants; that, despite his qualifications, he was rejected; and that after his rejection, the position remained open and the employer continued to seek applicants from persons of the complainant's qualification.[52]

The plaintiff's initial burden of proof in disparate treatment cases involving race or national origin is illustrated in a number of cases in which higher education institutions were defendants. In one case, an African American environmental research analyst was given a negative performance rating by a white supervisor. The analyst was subject to disciplinary measures that included restrictions on funding for professional conferences and the requirement to maintain daily written logs of his activity. His white male supervisor called him "space pilgrim," "lazy," and accused him of "shifting positions all the time." Alleging that these comments were racial slurs, the analyst filed an internal grievance alleging discrimination by the supervisor. On the recommendation of the university's grievance committee, the analyst was reassigned to another supervisor, but negative evaluations of his performance continued. When he was terminated in what the institution described as a layoff occasioned by a reduction-in-force, he filed a claim alleging disparate treatment. A federal appeals court affirmed a summary judgment motion for the university, concluding that the analyst failed to establish a prima facie claim of disparate

---

[50] *See* Ben-Kotel v. Howard Univ., 319 F.3d 532 (D.C. Cir. 2003) in which a claim of direct evidence of discrimination under Title VII was dismissed on appeal because the plaintiff, a national origin minority, failed to argue this claim in the district court.

[51] *See* Int'l Brotherhood of Teamsters v. United States, 431 U.S. 324, 355 (1977). The court noted, "proof of discriminatory motive is critical, although it can in some situations be inferred from the mere fact of difference in treatment."

[52] 411 U.S. at 802.

treatment.[53] The appeals court found that the analyst relied on his own perceptions and the findings of the institution's grievance committee in building his
case, but reasoned that his perceptions were not evidence and the grievance
report failed to provide the required inference of bias behind the institution's
actions, stipulating only that personality conflicts appeared to motivate the
supervisor's actions.

In another case, the Eighth Circuit applied the *McDonnell Douglas* test
in granting summary judgment to a higher education institution. An African
American chair and professor claimed direct evidence of racial discrimination,
as well as disparate treatment, when his institution failed to promote him to a
position as dean and hired a white applicant from outside the institution. The
professor had not applied for the position at the time it was filled and claimed
that the institution had not provided a definitive application process, yet had
a history of appointing from within. The federal appeals court found that the
circumstances provided no direct evidence of discrimination, but the court
proceeded to evaluate the professor's claim under the shifting burden of proof.
Despite the fact that the institution had hired several senior administrators
from within, the court adopted the view that many positions at universities
are necessarily filled in different ways, depending on the nature of a position,
its responsibilities, and other factors. The court concluded that a reasonable
fact-finder could not infer intentional race discrimination from the decision to
consider outside applicants when seeking a qualified individual for a position
as dean, and given the professor's failure to make timely application for the
position, summary judgment was granted in favor of the university.[54]

If the plaintiff is successful in establishing a prima facie case, the burden
then shifts to the employer to articulate a legitimate, nondiscriminatory reason
for the employment action.[55] Although a higher education institution must
articulate a legitimate, nondiscriminatory reason for its employment decision,
given the subjective and scholarly nature of judgments that typically apply to
employment decisions in academe and the reluctance of courts to intervene
in employment decisions that involve faculty qualifications, an institution
generally meets this requirement. For example, in a case in which a former
business professor, who is an African male of Ethiopian origin, contended his
nonrenewal was a pretext for Title VII disparate treatment, the institution prevailed by articulating a legitimate, nondiscriminatory reason for nonrenewal,
namely, student evaluations of the professor's instructional performance that
were regarded as below college standards.[56]

---

[53] Pilgrim v. Trs. of Tufts College, 118 F.3d 864 (1st Cir. 1997).
[54] Lockridge v. Bd. of Trs. of the Univ. of Ark., 294 F.3d 1010 (8th Cir. 2002).
[55] Texas Dep't of Cmty Affairs v. Burdine, 450 U.S. 248, 254 (1981).
[56] Girma v. Skidmore College, 180 F.Supp.2d 326 (N.D.N.Y. 2001). *See* Nguyen and Ward, *supra* note 12. (Case study examining this specific case utilizing a Critical Race Theory lens and its implications on "fit").

In *Guseh v. North Carolina Central University*,[57] a tenured professor who is a Liberian native and naturalized American citizen alleged that administrators at his university denied him a department chairmanship due to national origin. In each of the four times the department position became available, it was given to someone native to the United States and from outside the department. Further, the plaintiff alleged that each individual selected for the position was less qualified than he. The defendants acknowledged the plaintiff's qualifications, but argued that the appointed candidates were selected because the consensual scholarly and subjective judgment of the defendants was that the selected individuals would make better administrators. In rebuttal, the plaintiff simply offered a reiteration that his academic credentials surpassed those of the other candidates. As a result, the University moved to have the claims dismissed.

In considering the case, the United States District Court for the Middle District of North Carolina assumed for argument's sake that the plaintiff had established a prima facie case. When the university then provided legitimate, nondiscriminatory reasons for the employment action, the burden shifted back to the plaintiff to show that those reasons were simply pretexts for discrimination. As the plaintiff's rationale that he was better qualified did not meet that burden, and the courts generally tend to avoid becoming entangled in reasonable employment decisions, particularly those in academe, the court dismissed the plaintiff's claims.

To compound the plaintiff's difficulties, once the institution articulates its reason for the adverse employment decision, the burden shifts back to the plaintiff to persuade the court that he or she has been the victim of intentional discrimination and that the institution's proffered reason is a veil to disguise the intent to discriminate. For lower federal courts, it has frequently not been enough for the plaintiff to prove that the employer's legitimate, nondiscriminatory reason is pretextual; the plaintiff must also show that it is a pretext concealing a discriminatory motivation. This standard has led some federal courts to require a proof of discriminatory intent, while other courts have adopted the position that if the employer's reason is unworthy of belief, it can be assumed to be a disguise of a discriminatory motivation.

By way of illustration, a candidate for a position as director of a language program at a New York university challenged the decision of a selection committee that rejected his candidacy in favor of an external candidate. The candidate, who was on the institution's faculty and had served in the role of interim director, met the burden to establish a prima facie case under Title VII and challenged the institution's proffered reason for the hiring decision, which related to teaching effectiveness. The rejected candidate contended that the institution's claim that it simply appointed the best candidate was pretextual, in light of evidence that the process of recruitment and selection deviated from normal institutional procedures; the search committee was made up of individu-

---

[57] 423 F. Supp. 2d 550; 2005 U.S. Dist. LEXIS 41126.

als who could not speak Spanish, yet was charged to assess the candidates on the basis of their teaching competence in a model Spanish lesson; and that this atypical search committee was created because of the administration's belief that the interim director would likely win the position if normal procedures were followed. Although a federal district court granted summary judgment to the institution, a federal appeals court reversed, noting that the plaintiff's evidence permitted an inference of discrimination on the basis of national origin, and remanding for further findings. The court noted that the articulated reason for the employment decision was that an evaluation had been made that one candidate was better than another, yet the challenged decision was made only after the institution had deviated from its normal selection procedures, had appointed advisors who lacked proficiency in the skills they were asked to evaluate, and had informed another potential candidate that the interim director's candidacy would not be considered seriously. From this evidence, the appeals court concluded that there were genuine issues of fact as to whether the institution's explanation was a pretext to mask unlawful discrimination.[58]

The fact-intensive inquiry involved in the tripartite test is illustrated in a case in which a black assistant professor from the West Indies, who was hired on a tenure track, was issued a one-year contract and ultimately released by the institution. The trial court held the assistant professor met his initial burden of proof and went on to consider whether the institution articulated a legitimate, nondiscriminatory reason and assess whether that reason was pretextual. The institution defended its decision by presenting evidence of substandard performance evaluations, negative student evaluations, and failure to produce scholarly work and obtain the doctoral degree, which was expressly determined to be a requirement for maintaining the assistant professor's tenure-track position. The assistant professor presented evidence to rebut the institution's articulated reasons for the adverse employment decision, including evidence that the college had retained a white professor who did not have his doctorate and that student evaluations of teaching were tainted by a conspiracy among white students. While the trial court ruled in favor of the black professor, the federal appeals court reversed this ruling on the basis that the court's factual findings were clearly erroneous. The Fourth Circuit Court of Appeals held that the comparison with the white professor was inappropriate because he had been hired at an earlier time when the requirement for an advanced degree was not required. It also concluded that the trial court erred in inferring that the student evaluations were tainted, finding, for example, that student expressions indicating the assistant professor was difficult to understand might reasonably be interpreted as expressing a concern about effective communication, rather than discriminatory animus based on race or national origin.[59]

In *Mezu v. Morgan State University*,[60] the U.S. Court of Appeals for the Fourth Circuit dismissed a professor's untimely discrimination claim, finding

---

[58] Stern v. Trs of Columbia Univ. in the City of New York, 131 F.3d 305 (2d Cir. 1997).

[59] Jimenez v. Mary Washington College, 57 F. 3d 369 (4th Cir.1995).

[60] 2010 U.S. App. LEXIS 3301 (4th Cir. Feb. 19, 2010).

that a pending internal appeal did not halt the statute of limitations from running. Mezu, an African American woman of Nigerian origin, began teaching as a non-tenure-track lecturer and five years later earned a position as an associate professor. Four years later, in 2002, she applied for a promotion to full professor. Upon denial of the promotion, Mezu filed a complaint with the U.S. Equal Employment Opportunity Commission (EEOC) and suit in federal court, alleging discrimination based on race and national origin. The district court dismissed the claim, and the Fourth Circuit affirmed that decision.

In 2004, she applied a second time for full professor and was denied. In 2005, she applied a third time for full professor and, although the departmental promotion committee recommended promoting her to full professor, the chair recommended against promotion and advised that additional scholarly publication should be pursued. On April 6, 2006, she was informed of the fact that she was denied promotion and of her right to appeal the decision, which she did within a few days. The university did not act and, in the belief that it would not comply with the appeal procedures, she filed a second EEOC claim on March 25, 2007, followed by a suit in federal court. The district court dismissed the claim as untimely, as did the Fourth Circuit on appeal, which found that the letter of April 6, 2006, triggered the limitations period, despite the pending internal appeal. As such, the *Mezu* decision makes clear the imperative nature of awareness of the actual calendar of the limitations period.

Religious Discrimination

Private religious schools are often exempt from some of the religious restrictions imposed by Title VII.[61] It is also important to note that Title VII prohibitions on disparate treatment also extend to religious discrimination,[62] although religious institutions that are owned, supported, controlled, or managed by a religious organization, or that have a curriculum that is generally directed toward the propagation of a particular religion, are permitted to exercise religious preferences. Issues of religious discrimination have prompted several cases at religious institutions. A Catholic faculty member was fired from a Presbyterian college for conducting surveys of other faculty members. After the survey incident, he allegedly did not receive raises, or received less than the average faculty member, for seven years. He sued, and the court dismissed his suit. The court held that if the college discharged him because of his religious views, it could lawfully do so under Title VII.[63] In a similar situation, a private university that established a divinity school hired a professor to teach in both the divinity school and in the departments of religion and English. Differing theological views came between the professor and the dean of the divinity school, causing the professor to be released from his position

---

[61] *See* Hosanna-Tabor Evangelical Lutheran Church v. EEOC, 132 S. Ct. 694 (2012) (recognizing a ministerial exception to Title VII).

[62] 42 U.S.C. § 2000e-2(e).

[63] Wirth v. College of the Ozarks, 26 F. Supp. 2d 1185 (W. D. Mo. 1998).

there. The professor filed suit under Title VII.[64] As the university received a portion of its annual budget from the Alabama Baptist Convention, the court held that the university qualified as an educational institution protected by the exemptions of Title VII.[65]

The issue of preferential hiring by religious or religiously affiliated institutions has been the subject of several lawsuits. For example, when preferential treatment was used for hiring by a religious university, the university was challenged by a Jewish faculty member. In this instance, a Jewish part-time lecturer in the university's philosophy department objected when the university began requiring that seven of the department's thirty-one, tenure-track faculty positions be held by Jesuit priests, arguing that their presence enhanced the character of the university. The court found that membership in a preferred religious denomination can be a bona fide occupational qualification falling within the meaning of Title VII.[66] In a related case at another Catholic university, a rejected applicant for a theology position claimed the university's actions constituted sex discrimination. Twenty-seven, full-time faculty positions in the theology department were held by Jesuits. The court ruled that its action fell within Title VII's Section 702 exemption allowing religious schools/groups to hire employees of a particular religion, here Catholic. The trial court dismissed the case and the appellate court affirmed, based on the plaintiff's failure to establish a prima facie case of sex discrimination.[67]

In cases where Title VII's exemptions for religious institutions are not applicable, employees may assert alternative theories of religious discrimination: disparate treatment and failure to accommodate. In general, higher education institutions are required to reasonably accommodate an employee's religion unless the employer can demonstrate an undue hardship.[68] The Equal Employment Opportunity Commission has issued guidelines on the duty employers have under Title VII to provide reasonable accommodation for religious practices of their employees and applicants.[69] A non-higher-education case offers guidance relative to the employer's burden in cases involving religious accommodation. A public-school teacher requested to use the personal days provided in the union contract agreement allowing for paid leave for religious holiday observance. Additional days for religious observance would be afforded, but the employer would grant the additional days as unpaid leave. The schoolteacher sued the board of education, arguing religious accommodation should include additional days of paid leave. The United States Supreme Court held that an employer does not need to accede to the preferred accommoda-

---

[64] Killinger v. Samford Univ., 113 F. 3d 196 (11th Cir 1997).

[65] § 703(e)(2) of Title VII of the Civil Rights Act of 1964.

[66] Pime v. Loyola Univ. of Chicago, 803 F. 2d 351 (7th Cir. 1986).

[67] Maguire v. Marquette Univ., 814 F. 2d 1213 (7th Cir 1987).

[68] 42 U.S.C. § 2000e(j).

[69] 29 C.F.R. Part 1605.

tions of the employee and may offer its own accommodations, as long as they meet a standard of reasonableness.[70]

To prove a claim of religious discrimination under the disparate treatment theory, the evidentiary burdens of an employee alleging religious discrimination mirror those of an employee alleging race or national origin discrimination. In *Rubinstein v. Administrators of the Tulane Educational Fund,*[71] a plaintiff, who was Russian and Jewish, had been denied salary increases and promotion to full professor. The associate professor established his prima facie case and presented evidence that a senior faculty member within the department referred to him as a "Russian Yankee" and made an antisemitic remark concerning Jewish frugality. The institution justified the employment decisions on the basis that the professor's teaching evaluations were low and his service record was inadequate.

The appeals court affirmed summary judgment on the disparate treatment claim for the institution, finding that the evidence of student evaluations demonstrated that the associate professor was a poor teacher and was not entitled to the promotions he sought. The court reasoned that since salary increases were predicated upon merit and the available funds were limited, it was not improper for the institution to rely on these evaluations, together with memoranda and faculty reviews substantiating the professor's ineffective mentoring of students and his low participation rate on faculty committees, as a basis for denying him salary increases. The appeals court's judgment ultimately turned on the professor's failure to substantiate that the institution's articulated reasons for denying him promotion and salary increases were a pretext for discrimination. The appeals court agreed with the district court that the evidence of poor teaching performance was so overwhelming that the suggestion that some of the evaluations had been tampered with could not overcome the manifest weight of the evidence. As to the lack of service on committees, the appeals court recognized that discriminatory animus on the part of the department chair might have influenced the associate professor's opportunities for committee assignments, but this was not regarded as sufficient evidence of discriminatory intent. The court also concluded that the discriminatory comments by a faculty member who served on the promotion and pay raise committees would not defeat summary judgment on the claims of discrimination. In this case, the comments of the faculty member, alluding to the associate professor as a "Russian Yankee" and stating that "Jews are thrifty," were stray remarks not shown to be proximate in time or otherwise related to the employment decisions at issue.

However, there are instances in which an institution's articulated reasons may permit an inference that the employment decision was motivated by a discriminatory intent. In a representative case, *Abramson v. William Paterson College of New Jersey,*[72] the college hired the plaintiff, an Orthodox Jew, as a

---

[70] Ansonia Bd. of Educ. v. Philbrook, 479 U.S. 60 (1986).

[71] 218 F.3d 392 (5th Cir. 2000).

[72] 260 F.3d 265 (3d Cir 2001).

tenure-track associate professor. At the beginning of her first year at the college, the professor informed her department chair that she would not be able to teach on Jewish holidays, and accommodations in her teaching schedule were permitted. However, a new department chair took exception to the arrangement, and this issue became a matter of contention between the administration and the professor as she progressed toward a tenure decision. Relations with the department chair and dean continued to strain over the issue of the professor's religious absences, leading to a recommendation to discontinue the professor's employment. After filing a grievance under the institution's guidelines and initiating a complaint with the EEOC, the professor litigated under Title VII.

The Third Circuit Court of Appeals reversed a lower federal court decision granting summary judgment to the institution. In addition to establishing a claim based on a hostile work environment, the professor succeeded in convincing the appeals court that she met the requirements for a prima facie case under disparate treatment and that the institution's articulated reason for the adverse employment decision had shifted in the course of her dismissal. The appellate court stated that if a plaintiff demonstrates that the reasons given for termination do not remain consistent, beginning at the time they are proffered and continuing throughout the administrative proceedings, this may be viewed as evidence tending to demonstrate pretext. Based on the record as a whole, the appellate court ruled that the professor successfully established that the college's justification for tenure denial was sufficiently implausible and inconsistent enough that a fact-finder could reasonably disbelieve the articulated reasons.

Sex Discrimination

The shifting burden of proof in employment discrimination cases has application to claims of disparate treatment based on gender discrimination. A substantial number of these cases have involved allegations of gender discrimination in tenure denial. Institutions prevail in many of these cases on the basis that the proffered reasons for denying promotion and tenure were not pretextual. The college or university's rationale for tenure denial typically involves a judgment of faculty and administrative leadership that courts are reluctant to overturn in the absence of compelling evidence of pretext.[73] It is also unlikely that irregularities in the tenure review process will invalidate an adverse decision. While some irregularities, such as falsifying hiring criteria or documentary records, might lead to an inference of discrimination, subjective evaluative criteria, changes in the criteria over time, or lack of uniformity in procedures have been regarded as insufficient to establish pretext.[74] However, while institutions enjoy substantial discretion and judicial deference in making tenure and promotion decisions, institutional policies should be refined to

---

[73] *See*, for example, Lawrence v. Curators of the Univ. of Missouri, 204 F.2d 807 (8th Cir. 2000) in which subjective faculty assessments about the "quality of research" were largely unscrutinized by the reviewing court, despite a vigorous dissent by the chief judge of the appeals court.

[74] Aquilino v. Univ. of Kansas, 83 F.Supp. 1248 (D.Kan. 2000).

reduce the possibility of unequal treatment and to insure a documentary record that will provide evidence of consistency in the evaluation process. Standards of quality should not be so subjective that they cannot be effectively communicated and consistently assessed at any stage of the faculty evaluation process.

Evidence of lack of uniformity in the treatment of similarly situated male and female candidates can be a significant factor in judging the likelihood of discriminatory intent under Title VII. Evidence substantiating discrimination based on gender in tenure and promotion decisions has included a showing that similarly situated male candidates received counseling to assist them in the tenure process and were advised of a requirement for a terminal degree when the female candidate was not so advised.[75] In another instance, a court upheld the claim of an assistant professor and awarded tenure to her based on a finding that the university president's sexist remarks about the English department had established gender bias.[76] The university, in this latter case, had denied tenure despite unanimously favorable endorsement from department colleagues and support at administrative levels.

In *Leibowitz v. Cornell University*,[77] a federal appeals court vacated summary judgment on a strong demonstration of pretext and held that the nonrenewal of a teaching contract, even that of a nontenured individual, could form the basis for a Title VII claim. Leibowitz was a nontenured Senior Extension Associate, who had been teaching with the university since 1983. Although the program is based in Ithaca, she was teaching in Cornell's extension facilities in New York City. While in a dispute regarding reimbursement of her travel expenses, the university did not renew her contract in 2002, citing "budgetary exigencies."[78] Although she was allowed to continue teaching in 2002-03, she retired in December 2002 to preserve her benefits. She filed suit under Title VII, the ADEA, and state and local law.

Leibowitz presented evidence that supported her claim that Cornell's stated budgetary concerns were merely a pretext for discrimination. Specifically, she asserted that the budgetary concerns stated in 2002 had diminished over that year and the school was in "solid financial shape" by 2003[79]; the Extension Division had enough money to hire twelve new employees during the relevant time period; although the school laid off six employees, these employees were all women over age 50; although her requests for reimbursement of travel funds was cited as one reason for nonrenewal of her contract, negotiation for reimbursement of such funds was common practice among her male counterparts, and none of them were faced with nonrenewal or termination; she was not considered for positions that became vacant following her nonrenewal; a younger male was hired to fill a vacant teaching position in 2002; and she

---

[75] Kunda v. Muhlenberg College, 621 F. 2d 531 (2d Cir. 1980).
[76] Brown v. Trustees of Boston Univ., 891 F. 2d 337 (1st Cir. 1989).
[77] Leibowitz v. Cornell Univ., 584 F.3d 487 (2d Cir. 2009).
[78] *Id.* at 494.
[79] *Id.* at 504.

was also not considered for an opening in 2003.[80] Although the court makes reference to unequal treatment among male and female instructors, as well as among younger and older employees, the gender and age components were not specifically underscored as part of the decision. The Second Circuit reversed the district court's award of summary judgment and rejected its holding that a teacher could only show adverse employment action by offering proof that she held a tenured position.[81]

In general, an institution's tenure and promotion process is extensive and multi-layered. It will require distinction in research or teaching, depending on institutional mission, and no evidence of significant deficiencies in any of the three relevant categories of research, teaching, and service. While plaintiffs in these cases may raise a number of issues, the burden to establish sufficient evidence that the institution's proffered reason is a pretext for discrimination is difficult to carry. For example, in *Bickerstaff v. Vassar College*,[82] a female African American associate professor challenged the institution's decision to deny her promotion to full professor. Because the associate professor held positions in both the African studies and education departments, institutional policy required two separate advisory committees to make recommendations on promotion, with one committee voting for the candidate's promotion and the other rejecting it. Based on internal and external appraisals of the candidate's research and evidence from student evaluations, the institution denied her promotion. The candidate presented statistical evidence indicating differences in salary paid to faculty based on sex and race, as well as further statistical evidence tending to show that racial bias influenced student evaluations of her performance. Affirming summary judgment for the institution, the federal appeals court reasoned that the candidate failed to demonstrate "that the proffered reason was not the true reason for the employment decision and that race was."[83] In the appeals court's view, the associate professor's burden was to persuade the trier of fact that she was the victim of intentional discrimination in that an illegal discriminatory reason played a motivating role in the decision not to promote. On this question, the court found that no genuine issue of material fact existed that would support the associate professor's claim of intentional discrimination.

The appeals court emphasized that while statistical reports may establish an inference of discrimination, the statistical evidence in this case was so incomplete that it was inadmissible, as well as irrelevant since it failed to account for all the applicable variables that might account for the perceived disparities in salary and evaluation outcomes. Although reliance on these student evaluations of instruction may involve subjective judgments and hair-splitting when it comes to determining the point at which evaluations indicate "marked distinction," the appeals court noted first that the institution possessed

---

[80] *Id.* at 505.
[81] *Id.* at 510.
[82] 196 F.3d 435 (2d Cir. 1999).
[83] *Id.* at 446.

the expertise and the discretion to make such judgments, and second that the evidence in this case clearly reflected the candidate's declining effectiveness in the classroom.

The court reviewed evidence from a visiting faculty report that concluded there was opposition to the African studies program at the college and that the program was subject to hostility by some departments. However, when the full report was reviewed, the court noted that the visiting faculty had commented favorably on the program's support from the college administration and from other departments on the campus. Moreover, the court emphasized that any perceived resistance to the African studies program could not have established discriminatory intent in the candidate's promotion process.

In cases involving disparities in compensation, statistical evidence may play a role in establishing a plaintiff's prima facie case and meeting the burden to show the institution's reason is a pretext to mask discrimination.[84] When a female professor in a medical science field challenged the institution's decision to pay a similarly situated male professor at a significantly higher level of compensation, she presented two statistical studies that indicated gender significantly affected faculty salaries at the university. After adjusting for factors such as rank, degree, tenure, duration at the institution, and age, women tended to earn lower salaries than men. The institution countered that the studies failed to distinguish faculty salaries among medical specialties.

When a jury subsequently returned a verdict for the plaintiff on the issues of sex discrimination under Title VII and unequal pay under the Equal Pay Act (EPA), a federal appeals court reasoned that statistics evidencing an employer's pattern and practice of discriminatory conduct, though not determinative of an employer's reason for the action, are still helpful to confirm a general pattern of discrimination. Since the university failed to present evidence at trial rebutting the conclusions of the reports, the reports were sufficient to establish a prima facie case of sex discrimination.

The plaintiff, having met the initial burden of proof, then rebutted the university's affirmative defenses to explain the wage differential. The university first contended that the newly hired male professor was more productive in his ability to secure grants than the plaintiff, but the female professor established pretext by showing that the amount of grant funding she generated exceeded that of the new professor. As a second articulated reason for the disparity in compensation, the institution asserted the new male professor was offered a higher salary than that of the plaintiff as an incentive to retain the male professor's wife based on market forces. However, the appeals court rejected this defense as well by noting that market forces were not a tenable argument in

---

[84] Cases involving claims of sex discrimination that involve disparities in compensation often involve both Title VII and the Equal Pay Act. As one federal appeals court has noted, the Equal Pay Act and Title VII must be "construed in harmony, particularly where claims made under the two statutes arise out of the same discriminatory pay policies." Lavin-McEleney v. Marist College, 239 F.3d 476, 481 (2d Cir. 2001).

this case, since they simply served to perpetuate the salary discrimination that Congress sought to alleviate in both Title VII and the EPA.[85]

While both Title VII and the EPA apply the same burden-shifting standard articulated in *McDonnell Douglas*, if the plaintiff is successful in demonstrating a prima facie case under the EPA, the employer may then respond with an affirmative defense to establish that the pay differential is due to a seniority system, a merit system, a system measuring earnings by quantity or quality of production, or any factor other than gender. For example, in *Markel v. Board of Regents of University of Wisconsin*,[86] a plaintiff successfully demonstrated a pay disparity between herself and a similarly situated male consultant, thus establishing a prima facie case. The burden then shifted to the institution to provide evidence to justify the disparity in compensation, and the university explained that the male colleague's pay was based on the longer number of years he had worked for the institution and the fact that he had held a higher position. This was a legitimate rationale, not based on gender, for the disparity in compensation, a finding that harmonized both the requirements of the EPA and Title VII.

Statistical models tend to show that disparities in compensation between a plaintiff and a class of institutional employees are not typically sufficient to establish a claim of disparate treatment unless the plaintiff can also produce an actual opposite-sex comparator for purposes of the Title VII or EPA claim.[87] However, once the plaintiff has identified an actual opposite-sex comparator, statistical models may be employed to show disparities, provided that the analysis incorporates relevant variables that could account for salary disparities on the basis of factors unrelated to gender bias.[88]

In recent years, the Lilly Ledbetter Fair Pay Act of 2009,[89] discussed earlier, has come into play in sex discrimination cases. For example, in *Gentry v. Jackson State University*,[90] a federal district court upheld a professor's discrimination claim in reliance on an expansively interpreted Ledbetter Act, finding that an otherwise untimely denial of tenure claim is permitted when intertwined with a successful demonstration of a discriminatory compensation decision, as a Title VII violation can occur each time a discriminatory paycheck is issued. In *Gentry*, a professor initially filed a discrimination claim with the EEOC in 2006 after being denied tenure in 2004. She alleged that tenure was denied due to her gender. She later filed suit in U.S. District Court, further alleging that the denial of tenure and resulting discriminatory pay violated Title VII, as well as claiming that the university retaliated against her for filing the EEOC claim. The university argued that her claim was untimely, as her EEOC claim was filed two years after the denial of tenure, and filed a motion for sum-

---

[85] Siler-Khodr v. University of Texas Health Science, 261 F.3d 542 (5th Cir. 2001).

[86] *See* Markel v. Bd. of Regents of Univ. of Wisconsin, 276 F.3d 906 (7th Cir. 2002).

[87] *See* Houck v. Virginia Polytechnic Institute and State Univ., 10 F.3d 204 (4th Cir. 1993).

[88] Lavin-McEleney v. Marist College, 239 F.3d 476 (2nd Cir. 2001).

[89] Ledbetter Act, Pub. L. No. 111-2, 123 Stat. 5 (2009).

[90] 610 F. Supp. 2d 564 (S.D. Miss. 2009).

mary judgment. Gentry responded that in fact it was timely, as it qualified as a compensation decision under the Ledbetter Act. The district court agreed with the professor and denied the motion for summary judgment.

The university also filed motions for summary judgment on the professor's claim of gender discrimination related to pay disparity, as it alleged she was unable to identify a male comparator, as well as for summary judgment on her retaliation claim. The district court also denied these motions based on factual disputes for later resolution at trial and because the claim grew out of the unequal pay claim, respectively. At subsequent trial, the professor was awarded $100,000 on the retaliation claim and, while the jury rejected her sex discrimination claim (for denial of tenure and disparate pay), it awarded her the total damages requested under all claims.

Sexual Orientation and Gender Identity Discrimination

Sexual orientation discrimination law under Title VII is emerging. While sexual orientation discrimination is not prohibited by Title VII nationally, nor is there any federal law directed at such discrimination, there is a circuit split on interpretations of Title VII and sexual orientation-based claims. Many states and municipalities have passed state legislation or ordinances prohibiting employment discrimination on the basis of sexual orientation in both public and private sectors, and many have even added protections for gender identity and expressions. Issues related to sexual orientation go beyond discipline, hiring, discharge, and promotion; they also include access to benefits for unmarried same-sex partners and housing reserved for heterosexual couples.

Sexual orientation discrimination claims can be brought to the EEOC, and many states have been responsive to these claims bringing them under 42 U.S.C. § 1983 violations of the Fourteenth Amendment's Equal Protection Clause. For example, in *Miguel v. Guess*,[91] the state appellate court denied the employer's motion to dismiss a claim brought by the hospital employee alleging a Section 1983 claim that her dismissal was a result of her sexual orientation. Although the employee was allowed to move forward with her claim, she lost on public policy grounds because the state had not yet enacted law in this area. In *Lovell v. Comsewogue School District*,[92] the federal district court found that the basis of sexual orientation discrimination was different than the other types and, if proven, would be an Equal Protection Clause violation and actionable under Section 1983.

Plaintiffs have also been fruitful in their claims of sexual orientation discrimination using the Supreme Court's *Price Waterhouse* standard on sex stereotyping. Under this standard, plaintiffs allege that they were harassed, discharged, or not hired because they did not fit the image of a "typical" man

---

[91]   51 P.3d. 89 (Wash. Ct. App. 2002).

[92]   214 F. Supp. 2d. 319 (E.D.N.Y. 2002).

or woman. For example, in *Lewis v. Heartland Inns of America*,[93] the plaintiff claimed that she was denied a position as a front desk clerk of a hotel because she looked like Ellen DeGeneres, who is a prominent gay celebrity, rather than a "Midwestern" girl. The appellate court reversed a summary judgment for the employer, ruling that the plaintiff presented sufficient evidence of sex discrimination to proceed to trial.

Although there is no federal law prohibiting employment discrimination on the basis of gender identity or expression, commonly known as transgender status, many states and municipalities have adopted laws to recognize this kind of discrimination. The EEOC has ruled that discrimination based on gender identity/transgender status is a form of sex discrimination and violates Title VII.[94] Although Title VII does not specifically provide protection for trans-gendered individuals, some have had success challenging their discrimination under the *Price Waterhouse* theory of sex stereotyping.[95]

For example, in *Schroer v. Billington,* the plaintiff applied for a position at the Library of Congress. The plaintiff presented as a male during the job interview and was later offered the job.[96] However, when the plaintiff informed his prospective supervisor that he would be transitioning into the female gender, the offer was rescinded. The individual had an extensive career and was well qualified for the position, but the supervisor stated that she did not believe the plaintiff could be effective in the position as a transgender person. The court applied the *Price Waterhouse* standard and Title VII, and allowed the plaintiff to state a claim of sex discrimination and sexual stereotyping. The court ruled that the Library of Congress' reasons for rescinding the offer were pretextual and facially discriminatory. The plaintiff was awarded over $500,000 in compensatory damages.[97]

Transgender individuals can also state claims under the Equal Protection Clause.[98] Also, claims of harassment of transgendered individuals can be made

---

[93] 591 F.3d 1033 (8th Cir. 2010). *See also* Prowel v. Wise Business Forms, Inc., 579 F.3d 285 (3d Cir. 2009) a federal appellate court reversed a summary judgment for employer in a claim brought by a male employee who claimed that he was harassed because he was perceived to be gay.

[94] *See* Macy v. Holder, EEOC Appeal No. 0120120821 (April 20, 2012). *See also* Schroer v. Billington. 577 F. Supp. 2d 293 (D.D.C. 2008).

[95] *See* Smith v. City of Salem, Ohio, 378 F.3d 566 (6th Cir. 2004), where male firefighter was able to state a claim for being disciplined after he began sex reassignment. *See also* Barnes v. Cincinnati, 401 F.3d 729 (6th Cir. 2005), where federal appellate court affirmed jury verdict for police officer who alleged transgendered discrimination.

[96] 577 F. Supp. 2d 293 (D.D.C. 2008).

[97] *See also* Lopez v. River Oaks Imaging & Diagnostic Group, 542 F.Supp. 2d 653 (S.D. Tex. 2008) where the court denied summary judgment because "Title VII is violated when an employer discriminates against any employee, transsexual or not, because he or she has failed to act or appear sufficiently masculine or feminine enough for an employer."

[98] *See* Glenn v. Brumby, 724 F. Supp. 2d 1284 (N.D. Ga. 2010) where a biological male employee had begun the transition to the female gender and was dismissed. Manager stated that it was "inappropriate" and the court determined that the plaintiff established a prima facie case of sex discrimination.

under Title VII on the basis of gender identity or expression and under state law.[99] Although some states do not afford legal protections against discrimination based on sexual orientation and identity/expression, many colleges and universities have included these populations as protected categories in their policies. Laws and policies in this area are ever-changing. In 2012, the U.S. Equal Employment Opportunity Commission found that discrimination on the basis of gender identity, change of sex, or transgender status is a form of sex discrimination and a violation of Title VII.[100]

As mentioned above, there is a circuit split whether or not sexual orientation-based claims can be brought under Title VII.[101] While the Eleventh Circuit held that sexual orientation-based claims were not actionable under Title VII, the Second and Seventh Circuits held otherwise. In the Eleventh Circuit, the plaintiff claimed employment discrimination resulting from her sexual orientation.[102] The district court dismissed both claims, and the Eleventh Circuit Court of Appeals reversed regarding the gender-conformity claim because under *Price Waterhouse v. Hopkins[103]* discrimination based on an employee's failure to conform to a gender stereotype is sex-based discrimination. The appeals court, however, affirmed dismissal regarding the sexual orientation-based claim. The Eleventh Circuit cited that "[d]ischarge for homosexuality is not prohibited by Title VII."[104]

After *Evans*, the Seventh Circuit ruled a different conclusion in *Hively v. Ivy Tech Community College of Indiana*,[105] *where the* plaintiff alleged discrimination based on sexual orientation. Because of precedence, the trial court dismissed her claim and the original appellate panel affirmed. En banc, the court reversed and overruled prior precedent and offered two justifications why sexual orientation discrimination is sex discrimination. First of all, using the "comparative method," the plaintiff being a lesbian epitomizes the fundamental case of failure to conform to the female stereotype because she is attracted to other women, not men. Secondly, from the "associational theory," the court contrasted the facts to cases of interracial couples, who are protected from race-based discrimination under Title VII. As a result, the

---

[99] *See* Mitchell v. Axcan Scandipharm, Inc., 2006 U.S. Dist. LEXIS 6521 (W.D. Pa. 2006) (finding that the *Price Waterhouse* standard precludes dismissal of the plaintiff's sexual harassment and discrimination claims under Title VII). *See also* Del Piano v. Atlantic County, 2005 Dist. LEXIS 20250 (D.N.J. 2005) (finding that a cause of action exists under state law for a corrections worker who was allegedly harassed and discriminated against for cross-dressing on his own time).

[100] *See* Macy v. Holder, EEOC Appeal No. 0120120821 (April 21, 2012).

[101] *See generally* J. Dalton Courson, *Circuits Split on Interpretations of Title VII and Sexual-Orietntation-Based Claims*, AMER. BAR ASSOC. (Mar. 19, 2018), *available at* https://www. americanbar.org/groups/litigation/committees/civil-rights/practice/2018/circuits-split-on-interpretations-of-title-vii-and-sexual-orientation-based-claims/.

[102] *See* Evans v. Georgia Regional Hospital, 850 F.3d 1238 (2017), *cert. denied*, 138 S. Ct. 557 (2017).

[103] 490 U.S. 228 (1989).

[104] *See* Blum v. Gulf Oil Corp., 587 F.2d 936 (5th Cir. 1979)).

[105] 853 F.3d 339 (7th Cir. 2017) (en banc).

court found that discrimination against gays and lesbians implicates sex in the same manner that discrimination against a member of an interracial couple implicates race. Also, Title VII must be interpreted in light of Supreme Court cases recognizing that certain kinds of discrimination on the basis of sexual orientation are unconstitutional.[106]

More recently, the en banc Second Circuit issued *Zarda v. Altitude Express, Inc.*[107] *Zarda* agreed with *Hively* and overruled contrary precedent. The court found that sexual orientation discrimination is a form of sex discrimination because one cannot fully define a person's sexual orientation without identifying his or her sex; as a result, sexual orientation is a function of sex. The court also found that sexual orientation is doubly delineated by sex because it is a function of both a person's sex and the sex of those to whom he or she is attracted. It is likely that other appeals courts may be called to address this issue, and the Supreme Court may be requested to resolve the split.

Retaliation

Punishing an employee for exercising the right to challenge an employment decision under Title VII is prohibited.[108] However, lower federal courts have been divided on the degree of harm the employee must suffer before retaliation claims are actionable. As to retaliation claims, the United States Court of Appeals for the Ninth Circuit, in *Ray v. Henderson*,[109] explained that the federal circuits have developed different standards for assessing the severity of an adverse employment decision. As the Ninth Circuit characterized the issue, the circuits have aligned themselves with either a broad, restrictive, or intermediate position as to what constitutes an adverse employment decision actionable under Title VII.[110] In addition, employees must establish the causal connection between any adverse employment decision and the exercise of rights under Title VII.[111] Previously, the close temporal proximity between an employer's knowledge of a protected activity (filing a Title VII claim) and an adverse employment action will be sufficient to establish causality. Also, a material employment action might have included situations for graduate student assistants involving "retaliatory conduct that does not relate to employment or which occurred outside the ... graduate student assistant workplace" that "could well dissuade a reasonable ... graduate student, TA, or research assistant from making or supporting a charge of discrimination."[112] Further, it was held that anti-retaliation provisions also extended to those employees who may respond

---

[106] *See generally* Romer v. Evans, 517 U.S. 620 (1990); Lawrence v. Texas, 539 U.S. 558 (2003); U.S. v. Windsor, 570 U.S. 744 (2013); Obergefell v. Hodges, 576 U.S. ___ (2015).

[107] No. 15-3775, 2018 U.S. App. LEXIS 4608 (2d Cir. Feb. 26, 2018) (en banc).

[108] 42 U.S.C. 2000e-3(a). The retaliation provision makes it "an unlawful employment practice for an employer to discriminate" against someone who has opposed an employer's unlawful behavior or participated in a Title VII proceeding.

[109] 217 F.3d 1234 (9th Cir. 2000).

[110] *Id.* at 1240-41.

[111] Clark Cty Sch. Dist. v. Breeden, 532 U.S. 268 (2001).

[112] Kovacevich v. Vanderbilt Univ., 2010 U.S. Dist. LEXIS 36054 (M.D. Tenn. April 12, 2010).

to questions posed regarding discriminatory activity as part of an employer's internal investigation,[113] as well as third-parties claiming retaliation resulting from the actions of another.[114]

More recently, the Court in *University of Texas Southwestern Medical Center v. Nasser* narrowed this causal connection standard and ruled that the higher but-for causation standard used in ADEA non-retaliation cases should also apply to Title VII retaliation cases.[115] In this case, Dr. Naiel Nasser was a physician of Middle Eastern descent who was a specialist in infectious diseases and HIV/AIDS treatment. From 1995 to 1998 and 2001 to 2006, he served on the faculty of the University of Texas Southwestern Medical Center and was also a member of the medical staff of the hospital. He also served as Associate Medical Director of the hospital's Amelia Court Clinic. After the hospital hired Dr. Beth Levine to direct the clinic and supervise Nasser, Dr. Nasser complained several times about Dr. Levine's treatment of him, claiming that she treated him differently than the rest of the medical staff. Dr. Levine said, in Nasser's presence, "Middle Easterners are lazy." He met often with Dr. Gregory Fitz, the medical school's Chair of Internal Medicine and Levine's supervisor, to complain of her behavior. Levine encouraged Nasser to apply for promotion to associate professor, which he received, but he continued to claim harassment. Because of his continued discontentment, Nasser tried to become an employee of the hospital instead of just being on its medical staff. As a result, he would have to resign from the medical school faculty. When Nasser resigned, he cited Levine's discrimination as a cause in his resignation letter to Fitz. In order to exonerate Levine, Fitz moved to block Nasser's employment at the hospital.[116] Nasser claimed this block of employment at the hospital was retaliation for his claim of harassment by Levine; however, Fitz claimed that physician positions at the hospital were first priority for faculty members.

Justice Anthony Kennedy wrote that when Congress added Section 2000e-2(m) to Title VII in 1991, it did so only for the five status claims and not for retaliation claims. As a result, the Court found that under Title VII retaliation claims, they must be proved under traditional principles of but-for causation and not the lessened causation standard outlines in Section 2000e-2(m). This higher standard requires proof that the unlawful retaliation would not have occurred in the absence of the alleged wrongdoing by the employer. This is key, since proving that retaliation is the but-for cause of an employment action is the most difficult form of causation to prove. Justice Ruth Bader Ginsburg filed a dissenting opinion, arguing that the retaliation for complaining is closely associated to the core prohibition of the status-based discrimination.

In it, the retaliation provision of Title VII has been interpreted to focus on whether the employer's conduct, even if it falls short of a termination or tangible act, would deter the reasonable person from engaging in protected

---

[113] Crawford v. Metropolitan Government of Nashville, 555 U.S. 271 (2009).

[114] Thompson v. North American Stainless, LP, 562 U.S. 170 (2011).

[115] 135 S. Ct. 2517 (2013).

[116] Nasser v. Univ. of Tex. Sw. Med. Ctr., 674 F.3d. 448 (5th Cir. 2012).

activity.[117] Although the EEOC's interpretation of Title VII does not have the force of law, it is considered persuasive evidence of congressional intent. The manual explains that "[t]here is no requirement that the adverse action materially affect the terms, conditions, or privileges of employment."[118]

The question of how much harm the employee must have experienced as a result of an employer's retaliatory action was addressed in *Stavropoulos v. Firestone*,[119] in which the Eleventh Circuit, in considering a First Amendment claim, emphasized that the retaliatory action "must involve an important condition of employment."[120] In that case, the plaintiff alleged she suffered emotional distress when University of Georgia officials sent her negative memos, including a mental illness memo, and encouraged faculty members with negative comments about the plaintiff to come forward. Relying on Title VII case precedent, the federal appeals court concluded that the alleged harm was too insubstantial because other agents of the university eventually overrode the decision.

On the other hand, what constitutes an adverse employment action that rises to the level of retaliation under Title VII may include actions that fall short of termination. In *Mota v. University of Texas Houston Health Science*,[121] the university argued, first, that a professor who alleged same-sex harassment did not demonstrate the existence of an adverse employment action. The United States Court of Appeals for the Fifth Circuit disagreed, however, stating that in finding that the university had retaliated against the professor, the jury implicitly found that an adverse employment action had been taken. A rational jury, according to the court, could have concluded both that no tangible employment action resulted from the sexual harassment and that the university subsequently retaliated against the professor for filing a complaint concerning the harassment. In this case, the professor did not lose any job benefits when he refused to comply with requests for sexual favors from his department chair, but he was subjected to unfavorable assignments, denied a paid leave, stripped of a stipend he regularly received, removed as the principal investigator on certain grants, and subjected to ridicule when he filed an internal complaint about the harassment.

The university argued that many of the actions asserted by the professor did not rise to the level of "adverse employment actions." The professor proffered eleven separate examples of events that he contended were causally linked to the filing of his complaints with the university. Although the court of appeals found that some of them did not qualify as "ultimate employment decisions," it concluded that at least four of the actions allegedly taken by the university

---

[117] U.S. Equal Employment Opportunity Comm'n, No. 915.003 Compliance Manual 8-II(D)(3) (1998), available at http://www.eeoc.gov/docs/retal.pdf

[118] *Id.* 8, at IV.

[119] 361 F.3d 610 (11th Cir. 2004).

[120] *Id.* at 619.

[121] 261 F.3d 512 (5th Cir. 2001).

met this definition, giving particular attention to the denial of paid leave and the loss of a stipend he regularly received.[122]

In *Russell v. Board of Trustees of University of Illinois*,[123] the plaintiff alleged that the university hospital in which she worked suspended her for five days in retaliation for her complaints about her supervisor and his treatment of female staff members. She brought the complaints against her supervisor after he initiated a disciplinary proceeding against her for inaccurately completing timecards. The plaintiff, in a disciplinary meeting, was subsequently found to have violated hospital policy and was suspended without pay for five days. She appealed the suspension, arguing that the decision to discipline her was tantamount to sexual harassment in retaliation for her complaints about her supervisor and his treatment of female staff members.

The federal appeals court reasoned that in order to establish a prima facie case of retaliation under Title VII, the plaintiff must present sufficient evidence that she engaged in statutorily protected activity, that she suffered an adverse employment action, and there exists a causal link between the protected expression and the adverse employment action. Although the appeals court found that a five-day suspension was a sufficiently adverse employment decision to invoke Title VII's retaliation standards, the court found no evidence of a causal link between the punishment and the protected activity. The court affirmed a finding that there was no evidence the members of the institution's disciplinary committee had any reason to believe that the supervisor triggered the disciplinary proceedings for reasons turning on retaliation, nor was there any record that they were aware of the plaintiff's complaint. Thus, the appellate court ruled in favor of the university, concluding that it could not be liable under a theory of retaliation because the plaintiff failed to meet the third prong of a prima facie proof, presentation of evidence of a causal link between the employee's actions and the adverse employment action.

In *Rubinstein v. Administrators of the Tulane Educational Fund*,[124] the Fifth Circuit Court of Appeals affirmed a district court's determination that the evidence of retaliation for filing a discrimination claim was sufficient to overcome a summary judgment claim for the denial of a pay raise. The associate professor's testimony that his dean had advised him that filing a discrimination claim was not a step a "good colleague" would take was corroborated in part by the testimony of the dean, who, although he attempted to distance himself from the meaning of the comment, admitted that he had urged the associate not to bring suit. In the view of the appeals court, this evidence was sufficient to allow a jury to conclude that the institution illegally retaliated against the associate professor.

Similarly, in *Abramson v. William Paterson College of New Jersey*,[125] a federal appeals court found that a professor's complaints of religious discrimi-

---

[122] *Id.* at 522-523.
[123] 243 F.3d 336 (7th Cir. 2001).
[124] 218 F.3d 392 (5th Cir. 2000).
[125] 260 F.3d 265 (3d Cir 2001).

nation and harassment to the college, formal or informal, oral and written, were sufficient to satisfy the first prong of the prima facie case for retaliation. Further, the professor's termination constituted an obvious adverse employment action. In light of the timing of her termination and the demonstration of ongoing administrative antagonism that established a causal nexus between the adverse employment action and the protected activity, the court of appeals concluded there was ample evidence from which a reasonable jury could draw inferences establishing a prima facie case for retaliation. In *Crawford v. Nashville*,[126] the Supreme Court reversed district and circuit court decisions and held that the protection of the antiretaliation provision extends to an employee who simply reports discrimination as part of an employer's internal investigation, even when that action is not taken on her own initiative and is, rather, the result of an investigation of complaints made by others. In this case, a school district was investigating rumors of sexual harassment by its employee relations director. As part of the investigation, the plaintiff was asked if she witnessed any inappropriate behavior.[127] She provided details in the affirmative. Shortly following the conclusion of the investigation, she and two other employees were terminated. The district court granted summary judgment for the school district, holding that the opposition clause of Title VII could not be satisfied because she had not initiated the complaint, and the Sixth Circuit Court of Appeals affirmed the decision. Noting that "nothing in the statute requires a freakish rule protecting an employee who reports discrimination on her own initiative but not one who reports the same discrimination in the same words when her boss asks a question,"[128] the Supreme Court ruled that an employee need not initiate a complaint or report of discrimination in order to receive protection under the opposition clause of Title VII. However, in *Mato v. Baldauf*,[129] the Fifth Circuit rejected a claim based on an employee's assertion that her termination in the course of a reorganization was based on her protected activity. The protected activity that the plaintiff alleged involved encouraging and assisting other women to file sexual harassment complaints. The court noted that approximately a year and a half passed between the last sexual harassment complaint and the plaintiff's termination, a time period that did not support an inference of retaliation. Moreover, she failed to present any evidence that the director who initiated the reorganization even knew that she had aided female coworkers in filing sexual harassment claims, all five incidents of which took place before the director began working for institution. The plaintiff contended that the institution's decision to require a Ph.D. for the curator's position, and the consequential termination of her employment in the reorganization, was the act of retaliation. However, the appellate court found that the plaintiff failed to present sufficient evidence that would allow a jury to conclude that the reorganization decision was a pretext to retaliate against her.

[126] 555 U.S. 271 (2009).
[127] *Id.*
[128] *Id.* at 278.
[129] 267 F.3d 444 (5th Cir. 2001).

The court stated that the first step was to determine whether the director acted independently in deciding that the new curator would be required to hold the Ph.D. degree, or whether he was prevailed upon by others in the organization who were motivated by a retaliatory animus to create this requirement as a pretext for terminating the plaintiff's employment. The court ruled that the plaintiff produced no evidence which would allow a jury to conclude that a retaliatory animus was the impetus for this action.

The Supreme Court once again expanded the scope of retaliation claims in *Thompson v. North American Stainless, LP*,[130] with its unanimous decision to afford protection to those employees who have not engaged in protected activity themselves but who claim to have been retaliated against for the protected activity of another. In it, a female employee filed a sex discrimination complaint against her employer with the EEOC. Her fiancé, Thompson, who also worked for the same employer, was subsequently terminated; he claimed that his termination was in violation of Title VII, as it was in retaliation for her filed charges. As stated by the Court, such third-party retaliation claims are limited to those who fall "within the zone of interests sought to be protected by Title VII."[131]

Although it is difficult to establish specific guidelines for which relationships would be protected in a third-party situation, it is reasonable to infer that termination of a close relative of an employee engaging in a protected activity will almost always rise to the level of unlawful retaliation under Title VII. In its reasoning, the Court relied on its prior holding in *Burlington Northern & Santa Fe Railway Co. v. White*,[132] in that "Title VII's anti-retaliation provision must be construed to cover a broad range of employer conduct"[133] and that "the anti-retaliation provision, unlike the substantive provision, is not limited to discriminatory actions that affect the terms and conditions of employment,"[134] but rather prohibits action that "well might have dissuaded a reasonable worker from making or supporting a charge of discrimination."[135] In the immediate case, Thompson's termination rose to the level of unlawful retaliation, as a reasonable employee might well have been dissuaded from engaging in the protected activity of filing the discrimination charge if she were aware that her fiancé would risk termination. Ultimately, the Court reiterated its *Burlington* reasoning that "the significance of any given act of retaliation will often depend upon the particular circumstances."[136]

---

[130] 562 U.S. 1041 (2011).

[131] *Id.*

[132] 548 U.S. 53 (2006).

[133] *Id.*

[134] *Id.* at 64.

[135] *Id.* at 68.

[136] *Id.* at 69. Although the *Thompson* decision creates some uncertainty, as the Court declines to provide a precise list of relationships that fall within the "zone of interests," an employer's best course of action to minimize potential impact remains consistent application of well-vetted policies and procedures, and detailed documentation related to adverse employment decisions.

Reverse Discrimination/Affirmative Action

The passage of Title VII as part of the Civil Rights Act of 1964 would suggest that it was primarily intended to protect minorities and women from discrimination in the workplace. However, the provisions of the law have also been characterized as applying to all races, religious groups, and people of both genders. In 1976, the United States Supreme Court addressed a case of reverse discrimination in which it concluded that Title VII "was intended to cover white men and women and all Americans."[137] The Court applied Title VII to a case in which two white workers had been fired by their employer for stealing, but a third employee caught stealing, who was black, was not fired. When the two white workers brought suit, the Court stated that Title VII's "terms are not limited to discrimination against members of any particular race."[138] This concept is supported in the 2009 Supreme Court decision in *Ricci v. DeStefano*,[139] discussed in detail later in this chapter.

However, the Court also addressed an affirmative action plan based on a collective bargaining agreement between the United Steelworkers of America and Kaiser Aluminum & Chemical Corporation that seemed to undercut the "colorblind" reading of Title VII. In *United Steelworkers of America v. Weber*,[140] the Court examined a bargaining agreement that called for company training programs in an effort to promote more black workers, and earmarked a percentage of available slots in the training programs for these employees. The plaintiff in this case was a white worker who was denied a place in the training program, despite the fact that he was a more senior employee than any of the black employees selected. In deciding *Weber*, a majority of the Supreme Court rejected the view that the private company's affirmative action program negotiated with a union violated Title VII's prohibitions against racial discrimination in employment. The majority reasoned that Congress did not intend to condemn all private, voluntary, race-conscious affirmative action plans, and the affirmative action plan under consideration, which was designed to eliminate traditional patterns of conspicuous racial segregation, was permissible under Title VII. The Court's decision was influenced in part by the fact that the affirmative action plan did not require the discharge of white workers, its replacement with new black hirees did not create an absolute bar to the advancement of white employees, and the plan was a temporary measure not intended to maintain racial balance but simply to eliminate a manifest racial imbalance.[141]

As these differing opinions would suggest, the application of Title VII has not been easily adapted to claims of reverse discrimination. Claims in which a white male seeks redress under Title VII have resulted in agreement that

---

[137] McDonald v. Sante Fe Trail Transp. Co., 427 U.S. 273, 280 (1976).
[138] *Id.* at 276.
[139] 557 U.S. 557 (2009).
[140] 443 U.S. 193 (1979).
[141] *Id.* at 205-206.

the reverse discrimination plaintiff may establish a claim under the "direct evidence" standard. Lower courts, however, have not uniformly adopted a similar approach in instances where the reverse discrimination plaintiff has asserted disparate treatment based on circumstantial evidence. Direct evidence of discrimination could be shown by the employer's admissions of a discriminatory intent, but the likelihood of such an admission against interest seems remote in the more sophisticated academic setting in which subjective hiring and promotion decisions would veil direct evidence of discrimination.

When whites or men are the "minorities" in the institution in which they work, the shifting burden of proof in disparate treatment tends to work in the same way as it would in a traditional *McDonnell Douglas* context. In these cases, a majority plaintiff may show "intentionally disparate treatment when background circumstances support the suspicion that the defendant is that unusual employer who discriminates against the majority."[142] In an illustrative case, a white female professor of home economics at a historically black college established a prima facie case of racial discrimination under Title VII. The faculty member, who was in a racial minority at an institution where blacks outnumbered whites approximately two-to-one, both on the faculty and in the student body, claimed constructive discharge in that her decision not to continue at the institution was predicated on the hostility of her superiors. Although the institution insisted that nonrenewal would have been justified based upon charges of incompetence and lack of rapport with students, the faculty member presented compelling evidence that her superior had rejected claims of academic deficiencies and that department faculty had engaged in a systematic campaign to remove her from the department. This evidence included instigating student unrest and coercing students to sign a petition opposing the white professor's continued employment. When these findings were combined with evidence of the hiring of an African American faculty member to replace the white professor, the federal appeals court affirmed a lower court decision that because of her race, the white professor's failings were treated more harshly than similar failings in a black teacher would have been, and that her contract would have been renewed but for the fact that she was white.[143]

When background circumstances confirm that a white employee is suing a predominately white higher education institution under Title VII, different proof would appear to be required. Clearly, the plaintiff is unlikely to establish that the institution typically discriminates against the majority. Initially, the reverse discrimination plaintiff must establish a prima facie case, including a showing that the plaintiff is a member of a protected class under Title VII. Even if this hurdle is overcome, the *McDonnell Douglas* shifting burden of proof has emphasized that an institution of higher education need only meet a burden of production, insofar as the employer must articulate a legitimate, nondiscriminatory reason for its employment decision. The plaintiff-employee, however, must meet a burden of persuasion in which the ultimate burden is to

---

[142] Parker v. Baltimore & Ohio Railroad Co., 652 F.2d 1012, 1017 (D.C. Cir. 1981).
[143] Lincoln v. Bd. of Regents, 697 F.2d 928 (11th Cir. 1983).

persuade the court that the challenged decision was the result of discriminatory motivation.

In some cases, the minority or female plaintiff's proof that the articulated reason put into evidence by the institution was not the true reason is sufficient for the fact-finder to draw the inference that the true reason involved a discriminatory purpose. This inference is plausible because the institution's failure to put into evidence a credible nondiscriminatory reason may suggest that the real reason is discrimination, given the history of societal prejudice against minorities and women. However, when a white male plaintiff challenges an employment decision against a predominantly white higher education institution, it is more difficult to draw the inference that the employer acted because of discrimination against white males, even where a legitimate reason for the adverse employment decision has been negated. For example, a male assistant professor sued when he was denied tenure for failure to publish sufficiently, alleging that women were held to a lesser standard. The jury agreed and found a violation of Title VII, and the predominately white university appealed. On the issue of direct discrimination, the appellate court held that statements by the interim dean, that females and males were judged on different standards, was not probative evidence that the tenure decision was motivated by gender. In addition, the court concluded that the plaintiff did not establish either that he was qualified for tenure or that he was denied tenure in circumstances permitting an inference of discrimination. Because the evidence, in the view of the appeals court, did not support the jury's findings, the case was reversed and remanded.[144]

Many reverse discrimination cases arise in the context of institutionally adopted affirmative action plans designed to increase the representation of minorities and women in the workforce, or to correct alleged inequities in pay and promotion. When these plans are challenged under Title VII, the majority plaintiff can meet the prima facie burden to show unequal treatment, since the institution's plan consciously uses race or gender to advance the employment opportunities of minorities and women. However, if the institution's plan is valid, the institution can advance a legitimate reason for the use of race or sex in employment decisions. This rationale requires a reverse discrimination plaintiff to show that the institution's plan discriminates against the plaintiff and that the plan itself is invalid. In many of these cases, the plaintiff will challenge the plan on both equal protection and Title VII grounds. The United States Supreme Court has applied a standard of strict scrutiny to recent cases

---

[144] Krystek v. Univ. of S. Mississippi, 164 F. 3d 251 (5th Cir 1999).

in which a public employer has adopted an affirmative action plan favoring minorities.[145]

Reverse discrimination cases in higher education suggest that federal courts may be predisposed to recognize instances of reverse discrimination in affirmative action plans. In 1980 and 1989, as part of a settlement for gender-based discrimination claims, the University of Minnesota entered into consent decrees. The 1989 decree required female faculty members to take part in the distribution of $3 million. A male professor argued that the provisions of the consent decree discriminated against him because of his sex and sought damages by filing a Title VII and equal protection claim. The case was complicated, because the plan in question was implemented pursuant to a consent decree and was not a voluntary affirmative action plan. However, it was established that the plan mandated by the consent decree was not imposed after a judicial finding of intentional discrimination on the part of the university. After considering three statistical models measuring the differences in salaries between females and males, the district court granted summary judgment to the university on the male professor's claims. However, the appellate court reversed the summary judgment. The male professor met his burden to demonstrate that there was a genuine issue of material fact on the question of whether the variety of statistical models established a manifest or conspicuous imbalance in faculty salaries based on gender. Although this ruling left unanswered the question of whether the salary plan unreasonably discriminated against the male faculty member, the ruling established that the white professor was entitled to pursue his Title VII discrimination claim.[146]

In *Hill v. Ross*,[147] a college dean raised objections to the appointment of a male candidate for a faculty position, insisting that the department fill the position with a female. The dean had imposed hiring goals on the department that included increasing the number of women and minority faculty. He stipulated in e-mail communications that he was unwilling to send male candidates forward, and he ultimately refused to forward the name of the male candidate selected by the faculty. The university defended its decision to leave the position vacant, rather than hire the professor, on the basis that the dean's decision was made pursuant to a valid affirmative action plan.

The Seventh Circuit Court of Appeals reversed a district court's grant of summary judgment, noting three factors in the record that suggested a possible violation of Title VII. First, the appeals court was persuaded that a jury might reasonably conclude that the dean of the college used sex as the sole criterion for his decision not to recommend hiring the male applicant. Reasoning that

---

[145] *See* Adarand Constructors v. Pena, 515 U.S. 200 (1995) in which the Court held that all racial classifications developed as part of an affirmative action plan by any government —state, local or federal—are to be strictly scrutinized, and Richmond v. J.A. Croson, 488 U.S. 469 (1989), in which the Court applied strict scrutiny under the Fourteenth Amendment's Equal Protection Clause to a city's affirmative action program requiring a 30% set-aside for minority subcontractors.

[146] Maitland v. Univ. of Minnesota, 155 F.3d 1013, 1019 (8th Cir. 1998).

[147] 183 F.3d 586 (7th Cir. 1999).

the dean's imposition of hiring goals involving minorities and women might have exceeded the permissible application of an affirmative action plan, the court noted that the university did not contend its affirmative action plan, which was essential to the eradication of the consequences of past discrimination, either in the academic department or elsewhere in the institution. Second, the existing affirmative action plan at the institution did not require that the dean insist upon the hiring of a female candidate. Finally, the court emphasized that the plaintiff carried the burden to show that reliance on the affirmative action plan might be pretextual. By presenting evidence that the express terms of the affirmative action plan did not support the dean's decision to block the appointment, coupled with the university's admission that it had not engaged in past discrimination, the plaintiff effectively shifted the burden to the institution to come forth with a justification for the use of sex in the hiring decision. Since neither the university's plan nor its brief addressed that justification, it was compelled to offer an "exceedingly persuasive justification." The plaintiff then could have borne the burden of overcoming it.

In deciding *Ricci v. DeStefano*,[148] the Supreme Court set a new rule of law on when an employer can intentionally discriminate to avoid a lawsuit. In *Ricci*, a test was given by the city to determine which firefighters would advance to vacant lieutenant and captain positions. Upon receipt of the results, it was discovered that the white candidates had outperformed the minority candidates, and the city discarded the results to avoid a potential lawsuit due to the disparate impact of the test on minority candidates. As a result, the white and Hispanic firefighters who passed the test sued in federal court, alleging racial discrimination. The trial court ruled for the city, reasoning that if the city had gone through with certifying the test results, it may have been liable under Title VII for adopting a practice resulting in disparate impact on the minority firefighters, and the appeals court affirmed. However, a five-person majority of the Supreme Court reversed, remanded, and ultimately held that the city had improperly discarded employment test results on which minority candidates had underperformed disproportionately.

As Title VII not only prohibits intentional acts of discrimination but also policies and practices not intended to be discriminatory that nevertheless disproportionately impact a protected group, the Supreme Court recognized that the City found itself in an untenable situation. It essentially was faced with a choice to impose disparate impact on the minority firefighters, or effect disparate treatment on the firefighters who would have been eligible for promotion given the results of the test. The Court, therefore, was presented with considering whether intentional action to avoid disparate impact liability for one group under Title VII outweighs the possibility of that action resulting in disparate treatment discrimination for another.

The Court determined that the disparate treatment would only be justified if there were a "strong basis in evidence" that test certification would have

---

[148] 557 U.S. 557 (2009).

created liability for disparate impact. Because the court reasoned that the City undertook significant care in developing the test, and thus could have shown it to be "job related" and consistent with "business necessity," it held that there was not enough evidence to support the theory that the city would have faced liability if it had certified the test results.[149] Further, the Court argued that an equally valid, less discriminatory alternative could not have been identified by the minority candidates. In ordering the city to reinstate the test results, the Court warned that "fear of litigation alone cannot justify an employer's reliance on race to the detriment of individuals who passed the examinations and qualified for promotions."[150]

Filing a Complaint with the Equal Employment Opportunity Commission (EEOC)

An individual who has experienced discrimination based on the various protected classes mentioned above may file a complaint with the Equal Employment Opportunity Commission (EEOC), which enforces Title VII. The EEOC may receive, investigate, and resolve complaints of unlawful employment discrimination, and it may also initiate lawsuits against violators or issue right-to-sue letters to complainants. Employees have two possible causes of action, disparate impact or disparate treatment. Disparate treatment is more common in postsecondary education. This manifests when an individual is denied a job, promotion, or tenure or claims to be treated less favorably than their colleagues because of their race, sex, national origin, or religion, and is subjected to a detrimental working condition. All employment discrimination laws that are enforced by the EEOC, except for the Equal Pay Act, require complaints to be filed with the EEOC before civil lawsuits may be commenced against the alleged discriminator. It is critical to note that a complainant has to file a complaint with the EEOC within 180 days of the incident.

While complaints can be filed with the EEOC, Carbado and Gulati argued there are three problems with antidiscrimination law in proving discrimination in the workplace.[151] First, courts do not give credence to applicants who are members of marginalized populations and how their positionality subjects them to stereotypes and misconceptions regardless of the applicant's credentials. Because evidence, direct or circumstantial, is expected to support claims of discrimination, it is challenging to establish fault with an individual or the organization, especially because institutions will rely on their nondiscriminatory policies.

Secondly, when producing evidence to support the claim, institutions of higher education have established policies and programs that portray a persona of being inclusive and nondiscriminating environments. Since an applicant will

---

[149] *Id.* at 559.

[150] *Id.* at 592.

[151] *See generally* Carbado & Gulati, *supra* note 17.

only have limited interactions with the institution during the interview process, it may be difficult to show how a person was not hired unless someone says or does something that is deemed discriminatory.

The third and final question that must be answered for all discriminatory claims is: "Was there intentional discrimination based on the plaintiff's membership in a protected class, such as race, gender, or disability?" So long as an employer can show nondiscriminatory reasons, this is difficult to prove. If there is evidence that hiring officials said or did something discriminatory, "fit" will be couched in nondiscriminatory language despite the candidate knowing what they experienced. Plaintiffs in most cases have to rely on circumstantial evidence of intentional discrimination, and evidence would need to illustrate the alleged discrimination similarly to the assertion made by the applicant.

Re-examining Plaintiff's Burden

In *Desert Palace, Inc. v. Costa,*[152] a unanimous United States Supreme Court concluded that the 1991 amendments to Title VII allow a plaintiff to advance a mixed- motive discrimination claim against an employer. The essence of a mixed-motive claim is that the plaintiff alleges the employer's adverse employment action is predicated on both legitimate and illegitimate motives. The decision contradicts the generally accepted presumption associated with *Price Waterhouse v. Hopkins*[153] that precludes a finding of mixed-motive discrimination if the employer could prove it would have made the same employment decision with regard to the employee in the absence of discrimination. The essence of the *Costa* decision is that a plaintiff could prevail on a Title VII claim by showing, through a preponderance of direct or circumstantial evidence, that a discriminatory purpose was a motivating factor in the challenged employment decision.

In *Costa*, the Supreme Court held that the changes in Title VII make no mention of a heightened direct-evidence requirement for a plaintiff.[154] The Court read the statute to require that a plaintiff "demonstrate that an employer used a forbidden consideration with respect to any employment practice."[155] The Court noted, "[I]n order to obtain an instruction under § 2000e-2(m), a plaintiff need only present sufficient evidence for a reasonable jury to conclude, by a preponderance of the evidence, that race, color, religion, sex, or national origin was a motivating factor for any employment practice."[156] The requirement for "sufficient evidence" does not contemplate the necessity for "direct evidence" and would permit a plaintiff in a Title VII action to prove discrimination on the basis of circumstantial evidence. By allowing plaintiffs to proceed with a Title VII mixed-motive discrimination claim solely on the

---

[152] 539 U.S. 90 (2003).
[153] 490 U.S. 228 (1989).
[154] *Id.* at 2153.
[155] *Id.* (quoting 42 U.S.C. § 2000e-2(m) (2002)).
[156] *Id.* at 2154-55.

basis of circumstantial evidence, the Court's decision in *Costa* may make it easier for plaintiffs to succeed against employers in some cases.

While this decision appears to compromise *Price Waterhouse, Costa* does not modify the shifting burden of proof in *McDonnell Douglas*. The decision does not change the plaintiff's ultimate burden of persuading the fact-finder that he or she was a victim of intentional discrimination. However, the plaintiff may now succeed in this proof either directly, by persuading the fact-finder that a discriminatory reason more likely motivated the employer, or indirectly, by showing that the employer's proffered explanation is unworthy of credence.[157] Whether *Costa* will be interpreted by lower courts to reduce the plaintiff's ultimate burden of persuasion in Title VII cases has yet to be determined, but lower federal courts will be tasked to make that determination on a case-by-case basis.

In one such decision, *Rachid v. Jack in the Box, Inc.*,[158] the Fifth Circuit Court of Appeals applied a new analysis that leaves the initial stages of *McDonnell Douglas* intact. In this modified or merged proof structure, the plaintiff must establish a prima facie case, and the defendant must articulate a legitimate, nondiscriminatory reason for the adverse employment action. The Fifth Circuit then proposed that a plaintiff must produce sufficient evidence to create a genuine issue of material fact either that the defendant's articulated reason was a pretext for discrimination (a pretext alternative), or that the defendant's reason is true but another motivating factor for the decision was discrimination based on a protected characteristic (a mixed-motives alternative).[159]

Conclusion

Title VII remains the principal vehicle for pursuing claims of employment discrimination involving race, religion, national origin, and gender. Particularly in cases involving disparate treatment, the shifting burden of proof applicable to Title VII claims has been adopted as the appropriate standard when pursuing claims under the provisions of other federal and state antidiscrimination laws. However, federal and state courts will continue to refine the shifting burden in response to case-by-case analyses and legislative modifications of Title VII.

Two emergent issues will occupy federal courts in the immediate future. First, judges will be compelled to determine the extent to which claims of reverse discrimination will be actionable when brought against predominantly white institutions. It should be anticipated that challenges to affirmative action hiring and promotion plans will be among the challenges brought by white males under the auspices of both Title VII and the Fourteenth Amendment's Equal Protection Clause. In a larger sense, courts must ultimately assess whether differing standards in reverse discrimination suits are constitutional under the Fourteenth Amendment. Second, the shifting burden of proof as

---

[157] Tex. Dept. of Cmty. Affairs v. Burdine, 450 U.S. 248, 256 (1981).

[158] 376 F.3d 305 (5th Cir. 2004).

[159] *Id.* at 312.

established in *McDonnell Douglas* seems destined for revision in light of new Supreme Court decisions interpreting legislative changes to federal antidiscrimination law.

Discussion Questions

1. Title VII covers what kinds of employment discrimination?

2. What kinds of discrimination claims may employees assert against their employer?

3. How may employees assert claims against their employer for sexual orientation discrimination? How about gender identity or transgendered status discrimination? Do the laws apply the same everywhere nationally?

4. What are some of the arguments raised in cases alleging reverse discrimination?

5. Besides Title VII of the Civil Rights Act of 1964, list five other federal statutes that aim to curtail employment discrimination.

8 Sexual Harassment

Suzanne E. Eckes, J.D., Ph.D.
Indiana University

Martha M. McCarthy, Ph.D.
Loyola Marymount University

Introduction

In 2019, the U.S. Department of Education accused Michigan State University of displaying "a lack of institutional control" and asserted that university officials violated campus safety laws by how they handled the Larry Nassar scandal.[1] To be certain, ongoing controversies have increased national attention on sexual harassment and, as a result, universities are revisiting their policies and procedures. Institutions of higher education have an obligation to adopt policies to prohibit sex discrimination and to provide reporting procedures for students and employees who have been harassed on campus. For example, Stanford University's website states: "Stanford University strives to provide a place of work and study free of sexual harassment, intimidation or exploitation."[2] Like most university websites, Stanford's includes explicit policies related to preventing and responding to sexual harassment. Also illustrative is Northwestern University, which "prohibits all forms of sexual misconduct, including but not limited to, sexual assault, sexual exploitation, stalking, dating or domestic violence, and sexual harassment."[3]

From a legal perspective, sexual harassment is considered unwelcome sexual conduct or expression that interferes with an employee's ability to perform his or her job or with a student's ability to benefit from the educational program.[4] Only a small proportion of college students *report* episodes

---

[1] Kate Wells, *Michigan State Faulted for Handling of Sexual Abuse Cases*, NAT'L PUB. RADIO (Jan. 31, 2019), *available at* https://www.npr.org/2019/01/31/690230705/michigan-state-faulted-for-handling-of-sexual-abuse-cases. Michigan State was fined $4.5 million by the U.S. Dep't of Education in 2019. *See* Colin Dwyer, Michigan State University to Pay $4.5 Million Fine Over Larry Nassar Scandal (Sept. 5, 2019), *available at* https://www.npr.org/2019/09/05/757909245/michigan-state-university-to-pay-4-5-million-fine-over-larry-nassar-scandal.

[2] Sexual Harassment Policy Office, *Stanford Administrative Guide* (Aug. 2, 2016), *available at* https://adminguide.stanford.edu/chapter-1/subchapter-7/policy-1-7-1.

[3] Northwestern Univ., *Comprehensive Policy on Sexual Misconduct* (Sept. 10, 2018), *available at* file:///C:/Users/seckes/Downloads/Northwestern%20Policy.pdf.

[4] *See* U.S. DEPT. OF EDUC., OFFICE FOR CIVIL RIGHTS, SEXUAL HARASSMENT: IT'S NOT ACADEMIC (2008), *available at* http://www2.ed.gov/about/offices/list/ocr/docs/ocrshpam.html#_t1a.

of sexual harassment, but many have *experienced* it.[5] Women on campus are disproportionately affected.[6] Although it is difficult to track the data because many sexual assaults go unreported, it is estimated that one in five women will be a victim of sexual assault while in college.[7] Another report from the Campus Accountability Project similarly highlights the high number of incidents of sexual harassment and assault on campuses.[8]

After explaining some of the recent issues, particularly related to federal oversight and guidance regarding allegations of sexual harassment and sexual assault, this chapter examines the legal context in higher education. Given the amount of litigation in the higher education context, this chapter examines a number of illustrative cases and developments related to student and employee harassment. This chapter concludes with guidance for university personnel whose responsibility it is to adopt appropriate institutional policies and procedures that are focused on curtailing sexual harassment and sexual assault across university campuses.

Recent Issues

Given the prevalence of sexual harassment at colleges and universities, the U.S. Department of Education issued a *Dear Colleague Letter* in 2011.[9] This letter discussed federal legal requirements pertaining to student-on-student sexual harassment, including sexual violence. The letter also explained institutions' responsibilities "to take immediate and effective steps to end sexual harassment and violence."[10] Also, the Office for Civil Rights (OCR) in 2014 released a document responding to more than fifty questions about requirements under Title IX of the Education Amendments of 1972 to assist institutions in reducing sexual violence and remedying the effects of such violence on

---

[5] *See* Nancy Chi Cantalupo, *Burying Our Heads in the Sand: Lack of Knowledge, Knowledge Avoidance, and the Persistent Problem of Campus Peer Sexual Violence*, 43 LOY. U. CHI. L.J. 205, 205 (2011) (identifying high rates of non-reporting of sexual violence at colleges and universities).

[6] Amer. Assoc. Univ. Women, *Know your Rights: Sexual Harassment & Sexual Assault Under Title IX, available at* https://www.aauw.org/what-we-do/legal-resources/know-your-rights-on-campus/campus-sexual-assault/.

[7] Lee Winerman,, *Making Campuses Safer*, AMER. PSCYH. ASSOC. (Oct. 2018), *available at* https://www.apa.org/monitor/2018/10/campuses-safer.

[8] CAMPUS ACCOUNTABILITY PROJECT, MAKING THE GRADE? FINDINGS FROM THE CAMPUS ACCOUNTABILITY PROJECT ON SEXUAL ASSAULT POLICIES (2013), *available at* http://www.safercampus.org/blog/wp-content/uploads/2013/10/2013-Campus-Accountability-Project-Full-Report.pdf; *see also*, Mark Keierleber, Overshadowed by the College Sexual Assault Debate, 154 Open Title IX Investigations at K-12 Schools, THE 74 (Aug. 9, 2017), *available at* https://www.the74million.org/article/forgotten-in-the-devos-debate-over-campus-sex-assaults-the-154-pending-k-12-investigations/ (noting that the Office for Civil Rights has 350 open investigations at the university level).

[9] U.S. DEP'T OF EDUC, DEAR COLLEAGUE LETTER (2011, Apr. 4), *available at* http://www2.ed.gov/about/offices/list/ocr/letters/colleague-201104.html.

[10] *Id.* at 2.

campus.[11] This document specified that Title IX prohibits violence based on sexual orientation or gender identity, and it placed more emphasis on services for victims than prior documents had done. The 2011 *Dear Colleague Letter* and the 2014 OCR *Questions and Answers on Title IX and Sexual Violence* were considered "significant guidance documents,"[12] and they were being used nationally to assist colleges and universities in understanding their harassment-related obligations. Also, the *White House Task Force to Protect Students from Sexual Assault* issued its 2014 report declaring that colleges and universities must take action to curb violence against women.[13]

In 2017, the U.S. Department of Education, under the Trump administration, rescinded the 2011 and 2014 sexual assault guidance, and there is new interim guidance in place.[14] In 2018, the Department proposed new regulations to Title IX that change many of the above requirements, including the definition of sexual harassment.[15] The interim guidance is in effect until the regulations are enacted.[16] If they become law, many universities would need to handle allegations of sexual harassment in a different way. The draft regulations, for example, propose that complainants face cross-examination during campus hearings, and institutions may be able to limit the scope of what constitutes sexual harassment. Other changes include giving universities the option of using the "clear and convincing" standard of evidence instead of the lower "preponderance of the evidence" standard.[17] The proposed regulations attempt to bolster the rights of the accused. Assuming these changes and others become law, campuses will need to adjust accordingly.

---

[11] Catherine E. Lhamon, QUESTIONS AND ANSWERS ON TITLE IX AND SEXUAL VIOLENCE, U.S. Dept of Educ., Washington, DC (Apr. 28, 2014); *see also* NASPA, *NASPA and ELA React to OCR Guidance on Title IX: A First Take,* NASPA (Apr. 30, 2014), *available at* http://www.naspa.org/rpi/posts/naspa-and-ela-react-to-ocr-guidance-on-title-ix-a-first-take.

[12] The Department of Education has designated both to be "significant guidance documents" according to the Office of Management and Budget, 72 Fed. Reg. 3432.

[13] White House Task Force, WHITE HOUSE TASK FORCE TO PROTECT STUDENTS FROM SEXUAL ASSAULT (APR. 2014), *available at* http://apps.washingtonpost.com/g/documents/local/white-house-report-on-campus-sex-assault/960/

[14] Nat'l Assoc. of Indep. College & Universities, *Sexual Assault on Campus* (n.d.), *available at* https://www.naicu.edu/policy-advocacy/issue-brief-index/regulation/sexual-assault-on-campus.

[15] Laura Mecler, Betsy DeVos Releases Sexual Assault Rules She Hails as Balancing Rights of Victims, Accused, WASH. POST (Nov. 16, 2018), *available at* https://www.washingtonpost.com/local/education/betsy-devos-releases-sexual-assault-rules-she-hails-as-balancing-rights-of-victims-accused/2018/11/16/4aa136d4-e962-11e8-a939-9469f1166f9d_story.html?utm_term=.5ff72a616afb.

[16] *Nondiscrimination on the Basis of Sex in Education Programs or Activities Receiving Federal Financial Assistance*, 34 C.F.R. 106 (2018).

[17] Caroline Kitchener & Adam Harris, *A Step-by-Step Guide to Trump's New College Sexual Assault Policy*, ATLANTIC (Aug. 30, 2018), *available at* https://www.theatlantic.com/education/archive/2018/08/a-guide-to-how-the-new-rules-on-campus-; *see also*, U.S. Dep't of Educ., Press Release, *FAQs on Updated Campus Sexual Misconduct Guidance* (Sept. 22, 2017).

Legal Context

If a student on campus experiences sexual harassment or sexual violence, the student can file an internal complaint with the university, and the university can take steps to prevent any additional harassment. Some approaches that university officials may take include changing a student's class schedule to taking disciplinary action against the perpetrator. Schools should have someone who monitors compliance with the law and responds to sexual harassment or violence. This official is often known as the Title IX coordinator. If a student is unsatisfied, a complaint could be filed with the OCR. OCR complaints must generally be filed within 180 days of the incident. It is the student's choice whether or not to include law enforcement to address the matter. Students might also seek redress in courts. This section provides a framework for the subsequent discussion of sexual harassment claims initiated by employees and students in higher education. Specifically, the U.S. Supreme Court's interpretations of the central grounds to challenge sexual harassment in colleges and universities are reviewed.

Title VII of the Civil Rights Act of 1964

During the past few decades, substantial attention has focused on sexual harassment in the workplace. Most of the sexual harassment cases involving employees have been brought under Title VII of the Civil Rights Act of 1964, which bars public and private employers from discriminating against employees based on various characteristics, including sex.[18] Initially, courts recognized that individuals could get relief under Title VII for *quid pro quo* sexual harassment—repeated and unwelcome sexual advances or derogatory statements, gestures, or actions based on sex—if pay raises, promotions, or other benefits were conditioned on submission to the sexual advances.[19]

In 1986, the Supreme Court, in *Meritor Savings Bank v. Vinson*, recognized that a second type of sexual harassment is actionable under Title VII.[20] The Court held that severe and persistent harassment, such as sexual advances, abusive language, or demeaning behavior based on sex, resulting in a *hostile work environment*, could also be the basis for a successful Title VII claim. Citing the 1980 guidelines issued by the Equal Employment Opportunity Commission,[21] the Court ruled that employers could be liable for hostile environment harassment without evidence that the victims have suffered economic

---

[18] 42 U.S.C. § 2000e (2014). Title VII specifically prohibits employers with fifteen or more employees from discriminating on the basis of race, color, religion, gender, or national origin in hiring, promotion, and compensation practices including fringe benefits and other terms and conditions of employment. Title VII is enforced by the Equal Employment Opportunity Commission, and individuals can bring suits for remedies including compensatory and punitive damages.

[19] *See, e.g.,* Miller v. Bank of Am., 600 F.2d 211 (9th Cir. 1979); Barnes v. Costle, 561 F.2d 983 (D.C. Cir. 1977); Tomkins v. Public Serv. Elec. and Gas Co., 568 F.2d 1044 (3d Cir. 1977).

[20] 477 U.S. 57 (1986).

[21] 29 C.F.R. § 1604.11(a) (2014).

or other tangible losses.[22] The Court further noted that simply because the victim submits to sex-related conduct does not necessarily mean it was welcomed.[23]

Subsequently, the Court held in *Harris v. Forklift Systems* that the hostile environment does not have to cause a diagnosed psychological injury to be actionable under Title VII.[24] In this case, the Court identified factors to use in judging whether an environment is sufficiently hostile to abridge Title VII. These factors include the persistence or severity of the harassing conduct, whether it is physically threatening or humiliating, and the conduct's interference with an employee's work performance.[25] Until 1998, in order to obtain relief under Title VII, the aggrieved employee at least had to substantiate the employer's negligence by showing that the employer knew or should have been aware of the harassment (constructive notice) and failed to take corrective action.[26]

Then, in a trilogy of sexual harassment cases in 1998, the Supreme Court made it easier for victims to secure damages from their employers. In two of these cases, *Burlington Industries v. Ellerth* and *Faragher v. City of Boca Raton*, the Supreme Court held that the employer's intentional acts or negligence are not always required for liability to be assessed; under certain circumstances, the employer can be liable for sexual harassment initiated by supervisors against subordinates without any showing of negligence or fault.[27] Recognizing that the employer includes its agents, such as supervisors, for Title VII purposes, the Court concluded that the employer can be liable for a supervisor's harassment if the supervisor purports to act on behalf of the employer, relies on apparent authority, or is aided in accomplishing the harassment by the employment relationship.[28]

However, the Court held that if the employee experiences no tangible loss or change in job status, employers can avoid liability by demonstrating that they exercised reasonable care to prevent the harassment and took prompt corrective action and that the employee unreasonably failed to use the internal grievance procedures. If the victim experiences tangible loss, such as demotion or dismissal, the employer is strictly liable for the supervisor's behavior and cannot assert the defense that reasonable precautions were taken. Thus, employers who have acted appropriately are not completely vulnerable to liability for harassment initiated by their supervisors,[29] and employer liability for harassment among coworkers continues to be evaluated based on the "knew or should have known" constructive notice standard.[30]

---

[22] *See Meritor*, 477 U.S. at 69-71.

[23] *Id*. at 68.

[24] 510 U.S. 17 (1993).

[25] *Id*. at 22-23.

[26] *See, e.g., Meritor,* 477 U.S. at 70-73.

[27] Burlington Indus., Inc. v. Ellerth, 524 U.S. 742 (1998); Faragher v. City of Boca Raton, 524 U.S. 775 (1998).

[28] *See Burlington,* 524 U.S. at 742; *Faragher,* 524 U.S. at 775.

[29] *See Burlington,* 524 U.S. at 765; *Faragher*, 524 U.S. at 805-08.

[30] *See* 29 C.F.R. § 1604.11(d) (2014).

In the third Supreme Court decision rendered in 1998, *Oncale v. Sundowner Offshore Services*, the Court held that Title VII's prohibition of discrimination based on sex does not preclude a same-sex harassment claim.[31] The court further noted that while the harassment must be severe and persistent to be actionable under Title VII, it does not have to be motivated by sexual desire. As a result of *Oncale*, same-sex harassment suits can be initiated under Title VII if they meet the standards of proof applicable to sexual harassment claims generally. Taken together, these three 1998 rulings made it easier for employees to establish that they are victims of actionable sexual harassment and have made it more difficult for employers to build a defense. In 2019, the U.S. Supreme Court granted certiorari in several cases and will decide whether discrimination based on sex also includes sexual orientation and gender identity.[32]

While the terms *quid pro quo* harassment and *hostile environment* harassment are still used in Title VII cases, the difference between the two types of harassment has become less distinct. The Supreme Court in 1998 cast some doubt on continuing to use these categories, recognizing the "limited utility" of distinguishing "threats that are carried out" from "bothersome attentions" that are so persistent and severe that they create a hostile work environment.[33] The Office for Civil Rights (OCR) in the Department of Education also acknowledged in its *Sexual Harassment Guidance* that "in many cases the line between *quid pro quo* and hostile environment discrimination will be blurred."[34]

Title IX of the Education Amendments of 1972

Since Title VII remedies are confined to employment discrimination, some student harassment victims may use this provision if they are employed by their college or university in capacities such as research associates or teaching assistants. But in the absence of an employment relationship, students must find other grounds to use in challenging sexual harassment. The most commonly used provision is Title IX of the Education Amendments of 1972. Title IX specifies that "no person in the United States shall, on the basis of sex, be excluded from participation in, be denied the benefits of, or be subjected to discrimination under any education program or activity receiving federal financial assistance."[35] Student victims of sexual harassment may assert Title IX claims against education institutions by (1) suing the institution for money damages, (2) suing the institution for injunctive or declaratory relief, and (3) seeking

---

[31] 523 U.S. 75 (1998).

[32] *See* Bostock v. Clayton Cty.; 139 S.Ct. 1599 (2019); EEOC v. R.G. & G.R. Harris Funeral Homes, Inc., 884 F.3d 560 (6th Cir. 2019); Altitude Express, Inc. v. Zarda, 139 S. Ct. 1599 (2019); *see also* Adam Liptak, *Supreme Court to Decide Whether Landmark Civil Rights Law Applies to Gay and Transgender Workers*, N.Y. Times (April 22, 2019), *available at* https://www.nytimes.com/2019/04/22/us/politics/supreme-court-gay-transgender-employees.html.

[33] *Burlington*, 524 U.S. at 751.

[34] Sexual Harassment Guidance: Harassment of Students by School Employees, Other Students or Third Parties, 62 Fed. Reg. 12034, 12039 (1997, rev'd 2001).

[35] 20 U.S.C. § 1681 *et seq.* (2014).

administrative compliance by filing a complaint against the institution through an internal grievance process or with the U.S. Department of Education.[36]

Title IX covers both sexual harassment and sexual violence. It has generated a number of Supreme Court rulings interpreting congressional intent in enacting the law, and some of these rulings have, in turn, evoked congressional responses.[37] Also, questions have been raised regarding how Eleventh Amendment restrictions apply in Title IX disputes. The Eleventh Amendment provides that states are immune from suit except where Congress abrogates state immunity, states waive their own sovereign immunity, or in other limited circumstances. Congress attempted to clarify this issue by abrogating state immunity from Title IX suits in a 1986 law.[38]

In 1992, the Supreme Court delivered a significant decision, *Franklin v. Gwinnett Public Schools*, holding for the first time that students can use Title IX to seek monetary damages from school districts for sexual harassment by school personnel.[39] In this case, a female student alleged that school authorities took no action even though they were aware that a teacher/coach was harassing her, which included coercive intercourse on school grounds. The student further asserted that school personnel discouraged her from pressing charges against the teacher/coach. The unanimous Supreme Court held that Congress did not intend to restrict the remedies available to individuals for Title IX violations and, therefore, students could use Title IX to seek monetary damages for sex discrimination in the form of sexual harassment by school employees.[40] But

---

[36] William A. Kaplan, *A Typology and Critique of Title IX Sexual Harassment Law After Gebser and Davis,* 26 J.C. & U.L. 615, 636 (2000).

[37] *See* Grove City Coll. v. Bell, 465 U.S. 555 (1984) (finding Title IX program specific in that it applied only to educational programs directly receiving federal aid); North Haven Bd. of Educ. v. Bell, 456 U.S. 512 (1982) (clarifying that Title IX protects employees as well as students, since both are "beneficiaries" of educational programs); Cannon v. Univ. of Chicago, 441 U.S. 677 (1979) (recognizing a private right to bring suit under Title IX). Congress responded to the Supreme Court's misinterpretation of Title IX in *Grove City* by clarifying that this law and three other similarly worded federal laws cover entire institutions if any of their programs receive federal aid, Civil Rights Restoration Act of 1987, 20 U.S.C. § 1687 (2014).

[38] In Litman v. George Mason Univ., 186 F.3d 544, 548-57 (4th Cir. 1999), the federal appellate court discussed at length why it was an appropriate exercise of congressional power to enact the Civil Rights Remedies Equalization Act, 42 U.S.C. § 2000d-7(a)(1) (2014), amending Title IX as well as several other laws to make explicit that states are not immune under the Eleventh Amendment from suits alleging Title IX violations. The court reasoned that states and their political subdivisions know that as a consequence of accepting federal funds they must comply with Title IX's antidiscrimination provisions and must consent to federal suits to resolve disputes. *Id.* at 551-52. In addition to congressional authority to abrogate states' immunity under its powers granted by Section 5 of the Fourteenth Amendment, states can waive their immunity by consenting to be sued in federal court. For a discussion of whether Congress can attach a waiver of immunity to states' receipt of federal aid under its Article I spending powers, see Martha McCarthy, *Students as Targets and Perpetrators of Sexual Harassment: Title IX and Beyond,* 12 Hastings Women's L. J. 177, 181-82, n. 23 (2001).

[39] 503 U.S. 60 (1992).

[40] *Id.* at 70.

the Court was not precise as to the conditions that abridge Title IX, spawning a range of lower court decisions.[41]

In 1998, the Supreme Court finally clarified the Title IX standard in *Gebser v. Lago Vista Independent School District*, holding that school officials with authority to take corrective action must have actual knowledge of the harassment and be deliberately indifferent toward the victim to establish a Title IX violation.[42] The Court ruled that Title IX essentially entails a contract in that school districts promise not to discriminate based on gender in educational programs receiving federal funds. Since Title IX attaches conditions to the receipt of federal aid, the Court concluded that educational institutions must be aware of any requirements accompanying such funds. The Court further held that the school district's failure to adopt a sexual harassment policy and effective grievance procedure did not necessarily constitute a Title IX violation, even though the U.S. Department of Education guidelines for Title IX require such policies and procedures.[43]

In *Gebser*, a female student sued the school district for failing to stop her long-term sexual relationship with a teacher. The student did not report the relationship to school officials, but after a policeman caught the teacher and student having sexual relations, the teacher subsequently was terminated. The Supreme Court concluded that the student's claim did not satisfy the threshold of "actual knowledge" and "deliberate indifference" on the part of school authorities. The Supreme Court majority rejected basing Title IX liability on a constructive notice standard (i.e., the employer should have known of the inappropriate behavior) or on a theory of vicarious liability (i.e., the school district is liable for intentional acts of its teachers, regardless of the employer's fault) that is used to assess Title VII claims of sexual harassment in employment.

The Court emphasized the distinction between Title IX, a conditional spending law, and Title VII, a regulatory law that includes a direct prohibition on gender discrimination in employment. However, a number of commentators have questioned whether such structural differences justify the significantly different liability standards the Supreme Court has articulated for the two laws. For example, William Kaplan has asserted: "In particular, nothing about these acknowledged differences between Title IX and Title VII undermines the basic point . . . that in terms of public policy and statutory purposes (and, it might be added, common sense) it is unlikely that Congress would have contemplated or intentionally provided for such a divergence between the protections for students and the protections for employees."[44]

The most recent Supreme Court decision addressing sexual harassment against students, *Davis v. Monroe County Board of Education*, pertains to student-to-student harassment.[45] The Court, in this 1999 ruling, held that

---

[41] For a discussion of these cases, see McCarthy, *supra* note 38, at 184-87.

[42] 524 U.S. 274 (1998).

[43] *Id.* at 291-92; *see also* 34 C.F.R. § 106.8(b) (2014).

[44] Kaplan, *supra* note 36, at 624.

[45] 526 U.S. 629 (1999).

education institutions can be liable for damages under Title IX in connection with peer sexual harassment, but adopted the high threshold that it announced in *Gebser*. In short, educational institutions have an affirmative duty to protect students from sexual harassment inflicted by their peers if school personnel with the power to do something about the harassment have actual knowledge of the behavior and exhibit deliberate indifference toward the rights of the victim.

To establish a Title IX violation for peer harassment, the education institution must exercise substantial control over both the harasser and the environment in which the known harassment takes place, and the inaction of school personnel must at least make the victim more vulnerable to the harassment. The Supreme Court held that this duty is triggered only if the harassment is severe and persistent, and if it interferes with the victim's ability to benefit from educational opportunities. This is a heavy burden of proof for student victims of peer harassment to secure damages under Title IX, but this burden can be met, just as it can in cases involving employee-to-student harassment. It is also important to note that same-sex harassment is actionable under Title IX, like Title VII, as long as the harassment is based on sex.[46]

Both *Gebser* and *Davis* were five-to-four decisions, and only Justice O'Connor, who wrote both majority opinions, was in the majority in both cases.[47] The other four in the majority in *Gebser*, who supported the "actual knowledge" and "deliberate indifference" standards to award damages, were not convinced that similar criteria should be used to evaluate peer-harassment claims. The *Davis* dissenters contended that Title IX was not designed to make educational institutions liable for third-party peer harassment, which may make them vulnerable to frivolous peer-harassment suits.[48] But this has not happened, given plaintiffs' heavy burden of proof. Nonetheless, these decisions left unresolved issues as to precisely how indifferent the response of school authorities must be to abridge Title IX. Also, some ambiguity remains regarding the identification of educational personnel who are authorized to take corrective action, especially in connection with peer harassment.

Gebser and *Davis* involved elementary and secondary school students, but the Title IX principles developed in the majority opinions apply to higher education, as well. However, colleges and universities will have less risk of liability for peer harassment under Title IX because they generally exert less control over students and the environment than is the case in elementary and secondary schools.[49] Another issue complicating the applicability of *Davis* in higher education pertains to free speech protections. In *Davis*, the dissenting justices noted the potential conflict between protecting college students' First

---

[46] *See* Nabozny v. Podlesny, 92 F.3d 446 (7th Cir. 1996) (distinguishing between gender discrimination and sexual orientation discrimination); *see also* Oncale v. Sundowner Offshore Serv., 523 U.S. 75 (1998); *supra* text accompanying note 32.

[47] *Davis,* 526 U.S. at 654 (Kennedy, J., dissenting). Chief Justice Rehnquist and Justices Thomas and Scalia joined the dissent.

[48] *Id.* at 672-77.

[49] *See infra* text accompanying note 112.

Amendment free speech rights and shielding them from peer harassment, and they emphasized that the university's "power to discipline its students for speech that may constitute sexual harassment is also circumscribed by the First Amendment." [50]

Even though harassment and hate-speech policies have been struck down in institutions of higher education because the provisions have been vague or overly broad,[51] unlawful sexual harassment is not always shielded by free speech protections.[52] In an Iowa case, for example, a graduate student was not successful in using the First Amendment to contest his suspension from the Iowa State University engineering program for electronically harassing another student, after being warned to stop sending the harassing email messages.[53] The Iowa appeals court ruled that his suspension did not violate the student's free speech rights.

Other Grounds to Challenge Sexual Harassment

Although sexual harassment victims who are employees in higher education usually seek remedies under Title VII, and students seek relief under Title IX, there are other legal avenues for relief. For example, state tort cases may be initiated for intentional acts or if negligent supervision results in such harassment.[54] To establish negligence, the plaintiff must show that the defendant breached a duty to protect the plaintiff that resulted in harm. This burden was satisfied in a negligence suit against a Louisiana community college that was required to pay damages to a student because she was raped by the culinary arts supervisor, who was a convicted felon.[55] Additionally, state statutes prohibiting employment discrimination might be available to plaintiffs alleging sexual harassment.

Plaintiffs can also initiate suits claiming that sexual harassment implicates their Fourteenth Amendment rights if state actors are involved, asserting that such behavior impairs their equal protection rights to be free from purposeful governmental discrimination, or their substantive due process rights to bodily security. Usually such constitutional claims are initiated under Section 1 of the

---

[50] 526 U.S. at 668-69 (Kennedy, J., dissenting).

[51] *See, e.g.*, Dambrot v. Cent. Mich. Univ., 55 F.3d 1177 (6th Cir. 1995) (striking down university harassment policy as overbroad and vague, but holding that the coach's use of the term "nigger" during locker-room talk was not protected by the First Amendment); UWM Post, Inc. v. Bd. of Regents of Univ. of Wis. Sys., 774 F. Supp. 1163 (E.D. Wis. 1991) (striking down university speech code that prohibited the creation of an intimidating, hostile, or demeaning educational environment).

[52] *See* Gregory M. Petouvis, *Student-on-Student Sexual Harassment in Higher Education: The Effect of Davis v. Monroe County Board of Education*, 8 Va J. Soc. Pol'y & L. 397 (2001).

[53] Brewbaker v. State Bd. of Regents, 843 N.W.2d 466 (Iowa Ct. App. 2013).

[54] In Gebser v. Lago Vista Indep. Sch. Dist., 524 U.S. 274, 292 (1998), the Supreme Court observed that the stringent standard it adopted for relief under Title IX "does not affect any right of recovery than an individual may have. . . as a matter of state law."

[55] Harrington v. La. State Bd. of Elem. & Secondary Educ., 714 So. 2d 845 (La. Ct. App. 1998) (finding institutional negligence for failing to conduct a proper background check prior to hiring the felon).

Civil Rights Act of 1871, codified as 42 U.S.C. Section 1983 and commonly referred to as "Section 1983." This law does not create substantive rights, but instead provides a remedy when a state official, acting under color of state law, deprives an individual of federally protected rights.[56]

The standards that are applied in Title IX sexual harassment cases are comparable to the standards used under Section 1983.[57] A defendant can be liable under Section 1983 if the plaintiff can prove that the state actor had notice of a pattern of unconstitutional acts and reflected deliberate indifference to, or tacit authorization of, the offensive acts without taking sufficient remedial action.[58] Section 1983 suits are appealing in some situations because they can be directed toward individuals as well as the educational institution, whereas Title IX damages suits can be brought against only the institutional grant recipients. In a Section 1983 suit, individual defendants can assert the defense of qualified (good faith) immunity unless the actions violate clearly established federal rights.[59] The qualified immunity defense is available only to individuals, however, and cannot be used by the educational institutions.[60]

Whether claimants can bring suit under both Title IX and Section 1983 remained controversial until the 2009 decision, *Fitzgerald v. Barnstable.*[61] In this case, the Supreme Court held that Title IX does not preclude a Section 1983 action that alleges unconstitutional sex discrimination in schools. Until the *Fitzgerald* decision, the circuit courts were split regarding whether Title IX supplants Section 1983 suits against school officials responsible for a policy or practice that allegedly violates Title IX.[62] The Supreme Court has now clarified that it does not.

---

[56] 42 U.S.C.S. § 1983 (2014).

[57] *See* Hendrichsen v. Ball State Univ., No. IP 01-1630-C-B/S, 2003 U.S. Dist. LEXIS 3710 (S.D. Ind. Mar. 12, 2003).

[58] *See* Kinman v. Omaha Pub. Sch. Dist., 94 F.3d 463 (8th Cir. 1996).

[59] *See* Harlow v. Fitzgerald, 457 U.S. 800, 815-19 (1982); Bruneau v. South Kortright Cent. Sch. Dist., 163 F.3d 749, 755-56 (2d Cir. 1998); Crawford v. Davis, 109 F.3d 1281, 1284 (8th Cir. 1997); *see also* Oona, R.-S. v. McCaffrey, 143 F.3d 473, 477-78 (9th Cir. 1998) (recognizing that failure to take reasonable steps to curtail sexual harassment of students represents bad faith, because the law in this regard has been clearly established at least since 1992); Kimberly Bingaman, *Fourth Annual Review of Gender and Sexuality Law,* 4 GEO. J. GENDER & L. 329 (2002).

[60] Owen v. City of Independence, Mo., 445 U.S. 622 (1980). Courts have reasoned that public universities are immune from section 1983 claims because they are arms of state government and therefore are subject to Eleventh Amendment prohibitions on federal suits against states. *See* Johnson v. Univ. of Cincinnati, 215 F.3d 561 (6th Cir. 2000) (affirming summary judgment to the university on Eleventh Amendment immunity grounds for Section 1983 claims); Rounds v. Ore. State Bd. of Higher Educ., 166 F.3d 1032 (9th Cir. 1998) (reasoning that because the defendant was a state university, it was entitled to immunity on a section 1983 claim).

[61] 555 U.S. 246 (2009).

[62] *See* Delgado v. Stegall, 367 F.3d 668 (7th Cir. 2004). *Compare* Pfeiffer v. Marion Ctr. Area Sch. Dist., 917 F.2d 779, 789 (3d Cir. 1990); *and* Bruneau v. S. Kortright Cent. Sch. Dist., 163 F.3d 749 (2d Cir. 1998); *with* Crawford v. Davis, 109 F.3d 1281 (8th Cir. 1997); Seamons v. Snow, 84 F.3d 1226, 1233-34 (10th Cir. 1996); *and* Lillard v. Shelby Cty. Bd. of Educ., 76 F.3d 716, 722-24 (6th Cir. 1996).

Litigation Involving Higher Education

During the 1980s, sexual harassment in university settings typically involved male faculty members harassing female students.[63] While this form of harassment continues to be prevalent, charges of sexual harassment now involve a wider range of abuses of power.[64] This section addresses litigation involving both employees and students as victims. Due to the amount of litigation surrounding these issues, only selected cases are highlighted to illustrate the most frequently cited issues.

Claims Brought by Employees

Employees in higher education have brought both *quid pro quo* and hostile environment harassment claims under Title VII. The vast majority of these cases are brought by female plaintiffs, though some claims have been initiated by men. Despite the evidence of sexist university power structures and evolving legal standards more favorable to harassment victims, most university employees have been unsuccessful in their sexual harassment claims.[65]

To illustrate, in *Holly D. v. California Institute of Technology*, an administrative secretary at the California Institute of Technology (CIT) alleged that a faculty member engaged in unwelcome sexual advances toward her.[66] The employee brought suit under Title VII against both the university and the faculty member. The Ninth Circuit affirmed the district court's grant of summary judgment to the defendants. The appeals court noted that the employee produced no evidence demonstrating a connection between her job duties and the faculty member's requests that she engage in sexual acts with him.[67] However, the court did recognize that the employee's allegations against the university properly would have supported a hostile environment claim under Title VII, but the university established that it had taken reasonable care to prevent the sexually harassing behavior, which is an affirmative defense. Specifically, the court recognized that CIT implemented a written harassment policy with detailed procedures. The court also reasoned that since Title VII addresses actions of employers in responding to the harassment, the victim in this case could not use Title VII to get damages from the faculty member who was the actual harasser.

In *Okruhlik v. University of Arkansas*, a female faculty member also was unsuccessful in challenging the alleged hostile work environment.[68] She and three other faculty members complained to the dean about tension with

---

[63] *See generally* Linda Eyre, *The Discursive Faming of Sexual Harassment in a University Community*, 12 GENDER & EDUC. 3 (2000).

[64] *See id.*

[65] *See* Mark Bartholomew, *Judicial Deference and Sexual Discrimination in the University*, 8 BUFF. WOMEN'S L.J. 55, 57 (1999).

[66] Holly D. v. Cal. Inst. of Tech., 339 F.3d 1158 (9th Cir. 2003).

[67] *Id.* at 1181.

[68] Okruhlik v. Univ. of Ark., 395 F.3d 872 (8th Cir. 2005).

some of the program's male faculty and administrators. The dean then initiated an investigation, but the alleged harassment continued; in one instance, the female faculty member overheard dirty jokes and negative comments about her. Eventually, she took a leave because of the alleged emotional and psychological impact of the harassment. After being denied tenure, which she claimed was a form of retaliation, she filed a lawsuit against the university, the dean, and others for retaliation and a hostile work environment. Although the jury returned a verdict in favor of the female faculty member on both claims, the district court entered a judgment for the university and dean. The court reasoned that since the plaintiff did not appeal the tenure denial and did not report some of the alleged harassment in a timely manner, and since the dean pursued an investigation of the harassment, the jury's findings were in error. The Eighth Circuit affirmed this decision.[69]

Despite the poor record of plaintiffs prevailing in such suits, they have been successful in some cases. In one case, a tenured faculty member at the University of Iowa alleged a hostile work environment, denial of promotion, and retaliation for making a sexual harassment claim.[70] She contended that there were false rumors created by male faculty about her receiving beneficial treatment from the university's department head because of her sexual relationship with him. The federal district court agreed with the female faculty member, finding that she was the victim of unwanted sexual harassment based on her sex. The district court reasoned that a hostile environment was created by cartoons posted outside a classroom concerning the alleged sexual liaison and, in several other instances, by remarks concerning the sexual affair.[71] The university attempted to avoid liability by relying on the First Amendment, but the court was not persuaded. It stated:

> [f]ree speech and academic freedom considerations might preclude Title VII liability if the sexual relationship rumors were true, but ...[they] were not true. Rights of free speech and academic freedom do not immunize professors from liability for slander or their universities from Title VII liability for a hostile work environment generated by sexual-based slander.[72]

As noted, there have also been a few cases where male employees allegedly have been victims of harassment inflicted by women or other men. In *Bowman v. Shawnee State University* (SSU), a male former instructor filed a suit against the university and its former dean of education, alleging sexual harassment, discrimination, and retaliation.[73] Among causes of action, the plaintiff brought suit under Title VII, claiming that the female dean had touched him inappropriately, made several sexual remarks, and frequently telephoned

---

[69] *See id.* at 876.

[70] Jew v. Univ. of Iowa, 749 F. Supp. 946 (S.D. Iowa 1990).

[71] *Id.* at 958-63.

[72] *Id.* at 961.

[73] 220 F.3d 456, 458 (6th Cir. 2000).

him. The district court dismissed the case in favor of the university. On appeal, the Sixth Circuit affirmed, holding that the male former instructor had suffered no adverse employment action while at the university. The appellate court also reasoned that even though the alleged incidents did constitute sexual harassment, taken together, they were not severe or pervasive enough to create a hostile work environment.[74]

There have also been a few same-sex harassment cases filed. In *Mota v. University of Texas at Houston Health Science Center*, a male faculty member sued the university, alleging same-sex harassment and retaliation under Title VII.[75] He contended that he was harassed by his male supervisor and that the university retaliated against him for making complaints with both the university and the Equal Employment Opportunity Commission. He described the harassment by the supervisor as "unwanted and offensive sexual conduct." The Fifth Circuit affirmed the district court's holding that the faculty member had been harassed and experienced retaliation.[76]

It is also important to note that university employees who experience retaliation after complaining about sex discrimination have greater protections as a result of the 2005 *Jackson v. Birmingham Board of Education* decision.[77] In this case, the Supreme Court held that Title IX's private right of action includes claims of retaliation against someone who has complained about sex discrimination. Several university employees have initiated litigation against universities as a result of the *Jackson* decision,[78] and some scholars contend that such Title IX retaliation claims against universities are likely to increase.[79]

Claims Brought by Students

University students can be victims of harassment by university employees or by other students. Several cases have addressed faculty-to-student harassment, and most have involved allegations of Title IX violations. Since appropriate university officials must have actual notice of the harassment for a Title IX claim to succeed, questions have arisen regarding who in the university setting has authority to take corrective action. One federal district court found that the director of financial aid and the director of the graduate history program were not officials with the proper authority to take corrective action against the alleged harassment of a graduate student, even though the student argued that both were aware of her relationship with a faculty member.[80] The court found that the financial aid officer was aware only that the student and

---

[74] *Id.* at 463-66.

[75] 261 F.3d 512, 515 (5th Cir. 2001).

[76] *Id.* at 530.

[77] 544 U.S. 167 (2005).

[78] *See, e.g.,* Atkinson v. LaFayette Coll., 653 F. Supp. 2d 581 (E.D. Pa. 2009) (claiming retaliation for criticizing university athletic programs); Burch v. Regents of Univ. of Cal., 433 F. Supp. 2d 1110 (E.D. Cal. 2006) (claiming retaliation for advocating on behalf of female athletes).

[79] Kerry Brian Melear, *Title IX and Retaliation: The Impact of Jackson v. Birmingham Board of Education on Higher Education,* J. PERSONNEL EVALUATION EDUC., 91 (2007).

[80] Liu v. Striuli, 36 F. Supp. 2d 452, 466 (D.R.I. 1999).

faculty member were casually seeing each other. Also, there was insufficient evidence regarding whether the director of the graduate history program knew of the relationship.[81]

In *Pociute v. West Chester University*, a student claimed that she was harassed by a faculty member while she was enrolled at West Chester University (WCU).[82] The student brought suit against WCU, the faculty member, and the WCU president. During discovery, the district court dismissed all claims against the president but allowed the student to proceed with a Title IX claim and a state law claim against WCU. The jury returned a verdict in favor of WCU, concluding that the student had failed to inform "an appropriate person with authority to institute corrective measures at [WCU]."[83] On appeal, the Third Circuit affirmed the district court's decision. The appeals court reasoned that the student victim had not established either prior notice or a lack of appropriate response on the university's part.[84] In contrast, a New York federal district court, in *Esposito v. Hofstra*, denied a university's motion to dismiss a student's Title IX claim.[85] While the university argued that there was no notice of anything inappropriate between the professor and the student, the court found that the student's allegations were sufficient enough for her to proceed with her claim.

Some cases have focused on the "deliberate indifference" aspect of the Title IX standard. Specifically, once it is established that university authorities had actual notice, courts will consider if the university acted with deliberate indifference to the allegations of sexual harassment. In a case where a college investigated a student's claim that she was harassed by a faculty member, the federal district court held that the student failed to demonstrate that the college acted with deliberate indifference.[86] Similarly, in *Wills v. Brown University*, the First Circuit found the university's "reasonably firm" reprimand of a faculty member charged with sexually harassing a student to be sufficient for Brown to avoid liability under the "deliberate indifference" standard.[87] The court upheld the inadmissibility of evidence regarding the university's responses to other harassment allegations against the same faculty member. Finally, in *Hayut v. State University of New York*, a university student alleged that she was harassed by a professor who made several sexually inappropriate comments to her throughout the semester. The Second Circuit Court of Appeals found that although the professor could be liable in his individual capacity, the university officials were not liable under Title IX because they properly responded to the student's complaints.[88] In examining whether university of-

---

[81] *Id.*

[82] 117 Fed. App'x 832 (3d Cir. 2004).

[83] *Id.* at 834.

[84] *Id.* at 835-36.

[85] 2012 U.S. Dist. LEXIS 23971 (E.D. N.Y. 2012).

[86] Frederick v. Simpson Coll., 149 F. Supp.2d 826, 839-41 (S.D. Iowa 2001).

[87] 184 F.3d 20 (1st Cir. 1999); *but see* Chantos v. Rhea, 29 F. Supp. 2d 931, 934-38 (N.D. Ill. 1998) (finding a genuine issue of fact as to deliberate indifference where university had notice of professor's reputation for inappropriate conduct toward female students).

[88] Hayut v. State Univ. of N.Y., 352 F.3d 733 (2d Cir. 2003).

ficials were deliberately indifferent, the court held that the university officials acted "expeditiously and reasonably, and exhibited no indifference at all" to the student's allegations.[89]

Sometimes there may be viable claims against a university, but the court reviewing the claims may dismiss the case for other reasons. For example, in two cases students alleged that they experienced sexual harassment by a university instructor, but both plaintiffs filed their lawsuits outside the statute of limitations requirements.[90]

As with cases where employees are victims, some harassment cases involving student victims also have included First Amendment issues. In a Virginia case, a student alleged that a faculty member had sexually harassed her on several occasions and that some of the harassing statements were made during class.[91] The court dismissed the idea that judicial interference in a professor-to-student interaction could stifle academic speech.[92] The court noted that "[a]cademic freedom, while intended to encourage creativity, should never be used to shield illegal, discriminatory conduct."[93] Other courts have recognized that universities exercise broad authority over faculty members' classroom expression, which represents the institution.[94]

In addition to students bringing claims against faculty members, there have also been a series of cases involving coaches. In *Klemencic v. Ohio State University*, a former track and cross-country athlete for Ohio State filed a sexual harassment lawsuit against her coach and the university.[95] The coach in this case attempted to establish a romantic relationship with the plaintiff while she was still training with the team. Later that year, the student alleged that the coach prevented her from team training because she refused to date him, which amounted to *quid pro quo* sexual harassment. She brought these grievances to the attention of the athletic director, who reprimanded and admonished the coach and also provided the student with psychological services.

---

[89] *Id.* at 752.

[90] *See* Williams v. Columbia Univ., 2014 N.Y. Misc. LEXIS 109 (N.Y. 2014) (female students alleged that they had been harassed by a professor and were retaliated against by university officials after they reported the incidents); Gjenka v. Delaware Cty. Comm. Coll., 2013 U.S. Dist. LEXIS 73054 (E.D. Pa. 2013) (female student sued instructor and college for sexual harassment).

[91] Kadiki v. Va. Commonwealth Univ., 892 F. Supp. 746 (E.D. Va. 1995).

[92] Bartholomew, *supra* note 65, at 64.

[93] *Kadiki*, 892 F. Supp. at 755.

[94] *See, e.g.,* Bishop v. Aronov, 926 F.2d 1066 (11th Cir. 1991) (holding that university classrooms are not an open forum and faculty members can be prohibited from expressing their religious viewpoints in the classroom). Several courts have relied on a K-12 decision, *Hazelwood Sch. Dist. v. Kuhlmeier*, 484 U.S. 260 (1988), to conclude that faculty members' classroom expression represents the institution and can be regulated for pedagogical reasons. *See, e.g.,* Vanderhurst v. Colo. Mt. Coll. Dist., 208 F.3d 908 (10th Cir. 2000) (recognizing that professors at public institutions of higher education do not have a First Amendment right to decide what will be taught in the classroom, but finding that the defendant college waived appellate review because it had failed to assert before the district court that the faculty member's termination was based on legitimate pedagogical concerns).

[95] 263 F.3d 504, 507 (6th Cir. 2001).

Unhappy with this result, the student filed a sexual harassment claim in district court against Ohio State, the coach, and the athletic director in their official capacities. She alleged that she was a victim of *quid pro quo* harassment and a hostile work environment under Title IX. She also charged that both the coach and the athletic director were liable within their individual capacities under Section 1983. The district court entered final judgment in favor of the coach and granted summary judgment to the university. The Sixth Circuit Court of Appeals affirmed.[96]

In higher education, the line is not as clear between employee-to-student and peer harassment as it is at the K-12 level. For example, graduate students often are also university employees. In an illustrative case, *Morse v. Regents of the University of Colorado*, two female students at the University of Colorado at Colorado Springs (UCCS) claimed that they were subjected to harassment committed by both a higher-ranking cadet and an ROTC officer while they were participating in the ROTC program.[97] The female students alleged that such harassment created a sexually hostile environment, and they reported the harassment to UCCS representatives. Unsatisfied with the response, the female students filed a claim in district court under Title IX, Section 1983, and other grounds. UCCS argued that it did not exercise control over the ROTC department. The district court agreed and dismissed the Title IX and other claims against the university. However, on appeal, the Tenth Circuit found that the district court erred in failing to consider documents provided by the female students in response to UCCS's contention that it had no control over the alleged harassers. The appeals court reasoned that the ROTC program was offered and sanctioned by UCCS; thus, the university was liable for the hostile environment created by the fellow student and the ROTC instructor because UCCS knew of the harassment and did not adequately respond.[98]

The Supreme Court's *Davis* decision left questions regarding how its opinion would apply to peer harassment in the higher education context.[99] Since universities do not exert the degree of control over students that is evident at the K-12 level, it is not surprising that peer-harassment claims are not as prevalent among higher education students. However, there have been some cases involving allegations that colleges and universities are responsible for peer harassment or assault both on[100] and off campus.[101]

---

[96] *Id.*

[97] 154 F.3d 1124, 1126 (10th Cir. 1998).

[98] *Id.* at 1128.

[99] *See* Karen E. Edmonson, *Davis v. Monroe County Board of Education Goes to College: Holding Post-Secondary Institutions Liable Under Title IX for Peer Sexual Harassment*, 75 Notre Dame L. Rev. 1203 (2000).

[100] *See* Doe v. Brown Univ., 304 F. Supp. 3d 252 (D.R.I. 2018).

[101] Molly McCafferty, *Student Who Sued Harvard for Investigating Alleged Off-Campus Sexual Assault Voluntarily Dismisses Case,* Harvard Crimson (Jan. 9, 2019), *available at* https://www.thecrimson.com/article/2019/1/9/title-ix-lawsuit-dismissed/.

Likewise, media reports[102] and research[103] remind us that peer sexual harassment remains a problem on university campuses. And courts continue to address students' allegations that university officials have not adequately responded to claims of harassment.[104]

In *Adusumilli v. Illinois Institute of Technology* (IIT), a female student alleged that six male students and four male faculty members had sexually harassed her. The student had reported two of the student incidents to school officials. In her lawsuit, she claimed that the school knew and refused to respond to this harassment. She also contended that the school responded to her allegations with retaliation, such as unfair grades. Applying *Davis*, the Seventh Circuit concluded that despite the student's assertion that there were twelve incidents of sexual harassment, only two of those were reported to IIT. Of the two incidents reported, only one was given to a school official with authority to take corrective action; as a result, actual knowledge was not established. Additionally, the court did not find the harassment to be severe, pervasive, and objectively offensive.[105]

Likewise, a Kansas federal district court did not find challenged harassment to be severe enough to evoke liability under the *Davis* standard. In this case, a student alleged that another student touched her once in the mid-thigh area and three times on her shoulder or back area.[106] The female student alleged that the college was deliberately indifferent to her complaints. A college official told her that she could not file a complaint just because a classmate was "creeping" her out. The student, unhappy with this reaction, wrote a note to the vice president of the college, who organized a meeting with her to discuss the harassment. During this meeting, the vice president said he would speak with the alleged harasser. Although the college officials met with the male student and took measures to prevent further harassment, the female student still was not satisfied and sought his suspension from school.[107] The court did not find that the college acted with deliberate indifference because its officials met with the alleged harasser, notified the students' instructors, and took measures

---

[102] *See* Marta Figlerowicz & Ayeha Ramachandran, *No More Toughing it Out: Let's End Sexual Harassment on Campus*, Wash. Post (Nov. 29, 2017), *available at* https://www.washingtonpost. com/news/grade-point/wp/2017/11/29/no-more-toughing-it-out-lets-end-sexual-harassment-on-campus/?utm_term=.cda3ae86bc32; Dawn Rhodes, Ex-University of Illinois Professor Sued for Sexual Assault, Harassment of Students, Chic. Trib. (Sept. 11, 2019), *available at* https://www.chicagotribune.com/news/ct-university-of-illinois-professor-lawsuit-20190911-m6pv3r3a4rc3pfvqyeyjnwfgwi-story.html

[103] *See* Matthew R. Triplett, *Sexual Assault on College Campuses: Seeking the Appropriate Balance Between Due Process and Victim Protection*, 62 Duke L.J. 487 (2012); Stephen Henrick, *A Hostile Environment for Student Defendants: Title IX and Sexual Assault on College Campuses*, 40 N. Ky. L. Rev. 49 (2013); Nancy Chi Catalupo & William Kidder, *A Systematic Look at a Serial Problem: Sexual Harassment of Students by University Faculty*, 2018 Utah L. Rev. 671 (2018).

[104] *See* Foster v. Univ. of Mich., 2019 U.S. Dist. LEXIS 27434 (E.D. Mich. 2019).

[105] 191 F.3d 455 (7th Cir. 1999) (unpublished decision); *see also* Adusumilli v. Illinois Inst. of Tech., No. 97 C8 8507, 1998 U.S. Dist. LEXIS 14413 (N.D. Ill. Sept. 08, 1998).

[106] Cubie v. Bryan Career Coll., 244 F. Supp. 2d 1191 (D. Kan. 2003).

[107] *Id.* at 1202-04.

to prevent encounters between the two students. The court further found that the four instances of unwelcome touching did not rise to the level of severe and pervasive harassment.[108]

It is not impossible, however, for university students to be successful in peer-harassment lawsuits under Title IX. For example, Yale University was denied summary judgment where a student argued that the university created a hostile environment in the aftermath of her complaints that she was raped by a male student.[109] The victim filed a complaint with the Sexual Harassment Committee, requesting that the committee remove the male student from the course in which they both were enrolled. In accordance with its written grievance procedures, the committee researched the incident and recommended that the male student be required to take a leave of absence until the female student graduated. Throughout the grievance process, the female student contended that she made repeated requests for academic accommodations and that Yale never responded to these requests, thus creating a hostile environment in violation of Title IX. The court reasoned that although Yale was not liable for the rape, of which it had no notice, a reasonable jury could conclude that further encounters of any sort between the rape victim and her attacker could create an environment sufficiently hostile to deprive the victim access to educational opportunities provided by the university. The female student, therefore, raised an issue of material fact, and the court denied Yale's motion for summary judgment under Title IX.[110]

A female student similarly was successful in a New York case. In *Zakrzewska v. New School*, the student plaintiff, who was also a university employee, exchanged emails, had dinner, and attended the opera with another university employee.[111] After spending a significant amount of time together, the student worker alleged that she was sexually harassed by the university employee. School officials responded by telling the university employee to have no further contact with the student. The student worker was dissatisfied with the university's response and filed suit under the New York State Human Rights Law. The federal district court denied the university's motion for summary judgment because the New York law creates vicarious liability for managerial or supervisory employees even when the employer exercised reasonable care to prevent discriminatory actions.

Those who have been accused of sexual misconduct have also sued colleges and universities for not providing them their due process rights, among other claims. In one case against Vanderbilt University, the male student alleged that the university did not follow its own discipline policies and denied

---

[108] *Id.; see also*, Doe v. Miami Univ., 882 F.3d 579 (6th Cir. 2018) (finding the deliberate indifference claim failed).

[109] Kelly v. Yale Univ., No. 3:01-CV-1591, 2003 U.S. Dist. LEXIS 4543 (D. Conn. Mar. 26, 2003).

[110] *Id.* at *17; *see also*, Farmer v. Kan. State Univ., 918 F.3d 1094 (10th Cir. 2019) (students properly asserted Title IX claim against university).

[111] Zakrzewska v. New Sch., 598 F.Supp. 2d 426 (S.D.N.Y. 2009).

him the right to confront his accuser. His claims were dismissed.[112] Another student was unsuccessful in his disparate impact claim against the university where he alleged that the university's policy against men accused of sexual misconduct was unfair.[113] One court did, however, find that a male student was denied a fair hearing when he was expelled for allegedly raping another student.[114] Most recently, the Seventh Circuit reinstated a case involving a male student who had been accused of sexual assault. The court found that he adequately alleged violations of the Fourteenth Amendment and Title IX.[115]

From the growth in sexual harassment litigation in higher education since the early 1990s, one might think that the incidents of such harassment involving students have increased dramatically. The expansion of lawsuits, however, might be attributed to the Supreme Court's recognition in 1992 that individuals can use Title IX to sue educational institutions for sexual harassment.[116] Greater campus awareness and attention to the issue in recent years may also have encouraged more victims to come forward. The #MeToo movement has arguably generated increased public attention about harassment and assault as well. It should also be noted that many of the complaints filed at the university-level that involve a Title IX investigation, for example, do not lead to litigation.[117]

At the same time, some male students have alleged that there is a bias toward accusers in these types of cases.[118] Perhaps the threat of legal action will cause institutions of higher education to become more assertive in trying to prevent sexual harassment on campus. As discussed, courts continue to examine this issue, including campus discipline policies[119] and due process rights.[120]

Guidance for University Personnel

It is important for faculty, administrators, and students in institutions of higher education to understand the new approach that the current administration has taken when addressing campus assault and violence. University officials also need to know the legal requirements under Title VII and Title IX and to comply with them. In addition, the Campus Sexual Violence Elimination Act (SaVE) of 2013 has required colleges and universities to initiate education

---

[112] Z.J. v. Vanderbilt Univ., 355 F.Supp. 3d 646 (M.D. Tenn. 2018). *But see supra* text accompanying note 17.

[113] Pacheco v. St. Mary's Univ., 2017 U.S. Dist. LEXIS 94510 (W.D. Tex. June 20, 2017).

[114] Doe v. Univ. of S. Cal., 241 Cal. Rptr. 3d 146 (Cal. Ct. App. 2018); *see also* Marshall v. Indiana Univ., 170 F.Supp. 3d 1201 (S.D. Ind. 2016) (finding dismissal of student's due process claim was warranted).

[115] Doe v. Purdue Univ., 928 F.3d 652 (7th Cir. 2019).

[116] *See* Franklin v. Gwinnett Pub. Schs., 503 U.S. 60 (1992); *supra* text accompanying note 41.

[117] *See* Tyler Kingkade, *Barnard College Joins List of 94 Colleges Under Title IX Investigations*, HUFFINGTON POST (Jan. 7, 2015), *available at* www.huffingtonpost.com/2015/01/07/barnard-college-title-ixinvestigations_n_6432596.html .

[118] *See Pacheco*, 2017 U.S. Dist. LEXIS 94510 (W.D. Tex. 2017).

[119] *See* Z.J. v. Vanderbilt Univ., 355 F.Supp. 3d 646 (M.D. Tenn. 2018).

[120] *See* Plummer v. Univ. of Houston, 2015 U.S. Dist. LEXIS 189229, 2015 WL 12734039 (S.D. Tex. May 28, 2015), *aff'd*, 860 F.3d 767 (5th Cir. 2017).

programs addressing sexual assault and harassment since 2014.[121] Moreover, institutional sexual harassment policies should clearly articulate what behaviors are prohibited and should include explicit employee and student grievance procedures. There must always be more than one avenue to file sexual harassment complaints to ensure that victims do not have to submit their claims to the alleged harasser. The policies should also be clear regarding who will investigate complaints, how investigations will be conducted, and what disciplinary action will be taken when harassment is substantiated.[122]

Adopting appropriate institutional policies and procedures is essential, but not sufficient to curtail sexual harassment. Such policies must be widely disseminated so that potential victims know their rights and potential perpetrators know what penalties they may face for engaging in sexual harassment. Edward Stoner and Catherine Ryan have observed that "all supervisors, including department chairs and professors, must be educated thoroughly on all aspects of the policy, emphasizing their special obligation not to engage in discrimination or harassment and to deal with, rather than to ignore, potential discrimination and harassment."[123]

The legal standards outlined by the Supreme Court under Title VII and Title IX should be viewed as the minimum institutional response.[124] There are many things colleges and universities should do to combat sexual harassment that may not be legally required. For example, college and university administrators should be aggressive in offering students, faculty, and staff educational programs regarding sexual harassment, such as assemblies and workshops.[125] These programs not only should address the legal requirements and complaint procedures, but also should focus on the negative consequences of sexual harassment for the individuals and institutions involved. Such educational efforts may discourage incidents of sexual harassment and reduce potential university liability.[126] Moreover, counseling programs should be in place for victims when harassment does occur.

Despite recent efforts to strengthen institutional policies and enhance educational programs and other preventive efforts, sexual harassment remains a significant problem on college and university campuses.[127] This is an important issue, and all members of the higher education community should feel a commitment, as well as a responsibility, to work toward the elimination of sexual harassment.

---

[121] Campus Violence Elimination Act, 157 Cong Rec § 4843 (2013).

[122] Each educational institution has a legal obligation to designate at least one employee to coordinate Title IX compliance. *See* 34 C.F.R.§ 106.8(a) (2014).

[123] Edward N. Stoner & Catherine S. Ryan, *Burlington, Faragher, Oncale, and Beyond: Recent Developments in Title VII Jurisprudence,* 26 J.C. & U.L. 645, 662 (2000).

[124] *See* Kaplan, *supra* note 36, at 641-42.

[125] *Id. at* 643; *see also* A.J. Bolan, *Deliberate Indifference: Why Universities Must Do More to Protect Students from Sexual Assault,* 86 Geo. Wash. L. Rev. 805 (2018).

[126] Eyre, *supra* note 68, at 3

[127] *See* Nikki C. Townsley & Patricia Geist, *The Discursive Enactment of Hegemony: Sexual Harassment and Academic Organizing,* 64 W. J. of Communication 190 (2000).

Discussion Questions:

1. University officials must have clear policies in place with regard to harassment in employment. The EEOC offers helpful model language in this regard. Please see http://www.eeoc.gov/federal/model_eeo_programs. cfm and discuss how this language might be adopted at your workplace.

2. Compare and contrast student sexual harassment policies at two different universities. How do the universities address complaint procedures and due process? Do you believe these policies align with what you know about the law in this area?

3. Title VII prohibits discrimination in the workplace. How has Title VII been cited in recent court decisions involving harassment based on sexual orientation and gender identity?

4. Federal investigations involving sexual harassment have taken place on several college campuses recently. Use the internet to find two articles that discuss these investigations. What can your university learn from these investigations?

5. If the 2018 proposed Title IX regulations are adopted, what changes will institutions of higher education have to make in handling sexual harassment allegations?

9 Federal Disability Laws

Susan C. Bon, J.D., Ph.D.
University of South Carolina

Janet S. Bubert, J.D.
Underwood Law Firm, P.C.

Introduction

Across higher education institutions, students and employees with disabilities are protected by federal laws that establish the essential rights of individuals with disabilities. These federal laws set forth numerous responsibilities of higher education institutions, including, for example, nondiscriminatory practices, reasonable accommodations, and accessible services. Furthermore, these laws apply to both public and private higher education institutions that receive federal funds. Section 504 of the Rehabilitation Act of 1973[1] (Rehabilitation Act) and the Americans with Disabilities Act Amendments Act[2] (ADA) are the primary sources of authority and protection for individuals with disabilities in higher education; however, the Office of Civil Rights and Department of Justice also provide federal guidelines to institutions. In addition, prominent higher education law cases are regularly decided in the courts and continue to impact higher education institutions and professionals.

This chapter focuses primarily on the various laws, cases, and general legal principles that inform the resolution of disability issues in higher education settings. We begin, however, with a brief review and discussion of the significant historical events that influenced educational opportunities for individuals with disabilities. Initially, war and national conflicts profoundly impacted the evolution of disability rights across higher education institutions and society through federal legislation to improve overall the lives and treatment of returning veterans. For example, World War I and the return of disabled veterans sparked federal initiatives to provide vocational rehabilitation opportunities. These war-related initiatives sparked awareness and changes across higher education institutions.

---

[1]   29 U.S.C. § 794.
[2]   42 U.S.C. § 12101, *et seq.*

History of Disability Rights in Education and Society

World War I played an important role in the growing awareness about individuals with disabilities, particularly with the return of many war veterans with physical disabilities related to their service for the country. The disabled war veterans had a great impact on Congress and the White House during the Depression era because of their significant numbers and need for opportunities to support their re-entry into civilian life after their service in war.[3] In 1944, the Servicemen's Readjustment Act,[4] notably referred to as the GI Bill of Rights,[5] introduced educational benefits, which led to expanded campus enrollments of student veterans who were typically married, older, and disabled.[6]

Higher education opportunities began to expand again for veterans in the late 1960s and early 1970s. For example, the Rehabilitation Act of 1973[7] and Vietnam Era Veterans' Readjustment Assistance Act (VEVRAA) of 1974[8] were especially influential for veterans and veterans with disabilities. While the Rehabilitation Act and VEVRAA both include protections from discrimination for veterans with disabilities, the VEVRAA focuses extensively on employment opportunities and the elimination of discrimination, whereas the Rehabilitation Act directly identifies the rights of veterans with disabilities to be protected from discrimination and granted access to educational opportunities. Together these legislative enactments enhanced opportunities for veterans with disabilities who suffered new challenges, as many of their disabling conditions related to the use of chemical weapons in the Vietnam conflict.[9]

Around the time that Vietnam veterans were beginning to gain access to higher education institutions, students with disabilities were also beginning to gain access to education in the K-12 system.[10] As awareness increased and legal protections for individuals with disabilities evolved, access to and opportunities across higher education institutions continued to emerge. In the higher education setting, two primary laws established both the rights and responsibilities which are especially relevant to education in higher education settings. As described in greater detail below, these laws, the Rehabilitation Act[11] and the ADA,[12] are the primary sources of authority and protection for individuals with disabilities in higher education.

---

[3]   John R. Thelin, History of American Higher Education (3rd ed. 2019).

[4]   Public Law 346.

[5]   Roger Geiger, American Higher Education Since World War II (2019).

[6]   *Id.* Thelin at 262-267.

[7]   42 U.S.C. § 12101, *et seq.*

[8]   38 U.S.C §. 4212.

[9]   Nancy J. Evans et. al., Disability in Higher Education: A Social Justice Approach (2017).

[10]   *Id.*

[11]   29 U.S.C. § 794.

[12]   42 U.S.C. § 12101, *et seq.*

Disability Laws

The Rehabilitation Act is a nondiscrimination statute that focuses on the rights of individuals with disabilities. It provides in pertinent part that no "otherwise qualified individual with a disability . . . shall, solely by reason of her or his disability, be excluded from the participation in, be denied the benefits of, or be subjected to discrimination under any program or activity receiving federal financial assistance...."[13] Although a college may be required to provide a disabled student additional services or auxiliary aids in order to comply with its obligations under the statute, the federal government provides no money to the institution to cover the provision of such services.

Similar in nature, the Americans with Disabilities Act (ADA) is a relatively recent law, enacted by Congress in 1990, that has significantly impacted accessibility across campus facilities. Reauthorization and amendments in 2008, have clarified how statutory terms should be interpreted through an expanded definition of substantially limits. The 2008 amendments also expanded the definition of major life activities by including two non-exhaustive lists and addressed the limits on consideration of mitigating measures other than "ordinary eyeglasses or contact lenses" that may be considered when assessing whether an individual has a disability.

The ADA also prohibits discrimination against an individual because of or on the basis of the individual's disability.[14] Title I of the ADA applies to all terms and conditions of employment engaged in by covered employers, which is defined to include private and public employers with fifteen or more employees. Title II prohibits discrimination against disabled persons by public entities providing services, programs, and activities, including public colleges. In contrast, Title III applies to private entities, including most private colleges that provide public accommodations, although private religious programs are exempt from compliance with Title III.[15]

Defining Individual with a Disability

Congress specifically focused on alignment of the two disability laws, ADA and the Rehabilitation Act, when passing the ADA Amendments Act of 2008. Explicitly, with the 2008 amendments, Congress reversed a Supreme Court opinion that had attempted to narrow the ADA's coverage.[16] Furthermore, Congress broadened the scope of impairments that will support a finding that an individual is disabled, and ultimately shifted the focus of an ADA claim to whether unlawful discrimination occurred, rather than an extensive analysis

---

[13] 29 U.S.C. § 794(a).

[14] 42 U.S.C. § 12101.

[15] Title III exempts private religious programs from compliance. 28 C.F.R. § 36.102(e). *See also* White v. Denver Seminary, 157 F. Supp. 2d 1171 (D. Colo. 2001) (holding that a seminary was pervasively sectarian and thus exempt from Title III).

[16] Toyota Motor Mfg., Kentucky, Inc. v. Williams, 435 U.S. 184 (2002).

of whether the plaintiff is disabled.[17] The amended act rejects the standards identified in *Toyota Motor Manufacturing v. Williams,* and, as a consequence, the focus of a case brought under the amended act is whether the employer complied with its obligations to a disabled employee, not whether the individual's impairment qualified as a disability. The broad scope of protection achieved by expanding the definition of disability through the ADA amendments also applies to Section 504.

We begin with a discussion of the standards an educational institution must apply when determining whether a student or employee is considered disabled for purposes of these disability laws. In the employment context, individuals who are disabled will generally be evaluated under the provisions of the ADA. For students, the disability determination is primarily based on the provisions of the Rehabilitation Act.

Qualified Individual with a Disability under the ADA

Many substantive portions of the ADA remained the same after the 2008 amendments. The definition of disabled, for example, remained mostly intact. Under the ADA, someone with a disability is an individual with a physical or mental impairment that substantially limits one or more of the major life activities,[18] who has a record of such an impairment, or is regarded as having such an impairment.[19] An individual may have a record of a disability if the individual has a history of, or has been misclassified as having, an impairment that substantially limits a major life activity.[20] For example, an employee who was hospitalized in the past for tuberculosis,[21] but who no longer suffers from the disease, has a record of an impairment. An individual may be regarded as having a disability if an employer subjects the individual to some kind of adverse action based on an actual or perceived physical or mental impairment.[22] For example, an applicant who is refused employment because he takes anti-seizure medication, even though the employer is unsure why the applicant takes the medication, may be regarded as having an impairment.[23] In such cases, the employer regarded the applicant as disabled, whether or not the applicant has an actual disability.

The ADA also prohibits discrimination on the basis of an association or relationship an employee or potential employee may have with a disabled person. An employer cannot refuse to hire an applicant because of a family, business, social, or other relationship with a person with a disability.[24] In related circumstances, courts have also recognized the viability of an ADA

---

[17] *Id.*
[18] 29 C.F.R. § 1630.2(g)(1).
[19] 42 U.S.C. § 12102(1); 29 C.F.R. § 1630.2(g)(3).
[20] 29 C.F.R. § 1630.2(k)(1).
[21] Sch. Bd. of Nassau Cnty. v. Arline, 480 U.S. 273 (1987).
[22] 29 C.F.R. § 1630.2(l)(1).
[23] 29 C.F.R. § 1630.2 (l)(2)(i).
[24] 29. C.F.R. § 1630.8.

retaliation claim by an employee advocating on behalf of disabled students.[25] The ADA prohibits employers from retaliating against employees who claim disability discrimination as a result of their actions on behalf of an individual with a disability.[26] Further, protected activity under the ADA may also include complaints to supervisors.[27]

Although many substantive portions of the ADA generally remained the same, the 2008 amendments changed the way in which the definition of disability is interpreted and applied. The stated purpose of the 2008 amendments is "to make it easier for people with disabilities to obtain protection under the ADA."[28] Therefore, the definition of disability must "be construed broadly, to the maximum extent permitted by the terms of the ADA."[29]

Currently, an impairment constitutes a disability if it substantially limits the ability of an individual to perform a major life activity as compared to most people in the general population. An individual alleging an ADA claim no longer must show that an impairment "prevents" or "significantly restricts" performing a major life activity. In fact, by amending the ADA, Congress intended to eliminate extensive analysis on the question of whether a person is disabled.

The scope of individuals who may be considered disabled expanded in 2008 through the adoption of a provision prohibiting an employer from considering the ameliorative effects of mitigating measures an employee uses to treat an impairment.[30] In addition, employers must treat impairments that are episodic or in remission as if they were active.[31] For example, employees with high blood pressure may take medication that corrects and maintains their blood pressure at normal levels.[32] However, when making a determination

---

[25] *See* Manigaulte v. C.W. Post of Long Island Univ., 659 F. Supp. 2d 367 (E.D.N.Y. 2009) (finding that Title I of the ADA does not allow relief for a teacher alleging an adverse employment action resulted from advocacy on behalf of his disabled students); *But see* Reinhardt v. Albuquerque Public Schools, 595 F.3d 1126 (10th Cir. 2010) (finding that advocating on behalf of disabled students raised a § 504 claim).

[26] *See* Ragusa v. Malverne Union Free Sch. Dist., 582 F. Supp. 2d 326, 347 (E.D.N.Y. 2008) (finding that retaliation claims survive dismissal of discrimination claims; thus, a plaintiff's standing to bring a retaliation claim based on alleged retaliation for reporting of alleged unlawful actions may proceed); *see also* 42 U.S.C. § 12203(a) ([n]o person shall discriminate against any individual because such individual has opposed any act or practice made unlawful by this chapter or because such individual made a charge, testified, assisted, or participated in any manner in an investigation, proceeding, or hearing under this chapter).

[27] *See* Felton v. Katonah Lewisboro Sch. Dist., No. 08-CV-9340, 2009 WL 2223853, at *6 (S.D.N.Y. July 27, 2009) (holding that complaints to supervisors are considered protected activity under the ADA).

[28] 29 C.F.R. § 1630.1(c)(4).

[29] 29 C.F.R. § 1630.1(c)(4).

[30] 42 U.S.C. § 12102(4)(E)(i); ADA Amendments Act of 2008, Pub. L. No. 110-325, § 2(b)(2) (rejecting the Supreme Court's holding in *Sutton v. United Air Lines, Inc.*, 527 U.S. 471(1999)).

[31] 42 U.S.C. § 12102(D).

[32] *See* Murphy v. U.P.S., 527 U.S. 516 (1999) in which the Supreme Court found that a truck driver's hypertension did not qualify as a disability because he functioned normally with medication.

about whether an employee is disabled, and therefore entitled to the protections provided by the ADA, the employer must evaluate those employees as if they were not taking medication, thus leading to more employees meeting the disability standard.

Almost all mitigating measures must be excluded from the disability determination: medication, prosthetics, hearing aids, oxygen therapy equipment, assistive technology, and auxiliary aids.[33] The 2008 amendments carved out one exception—ordinary eyeglasses or contact lenses.[34] Low-vision devices, however, which "magnify, enhance, or otherwise augment a visual image,"[35] may not be considered in determining disability. Therefore, employers must distinguish these devices from ordinary eyeglasses or contact lenses, which "are intended to fully correct visual acuity or eliminate refractive error."[36] Using qualification standards or selection criteria that are based on uncorrected vision is still prohibited, unless the standards are job-related and consistent with business necessity.[37]

Despite the broadened definition of disability, the ADA still specifically excludes certain characteristics from consideration as a qualifying impairment: physical characteristics such as eye color, hair color, left-handedness, height, weight, or muscle tone that is within "normal" range and is not the result of a psychological disorder; personality traits such as poor judgment or quick temper; environmental, cultural, or economic disadvantages; or advanced age.[38] Also excluded from the definition of "disability" are transvestism, transexualism, pedophilia, exhibitionism, voyeurism, gender identity disorders not resulting from physical impairments, or other sexual behavior disorders; compulsive gambling, kleptomania, or pyromania; psychoactive substance-use disorders resulting from current use of illegal drugs; or homosexuality or bisexuality.[39]

The ADA affords no protection to individuals who are the object of an adverse employment action on the basis of current illegal drug use.[40] However, the law does protect an individual who no longer uses illegal drugs and has completed a supervised drug-rehabilitation program or is currently enrolled in such a program.[41] An employer may conduct drug testing of an individual to ensure that the employee's illegal drug use is not current.

The federal regulations also identify examples of specific impairments that will consistently meet the definition of a disability, including deafness, blindness, intellectual disability, partially or completely missing limbs, mobility impairments requiring use of a wheelchair, autism, cancer, cerebral palsy, diabetes, epilepsy, HIV infection, multiple sclerosis, muscular dystrophy,

---

[33] 42 U.S.C. § 12102(4)(E)(i)(I)-(IV).
[34] 42 U.S.C. § 12102(4)(E)(ii).
[35] 42 U.S.C. § 12102(4)(E)(iii)(II).
[36] 42 U.S.C. § 12102(4)(E)(iii)(I).
[37] 42 U.S.C. § 12102(4)(E).
[38] 29 C.F.R. § 1630.2(h) Appx.
[39] 29 C.F.R. § 1630.3(d)-(e).
[40] 42 U.S.C. § 12210(a).
[41] 42 U.S.C. § 12210(b).

major depression, bipolar disorder, post-traumatic stress disorder, obsessive compulsive disorder, and schizophrenia.[42]

Numerous other impairments will also qualify as disabilities; the list provided by the federal regulations is meant only to be illustrative. Because of certain characteristics associated with the impairments listed, employers can quickly and easily conduct an assessment of the individual's limitations and reach the conclusion that the individual qualifies as disabled. Note, however, that even with an impairment that consistently meets the definition of a disability, it must still substantially limit the individual in a major life activity to qualify as a "disability."

The 2008 amendments also expanded the list of "activities" included in the definition of "major life activities."[43] An impairment that substantially limits at least one major life activity is sufficient to qualify an individual as disabled.[44] Generally, major life activities are basic activities that most people in the general population can perform with little or no difficulty.[45] The ADA states that major life activities "include, but are not limited to, caring for oneself, performing manual tasks, seeing, hearing, eating, sleeping, walking, standing, sitting, reaching, lifting, bending, speaking, breathing, learning, reading, concentrating, thinking, communicating, interacting with others, and working."[46]

In *Sutton v. United Air Lines*, the Supreme Court determined that to be "substantially limited" in the major life activity of working, an individual must be precluded from more than one type of job, a specialized job, or a desired job.[47] In essence, the Court found that just because an employee cannot perform one particular job does not mean the employee is substantially limited in the major life activity of working. The Court even hinted that an individual may need to be substantially limited in the major life activity of working, plus some other activity, in order to qualify as disabled.[48]

Congress disagreed with the conclusion in *Sutton v. United Air Lines* and included language in the 2008 amendments to the ADA to ensure a change in the consideration of limitations on working. The amended statute states that an "impairment that substantially limits one major life activity need not limit other major life activities in order to be considered a disability."[49] The federal regulations acknowledge that, following the 2008 amendments, someone with a disability will generally be substantially limited in a major life activity other than working, making reliance on "working" as the qualifying major life activity unnecessary.[50] The regulations further clarify that to be substantially

---

[42] 29 C.F.R. § 1630.2(j)(3).

[43] 29 C.F.R. § 1630.2(i).

[44] 29 C.F.R. § 1630.2(j)(1)(viii).

[45] 29 C.F.R. § 1630.2(i).

[46] 42 U.S.C. § 12102(2)(A).

[47] Sutton v. United Air Lines, 527 U.S. 471, 492 (1999).

[48] *Id.* (concluding that working should be viewed as a major life activity as a last resort, only if an individual is not substantially limited with respect to any other major life activity).

[49] 42 U.S.C. § 12102(4)(C).

[50] 29 C.F.R. § 1630.2(j) Appx.

limited in the major life activity of working, an individual must be limited in performing either a "class or broad range of jobs in various classes" rather than a "type of work."[51]

The ADA also includes the operation of major bodily functions as a major life activity, including "functions of the immune system, special sense organs and skin, normal cell growth, digestive, bowel, bladder, neurological, brain, respiratory, circulatory, cardiovascular, endocrine, hemic, lymphatic, musculoskeletal, and reproductive functions."[52] The list of major bodily functions is also illustrative, and many other systems and functions of the body may be covered. Additionally, the regulations state that the operation of a major bodily function includes the operation of an individual organ within a body system.[53] It would be nearly impossible for a regulatory agency to enumerate each potential impairment to a bodily function that qualifies as a disability—kidney disease may affect an individual's bladder function, cancer may affect normal cell growth, and rheumatoid arthritis affects musculoskeletal functions.

Qualifying as disabled is no longer the burden it once was for a plaintiff bringing an ADA claim. However, job applicants and employees must still meet job-related qualifications, which typically include education, experience, and skill levels. According to the ADA, an employer may refuse to hire an applicant who fails to achieve the job-related qualifications. An individual is a "qualified individual" if he or she "satisfies the requisite skill, experience, education, and other job-related requirements of the employment position" and can perform the essential functions of the job with or without reasonable accommodation.[54]

Qualified Individual with a Disability under the Rehabilitation Act

Generally, the same standards for determining whether an individual is disabled under the ADA also apply to a student asserting a disability under the Rehabilitation Act. The ADA Amendments Act expressly states that all of its changes also apply to the Rehabilitation Act. A college covered by the Rehabilitation Act is responsible for providing a qualified student with a disability an equal opportunity to participate in and benefit from educational programs to the same extent enjoyed by nondisabled peers.[55] The Rehabilitation Act does not guarantee success or a specific result in an educational program, only an equal opportunity to succeed.

A student is considered disabled under the Rehabilitation Act if the student (a) has a physical or mental impairment that substantially limits one or more major life activities, (b) has a record of such an impairment, or (c) is regarded

---

[51] 29 C.F.R. § 1630.2(j) Appx.

[52] 29 C.F.R. § 1630.2(i)(1)(ii).

[53] 29 C.F.R. § 1630.2(i)(1)(ii).

[54] 42 U.S.C. § 12111(8).

[55] 34 C.F.R. §104.4(b)(2).

as having such an impairment.[56] A student has a record of an impairment if a student has a history of a qualifying impairment.[57] For example, a student who had cancer and required additional time to complete assignments while undergoing chemotherapy may now be in recovery and no longer need accommodations, but the student is still considered a student with a disability who is entitled to protection from discrimination under the Rehabilitation Act.

A student may be regarded as disabled if the student has a physical or mental impairment that does not substantially limit a major life activity, but the student is treated by the college as having a limitation (e.g., a student who walks with a limp is denied the opportunity to participate in a physical activity due to the school's perception of an impairment), or a student who has a physical or mental impairment that substantially limits a major life activity only as a result of the attitudes of others toward the impairment (e.g., a student who is obese).[58] Students regarded as having an impairment are not entitled to accommodations, but may bring a discrimination claim against the college.

Colleges do not have a duty to identify students with disabilities. Students in institutions of postsecondary education are responsible for notifying school staff of their disability status if they are requesting accommodations or other disability services. Colleges are not required to conduct or pay for an evaluation to document a student's disability or need for an accommodation. Upon request, a student seeking accommodations must provide documentation that the student has a disability and that supports the need for an academic adjustment. The documentation should identify a 'major life activity' that is substantially limited as a result of the disability.[59]

The primary purpose of the documentation is to provide the information necessary for officials to work interactively with the student to identify appropriate services. Colleges may set their own requirements for documentation as long as they are reasonable and comply with the Rehabilitation Act and the ADA. The focus should be on whether the information adequately documents the existence of a current disability and a need for accommodations.

Disability Issues for Students and Applicants

Disability issues may arise across the entire span of the relationship between a college and a student with a disability. The Rehabilitation Act and the ADA protect a student with a disability beginning with an application for admission, request for accommodations, effort to gain access to programs and services, and through graduation.

---

[56] 34 C.F.R. §104.3(j)(1).

[57] 34 C.F.R. §104.3(j)(2)(iii).

[58] 34 C.F.R. § 104.3(j)(2)(iv).

[59] Bragdon v. Abbott, 524 U.S. 624 (1998).

Admission

An applicant with a disability must meet any essential requirements for admission that are applied to other students. A student has no obligation to inform a college about a disability. Colleges are not permitted to make pre-admission inquiries about an applicant's disability status. Preadmission inquiries are permitted only if the college is taking remedial action to correct the effects of past discrimination or taking voluntary action to overcome the effects of conditions that limited the participation of individuals with disabilities.[60] However, a college may inquire about an applicant's ability to meet essential program requirements provided that the inquiry is not designed to reveal disability status. For example, guidance from the U.S. Department of Education provides that, if lifting a certain amount is an essential requirement for a degree program in physical therapy, it is acceptable to ask an applicant whether she can lift 25 pounds with or without reasonable accommodation.[61]

College officials should strive to make the application process accessible. Most postsecondary institutions use a student's score on commercially available tests to make admission decisions; however, any entrance exams administered by the school are subject to requests for testing accommodations by a student with a disability. Such exams may not be selected or administered in a way that tests the impact of the disability rather than the prospective student's past academic achievement or aptitude.[62]

After the completion of an application file seeking admission, students with disabilities may be evaluated based on facially neutral criteria (both objective and subjective) that are administered uniformly (e.g., grade point average requirements, blind review of writing sample). Some requirements may have a disparate impact on disabled applicants (e.g., use of test scores when considering the admission of persons with learning disabilities); such requirements are permitted if shown to be valid predictors of success in the program. Students may be denied admission based on published criteria and not on stereotypical assumptions about what they may or may not be able to do.[63] All admitted students must meet essential program requirements, although disabled students may require reasonable accommodations and modifications in order to do so.[64]

---

[60] 34 C.F.R. § 104.42(b)-(c).

[61] U.S. Dep't of Educ., Transition of Students with Disabilities to Postsecondary Educ. (March 2011).

[62] 34 C.F.R. §104.42(b); 28 C.F.R. 35.130(b)(8).

[63] Corey v. W. Conn. State Univ., No. 3:03CV0763, 2004 U.S. Dist. LEXIS 3982 (D. Conn. March 10, 2004).

[64] 28 C.F.R. § 36.309(c)(2) (2010). Possible modifications include changes in length of time permitted for the completion of a course, substitution of specific requirements, or adaptation of the manner in which a course is conducted or materials distributed.

Accommodations and Modifications

The ADA and Section 504 require that reasonable modifications in policies, practices, or procedures be made for qualified individuals. However, under Section 504, postsecondary institutions are not required to provide an academic adjustment that would alter or waive essential academic requirements or any directly-related licensing requirement.[65] The U.S. Supreme Court determined that reasonable accommodations do not require an "educational institution to lower or to effect substantial modification of standards to accommodate a handicapped person."[66]

Under the ADA, postsecondary institutions also do not have to provide an academic adjustment that would fundamentally alter the nature of a service, program or activity or result in undue financial or administrative burdens considering the institution's resources as a whole.[67] For example, an appropriate academic adjustment may be to extend the time a student with a disability is allotted to take a test, but an institution is not required to change the substantive content of the test such that a student would be unable to pass a licensing exam. As another example, a postsecondary institution is not required to make modifications that would result in undue financial or administrative burdens such as providing a full-time tutor or one-on-one personal aide for a student.

Academic adjustments are defined in the Section 504 regulations as:

> [S]uch modifications to [the] academic requirements as are necessary to ensure that such requirements do not discriminate or have the effect of discriminating, on the basis of [disability] against a qualified ... applicant or student [with a disability]. Academic requirements that the recipient can demonstrate are essential to the instruction being pursued by such student or to any directly related licensing requirement will not be regarded as discriminatory within the meaning of this section. Modifications may include changes in the length of time permitted for the completion of degree requirements, substitution of specific courses required for the completion of degree requirements, and adaptation of the manner in which specific courses are conducted.[68]

Academic adjustments also may include a reduced course load, extended time on tests, and the provision of auxiliary aids and services. Auxiliary aids and services are defined in the Rehabilitation Act regulations and the Title II ADA regulations. They include note-takers; readers; recording devices; sign language interpreters; screen readers; voice recognition and other adaptive software or hardware for computers; and other devices designed to ensure the

---

[65] *See* 34 C.F.R. § 104.44(a).
[66] Se. Cmty. Coll. v. Davis, 442 U.S. 397 (1979).
[67] *See* 28 C.F.R. § 35.164.
[68] 34 CFR § 104.44(a).

participation of students with impaired sensory, manual, or speaking skills in an institution's programs and activities.[69]

Colleges are not required to provide personal devices and services, such as attendants; individually prescribed devices, such as eyeglasses; readers for personal use or study; or other services of a personal nature.[70] However, if institutions offer tutoring to the general student population, then they must ensure that tutoring services also are available to students with disabilities. Additional examples of reasonable accommodations recognized by courts for postsecondary institutions include additional time on tests, additional time to complete an academic program, the opportunity to retake failed exams, or the ability to write answers out.[71]

On the other hand, accommodations are not justified or reasonable if the student is not otherwise qualified. In an illustrative case from the Fourth Circuit Federal Court of Appeals, a medical student asserted disability discrimination when she was terminated from her medical school program. Contrary to the student's claims that she suffered disability discrimination on the basis of her ADHD and anxiety disorder, the medical school countered that she did not request accommodations until several years after engaging in unprofessional acts, including abusive treatment of staff and multiple unexcused absences. Further, the court determined that the student's requested accommodations (psychiatric treatment, participation in program for distressed physicians, and strict probation) were unreasonable because demonstrating professionalism was a fundamental aspect of the medical school program.[72]

Public postsecondary institutions are required to give primary consideration to the auxiliary aid or service requested by a student, but can opt to provide alternative aids or services if they are effective. They can also opt to provide an effective alternative if the requested auxiliary aid or service would fundamentally alter the nature of a service, program or activity or result in undue financial or administrative burdens. For example, guidance from the U.S. Department of Education provides that if it would be a fundamental alteration or undue burden to provide a disabled student's request for a note-taker for oral classroom presentations and discussions, and a tape recorder would be an effective alternative, a postsecondary institution may provide the student with a tape recorder instead of a note-taker.[73]

The aids, benefits, and services a college provides to a qualified student under Section 504 are not required to produce identical results or levels of achievement for disabled and nondisabled students. They must, however, af-

---

[69] 34 CFR § 104.44(d); 28 CFR § 35.104.

[70] 28 CFR § 35.135; 35 CFR § 104.44(d)(2).

[71] *See* Pirouzkar v. Regents of Univ. of Cal., B161327, 2004 Cal. App. Lexis 3678 (Cal. Ct. App. 2004); Frank v. Univ. of Toledo, No. 3:06 CV 1442, 2007 U.S. District Lexis 94993 (N.D. Ohio 2007); Raymond v. Univ. of Houston, 2009 WL 4604648 (S.D. Tex. 2009).

[72] Halpern v. Wake Forest Univ. Health Sciences, 669 F.3d 454 (4th Cir. 2012).

[73] U.S. DEP'T OF EDUC., TRANSITION OF STUDENTS WITH DISABILITIES TO POSTSECONDARY EDUC. (March 2011).

ford an equal opportunity for disabled students to achieve equal results.[74] Most often, requests for accommodations are reasonable and are provided without controversy, cost to the student, or delay. However, even then, it is important to clarify the scope of an agreed-upon accommodation. For example, if it is agreed that a student will have additional time for tests, the college should specify how much time.

Waiver of Degree and Program Requirements

Of all requested accommodations or modifications, arguably the most controversial is a request to waive a requirement outright or to substitute something that clearly does not reflect the same or even similar competency. Some requests are made soon after admission as incoming students learn of mandatory courses they anticipate may be difficult to complete (e.g., math, foreign language).[75]

In an illustrative case from the Sixth Circuit Federal Court of Appeals, an education major had to earn a grade of "C" or better in math to graduate. After four attempts, she was diagnosed with a math learning disability. She received accommodations, but still failed to earn a "C" in two additional efforts. She filed suit, claiming that the university should accept her "D" grade or waive the course outright, given the nature of her disability. Officials had provided a private testing room, a proctor to read exams, extended time, the use of a personal tutor, the use of manipulatives and other physical equipment during exams, the opportunity to repeat a course, and permission to begin student teaching despite her failure to complete the entire curriculum. The district court reasoned that educational institutions are not required to lower their standards to accommodate disabled students and ruled in favor of the university. The student appealed, arguing that the math course was not a state requirement and, therefore, should not be required by the university. The appellate court disagreed and affirmed the lower court's ruling, observing that deference should be given to educators when evaluating curriculum requirements.[76]

To avoid related litigation, program faculty should examine admission and program requirements and make a reasoned and thoughtful determination as to whether each criterion is essential. Substitutions should be allowed for current requirements that are only tangentially related to the program's mission but result in disparate impact on disabled students. However, requirements that are viewed as essential for all applicants and students should be maintained.

---

[74] 34 C.F.R. §104.4(b)(2).

[75] Gati v. W. Ky. Univ., 762 Fed. Appx. 246 (6th Cir. 2019) (concluding that an educational institution is not required to lower or substantially modify curriculum standards that were necessary to sustain institutions accreditation for the counseling program).

[76] Pangburn v. N. Ky. Univ., No. 99-5474, 2000 U.S. App. LEXIS 6413 (6th Cir. 2000), *cert. denied*, 531 U.S. 875 (2000). *See also* Dicks v. Thomas Moore Coll., 73 Fed. Appx. 149 (6th Cir. 2003) (determining that the College was not required to waive an algebra course for a student; college officials had provided plaintiff with numerous reasonable accommodations).

Duty to Investigate

Unreasonable accommodations may be rejected by campus programs, although such decisions should be made after first investigating whether there are possible options that would qualify as reasonable accommodations.[77] If there were no duty to investigate options, colleges may miss an opportunity to promote an inclusive campus for students with disabilities. Further if colleges are only required to provide only those accommodations that are specifically requested by students, such an approach may limit meaningful access to programs and activities by qualified students. Many college students know a great deal about their respective disabilities, but fewer are knowledgeable about college operations, adaptive technologies, methods of making materials available, and alternative teaching methodologies. As a result, in an effort to demonstrate good-faith compliance, it is recommended that officials explore realistic options with students.

At times, a college may determine that requested accommodations are unreasonable, or perhaps unrelated to the disability.[78] One court even observed that a plaintiff who wanted to use her personal notes while taking a test (in addition to numerous other accommodations that were provided) had a misunderstanding of disability laws, and that these laws do not create absolute rights to any and all accommodations demanded by the individual with a disability.[79]

Additionally, a university likely does not have a duty to provide an accommodation if it is able to demonstrate that a student may pose a threat to the campus community. In *Stebbins v. University of Arkansas*,[80] the university succeeded in proving that Stebbins posed a threat to the community given his past behaviors and the hostile statements he made to a number of campus officials.[81] The duty to provide a reasonable accommodation may also be judged

---

[77] Wynne v. Tufts Univ. Sch. of Med., 976 F.2d 791, 796 (1st Cir. 1992), *cert. denied*, 507 U.S. 1030 (1993); Nathanson v. Med. Coll. of Pa., 926 F.2d 1368, 1383 (3d Cir. 1991). *But see* Ohio Civil Rights Comm'n v. Case W. Reserve Univ., 666 N.E.2d 1376, 1387 (Ohio 1996) (finding no duty to investigate).

[78] Stern v. Univ. of Osteopathic Med. and Health Sci., 220 F.3d 906 (8th Cir. 2000), *rehearing denied*, No. 99-3312SIDM, 2000 U.S. App. LEXIS 23699 (8th Cir. Sept. 21. 2000) (finding that the requested accommodation of a student to supplement his multiple choice answers on exams with either an essay or with responses to oral questions were unrelated to his disability, dyslexia).

[79] Hoffman v. Contra Costa Coll., 21 Fed. Appx. 748 (9th Cir. 2001). *But see* Kenny v. Loyola Univ. of Chi., No. 02 C 1006, 2003 U.S. Dist. LEXIS 2597 (N.D. Ill. Feb. 20, 2003) (denying summary judgment where plaintiff was requesting a laptop computer with voice recognition software; visual fire alarm; TTD text phone; area for rescue assistance; power assisted door; wheelchair-accessible bathroom with tilted mirror, widened toilet stall with grab bars, a soap holder, a 63-inch hose, ADA compliant shower head, lever-style faucets, and a tub with a seat and grab bars; cafeteria alterations; and expedited cafeteria checkout).

[80] No. 11-2465 (8th Cir. 2011), *cert. denied*, 572 U.S. 1105 (2014) (noting the context of Stebbins' threats made directly after the Virginia Tech tragedy put campus administrators understandably on high alert regarding the need for campus safety and careful assessment of perceived risks.)

[81] *See* Sch. Bd. of Nassau Cnty., Fla. v. Arline, 480 U.S. 273, 287 (1987) (identifying threat assessment risk factors: the nature, duration, severity, and probability of the threat resulting in harm).

by the efforts made in response to such a request, as in the study abroad case that follows.

In a Ninth Circuit Federal Court of Appeals case, a wheelchair-confined student alleged that her college failed to reasonably accommodate her disabilities. On campus, the college had installed ramps at her dormitory, changed inside doors, remodeled the bathrooms, and reconfigured the biology lab. When the plaintiff enrolled in a field-based program designed to "explore" Australia, officials provided her with private taxis, air transportation (when others used buses and trains), and the use of an accessible van. Two students were hired to serve as her "helpers."

Staff purchased a sleeping cot manufactured to her specifications, a small narrow wheelchair for her improved maneuverability, and a special shower head for her use. They also provided more accessible housing when available and scheduled activities and selected sites for the group that ordinarily were not selected, but were more accessible to the plaintiff. The court noted that compliance with Title III is determined by viewing a program in its entirety, and that the occasional failure to accommodate will not necessarily result in a violation. The Ninth Circuit upheld the jury's finding that the student was provided with reasonable accommodation.[82]

Neither the ADA nor Rehabilitation Act creates a presumptive right for an individual to dictate all possible accommodations to be provided in an educational program. Accommodations should be limited to what is necessary to provide a student an equal opportunity to participate in the educational program, not to provide an advantage to a student. The important decisions to be made are whether or not the requested accommodations will fundamentally alter the nature of the education program or impose an undue hardship. If the college considers a requested accommodation unreasonable, officials should work collaboratively with the student to determine if a reasonable alternative is available.

Access

Public colleges are required to make services, programs, and activities readily accessible to and usable by disabled individuals,[83] while private colleges must make changes to existing structures that are readily achievable (i.e., easily accomplished, able to be performed without much difficulty or expense).[84] Renovations and new construction on both public and private campuses must comply with standards identified within the ADA. Nevertheless, disability law does not require that every building or every part of every building be acces-

---

[82] Bird v. Lewis & Clark Coll., 303 F. 3d 1015 (9th Cir. 2002), *cert. denied*, 538 U.S. 923 (2003). *See also,* Maczaczyj v. New York, 956 F. Supp. 403 (W.D.N.Y. 1997) (concluding that a College was not required to provide a student who has panic attacks, anxiety, and social phobia with an entire master's degree program in a distance learning format so that he would not be required to physically attend college).

[83] 28 C.F.R. § 35.150.

[84] 28 C.F.R. § 36.304(a).

sible at this time. Rather, the critical issue is whether the service, program, or activity housed within the structure can be accessed. The institution need not incur undue hardship in the process or deface historic structures.

Disability Issues Related to Animals on Campus

Service Animals On-Campus

Pursuant to the ADA, public entities are required to accommodate the use of service animals by individuals with disabilities in all areas that are open for public programs, services, and activities.[85] Although the use of a service animal is an essential tenet of the ADA and accompanying Department of Justice regulations, this right does not provide a blanket guarantee. Rather, the service animal regulations would not require a public entity to modify policies or practices that are designed to promote safety and health considerations regarding when and if service animals may accompany an individual with a disability in a public facility.[86]

Service animals are defined as "…any dog that is individually trained to do work or perform tasks for the benefit of an individual with a disability, including a physical, sensory, psychiatric, intellectual, or other mental disability."[87] The work or tasks performed by a service animal must be directly related to the handler's disability.[88] For example, a service animal might be trained to perform an array of tasks, including but not limited to assisting individuals who are blind, pulling a wheelchair, assisting an individual during a seizure, and helping persons with psychiatric and neurological disabilities by preventing or interrupting impulsive or destructive behaviors. Work tasks performed by a service animal may not include, however, emotional support, companionship, or comfort.

Although the use of a service animal is generally presumed to be reasonable, a service animal may be removed if it is out of control or if it is not housebroken.[89] Pursuant to federal regulatory guidance, a service animal shall be directly controlled via harness or other tether, unless the handler's control is achieved through voice signals or other effective means. Providing care or supervision for a service animal is not required by the institution; rather, the handler is solely responsible for such care or supervision.

Fair Housing Act's On-Campus Application

In 2015, a case and subsequent settlement agreement revealed the extent to which the Fair Housing Act[90] applies to on-campus housing. In the first,

---

[85] § 35.136(g).
[86] 28 C.F.R. § 36.208(a).
[87] 28 C.F.R. § 35.104.
[88] Id.
[89] 28 C.F.R. § 35.136
[90] 42 U.S.C. §§ 3601-3631.

fairly high profile civil rights lawsuit, the Justice Department and University of Nebraska at Kearney (UNK) reached a settlement agreement that affirmed the responsibility of UNK to allow emotional support animals (ESAs) in on-campus housing[91] consistent with the Fair Housing Act. Officially, UNK had adopted a no-pet policy with an exemption for service animals under the ADA and the pets of residence hall directors.

As a result of the court's interpretation that residence halls are dwellings subject to the Fair Housing Act, students living on-campus have legitimate expectations that their requests for ESAs are legally protected. To a degree, the consent order provided guidance regarding what may qualify as an appropriate housing policy with respect to ESAs. In other words, housing policies should permit individuals with "psychological disabilities to keep animals with them in university housing where such animals provide necessary therapeutic benefits."[92]

Dismissal or Removal

Generally, dismissal or removal of a student with a disability from a program or campus should follow the same procedures as are used for other students, whether the dismissal is for academic reasons or misconduct issues. While the court opinions in these cases vary, a determining factor includes whether or not the academic performance was related to a learning disability for which the student had sought an accommodation.

Academic Dismissal

Students with disabilities, like all other students, may be dismissed when they fail to meet academic requirements. To successfully challenge a college's decision to dismiss a student from its program, the student must show that (1) the standards had not been applied uniformly (e.g., that other students with lower performance were retained); (2) different, more difficult standards were used when assessing the plaintiff's performance; (3) grades were based at least in part on the student's disability; or (4) there was a miscalculation of the grades (i.e., simple error). Although there are examples of cases involving professor misconduct, discrimination, and error, the vast majority of claims challenging grades or academic dismissal have been unsuccessful.

In a Sixth Circuit case, a student with a diagnosed learning disability had to complete Latin 111, 112, and 113, prior to graduation. The plaintiff alleged that his Latin 112 professor refused to acknowledge his disability, changed the syllabus to cover more material, and gave a longer final exam than previously administered. He received a D- and subsequently failed Latin 113. He sued, demanding an "A" for each of the three classes, $100,000 from each defendant,

---

[91] United States v. Univ. of Neb. at Kearney, 4:11-CV-3209 (D. Neb. Sept. 4, 2015 (Consent Decree).

[92] Id.

plus reimbursement for all expenses incurred due to not graduating. The court dismissed the suit and noted that the Rehabilitation Act does not permit suits against individual defendants, and no proper claim was made supporting an institutional violation. Moreover, the student could not show discrimination based on his disability, given that the expanded course requirement affected all students.[93]

Similarly, when a student's extracurricular activities, anxiety, or poor study habits affect academic performance and are not related to learning disabilities, a student will be unlikely to demonstrate that her disability limited her learning, given the existence of other factors that accounted for insufficient performance.[94] On appeal, the court concluded that in order to establish a disability under the ADA, "a plaintiff must establish not only that she suffers from an impairment but also that the impairment causes a significant limitation on a major life activity."[95] The student's presentation of evidence that she suffered from a mental impairment did not sufficiently prove that such disability limited her learning, given the existence of other factors that accounted for her limited performance.

Behavior Dismissal

In the higher education setting, neither the ADA nor Rehabilitation Act stipulates that additional or different criteria must be used in determining an appropriate penalty for students with disabilities who violate codes of conduct.[96] When students exhibit inappropriate behavior that endangers others (or themselves), or disrupts the educational environment, they may be penalized by restrictions on activities or by removal from the campus, even if the behavior is shown to be a manifestation of the student's disability. Accordingly, courts are likely to conclude it is irrelevant that a student diagnosed with Tourette syndrome uses pervasively vulgar and sexually explicit language in the classroom, or that a student who is bipolar attacks his professor and then explains he was not taking his medication. Students remain responsible for their conduct and may receive an appropriate penalty.

Nonetheless, officials may elect to consider the effect of a student's disability as it relates to specific behavior at the penalty or "sentencing" stage of the discipline process. Based on the nature and extent of the disability, the administrator may consider whether the student represents a continuing risk to the campus community and whether the behavior is likely to be repeated.

---

[93] Bevington v. Ohio Univ., 93 Fed. Appx. 748 (6th Cir. 2004), *cert. denied,* 125 S. Ct. 306 (2004).

[94] Singh v. George Wash. Univ. Sch. of Med., 667 F.3d 1 (D.C. Cir. 2011).

[95] *Id.*

[96] Fedorov v. Bd. of Regents of Univ. of Ga., 194 F. Supp. 2d 1378 (S.D. Ga. 2002) (concluding that a dismissed student, who was caught in possession of illegal drugs, was not protected under federal law—the plaintiff entered rehabilitation only upon notice that police would be questioning him).

Whether a college will consider a student's disability in making discipline decisions should be incorporated into the school's published discipline policy.

Employment Issues for Colleges and Universities

Colleges and universities serve not only as educational institutions, but also as large employers. Initially, an employer must decide whether an individual asserting a claim under a disability law is, in fact, an employee. Although not decided in the context of the ADA, the U.S. Supreme Court determined the status of "employee" by simply identifying whether the claimant was on the employer's payroll at the time of the alleged discrimination, otherwise known as "the payroll method."[97] Many lower courts have accepted the payroll method for interpreting the ADA and other federal employment statutes. Under this simplistic approach, the relevant questions are, when was the employee placed on the payroll and when was the employee taken off the payroll? An individual suffering from alleged discrimination while on an employer's payroll qualifies as an "employee."

Even if a court determines a plaintiff is an "employee," a public college or university may still assert a defense of Eleventh Amendment immunity against a request for monetary damages.[98] However, a claimant may still obtain a non-monetary judgment against a school, such as an injunction to require or prohibit certain action by the school. Additionally, plaintiffs are still free to assert any state law claim that allows them to recover monetary damages.

The Hiring Process

The process of filling a vacant position depends greatly on variables such as the type of position, applicable collective bargaining agreements, and the number and quality of applicants. However, being proactive and following compliance procedures, such as those discussed below, may help avoid litigation. In 2009, the year the 2008 amendments took effect, the EEOC received 21,451 charges of disability discrimination.[99] Since then, the charges filed with the EEOC have increased, but also appear to be steadily declining for at least a few years, beginning with 28,073 filed in 2016, 26,838 in 2017, and 24,605 in 2018. Given the risk of litigation, campus officials are encouraged periodically to assess their hiring practices at each of the key employment phases, as described in the following sections.

Pre-employment
The pre-employment stage may be the most important part of the hiring process. It should involve identification of essential functions, preparation of job descriptions, advertising, and recruiting. Before posting an opening or

---

[97] Walters v. Metro. Educ. Enter., 519 U.S. 202 (1997).

[98] Bd. of Tr. of the Univ. of Ala. v. Garrett, 531 U.S. 356 (2001).

[99] EEOC statistics available at http://www.eeoc.gov/eeoc/statistics/enforcement/charges.cfm.

soliciting a resume or curriculum vitae, employers should identify the requirements for the position, even delineating between the essential and nonessential
functions of the job. The law defines "essential functions" as "the fundamental
job duties of the employment position the individual with a disability holds
or desires."[100] The term does not encompass the marginal functions of the
position. When determining what functions of a job are "essential," courts
will give deference to the employer's judgment, but it is not the only factor
that will play into the determination.[101] Courts may also examine written job
descriptions prepared before interviewing candidates, the amount of time
someone in the position would spend performing that function, the terms of
a collective bargaining agreement, the work experience of past employees in
the position at issue, the work experience of employees in similar positions,
and the consequences of not requiring an employee to perform a certain function.[102] All applicants warranting consideration should be able to perform all
the specified essential functions of the position with or without a reasonable
accommodation. Once the employer identifies the essential functions of the
position, preparation of a formal job description may take place.

Job descriptions should be specific and detailed as to qualifications, duties, and expectations. When creating the job description, it is essential to
ensure that a nexus exists between each qualification and the business necessity of the position. Criteria that disproportionately screen out job applicants
with disabilities may face particular scrutiny from courts.[103] For example,
if punctuality and regular attendance can be shown to be essential (e.g., an
elementary school teacher), it is irrelevant that an applicant has a sleeping,
anxiety, or emotional disorder that causes him or her to be routinely late or
absent from work. Although the employee's absence may, in fact, be a result
of the disorder, such a person is simply not qualified for the position. Once the
finished job description is complete and contains the essential functions of the
job, it should serve as the basis for creating interview questions, narrowing the
field of candidates, and ultimately making a hiring decision.

In addition to paper credentials, employers may require prospective employees to submit to nonmedical examination tests (e.g., computer skills test).
Physical agility and ability tests that are consistent with business necessity are
not considered medical examinations and may be given at any point in the
application or employment process, as long as such examinations are given
to all applicants. Only those applicants who meet the employer's legitimate
physical criteria for the job are "qualified" to receive confirmed offers of
employment and begin work.

---

[100] 29 C.F.R. § 1630.2(n).

[101] 42 U.S.C. § 12111(8); *see also* McBride v. BIC Consumer Products Mfg. Co., Inc., 583 F.3d
92, 98 (2nd Cir. 2009).

[102] 29 C.F.R. § 1630.2(n)(3).

[103] *See* 29 C.F.R. § 1630.10.

Interview and Screening

Once the employer begins to receive applications, the search committee or decision maker may make a first-round of cuts based on qualifications. Removing all applicants from the pool who do not meet the minimum criteria established in the job description can start narrowing the field. Eliminating applicants based on minimum qualifications alone though, will not likely create a manageable number of remaining applicants for interviews. Search committees must determine which remaining candidates it would like to consider based on a formal process such as ranking applicants or informally discussing remaining applicants' qualifications. There is no set method or formula that search committees must use, as long as their decision-making is not influenced by impermissible factors such as race, age, or disability.

Once the committee narrows the field of applicants to a manageable size, it may conduct interviews to determine a set of finalists. If the committee conducts in-person interviews, the disabilities of some applicants may be apparent. At this stage of the process, even if a disability is apparent, an employer generally should not inquire into the nature and extent of an applicant's disability; the exception to this being if the applicant requests some sort of accommodation for the interview. However, if an applicant requests an accommodation, an employer should make as limited an inquiry into the disability as is necessary to assess the accommodation request. An employer may request documentation to support the existence of a disability if the disability is not obvious to or known by the employer at the time of the interview.

While an employer should avoid asking any direct questions related to an applicants' disability, it must still obtain information relevant to the position during the interview. An applicant, whether disabled or not, should field questions related to education, work history, experience, and skills. An employer may direct questions to the applicant regarding the applicant's ability to perform job functions and as to how the applicant would perform certain tasks.[104] As long as an employer tailors all questions and pre-employment tests to the business necessity of the position and administers them equally to all candidates, the employer is not engaging in discrimination based on an individual's disability.

Making a Conditional Job Offer

After reviewing applications and completing interviews, the decision-making authority must select a candidate to fill the position. At this stage, an individual's disability should not be a part of the decision of whether to make an offer to that candidate. In selecting the best "qualified" individual for the position, it is important to note that the law demands nondiscrimination, not favoritism. Federal law does not require an employer to hire an individual who is unqualified for a position, one who is less qualified for a position, or even one who is equally qualified for a position. The employer should certainly tender an offer of employment to a disabled applicant if the applicant is the

---

[104] 29 C.F.R. § 1630.14(a).

best candidate, but there is no obligation to make an offer of employment to a disabled individual who is not qualified just because the applicant is a member of an underrepresented population. The employer may eliminate from consideration any candidate who does not meet minimum qualifications or possess the ability to perform the essential functions of the job, regardless of disability, at any stage of the process. If a search committee serves in an advisory capacity and makes a recommendation of employment to university administrators, the administrators should inform committee members of their decision. An administrator may then tender the conditional offer of employment, or if the administration is comfortable with the candidate, a final job offer.

Post-Offer Examinations and Confirmed Job Offer

Once an employer makes a conditional offer of employment, the employer might then require the applicant to undergo a medical examination and condition the offer on the results of the examination, as long as all entering employees in the same category must undergo a medical examination regardless of disability.[105] During this stage, the employer may also question the applicant regarding the applicant's general and physical health, as well as past uses of medical leave or workers' compensation. The medical examination does not need to be job-related or tied to business necessity unless certain criteria screen out employees with disabilities.[106] In that case, the criteria responsible for screening out employees with disabilities must be consistent with business necessity and the employee's ability to perform the essential functions of the job. As a part of the showing of business necessity, an employer would need to demonstrate that there is no reasonable accommodation that would allow the applicant to perform the essential functions of the job.[107]

If the applicant passes all post-offer examinations, the employer should then tender a final job offer. From the medical examination, the employer should be aware of any impairments the applicant may have, though the offer of employment may not be withdrawn simply because an employer discovers that an applicant has a physical or mental impairment that substantially limits a major life activity or has a need for a reasonable accommodation to perform essential job functions.

Reasonable Accommodations

The law regarding reasonable accommodations remained intact through the 2008 amendments, but colleges and universities may well see an increase in the number of individuals requiring accommodations. In the workplace, reasonable accommodations are modifications or adjustments that enable an employee with a disability to enjoy equal benefits and privileges of employ-

---

[105] 29 C.F.R. § 1630.14(b).
[106] 29 C.F.R. § 1630.14(b)(3).
[107] 29 C.F.R. § 1630.14(b) Appx.

ment as those enjoyed by similarly situated employees without disabilities.[108] A job applicant may also require a reasonable accommodation if the applicant is a qualified individual and the reasonable accommodation is necessary to enable the individual to be considered for the position.[109]

Reasonable accommodations may include such practices such as making facilities accessible and usable; restructuring jobs and work schedules; reassigning existing employees with disabilities to vacant positions; acquiring or modifying equipment; making adjustments or modifications to examinations, training materials, and policies; or providing readers or interpreters.[110]

Absent undue hardship, an employer must provide a reasonable accommodation to a qualified individual with a substantially limiting impairment or a record of such impairment.[111] An accommodation is only reasonable if it enables a qualified individual to perform the essential functions of the job.[112] Other requests are simply not reasonable for the position the employee holds. A professor cannot reasonably request that all faculty meetings which he attends be limited to twenty minutes due to his back pain.[113] Similarly, an employee cannot request indefinite leave as a reasonable accommodation.[114]

Interactive Process

To determine whether an accommodation is both appropriate and reasonable, it is necessary for the employer and the employee with the disability to engage in an informal process to discuss how the employee will perform the essential functions of the job. The expansive definition of "disabled" only heightens the importance of engaging in this interactive process with employees who are qualified individuals. A meaningful interactive process may take a series of meetings and ideas to create an accommodation both reasonable and enabling for the employee, and one that will be effective and economically feasible for the employer.

A single instance of requesting ideas for a reasonable accommodation from the employee will not suffice. Further, terminating an employee who was unable to immediately present a potential accommodation when questioned is not defensible.[115] An employer may ultimately select among different alternatives for accommodation, and although an individual with a disability is not required to accept the accommodations chosen by the employer, the

---

[108] 29 C.F.R. § 1630.2(o)(1)(iii).

[109] 29 C.F.R. § 1630.2(o)(1)(i).

[110] 42 U.S.C. § 12111(9); 29 C.F.R. § 1630.2(o)(2).

[111] 29 C.F.R. § 1630.2(o)(4).

[112] Cleveland v. Pol'y Mgmt. Sys. Corp., 526 U.S. 966 (1999).

[113] Windhauser v. Bd. of Supervisors for Louisiana State Univ. & Agric. & Mech. Coll., 360 Fed. Appx. 562 (5th Cir. 2010).

[114] Amsel v. Tex. Water Dev. Bd., 464 F.Appx. 395, 400 (5th Cir. 2012) (indefinite leave is not a reasonable accommodation). See also Fiumara v. Harvard Coll., 2009 WL 1163851 (1st Cir. 2009); Davis v. George Wash. Univ., 26 F. Supp. 3d 103 (D.D.C. 2014).

[115] Cutrera v. Bd. of Supervisors for La. State Univ. & Agric. & Mech. Coll., 429 F.3d 108 (5th Cir. 2005).

consequence of refusal may result in the employee not being able to perform the essential functions of the position. In such a case, the individual will not be considered qualified and may be removed from the position.

Undue Hardship

There may be accommodations that would enable an employee to perform the essential functions of the job, but they are simply financially or realistically impractical for the employer to provide. In these situations, implementing the accommodation would place an undue hardship on the employer.[116] Generally, an undue hardship occurs if an employer would undertake significant difficulty or expense relative to certain factors related to the employer's business.[117] These factors, which a court will consider when determining the validity of an employer's defense, include the nature and cost of the accommodation, the employer's overall size and budget, the effect of the accommodation on expenses and resources, the relationship of the affected facility to the employer, and the impact on the employer's ability to conduct business.[118] Because there is no fixed formula for determining if providing an accommodation would create an undue hardship, the same accommodation provided in different circumstances may be an undue hardship in one instance and not in another.

Terms of Employment

An employer's responsibility to ensure nondiscrimination does not stop after an employee is hired. Just as an employer cannot discriminate in making its hiring decision, it also may not discriminate in the management of its employees.

Compensation and Benefits

It is axiomatic that an employer may not pay a disabled employee less than other, nondisabled employees. Although this may not automatically ensure that a disabled employee will never earn less than nondisabled employees. Employers should compensate a disabled employee the same as any other individual, commensurate with experience, productivity, and whatever other nondiscriminatory criteria an employer chooses.

A disabled employee may require leave time to attend doctor appointments; physical, occupational, or another form of therapy; or any other type of treatment related to the disability. The ADA does not require disabled employees to receive more paid or unpaid leave than nondisabled employees, but the parties should work together in reaching a mutually favorable outcome, such as making leave for such medical purposes a reasonable accommodation. This is not to say that an employee with a disability should be entitled to leave in excess of what other employees receive. If an employee was absent from work enough to substantially impact the employee's productivity, the employee may not be

---

[116] 29 C.F.R. § 1630.15(d).

[117] 42 U.S.C. § 12111(10)(A); 29 C.F.R. § 1630.2(p).

[118] 42 U.S.C. § 12112(b)(5)(A); 42 U.S.C. § 12111(10)(B); 29 C.F.R. § 1630.2(p).

performing the essential functions of the job, or such an accommodation may be placing an undue hardship on the employer.

Reassignments

Reassignment may be a reasonable accommodation for existing personnel, but not for applicants. An applicant must be qualified for a position and be able to perform the essential functions of the position, even if performance requires use of accommodations. However, for existing employees, there may be occasions when reassignment to an open position may be necessary for continued employment. A person may have been qualified for his or her current position but have experienced a decline in mobility, manual dexterity, or vision such that he or she can no longer perform the essential functions of the position. In other words, the person is no longer qualified for the current job. But if the employment relationship is ongoing, then an employee with a disability usually should be reassigned if another appropriate position is vacant.[119] Generally, courts have held that it is the employee's responsibility to identify and request reassignment to a vacant position. However, federal law does not require employers to remove an existing employee to create an opening, establish a new position, reassign essential functions,[120] promote an employee to an open position that violates a seniority-based system, or violate collective bargaining agreements regarding "bumping" rights[121] in order to retain an employee who is no longer qualified because of a disability.

Adverse Employment Actions

Employees with disabilities succeed and fail in the workplace, just as individuals who are not disabled do. Occasionally, it is necessary to nonrenew, suspend, transfer, demote, refuse tenure, deny promotions, or even terminate an employee with a disability. Adverse employment action may be due to a violation of policies or directives, poor performance, nonperformance, inappropriate actions while on the job, inadequate skills, or even criminal activity.[122] Other times, an employee's disability was the basis for either an adverse decision

---

[119] Off. of the Architect of the Capitol v. Off. of Compliance, 361 F.3d 633 (Fed. Cir. 2004) (finding that transfer to an open position qualified as a reasonable accommodation).

[120] Phelps v. Optima Health & Catholic Med. Ctr., 251 F.3d 21 (1st Cir. 2001) (concluding that the ADA did not require reassignment of essential functions or creation of a new position to enable a nurse who could no longer lift clients to remain employed).

[121] Ozlowski v. Henderson, 237 F.3d 837 (7th Cir. 2001) (observing that an employer is not required to bump a current employee to allow a person with a disability to fill the position or to fill a vacant position it did not intend to fill for reasons independent of the employee's disability).

[122] See, e.g., Newberry v. E. Tex. State Univ., 161 F.3d 276 (5th Cir. 1998) (concluding that a professor was dismissed due to unprofessional conduct, failure to attend meetings, harassment of colleagues, and poor work ethic rather than disability); Curtis v. Univ. of Houston, 940 F. Supp. 1070 (S.D. Tex., 1996) (concluding that a former alcoholic professor was not discriminated against because of his poor academic performance), aff'd without published opinion, 127 F.3d 35 (5th Cir. 1997).

or the creation of an environment that was so hostile that the employee was forced to resign and may be considered constructively discharged.

If an adverse employment action is challenged, the employer's decision will be upheld if there is a legitimate, nondiscriminatory reason for the employment action, (e.g. insubordination, neglect of duty, immorality).[123] In order to prevail, the plaintiff must show that the proffered reason given by the employer for the decision is merely a pretext, and the true reason for the adverse action was a form of unlawful discrimination, such as a decision based on the individual's disability.[124]

Conclusion

As the educational rights of individuals with disabilities in higher education continue to evolve, higher education professionals should be prepared to adjust practices and ensure adherence to the numerous state and federal laws that protect disability rights and promote inclusive as well as nondiscriminatory practices. Given the lessons learned from past legal decisions, legislation, and policy directives, there are a number of practical steps that can be taken to ensure campus programs, services, facilities, and opportunities are nondiscriminatory and inclusive for students, staff, faculty, visitors, and community members.

The authors wish to recognize contributions made to earlier editions of this chapter by Jodi Bender, J.D., and Stephen Thomas.

---

[123] 29 C.F.R. § 1630.15(a).
[124] Reeves v. Sanderson Plumbing Prods., 530 U.S. 133 (2000).

10 Liability for Negligence

Scott R. Bauries, J.D., Ph.D.
University of Kentucky College of Law

Introduction

Tort law is a system of law through which parties seek compensation from other parties for wrongful acts. This system of law encompasses the three basic fault-based groupings of intentional torts—those in which the wrongdoer (or "tortfeasor") committed the wrongful act either intentionally or with reckless disregard of an extreme risk of harm (e.g., battery); strict liability torts—those in which public policy dictates assigning responsibility to a party even if that party personally did not do anything wrong (e.g., the strict vicarious liability of an employer for its employee's wrongful conduct); and negligence torts, the subject of this chapter.

Negligence is a form of tort liability in which a person's conduct falls below the duty of care established by law for the protection of others against unreasonable risk of harm. The generally applicable standard holds that a party has acted negligently if the party has departed from the conduct expected of a reasonably prudent person acting under circumstances similar to those in which an injury occurred. In order to establish negligence, an injured plaintiff or the plaintiff's representative must prove (1) the defendant owed a duty to the plaintiff; (2) the defendant breached that duty by failing to conform to the required standard of conduct; (3) the defendant's negligent conduct was the proximate cause of the harm to the plaintiff; and (4) the plaintiff suffered injury that would justify an award of damages.

As government or corporate business entities, higher education institutions can be liable for negligence in some cases. However, the landmark decision in *Bradshaw v. Rawlings*[1] significantly limited a higher education institution's duty to protect students from injury and harm based on negligence. The student plaintiff in *Bradshaw* was injured in an automobile accident that occurred

In previous versions of this chapter, Professor Joseph Beckham was listed as an author, and his prior work laid the foundations for this chapter in its current form. Professor Beckham has elected not to continue in this role. I wish to thank him for all of his prior contributions and research, and I hope that I can continue to uphold his high standards going forward.

[1] 612 F.2d 135 (3d Cir. 1979)..

while the student was returning to the campus. The car was driven by another student who was intoxicated with alcohol provided at an unsupervised, but college-sponsored, off-campus event. When a jury found the college negligent in its planning and supervision of the event, the college appealed. Rejecting the student's claim that his injuries were proximately caused by the institution's failure to supervise underage drinking at the event, the appeals court reasoned that the institution had no *in loco parentis* authority to control students and held that it had no duty to supervise them. Emphasizing that the "modern American college is not an insurer of the safety of its students,"[2] the federal appeals court dismissed the claim against the institution.

Since *Bradshaw*, the question of how and to what extent institutions of higher education could be held liable for negligence involving students has preoccupied the courts. Judges initially rejected the *in loco parentis* notion of the relationship between student and institution that has traditionally applied in P-12 education, relying on *Bradshaw* and its progeny to adopt a "no duty" standard for higher education institutions.[3] However, over time, judges have retreated from principles that effectively denied relief to injured student-plaintiffs and extended liability, initially in cases involving the inspection and maintenance of premises, and then in cases involving the duty of care associated with a landlord's responsibility to a tenant. In a limited number of cases, judges have imposed a special duty of care on institutions of higher education predicated on the relationship between the parties, the foreseeable risk of harm, and public policy considerations related to the changing role of colleges and universities.[4]

This chapter surveys the evolving nature of duty of care in the area of liability for negligence involving higher education institutions and students. It begins with an examination of the duty of care reflected in premises liability cases, then reviews contemporary case law related to third-party assaults. Following this analysis, the concept of a special duty of care is analyzed in the context of hazing, the unique duty of care applicable to intercollegiate athletics, and high-risk student activities such as alcohol use. Finally, student suicide as an area of emerging institutional duty of care is considered.

Premises Liability

The traditional common law of torts divides the parties entitled to recover from the owner or custodian of real property into three groups: invitees (sometimes termed "business invitees"), licensees, and trespassers. Invitees enter the property at the invitation of the owner or custodian, and are present there at least in part to further the interests of the owner or custodian. As a result, the

---

[2] *Id.* at 138.

[3] See Peter F. Lake, *The Rise of Duty and the Fall of* In loco parentis *and Other Protective Tort Doctrines in Higher Education Law*, 64 Mo. L. Rev. 1, 2 (1999).

[4] See Robert D. Bickel & Peter F. Lake, *The Emergence of New Paradigms in Student-University Relations: From '*In loco parentis*' to Bystander to Facilitator*, 23 J.C. & U. L. 755 (1997).

owner or custodian owes such parties an ordinary duty of care, including the duty to make reasonable inspections of the premises and to remedy dangerous conditions within a reasonable time.[5] Licensees enter the premises not pursuant to the invitation of the owner or custodian, but with that party's permission or acquiescence. They are present on the property for their own interests, and not for the interests of the property owner or custodian. As such, licensees accept their "license" to enter the property as they find it. The property owner or custodian is under no duty to inspect the premises or make them safe, but if the owner or custodian knows or should know of a dangerous condition that is concealed to the ordinary observer, then the owner or custodian must either make that condition safe or warn any licensees of it.[6] Trespassers enter the land contrary to the wishes of the owner or custodian, with no invitation or license. As such, they are owed no duty of care. The property owner must simply refrain from injuring them willfully or wantonly.[7]

In cases involving higher education institutions, some courts[8] have explicitly relied on the distinction between an invitee and a licensee[9] in determining whether a duty is owed, but the overwhelming majority of courts have treated those harmed on campus—especially students—as invitees. In determining the duty of the institution as owner, then, the standard is whether the institution's agents have acted reasonably in light of the probability of a risk of injury. However, the affirmative defense of "assumption of the risk" places a significant limitation on potential liability, even where an injured party is the invitee of the institution. Even an invitee assumes all the known risks attendant to the use of the premises, and an institution may avoid liability where a danger on the premises is open or obvious to a potential plaintiff, and the

---

[5] *See, e.g.*, Harris v. Univ. of S. Car., 391 S.C. 518, 523-24, 706 S.E.2d 45, 48 (S.C. Ct. App. 2011).

[6] *Harris*, 391 S.C. at 523, 706 S.E.2d at 47 ("A licensee is a social guest or 'a person who is privileged to enter upon land by virtue of the possessor's consent.'"). On college and university campuses, parents and other visitors are often considered licensees, and they accordingly rarely recover against the institution in tort suits. *See id.*

[7] Kline v. Ohio Univ., 62 Ohio Misc. 2d 704, 707, 610 N.E.2d 1205, 1207 (Ct. Cl. 1990).

[8] *See, e.g.*, Peery v. Cleveland State Univ., 2007 Ohio 5275, 2007 Ohio Misc. LEXIS 379 (Ohio Ct. Cl. 2007), in which a person injured approaching the stairs to a volleyball facility was characterized as a licensee who could not recover as the injury was not caused by a hidden dangerous condition but by an open and obvious condition that was not particularly hazardous.

[9] Light v. Ohio Univ., 28 Ohio St. 3d 66, 68, 28 Ohio B. 165, 502 N.E. 2d 611, 613 (1968).

plaintiff chooses to use the premises despite that known risk.[10] Put differently, a consenting participant who is aware of the risk, has an appreciation for the nature of the risk, and voluntarily assumes the risk cannot hold the institution liable for injury.

In general, however, a higher education institution has the duty to maintain its premises in a reasonably safe condition for those who enter the property at the invitation of the institution.[11] The duty imposes a responsibility to exercise ordinary care in managing the premises to avoid exposing persons to an unreasonable risk of harm.[12] Defining the nature and scope of the duty and the persons to whom it is owed requires consideration of the likelihood of injury to another from a dangerous condition on the property, the seriousness of the potential injury, the burden of avoiding the risk, and the foreseeability of a potential plaintiff's presence on the property.[13] An injured plaintiff must establish that a duty was owed, and that the institution either created the defective condition or had actual or constructive knowledge[14] of the defective condition for such a period of time that with the exercise of reasonable care, the manager should have corrected the condition. As an illustration of this latter requirement, in *Bowen v. City University of New York*,[15] the court rejected liability for a slip-and-fall injury following a snowstorm on campus, reasoning that the institution owed a duty "for a hazardous condition created on

---

[10] *See* Kanita v. Ohio Univ., 2009 Ohio 7187, 2009 Ohio Misc. LEXIS 507 (Ohio Ct. C. 2009) (rejecting a student's slip and fall claim because she admitted she could see water dripping from trays in a rack in the cafeteria. The appeals court reasoned that the student did not identify any attendant circumstances preventing her from noticing the water and the institution had no duty to protect or warn the student from such an open and obvious condition); Morgan State Univ. v. Walker, 919 A.2d 21 (Md. 2007) (denying recovery to a parent, who sued the university following a slip and fall in an icy university parking lot, on the basis that she acknowledged the lot was icy and potentially dangerous when she voluntarily crossed it and thus fully assumed the risk of injury). Some cases cast this assumption of the risk defense as a "no duty" rule, and although that distinction should be paid attention at the pleading stage, it makes no difference in the outcome. *See, e.g.*, Blust v. Berea Coll., 431 F. Supp. 2d 703, 705 (E.D. Ky. 2006) (recognizing that "the danger of slipping and falling from the edge of a such a cliff is open and obvious to one exercising ordinary care. The defendant had no duty to warn of such a danger, nor did it have a duty to make the property absolutely safe").

[11] In Varnell v. La. Tech Univ., 709 So.2d 890 (La. Ct. App. 1998), a parent visited a student's residence hall room and was injured in a slip and fall because of standing water near a window air conditioning unit. The state court determined that fault should be apportioned between the student, who failed to warn of the risk, and the institution, which had received numerous requests to correct the problem.

[12] *See, e.g.*, Radcliffe v. Hofstra Univ., 200 A.D.2d 562, 606 N.Y.S.2d 333 (1994).

[13] *See, e.g.*, Witherspoon v. Columbia Univ., 7 A.D.3d 702, 777 N.Y.S.2d 507 (2d Dept 2004) (recognizing that the presence of an alternative route on the campus did not relieve the institution of a duty to maintain a courtyard in reasonably safe condition).

[14] *See, e.g.*, Carlson v. Bd. of Regents, 47 Ill. Ct. Cl. 171; 1994 Ill. Ct. Cl. LEXIS 57 (Ill. Ct. Cl. 1994) (finding that a student's slip and fall on a wet tile floor in the exit passageway of a residence hall shower-bathroom was attributable to the institution's failure to maintain premises given constructive knowledge of a foreseeable risk based on student complaints of the standing water puddle in the passageway).

[15] 743 N.Y.S.2d 119, 294 A.D.2d 322 (A.D. 2 Dept. 2002).

its premises by precipitation only if the landowner had actual or constructive notice of the conditions and had a reasonably sufficient time from cessation of the precipitation to remedy the condition caused by it."[16]

A key consideration in these cases is whether the danger was foreseeable. Were the institution's agents aware of the danger? Were they aware that visitors and invitees to the campus would be in the area or using the facilities? Would reasonable inspection and maintenance policies have disclosed the danger or led to correction of the deficiency? In an illustrative case, *McDonald v. University of West Virginia Board of Trustees*,[17] a theater major who was enrolled in a stage-movement class brought a negligence claim against the university after she fell and broke her leg while running across a lawn on the campus. The professor had moved the class outdoors, and the assignment for students was to run across the lawn as if in fear for their lives. The student contended that the institution breached a duty to maintain the lawn. A state appeals court affirmed the trial court's judgment in favor of the institution, holding that the evidence did not support a breach of duty. The appeals court noted that the student-plaintiff failed to show that the institution had actual knowledge of any defect that might have caused the fall, and the record suggested the defect was so minor that it could not later be located.[18]

As the preceding case summary suggests, negligence cannot be presumed solely because an accident occurred on the institution's property. As long as the institution fulfills its duty to exercise reasonable care for the protection of participants from non-obvious or unreasonably increased risks, the institution is insulated from liability. For example, in *Baldauf v. Kent State University*,[19] a student-plaintiff asserted a negligence claim against the state university related to a slip-and-fall injury on dormitory steps. The student contended that lighting in the stairway was inadequate and the concrete steps were crumbling. Although no evidence of crumbling was adduced, the university did admit that the steps were in need of repair. However, the institution's agents testified they did not believe that the stairs constituted a dangerous condition. A state appeals court rejected the student's claim after finding that the university had no actual or constructive notice regarding the condition of the steps, and the defective nature of the steps did not rise to the level of being unreasonably dangerous.[20]

Similarly, it cannot be presumed that, even if a dangerous condition existed and caused an accident, the higher education institution should be liable for that condition. Returning to the distinctions between invitees, licensees, and trespassers, these classifications, though traditional, still have force in the recent cases involving higher education institutional negligence. For example,

---

[16] *Id.* at 120.

[17] 191 W. Va. 179, 444 S.E.2d 57 (W. Va. 1994).

[18] In considering the alternative theory that the professor's failure to adequately inspect the lawn was the proximate cause of the injury, the court noted that the professor had inspected the lawn and there was nothing to suggest that an inspection would have identified the minor defect. *Id.* at 183, 444 S.E.2d at 63.

[19] 49 Ohio App. 3d 46, 550 N.E.2d 517 (1988).

[20] *Id.* at 50, 550 N.E.2d at 521.

in *Harris v. University of South Carolina*,[21] a student's mother stayed overnight on University property in coastal South Carolina, ostensibly to participate in a University environmental initiative, and she slipped and broke her ankle badly on a boardwalk step while there. She contended at trial that she was a business invitee as a matter of law, and on appeal that it was error for the court to charge the jury that it must determine whether she was an invitee or a licensee. The jury had found that she was a licensee, based on her activities while there, which included sunbathing and reading, and the appellate court upheld the jury charge, as well as the verdict denying her compensation.[22] If the jury would have found her to be an invitee, the liability verdict would likely have been the opposite, so the traditional classification system can be very impactful.

Third-Party Assaults on Students

In general tort law, a party does not have the duty to protect another party from even foreseeable harm from third parties, unless there is a "special relationship" between the parties (i.e., one extending beyond an ordinary business or contractual relationship).[23] However, cases involving third-party assaults on the campus illustrate the erosion of this "no duty" standard. Drawing on the institution's responsibility to maintain the premises and the obligations of a landlord to a tenant, judges have derived a duty of reasonable care for the safety of students linked to a foreseeable risk of which the student may be unaware. In some instances, the duty arises based on previous instances of third-party assaults on the campus, while in other cases, judges take notice of a general foreseeable risk related to maintaining residence halls in, for example, a densely populated urban area with high crime rates. In a relative few cases, judges have concluded that the institution, through the implementation of security systems and warnings to students, has assumed the duty to provide safety and security on the campus predicated on acknowledging a known foreseeable risk implicit in its own policies.

The traditional "no duty" standard applicable to security in residence halls is reflected in the 1981 case of *Hall v. Board of Supervisors*.[24] In *Hall*, a student shot by a non-student in the lobby of her residence hall claimed that the institution had breached its duty to protect her (1) by requiring her to live on campus without warning her of the dangers to which she would be subjected, (2) by failing to maintain adequate security, and (3) by failing to bar her assailant from the campus. In its decision, the state appeals court asserted

---

[21] 391 S.C. 518, 706 S.E.2d 45 (Ct. App. 2011).

[22] Harris v. Univ. of S.C., 391 S.C. 518, 524-25, 706 S.E.2d 45, 48 (Ct. App. 2011) ("We find the jury was properly given the opportunity to determine whether or not Harris had an express invitation to visit the Island and whether or not her presence on the Island benefited the University. Thus, the trial court did not err in charging the jury the law regarding both licensees and invitees because Harris's status at the time of her injury was a question of fact for the jury.").

[23] Niece v. Elmview Grp. Home, 131 Wash. 2d 39, 43, 929 P.2d 420, 423 (1997).

[24] 405 So. 2d 1125 (La. Ct. App.1981).

that prior isolated criminal activities did not create a duty to warn residents of probable dangers, asserting there was "...no proof that living on campus increased the hazard above the ordinary."[25] The court held that in cases where spontaneous unforeseeable violence occurs, unless a causal relationship is established between security inadequacies on the college's part and an injury sustained to the student, negligence could not be established: "Even the most sophisticated security forces are powerless to prevent a spontaneous, sudden and unprovoked act of violence."[26]

Judicial opinions consistently emphasize that there is no duty to control the conduct of a third party or to prevent him or her from causing harm unless a special relationship exists that imposes such a duty. For example, in *Ruchalski v. Schenectady County Community College*,[27] a student who was injured when struck by a traffic cone thrown by another student in a college cafeteria could not recover damages on a theory that the college owed a special duty of care. The court noted that the college could not have foreseen the act that led to the injury and no special duty to protect the student could be established. The general rule derived from the case law is that there is no duty to protect a student from a third-party attack or injury unless the institution, based on a special duty relationship, had reason to foresee the likelihood of criminal conduct that would endanger the safety of the student-tenant.[28]

This standard was applied in *Rhaney v. University of Maryland Eastern Shore*,[29] despite a fact pattern that might suggest foreseeable risk. In *Rhaney*, a student was punched by his roommate in the residence hall room they shared during the fall term. The roommate had been in two fights on campus the previous spring and had been suspended in that term for one of those fights. After completing a counseling program, the roommate was readmitted and assigned to a room with the plaintiff student. The injured student contended that the university breached a duty of care in assigning him to a room with a student who had a dangerous propensity for violence and failing to warn him of the roommate's previous conduct. The court reasoned that a previous instance in which the institution had disciplined the roommate for fighting with other students in the common areas of the school did not establish a foreseeable risk that the roommate would assault the student plaintiff in the dorm room, and therefore, the college did not owe a duty to the plaintiff to protect him from his roommate.[30]

However, institutional negligence predicated on the landlord-tenant relationship was affirmed in *Nero v. Kansas State University*,[31] in which a female

---

[25] *Id.* at 1126.

[26] *Id.*

[27] 239 A.D.2d 687, 656 N.Y.S.2d 784 (1997).

[28] *See* Luina v. Katharine Gibbs Sch., 37 A.D.3d 555, 830 N.Y.S.2d 263 (App. Div. 2007) (denying recovery to a student, who had been struck in the face by a fellow student during a classroom altercation, on the basis that the college owed no duty for a sudden and unforeseeable act).

[29] 880 A.2d 357 (Md. 2005).

[30] *Id.* at 366.

[31] 861 P.2d 768 (Kan. 1993).

student who was sexually assaulted in her residence hall contended that the institution owed a duty of reasonable care to students in residence halls once it exercised its discretion to make such housing available to students. While declining to hold that the university-student relationship itself imposes a duty on institutions to protect students, the opinion emphasized that a university has a duty to regulate and supervise foreseeable dangers occurring on its property. In *Nero*, there was evidence that the student's assailant was reassigned to a coeducational residence for the summer after having been disciplined for a previous assault on a female student during the academic year. Finding that the trial court erred in granting summary judgment to the institution, the Supreme Court of Kansas reversed and remanded, emphasizing that the trial court must resolve the question of whether, at the time of the attack, the institution's agents should have foreseen the attack, based on knowledge of the assailant's prior history at the institution.

As attacks on students in residence halls received widespread national attention, judges, motivated by social policy concerns, began to place increased responsibility on institutions to protect students. Heightened institutional liability, predicated on an apparent judicial expansion of the scope of foreseeable risk, was evident in the case of *Mullins v. Pine Manor College*.[32] In *Mullins*, a female student who was raped on campus after being abducted from her residence hall room by an unidentified assailant prevailed in her claim that the college, as landlord, was negligent. The Supreme Judicial Court of Massachusetts affirmed the trial court's decision holding the college negligent and determined that the college had the duty to protect the student primarily because there was a general community consensus that the college would take steps to provide security despite prevailing perceptions of college students as adults.

> Of course, changes in college life, reflected in the general decline of the theory that the college stands *in loco parentis* to its students, arguably cut against this view. The fact that a college need not police the morals of its resident students, however, does not entitle it to abandon any effort to ensure their physical safety. Parents, students, and the general community still have a reasonable expectation, fostered in part by colleges themselves, that reasonable care will be exercised to protect resident students from foreseeable harm.[33]

The *Mullins* court reasoned that since the college had established a security force, it had an obligation to ensure a degree of care grounded in the theory that "...a duty voluntarily assumed must be performed with due care."[34] In addressing the college's argument that the incident was not foreseeable since there had not been any previous incidents of third-party assaults in campus residence halls, the court asserted that "(p)rior criminal acts are simply one factor among others that establish the foreseeability of the act of the third

---

[32] 449 N.E.2d 331 (Mass.1983).

[33] *Id*. at 335-336.

[34] *Id*. at 336.

party."[35] Because the college had routinely warned students during orientation of the dangers inherent in being housed near a larger urban metropolis, there was sufficient evidence that the risk of a criminal act was both foreseeable and foreseen by the college.

Several cases that followed *Mullins* support the contention that the landlord-tenant relationship creates a special duty to protect students residing in residence halls. In the case of *Cutler v. Board of Regents*,[36] a Florida appeals court allowed a female university student who was assaulted and raped in her residence hall room to amend her complaint, asserting that "recent Florida decisions have held that a landlord, who recognizes and assumes the duty to protect his tenants from foreseeable criminal conduct, may be liable if he fails to take reasonable precautions to prevent injury to his tenants from this conduct."[37] In *Miller v. State*,[38] the Court of Appeals of New York affirmed negligence on the part of the university for failing to protect a female student from rape in a residence hall. The appeals court noted:

> As a landowner, the State must act as a reasonable (person) in maintaining property in a reasonably safe condition in view of all the circumstances... Under this standard, a landlord has a duty to maintain minimal security measures, related to a specific building itself, in the face of foreseeable criminal intrusion upon tenants... Thus, defendant here had a duty to take the rather minimal security measure of keeping the dormitory doors locked when it had notice of the likelihood of criminal intrusions.[39]

The State Supreme Court of Maine relied heavily on the *Mullins* decision in reversing summary judgment for the University of Maine in another case involving a sexual assault in a residence hall. In *Stanton v. University of Maine*,[40] a student attending a pre-season summer soccer program was sexually assaulted in her campus residence hall after attending a fraternity party. The lower court had granted summary judgment in favor of the university based on the contention that the university owed no duty of care to the student and that even if it had owed a duty of care, it fulfilled that duty by providing a residence hall that was reasonably safe and secure. The state supreme court, in reversing the decision, determined that a duty founded on premises liability existed. In responding to the university's contention that the assault was not foreseeable, the court held that an assault in a residence hall room is clearly foreseeable as evidenced by the security measures the university had already put in place. In essence, the court concluded that foreseeability need not be dependent on prior criminal acts. The precautions taken by the institution to

---

[35] *Id.*
[36] 459 So.2d 413 (Fla. Dist. Ct. App.1984).
[37] *Id.* 414-415.
[38] 478 N.Y.S.2d 829, 467 N.E.2d 493 (App.Div. 1984).
[39] *Id.* at 833, 467 N.E.2d at 496.
[40] 773 A.2d 1045 (Me. 2001).

protect students against criminal activities were regarded as an acknowledgment that criminal activities were foreseeable.

Attacks on students that occur on the campus, but outside residence halls, present greater challenges for student-plaintiffs, both because the analogy to landlord-tenant relationships applicable to residence halls is less persuasive outside that context, and because it is more difficult to establish a foreseeable risk. This reluctance to impose a duty on colleges to protect students or control their behavior while on the campus is reflected in numerous cases. For example, in *Smith v. Day and Norwich University,*[41] an attempt was made to hold Norwich University responsible for injuries sustained by plaintiffs shot on campus by a cadet who attended the university. The plaintiffs argued that a special duty relationship existed between the student and the university because of the degree of control exerted by the university over its students via institutional rules and regulations. The Supreme Court of Vermont, however, agreed with earlier judicial opinions that creating such a duty would be contrary to public policy.

> In the instant case, compelling public policy reasons exist against extending the common law understanding of duty. First, most college students...are adults and must take full responsibility for their actions... Second, it is unrealistic to expect the modern American college to control all of the actions of its students... Third, making a university liable for this type of action would inevitably lead to repressive regulations and a loss of student freedoms, thus contravening a goal of higher education: "the maturation of students."[42]

In *Rabel v. Illinois Wesleyan University,*[43] an Illinois appeals court reviewed injuries sustained to a female student at Illinois Wesleyan University after a fraternity member forcibly grabbed her and attempted to run with her through a gauntlet of his fraternity peers. The plaintiff received serious injuries to the head when the male student tripped and dropped her onto a campus sidewalk. She alleged that the university, through policies, regulations, and handbooks provided to students, created a special duty of care to protect students from the misconduct of other students. However, the appeals court concluded that the imposition of such a duty on the university was unrealistic.

> (W)e have considered the likelihood of the injury from the existence of the condition here, the magnitude of guarding against it and the consequences of placing the burden on the defendant. Upon consideration, we do not believe that the university, by its handbook, regulations, or policies voluntarily assumed or placed itself in a

---

[41] 148 Vt. 595, 538 A.2d 157 (Vt. 1987).

[42] *Id.* at 599, 538 A.2d at 160. *See also* Adams v. State, 210 A.D.2d 285, 620 N.Y.S.2d 80 (App. Div. 1994) (rejecting a claim of special duty by an invitee on the campus, who was struck by a bullet allegedly fired from a residence hall, because institution had no duty to protect her while attending a cultural event sponsored by the institution).

[43] 514 N.E.2d 552 (Ill. App. Ct. 1987).

custodial relationship with its students, for purposes of imposing a duty to protect its students from the injury occasioned here. The university's responsibility to its students, as an institution of higher education, is to properly educate them. It would be unrealistic to impose upon a university the additional role of custodian over its adult students and to charge it with the responsibility for assuring their safety and the safety of others.[44]

Absent substantial evidence of a known foreseeable risk, judges have been unwilling to impose institutional liability based on the recognition of a special duty relationship to ensure safety and security on the campus. Two cases with dramatically different outcomes serve to illustrate this principle. In *Klobuchar v. Purdue University*,[45] a university student, who was injured after her husband kidnapped her from campus, brought an action against the university for failing to provide adequate security. An Indiana appeals court affirmed summary judgment in favor of the university after determining that there was no material fact that gave rise to a special duty to protect the plaintiff. In its decision, the court emphasized that even in light of a duty to the plaintiff that would be the same general duty afforded to the public, there was nothing that would have alerted the university to any possible danger as the plaintiff admitted that "...neither she, nor anyone else, told the University that her husband might be a threat to her."[46]

In contrast, in the case of *Sharkey v. Board of Regents*,[47] a state university was held to owe a duty of care to a husband and wife, both of whom were students, in an incident in which the husband was stabbed during a confrontation with another student. The confrontation arose from the third student's alleged harassment of the wife while on the campus, which had been reported to campus security. When campus security took no steps to address the harassment, the husband intervened and was stabbed in an attack. The Supreme Court of Nebraska reasoned that the institution's police force had been made aware of the harassing student's specific behavior on more than one occasion and knew of instances of criminal activity on the campus. The court found it reasonable to believe that the harassing behavior would escalate into violence and held that the institution had a duty of care to take reasonable, precautionary measures to protect the students as invitees.

When addressing student claims of negligence that involve injuries off campus, judges are disinclined to recognize a duty of care either to maintain a safe environment or to require the institution to warn students. This general rule is clearly applicable to instances when students leave the campus to engage in activities unrelated to the institution's sponsored programs or activities.[48]

---

[44] *Id.* at 360-361, 514 N.E.2d at 560.

[45] 553 N.E.2d 169 (Ind. Ct. App. 1990).

[46] *Id.* at 171.

[47] 615 N.W.2d 889 (Neb. 2000).

[48] *See* Conroy v. Marquette Univ., 582 N.W.2d 126 (Wis. Ct. App. 1998); Hartman v. Bethany Coll., 778 F. Supp. 286 (N.D.W.Va. 1991).

However, when the institution undertakes supervision and control of students off campus, a special duty relationship may be created.

For example, in *Rogers v. Delaware State University*,[49] a student sought to recover damages for injuries that resulted from a shooting at a motel the university was using as a supplemental housing facility to accommodate overflow from on-campus housing. The situation began when a male student and a female student friend were threatened in the parking lot of the motel by the female student's ex-boyfriend. After driving the female student to a local police station, the male student returned to the motel, where he was shot by the ex-boyfriend in the parking lot. The state supreme court, in rejecting a summary judgment for the institution, found material issues of fact existed regarding whether the attack was foreseeable and took the view that a reasonable juror could conclude that the failure of the state university to follow usual and customary student safety and security measures was a proximate cause of the student's injuries.

Whether the degree of supervision or control creating a special duty relationship extends to student participation in off-campus programs has been the subject of judicial speculation leading to mixed results. In *Bloss v. University of Minnesota*,[50] a taxi driver sexually assaulted a student participating in an international study-abroad program. Despite contentions that the sponsoring institution was negligent in failing to secure housing closer to the program site, failing to provide safe transportation for students, failing to inform of the risks to students, and failing to protect students from a foreseeable harm, the state appeals court affirmed summary judgment for the institution on the basis of qualified immunity. The court reasoned that the suit arose out of discretionary functions performed by state officials in planning and implementing an international program intended to provide cultural immersion for students. Similarly, in *McNeil v. Wagner College*,[51] a student injured in a slip and fall on ice while attending an overseas college program could not establish a claim for negligence based on an institutional employee's voluntary act of assisting her with medical care. In this case, the student alleged negligent supervision of her medical care when the director of the international program sought to act as an interpreter for her in the Austrian hospital where she was treated. The court rejected the claim based on the general principle that the *in loco parentis* doctrine does not apply at the college level. The court went on to rule the defendant had no obligation to supervise the plaintiff's care after the accident, and the mere fact that he acted as an interpreter was not sufficient to create this duty of care.

However, recent cases suggest that the liability for sponsoring off-campus programs can arise under circumstances in which a duty of care is applicable and the institution could or should reasonably foresee a risk of harm. In *Nova*

---

[49]   905 A.2d 747 (Del. 2006).
[50]   590 N.W.2d 661 (Minn. Ct. App. 1999).
[51]   246 A.D.2d 516, 667 N.Y.S.2d 397 (App.Div. 1998).

Southeastern University v. Gross,[52] the Supreme Court of Florida ruled that a university could be found negligent if it assigned a student to a mandatory off-campus internship site that institutional officials knew to be unreasonably dangerous. The graduate student was abducted from the parking lot of her assigned internship site robbed and assaulted. University officials had been made aware of a number of criminal assaults that had occurred at or near the internship site, but provided the student with no adequate warning of the danger. While refusing to adopt a general duty of supervision for the safety of students, the court found that the institution had a duty to use ordinary care in providing educational services and programs. Noting that the case was not based on premises liability, the court emphasized that the "special relationship" in this case was limited to the foreseeable risk involved, the institution's knowledge of that risk, and the failure to warn the student of the known danger.

> As Nova had control over the students' conduct by requiring them to do the practicum and by assigning them to a specific location, it also assumed the . . . correlative duty of acting reasonably in making those assignments. In a case such as this one, where the university had knowledge that the internship location was unreasonably dangerous, it should be up to the jury to determine whether the university acted reasonably in assigning students to do internships at that location.[53]

The institution's duty may also extend to instances of negligent hiring.[54] In *Harrington v. Louisiana State Board*,[55] a student in a culinary apprenticeship brought an action against a community college alleging that the director of the program had raped her. The director admitted that he had been arrested and convicted for raping the student in his car after taking her with him on a series of visits to arrange student internships with local restaurants. Finding that the institution's agents made no inquiries about the director's past criminal behavior before hiring him, which included several arrests and convictions, a state appeals court reversed a summary judgment motion on behalf of the college and held the institution was liable for negligently hiring the director.

Finally, an emerging issue in the area of premises liability is that of campus sexual assaults. Here again, the distinctions between invitees and licensees can be very impactful. For example, in *Leonardi v. Bradley University*,[56] a student was allegedly assaulted at an on-campus fraternity house, and she sued the University for failure to exercise due care in preventing sexual assaults. Because she was a tuition-paying student and was on campus at the time of the alleged assault, she contended that she was the business invitee of the University, and

---

[52] 758 So.2d 86 (Fla. 2000).

[53] *Id.* at 89.

[54] Oren R. Griffin, *Confronting the Evolving Safety and Security Challenge at Colleges and Universities*, 5 Pierce L. Rev. 413, 426-432 (2007).

[55] 714 So.2d 845 (La. Ct. App. 1998).

[56] 253 Ill. App. 3d 685, 691, 625 N.E.2d 431, 435 (1993).

that accordingly, the University owed her a duty of due care. But the court rejected that classification, holding that she was a licensee, because "There [were] no facts alleged in either complaint which show[ed] that plaintiff's location at the time of the assault was connected with any activity conducted or sponsored by Bradley or that Bradley received any benefit from her presence at the fraternity house."[57] Thus, the student's complaint was dismissed for failure to properly allege the duty element of the negligence claim. Other cases have come out differently on similar questions, but the duty issue is central to imposing liability for negligent management of a higher education institution's premises.[58]

Hazing Activities

Institutional liability for hazing activities increases with the degree of foreseeable risk involved. Recent cases in which individuals and their fraternities have been subject to suit for hazing that resulted in injuries to students may presage a heightened risk of liability for institutions.[59] Several decisions involving student injuries caused by hazing have departed from the negligence law presumption that institutions owe no duty to students to protect them from harm by others. In *Furek v. University of Delaware*,[60] the Supreme Court of Delaware determined that the magnitude of the foreseeable risk and the institution's policies toward hazing imposed a duty of reasonable care for the safety of students. *Furek* involved a student injured in a hazing-related accident at a fraternity on the University of Delaware campus. In its decision, the court emphasized that judges have been reluctant to impose institutional liability because higher education institutions are not insurers of students' safety. However, the *Furek* court reasoned that the university's policies against hazing (which reflected state law mandates), the security system in place to

---

[57] *Id.*

[58] *See, e.g.*, Peterson v. San Francisco Community Coll. Dist., 36 Cal. 3d 799, 685 P.2d 1193, 1198 (Cal. 1984) (holding to be a business invitee a student who paid a fee to use the college's parking lot and was then assaulted while climbing an internal stairway); Rawlings v. Angelo State University, 648 S.W.2d 430, 431–32 (Tex. Ct. App.1983) (holding to be a business invitee a student who tripped over a hose placed across a campus sidewalk near the university library while the student was on her way to the library to study); Brown v. North Carolina Wesleyan Coll., Inc., 65 N.C. App. 579, 309 S.E.2d 701 (1983) (holding a cheerleader to be a business invitee of the college at the time she was abducted following a basketball game on the college's campus); Relyea v. State, 385 So.2d 1378, 1380–83 (Fla. Dist. Ct. App.1980) (holding two Florida Atlantic University students to be business invitees when they were walking to their car after attending classes, at which time they were physically battered).

[59] *See* Nisbet v. Bucher, 949 S.W.2d 111 (Mo. Ct. App. 1997) (finding proximate cause was established by allegation student was forced to drink excessive amount of alcohol and was abandoned in a state of excessive intoxication by fraternity members.); Oja v. Grand Chapter of Theta Chi Fraternity, 667 N.Y.S.2d 650 (Sup. Ct. 1997) (ruling summary judgment was precluded by allegation that pledge's drinking was imposed upon pledges as an implied condition of membership).

[60] 594 A.2d 506 (Del. 1991).

protect students, and the university's knowledge of previous hazing incidents in fraternities created such a duty.

> The evidence in this record, however, strongly suggests that the university not only was knowledgeable of the dangers of hazing but, in repeated communications to students in general and fraternities in particular, emphasized the university policy of discipline for hazing infractions. The university's policy against hazing, like its overall commitment to provide security on its campus, thus constituted an assumed duty which became "an indispensable part of the bundle of services which colleges...afford their students."[61]

The *Furek* decision concluded that changing societal attitudes toward hazing suggest that institutions are not free from all obligations to protect their students. On balance, the court found the likelihood of injury during hazing activities occurring on university campuses to be greater than the utility of university inaction. Imposing liability on the institution was based on the belief that the university had a degree of control over its premises, including the fraternity house, which was supported by its involvement in the regulation of fraternity life. This control, combined with the cumulative evidence that the incident was foreseeable, created a duty to protect the student from harm.

The Supreme Court of Nebraska used reasoning that paralleled the *Furek* decision in *Knoll v. Board of Regents.*[62] In *Knoll*, a student who was injured in a hazing activity filed suit against the university, alleging that it acted negligently in failing to enforce prohibitions against hazing, consumption of alcohol, and physically abusive behavior. The state supreme court reversed a grant of summary judgment to the university, finding that the hazing activities were foreseeable by the university, which had knowledge of previous instances of hazing by other fraternities and of specific instances of possession of alcohol, alcohol abuse, and assaults involving the fraternity that had subjected the student to hazing. The court adopted the view that whether the risk can reasonably be perceived determines whether a duty is owed.

Adopting a different rationale justifying institutional liability for hazing, the Vermont Supreme Court, in *Brueckner v. Norwich University*,[63] examined the experience of a student attending a military college who was subjected to incidents of hazing that included verbal and physical harassment by upperclassmen known as "the cadre." The student reported the hazing incidents to university officials but eventually withdrew from the institution, thinking that his situation would not improve. His scholarship was terminated, and he brought suit against the institution. A lower court found the institution liable

---

[61] *Id.* at 520.

[62] 601 N.E.2d 757 (Neb. 1999).

[63] 169 Vt. 118, 730 A.2d 1086 (Vt. 1999). *But see* Alton v. Texas A & M Univ., 168 F.3d 196 (5th Cir. 1999) (rejecting a claim that hazing by members of a university's military training organization violated a student's Fourteenth Amendment due process rights).

for assault and battery, negligent infliction of emotional distress, intentional infliction of emotional distress, and negligent supervision.

The Vermont Supreme Court affirmed the lower court's decision holding the institution liable for the tortious conduct of the cadre and affirmed an award of compensatory damages.

Applying the doctrine of *respondeat superior*, the court ruled that the university would be vicariously liable for the actions of the cadre if these cadets were acting within the scope of employment as agents of the institution. Although the institution had adopted policies against hazing, it had charged the cadre members with indoctrinating and orienting new students. The court reasoned that a jury could find that the members of the cadre were performing a general duty to indoctrinate and orient on behalf of the institution and the cadre's hazing activities were within the scope of employment. The institution was liable for the tortious acts of the cadre both because the institution had authorized the indoctrination and orientation and because the institution was negligent in meeting a duty of reasonable care to control and supervise the cadre.

However, recent cases are not uniform on these trends. For example, in *Yost v. Wabash College*, the court upheld summary judgment in favor of the College on a student fraternity pledge's claim for negligence in connection with an alleged hazing incident at a campus-leased fraternity house. In denying the student's claim, the court relied on two rationales. First, since the house was leased by the fraternity (as most on-campus fraternity houses are), it was the fraternity—the custodian of the property—that owed a duty of care to the plaintiff. Second, in response to the student's argument that, in promulgating a strong anti-hazing and student conduct policy, the College had assumed the duty to protect the student, the court held, "Thus, even assuming that Yost was injured in the course of an incident of 'hazing'—a characterization in vigorous dispute among the parties—the conduct of Wabash relied upon by Yost evinces no more than a general intent to elicit good behavior from and maintain general order among the student body."[64] Thus, while hazing incidents can give rise to institutional liability, courts will generally base such liability on traditional doctrines, and will sometimes view with skepticism arguments that these traditional rules should be set aside.

Athletics and Related Programs

Student-institution relationships involving a high degree of institutional supervision or control may implicate a special duty relationship. For example, judges have recognized that higher education institutions owe a legal duty to students to provide proper instruction and adequate supervision in classroom or laboratory contexts that involve high risks, foreseeable harm, and the in-

---

[64] Yost v. Wabash Coll., No. 54S01-1303-CT-161, 2014 WL 575955 (Ind. Feb. 13, 2014) (slip opinion).

structor's special expertise.[65] Because of the degree of supervision and control exercised over school-sponsored intercollegiate athletic programs, several courts have imposed a special duty relationship in these contexts as well. In an illustrative case, *Kleinknecht v. Gettysburg College*,[66] a federal appeals court upheld liability specifically predicated on a special duty relationship. After a student who had been recruited to play lacrosse suffered a fatal heart attack during practice, the parents of the student brought a negligence action against the college, arguing that a special relationship existed between the student and the college by virtue of the student's status as a member of the intercollegiate athletic team. A federal appeals court agreed, reasoning that because the student was recruited to play lacrosse, and at the time of his heart attack he was participating in a scheduled athletic practice for a college-sponsored intercollegiate team, a special relationship existed that was sufficient to impose a duty of reasonable care.

Having determined that a special relationship existed, the court then reviewed the record to evaluate whether the incident was foreseeable and assess whether a duty of care was owed. The court determined that it was foreseeable that a member of the college's interscholastic lacrosse team could suffer a serious injury during an athletic event and concluded that the college owed a duty to the student to take precautions against the risks of injury. In making its determination, the federal court clearly intended to set limits on the class of students to which this decision would apply, stating:

> There is a distinction between a student injured while participating as an inter-collegiate athlete in a sport for which he was recruited and a student injured at a college while pursuing his private interests, scholastic or otherwise. This distinction serves to limit the class of students to whom a college owes the duty of care that arises here. Had [the student] been participating in a fraternity football game, for example, the College might not have owed him the same duty or perhaps any duty at all.[67]

Kleinknecht reflects the degree of control a university must have over the student in order to persuade a court to impose a special duty of care. The court recognized that the college had actively sought out the student's participation on the lacrosse team by recruiting him and that the student suffered the heart attack while participating in a scheduled and supervised lacrosse team practice. The court also implied that the student-athlete might more appropriately be characterized as a business invitee to whom a special duty of care was owed: "We cannot help but think that the College recruited [the student] for its own

---

[65] *See generally*, Fu v. State, 643 N.W.2d 659 (Neb. 2002) (explosion in chemistry laboratory); Garrett v. Northwest Miss. Junior Coll., 674 S.2d 1 (Miss. 1996) (injury in using milling machine) and Delbridge v. Maricopa County Cmty. Coll., 893 P.2d 55 (Ariz. Ct. App. 1994) (fall from utility pole in training class).

[66] 989 F.2d 1360 (3d Cir. 1993).

[67] *Id.* at 1368.

benefit, probably thinking that his skill at lacrosse would bring favorable attention and so aid the College in attracting other students."[68]

Following *Kleinknecht*, other courts recognized a special duty relationship applicable to circumstances in which the institution may be said to exercise a greater degree of control over students engaged in sponsored programs. For example, in *Searles v. Trustees of St. Joseph's College*,[69] the Supreme Court of Maine held that an institution may be liable for injuries to student-athletes in school-sponsored programs when college coaches or trainers are found to have breached a duty to exercise reasonable care for student-athlete safety. In this case, a member of a men's basketball team alleged that despite medical advice to the contrary, his college coach and an athletic trainer had insisted that the student continue to play basketball after several knee surgeries. The court reasoned that a duty of adequate supervision would arise from the level of control exercised by the coach and trainer over the athlete and returned the case to the trial court for a determination on whether the duty was breached.

The fact that an institution exercises a level of supervision and control over a student-athlete's training and participation in intercollegiate sports can create a duty of care to foresee potential risks. In *Moose v. Massachusetts Institute of Technology*,[70] a Massachusetts appeals court affirmed a jury verdict in favor of a student-athlete injured while attempting a pole vault while under the supervision of his coach. The student sustained the injury when his heels hooked on the back edge of the landing pit and his head struck the unprotected surface on the track. Using a comparative negligence standard, the jury apportioned the fault proximately causing the injury between the institution and the student, holding the institution partially liable. On appeal, the state court emphasized there was sufficient evidence for the jury to find that the risk of falling over the back of the padded landing pit was foreseeable and the coach's failure to evaluate the potential risk and take affirmative steps to reduce it was negligence. In a case with a similar result, *Trustees of Trinity College v. Ferris*,[71] a student-athlete participating in rowing practice was injured when his team's scull collided with a scull rowed by the women's team. The women's' scull was in the wrong lane at the time of the accident, violating a navigation rule. The institution appealed a jury verdict in favor of the student-athlete, contending that the student had assumed the risk of the activity and pointing to the fact that the student had signed a release before participating in the practices. The state appeals court rejected the institution's argument, ruling that the student athlete might have been aware of the general risks inherent in the sport, but a jury could find that he was not aware of and did not assume the specific risk or harm associated with his injury.

---

[68] *Id.*

[69] 695 A.2d 1206 (Me. 1997).

[70] 683 N.E.2d 706 (Mass. App. Ct.1997).

[71] 491 S.E.2d 909 (Ga. Ct. App. 1997).

Finding that school-sponsored cheerleading teams are comparable to other school-sponsored athletic programs,[72] a North Carolina appeals court reversed a decision of a state commission and ruled that the University of North Carolina had an affirmative duty of care toward a student-athlete who was injured during a cheerleading practice. In *Davidson v. University of North Carolina*,[73] a member of the junior varsity cheerleading squad was injured when she fell onto the hardwood floor while performing a stunt prior to a women's basketball game. Upon review, the appeals court determined that a duty of care existed based on several factors, one being that the university exerted a considerable degree of control over its cheerleaders and the cheerleading program. In its finding, the court noted that although the student-university relationship on its own did not constitute a duty of care, by voluntarily undertaking responsibilities for sponsoring, teaching, and advising the junior varsity cheerleaders, the university had established a duty based upon a special relationship. The court compared the institution's services and support for the varsity cheerleading team with that provided to the junior varsity and found the institution had not provided a level of safety and support congruent with its own policy for other student athletes.

Cases involving student-athletes typically involve a defense that the student assumed the risk of injury. For example, in *Nova University v. Katz*,[74] a student at Nova University who severely injured her foot during cheerleading practice brought an action against the university for negligence. The plaintiff alleged that the coach had failed to provide spotters for her when she fell while doing a cheerleading stunt and that he had generally failed to supervise the students. After the jury ruled in favor of the student, the university appealed, arguing that the claim should have been barred because the student assumed the known risks of participation in the activity.

Under the assumption of risk doctrine, participants in athletic events may be held to have consented, by their participation, to those injury-causing events that are known, apparent, or reasonably foreseeable consequences of participation. An institution, however, generally has a duty to exercise reasonable care to protect participants from concealed or unreasonably increased risks that could not have been assumed. In the *Katz* case, the state appeals court, while recognizing the risks inherent in cheerleading and assumed by students participating in the activity, pointed out that the assumption of risk defense did not release the university from its responsibility to continue to provide proper supervision and instruction during a practice.

> Here, the cheerleader's conduct in going ahead with a stunt even though she knew spotters were not present may be characterized as implied qualified assumption of the risk. While she may have

---

[72] *See* M. V. Johnson & Beth Easter, *Legal Liability for Cheerleading Injuries: Implications for Universities and Coaches*, 17 J. LEGAL ASPECTS OF SPORT 213 (2007) for a discussion of leading cases addressing institutional liability for cheerleading programs.

[73] 543 S.E.2d 920 (N.C. Ct. App. 2001).

[74] 636 So. 2d 729 (Fla. Dist. Ct. App. 1993).

waived risks inherent in the sport itself, those do not include the failure to have proper supervision and to have spotters. She did not absolve the school of its responsibility for proper instruction and to properly supervise the activity.[75]

However, the assumption of risk defense effectively insulated a state university from liability in *Schiffman v. Spring*.[76] In *Schiffman*, a student on the women's varsity soccer team was injured when her foot became stuck in the mud while playing in a soccer match. She alleged that the athletic director and coach were negligent by electing to hold a soccer match on a field that was wet, slippery, and muddy. The university prevailed on a summary judgment motion after the judge concluded that the plaintiff was fully aware of the condition of the field before she voluntarily agreed to participate in the soccer match, thus establishing an assumption of risk. The institution established that the plaintiff's injury was not the result of a breach of duty; rather, it was "a luckless accident arising from the vigorous voluntary participation in competitive inter-scholastic athletics."[77]

Release or waiver of liability forms are often used to establish an evidentiary basis for an assumption of risk defense.[78] These forms have had mixed utility for institutions of higher education. Although they may often dissuade a potential plaintiff from bringing a suit, the release may not be an effective bar to recovery in a negligence action either because such a release violates public policy or lacked sufficient specificity to establish that the student assumed the risk of the activity in question. For example, the West Virginia Supreme Court of Appeals refused to enforce an "anticipatory release" signed by a student as a condition of participating in a rugby club on campus.[79] Under the terms of the release, the student agreed to waive "any and all claims, both present and future, arising from my participation in rugby club activities, including but not

---

[75] *Id.* at 730.

[76] 202 A.D.2d 1007, 609 N.Y.S.2d 482 (App. Div. 1994).

[77] *Id.* at 483- 484. *See also* Rendine v. St. John's Univ., 289 A.D.2d 465, 735 N.Y.S.2d 173 (App. Div. 2001) (holding that a cheerleader, injured when she fell while performing a stunt, assumed the risk of the activity because she was under no compulsion to perform the stunt and had been advised that no spotter was available).

[78] *See, e.g.*, Roe v. Saint Louis Univ., No. 4:08CV1474 HEA, 2012 WL 6757558, at *5 (E.D. Mo. Dec. 31, 2012) *aff'd sub nom.* Roe v. St. Louis Univ., 746 F.3d 874 (8th Cir. 2014) (upholding and applying a release in a case involving a back injury to a student field hockey player, stating, "There is no question that the language above is clear and explicit. It unambiguously releases Defendant SLU from any and all liability, actions, cause of action, debts.").

[79] Kyriazis v. Univ. of W. Va., 450 S.E.2d 649, 651 (W.Va. 1994).

limited to negligence, property damage, personal injury, and wrongful death."[80] The appeals court reversed a trial court decision dismissing the suit against the institution, holding that the state university was performing a public service by sponsoring the rugby club and could not exculpate itself from tort liability. The state appeals court reasoned that university sponsorship of athletic and recreational activities were integral to the institution's mission and thus a duty of care was owed to students who participated in these activities. Furthermore, the court reasoned the university held a decisive bargaining advantage when it required the plaintiff to sign the anticipatory release as a condition of playing rugby. Because the university had the benefit of counsel in drafting the release, while the student had been compelled to sign the release as a condition of participation in the activity and had no guidance on its implications, the appeals court declared the release unenforceable.

However, in *Lemoine v. Cornell University*,[81] a New York appeals court affirmed the legal viability of a release of liability. In *Lemoine*, a student alleged the institution was negligently liable for injuries she suffered when she fell from a climbing wall during the first session of a rock-climbing course offered by the institution's outdoor recreation program. The student had signed a release agreeing to follow climbing wall safety policies and to hold the university harmless for any injuries from using the climbing wall, including injuries caused by the negligence of the institution's representatives. The university moved to dismiss the case, citing the negligence-release agreement the student signed, and the state appellate court ruled in favor of the university. The court reasoned that the release form was a contract the student signed, which unambiguously acknowledged the inherent risks of rock climbing and the use of climbing walls, and that the language holding the university harmless for injuries incurred during rock climbing instruction was legally enforceable.

Additional limits of institutional liability for negligence in the context of student-athlete injuries are illustrated in cases involving unsanctioned activities

---

[80] *Id*. at 652, n. 1. In other contexts, such as employment claim releases, parties have developed the tactic of securing both a prospective and retrospective release of claims and a covenant not to sue, which is, in effect, a contract that contains an executor prohibition on using the legal system against the opposing party, usually the employer. Where such a contract is not void as against public policy, it has the potential to be more effective than a release, since unlike a release, which simply forms the basis of an affirmative defense, a covenant not to sue can give rise to the defendant's claim against the plaintiff for damages for breach of the covenant. *See, e.g.*, Kristin L. Wright, Phelps v. Firebird Raceway, Inc.: *Establishing Express Assumption of Risk as a Question of Fact for the Jury*, 47 ARIZ. L. REV. 1081 (2005) (reviewing a case distinguishing between prospective releases, waivers (retrospective releases), and covenants not to sue). Higher education general counsels would do well to consider such strategies if their states permit them.

[81] 2 A.D.3d 1017, 769 N.Y.S.2d 313 (App. Div. 2003).

and intramural programs.[82] In *Rubtchinsky v. State University of New York*,[83] a student was injured in a game between first- and second-year students that was conducted as part of an orientation program. The court found that the student, who had been offered several orientation activities, chose to play the game and ruled that, by voluntarily participating in the game, he assumed the risks of his injury as a participant. Similarly, in *Ochoa v. California State University*,[84] a case involving a student who was struck by an opposing player in an intramural soccer game, a California appeals court ruled that the institution did not owe a duty to the student simply by organizing and sponsoring the game. The court took the position that soccer is a hazardous recreational activity and fisticuffs between participants were reasonably to be expected. Affirming summary judgment for the institution, the court emphasized:

> It is unclear how the policy of preventing future harm would be fostered by finding a special relationship between universities and the participants in their intramural events, since it is unclear how those events could proceed if every injury suffered by a participant might expose the university to liability... (T)he likely consequences to the community would be the abandonment of intramural sports by colleges and universities, which would serve no one's interest.[85]

These cases establish that, because of the degree of supervision and control associated with school-sponsored intercollegiate athletic programs, it is possible for a court to recognize a special duty relationship.[86] The university or college may be liable for an injury when it is clear that institutional officials did not exercise reasonable care to protect students from foreseeable injuries. To be foreseeable, the injury does not have to be specifically foreseen by the university, but need only fall into a general category of injuries likely to occur during participation in an athletic event. To reduce the risk of liability in these cases, colleges and universities must substantiate that students were warned and are aware of the risks inherent in engaging in athletic activities, although it is not necessary to provide notice of the specific manner in which an injury might occur. It is also essential that institutions provide up-to-date training and supervision commensurate with the risks involved in the activity.

---

[82] *See* Sarah K. Fields & Sarah J. Young, *Learning from the Past: An Analysis of Case Law Impacting Campus Recreational Sport Programs,* 20 J. LEGAL ASPECTS OF SPORT 75 (2010) in which the authors review decisions on institutional liability for campus recreation programs and conclude that risk management should include properly administered waivers and effective maintenance of facilities (at 88).

[83] 46 Misc. 2d 679, 260 N.Y.S.2d 256 (N.Y. Ct. Cl., 1965).

[84] 72 Cal. App. 4th 1300, 85 Cal. Rptr. 2d 768 (Cal. Ct. App. 1999).

[85] *Id.* 1302, 85 Cal. Rptr. 2d at 772.

[86] In one of the few cases rejecting a special duty involving student-athletes, Howell v. Clavert, 1 P.3d 310 (Kan. 2000), the Supreme Court of Kansas declined to impose a special duty to provide adequate supervision, instruction, warning, and safe premises for a required conditioning run that followed a route off campus and through automobile traffic. The decision, however, affirmed institutional liability under a comparative negligence standard in a case in which two student-athletes were struck from behind by a truck during the mandatory early morning run.

Alcohol-Related Cases

Although institutional liability for alcohol-related injuries is substantially influenced by state criminal law, judicial decisions confirm that an institution's general awareness of underage drinking on college campuses, or the adoption of university policies and regulations prohibiting such activities and providing for discipline for instances of misconduct, does not increase the risk of liability for these institutions. Dicta contained in decisions involving alcohol-related negligence claims reflect that appellate courts believe that imposing a duty on institutions to prevent underage drinking would, in effect, represent a step back toward the creation of an *in loco parentis* responsibility for students, a step appellate judges are unwilling to take because such an expectation is unrealistic and against public policy.

The leading case involving institutional liability for alcohol-related student injuries is *Bradshaw v. Rawlings*.[87] In *Bradshaw*, a federal appeals court held that there existed no special duty relationship between a college and a student that would impose upon the college a duty to control the conduct of a student operating a motor vehicle or to protect a student traveling to and from a class picnic. The injured student had been a passenger in the car of another student who had consumed alcohol at an off-campus college-sponsored function. When the student was injured in an automobile accident on the return trip to the campus, he joined the institution as one of several defendants in a negligence suit. In ruling that "the modern American college is not an insurer of the safety of its students,"[88] the federal appeals court emphasized that "college students today are no longer minors; they are now regarded as adults in almost every phase of community life."[89]

The *Bradshaw* rationale was followed in *Baldwin v. Zoradi*.[90] In this case, a student at California Polytechnic State University brought suit against the Trustees of the University and two of its residence hall staff members after she was seriously injured in an automobile accident involving several intoxicated students. The plaintiff alleged that the residence hall staff had created a dangerous situation in that they knowingly permitted the students to consume alcoholic beverages in the residence halls and failed to take appropriate steps to control the students. A California appeals court concluded that it would be impossible and, in some respects, improper, for the university to be expected to police and eradicate alcohol consumption on the campus.

> Although the consumption of alcoholic beverages by persons under 21 years of age is proscribed by law (citations omitted), the use of alcohol by college students is not so unusual or heinous by contemporary standards as to require special efforts by college

---

[87] 612 F.2d 135 (3d Cir. 1979).

[88] *Id.* at 138.

[89] *Id.* at 139.

[90] 123 Cal. App. 3d 275, 176 Cal. Rptr. 809 (Cal. Ct. App. 1981).

administrators to stamp it out. Although the university reserved to itself the right to take disciplinary action for drinking on campus, this merely follows state laws. The same may be said of the provisions of the license agreement prohibiting alcoholic beverages. We do not believe they created a mandatory duty.[91]

The Supreme Court of Colorado relied on *Bradshaw* and *Baldwin* in deciding *University of Denver v. Whitlock.*[92] *Whitlock* involved an intoxicated student who was injured after a trampoline accident in the front yard of a fraternity house leased from the university. The court examined both the relationship between the student and the university, as well as the lease between the university and the fraternity, to assess whether a special duty relationship existed. Ruling that no special relationship existed, the court reasoned that there was nothing in the university's handbook that "reflects an effort by the University to control the risk-taking decisions of its students in their private recreation,"[93] or anything in the lease that would provide a basis for establishing a special relationship between students and the institution. In affirming the general principle that to impose such a duty would run contrary to the expectations held by the public for colleges and their students, the court stated, "[A] conclusion that a special relationship existed between Whitlock and the University sufficient to warrant the imposition of liability for nonfeasance would directly contravene the competing social policy of fostering an educational environment of student autonomy and independence."[94]

Other precedents have followed a similar reasoning, denying liability in instances of alcohol use by students. In *Campbell v. Board of Trustees, Wabash College,*[95] an Indiana appeals court pointed out that there could be circumstances in which a third party could be held liable under Indiana law for injuries sustained relating to alcohol consumption but concluded that there was no basis for institutional liability absent evidence to suggest that the defendant college provided alcoholic beverages, knew that the student would be drinking that night, or that he would be driving an automobile after becoming intoxicated. The court emphasized that college students should and will be treated as adults under the law and, thus, as responsible for their own actions. In *Allen v. Rutgers State University of New Jersey,*[96] a New Jersey court affirmed a jury verdict in favor of the university, holding that the university's maintenance of a policy prohibiting alcohol consumption did not result in responsibility for injuries sustained as the result of its violation, nor was the institution under any common law or statutory duty to protect a student from his own voluntary intoxication.

---

[91] *Id.* 288, 176 Cal. Rptr. at 817.

[92] 744 P.2d 54 (Colo. 1987).

[93] *Id.* at 60.

[94] *Id.* at 62.

[95] 495 N.E.2d 227 (Ind. Ct. App.1986).

[96] 216 N.J.Super. 189, 523 A.2d 262 (N.J. App. 1987).

Similarly, in *Rothbard v. Colgate University*,[97] a student, who was injured when he fell out a window in his fraternity house following a party at which he consumed a large quantity of alcohol, did not prevail in a suit alleging that the university assumed a special duty of care. The New York appeals court affirmed a grant of summary judgment to the institution, rejecting the contention that the university had assumed the duty to control the behavior of students because its student handbook prohibited underage drinking and provided disciplinary penalties for misconduct. Noting that "this is not a case where the university encouraged its students to participate in an activity and took affirmative steps to supervise the activity,"[98] the court emphasized that the terms of the handbook expressly prohibited the conduct involved and reasoned that the plaintiff was not a child in need of supervision, but an adult who must take responsibility for his behavior.

Courts have also rejected the contention that a special duty of care is owed by the institution to students below the legal age for the purchase and consumption of alcohol. In *Booker v. Lehigh University*,[99] for example, a federal court held that the institution's implementation of a social policy prohibiting alcohol consumption did not give rise to a special duty to control the actions of underage drinkers and addressed the "adult" status of college students who may be underage for purposes of purchasing and consuming alcohol.

> At this point, we should explain the inter-relationship between plaintiff's adult, minor, and underage status. Plaintiff, being over the age of eighteen at the time of the incident, was an adult. For all facets of life, other than purchasing and consuming alcohol, she was an adult. As to purchasing and consuming alcohol, she would be considered by many to be a minor, i.e., she was legally incompetent to participate in such activities. We believe that a better description of this status is to call her "underage." There can be no question that she was competent, legally or otherwise, to decide, inter alia, whether to break the law, e.g., whether to drink alcohol. She thus makes such a decision as an adult who is merely under the legal age for consuming alcohol.[100]

Other courts have rejected an institutional duty of care in alcohol-related negligence cases even when the institution might have been regarded as having responsibilities for supervision and control of students. For example, in *Albano v. Colby College*,[101] a student, who was injured after becoming intoxicated while on a college-sponsored trip to Puerto Rico, alleged his tennis coach and the institution owed a special duty of care to protect him from the risks attendant to drinking alcohol. The federal court affirmed summary judgment for the

---

[97] 235 A.D.2d 675, 652 N.Y.S.2d 146 (Sup.Ct. 1997).
[98] *Id.* at 676, 652 N.Y.S.2d at 148.
[99] 800 F. Supp. 234 (E.D.Pa.1992).
[100] *Id.* at 238.
[101] 822 F. Supp. 840 (D. Me. 1993).

institution, finding that the student voluntarily chose to consume alcohol, the coach and institution did not provide the alcohol, and the consumption of the alcohol was unrelated to the tennis team's training or instruction. Similarly, the Supreme Court of Utah in *Beach v. University of Utah*[102] determined that a special duty relationship did not exist in a case involving a biology student's fall on a field trip that rendered the student a quadriplegic. The student in *Beach* contended that the university breached its affirmative duty to supervise and protect her once she became intoxicated on the field trip as her disorientation led to a fall from a cliff. The court maintained that whether an affirmative duty is owed to protect a student from his or her own actions is a matter that must be weighed in relation to the consequences for the parties and society at large. After reviewing the implications of recognizing such a duty and the nature of the college-student relationship, the court concluded there was no special relationship:

> We do not believe that Beach should be viewed as fragile and in need of protection simply because she had the luxury of attending an institution of higher education. Not only are students such as Beach adults, but also law and society have increasingly come to recognize their status as such in the past decade or two. Nowhere is this truer than in the relations between the students and institutions of higher education.[103]

While these cases clearly establish that appellate courts will not hold colleges and universities responsible for injuries sustained by students as a result of their illegal consumption of alcohol, changing social policies and awareness of the epidemic proportions of binge drinking may influence courts to re-examine institutional liability in this context. The basis for rejecting liability is the presumption that students are adults, and colleges and universities are not expected to act *in loco parentis* to police their alcohol consumption.

While courts thus far have been uniform in rejecting institutional liability, there are signs that institutions might be held to a duty of care when they exercise a degree of supervision and control over student activities. For example, in *Coghlan v. Beta Theta Pi Fraternity*,[104] the Supreme Court of Iowa considered a case in which an underage student was furnished alcohol at several fraternity parties. The student became intoxicated and later fell from a fire escape at her sorority house, sustaining permanent injuries. Among her claims was an assertion that university employees were present at the parties as supervisors and observed her and other minors being served alcoholic beverages in violation of state law and university policies. The court found the allegations sufficient to support an inference that the university assumed a duty to exercise reasonable care to safeguard the underage plaintiff from the criminal acts of third parties (furnishing alcohol to minors). In remanding the case, the court ruled

---

[102] 726 P.2d 413 (Utah 1986).
[103] *Id.* at 418.
[104] 987 P.2d 300 (Idaho 1999).

the lower court had erred in dismissing the claim but reached no conclusion that an assumed duty existed.

Suicide

Courts generally have declined to recognize negligence liability for college student suicide on the basis that no special duty of care was owed to the student and the student's intentional act was the proximate or intervening cause of the student's death.[105] In *Jain v. State*,[106] for example, a student asphyxiated himself by leaving his moped running in his locked room. The Iowa Supreme Court affirmed a trial court ruling granting summary judgment to the university because it found that the university neither increased the likelihood that the student would commit suicide nor led him to stop looking for help elsewhere. The *Jain* court also affirmed the general principle that suicide is an intervening act that supersedes any institutional liability.[107] Because the court determined that no special relationship existed between the university and the student, it did not allow for an exception to that principle.

Two recent cases have revived the possibility that institutions and their agents could be liable for student suicides taking place in residential living facilities maintained by the institution. In *Schieszler v. Ferrum College*,[108] a student hanged himself in his dormitory room after writing letters to friends indicating that he was depressed and thinking of committing suicide. A federal district court found that the plaintiff offered enough evidence to establish the existence of a special relationship because agents of the institution, including the Dean of Student Affairs and the student's resident advisor, knew of the student's problems. The court concluded that the university breached its duty of care,[109] but did not resolve the question of proximate cause. Prior to a trial on the merits of the wrongful death claim, the parties reached a settlement agreement.

In a case with a similar outcome, *Shin v. Massachusetts Institute of Technology*,[110] a student experienced psychiatric health problems for more than a year and received counseling and other support services while remaining enrolled at the institution. Psychiatrists and physicians employed by the institution, as well as several senior administrators, professors, campus police, and residence hall staff knew of the student's suicidal ideations and troubling behavior and had communicated with psychiatrists concerning her condition. Just before the student's suicide, administrators had conducted a "deans and psychs" meeting where they discussed the severity of the student's problems

---

[105] *See generally* Joy Blanchard, *University Tort Liability and Student Suicide: Case Review and Implications for Practice*, 36 J.L. & EDUC. 461 (2007).

[106] 617 N.W.2d 293, 300 (Iowa 2000).

[107] *Id.* at 300.

[108] 236 F. Supp. 2d 602 (W.D. Va. 2002).

[109] *Id.* at 610.

[110] 19 Mass. L. Rep. 570 (Mass. Super. Ct. 2005).

and arranged an appointment for her at a psychiatric treatment facility.[111] Before the referral could be implemented, however, the student set herself on fire in her dormitory room and died shortly thereafter. When the student's parents sued for wrongful death and negligence on the part of the institution and its agents, a state court granted summary judgment to the institution, but denied it to administrators on the theory that they had created a special duty of care. The existence of a special duty of care was based on knowledge of the severity of the student's psychological problems and the reasonably foreseeable risk that she would take her own life.[112] Before a jury could reach a verdict in the case, however, the parties reached a settlement agreement.

While the judges in both these cases rejected a "no-duty" position with regard to student suicide and recognized a special duty relationship that would ultimately turn on the issue of a reasonably foreseeable risk, settlements in both cases avoided a legal precedent finding institutional liability for student suicide. Conscious of the risk of legal liability, however, some institutions have adopted policies requiring students with severe psychological problems to withdraw or be evicted from residential housing. These policies, however, may violate provisions of federal law, including the Americans with Disabilities Act,[113] Section 504 of the Rehabilitation Act of 1973,[114] and, in the case of public institutions, the provisions of the Due Process Clause of the Fourteenth Amendment.[115]

While colleges and universities may not be under an all-inclusive duty to prevent student suicide, policies and practices may be viewed as exerting such a high degree of custody or control as to create a special duty relationship.[116] A Connecticut court denied a private college's summary judgment motion in a case in which a student, having complained of a panic attack, was dropped off at a public hospital by the institution's private security officers without securing medical attention for him. Once the officers departed, the student left the hospital and allegedly committed suicide. The court determined that a genuine issue of fact existed as to whether the institution had established a special duty to the student by asserting a level of control, through the actions of its security officers, which rendered the student vulnerable and dependent on those officers.[117] Furthermore, the court found that the factual dispute as to whether the student's suicide was reasonably foreseeable precluded summary judgment for the college.[118]

---

[111] *Id.* at 575.

[112] *Id.*

[113] 42 U.S.C. § 12101.

[114] 29 U.S.C. § 794(a) (2006).

[115] U.S. Const. amend. XIV, § 1.

[116] *See* Wallace v. Broyles, 961 W.S.2d 712 (Ark. 1998), for a case in which the Supreme Court of Arkansas determined that genuine issues of material fact precluded summary judgment in a case in which a student-athlete's suicide was alleged to have been proximately caused by the illegal and uncontrolled dispensing of prescription drugs by institutional employees.

[117] Leary v. Wesleyan Univ., 2009 Conn. Super. LEXIS 621 (Conn. Super. 2009).

[118] *Id.*

Legal commentators are divided on the nature of an institution's duty of care with regard to student suicide. Some commentators suggest that an institution's primary duty in instances involving a risk of student suicide is to notify parents, or a designated third party, as a means of shifting the risk and reducing the institution's burden.[119] Another commentator has suggested a collaborative approach that avoids liability for institutions, which necessitates that courts, legislatures, and institutions take unified and complementary actions to create a comprehensive strategy that combats what is characterized as a student suicide epidemic.[120] Other commentators emphasize that while institutions and their agents need to adopt sound risk-management strategies to mitigate the possibility of negligence liability that may arise from a mishandled institutional response, institutions are not in any immediate risk of a shift in the judicial landscape that would impose a special duty of care relative to student suicide.[121]

Tort Immunities and Alternative Claims Procedures

Notwithstanding the many doctrinal nuances discussed above, even plaintiffs meeting all of their strictures may find themselves without actionable claims for damages due to state sovereign immunity. In some instances, doctrines of sovereign or charitable immunity create legislated or judicially imposed barriers to a plaintiff's recovery in a negligence action. For example, a state may grant charitable immunity through legislative enactment, extending protections to higher education institutions that, when such provisions are liberally construed, insulate private religious, charitable, and educational institutions from liability to those who are beneficiaries of the services provided by the institution.[122] These same state entities may avoid litigating a negligence claim in a federal forum by advancing the defense of sovereign immunity under the Eleventh Amendment.[123]

By far, however, the most important set of immunities to negligence liability arise under state-law sovereign and governmental immunity doctrines. Negligence claims are most often filed and litigated in state courts, so

---

[119] Peter Lake & Nancy Tribbensee, *The Emerging Crisis of College Student Suicide: Law and Policy Responses to Serious Forms of Self-Inflicted Injury*, 32 STETSON L. REV. 125, 147 (2002).

[120] See Juhi Kaveeshvar, *Comment: Kicking the Rock and the Hard Place to the Curb: An Alternative and Integrated Approach to Suicidal Students in Higher Education*, 57 EMORY L.J. 651 (2008).

[121] Richard Fossey & Heather Moore, *University Tort Liability for Student Suicide: The Sky is Not Falling*, 39 J.L. & EDUC. 225 (2010).

[122] *See, e.g.*, Gilbert v. Seton Hall Univ., 332 F.3d 105 (2d Cir. 2003).

[123] *See, e.g.*, Walls v. Board of Regents of Southeast Missouri State Univ., 2009 U.S. Dist. LEXIS 62436 (E.D. Mo. 2009) (holding that the state university was immune from a negligence suit brought in a federal court under the doctrine of sovereign immunity. Under Missouri law, a state university is an arm of the state and therefore entitled to sovereign immunity under the 11th Amendment).

the strength or weakness of a particular state's sovereign and governmental immunity doctrines, as well as any legislative abrogation of these doctrines, often makes the difference between a successful or unsuccessful case. There are fifty different approaches to sovereign immunity among the fifty states, but some common features unite most of the states' approaches.

In most states, the doctrine of "sovereign immunity" is considered an inherent feature of state sovereignty, presupposed as of the date of the adoption of the state's constitution,[124] while in several, the doctrine is established explicitly by statute.[125] In the tort context, this immunity can have as many as three dimensions, depending on the state. The first, and most traditional, dimension of sovereign immunity is the absolute immunity of the state and its political subdivisions (some courts say "arms"), as well as officials of such entities, from tort suits for damages. As one recent lucid commentary on the topic points out:

> Sovereign immunity from tort actions does not imply that a tort has not been committed. Instead, immunity acts as a bar against liability, denying relief to any person harmed by the tortious conduct of the government where state sovereign immunity is mandated by the constitution.[126]

So, a plaintiff who sues a state, an "arm" of the state, or an official who works for either may not recover tort damages against that defendant, regardless of the harm or the fault of the state or its employees, unless the state or state entity consents to suit or prospectively waives its immunity.

The second dimension (often called "governmental immunity") applies when one sues a local government or local government official in his or her official capacity (i.e., as the representative of the local government that would otherwise be the defendant). Where this is the case, courts draw a distinction between "governmental functions," those that form the core of the government's service to the public, such as teaching students in an educational institution; and "proprietary functions," those in which any business might engage, such as selling concessions at an athletic event. If the former, then the government's immunity extends to the government official. If the latter, then the immunity does not transfer, and ordinary negligence rules apply.

The third dimension (often called "official immunity") applies where a local government official is sued in his or her individual capacity (i.e., as a

---

[124] *See, e.g.*, Withers v. Univ. of Kentucky, 939 S.W.2d 340, 343 (Ky. 1997) (holding the University of Kentucky to be absolutely immune from a medical negligence suit for damages in connection with the University Hospital, based on Section 231 of the Kentucky Constitution).

[125] *See, e.g.*, Conner v. Wright State Univ., 2013-Ohio-5701, ¶ 11 (elucidating statutory "public duty" immunity in the context of a negligence claim against officers who responded to a call relating to a student suicide attempt, and concluding that the exception to immunity of "special relationship" did not apply).

[126] Matthew T. Lockaby & JoAnna Hortillosa, *Government Tort Liability: A Survey Examination of Liability for Public Employers and Employees in Kentucky*, 36 N. Ky. L. Rev. 377, 386 (2009).

negligent party who happens to work for the government, and was in the scope of that employment at the time of the alleged negligence). If this is the case, then the courts generally distinguish between "discretionary duties," those which require or permit the exercise of decision-making authority over both ends and means; and "ministerial duties," those which permit only very limited discretion as to means, and none as to ends. If the former, then the official in question is able to claim the government's immunity as his own, but only in a qualified sense. If the plaintiff can show that the official in question acted arbitrarily, then the plaintiff may be able to succeed, despite the immunity. If the latter, then no immunity attaches, and ordinary negligence principles apply.

Because these doctrines can be quite complex, because courts have been known, for time to time, to misapply them, and because many consider them to be unfair, several states have enacted legislation establishing claims procedures for tort claims against state and local government entities.[127] The typical structure of such statutes consists of a limited waiver of the state's sovereign immunity for certain classes of tort suits; a claims process by which harmed parties can seek compensation, usually outside the court system through a board of claims or a similar entity; and the establishment of this adjudicatory entity and procedures that govern its review. Since most public colleges and universities are "arms of the state,"[128] and since the ones that are not are usually local government entities,[129] plaintiffs seeking to sue such entities for negligence must consult both case law and statutory law prior to filing to ensure (1) that their claims are actionable; and (2) if actionable, that the claims can be filed and litigated in a traditional court.

Emerging Issues

No area of potential liability is more troubling that the danger of third-party assaults on campus. While it remains true that a college or university, as a general rule, has no duty to protect a person from deliberate criminal attacks by a third person, emerging exceptions to this rule include the landlord-tenant relationship or other special circumstances[130] warranting a shift of responsibility for the student's safety from the student to the institution. On April 16, 2007, 23-year-old Seung-Hui Cho, a student at Virginia Tech University in

---

[127] *See, e.g.*, MISS. CODE ANN. § 11-46-1 et seq. (Supp. 1999); O.R.C. § 2744.03(A)(5); & S.C. Code Ann. § 15-78-60(25) (Supp. 1999).

[128] *See, e.g., Withers*, 939 S.W.2d at 343 (holding that the University of Kentucky is an arm of the state for the purposes of sovereign immunity).

[129] *See, e.g.*, Luciano v. Waubonsee Cmty. Coll., 245 Ill. App. 3d 1077, 1084, 614 N.E.2d 904, 908-09 (1993) (holding a community college to be a local government entity under the state's governmental immunity act).

[130] For example, in Tarasoff v. Regents of the Univ. of Cal., 17 Cal.3d 425, 551 P.2d 334 (1976) a university psychotherapist failed to warn his patient's victim of the patient's dangerous tendencies after the patient had stated he would kill the victim. When he did in fact kill the victim, the court held that the patient-therapist relationship created a duty of reasonable care to warn others of the foreseeable risks of the patient's homicidal threat.

Blacksburg, Virginia, shot to death thirty-two students and faculty members, wounded many more, and then committed suicide. In the aftermath of this tragedy, it was discovered that the student was an isolated individual with a history of psychiatric problems. Several of his professors noted that his writing had violent themes and had encouraged him to seek counseling. A psychiatrist evaluated Cho after he expressed suicidal thoughts to a roommate, and a probate judge found him to be mentally ill and ordered him to seek outpatient treatment. These events, when viewed together, may signal a foreseeable risk that could occasion institutional liability.

The Virginia Tech tragedy has sparked a nationwide reconsideration of threat-assessment mechanisms, risk-management processes, and incident-response systems that allow for early detection and effective response to emergencies.[131] Not only has the tragedy at Virginia Tech informed our thinking about steps institutions must take to reduce and manage risks in the campus setting, but there is also ample evidence that both state and federal legislation will impose new standards of care in the context of addressing campus safety and security in the modern era.[132] In addition, institutions must undertake comprehensive and continuous campus outreach efforts that inform faculty, staff, and students about potential threats, crime statistics, and emergency-response protocols.[133]

Several authorities have suggested the emergence of a new phase in the evolution of negligence liability involving higher education institutions and students. One perspective suggests that a higher education institution serves a facilitative role in student development that is based on education in the broadest sense, extending well beyond the classroom and the campus.[134] This perspective recognizes the breadth of the modern higher education institution's mission to educate students; acknowledges the need for mutual, shared responsibility for student educational development between student and institution; and proposes a range of factors that might guide judges in setting legal standards for negligence liability.[135] In another characterization, the relationship between institution and student creates an affirmative duty on the part of the institution "based on a student's detrimental, reasonable reliance on

---

[131] See Oren R. Griffin, *Constructing a Legal and Managerial Paradigm Applicable to the Modern-Day Safety and Security Challenge at Colleges and Universities*, 54 St. Louis L.J. 241 (2009).

[132] *Id.* at 258-265.

[133] The principal federal legislation designed to address security and safety in higher education is the Jeanne Clery Disclosure of Campus Security Policy and Campus Crime Statistics Act (Clery Act), a part of the Higher Education Act of 1965. 20 U.S.C. § 1092 (f) (2006). The Clery Act requires colleges and universities to disclose annual information about campus crime statistics, provide sexual assault victims with information about their option to notify law enforcement agencies of the crime against them and to notify victims that campus personnel will assist them in contacting these agencies, and give students and employees timely warnings about criminal activity that may constitute an ongoing threat to the campus community.

[134] Robert D. Bickel & Peter F. Lake, The Rights & Responsibilities of the Modern University 5 (1999).

[135] *Id.* at 203.

a college's act that is tangentially related to the college's overall mission."[136] The institution's affirmative duty arises out of "a relationship of reliance and trust between the college and its student body based on a student's desire to succeed academically and to contribute to the broad educational mission of the college community."[137] Under this conception, institutions would assume an affirmative duty to protect against foreseeable harm that would be balanced by an expectation that students exercise reasonable prudence. Under this characterization, it would not be reasonable for students to expect that an institution would "protect them from danger or injuries resulting solely from acts that a college had no reason to know about, acts the college had no power to protect against, or from the student's own patently irresponsible behavior."[138]

Adding a new dimension to these developments are the increasing moves within state legislatures to authorize the carrying of firearms on college and university campuses, often in response to tragedies such as the Virginia Tech tragedy.[139] The movement to allow such actions has not been universally successful, but it has gained momentum in several states, despite opposition from colleges and universities understandably concerned about accidents and student and faculty safety. It is almost a statistical inevitability that, at some point, an accidental discharge, or even an intentional one in the heat of the moment, will create a liability problem for a college or university,[140] and in states with laws explicitly allowing for the concealed carrying of firearms on campus, the challenges in preventing such risks are obvious. Higher education attorneys will be wise to monitor future developments in their respective states and work together to devise risk management strategies that do not impinge on these state policies.

---

[136] Kristen Peters, *Protecting the Millennial College Student*, 16 S. CAL. REV. L. & SOCIAL JUSTICE 431, 467 (2007).

[137] *Id.*

[138] *Id.* at 467-468.

[139] *See* NATIONAL CONFERENCE OF STATE LEGISLATURES, GUNS ON CAMPUS: AN OVERVIEW (Feb. 23, 2015), *available at* http://www.ncsl.org/research/education/guns-on-campus-overview.aspx (last visited Mar. 30, 2015) (explaining that seven states currently permit the carrying of concealed firearms on college campuses, most recently Idaho in March of 2014).

[140] The case of James v. Duquesne Univ., 936 F. Supp. 2d 618, 624 (W.D. Pa. 2013) illustrates how quickly verbal altercations can escalate when concealed firearms are present: "As plaintiff and his teammates proceeded the Eason group started to argue and curse at them. At least one of the teammates started to argue back. Plaintiff cautioned his teammates that they needed to maintain their composure because there could be repercussions if they were in a fight on campus. Plaintiff nudged one of his teammates and they then began to walk away by continuing down Academic Walk. Holmes and Lee pulled out handguns and opened fire on the basketball players. The shooting took place near or in front of the Duquesne Towers, one of the dormitories on campus, which is over 200 yards from the Student Union." Although in *James*, the University was held not to have the duty to protect against the "spontaneous shooting," *see id.* at 645, a small change in facts could have altered that outcome.

Conclusion

It remains true that the college or university is not an insurer of the safety of its students nor a policer of student morality. However, recent case law suggests that the "no duty" standard has been gradually eroded, and a special duty relationship is possible, particularly in cases that involve third-party assaults on students, hazing, and injuries in institutionally sponsored activities involving a high degree of supervision. It is possible that public policy will influence judges to recognize liability in other contexts as well, particularly in cases involving student alcohol abuse and student suicide. The emerging duty of care imposed on institutions has been influenced by a range of factors, including the relationship between the parties, awareness of the degree of risk involved, the foreseeable nature of the harm incurred, and the public policy consequences that will result from a precedent extending or expanding liability.

Recognizing that learning experiences transcend the classroom, higher education administrators and faculty have expanded the range of educational programs for students well beyond the classroom, laboratory, or lecture hall. Institutions of higher education seek to attract students through the provision of a range of programs and services that are often described in institutional brochures and guides as key elements in student development and socialization. Adopting a holistic approach to higher education has led to the introduction of community service programs, off-campus internships, study abroad, and a host of other educational experiences sponsored by the institution and made available to students as an integral part of a diverse learning environment.

Judges have made clear that it is possible to create a duty if one voluntarily undertakes to perform an act, and to find that a duty is breached when the act is performed in a negligent manner. Although judicial recognition of a special duty relationship has been limited, institutional administrators should emphasize their responsibility to educate students about the risks inherent in activities, take affirmative steps to reduce risks, and adopt risk-management and risk-avoidance practices[141] commensurate with the known dangers that can result from institutional programs.

Discussion Questions

1. Student handbooks and codes of conduct (often embedded in college catalogs or websites) are ubiquitous features of higher education life. As you can see from the above discussion, though, they can also be sources to which courts will look, once a lawsuit arises, to determine how foreseeable particular risks would have been. Choose student conduct codes from two higher education institutions, and evaluate them for whether their language or provisions could create unintended liability consequences for

---

[141] *See* WILLIAM A. KAPLAN & BARBARA A. LEE, THE LAW OF HIGHER EDUCATION 152-157 (4th ed. 2006) for a discussion of the three principal approaches to risk transfer: liability insurance, hold harmless and indemnification agreements, and releases and waivers.

the institution. Compare and contrast their provisions. Which strikes the best balance between managing student behavior and protecting against expansion of the institution's duty of care?

2. Tort law is a basic form of common law, and it interacts with numerous provisions of statutory law at both the state and federal level. Choose a subtopic from the discussion above, and conduct research on search databases (e.g., Lexis, Westlaw, Google Scholar, etc.) to determine whether any federal or state statutory schemes are relevant to it. If so, do the statutory provisions in question alter the tort landscape, or complement/coexist with it?

3. Review the material above on tort immunities. Is this legal doctrine just? Place yourself and a partner on either side of this question and debate it, with one of you attacking the doctrine and the other defending it. To argue and debate effectively, you will have to first think carefully about the public policy considerations that underlie sovereign and governmental immunities.

11

Defamation and Intentional Torts

Richard Fossey, J.D., Ed.D.
University of Louisiana at Lafayette
Kerry B. Melear, J.D., Ph.D.
University of Mississippi

Liability for injuries caused by negligence is a consistent concern for all colleges and universities, but campus leaders need to be aware of other torts as well. In particular, they should be aware of the basic principles of defamation law to avoid liability arising from a thoughtlessly expressed false statement or carelessly written document. In addition, the common law recognizes several intentional torts: assault, battery, false imprisonment, fraud, and intentional infliction of emotional distress. Although case law concerning intentional torts is less frequent in the higher education sector, all college and university officials who have risk- management responsibilities should be knowledgeable about the essential element of these torts.

Defamation

Defamation is the publication, either orally or in writing, of a false communication about a person that injures that person's reputation or standing in the community.[1] A written defamation is defined as libel, while defamations that are expressed orally or through gestures are referred to as slander.[2] To be liable for defamation, the defamatory remark must be published to a third party[3]. A false statement made only to the defamed person is not actionable in a defamation suit, no matter how scurrilous or insulting.

At common law, there are two forms of defamation—those that are defamatory *per se* and those that are defamatory *per quod*. Statements are defamatory *per se* if they are injurious to an individual's reputation by their very nature, and the injured party need not show special damages when bringing suit. A publication is defamatory *per se* if it 1) imputes conduct to the plaintiff that

---

[1] RESTATEMENT (SECOND) OF TORTS §559.

[2] *Id. at* § 568.

[3] W. PAGE KEETON, PROSSER & KEETON ON THE LAW OF TORTS 771(5th ed. 1984) [hereinafter PROSSER & KEETON] (defamation requires publication to a party other than the person defamed).

constitutes a criminal offense punishable by imprisonment or a crime of moral turpitude[4]; 2) imputes that the plaintiff has a "loathsome" disease such as a venereal or other communicable disease[5]; 3) ascribes "conduct, characteristics or a condition that would adversely affect [the plaintiff's] fitness for the proper conduct of his lawful business, trade or profession, or his public or private office"[6]; or 4) involves words that impute serious sexual misconduct.[7]

All other defamatory communications, no matter how gross or insulting, are defamatory per quod and are not actionable unless the plaintiff can prove actual damages. For example, referring to someone as a "bastard," imputing canine ancestry, or calling someone a "crook," a "damn liar," or a "Communist" are not actionable as defamation unless the offended individual can show some actual damage.[8] Similarly, a Pennsylvania court ruled that a student's statement, given at a college judicial board hearing, that a student told classmates "that she was still drunk," was simply not defamatory.[9] "College students drinking before class or coming to class hung over, as untoward as it may be, is not something that would rise to the level of defamatory in the mind of the average college student," the court observed.[10]

Defenses to Defamation

Truth

Falsity is an absolute requirement in a defamation suit.[11] If the defendant can show that the published statement is true, the plaintiff's defamation claim must fail.[12] For example, in a Louisiana case,[13] Glynn Cyprien, an applicant for the varsity basketball coach's position at Louisiana University at Lafayette (ULL), represented on his resume that he had a Bachelor of Science degree from the University of Texas at San Antonio (UTSA). In fact, although he had been a student at UTSA, he did not have a degree from that institution. The university hired Cyprien for the coach's position, and he accurately indicated that he graduated from Lacrosse University on a form he filled out during the hiring process.

About two months after he began working at ULL, a newspaper reported that Cyprien "did not graduate from the University of Texas at San Antonio as he claimed on his resume, according to the university registrar's office."[14]

---

[4]   RESTATEMENT (SECOND) OF TORTS § 571.

[5]   *Id. at* § 572.

[6]   *Id. at* § 573.

[7]   *Id. at* § 574.

[8]   PROSSER & KEETON, *supra* note 3 at 793.

[9]   Reardon v. Allegheny Coll., 926 A.2d 477, 485 (Pa. Sup. Ct. 2007).

[10] *Id.*

[11] *Id.* at §581A ("One who publishes a defamatory statement of fact is not subject to liability for defamation if the statement is true.").

[12] *See, e.g.*, Collins v. Purdue Univ., 703 F. Supp. 2d 862, 876 (N.D. Ind.) (newspaper's publication of criminal charge of false informing was not false and therefore not defamatory).

[13] Cyprien v. Bd. of Supervisors for the Univ. of La. Sys., 5 So. 2d 862 (La. 2009).

[14] *Id.* at 864 (internal pagination omitted).

On the same day the article appeared, ULL fired Cyprien "on the ground that he lied about his academic credentials on his resume."[15]

Cyprien sued ULL for defamation and bad faith breach of contract, but the Louisiana Supreme Court sided with the university. "ULL has established as an undisputed fact that Mr. Cyprien sent in a resume that falsely represented that he received a Bachelor of Science degree from UTSA," the court pointed out.[16] "Thus, ULL has demonstrated that Mr. Cyprien will be unable to establish an essential element of his defamation claim—namely, that ULL made a false statement."[17]

Likewise, in *Wynne v. Loyola University of Chicago*,[18] Martha Ellen Wynne, a faculty member in Loyola's School of Education, sued a colleague for comments made in a memorandum to a senior faculty member expressing concern about Wynne becoming department chair of a new department. The memorandum stated that Wynne had brought personal problems, such as infertility and psychiatric issues related to a sleep disorder, into the workplace and expressed the view that Wynne lacked leadership ability. Wynne sued for defamation but admitted many of the assertions in her colleague's memorandum. Upholding a trial court's decision to dismiss her case, an Illinois appellate court concluded that "[i]nasmuch as Wynne admits the foregoing facts, and inasmuch as the contents of the Rogers memorandum are 'substantially true,' her defamation claims must fail."[19]

In *Walker v. President and Fellows of Harvard College*,[20] a law student was accused of plagiarism based on a manuscript she submitted to one of Harvard Law School's scholarly journals. A hearing was held on the matter, and a statement was placed on her transcript noting that she had been "issued a letter of Reprimand by the Administrative Board" based on the plagiarism incident.

The student sued for defamation and breach of contract, but a federal district court entered summary judgment against her. Truth is a defense to a defamation claim, the court pointed out. Thus, [b]ecause the plaintiff committed plagiarism within the meaning of Harvard's Student Handbook . . ., the publications of fact she alleges libelous are true, and she cannot recover."[21] The court dismissed her breach of contract claim as well.

Privileged Communications

Courts have long recognized that the public interest requires individuals to be able to speak freely in certain settings without undue fear of being sued for defamation. Thus, the law has identified privileged communications that are protected from lawsuits based in libel or slander. Statements made in judicial

---

[15] *Id.*
[16] *Id.* at 867.
[17] *Id.*
[18] 741 N.E.2d 669 (Ill. Ct. App. 2000).
[19] *Id.* at 676.
[20] Civil Action No. 12-10811-RWZ, 2014 U.S. Dist. LEXIS (Dec. 30, 2014).
[21] *Id.* at *16.

proceedings, for example, whether made by the judge, attorneys, or witnesses who testify at trial, are absolutely privileged. Statements made in open court or in court pleadings enjoy complete protection from defamation suits.[22]

In some jurisdictions, courts recognize an absolute privilege for communications made in quasi-judicial proceedings like administrative hearings or college student disciplinary hearings. For example, a federal court in Oregon ruled that a law student's testimony at an honor code committee hearing about another student's alleged plagiarism were absolutely privileged and could not form the basis of a defamation suit.[23]

A federal court in Texas applied the judicial privilege to dismiss a defamation case brought by a former student against a community college. The college sought a temporary restraining order and an injunction against her based on the college's allegations that she had made threatening statements in a judicial pleading that she had filed in a case against the college.[24] The court ruled that Texas had long recognized a "litigation privilege" that was an absolute bar to a defamation claim.[25] As described by the court, the Texas litigation privilege is comprehensive and "extends to any statement made by the judge, jurors, counsel, parties or witnesses, and attaches to all aspects of [judicial] proceedings, including statements made in open court, pre-trial hearings, depositions, affidavits, and any of the pleadings or other papers in the case."[26]

Although the judicial privilege is absolute, courts have recognized other privileged communications that are conditional, such as the privilege of fair comment or criticism,[27] particularly when the party speaking has an interest in the subject matter being discussed, or a legal, moral, or social duty to communicate on a topic.[28] Any person who claims such a privilege must have published the defamatory statement in good faith and without abusing the privilege by circulating the defamation outside the scope and purpose of the privilege.[29] For example, courts have recognized that faculty members and college administrators have a common interest in sharing information

---

[22] PROSSER & KEETON, *supra* note 3 at 816-817.

[23] Singh v. Tong, 2006 U.S. Dist. LEXIS 78228 (D. Or. 2006).

[24] O'Neal v. Alamo Comm. Coll. Dist., Civil Action No. SA-08-CA-1031-XR, 2101 U.S. Dist. LEXIS 6637, *5 (W.D. Tex. Jan. 27, 2010).

[25] *Id.* at *46.

[26] *Id.* at *46-47, citing Jenevein v. Friedman, 114 S.W.3d 743, 745-46 (Tex. App. 2003) (internal citations and quotation marks omitted).

[27] WILLIAM A. KAPLIN & BARBARA A. LEE, THE LAW OF HIGHER EDUC. 248 (5th ed.2013) [hereinafter KAPLIN & LEE] (One of the most important defenses to a defamation action is the conditional or qualified privilege of fair comment and criticism.").

[28] *See, e.g.,* Olsson v. Ind. Univ. Bd. of Trs, 571 N.E.2d 585, 587 (Ind. Ct. App. 1991) ("Under the qualified privilege rule (or common interest rule), a communication is privileged if made in good faith on any subject matter in which the party making the communication has an interest or in reference to which he has a duty either public or private, whether legal, moral, or social, if made to a person having a corresponding interest or duty.").

[29] See RESTATEMENT (SECOND) OF TORTS § 604, comment a ("Ordinarily, a privilege is abused by speaking defamatory words in the presence of persons whose knowledge of them is unnecessary to the protection of the interest in question.").

about the qualifications of students, former students, and scholars who are seeking employment or promotion.[30] Therefore, communications pertaining to the qualifications and skills of others in the academic setting usually enjoy conditional immunity from defamation suits.[31]

This principle is illustrated in *Olsson v. Indiana University Board of Trustees*,[32] which involved a university professor's negative evaluation letter about a former student. Janet Olsson, a student in the School of Education at Indiana University (IU), performed her student teaching under the supervision of Linda Null, an IU professor. After her student teaching assignment was over, Olsson sought a full-time job at an elementary school; James Lundy, the school's principal, asked Null for a written evaluation of Olsson's overall teaching ability. In response to Lundy's request, Null wrote a letter in which she stated that Olsson was a "marginal student teacher."[33] Olsson did not get the job she applied for or any other teaching job, and she sued IU for defamation based on Null's letter.

A trial court awarded summary judgment to the university, and an Indiana intermediate appellate court affirmed. "The subject matter of the letter was information IU had a duty to report to school administrators," the court ruled;[34] thus, Null enjoyed a qualified privilege to write it.

Furthermore, the court added that Olsson had produced no material evidence that Null had abused her qualified privilege to write Lundy about Olsson's teaching performance. Olsson had not shown that Null was motivated by ill will when she wrote the letter, had engaged in excessive publication of the letter, or had written the letter without believing that what she wrote was true.

In *Havlik v. Johnson & Wales University*,[35] the First Circuit Court of Appeals considered whether a private Rhode Island university enjoyed a qualified privilege to notify the campus community about an incident that initially appeared to be a crime, as required by the Clery Act.[36] In that case, Christopher

---

[30] *See, e.g.*, Taggart v. Drake Univ., 549 N.W.2d 796 (Iowa 1996) (department chair has qualified privilege to evaluate a faculty member).

[31] *See, e.g.*, Tacka v. Georgetown Univ., 103 F. Supp. 2d 43 (D.D.C. 2001) (although department chair enjoyed qualified to share negative external reviewer's evaluation to tenure committee in connection with a professor's tenure application, fact issues existed concerning whether chair's conduct was motivated by malice); El Deeb v. Univ. of Minn., 60 F.3d 423 (8th Cir. 1995) (department chair's letter to dean asserting inconsistencies in a professor's vita with regard to grant activity and publications was protected by qualified privilege); Rosenthal v. Regents of Univ. of Cal., 269 Cal. Rptr. 788 (Cal. Ct. App. 1990) (university committee charged with evaluating undergraduate programs had qualified privilege to criticize leadership by department chair in report circulated to faculty and students at institution).

[32] 571 N.E.2d 585 (Ind. Ct. App. 1991).

[33] *Id.* at 486.

[34] *Id.* at 588.

[35] 509 F.3d 25 (1st Cir. 2007).

[36] The Clery Act requires all colleges and universities that receive federal funds to make "timely reports to the campus community on [certain] crimes considered to be a threat to other students and employees . . . that are reported to campus security or local law police agencies." 20 U.S.C. § 1092(f)(3).

Havlik sued Johnson & Wales University after officials issued a "crime alert" notifying the university's constituencies about a physical altercation between Havlik and another student. The alert mentioned Havlik's name and incorrectly stated that a knife had been brandished.

Havlik sued the university for defamation, arguing that university personnel circulated false information about him in the crime alert. A federal trial court dismissed his case on the university's motion for summary judgment. Assuming the crime alert was defamatory, the trial court reasoned, the university enjoyed a qualified privilege to publish it within the university, stemming from its legal obligation under the Clery Act to notify the campus community when designated serious crimes are reported.

On appeal, Havlik maintained that the altercation that triggered the university's crime alert had occurred off campus. The university had no legal obligation to issue a crime alert under the Clery Act, Havlik argued; thus, it was not entitled to qualified immunity from his defamation claim.

The First Circuit rejected this line of attack. The goal of the Clery Act's crime notification requirement, the court noted, "is to protect members of the constituent campus communities by 'aid[ing] in the prevention of similar occurrences.'"[37] To comply with the act, "school officials must act expeditiously," the court reasoned, and a reasonable belief that a crime alert should be issued is all that is required for the qualified privilege to apply.[38] Nor, in the court's opinion, was there any evidence that the university had abused its qualified privilege by acting with malice.

Similarly, in *Slovinec v. American University*, [39] a university issued a "barring notice" against Joseph Slovinec due to concerns about what the university police chief described as Slovinec's "unpredictable and disruptive behavior." [40] The notice, which contained a photograph of Slovinec, advised that Slovinec would be arrested and charged with unlawful entry if he came on campus, but it gave no details about the university's concerns and was distributed only to safety officers and administrators who had a duty to protect university students and staff.

Slovinec sued for defamation, but a federal court dismissed the claim on two grounds. First, the court ruled that the university had issued the barring notice in good faith and had only distributed it to university personnel charged with protecting staff and students. Thus, the notice was privileged.[41] In addition, the court ruled that the notice was not defamatory. The court pointed out that the notice did not disclose the circumstances leading up to its issuance. Rather it merely advised that Slovinec was subject to arrest if he appeared on campus.

In *Olssen*, *Havlik*, and *Slovinec*, universities defeated defamation claims based on court findings that their supposedly defamatory communications were

---

[37] *Id.* at 30.

[38] *Id.* at 32.

[39] Slovinec v. Am. Univ., 565 F. Supp. 2d 114, 116 (D.D.C. 2008).

[40] *Id.* at 116.

[41] *Id.* at 119.

protected by a qualified privilege.[42] In *Melton v. Bow*,[43] however, the Georgia Supreme Court upheld a jury verdict against Charles Melton, a University of Georgia professor who had been sued for libel and slander by Michael Bow, a student worker at the university. The court acknowledged that Professor Melton had a limited privilege to communicate information about Bow as part of an investigation of a report that Bow had received a W-2 form for earnings as a student worker at a time he was no longer working at the university. Subsequently, however, university investigators determined that Bow was guilty of no wrongdoing and that the discrepancy in accounts was the work of an embezzler in Melton's department.

In upholding the jury's verdict, the Georgia Supreme Court noted that the evidence showed that Melton made defamatory remarks and published defamatory reports about Bow to numerous people not involved in the investigation and that he continued to make defamatory statements about Bow after he had been cleared of any wrongdoing. "Dr. Melton, by oral and written statements, accused Bow of the theft of hotplates from the chemistry laboratory where he had worked. He called Bow a liar, stated that Bow was in trouble with the IRS, and made many other derogatory remarks about him."[44]

Melton argued that Bow had not been injured by Melton's remarks since Bow continued to enjoy an excellent reputation, but the Georgia Supreme Court rejected this argument as being inconsistent with Georgia defamation law. "To impute the crime of theft to a person is actionable per se without proof of special damages," the court pointed out. "Bow had no burden to prove that his reputation had been damaged by the statements imputing a crime to him. The law infers injury to his reputation."[45]

Likewise, in *Doe v. Gonzaga University*,[46] the Washington Supreme Court upheld a jury verdict of more than one million dollars against university employees who had communicated an allegation of sexual misconduct about a student outside the scope of their employment. The defendants were not protected by a conditional "common interest" privilege, the court ruled, and could be held liable for their defamatory statements.

Satire, Jest, and Hyperbole

Defamation by definition is a false statement of fact. Courts have ruled consistently that a statement that is outrageous, offensive, and vulgar is not actionable under defamation law if no reasonable person would interpret the communication as being a statement of fact. For example, calling someone a

---

[42] *See also* Dupree v. Saunders, 588 F.3d 282, 291 (5th Cir. 2009) (professor's defamation claim against president of university based on actions taken in response to report of professor's allegedly disruptive behavior could not survive summary judgment as there was no evidence that the president published or revealed any charges against the professor).

[43] 247 S.E.2d 100 (Ga. 1978).

[44] *Id.* at 101.

[45] *Id.*

[46] 24 P.3d 390 (Wash. 2001), *rev'd on other grounds*, Gonzaga Univ. v. Doe, 536 U.S. 273 (2002).

"traitor" or a person engaged in blackmail is not defamatory when reasonable people would understand those appellations to be hyperbole.[47] Likewise, communications that would only be understood as "good-natured fun" and not to be taken seriously are not defamatory.[48]

This point of law has been illustrated several times in the context of public education. For example, in *Salek v. Passaic Collegiate School*,[49] students published a school yearbook containing a photo of Sylvia Salek and a male teacher next to a caption that read, "Not tonight, Ms. Salek, I have a headache."[50] Salek claimed that the average reader who saw the photo and read the caption would conclude that Salek was in a sexual relationship with the teacher; she sued for defamation, false light, infliction of emotional distress, and negligent supervision.

A New Jersey court ruled as a matter of law that the objectionable material "is susceptible of only non-defamatory meaning and is clearly understood as being parody, satire, humor, or fantasy."[51] The court rejected all of Salek's other tort theories as well.

In *Walko v. Kean College of New Jersey*,[52] college students published a "spoof" edition of the student newspaper that included phony advertisements. One fake advertisement purportedly announced a "whoreline," and listed Ann Walko and several other well-known campus figures as being available for "good telephone sex."[53]

As in the *Salek* case, the court dismissed Walko's defamation claim as a matter of law. "Given all of the surrounding circumstances," the court concluded, "virtually everyone who read Ann Walko's name in the 'Whoreline' ad would know that it was a joke" and not to be interpreted as an assertion of fact that anyone would take seriously.[54]

In a more recent case, *Yeagle v. Collegiate Times*,[55] the Virginia Supreme Court considered whether the student newspaper at a state university had defamed Sharon Yeagle, a university administrator, when it published an article that contained a block quotation attributed to her and the phrase "Director of Butt Licking" under her name.

Yeagle sued the newspaper for defamation, arguing that the phrase "Director of Butt Licking" was defamatory per se, since a literal interpretation of that phrase imputed that she was guilty of a criminal offense involving moral

---

[47] Greenbelt Coop. Publ'g Assn. v. Bresler, 398 U.S. 6, 14 (1970). (most readers would understand use of word "blackmail" to "no more than rhetorical hyperbole"); Letter Carriers v. Austin, 418 U.S. 264, 286 (1974) (impossible for reasonable reader of newsletter to conclude that nonunion members had committed the criminal offense of treason).

[48] RESTATEMENT (SECOND) OF TORTS § 566, comment d.

[49] 605 A.2d 276 (N.J. Sup. Ct. App. Div. 1992).

[50] *Id*. at 278.

[51] *Id*.

[52] 561 A.2d 680 (N.J. Sup. Ct. Law Div. 1988.

[53] *Id*. at 683.

[54] *Id*. at 684.

[55] 497 S.E.2d 136 (Va. 1998).

turpitude under Virginia's sodomy statute.[56] In defense, Yeagle argued that the offensive phrase implied "that she curries favor with others by disingenuous behavior or directs others to do so."[57] This implication was also defamatory per se because it suggested that she performed her job "in an artificial, shallow, or other manner that generally lacks integrity."[58]

As in *Salek* and *Walko*, the court concluded that Yeagle had not stated a defamation claim. In the court's opinion, the phrase "Director of Butt Licking," while offensive and in extremely bad taste, was no more than "rhetorical hyperbole" that could not be reasonably understood as an assertion that she had committed a crime of moral turpitude or had performed her job in a way that lacked integrity.[59]

Finally, *Mink v. Knox*,[60] decided by the Tenth Circuit Court of Appeals in 2010, suggests that an overly harsh reaction to a college student's web-based parody might be a violation of the student's constitutional rights. Thomas Mink, a student at the University of Northern Colorado (UNC), created a fictional character named "Junius Puke" for the editorial column of his internet-based journal, *The Howling Pig*. The column displayed an altered photograph of a real individual, Junius Peake, a UNC professor. According to the court, Mink's column asserted views that were diametrically opposed to Professor Peake's views.[61]

Professor Peake, unhappy about the parody, contacted the local police, who began investigating Mink for a possible violation of Colorado's criminal libel statute. At some point, Susan Knox, a deputy district attorney, approved a search warrant affidavit prepared by a police officer, and a judge issued a warrant to search the home where Mink lived with his mother. During the search, police seized Mink's personal computer and some written materials referencing the *Howling Pig*.[62]

Mink and his mother filed suit and obtained a temporary restraining order and a court order directing the police to return the items they had seized, including Mink's computer. The district attorney subsequently dropped the criminal investigation, concluding that Mink's writings in the *Howling Pig* could not be prosecuted for criminal libel.

Mink then sued Knox, arguing that she had violated his constitutional rights under the First and Fourth Amendments. A federal trial court dismissed the case, ruling that Knox was entitled to qualified immunity since a reasonable prosecutor might believe that Mink's statements in the *Howling Pig* were not protected under the First Amendment.

---

[56] *Id.* at 138.
[57] *Id.*
[58] *Id.*
[59] *Id.*
[60] 613 F.3d 995 (10th Cir. 2010).
[61] *Id.* at 998.
[62] *Id.* at 999.

On appeal, the Tenth Circuit reversed. In the appellate court's opinion, no reasonable person would have attributed statements made in the *Howling Pig* to Professor Peake or understood them as anything other than hyperbole or satire. Thus, no reasonable prosecutor would take the *Howling Pig* commentary as statements of fact or conclude that the statements constituted a crime that would justify a warrant to search Mink's property.[63]

In summary, *Salek, Walko, and Yeagle* establish that students may not be sued for defamation based on statements that most people would interpret as parody or satire—no matter how tasteless and offensive those statements might be. The Tenth Circuit went further in *Mink* to indicate that harsh punitive action taken against a college student engaged in satire or parody might be a violation of the student's constitutional rights.

Opinion

Under the common law, a person may not be sued for a defamatory statement expressed as an opinion unless the statement "implies the allegation of undisclosed defamatory facts as the basis for that opinion."[64] According to Prosser and Keeton's treatise on tort law, "This position is based on the notion that the constitutional privileges of freedom of the press and speech have now rendered actions for defamation based on pure opinions as unconstitutional."[65]

In *Reardon v. Allegheny College*,[66] a Pennsylvania court applied this principle when it ruled that a professor's testimony about a student in a judicial board hearing consisted of opinions that were not actionable in a defamation suit. Likewise in *Pavlica v. Behr*,[67] a court ruled that a professor's email statements describing a "disastrous year" and commenting on a colleague's "insensitivity and lack of judgment in dealing with others" were subjective opinions that did not assert or imply objective facts. Similarly in *Avins v. White*,[68] a former law-school dean could not maintain a defamation action based on language in a summary accreditation report that described the law school environment by such intangible phrases as "academic ennui" and lack of "intellectual spark." These criticisms were aimed more at the institution than an individual, a federal appellate court ruled, and were not factual statements. [69]

On the other hand, in *Milkovich v. Lorain Journal Company*,[70] the Supreme Court made clear that a defendant cannot escape liability for defamation simply by adding the phrase "in my opinion" to an otherwise slanderous or libelous

---

[63] *Id.*

[64] PROSSER & KEETON *supra*, note 3 at 814. See also RESTATEMENT (SECOND) OF TORTS § 566 ("A defamatory communication may consist of a statement in the form of an opinion, but a statement of this nature is actionable only if it implies the allegation of undisclosed defamatory facts as the basis for the opinion.").

[65] *Id.*

[66] 926 A.2d 477 (Pa. Super. Ct. 2007).

[67] 2006 U.S. LEXIS 38710, *17 (S.D.N.Y. 2006).

[68] 727 F.2d 637, 643 (3d Cir.), *cert. denied*, 449 U.S. 982 (1980).

[69] *Id.*

[70] 497 U.S. 1 (1990).

statement. The Court made clear that it was unwilling to grant "a wholesale defamation exemption" for anything that can be labeled as an opinion.[71] On the contrary, a statement that implies a false assertion of fact is actionable in defamation, even if couched as a statement of opinion, since the statement, "'In my opinion Jones is a liar' can cause as much damage to reputation as the statement, 'Jones is a liar.'"[72]

In the light of the *Milkovich* decision, college administrators and faculty members would be wise not to put too much confidence in common law defenses against a defamation suit based on a right to fair comment or the right to express an opinion. *Milkovich* makes clear that any statement that implies that a person engaged in serious misconduct, such as lying in a judicial proceeding, is actionable in defamation if the statement implies a factual basis and is not true.

Public Officials and Public Figures

Although the Supreme Court declined to recognize a constitutional privilege to express all opinions, it has put constitutional limitations on defamation suits brought by public officials and public figures. In *New York Times v. Sullivan*,[73] the Court issued its landmark decision in a defamation case brought by L. B. Sullivan, Commissioner of Public Affairs for the city of Montgomery, Alabama, against the *New York Times* and other defendants arising from an advertisement published in the *Times* protesting civil rights abuses in Alabama. Although Sullivan was not mentioned in the advertisement, he sued in an Alabama court, claiming the advertisement defamed him personally. An Alabama jury agreed and awarded him a judgment of half a million dollars. The Alabama Supreme Court affirmed.

The *New York Times* appealed to the United States Supreme Court. The Court reversed the judgment and crafted a constitutional limitation on defamation suits brought by public officials based on criticisms of their official conduct. Constitutional guarantees require, the Court declared, "a federal rule that prohibits a public official from recovering damages for a defamatory falsehood relating to his official conduct unless he proves that the statement was made with 'actual malice'—that is, with knowledge that it was false or with reckless disregard of whether it was false or not."[74] Reviewing the record, the Court concluded that it would be impossible to sustain a libel judgment against the *New York Times* or the other defendants under the constitutional standard that the Court had articulated.

---

[71] *Id*. at 17.
[72] *Id*. at 19.
[73] 376 U.S. 254 (1964).
[74] *Id*. at 279-280.

In a later decision, the Supreme Court placed constitutional restrictions on defamation suits "brought not by public officials but by public figures,"[75] and in yet another decision, the Court explained that a public figure could be of two types: individuals who are public figures for all purposes, and individuals who inject themselves or are drawn into particular controversies.[76] Thus, in a series of holdings, the Court crafted constitutional standards that require public officials and public figures to prove that defamatory statements made against them were made with malice.[77]

New York Times v. Sullivan and its progeny have been applied in numerous cases involving defamation cases in the higher education arena. In *Avins v. White*,[78] the Third Circuit Court of Appeals determined that a dean was a public figure for a limited purpose because he had voluntarily injected himself into a controversy about the accreditation of the Delaware Law School. Likewise, in *McGarry v. University of San Diego*,[79] a football coach who had been terminated by the University of San Diego was a "limited purpose public figure," and he was required to show that allegedly false statements made about his termination had been made with malice. "McGarry voluntarily entered the public arena as a college football coach," the court noted, "and the [allegedly defamatory] statements dealt exclusively with his performance of the public role he voluntarily undertook."[80] And in *Alaniz v. Hoyt*,[81] a college's chief financial officer was found to be a public figure by a Texas appellate court and was thus compelled to show actual malice on the part of a professor who made statements suggesting that the financial administrator had improperly diverted college funds.

On the other hand, in *Dobkin v. Johns Hopkins University*,[82] an unpublished opinion, the Fourth Circuit Court of Appeals held that Pearl German, a gerontology professor, and Estelle Fishbein, Vice President and General Counsel at Johns Hopkins University (JHU), were not public figures. Thus, the

---

[75] Curtis Publ'g. Co. v. Butts, 388 U.S. 130, 155 (1967) (holding that public figures who are not public officials "may also recover damages for a defamatory falsehood whose substance makes substantial danger to reputation apparent, on a showing of highly unreasonable conduct constituting an extreme departure from the standards of investigation and reporting ordinarily adhered to by responsible publishers").

[76] Gertz v. Robert Welch, Inc., 418 U.S. 323, 351 (1974).

[77] *See* KERN ALEXANDER & M. DAVID ALEXANDER, AMERICAN PUBLIC SCHOOL LAW 697 (8th ed. 2012) ("If a plaintiff is adjudged to be a public official or a public figure, the publisher of the defamation is protected by a privilege that requires a showing of malice to be overcome. The burden of proof is on the plaintiff to give evidence of malicious intent on the part of the defendant, a burden that has in most cases been very difficult to sustain."); *see also* KAPLIN & LEE, *supra* note 25 at 250 ("If the plaintiff is a 'public figure,' he or she must prove that the defendant acted with 'actual malice,' and the privilege to defame is thus broader than it would be if the plaintiff were a 'private figure.'").

[78] 627 F.2d 637, 646-648 (3d Cir. 1980).

[79] 64 Cal. Rptr. 3d 467 (Cal. Ct. App. 2007).

[80] *Id.* at 481.

[81] 105 S.W.3d 330 (Tex. App. 2003).

[82] No. 96-1715, No. 96-1716, 1999 U.S. LEXIS 725 (4th Cir. Jan. 21, 1999).

court ruled, German and Fishbein were not required to prove malice in their defamation counterclaim against Robert Dobkin, a JHU graduate student who had sued them and the university for defamation after his graduate traineeship grant was terminated.[83]

In *Nadel v. Regents of the University of California*,[84] involving protests at the University of California's Berkeley campus, a California appellate court ruled that the malice standard set forth in *New York Times v. Sullivan*, which required a public official or public figure to prove knowledge of falsity or reckless disregard of the truth in a defamation action, could be invoked by university officials who had been sued for defamation. David Nadel and Carol Ruth Denney were members of a group of protesters called the People's Park Defense Union, which opposed a plan by the University of California to construct volleyball courts in People's Park. As construction on the volleyball courts commenced, protests escalated, eventually culminating in vandalism and rioting. In due course, UC sued the Union, Nadel, Denney and two other activists for damages and injunctive relief and obtained a temporary restraining order enjoining them from committing acts of violence and vandalism against university employees and university property. In several communications, four university employees publicly explained why the university had filed the lawsuit. For example, Vice Chancellor Daniel Boggan stated in a press release that the university was pursuing litigation "to deter perpetrators of violent and destructive acts."[85] University attorney Christine Helwick was quoted as saying, "We are not after anyone except those who have a history of violent conduct."[86]

In a separate lawsuit, Nadel and Denney sued UC, Boggan, Helwick, and two other university employees for civil rights violations and defamation. The university defendants moved for summary judgment, arguing that Nadel and Denney were public figures and could not prove that the UC employees' statements had been motivated by malice. A trial court granted their motion, finding that Nadel and Denney were limited-purpose public figures who had "thrust themselves to the forefront of the People's Park controversy."[87]

On appeal, a California intermediate appellate court affirmed. After a lengthy analysis, the court ruled that the UC defendants were entitled to invoke the malice standard of *New York Times v. Sullivan* and its progeny and that Nadel and Denney were public figures. The court found no evidence that the UC spokespeople had made statements about the litigation against Nadel and Denney that showed malice or reckless disregard of the truth. On the contrary, UC employees had presented declarations in UC's application for a temporary restraining order (TRO) that described "several acts of vandalism and battery by Nadel and Denney," some of which were enumerated by the court.[88]

---

[83] *Id.* at *18.

[84] 34 Cal. Rptr. 2d 188 (Cal. Ct. App. 1994).

[85] *Id.* at 191.

[86] *Id.*

[87] *Id.*, quoting the trial court (internal quotation marks omitted).

[88] *Id.* at 199.

In summary, the court found that the UC defendants had not spoken recklessly in their characterizations of Nadel and Denney. "Those characterizations might have been untrue, or at least exaggerated," the court concluded, "but their support in the record precludes any determination that they were asserted with reckless disregard as to their truth."[89]

In *Thomas M. Cooley Law School v. Kurzon Straus, LLP*,[90] the Sixth Circuit Court of Appeals ruled that Thomas M. Cooley Law School (Cooley) was a public figure in the context of a defamation suit the law school had filed against a law firm and two individual attorneys. Cooley accused the law firm of posting false accusations about the law school on a web site and in a draft complaint of a proposed lawsuit that eventually appeared on the web. Specifically, Cooley alleged the defendants had falsely claimed that Cooley had misrepresented employment statistics of its graduates and had engaged in "Enron-style" accounting techniques.[91]

Although the law firm later retracted at least some of its allegations,[92] the law school sued the firm and two attorneys alleging defamation and other tortious conduct. A federal trial judge dismissed the case, however, ruling that the law school was a public figure for purposes of a defamation lawsuit, requiring it to show that the defendants' communications about it had been made with actual malice.

On appeal, the Sixth Circuit upheld the trial court's dismissal, concluding that Cooley was a limited-purpose public figure that could not prevail on its defamation claim absent a showing of actual malice. In the Sixth Circuit's view, Cooley had been unable to "demonstrate that a reasonable jury could find that defendants published [their comments about Cooley] with actual malice."[93] In the court's view, there was simply no evidence showing that the defendants subjectively doubted the truth of their challenged statements or that they had published any allegedly defamatory statements about Cooley with the knowledge that the statements were false.

Immunity

In many states, public colleges and universities enjoy substantial immunity protection from lawsuits in tort, including lawsuits for defamation. Originally, governmental immunity was rooted in the common law principle that "the king could do no wrong."[94] Gradually, states have abandoned sovereign immunity

---

[89] *Id.* at 200.

[90] 759 F.3d 522 (6th Cir. 2014).

[91] *Id.* at 527.

[92] *Id.* at 526.

[93] *Id.* at 532.

[94] Prosser & Keeton, *supra* note 3 at 1043.

as a judicial doctrine and replaced it with governmental immunity defined by statute.[95]

In *Leatherwood v. Prairie View A&M University*,[96] Anthony Leatherwood sued Prairie View A&M University and several individuals for defamation and retaliation under the Texas Whistleblower Act. Leatherwood's defamation claim was based on a one-page letter written by his supervisor that described five alleged "behavioral conflicts" between Leatherwood and several coworkers.[97] A Texas trial court dismissed his suit, and a Texas appellate court affirmed.

Without describing the substance of the reputedly defamatory letter, the appellate court ruled that state agencies were shielded from tort claims, including defamation, unless the state legislature waived immunity by statute.[98] Under the Texas Tort Claims Act, the court continued, the Texas legislature had waived sovereign immunity in only three circumstances: injuries arising from the operation of a publicly owned vehicle, premises defects, or the use or misuse of university property.[99] Since Leatherwood had not claimed that his supervisor's letter related to any of these statutory exceptions, the court upheld the trial court's decision to dismiss his defamation claim. In addition, the court ruled, intentional torts such as defamation do not fall within the scope of the waiver provisions of the Tort Claims Act, and this finding provided a second ground for dismissing Leatherwood's defamation claim.[100] The court also determined that Leatherwood's pleading concerning his Whistleblower Act claim was defective and dismissed that claim as well, although the court gave him leave to amend his pleadings.[101]

Likewise, in *Genetzky v. Iowa State University*,[102] the Iowa Supreme Court upheld the dismissal of a veterinary medicine professor's defamation clam, which he filed as part of a lawsuit challenging Iowa State University's decision not to grant him tenure. The professor maintained that the university's conduct had "cause severe damage to [his] reputation as a professional in the

---

[95] *See, generally*, Peter J. Maher, Kelly Price, & Perry A. Zirkel, *Governmental and Official Immunity for School Districts and Their Employees: Alive and Well*, 19 KAN. J. L. & PUB. POL'Y 234, 247 (2010) (overview of statutory immunity protections for school districts and employees, concluding that governmental and official immunity was a "robust" defense to tort suits against school districts and employees); see also, generally, Nate Carman & Richard Fossey, *Statutory Immunity for Teachers and Administrators in Texas Public Schools: Texas Educators Enjoy Strong Protection Against Defamation Suits*, 247 Educ. L. Rep. [581] (2009).

[96] No. 01-02-01334-CV, 2004 Tex. App. LEXIS 1455 (Tex. Ct. App. Feb. 12, 2004).

[97] *Id.* at *2.

[98] *Id.* at *6.

[99] *Id.*, citing the Texas Tort Claims Act, TEX. CIV. PRAC. & REM. CODE ANN. § 101.021 (Vernon 1997).

[100] *Id.* at *7-8.

[101] *See also* Crouch v. Trinque, 262 S.W.3d 417, 422 (Tex. Ct. App. 2008) (ruling that state university administrator enjoyed a qualified privilege when commenting on a subordinate but that this privilege must be exercised in good faith and not addressing the issue of sovereign immunity).

[102] 480 N.W.2d 858 (Iowa 1992).

field of veterinary clinical sciences."[103] Without examining the substance of the professor's defamation claim, the court merely upheld the trial court's ruling "that the State does not waive sovereign immunity as to this type of action."[104]

Finally, in *Slack v. Stream*,[105] involving a department chair's plagiarism investigation of an assistant professor, the Alabama Supreme Court ruled that the department chair was not entitled to state-agent immunity under Alabama law and upheld a jury award of $662,000 in a defamation suit brought by the professor. Assistant Professor Christopher Stream submitted a coauthored manuscript to a journal that apparently included some material that had been taken from an unattributed source. In an email message, the journal editor rejected the manuscript and forwarded a message from of one of the manuscript's reviewers, who noted "several instances of plagiarism."[106]

Several months later, Stream accepted an offer to work at the University of Nevada at Las Vegas (UNLV) and the coauthor of the rejected manuscript revealed the plagiarism allegation to Stream's department chair, James Slack.

After conducting an investigation, Slack confronted Stream with the plagiarism charge and wrote Stream a harsh reprimand in which he referred to plagiarism as "intellectual theft" and the "rape of the academy."[107] Acknowledging that Stream had obtained a new job at UNLV, Slack informed Stream that had he not resigned to accept the new post, he would have recommended termination.

On the same day he wrote Stream the letter of reprimand, Slack called the chair of Stream's new department at UNLV and asked the chair if he knew he was hiring a plagiarist. Slack then faxed various materials to the chair, including the letter of reprimand. In addition, Slack sent copies of the reprimand to the chair of the Department of Government at Florida State University, where Stream had received his doctoral degree and to the editors of eight scholarly journals.

UNLV investigated Slack's plagiarism allegations and concluded that the incident constituted "sloppy scholarship," but not intentional plagiarism.[108] UNLV did not rescind its job offer to Stream, and he began teaching at UNLV that fall.

An investigative committee at UAB also investigated Slack's charges and Stream. Although it concluded that Stream's manuscript had some unattributed quotes, it found extenuating circumstances. It also concluded that Slack had not handled the matter in accordance with UAB policy. Slack's dean required him to tender his resignation as department chair, and UAB's provost described Slack's actions as unacceptable and "callously precipitous."[109]

---

[103] *Id.* at 861.
[104] *Id.*
[105] 988 So. 2d 516 (Ala. 2008).
[106] *Id.* at 518.
[107] *Id.* at 521.
[108] *Id.* at 523.
[109] *Id.* at 525.

Stream sued Slack and UAB for defamation, invasion of privacy, and intentional interference with a business contract. Slack counterclaimed, accusing Stream of defaming him. All claims against UAB were dismissed on sovereign immunity grounds. Slack moved for dismissal of Stream's suit against him dismissed based on state-agent immunity, but the trial court denied the motion. After a trial, a jury awarded Stream $212,000 in damages and $450,000 in punitive damages. The jury also ruled in Stream's favor on Slack's defamation counterclaim.

On appeal, Slack argued that he was entitled to state-agent immunity under Alabama law, but the Alabama Supreme Court disagreed. First, the court ruled that Slack had not conducted his plagiarism investigation in accordance with UAB policy. Slack argued that he did not know about the policy, but the court was unsympathetic. "[W]e decline to extend State-agent immunity to individuals who are ignorant of the rules and regulations of the State agency with which they are employed."[110] Furthermore, the court added, "Because Slack acted willfully and maliciously in disseminating the letter of reprimand concerning Stream, as well as beyond the scope of his authority, he is not entitled to state-agent immunity."[111]

Together, *Leatherwood*, *Genetzky*, *Moran*, and *Slack* demonstrate the importance of governmental and official immunity in defamation lawsuits brought against public higher education institutions and their employees. In most states, immunity protection is defined in statutes, and these statutory provisions vary greatly from jurisdiction to jurisdiction.[112] Moreover, as these cases demonstrate, judicial interpretations of immunity provisions differ from state to state. *Leatherwood* and *Genetzky* show how statutory immunity provisions can be a formidable barrier in defamation cases brought against public colleges or universities and their employees. On the other hand, *Slack v. Stream* shows that defamation defendants cannot rely on state immunity provisions as a blanket protection from a defamation suit if they published defamatory matter beyond the bounds of a legitimate work-related interest.

Summary of Defamation Law

In summary, defamation law, although firmly rooted in the common law, varies from state to state. State immunity statutes have a substantial impact on the potential liability of public universities and their employees, and the Supreme Court has identified constitutional dimensions to defamation actions brought by public officials and public figures. Nevertheless, certain general principles are generally applicable across jurisdictions.

---

[110] *Id*. at 530.

[111] *Id*. at 531.

[112] See PROSSER & KEETON, *supra* note 3 at 10443-1051 for a description of the different kinds of immunity provisions that have been adopted under the laws of the various states.

First, truth is an absolute defense to defamation. Thus, persons who speak and write truthfully, prudently, and discreetly or discretely can significantly limit their exposure to libel or slander lawsuits.

Second, courts have consistently ruled that communications that no reasonable person would interpret as a statement of fact are not defamatory, no matter how outrageous or insulting. This principle was dramatically demonstrated in *Yeagle v. Collegiate Times*,[113] in which a university administrator was identified as "Director of Butt Licking." Litigation over sophomoric student writings is generally fruitless, and a university that seeks to punish a student journalist or student newspaper for offensive expressions risks violating the First Amendment.

Third, the Supreme Court has placed constitutional hurdles that public officials and public figures must overcome when bringing defamation suits that pertain to their public functions. Unless such individuals can show that the defendant made the defamatory statement with actual malice, they cannot prevail in a libel or slander lawsuit.

Fourth, many states provide public universities and their officials with very strong protection against defamation suits that concern public officials' discretionary duties and functions. In some jurisdictions, statutory protection may almost completely bar defamation suits against the employees of public colleges and universities if those suits are based on statements made as part of their official duties.

Finally, although college administrators and professors often enjoy a qualified privilege to communicate on sensitive matters within their institutions, that privilege does not permit them to make defamatory statements to the general public. *Melton v. Bow* and *Slack v. Stream* offer two dramatic examples of the danger of publishing slanderous or libelous statements that have no legitimate work-related purpose.

Other Intentional Torts

While defamation claims remain the most frequently litigated of the intentional torts in higher education, other intentional tort claims are regularly forwarded against colleges and universities. Claims such as fraud, intentional infliction of emotional distress, assault, false arrest, false imprisonment, or tortious interference with contract are filed against postsecondary institutions, but plaintiffs do not often meet with success because of failure to establish the requisite elements of such claims. This section will briefly discuss examples of intentional torts other than defamation that fall within these categories.

Fraud and Misrepresentation

Fraud claims against institutions of higher education remain robust, and while no sector is insulated, the profit-driven proprietary sector is particularly

---

[113] 497 S.E.2d 136 (Va. 1998).

vulnerable to student assertions that some element of the educational experience was misrepresented to induce enrollment.[114] In the nonprofit sector, colleges and universities can fall prey to misrepresentation claims when institutional representatives negligently make statements that fall outside the scope of truth or are made with disregard for their veracity.[115]

Claims of fraud brought against colleges and universities require that a plaintiff prove that (1) the institution or representative made a statement that misrepresented a material fact; (2) the statement was made to willfully deceive, or was made recklessly and with disregard for knowledge of its truth; (3) the plaintiff justifiably relied on the statement under the circumstances; and (4) reliance was the proximate cause of damages to the plaintiff.[116]

Courts have generally rejected allegations of fraud because the proof of justifiable reliance on a false assertion of fact leading to actual injury is difficult to establish, particularly in the context of the nonprofit university. For example, in *Rodi v. Southern New England School of Law*,[117] a law school graduate whose institution failed to receive American Bar Association accreditation during his enrollment filed suit against the institution for fraudulent misrepresentation. He asserted that two successive deans of the law school made statements suggesting that the institution would receive accreditation and that these statements misled him into remaining enrolled there. A federal district court dismissed his claims, and the United States Court of Appeals for the First Circuit affirmed.[118] The student had made applications for transfer to other institutions that he never rescinded, which suggested a lack of reliance on the deans' statements.[119] Further, the school's catalog clearly stated that accreditation was an external issue controlled by a party independent of the law school.[120] Thus, the First Circuit concluded that no reasonable jury would find that the student relied on the deans' statements or, if he did, that his reliance was reasonable.[121] The United States Supreme Court denied certiorari in 2009.

Lack of reliance on an institutional statement resulted in the dismissal of a fraud claim leveled against the University of Kentucky by a former coach.[122] The assistant football coach resigned in 2000 amid speculation of NCAA infractions related to recruiting and academic violations. He filed suit against the

---

[114] *See* Osamudia R. James, *Predatory Ed.: The Conflict Between Public Good and For-Profit Higher Education*, 38 J.C.&U.L. 45 (2011). *See also* Urquilla-Diaz v. Kaplan University, 780 F.3d 1039 (2015).

[115] *See* Aaron O. Taylor, *Ending the Higher Education Sucker Sale: Toward an Expanded Theory of Tort Liability for Recruitment Deception*, 2015 Utah L. Rev. 425 (2015). *See also* United States of America v. Sanford Brown, Ltd., 788 F. 3d 696 (7th Cir. 2015).

[116] Blane v. Alabama Comm. Coll., 585 So.2d 866 (Ala. 1991).

[117] 532 F.3d 11 (1st Cir. 2008), *cert. denied*, 129 S.Ct. 1373 (2009).

[118] *Id.*

[119] *Id.* at 16.

[120] *Id.* at 13.

[121] *Id.* at 17. *See also* Lidecker v. Kendall College, 550 N.E.2d (Ill. App. Ct. 1990) (nursing students failed to establish fraud claim when institution did not receive accreditation asserted by administrators).

[122] Bassett v. National Collegiate Athletic Ass'n, 528 F.3d 426 (6th Cir. 2008).

university for fraud, among other charges, contending that the athletic director lied when he informed the coach that there would be no further investigation against him if he resigned.[123] A federal district court dismissed the fraud claim, concluding that the coach failed to demonstrate reasonable reliance on the athletic director's statement.[124] The United States Court of Appeals for the Sixth Circuit upheld that decision, reasoning that the coach's own knowledge of NCAA procedures defeated any reasonable reliance he might have placed on the athletic director's statement.[125] His injury was therefore the result of his own conduct, not reliance on the athletic director's assurance that no further investigation would take place.

For-profit institutions, however, have remained vulnerable to fraud claims because their profit-generating mission likens them more closely to private sector organizations. Statements made by for-profit institutions that are intended to encourage students to enroll may lead to misrepresentation of programs or services available to students, resulting in an action for fraud. Successful claims for fraudulent misrepresentation must be based on specific and clear representations known to be false or made with reckless disregard for their veracity. Generalizations about curriculum or mere assertions that an institution did not provide the educational experience it represented are generally rejected by the courts as attempts to plead educational malpractice, which courts refuse to hear for policy reasons.

Such was the circumstance in *Jamieson v. Vatterott Educational Center, Inc.*,[126] in which a group of students filed suit against Vatterott College, a for-profit institution that provides vocational training in courses of study such as computer programming, medical office employment, and electrical mechanics. The students alleged that they did not receive the instruction the institution promised, that the college knowingly or recklessly misrepresented numerous factors to induce them to enroll, and that they relied on those statements in doing so.[127] The college moved for summary judgment on all of the students' claims, and a federal district court granted the college's motion on several counts, concluding that the students' arguments were tantamount to claims of educational malpractice, which courts do not hear. However, the court denied the motion on several counts that alleged specific instances of misrepresentation, concluding that a jury should determine whether the college misrepresented whether various local employers "actively and regularly

---

[123] *Id.* at 429.
[124] *Id.*
[125] *Id.* at 436-437.
[126] 259 F.R.D. 520 (D. Kan. 2009).
[127] *Id.* at 524-25.

sought Vatterott graduates"[128] or that the institution would provide hands-on training in some subjects.[129]

More recently, a Missouri appellate court upheld a damages award against the same institution for violation of the Missouri Merchandise Practices Act. A jury found that Vatterott College had engaged in deceitful practices in selling one of its programs to students.[130] On appeal, the court upheld an award for $27,000 in compensatory damages and a punitive damages award of more than $2 million.

In *Craig v. Forest Institute of Psychology*,[131] student-plaintiffs presented evidence that the institute represented that the students would be able to obtain graduate degrees in psychology and become licensed in Alabama if they enrolled. The students argued that the representatives of the institute knew that it could not continue operating the branch campus at which the students were enrolled when enrollments fell, but that representatives continued to recruit students without disclosing the institute's precarious financial condition. These allegations and the evidence on which they were based created a question of whether the representatives had defrauded the students and justified returning the question to the trial court for further proceedings.

Similarly, students filed suit against a New York for-profit institution alleging that it marketed itself as a respectable vocational school well-equipped to train students for active employment, but that it failed to keep those promises.[132] The students asserted that the institution made fraudulent representations to induce them to enroll, which they did, financing the experience through federal student loans. A federal district court concluded that the students properly established a case for fraud by proving their reliance on specific statements made by the institution's recruiters and catalog concerning federal funding, educational facilities, and job placement opportunities. However, in *Villarreal v. Art Institute of Houston*,[133] a student's claims for fraud and breach of contract were dismissed because she failed to present evidence of reliance on specific promises resulting in injury.

Allegations of fraudulent activity faced by colleges and universities continue to increase, especially as society becomes more litigious and courts more willing to hold higher education institutions accountable for their statements and actions.[134] Institutional representatives, especially those who recruit students or have apparent authority to bind the institution through their

---

[128] *Id.* at 527.

[129] *Id.* at 537-38. *See also* Alsides v. Brown Institute, Ltd., 592 N.W.2d 468 (Minn. Ct. App. 1999) (concluding that a student may file suit against an institution for fraud or fraudulent misrepresentation if the claim focused on specific allegations of failed performance and not a general assertion concerning the educational process).

[130] Kerr v. Vatterott Educational Centers, Inc., 439 S.W.3d 802 (Mo. Ct. App. 2014).

[131] 713 So.2d 967 (Ala. Ct. App. 1997).

[132] Moy v. Adelphi Institute, 866 F. Supp. 696 (E.D.N.Y. 1994).

[133] 20 S.W.3d 792 (Tex. Ct. App. 2000).

[134] *See* Kelly A. Bednarz, *Higher Education Law: The Negative Effects of Student Loans: A Plea for Impacted Students*, 40 W. New Eng. L. Rev. 101 (2018).

statements, should take care to provide accurate and reliable information to applicants, employees, or other members of the academic community to avoid institutional or personal liability.[135]

Intentional Infliction of Emotional Distress

Claims for intentional infliction of emotional distress are regularly filed against colleges and their employees, but rarely as the primary claim. Rather, intentional infliction of emotional distress is typically filed as a claim accompanying others, such as sexual harassment or employment discrimination. The standard required in most states to reach the threshold of intentional infliction of emotional distress directs that the conduct must be sufficiently outrageous, which is difficult for plaintiffs to establish.[136] As such, postsecondary institutions regularly prevail when faced with such claims.

In order to establish a claim for intentional infliction of emotional distress, a plaintiff must prove that (1) the defendant's intent was to inflict emotional distress; (2) the defendant's conduct was outrageous or extreme, beyond the bounds of decency; (3) the defendant's actions caused the plaintiff's distress; and (4) the resulting emotional distress was severe in nature.[137]

In *Gary v. New York University*,[138] the student-plaintiff who pursued a claim of intentional infliction of emotional distress was unsuccessful because she was academically dismissed and failed to establish that the comments made by administrators and faculty about her academic performance were sufficiently outrageous. Similarly, an annual gifts officer at Tarleton State University in Texas filed suit when her employment was terminated for being allegedly hostile and confrontational.[139] While the employee prevailed on some claims, a Texas appellate court dismissed her intentional infliction of emotional distress claim because she could not establish that the administrative conduct preceding her dismissal was not sufficiently extreme or outrageous. In *Austin v. The University of Oregon*,[140] a federal district court found that found that a public university did not commit intentional infliction of emotional distress upon disciplining student athletes who were accused of sexual assault, holding that "the conduct at issue does not constitute an extraordinary transgression of socially tolerable conduct."[141]

---

[135] *See* Minger v. Green, 239 F.3d 793 (6th Cir. 2001) (parents' allegations that housing administrator failed to disclose fire safety issues leading to the death of a student were sufficient to state a claims for intentional misrepresentation).

[136] *See* Frank J. Cavico, *The Tort of Intentional Infliction of Emotional Distress in the Private Employment Sector*, 21 HOFSTRA LAB. & EMP. L. J. 109, 112 (2003).

[137] DAN B. DOBBS, THE LAW OF TORTS § 303 (2000).

[138] 850 N.Y.S.2d 433 (N.Y.App. 2008).

[139] Crouch v. Trinque, 262 S.W.3d 417 (Tex. Ct. App. 2008).

[140] 205 F. Supp. 3d 1214 (D.Org. 2016).

[141] *Id.* at 1230. *See also* Bd. of Trs. of Purdue Univ. v. Eisenstein, 87 N.E. 3d 481 (Ind. Ct. App. 2017); Nungesser v. Columbia Univ., 169 F. Supp. 3d 353 (S.D.N.Y. 2016); and Doe v. Salisbury Univ., 123 F. Supp. 3d. 748 (2015).

However, it is not impossible to establish an intentional infliction of emotional distress claim against a postsecondary institution. For example, a medical professor was successful in stating a claim in an Oklahoma case in which the professor, a naturalized American citizen born in Egypt, allegedly endured a pattern of discrimination by his colleagues that he found sufficient to cause his resignation.[142] He sued these colleagues and the university, and a federal district court concluded that the Oklahoma tort claims act only shielded employees acting within the scope of their duties. Here, the court noted that the professor's colleagues reputedly acted with bad faith and malice, placing their actions outside of the scope of their employment.

Miscellaneous Other Intentional Torts

Various other intentional tort claims, such as invasion of privacy, assault, false arrest, or tortuous interference with contract, are occasionally filed against colleges and their employees. These claims are often fact-intensive, irregular, and subject to jurisdictional constraints. For example, employees at the University of Georgia faced an invasion of privacy claim when they reported that their supervisor engaged in a prohibited sexual relationship with the university's vice chancellor responsible for their division. A Georgia appellate court concluded that the employees were acting within the scope of their employment when they reported the relationship and dismissed the claim.[143]

George Washington University prevailed on claims of false arrest and false imprisonment asserted by a faculty member who was escorted from campus by university police.[144] The professor had been barred from campus for various reasons, yet defied that order and arrived to teach a class and was removed from campus. A federal district court concluded that his false arrest and imprisonment claims failed because he was never actually detained or even touched— simply escorted from campus. However, the City University of New York did not prevail on an assault charge leveled when a plaintiff sued and successfully demonstrated use of excessive force after being treated roughly by a campus police officer.[145]

A disgruntled graduate student failed to state a claim for tortuous interference with contract when an Arizona appellate court concluded that his advisor

---

[142] Dashan v. Oklahoma, ex rel. Bd. of Regents of Univ. of Oklahoma, 2008 WL 4899240. *See also* McGrath v. Dominican College, 672 F. Supp. 2d 477 (S.D.N.Y. 2009) (parent of student who committed suicide after being raped established claim for intentional infliction of emotional distress). *See also* Richard Fossey, *McGrath v. Dominican College: Deliberate Indifference to Gang Rape in a College Residence Hall May Violate Title IX*, TEACHERS COLLEGE RECORD 2010. Available http://www.tcrecord.org.

[143] Massey v. Roth, 659 S.E.2d 872 (Ga. Ct. App. 2008). *Cf.* Saha v. Lehman, 537 F.Supp.3d 122 (D.D.C. 2008) (professor did not establish invasion of privacy claim).

[144] Saha v. Lehman, 537 F.Supp.2d 122 (D.D.C. 2008). *See also* Maniaci v. Marquette Univ., 184 N.W.2d 168 (Wisc. 1971); White v. Univ. of Idaho, 797 P.2d 108 (Id. 1990); and Wishnatsky v. Bergquist, 550 N.W.2d 394 (N.D. 1996).

[145] Rister v. City Univ. of N.Y., 858 N.Y.S.2d 528 (N.Y. Ct. Cl. 2008).

did not interfere with his degree completion.[146] An untenured medical professor at Marshall University also failed to state such a claim when he was terminated for proper reasons.[147]

Actions for false imprisonment are rare in the higher education context, and most involve allegations of misconduct against university police departments or hospitals that have confined individuals against their will.

At common law, a defendant is liable for false imprisonment if the defendant acts with the intention of confining another person, the defendant's actions directly or indirectly results in the confinement of a person, and the confined person is conscious of the confinement or is harmed by it.[148]

A North Dakota case gives the general flavor of false imprisonment litigation in the higher education community. In *Wishnatsky v. Bergquist*,[149] Martin Wishnatsky, who was not a student, entered the student newspaper office of the *Spectrum*, the student newspaper at North Dakota State University (NDSU), to see if the *Spectrum* had printed his anti-abortion advertisement. After a brief encounter with Paul Bergquist, editor of the *Spectrum*, Bergquist asked Wishnatsky to leave the *Spectrum* offices. When Wishnatsky refused to leave, Bergquist called the campus police.[150]

Before the campus police arrived, Wishnatsky left the *Spectrum* offices and sat down in a student lounge located in the same building. Bergquist made two more calls to campus police. In the second call, he informed the police that Wishnatsky had left the *Spectrum* offices. In the third call, he informed police that Wishnatsky was still in the building.

Two police officers arrived and asked Wishnatsky to identify himself and say whether he had any legitimate business on campus. Wishnatsky refused to answer. One officer told Wishnatsky that NDSU had a trespassing policy for nonstudents who had no legitimate business on the campus and advised Wishnatsky that he would give him a "warning card." The officer gave Wishnatsky a copy of the NDSU trespassing policy and showed him a trespass warning card that stated, "I must ask you to leave the university campus and if you refuse or return you may be arrested for trespassing."[151] Wishnatsky still refused to provide his name or answer the officers' questions.

What happened next, according to the North Dakota Supreme Court, was disputed. The officers stated that they asked Wishnatsky to come to the campus police station and he voluntarily complied. Wishnatsky stated in an affidavit that the officers told him they would take him into custody if he refused to give his name and then "laid hands upon [him]" and "escorted [him] out of the building to the police car outside."[152] Wishnatsky was taken to the police

---

[146] Dube v. Desai, 186 P.3d 587 (Ariz. Ct. App. 2008).

[147] Yoak v. Marshall Univ. Bd. of Governors, 672 S.E.2d 191 (W.Va. 2008).

[148] RESTATEMENT (SECOND) OF TORTS § 35.

[149] 550 N.W.2d 394 (N.D. 1996).

[150] *Id.* at 396.

[151] *Id.*

[152] *Id.*

station, where he met with the campus police chief. After a brief discussion, he left the campus.

Not long after this incident, Wishnatsky sued Bergquist, the two officers who took him to the police station, the campus police chief, and the president of NDSU, alleging a variety of legal claims. Assuming that Wishnatsky was arrested, the court ruled that the police officials enjoyed qualified immunity from suit because they reasonably believed that they had probable cause to make the arrest. They also enjoyed statutory immunity under North Dakota law because there was no evidence to suggest that they acted recklessly or were grossly negligent in their encounter with Wishnatsky.

As for Bergquist, the *Spectrum* editor, the court ruled that the false imprisonment claim against him must be dismissed. A private citizen cannot be held liable for false arrest, the court ruled, when the citizen "merely provides information to the police and leaves the decision whether to arrest to the officer's judgment and discretion."[153] Moreover, there was no evidence to suggest that Bergquist gave false information to the police, so there could be no liability on that ground.

Conclusion

With the exception of negligence, the most common tort claim in the higher education sector is defamation. In many of these cases, a plaintiff files suit claiming that a college administrator or professor made a defamatory communication during the course of some evaluative or disciplinary process. College personnel usually enjoy a conditional privilege to express negative views about faculty members, students, and college employees if necessary to carry out their jobs or to further their institution's legitimate interests.

In *New York Times v. Sullivan* and subsequent decisions, the United States Supreme Court has placed constitutional limitations on defamation suits brought by public officials and public figures, who can only recover if they can show that the defendant acted maliciously in publishing a false communication. Truth is an absolute defense to a defamation claim, and courts have ruled consistently that satire, hyperbole, and humorous comments cannot form the basis for a defamation claim if no reasonable person would interpret such comments as statements of fact. University personnel can limit their exposure to defamation claims by expressing all negative opinions objectively, fairly, and accurately, and by not communicating these opinions beyond the bounds of what is necessary to carry out their job duties.

There are many other intentional tort claims filed against universities and their employees, and this brief discussion is not an exhaustive treatment. As noted, such claims are bound by jurisdiction and circumstance, and may even be criminal in nature, such as assault or battery. This overview is intended to

---

[153] *Id.* at 399.

illustrate the breadth of such claims, as well as the need to maintain an atmosphere of safety and civility on campus.

Apart from defamation, the most frequently litigated intentional tort claim is fraud. Typically, students who bring fraud claims allege that a for-profit institution induced them to enroll in a particular academic or job-skills program based on false or misleading representation.

For-profit institutions have the most exposure to fraud claims. Administrators, recruiters, and student-services personnel at for-profit institutions should be particularly careful not make false or misleading representations about the value of a particular program or a program's accreditation status. Other intentional tort claims are less frequent, but it remains important for members of the higher education community to become familiar with the risks associated with daily operations.

Discussion Questions

1. Why do the courts distinguish between false communications that are defamatory *per se* and those that are defamatory *per quod*?

2. In *Yeagle v. Collegiate Times*, the Virginia Supreme Court ruled that a university administrator could not pursue a defamation claim against the campus newspaper even though she had been described as "Director of Butt Licking" in a newspaper article. Do you agree with the court's decision?

3. The U.S. Supreme Court has ruled that certain public figures and public officials must prove that a defamatory statement was made with malice in order to recover in a defamation action. Why did the Court fashion this constitutional rule for the tort of defamation?

4. Some states provide statutory immunity against defamation claims for public officials. What is the policy justification for providing such immunity?

5. What are the elements of a fraud claim? How can colleges make sure their employees do not make false statements to prospective students about the nature of academic programs?

12

Student Rights to Due Process

Richard Fossey, J.D., Ed.D.
University of Louisiana at Lafayette

Introduction

Under the Fourteenth Amendment to the United States Constitution, no state may "deprive any person of life, liberty, or property without due process of law."[1] Although the United States Supreme Court has never ruled directly that students enrolled at public universities have a constitutionally protected property interest in continuing their education, the Court has assumed this is so.[2] Numerous federal courts have ruled that students at public institutions of higher education are entitled to some level of procedural due process before they can be suspended or expelled for a disciplinary offense.[3] Courts have not ruled consistently with regard to the exact contours of a student's right to procedural due process, but they are in broad agreement that a student facing suspension or expulsion at a public college or university for a disciplinary offense is entitled to notice of charges, an opportunity for a hearing that includes some right to confront adverse witnesses and present exculpatory evidence, and a fair tribunal.

Of course, private colleges and universities are not constrained by the Fourteenth Amendment, and they have no constitutional obligation to provide students with procedural due process prior to suspending or expelling them. Nevertheless, the courts have consistently ruled that students at private colleges and universities are entitled to some sort of fair process before they can be ousted from their studies. Often the courts have found that a private college has a contractual obligation to provide students with procedural due process

---

[1] U.S. Const. amend. XIV, § 1.
[2] *See* Bd. of Curators of Univ. of Mo. v. Horowitz, 435 U.S. 78, 8591978); Regents of Univ. of Mich. v. Ewing, 474 U.S. 214, 223 (accepting university's invitation to assume the existence of a constitutionally protected property interest in continued enrollment in medical school).
[3] *See, e.g.*, Dixon v. Ala. State Bd. of Educ., 294 F.2d 150 (5th Cir. 1961).

in disciplinary proceedings,[4] and they have ruled that the dismissal process at private colleges must comply with basic fairness.[5]

When students receive an academic sanction—removal from a program of study based on academic deficiencies, for example—they are not entitled to an adversarial due process hearing. The United States Supreme Court has spoken twice regarding a student's right to due process when an institution makes an adverse academic decision about a student, both times involving dismissal of a student from medical school.[6] The Court has emphasized that the judiciary should not interfere with the academic decisions of public colleges and universities as long as those decisions are made within the bounds of academic norms and are not arbitrary or capricious.[7]

This chapter is divided into four parts. The first part discusses the requirements of procedural due process at public colleges and universities when a student faces severe disciplinary sanctions such as expulsion or suspension. Second, the chapter reviews cases involving students who are suspended or expelled at private institutions based on charges of misconduct. Third, the chapter explores a student's entitlement to due process when challenging an adverse academic decision. Finally, the chapter examines a college or university's authority to revoke a degree that has already been granted.

A Student's Right to Due Process Before Being Suspended from a Public College

Dixon v. Alabama State Board of Education,[8] decided in the crucible of the civil rights struggle in Alabama during the early 1960s, is the first federal appellate court opinion to hold that students at a public university are entitled to procedural due process prior to being expelled for a disciplinary infraction. The plaintiffs, six African American students at Alabama State College, participated in a demonstration against a segregated lunchroom located in the basement of the county courthouse in Montgomery, Alabama. On the day this demonstration took place, the governor of Alabama called the president of the

---

[4] See WILLIAM A. KAPLIN & BARBARA A. LEE, THE LAW OF HIGHER EDUCATION 1195 (5th ed. 2013) (courts tend "to find a contractual relationship between the college and the student with respect to serious discipline (suspension, expulsion").

[5] *See, e.g.,* Ahlum v. Admin. of Tulane Educ. Fund, 617 So. 2d. 96 (La. Ct. App. 1993) (court reviewed private university's suspension of student for sexual misconduct for determination as to whether suspension was arbitrary or capricious).

[6] Bd. of Curators of Univ. of Mo. v. Horowitz, 435 U.S. 78, 85 (assuming without deciding that medical student has liberty or property interest implicated by dismissal from medical school); Regents of Univ. of Mich. v. Ewing, 474 U.S. 214, 223 (1985) (accepting university's invitation to assume existence of constitutionally protected right to continued enrollment in medical school).

[7] *See* Regents of Univ. of Mich. v. Ewing, 474 U.S. 214, 227 (when reviewing medical school's decision to dismiss student, narrow focus of judicial review is limited to determination of whether decision was "substantial departure from accepted academic norms as to demonstrate the faculty did not exercise professional judgment").

[8] 294 F.2d 150 (5th Cir. 1961).

college and said that if he were in the president's position, he would consider expelling students who participated in the demonstration.[9]

Later, the governor's office presented the college president with reports that at least some of the plaintiffs had participated in other mass civil rights demonstrations and were among the "ringleaders" in these demonstrations.[10] The Alabama State Board of Education, after hearing these reports, voted unanimously to expel nine students from Alabama State College, including the six plaintiffs, and to place twenty students on probation. The six expelled students sued in federal court, alleging a violation of due process. An Alabama trial judge dismissed their case, concluding that the plaintiffs' conduct was calculated to create disruption on the college campus. In the trial court's opinion, the state board of education had acted in good faith when it expelled the students, and they had suffered no violation of their constitutional rights.[11]

On appeal, the Fifth Circuit reversed. Students have a constitutionally protected interest in remaining at a public college where they were enrolled in good standing, the court determined, entitling them to due process before they are expelled. "We are confident," the court stated, "that precedent as well as a most fundamental constitutional principle support our holding that due process requires notice and some opportunity for hearing before a student at a tax-supported college is expelled for misconduct."[12]

The Fifth Circuit then went on to spell out the requirements of procedural due process in a case involving allegations of student misconduct. First, students are entitled to notice, which should contain "a statement of the specific charges and grounds which, if proven, would justify expulsion under the regulations of the Board of Education."[13] Second, students are entitled to a hearing, which "requires something more than an informal interview with an administrative authority of the college."[14] At an expulsion hearing for misconduct, the court said, the hearing body must have "an opportunity to hear both sides in considerable detail."[15] The court cautioned that a "full-dress judicial hearing, with the right to cross-examine witnesses" was not required. "Nevertheless, the rudiments of an adversary proceeding may be preserved without encroaching upon the interests of the college."[16] In a case like the one before it, involving allegations of misconduct, the defending students were entitled to be given the names of witnesses "and an oral or written report on the facts to which each witness testifies."[17] In addition, the defending student has the right to present a defense to the charge to the administrative hearing

---

[9] Dixon v. Ala. State Bd. of Educ., 186 F. Supp. 945, 947 (M.D. Ala. 1960), *rev'd*, 294 F.2d 150 (5th Cir. 1961).

[10] *Id.* at 948.

[11] *Id.* at 952.

[12] *Id.* at 158.

[13] *Id.*

[14] *Id.*

[15] *Id.* at 159.

[16] *Id.*

[17] *Id.*

body and to "produce either oral testimony or written affidavits of witnesses on his behalf." Finally, the court instructed, "If the hearing is not before the Board directly, the results and findings of the hearing should be presented in a report open to the student's inspection."[18] These "rudiments of fair play," the court concluded, are necessary to meet the requirements of due process in a disciplinary proceeding such as the one involving the six plaintiffs.[19]

As Kaplin and Lee pointed out,[20] the post-*Dixon* court decision that spells out a public college's procedural process obligations in the most detail is the trial court's opinion in *Estaban v. Central Missouri State College.*[21] In that case, a state college suspended two students for participating in events that were variously described as "disturbances," "incidents," or "riots" after providing them with only very informal proceedings. Essentially, the college's dean of men orally informed both students of the charges against them and gave them an opportunity to explain their version of the events. The dean recommended suspension, and the students then appealed unsuccessfully to the college's president.

Both students sued the college in federal court, arguing they were denied due process. The court determined that due process had, indeed, been deficient and ordered the college to grant the students a new hearing. At the new hearing, the court directed that the college was to include eight specific procedural features:

1. Students are entitled to a written statement of the charges, furnished at least ten days before the hearing.
2. The hearing should be conducted by the body or person having the power to suspend or expel.
3. Students have the right to advance inspection of affidavits and exhibits that the college intends to present at the hearing.
4. Students shall have the right to have legal counsel with them at the hearing to advise them.
5. Students have the right to present their own version of events and to present witnesses, affidavits, and exhibits to support their defense.
6. Students have the right to hear the evidence presented against them and to question adverse witnesses.
7. The hearing body shall make a decision based solely on the evidence presented and shall render the disciplinary decision in writing.
8. Both sides have the right to make a written record of the hearing at their own expense.[22]

Numerous federal court decisions have ruled on most of the procedural guidelines enumerated in *Dixon* and *Estaban*, and they are not in total agreement about what constitutes adequate procedural due process when a student

---

[18] *Id.*
[19] *Id.*
[20] KAPLIN & LEE, *supra*, note 4 at 1181.
[21] 277 F. Supp. 649 (W.D. Mo. 1967).
[22] *Id.* at 651-52.

faces expulsion or suspension for a disciplinary offense. Nevertheless, it is fair to say that most of the decisions follow the broad procedural guidelines outlined in *Dixon* and *Estaban*. The following discussion outlines what the courts have said about various aspects of a student's right to procedural due process when facing suspension or expulsion.

Adequacy of Notice

In *Dixon*, the court held that a student charged with a disciplinary violation is entitled to notice of the "specific charges and grounds" that would justify discipline, indicating that a charge of misconduct must be stated with some particularity.[23] Nevertheless, a public university's notice to a student of a disciplinary infraction need not be as specific as the language of a criminal indictment. As found in several cases following *Dixon* and *Estaban*, the due process protections for students facing disciplinary charges are not at the same level as protections that must be afforded to defendants in criminal court proceedings.

In *Jenkins v. Louisiana State Board of Education*,[24] for example, Louisiana State University disciplined students for organizing campus protests that turned violent. On appeal, the students claimed that the university had not given them adequate notice that they were being charged with conspiracy. The Fifth Circuit rejected this argument, stating, "College administrators should not be held to the strict requirements of criminal law relating to giving notice of conspiracy."[25] The court acknowledged that the university might have drafted its notice of charges with more specificity. Nevertheless, the record revealed that the students understood the nature of the charges against them.

Similarly, in *Nash v. Auburn University*,[26] two students found guilty of cheating on an exam challenged the adequacy of the notice they received prior to their disciplinary hearing on a charge of academic dishonesty. Specifically, the students argued that they were entitled to a summary of the testimony expected from a professor and other accusing witnesses at the hearing, because such notice would protect them from being surprised by the testimony of adverse witnesses and enable them to have a fair opportunity to respond. To support their argument, the students relied in part on the *Dixon* decision, in which the Fifth Circuit had ruled that students facing expulsion for misconduct were entitled to a "report" of the testimony of adverse witnesses.

Although the Eleventh Circuit Court of Appeals expressed some sympathy for the students, the court ruled that they had received adequate notice of the charges against them. According to the Eleventh Circuit, *Dixon* had required that students facing expulsion in that case receive a report of witnesses' testimony because the students themselves were not present to hear the testimony. Students were not constitutionally entitled to advance notice of statements by witnesses whom the defending students would hear testify at the hearing.

---

[23] *Dixon*, 294 F.2d at 158.
[24] 506 F.2d 992 (5th Cir. 1975).
[25] *Id.* at 1000.
[26] 812 F.2d 665 (11th Cir. 1987).

In a Sixth Circuit opinion, *Flaim v. Medical College of Ohio*,[27] a medical student expelled from medical school for a felony drug conviction argued that he had received inadequate notice of the charges against him in the medical school's disciplinary proceeding, in part because the notice did not fully inform him of the evidence and testimony that would be used against him. The Sixth Circuit had little sympathy for this argument. The student had already been convicted of a drug offense, the court pointed out, and the medical school's failure to produce a list of witnesses and copies of documents that would be presented at the hearing did not increase the risk of an erroneous outcome.

Disciplinary rules at public universities are not expected to provide the same level of detail as found in criminal codes. In the *Estaban* case discussed above, students Roberds and Estaban appealed their college's second suspension process, even though the college followed the procedural guidelines that had been spelled out by the trial court. On appeal, the two argued that the college's regulations were overbroad and had not given them fair notice that they could be suspended for participating in a campus demonstration.

The Eighth Circuit Court of Appeals was extremely unsympathetic to this argument. "[W]e see little basically or constitutionally wrong with flexibility and reasonable breadth, rather than meticulous specificity, in college regulations related to conduct," the court wrote. "Certainly these regulations are not to be compared with the criminal statutes."[28] College student conduct regulations were "codes of general conduct," the court emphasized, that could "be expressed in general rather than specific terms."[29] In the court's view, Roberds and Estaban would have known their conduct could lead to suspension if they had simply read the regulations and exercised common sense.[30]

Right to Confront Witnesses

Although students at a public college are entitled to a hearing to contest charges that might lead to expulsion, courts do not require the hearing to approach the formality of a criminal trial. In particular, although a student has a right to confront adverse witnesses, "the right to unlimited cross-examination has not been deemed an essential requirement of due process in school disciplinary cases."[31]

In *Flaim v. Medical College of Ohio*,[32] already discussed, a medical school expelled a student because he had been convicted of a felony drug crime and did not permit the student to cross-examine the arresting officer. The Sixth Circuit ruled that the student had no constitutional right to cross examine his accuser at the hearing. The court pointed out that the critical fact at the hearing, his conviction for a drug offense, was not contested. The student

---

[27] 418 F.3d 629 (6th Cir. 2005).

[28] *Id*. at 1088.

[29] *Id*.

[30] *Id*.

[31] Gorman v. Univ. of R.I., 837 F.2d 7, 16 (1st Cir. 1988).

[32] 418 F.3d 629 (6th Cir. 2005).

was able to listen to the officer testify and to point out any inconsistencies in the officer's testimony in the student's own testimony. In the court's opinion, cross-examining the officer would have been a fruitless exercise."[33]

More recently, however, the Sixth Circuit backed away from its precedent in *Flaim* when it ruled emphatically that a student charged with sexual misconduct at a college disciplinary hearing has the right to confront his accuser. In *Doe v. University of Cincinnati*,[34] decided in 2017, a male student identified as John Doe, was suspended from his studies based on a finding he had sexually assaulted Jane Roe, a female student. Roe did not appear at the disciplinary hearing; rather, her unsworn accusation was merely read into the record of the proceedings. Thus, the hearing panel decided Doe's fate without hearing from Roe at all. "That is disturbing," the Sixth Circuit," wrote, "and, in this case, a denial of due process."[35]

Almost exactly one year later, in *Doe v. Baum*,[36] the Sixth Circuit reiterated its ruling that a university student accused of sexual assault has a constitutional right to confront his accuser at a disciplinary hearing. In *Baum*, Jane Roe, a first-year student at the University of Michigan, accused John Doe, a male student, of sexually assaulting her during a fraternity party. Numerous students saw Roe and Doe dancing together and kissing; later, the two went to Doe's room, where they engaged in sexual intercourse. Two days later, Roe filed a sexual misconduct complaint against Doe, claiming she was too drunk to consent to having sex with him. The university launched an investigation, and a university investigator interviewed twenty-three witnesses over the course of three months.

As the investigator noted in his report, almost all the male witnesses corroborated Doe's claim that the sexual encounter was consensual. In contrast, all the female witnesses corroborated Roe's version of events. Given the sharp conflict among the witnesses, the investigator concluded that the evidence supporting a sexual misconduct charge was no more convincing than the evidence supporting Doe's claim that he was innocent. "So," the Sixth Circuit court summarized, "after three months of thorough fact-finding, the investigator was unable to say that Roe exhibited outwards signs of incapacitation that Doe would have noticed before initiating sexual activity."[37] Based on these findings, the investigator recommended that the university rule in Doe's favor and close the case. Roe appealed the investigator's recommendation to the university's Appeal Board, which reviewed the investigator's findings. After meeting in two closed sessions and without reviewing any new evidence or interviewing any witnesses, the Appeal Board reversed.

---

[33] *Id.* at 641 (internal citation omitted).

[34] Doe v. Univ. of Cincinnati, 872 F.3d 393 (6th Cir. 2017). *See also*, Richard Fossey & Todd DeMitchell, Doe v. University of Cincinnati: *A College Student Accused of Sexual Assault Has a Constitutional Right to Confront His Accuser at a University Disciplinary Hearing*, TEACHERS COLL. REC. (March 12, 2018), tcrecord.org. ID Number: 22303.

[35] *Id.* at 402.

[36] 872 F.3d 393 (6th Cir. 2017).

[37] *Id.* at 580.

As the Sixth Circuit observed, in finding in favor of Jane Roe, "the Board credited exclusively female testimony (from Roe and her witnesses) and rejected all of the male testimony (from Doe and his witnesses)."[38] The Board justified its decision by explaining that Doe's witnesses lacked credibility because many of them were Doe's fraternity brothers. But, the Sixth Circuit pointed out, "the Board did not similarly note that several of Roe's witnesses were her sorority sisters, nor did it note that they were female."[39] Doe sued the University of Michigan alleging that the University's disciplinary process violated his right to due process and was gender-biased in violation of Title IX. A federal trial court dismissed Doe's claims in response to the University's motion to dismiss. Doe appealed, and the Sixth Circuit Court of Appeals reversed.

The Sixth Circuit began its analysis by reaffirming prior decisions in which it had upheld the right of a student to cross-examination at university disciplinary hearings where credibility was at issue. According to the Sixth Circuit Court of Appeals "... if a public university has to choose between competing narratives to resolve a case, the university must give the accused student or his agent an opportunity to cross-examine the accuser and adverse witnesses in the presence of a neutral fact-finder. Because the University of Michigan failed to comply with this rule, we reverse."[40]

Furthermore, "[d]ue process requires cross-examination in circumstances like these," the Sixth Circuit emphasized, "because it is the greatest legal engine ever invented for uncovering the truth."[41] Cross-examination not only allows the accused to identify inconsistencies in the accuser's story, the court stated, "but it also gives the fact-finder an opportunity to assess a witness's demeanor and determine who can be trusted."[42] Thus, "if a university is faced with competing narratives about potential misconduct, the administration must facilitate some form of cross-examination in order to satisfy due process."[43]

By denying Doe the opportunity to cross-examine Roe and her witnesses, the court continued, the University created "a significant risk" of an erroneous decision regarding Roe's complaint. In the court's view, this risk was all the more troubling given the significance of Doe's interest and the minimal burden to the university of giving Doe the right of cross-examination. Recognizing the severity and stigma of being found responsible for sexual misconduct, the Sixth Circuit Court noted "students have a substantial interest at stake when it comes to school disciplinary hearings for sexual misconduct."[44] The court further reasoned that, "[b]eing labeled a sex offender by a university has both an immediate and lasting impact on a student's life."[45] Such a label may force

---

[38] *Id*. at 586.

[39] *Id.*

[40] *Id*. at 578.

[41] *Id*. at 581 (internal punctuation and citation omitted).

[42] *Id.*

[43] *Id.*

[44] *Id.* at 582.

[45] *Id.*

a student to withdraw from classes or move out of university housing, and it could jeopardize future educational and job opportunities.

In contrast, the court pointed out, giving Doe the opportunity to cross-examine adverse witnesses would have cost the university little. Indeed, the university already had the resources in place to facilitate cross-examination in disciplinary proceedings and had identified no substantial burden it would suffer if it gave Doe the right to cross-examine his accuser.

It is important to point out, however, that the court emphasized that the right to cross-examination does not mean that a university must allow an accused student "to *personally* confront his accuser" in sexual misconduct cases.[46] After all, the court acknowledged, "[u]niversities have a legitimate interest in avoiding procedures that may subject an alleged victim to further harm or harassment."[47] In its *University of Cincinnati* decision, the Sixth Circuit had approved a procedure whereby the accusing student could testify via "modern technology" such as Skype.[48] Alternatively, a hearing panel might insist that the accused student's agent, not the student himself, direct questions to an accuser.[49] But the right of cross-examination cannot be dispensed with altogether.

Right to Representation by an Attorney

Although some older cases have ruled that students are entitled to legal representation at college disciplinary proceedings,[50] more recent decisions have not imposed this requirement. *Osteen v. Henley*,[51] a Seventh Circuit decision, involved a varsity football player who was suspended from Northern Illinois University for a physical altercation outside a bar. The football player argued that the hearing procedure violated due process in several regards, including the fact that he was deprived of the right to be represented by counsel.

In rejecting the ousted football player's claims, the court articulated strong policy arguments for disallowing legal representation at student disciplinary hearings. As the Seventh Circuit observed, recognizing the right to legal representation "would force student disciplinary proceedings into the mold of adversary litigation. The university would have to hire its own lawyer to prosecute these cases and no doubt lawyers would also be dragged in—from the law faculty or elsewhere—to serve as judges."[52] The court also expressed concern about the cost and complexity of student judicial hearings if students were represented by counsel, as well as the danger of encroaching bureaucratization of higher education. In addition, the court viewed the introduction of attorneys into the realm of student discipline as an encroachment on universi-

---

[46] *Id.* at 583.

[47] *Id.*

[48] Doe v. Univ. of Cincinnati, 872 F.3d at 406.

[49] Doe v. Baum, 903 F.3d at 583.

[50] *See, e.g.*, Mills v. Bd. of Educ. of D.C., 384 F. Supp. 866, 881 (D.D.C. 1972); Givens v. Poe, 346 F. Supp. 202, 209 (W.D.N.C. 1972).

[51] 13 F.3d 221 (7th Cir. 1993).

[52] *Id.* at 225.

ties' academic freedom. Furthermore, in the *Osteen* court's view, the risk of unfair student suspensions if attorneys were barred from representing students in disciplinary hearings was slight. A public university, in the court's opinion, had no incentive to engage in an "orgy of expulsions."[53]

A persuasive older case, *Gabrilowitz v. Newman*,[54] ruled that a student who is facing criminal prosecution for the same conduct that forms the basis of a university's disciplinary hearing has a constitutional right to consult with an attorney in the university's proceeding, but not the right to full attorney representation. In that case, local police charged a University of Rhode Island student with intent to commit rape on another student; the student faced suspension from his university based on the same allegation.[55] He wanted to defend himself in the university proceedings, but he feared he would jeopardize his defense in a subsequent criminal trial if he appeared at the university's disciplinary hearing without a lawyer.

The First Circuit, recognizing the student's obvious need for legal counsel under those circumstances, granted the student the right to consult with lawyer at the university's hearing. In the court's opinion, the lawyer's role would not be very intrusive. "Counsel would be present only to safeguard [the student's] rights at the criminal proceeding," the court emphasized, "not to affect the outcome of the disciplinary hearing."[56] The attorney's principal function would simply be to advise the student whether or not he should answer questions and safeguard the student's right not to incriminate himself.

Gabrilowitz's compromise position—giving students the right to consult with their attorneys at college disciplinary hearings if they face criminal charges—makes sense for any disciplinary proceeding involving a charge of serious misconduct that might also constitute a crime. One commentator has argued that students in such situations ought to have the right to full representation by a lawyer at their disciplinary hearings because "the stakes are enormous."[57] In recent years, however, the courts have not so held. The most a student facing expulsion can reasonably expect with regard to legal representation at a disciplinary hearing is the right to consult with an attorney while the proceedings are taking place.[58]

---

[53] *Id*. at 226.

[54] 582 F.2d 100 (1st Cir. 1978).

[55] *Id*. at 101-102.

[56] *Id*. at 106.

[57] Lisa Tenerowicz, Note: *Student Misconduct at Private Colleges and Universities: A Roadmap for "Fundamental Fairness" in Disciplinary Proceedings*, B. C. L. Rev. 653, 692 (2001).

[58] For a vigorous argument that students should have the right to full representation by legal counsel at any disciplinary hearing that might end in suspension or expulsion, see Robert B. Groholski, *The Right to Representation by Counsel in University Disciplinary Proceedings: A Denial of Due Process of Law*, 19 N. Ill. U. L. Rev. 739 (1999).

Right to a Fair Judicial Tribunal

In the venerable case of *Tumey v. Ohio*,[59] the Supreme Court ruled that a fair judge is an essential component of due process. In that case, an Ohio village mayor who also served as a judge was paid a portion of the fines he collected when he found defendants guilty of a crime, but was paid nothing when he found defendants innocent. This state of affairs violated due process, the court said, for the defendant "had a right to an impartial judge." [60]

In an administrative setting, however, a person often occupies dual roles, serving primarily as an administrator or executive, but occasionally serving as a quasi-judicial officer. The Supreme Court ruled in *Hortonville Joint District No. 1 v. Hortonville Education Association*[61] that school board members who served primarily in an executive role were not automatically incapacitated from serving a judicial function. In that case, a Wisconsin school board had been engaged in acrimonious contract negotiations with the teachers union. At some point, the teachers went on strike in violation of Wisconsin law, and the school district began dismissal proceedings against them. Under Wisconsin law, teachers were entitled to a hearing when faced with dismissal, but the designated hearing body was the school board.

The teachers union argued that the Fourteenth Amendment prohibited the school board from sitting as a hearing body for teachers being fired, because board members could not be impartial. The Supreme Court rejected this argument. There was no evidence that the school board members had a personal or financial stake in the dismissal hearing, the Court pointed out. Furthermore, the fact that the school board members were familiar with the facts leading up to the illegal strike did not disqualify them from serving in a quasi-judicial role at teacher dismissal hearings. A mere showing that school board members were "involved" in events leading up to the dismissals "is not enough to overcome the presumption of honesty and integrity in policymakers with decisionmaking powers," the Court ruled. [62] The Due Process Clause did not require the dismissal hearings to be heard by some party other than the school board.

In several cases, university students have challenged the impartiality of their judicial hearing bodies in disciplinary proceedings. In the previously discussed *Osteen v. Henley*,[63] for example, a suspended varsity football player challenged the impartiality of the assistant judicial officer who suspended him. The football player pointed out that the person who presented—in essence, prosecuted—his case was the superior of the person who rendered the suspension decision. Not surprisingly, the assistant accepted her superior's recommendation for a two-year suspension. In very few words, the *Osteen* court rejected the argument that his arrangement was fundamentally unfair. The court merely observed that this kind of conflict of interest "has not been

---

[59] 273 U.S. 510 (1927).

[60] *Id.* at 535.

[61] 426 U.S. 482 (1976).

[62] *Id.* at 497.

[63] 13 F.3d 221 (7th Cir. 1993).

thought in the previous cases involving school disciplinary action to violate due process."[64]

In summary, although federal courts affirm that universities' student conduct hearing bodies must be unbiased, they require a student to show substantive evidence of prejudice before they will find that a hearing body's bias constitutes a denial of due process. A participant in a university student disciplinary matter may play multiple roles, as Weisinger did in the *Gorman* case, and a judicial officer may even present a case to his own assistant, as occurred in *Osteen*. These practices would be impermissible in a civil court proceeding, but they are tolerated in student disciplinary hearings unless the affected student has good evidence of actual prejudice.

Procedural Due Process for Students Who Are Suspected of Being Dangerous

In recent years, colleges and universities have become more and more concerned about students who show signs of being dangerous, either to themselves or to others. For example, in the fall of 2010, officials at Pima Community College suspended student Jared Loughner based on concerns about his bizarre behavior. In January 2011, only a few months after his suspension, Loughner shot and killed six people and wounded thirteen others in a Tucson, Arizona grocery store.[65]

These acts of student violence may cause campus administers to ask whether they may legally suspend or expel students they suspect of being dangerous without affording the affected students procedural due process. According to *Barnes v. Zaccari*,[66] an Eleventh Circuit decision issued in 2012, the answer to that question is no. In the *Zaccari* case, Thomas Barnes, a student at Valdosta State University, came into conflict with the university president, Ronald Zaccari, when Barnes opposed the construction of a campus parking garage.[67] Barnes expressed his opposition in e-mail messages to university officials, the student newspaper, and his Facebook webpage. He also contacted members of Valdosta's board of regents, and he wrote three e-mail messages to President Zaccari about the proposed facility. As the Eleventh Circuit observed, "These emails show Barnes was passionate about environmental issues," but the messages contained no threats or any indication that he might harm someone.[68]

---

[64] *Id.* at 226.

[65] Richard Fossey, *A Salute to Pima Community College in the Wake of the Tucson Shootings*, TEACHERS COLL. RECORD (Jan. 19, 2011), http://www.tcrecord.org/content.asp?contentid=16294.

[66] 669 F.3d 1295 (11th Cir. 2012).

[67] Much of the discussion of Barnes v. Zaccari is taken from the author's 2012 article in *Teachers College Record. See* Richard Fossey, *Barnes v. Zaccari: A Public University Cannot Expel a Student Without Offering a Due Process Hearing—Even if the Student is Suspected of Being Dangerous* TEACHERS COLL. RECORD (June 4, 2012), http://www.tcrecord.org/content.asp?contentid=16792.

[68] *Id.* at 1299.

Barnes and President Zaccari met about the parking garage issue on April 16, 2007. Apparently, Zaccari attempted to persuade Barnes to drop his opposition to the construction project, but his efforts were unsuccessful. Immediately after that meeting, according to the Eleventh Circuit opinion, "Zaccari began looking for a way to get Barnes off the Valdosta campus."[69] Zaccari examined Barnes' academic record, and he met with Valdosta campus administrators to explore ways that Barnes might be removed from the university. Two campus mental health professionals "repeatedly told Zaccari that Barnes was not a threat to himself or others," and other administrators concluded that Zaccari was overreacting.[70]

Nevertheless, Zaccari explored several avenues for kicking Barnes off campus, but all university procedures required that Barnes be afforded some type of hearing. "Zaccari ultimately rejected these options as too 'cumbersome.'"[71] In the end, Zaccari decided that he could "administratively withdraw" Barnes from Valdosta on the grounds that Barnes presented "a clear and present danger to the campus."[72] On May 7, 2007, university police officers slipped a letter under Barnes' dormitory room door, notifying him that he was being administratively withdrawn from the university. The letter also informed Barnes that he could not return to the Valdosta campus until he had obtained two letters from mental health professionals certifying that he was not a danger to himself or others, and that he would receive therapy while he was enrolled. Barnes obtained the letters, but the university did not reinstate him. He also asked for a hearing, but six months after making this request, he had not been given a hearing.

In 2008, Barnes sued Zaccari and the Board of Regents of the University System of Georgia, alleging a violation of due process. Zaccari moved for summary judgment, but a trial court denied the motion, and Zaccari appealed to the Eleventh Circuit. On appeal, the Eleventh Circuit upheld the trial court's decision and stated plainly that Barnes had a right to a due process hearing before being removed from Valdosta State University. As the Eleventh Circuit opined, "no tenet of constitutional law is more clearly established than the rule that a property interest in a state school is an important entitlement protected by the Due Process Clause of the Fourteenth Amendment."[73] The court pointed out that this principle had been articulated fifty years earlier in the 1961 case of *Dixon v. Alabama State Board of Education*.[74]

Zaccari argued that Barnes presented the university with an emergency that entitled him to suspend Barnes from his studies without a hearing. The Eleventh Circuit acknowledged that an actual or reasonably perceived emergency might justify removing a student without first giving the student a

---

[69] *Id.* at 1301.

[70] *Id.* at 1300.

[71] *Id.* at 1301.

[72] *Id.*

[73] *Id.* at 1305, citing Goss v. Lopez, 419 U.S. 565, 574, 576 n.8 (1975).

[74] 294 F.2d 150 (5th Cir. 1961).

pre-deprivation hearing; however, in the case before it, no emergency existed. In fact, the Eleventh Circuit court said, any fear that Zaccari might have had about Barnes was unreasonable.

The *Zaccari* decision affirms the clear principle that a public university cannot suspend or expel a student without affording the student some kind of due process hearing, even if university officials believe the student constitutes "a clear and present danger" to the university community. Of course, there may be circumstances in which campus officials reasonably believe a student is so violent or dangerous that they can remove the student unilaterally without giving the student a pre-expulsion hearing. Even in those instances, however, the university is obligated to provide a hearing as soon as reasonably possible after the expulsion in a setting that will protect all parties' safety.[75] But, a student's right to challenge a suspension or expulsion in a due process hearing cannot be dispensed with altogether.

A Student's Right to a Fair Process Before Being Suspended or Expelled from a Private College

Private colleges and universities are not state actors and are not constitutionally obliged to provide students with due process prior to discipline or expulsion. Indeed, in early cases, courts would permit private institutions to expel students for purely arbitrary reasons. In a 1928 decision, for example, a New York court permitted Syracuse University to dismiss a young woman from her studies in Home Economics on the grounds that she was rumored to be a troublemaker and was not "a typical Syracuse girl."[76] And as late as 1967, in a case involving Howard University, a federal court stated that courts should not interject themselves into matters of school discipline at a private university.[77]

Today, however, most courts recognize that private colleges are obligated to abide by some type of fair process when suspending or expelling their students.[78] " As a general rule, courts will require a private college to follow

---

[75] *See* Goss v. Lopez, 419 U.sl 565 (1975) (acknowledging some circumstances in which it is reasonable for school officials to remove a disruptive student from the school environment without first providing a due process hearing but noting that the hearing should be conducted at a later time).

[76] Anthony v. Syracuse Univ., 231 N.Y.S. 435, 437(App. Div. 1928).

[77] Greene v. Howard Univ., 271 F. Supp. 609, 613 (D.D.C. 1967). On appeal, the students' suit was dismissed for mootness although the appellate court ruled that faculty members who had joined students in the suit had a valid cause of action. Greene v Howard Univ., 412 F.2d 1128 (D.C. Cir. 1969).

[78] As one commentator stated, "It seems unthinkable that a private school would even consider guaranteeing fewer rights for their students than the minimum rights the Constitution exacts from public schools." Tenerowicz, *supra* note 32 at 684-85.

their own rules when conducting disciplinary proceedings and to conduct those proceedings in a way that is fundamentally fair.[79]

For example, in *Ahlum v. Administrators of Tulane Educational Fund,*[80] Tulane University suspended freshman Sean Ahlum for having non-consensual sex with an inebriated freshman woman in his residence hall. Initially, a hearing board made up of two faculty members, two students, and the Associate Vice President for Student Affairs concluded unanimously that Ahlum had violated Tulane's code of student conduct. Ahlum appealed this decision to an appellate committee, which overturned the board on the grounds that a copy of Louisiana's rape statute had been placed into the record before the hearing without Ahlum's knowledge. A second hearing was held; again, the hearing board unanimously concluded that Ahlum had violated Tulane's code of conduct.

Because a tape recorder malfunctioned, no record of the second hearing was preserved for review. Nevertheless, Tulane's Vice President for Student Affairs accepted the second hearing board's decision and suspended Ahlum for the spring 1992 semester. Before being readmitted, Ahlum was required to participate in an "awareness raising program" and prepare a 30-minute video training session for residence hall advisors about how to deal with sexual assault.[81]

Ahlum appealed his suspension in a Louisiana court, where he obtained a restraining order against Tulane. The court ordered Tulane to hold a third hearing and to make a written record of it. Tulane then appealed the trial court's decision, arguing that courts had no power to intervene in a private university's internal disciplinary proceedings. The appellate court rejected this argument, however, stating that a policy of judicial restraint does not mean that the actions of private institutions are inviolate or that they could ignore due process standards altogether. Although courts would exercise restraint when reviewing the conduct of a private institution, the court said, "[t]he disciplinary decisions of a private school may be reviewed for arbitrary and capricious action."[82]

Having reserved to itself the right to review Tulane's suspension decision, the court went on to conclude that Tulane's dismissal process was adequate. Ahlum had received two separate hearings and appeals prior to filing his lawsuit, the court pointed out; and the court found no basis for concluding that Tulane's suspension decision was "unreasoned" or "thoughtless."[83]

Likewise, in *Cloud v. Trustees of Boston University,*[84] a law student expelled for sexual misconduct failed to persuade a court that he had been

---

[79] *See, e.g.,* Rensselaer Soc. of Engineers v. Rensselaer Polytechnic Inst., 260 A.D.2d 992, 993, 689 N.Y.S.2d 292, 295 (N.Y. App. Div. 1999) (judicial review of private university's discipline of fraternity is determination of whether university's action was arbitrary or capricious): Ahlum v. Admin. of Tulane Educ. Fund, 617 So. 2d 96, 99 (La. Ct. App. 1993) (judicial review of private university's disciplinary action will be reviewed for arbitrary or capricious action).

[80] 617 So. 2d 96 (La. Ct. App. 1993).

[81] *Id.* at 97-98.

[82] *Id.* at 99.

[83] *Id.*

[84] 720 F.2d 721 (1st Cir. 1983).

treated unfairly. Cloud went before a judicial committee based on charges that he had crept under tables in the university library and peeked under women's skirts. At his hearing, which was conducted under BU's Provisional Student Code (PSC), the hearing examiner permitted one nervous female witness to testify anonymously behind a screen outside Cloud's view. In addition, Cloud had previously been convicted of rape, and a transcript of this conviction was placed in evidence before the hearing tribunal. Cloud was represented by legal counsel during the hearing, which lasted 20 hours, and his counsel called nine witnesses on his behalf. At the hearing's conclusion, the judicial committee found Cloud guilty of misconduct and expelled him. Cloud appealed the decision to BU's president, who upheld the expulsion.

Cloud sued, arguing that the hearing was conducted in violation of his contract right to a fair hearing under BU's own rules. Specifically, Cloud argued that the hearing officer should not have permitted a witness to testify anonymously. He also argued that his hearing should have been conducted under the law school's disciplinary rules and not the general university disciplinary code. He accused the hearing examiner of bias, thereby depriving of his right to a fair hearing, and he argued that he had been deprived of his right to call witnesses because BU failed to produce some employees to testify as Cloud had requested. Finally Cloud argued that his legal right to privacy under Massachusetts law had been violated by the disclosure of his rape conviction at the hearing.

In reviewing Cloud's appeal, the First Circuit stated that it would review BU's dismissal process to determine whether the university followed its own rules as determined by the reasonable reading of those rules and whether the hearing process comported with "basic fairness."[85] According to the First Circuit, all of Cloud's arguments were insubstantial. In particular, the hearing officer's decision to allow one witness to testify anonymously did not render the hearing unfair. The rape conviction, the court pointed out, was a matter of public record that Cloud himself had publicly disclosed. In the court's view, BU properly used the university's general discipline code in Cloud's proceeding rather than the law school's rules because the charges involved his behavior in the university library, not the law school. The court found no evidence of bias by the hearing examiner and BU's failure to obtain witnesses that Cloud requested did not render the hearing unfair.

More recent decisions show that courts will require private colleges to follow a fair process when deciding whether to impose severe sanctions on their students for sexual misconduct. In *Doe v. Claremont McKenna College*, for example, a California appellate court ruled that a male student charge with sexual misconduct (engaging in unprotected sex over his partner's objections) must be afforded the right to confront his accuser.[86] After examining relevant case law, the court wrote:

---

[85] *Id.* at 725.
[86] 25 Cal. App.5th 1055 (Cal. Ct. App. 2018).

We concluded that these cases distill to a set of core principles applicable to cases where the accused student faces a severe penalty and the school's determination turns on the complaining witness's credibility. First, the accused student is entitled to a process by which the respondent may question, if even indirectly, the complainant. Second, the complaining witness must be before the finder of fact to assess the complaining witness's credibility in responding to its own questions or those proposed by the accused student.[87]

Likewise, in *Doe v. Brandeis University*,[88] a federal court spelled out specific procedural protections that must be afforded a student accused of sexual misconduct in order to assure disciplinary hearings are "conducted with basic fairness."[89] These protections include: the right to notice of charges; the right to counsel, at least when the institution is assisted by legal counsel; the right to confront the accuser; the right to cross-examine witnesses, the right to examine evidence and witness statements; an unimpaired right to call witnesses and present evidence; the right to see the investigative report forming the basis of the accusation, the right to a separation of the institution's investigatory, prosecution, and adjudication functions when pursuing disciplinary sanctions; and the right to an effective appeal.[90]

Interestingly, the *Brandeis* decision questioned the propriety of applying the preponderance-of-the-evidence" standard in the disciplinary proceedings against Doe. Although the court acknowledged that the preponderance-of-the-evidence standard is commonly used in civil proceedings, Brandeis utilized a higher standard of proof for almost all disciplinary matters except charges of sexual misconduct. In the court's view, "the lowering of the standard appears to have been a deliberate choice by the university to make cases of sexual misconduct easier to prove—and thus more difficult to defend, both for guilty and innocent students alike."[91] Thus, the lower standard could be seen "as part of an effort to tilt the playing field against accused students, which is particularly troublesome in light of the elimination of other basic rights of the accused."[92]

In sum, then, a line of cases demonstrates that courts obligate private colleges to conduct disciplinary proceedings against their students in a manner that is fundamentally fair. Moreover, these cases show that courts require private institutions to offer procedural protections to accused students that are virtually identical to the elements of procedural due process that are constitutionally imposed on public universities.

---

[87] *Id.* at 1070 (internal citations and punctuation omitted).

[88] 177 F.Supp.3d 561 (D. Mass. 2016).

[89] *Id.* at 601.

[90] *Id.* at 602-607.

[91] *Id.* at 607.

[92] *Id.*

Due Process When a Public College Dismisses a Student for Academic Deficiencies

As we have seen, students at public colleges or universities are entitled to procedural due process before being suspended or expelled for a disciplinary violation. A student facing dismissal from a public institution for academic deficiencies, however, is entitled to substantially less protection under the Fourteenth Amendment's Due Process Clause, as the Supreme Court made clear in two important decisions.

In *Board of Curators of the University of Missouri v. Horowitz*,[93] a medical school dismissed student Charlotte Horowitz during the clinical phase of her education based on poor faculty reviews, poor relationships with patients and fellow students, and poor personal hygiene. Horowtiz had done fine in her academic course work, but her professors were unhappy with her performance during her pediatrics rotation, and a council on evaluation recommended that she be admitted to her final year of medical school on a probationary basis.

Horowitz was not able to overcome concerns about her clinical performance during her final year of medical school, and the council on evaluations recommended that she not be permitted to graduate. As part of a process appealing that recommendation, Horowitz spent time with seven practicing physicians, two of whom recommended that she be permitted to graduate on schedule, two recommended that she be dropped from medical school, and three recommended that she be continued on probation.

Following the physicians' evaluations, the council met again and recommended that Horowitz be dropped from medical school. A coordinating committee made up solely of faculty members and the medical school's dean approved the council's recommendation and dismissed her. Horowitz sued, and the Eighth Circuit ruled that she had a constitutionally protected interest in her medical education and could not be dismissed without being afforded procedural due process.

On appeal, the Supreme Court reversed. Assuming Horowitz had a property interest in her education, the Court ruled, she had been afforded full due process. In fact, the Court stated, the medical school had given Horowitz more due process than the Constitution required. In so ruling, the Court articulated a clear distinction between a dismissal based on a disciplinary violation and a dismissal triggered by academic deficiencies:

> Academic evaluations of a student, in contrast to disciplinary determinations, bear little resemblance to the judicial and administrative fact-finding proceedings to which we have traditionally attached a full hearing requirement. . . .The decision to dismiss [Horowitz], by comparison, rested on the academic judgment of school officials that she did not have the necessary clinical ability to perform adequately as a medical doctor and was making insufficient progress

---

[93] 435 U.S. 78 (1978).

toward that goal. Such a judgment is by its nature more subjective and evaluative than the typical factual questions presented in the average disciplinary decision. Like the decision of an individual professor as to the proper grade for a student in his course, the determination whether to dismiss a student for academic reasons requires an expert evaluation of cumulative information and is not readily adapted to the procedural tools of judicial or administrative decision making.[94]

Thus, the Supreme Court made clear that students are not entitled to an adversarial hearing when facing dismissal from a public university on academic grounds. In the Court's view, the medical school's decision was "careful and deliberate"[95] and no formal hearing was required. Even assuming Horowitz had a substantive right to due process which would bar the school from dismissing her capriciously or arbitrarily, she could not prevail, the Court added. There was no showing the school had acted arbitrarily or capriciously when it decided to dismiss Horowitz from medical school.

In a later decision, the Supreme Court spelled out the requirements of substantive due process in academic decisions. In *Regents of the University of Michigan v. Ewing*,[96] a medical school's promotion and review board dropped a student from medical school after he failed a standardized examination and was not permitted to retake it. Ewing appealed to the medical school's executive committee, which upheld the dismissal. The student then asked for a leave of absence in order to retake the exam, but his request was denied. Ewing sued, arguing that the medical school had acted arbitrarily and capriciously in violation of his right to substantive due process. The trial court dismissed his claim, but the Sixth Circuit Court of Appeals reversed, ordering the medical school to allow Ewing to retake the exam and, if he passed, to reinstate him.

On appeal to the Supreme Court, the Sixth Circuit's decision was reversed. Even if Ewing had a property interest in his medical education that gave him the right to substantive due process, the Court ruled, the record revealed that the medical school's action was not arbitrary. The school's dismissal decision must be upheld, the Court instructed, unless it could be shown that its conduct "was such a substantial departure from accepted academic norms as to demonstrate that the faculty did not exercise professional judgment." [97] Unless an academic decision falls outside accepted academic norms, courts will not overturn a public university's decision about a student that is clearly an academic dismissal.

Sylvester v. Southern University,[98] however, shows that a student can get a federal court to change a grade under exceptional circumstances. In that case, Karen Sylvester, a third-year law student at Thurgood Marshall School of Law,

---

[94] *Id.* at 89-90.

[95] *Id.* at 85.

[96] 474 U.S. 214 (1985).

[97] *Id.* at 227.

[98] 957 F. Supp. 944 (S.D. Tex. 1997).

received a D in her wills and trust course, which dropped her class standing from first to third place. Sylvester protested her grade to the associate dean, and she asked the law school's academic standards committee to review her grade. When she got no response, she filed suit in federal court. A federal judge ordered the academic standards committee to review Sylvester's grade. The committee was made up of both faculty and students, but the faculty members expelled the students from the committee and then submitted a report saying it had reviewed Sylvester's examination and found no inconsistencies in the way her professor had graded the examinations.

Based on these events and the professor's behavior, which the court described as "recalcitrant" and "defiant,"[99] the court made an equitable adjustment in Sylvester's grade, changing it from a D to a pass. This change reinstated her to her ranking as first in her class, which the court said she would share with the class valedictorian. In the court's opinion, Sylvester was entitled to both procedural and substantive due process, and she had received neither.

Sometimes the distinction between a university's academic sanctions and disciplinary sanctions is easy to see. *Sylvester* clearly involved an academic dispute about a grade, while a student charged with sexual misconduct is obviously involved in a disciplinary dispute. Other times, the distinction between an academic dispute and a disciplinary dispute is not clear, as when a student's academic deficiency is based on misconduct like cheating or plagiarism. Kaplin and Lee advise universities to provide a student with procedural due process any time a sanction against a student requires university officials to make a judgment on disputed factual issues.[100] "Indeed," they write, "there may be good reason to provide some form of hearing prior to academic dismissal whenever the student has some basis for claiming that the academic judgment was arbitrary, in bad faith, or discriminatory."[101]

Degree Revocation at Public and Private Colleges

Colleges and universities, whether public or private, may revoke a degree already awarded if a degree recipient is found to have committed fraud or academic dishonesty during the course of studies.[102] In the oft-cited case of *Waliga v. Kent State University*,[103] the Ohio Supreme Court explained the rationale for giving higher education institutions the authority to revoke academic credentials already awarded:

> We consider it self-evident that a college or university acting through its board of trustees does have the inherent authority to

---

[99] *Id.* at 946.

[100] KAPLIN & LEE, *supra* note 4 at 987.

[101] *Id.*

[102] KAPLIN & LEE, *supra* note 4 938 ("Generally, both public and private colleges and universities have authority to revoke improperly awarded degrees when cause for doing so, such as the discovery of fraud or misrepresentation, is shown.").

[103] 488 N.E. 2d 850 (Ohio 1986).

revoke an improperly awarded degree where (1) good cause, such as fraud, deceit, or error is shown, and (2) the degree-holder is afforded a fair hearing at which he can present evidence and protect his interest. Academic degrees are a university's certification to the world at large of the recipient's educational achievement and fulfillment of the institution's standards. To hold that a university may never withdraw a degree, effectively requires the university to continue making a false certification to the public at large of the accomplishment of persons who in fact lack the very qualifications that are certified.[104]

When a public university revokes a graduate's degree, procedural due process must be afforded just as when students are suspended or expelled while their studies are still ongoing. Indeed, some commentators have observed that courts seem inclined to require more due process when a public university revokes a degree than is required when the university expels a student.[105] Nevertheless, even in degree-revocation proceedings, procedural due process protections need not approach the formality of a criminal trial.

In *Crook v. Baker*,[106] a 1987 decision, the Sixth Circuit considered due process claims of an individual who lost his master's degree in geology from the University of Michigan based on the university's finding that the data he used in his thesis had been fabricated. Upon discovering that Crook may have procured his degree by fraud, the university notified him that a hearing would be held on the charges, which, if sustained, would lead to revocation of Crook's degree. The university then impaneled an ad hoc disciplinary committee of university professors to hear the charges, and sent Crook copies of documents that allegedly supported the charges. At the hearing, which lasted eight hours, Crook was accompanied by his lawyer, who supplied an experienced court reporter to transcribe the proceedings.[107] Although the lawyer was denied the right to cross-examine witnesses, Crook questioned witnesses himself and was free to consult with his lawyer and an expert. The disciplinary committee concluded that Crook had fabricated his data, and ultimately the Board of Regents voted to revoke his degree.

Crook sued to enjoin the revocation, arguing the university had no authority to rescind his degree and that the disciplinary hearing violated due process. After a nine-day hearing, a federal court ruled in Crook's favor, finding that

---

[104] *Id.* at 852.

[105] Charles Russo & William Thro, *Student Equal Protection and Due Process*, in CONTEMPORARY ISSUES IN HIGHER EDUCATION LAW 268 (Joseph Beckham & David Dagley, eds, 2005) ("Courts apply a higher level of scrutiny in degree revocation cases and show less deference to academic decision-making because the revocation of a degree is the most severe penalty that an institution can take against a former student."); Jayme L. Butcher, MIT v. Yoo: *Revocation of Academic Degrees for Nonacademic Reasons*, 51 CASE W. RES. 749, 758 (2001) ("Courts apply a higher level of scrutiny in degree revocation cases, showing much less deference than in the suspension, expulsion, and even degree withholding cases.").

[106] 813 F.2d 88 (6th Cir. 1987).

[107] *Id.* at 94.

Crook had been denied both substantive and procedural due process. Specifically, the judge ruled that Crook had not received adequate notice and an opportunity to plead his case.[108] She also concluded that university officials involved in the dispute, from the professors making up the hearing committee to the University of Michigan Regents, were partial, and that there was no rational basis for concluding that Crook had fabricated data.

On appeal, the Sixth Circuit reversed. Relying partly on the Ohio Supreme Court's decision in *Waliga*, the Sixth Circuit concluded that the university did indeed have the authority to revoke Crook's degree. As for Crook's procedural due process claims, the Sixth Circuit ruled that Crook had received adequate notice of the charge against him, as evidenced by a document he filed in response to the charge. Moreover, the Sixth Circuit found that Crook had received an adequate opportunity to defend himself at the hearing. Both Crook and his counsel made an opening statement, Crook was permitted the right to consult with his attorney during the hearing, and Crook questioned witnesses and called his own witnesses. Although the trial court had described the hearing as a "circus-like free-for-all," the Sixth Circuit disagreed, finding the proceedings merely informal.[109]

Nor was Crook denied due process because the hearing procedures prohibited Crook's attorney from examining and cross-examining witnesses. The court pointed out that Crook himself had examined and cross-examined the witnesses, and that he was a highly educated person with expertise in the field that was the subject of investigation. Accordingly, the Sixth Circuit rejected the trial court's finding that Crook had been denied substantive process because the university had no rational basis for concluding that Crook had fabricated data. On the contrary, the Sixth Circuit made clear, the university decision makers had used their professional judgment when they reached their decision, which had been based on clear and convincing evidence.[110]*Crook* illustrates the non-controversial principle that a university may revoke a graduate's degree if the degree was obtained by fraud or some other kind of academic misconduct, such as plagiarism.[111]

May a university revoke a student's degree or withhold a degree based on non-academic misconduct? Several courts have ruled that colleges have this authority. In *Harwood v. Johns Hopkins University*, for example, a court upheld a private university's decision to deny a degree to a student who murdered another student after completing his course requirements but before his degree was awarded.[112]

Harvard University's decision to suspend two students for one year based on a finding they had misappropriated money from a student-run enterprise

---

[108] *Id.* at 97.

[109] *Id.* at 98.

[110] *Id.* at 100.

[111] *See, e.g.*, Abalkhail v. Claremont Univ. Ctr., 2d Civ. No. B014012 (Cal. Ct. App. 1986) (degree revoked for plagiarism).

[112] Harwood v. Johns Hopkins Univ., 747 A.2d 205 (Md. Ct. Spec. App. 2000).

was likewise upheld even though the students argue that they had completed all their degree requirements and should be awarded their diplomas.[113] Of course, a college, whether public or private, may not act "maliciously and in bad faith" by refusing to award a degree to a student who has met all the academic requirements for graduation. [114]

One author has argued persuasively that graduates faced with revocation of their degrees based on nonacademic misconduct should be entitled to a very high level of procedural due process, and that procedural protections should be the same whether the university is public or private. The commentator also recommended that universities be required to create a list of nonacademic reasons that could trigger a degree revocation.[115]

Due Process Standards in Campus Proceedings Involving Allegations of Sexual Misconduct

In recent years, colleges and universities have been sued repeatedly by male students who were suspended from their studies based on a ruling by a campus disciplinary panel that they had committed an act of sexual violence against a female student. Indeed, a review of this litigation described this trend as an "assembly line" of cases in which male college students argue that their disciplinary hearings were mishandled.[116] In many of these cases, the male plaintiffs alleged they had been denied due process or that findings against them were motivated by illegal bias.

Although it is beyond the scope of this chapter to review this tide of litigation, an illustrative case is presented to give the flavor of these lawsuits. For more in-depth treatment than is provided herein, readers are encouraged to review chapter 8 for a comprehensive discussion of sexual harassment cases in higher education. In 2019, the Seventh Circuit court ruled in *Doe v. Purdue University*[117] that a college disciplinary panel failed to ensure the fundamental rubrics of due process before finding a male college student responsible for sexual violence. John Doe, an undergraduate at Purdue University, was suspended from the university for one year based on a finding by a university disciplinary panel that he had committed an act of sexual violence against Jane Roe. As a result of the panel's decision, Mr. Doe was also expelled from

---

[113] Dinu v. President & Fellows of Harvard Coll., 56 F. Supp. 2d 129 (D. Mass. 1999).

[114] Johnson v. Lincoln Christian Coll., 501 N.E.2d 1380, 1384 (Ill. Ct. App. 1986) (degree revocation based on rumor that student was a homosexual).

[115] Butcher, *supra* note 117 at 773. See also Stephen B. Thomas & Deborah L. Barber, *The Right to Rescind a Degree*, 33 Educ. L. Rep. [1], 2-3 (1986) (arguing that due process is typically required any time a college or university revokes a degree because revocation "generally alleges misconduct, fraud, cheating, misrepresentation, or the like").

[116] Dianne Heckman, *The Assembly Line of Title IX Mishandling Cases Concerning Sexual Violence on College Campuses*. 336 Educ. L. Rep. 619 (2016).

[117] Doe v. Purdue Univ., 928 F.3d 652 (7th Cir. 2019).

the university's Navy ROTC program, which terminated his plans to pursue a career in the Navy.[118]

Doe sued Purdue and several university administrators in 2017, charging the defendants with violating his right to due process under the Fifth Amendment and a violation of Title IX of the Education Amendments of 1972. A magistrate dismissed Doe's lawsuit on Purdue's motion for dismissal, but the decision was reversed on appeal to the Seventh Circuit. In a lengthy opinion, the Seventh Circuit concluded that Doe's allegations were sufficient to state a cause of action against Purdue University. As outlined by the appellate court, Jane Roe, a female Purdue student, accused Doe of groping her over her clothes while she was sleeping with him in Doe's dormitory room. Roe did not file a formal complaint against Doe, but Katherine Sermersheim, Purdue's Dean of Students, elected to pursue an investigation against him and assigned two investigators to look into the matter.[119]

Doe denied Roe's accusations and set forth evidence, which, he maintained, was inconsistent with Roe's assault claim. Specifically, Doe argued, Roe had texted and talked to him after the alleged assault took place; and Roe had sent Doe's family a package of homemade Christmas cookies. In addition, Doe offered his roommate's testimony to refute Roe's accusations. This roommate, Doe said, was present when the alleged assault took place and could testify that an assault never happened.[120] In due time, the investigators prepared a report on Roe's accusations, but Sermersheim did not give Doe a copy of the report and did not share its contents with him. Later, Doe appeared at a meeting before a three-member "Advisory Committee." Just before the meeting, Doe and his ROTC representative were allowed to see a redacted copy of the investigators' report, which, Doe maintained, falsely said he had confessed to Roe's accusations.

As the Seventh Circuit noted, the subsequent meeting with the Advisory Committee "did not go well for John."[121] Two committee members confessed they had not read the investigators' report. The panel refused to allow Doe to present witnesses in his defense, including his roommate who was prepared to testify that he was in the room when the alleged assault took place and that that Roe's "rendition of events was false."[122] In concluding that Doe had made out a cause of action for violation of his right to due process, the Seventh Circuit identified these deficiencies in the way Purdue administrators had assessed Jane Roe's assault claims. First, "two of the three panel members candidly admitted that they had not read the investigate report, which suggest that they decided that John was guilty based on the accusation rather than the evidence."[123] Second, Doe's roommate, a crucial witness, was not allowed to testify. Third, the

---

[118] *Id*. at 656.

[119] *Id*. at 657.

[120] *Id*. at 658.

[121] *Id*.

[122] *Id*.

[123] *Id*.

panel found in favor of Jane Roe without even reviewing a written statement by her and without Roe being present at the hearing. "It is unclear, to say the least," the Seventh Circuit court observed, "how Sermersheim and the committee could have evaluated Jane's credibility."[124]

Doe v. Purdue University is but one of several federal appellate court decisions that have examined whether a college disciplinary panel complied with the fundamental rubrics of due process before finding a male college student responsible for sexual violence or assault. In two separate opinions discussed earlier in this chapter, the Sixth Court of Appeals ruled emphatically that a student accused of sexual misconduct has a constitutional right to confront his accuser before being suspended or expelled from the university.[125] In the years to come, the federal courts will undoubtedly continue to sketch out the minimal requirements of procedure due process that a university must follow before disciplining a student based on a finding that the student committed a sexual assault.

Conclusion

Under the Fourteenth Amendment, students are entitled to fair procedures when faced with suspension or expulsion from a public college or university, as first articulated in *Dixon v. Alabama State Board of Education*[126] and reaffirmed by a string of federal court decisions. Those procedures need not approach the formality of a criminal trial, but the student must be given notice of charges, a fair opportunity to contest the charges in an adversarial proceeding, and an unbiased tribunal. College students at private institutions are also entitled to fair procedures before being suspended or expelled, with the courts generally grounding this right in contract law or a duty on the private institution's part not to act arbitrarily or capriciously.

Students are entitled to much less procedural protection when challenging a college's academic decisions, and the Supreme Court has made clear that a public university is not required to provide an adversarial hearing when making an adverse academic decision against a student.[127] A university's academic decisions will be upheld if they comply with academic norms and are not arbitrary or capricious. Sanctions for an academic deficiency that is grounded in a charge of dishonesty or fraud require more procedural due process, something akin to due process requirements when a disciplinary sanction is imposed.

A college or university is required to provide procedural protections when revoking a graduate's degree, but those procedures need not be as formal as a criminal trial, as the *Crook* decision illustrates.[128] Colleges clearly have the

---

[124] *Id.* at 664.

[125] Doe v. Univ. of Cincinnati, 872 F.3d 393 (6th Cir. 2017) ; Doe v. Baum, 903 F.3d 575 (6th Cir. 2018).

[126] 294 F.2d150 (5th Cir. 1961).

[127] Bd. of Curators of Univ. of Mo. v. Horowitz, 435 U.S. 78 (1978).

[128] Crook v. Baker, 813 F.2d 88 (6th Cir. 1987).

authority to revoke degrees based on findings of fraud or plagiarism, and to withhold a degree based on nonacademic misconduct that violates university rules and takes place before graduation.

In summary, whether a college is public or private, it must provide students with a fair process before suspending or expelling them for nonacademic misconduct or an academic deficiency containing elements of fraud or dishonesty. When a university sanctions a student for a purely academic deficiency, no adversarial process is required. Courts are extremely deferential to an institution's academic decisions and will not overturn them absent good evidence of arbitrary or capricious conduct.

Discussion Questions

1. The courts are not in total agreement about the contours of procedural due process when students are charged with disciplinary infractions. What are the minimal requirements of procedural due process as outlined in the *Dixon* case?

2. Why have the courts articulated different due process requirements for students facing academic penalties as opposed to sanctions for a disciplinary violation? In your opinion, is the distinction between academic sanctions and disciplinary sanctions valid?

3. The chapter indicated that a university can legally revoke a student's degree after it has been conferred under certain circumstances. What are those circumstances?

4. How should a university meet its constitutional obligation to afford due process when university officials believe a student constitutes a danger to the campus community and needs to be removed immediately?

5. Private colleges and universities are not constitutionally obligated to provide students with procedural due process before students are suspended from their studies, or expelled. Nevertheless, the courts have required private institutions to conduct suspension and expulsion proceedings in a fair manner. What legal principles have courts invoked when they have ruled that private colleges and universities have an obligation to be fair to students who face suspension or expulsion?

13 Student Speech and Expression

Jennifer Rippner, J.D., Ph.D.
Indiana University
Mark A. Paige, J.D., Ph.D.
University of Massachusetts-Dartmouth

One of the most pressing and engaging legal issues in higher education concerns student expression, namely speech. Important and intriguing questions include: May students invite controversial speakers to campus? May other students protest those speakers and prevent their speech? Do students have the right to say hateful things? Do students have a right to protest anywhere, anytime on campus? What makes these and other questions so fascinating is that the campus truly acts as a laboratory for our larger democracy. These questions relate to matters beyond college campuses. Indeed, these discussions impact the rules and norms for society as a whole.

The issue of speech on campus certainly has political as well as legal implications. This chapter provides an introduction to the existing legal foundation, rather than focusing on the politics. We do not attempt to tip the scales on behalf of increased freedom of speech nor greater protections for student sensitivity. The balancing of these important imperatives is best done by those intimately familiar with the culture and context of their particular institution. We provide this chapter to help with this important task.

The First Amendment

State and federal courts frequently address controversies between students and public higher education institutions involving the First Amendment. The First Amendment to the United States Constitution provides, in relevant part, that "Congress shall make no law . . . abridging the freedom of speech, or of the press."[1] This clause extends to state and local government entities.[2] Conse-

---

[1] U.S. CONST. amend. 1.
[2] Gitlo v. New York, 268 U.S. 652, 666 (1925) (interpreting the First Amendment Rights to be among those protected under the Fourteenth Amendment's Due Process Clause and applicable to states).

quently, the First Amendment is applicable to public colleges and universities because they are state entities[3].

The United States Supreme Court has reasoned that "if there is a bedrock principle underlying the First Amendment, it is that the government may not prohibit the expression of an idea simply because society finds the idea itself offensive or disagreeable."[4] Yet, it also has emphasized that "the protections afforded by the First Amendment are not absolute, and we have long recognized that the government may regulate certain categories of expression consistent with the Constitution."[5] Thus, there are limits to freedom of expression. This chapter explores the range of First Amendment claims involving students in higher education settings including student protests, inviting speakers on campus, student publications, student advocacy, student organizations, and hate speech.

Protected Speech

In evaluating First Amendment free speech claims by students attending public colleges and universities, judicial inquiry begins with a determination of whether the particular speech enjoys First Amendment protection. Only a few narrow exceptions to protected free speech have been identified as speech that falls outside the scope of First Amendment protection. Notably, fighting words,[6] true threats,[7] incitement,[8] obscenity,[9] and defamation[10] constitute potential exceptions to the expansive protection offered by the First Amendment.

---

[3] Private institutions of higher education are not state actors and therefore the First Amendment does not apply in that context. Students at private institutions are only entitled to the First Amendment rights granted through institutional policies and contracts.

[4] Texas v. Johnson, 491 U.S. 397, 414 (1989).

[5] Virginia v. Black, 538 U.S. 343, 358 (2003).

[6] *See* Texas v. Johnson, 491 U.S. 397 (1989) (ruling that burning of an American flag was protected speech); Gooding v. Wilson, 405 U.S. 518 (1972); Chaplinsky v. New Hampshire, 315 U.S. 568 (1942).

[7] *See* Watts v. United States, 394 U.S. 705, 708 (1969) (per curiam) (emphasizing that true threats must be distinguished from "political hyperbole").

[8] *See* Virginia v. Black, 538 U.S. 343, 359 (2003) (interpreting the constitutionality of a state law restricting cross burning). See also, Tinker v. Des Moines Indep. Cnty. Sch. Dist., 393 U.S. 503, 508 (1969), in which the Court noted that "undifferentiated fear or apprehension of disturbance . . . is not enough to overcome the right to freedom of expression."

[9] *See* Miller v. California, 401 U.S. 15 (1973), in which the Court emphasized the offense "must be limited to works which, taken as a whole, appeal to the prurient interest in sex, which portray sexual conduct in a patently offensive way, and which, taken as a whole, do not have serious literary, artistic, political, or scientific value; Cohen v. California, 403 U.S. 15, 26 (1971), in which the Court noted "it is largely because governmental officials cannot make principled distinctions in this area that the Constitution leaves matters of taste and style so largely to the individual."

[10] *See* Milkovich v. Lorain Journal, 497 U.S. 1, 18 (1990) (holding that when an expression of opinion contains implied assertions of underlying objective fact, the statement may be an actionable defamation).

Figure 1: Types of Speech Not Protected By the First Amendment

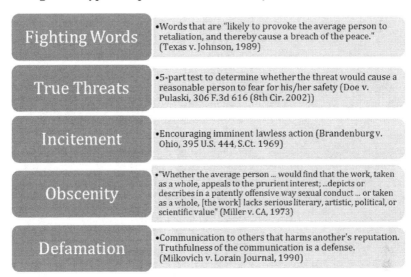

Fighting Words	•Words that are "likely to provoke the average person to retaliation, and thereby cause a breach of the peace." (Texas v. Johnson, 1989)
True Threats	•5-part test to determine whether the threat would cause a reasonable person to fear for his/her safety (Doe v. Pulaski, 306 F.3d 616 (8th Cir. 2002))
Incitement	•Encouraging imminent lawless action (Brandenburg v. Ohio, 395 U.S. 444, S.Ct. 1969)
Obscenity	•"Whether the average person ... would find that the work, taken as a whole, appeals to the prurient interest; ...depicts or describes in a patently offensive way sexual conduct ... or taken as a whole, [the work] lacks serious literary, artistic, political, or scientific value" (Miller v. CA, 1973)
Defamation	•Communication to others that harms another's reputation. Truthfulness of the communication is a defense. (Milkovich v. Lorain Journal, 1990)

Although narrow exceptions to free speech exist, as noted above, the protection afforded speech extends to religious, political, or philosophic speech in a variety of expressive forms, including "offensive" speech. The United States Supreme Court considered the "offensive" content of student speech in *Papish v. Board of Curators of the University of Missouri.*[11] In *Papish,* a graduate student challenged his expulsion from a public university for violating an institutional policy prohibiting the publication and distribution of indecent speech. The student distributed an "underground" newspaper on campus that included a front cover cartoon representing policemen raping the Statute of Liberty and Lady Justice. The accompanying caption read, "With Liberty and Justice for All." The Court ruled in favor of the student, reasoning that "dissemination of ideas—no matter how offensive to good taste—on a state university campus may not be shut off in the name alone of 'conventions of decency.'"[12]As the decision in *Papish* suggests, the fact that student speech may be offensive to others does not necessarily mean it can be suppressed. For example, in *Iota Xi Chapter of Sigma Chi Fraternity v. George Mason University,*[13] a federal appeals court struck down a public university's attempt to punish student speech that offended provisions of a campus civility code. In *Iota,* a university fraternity staged an "ugly women" skit in the student union cafeteria that included a student painted in blackface and crude gender- and race-based humor. The Fourth Circuit Court of Appeals affirmed a preliminary injunction barring application of the institution's penalty for this conduct,

---

[11] 410 U.S. 667 (1973).

[12] *Id.* at 670.

[13] 993 F.2d 386 (4th Cir. 1993).

emphasizing that the speech constituted parody and was protected by the Free Speech Clause of the First Amendment.

So then, where is the line between merely offensive speech and speech that universities can curtail under the First Amendment in the name of protecting students? The Fourth Circuit Court of Appeals recently dismissed a public university's claim that the First Amendment barred them from taking action on student-to-student cyberbullying. In *Feminist Majority Foundation v. Hurley,*[14] members of the University of Mary Washington (Virginia) feminist group claimed, among other things, that university administrators were deliberately indifferent to sexual harassment occurring over the social network Yik Yak. By one account, there were over 700 threatening and harassing "Yaks" directed at the feminist group and specific individuals within that group. Administrators held "listening circles" and issued rather tepid campus-wide e-mails chastising the harassing behavior, but did little else to address the students' numerous pleas for protection and safety. The court reasoned that true threats are not protected speech and that the university had several avenues to respond to the harassing behavior (as required by Title IX[15]) that did not violate the First Amendment. Further, the threats on Yik Yak constituted criminal conduct and the university should have investigated the student authors of the threatening Yaks, even if, on their face, they were posted anonymously.[16]

In another recent Fourth Circuit Court of Appeals case, students claimed that a university's investigative action violated their First Amendment rights. In *Abbott v. Pastides,*[17] a student group of the University of South Carolina lawfully held a campus event to highlight perceived threats to free expression on college campuses. University administrators knew that this event would include displays of controversial symbols such as a swastika. Subsequently, some students complained to university administrators that the event included sexist and racist statements and symbols. An administrator requested that one of the student sponsors of the event meet with him to review the complaint and determine whether further action was warranted. After the meeting, the official determined no further action was needed and the matter was dropped. The student sponsors of the event claimed that their First Amendment rights were violated when they were required to attend the meeting with the university official. The court dismissed this allegation and found that the university was "prompt and minimally intrusive" in its investigation of the student complaints.[18]

College administrators admittedly have a tough job in balancing the need for a welcoming and conducive learning environment for all students and ac-

---

[14] 911 F.3d 674 (4th Cir. 2018).

[15] 20 U.S.C. § 1681 *et seq.* (2014).

[16] The court determined that at least some of the Yaks were posted utilizing the school's website server and "it is widely known that a university can control activities that occur on its own network." (688).

[17] 900 F.3d 160 (4th Cir. 2018).

[18] *Id.* at 163.

knowledging constitutional speech rights. Sometimes it may feel like the law tries to baffle administrators with seemingly contradictory aims, such as the simultaneous requirements to protect student rights under *both* Title IX and the First Amendment. However, there are ways that university administrators can address offensive speech without violating speech rights. First, criminal harassment (as defined in federal and/or state law) is not protected speech and can be punished. Second, the use of top officials' bully pulpit is an important tool. Administrators may admonish the behavior or statements of students without repressing students' right to the expression. In addition, administrators may hold information sessions on why particular speech is harmful and reiterate the values of the institution and its community.

Nature of the Forum

The context or place in which the speech occurs may influence the extent of free speech protections. A public sidewalk on the periphery of a campus has been acknowledged as an open, or public, forum, subject only to limitations designed to avoid substantial disruption or material interference with the rights of pedestrians to access campus buildings.[19] In this, as in other traditional public forums such as public streets or parks, the government must accommodate broad access to the forum. It may only impose restrictions if they are content-neutral, narrowly drawn to serve a significant interest, and leave open alternative channels of communication. If the restrictions are content-specific, then judges may require that the institution show a compelling state interest for the policy.

Nonpublic[20] Forums

If the forum is exclusively dedicated to the institution's specific educational objectives, it may be regarded as nonpublic, and the institution may promulgate reasonable rules that restrict speech in order to preserve the setting for its intended educational purpose. Classrooms, libraries, lecture halls, theaters, laboratories, and even Internet platforms[21] are typically set aside on the public institution's campus for educational purposes, and judges consistently apply

---

[19] Brister v. Faulkner, 214 F. 3d 675 (5th Cir. 2000). The 5th Circuit later limited *Brister*, noting that it was fact-specific; the property in question was for constitutional purposes "indistinguishable" from the city sidewalk. *Id.* at 683. *See also* Borgault v. Yudof, 316 F. Supp.2d 411 (N.D. Tex. 2004) (announcing that *Brister* does not stand for the principle that the entire university is a public forum).

[20] Non-public forums may also be called closed forums.

[21] *See, e.g.,* Loving v. Boren, 956 F. Supp. 953 (W.D. Okla. 1997) (holding institution's computer and Internet services do not constitute a public forum because they are lawfully dedicated to academic and research uses); Buffalo Ventures v. Univ. of Tex. at Austin, 2004 U.S. Dist. LEXIS 19152 (W.D. Texas 2004) (ruling institution's Internet nonsolicitation rules and anti-spam policy were valid under a test for constitutionality of commercial speech regulation).

analysis associated with a nonpublic forum to these settings.[22] When the venue serves a specific institutional purpose that is closely aligned with its educational mission, the institution may properly assert that its primary use is incompatible with extending broad free speech protections, as long as legitimate pedagogical concerns support the nonpublic forum policy.

When a nonpublic forum has been judicially recognized, institutions need only articulate a legitimate pedagogical basis for restricting free speech.[23] One federal appeals court found that a drama classroom constituted a nonpublic forum and reasoned that because a student's speech occurred as part of a curricular assignment during class time and in the classroom setting, it was not protected under the First Amendment.[24] Similarly, a university did not violate a graduate student's free speech rights when it refused to include his thesis in its library holdings because he had written a "disacknowledgments" section in the document using profane language to attack those he felt had interfered with his completion of the degree.[25] The court emphasized that the university could enforce reasonable standards to prohibit objectionable content in a student's academic work since the institution's decision was held to be reasonably related to a legitimate pedagogical objective of teaching the student the proper format for a scientific paper.[26]

A recent case from the Tenth Circuit Court of Appeals also gives institutions wide latitude to regulate speech in the classroom if there is a legitimate pedagogical concern. In *Pompeo v. Board of Regents*,[28] a student brought suit against a public university after an instructor and administrators required her to revise a paper that was critical of lesbians. In the paper, the student provided several opinions about lesbians, including describing them as "perverse" and "barren" without providing any citations or other support that would be accepted practice in an academic paper. Ultimately, the student chose not

---

[22] *See* Salehpour v. Univ. of Tenn., 159 F. 3d 199 (6th Cir. 1998), *cert. denied,* 526 U.S. 1115 (1999) (upholding the discipline of a dental student who sat in one of the last two rows of class, in violation of professors' rules); Furumoto v. Lyman 362 F. Supp. 1267 (N.D. Cal. 1973) (upholding discipline of students who disrupted engineering class to demand that allegedly racist professor publicly debate his views on genetics); Adibi-Sadeh v. Bee County Coll., 454 F. Supp. 552 (S.D. Tex. 1978) (finding that arrest of student who refused to disperse from gym classroom did not violate free speech).

[23] *See, e.g.*, Heenan v. Rhoades, 757 F. Supp. 2d 1229 (M.D. Ala. 2010) (holding nursing student's criticism of point system for awarding grades did not support a First Amendment claim because it was directed at pedagogical and curricular concerns that reflected an effort to obtain judicial review of her academic performance); Keeton v. Anderson-Wiley, 733 F. Supp. 2d 1368 (S.D. Ga. 2010) (holding that a counseling student's imposition of her moral viewpoint on counselees in a state university's counseling program was not constitutionally protected free speech and the student's refusal to adhere to professional ethics constituted a refusal to complete curricular requirements). Similarly, at least one court frowned upon student attempts to bootstrap a challenge to their grades through a First Amendment claim. *See, e.g.,* Stephenson v. Central Michigan University, 897 F.Supp.2d 556, 566 (E.D. Mich. 2012) (finding that "gripes" about grades are not protected under the First Amendment) (citations omitted).

[24] Axson-Flynn v. Johnson, 356 F. 3d 1277 (10th Cir. 2004).

[25] Brown v. Li, 308 F.3d 939 (9th Cir. 2002).

[26] *Id.* at 952.

to revise the paper or complete another assignment and filed suit. The court determined that the instructor and the university had a legitimate pedagogical reason to exercise viewpoint discrimination in the classroom assignment in order to encourage students to submit academic, and not merely opinionated, work. Further, the instructor's legitimate pedagogical purpose did not appear to be a pretext for some other impermissible motive.

Yet, a nonpublic forum cannot be created in a veiled attempt to suppress ideas. For example, in *Brown v. Board of Regents of the University of Nebraska*,[27] a state legislator objected to the showing of a controversial film at the university's film theatre, and university officials cancelled the event. Students sued the university claiming a violation of their right to receive ideas, a right they argued was fundamental to the meaningful exercise of free speech. The federal district court determined that the decision of university officials did not meet the test for a reasonable regulation. In the court's view, the film was unconstitutionally suppressed, not because it was inappropriate for the closed forum of the university film series, but rather because it was at odds with the religious views of a state legislator who intervened to have it canceled.[28]

Facilities such as residence halls have typically been regarded as nonpublic forums, thus requiring a reasonableness standard for regulation of speech[29]. In an illustrative case, *Chapman v. Thomas*,[30] a federal appeals court placed campus dormitories in the category of nonpublic forums and determined that an institution's restrictions on solicitation would be subject to a test of reasonableness. The public university's policy prohibited door-to-door solicitation in residence halls, but provided an exception for door-to-door campaigning for student government elections. The appeals court ruled in favor of the university, recognizing that the university had a legitimate interest in protecting students in its residence halls from "unwanted, indiscriminate door-to-door solicitation by whoever might choose to descend uninvited upon them at whatever time and for whatever purpose."[31] The policy was reasonable, and the exception for political activity was narrowly drawn to encourage participation in student government politics. Moreover, the solicitation policy did not prevent students from using lobbies and waiting areas to reach students, leaving open alternative

---

[27] 640 F. Supp. 674 (D. Neb. 1986).

[28] *See also* Linnemeir v. Bd. of Tr. of Purdue Univ., 260 F. 3d 757 (7th Cir. 2001) (affirming denial of a requested injunction on the basis that the First Amendment does not forbid a state university from providing a venue, albeit a nonpublic forum, for the expression of viewpoints antagonistic to conventional religious beliefs).

[29] Note that a legitimate pedagogical concern may constitute a *reasonable* restriction which would satisfy the forum analysis.

[30] 743 F.2d 1056 (4th Cir. 1984).

[31] *Id.* at 1059.

channels of communication that did not operate as a total ban on speech.[32] Also related to residence halls, institutions must be careful to develop policies that do not discriminate according to viewpoint. For instance, if a residence hall allows residents to post material on the outside of their room door or on their window, the institution cannot then decide what type of speech can be put on a door or window. It must all be allowed or not.[33]

The concept of a closed forum appears to apply to online class discussions.[34] In this case, a student was initially warned and then disciplined for his discussion board postings under an institutional policy that prohibited "disruption, obstruction or interference with educational activities in classrooms," including "displaying defiance or disrespect of others."[35] In affirming the institution's policy and the discipline imposed, a federal district court distinguished the unique context of the classroom and then noted the content of the student's speech:

> Plaintiff argues that because his objectionable speech is connected in some way, even tangentially, to his personal political convictions, he is entitled to express himself in any way he chooses. It is possible, however, for Plaintiff to express his political views without insulting other students. The right to express his political views is not infringed with the requirement that he refrain from disrupting class and interfering with the course objectives by being disrespectful and inhibiting discussion[36]

Limited or Designated "Open" Forums

Most controversies involving student speech fall within the context of a designated or limited open forum, whether created by the institution's express designation[37] or as a function of custom and practice. A public institution's creation of a forum for student speech was examined in a case involving a student organization's use of campus facilities in *Widmar v. Vincent*.[38] In *Widmar*,

---

[32] In this case and others where courts have construed residence halls to be nonpublic forums, federal courts have upheld restrictions on solicitation provided the restrictions were reasonable and alternative channels were available to communicate with students. *See* Fox v. Bd. of Tr., 492 U.S. 469 (1989), *on remand*, 42 F.3d 135 (2d Cir. 1994), *cert. denied*, 515 U.S. 1169 (1995); Brush v. Penn State Univ., 414 A. 2d 48 (Pa. 1980); Nat'l Movement for Student Vote v. Regents of the Univ. of Cal., 123 Cal. Rptr. 141 (Ct. App. 1975).

[33] Of course, speech not protected by the First Amendment, as discussed earlier in the chapter, may be censored.

[34] Harrell v. Southern Oregon Univ., 2009 WL 3562732 (D. Or. 2009). *See also* Feine v. Parkland College, 2010 WL 1524201 (C.D. Ill. 2010).

[35] *Id.* at 4.

[36] *Id.* at 20-21.

[37] *See* Yates v. Fithian, 2010 WL 3788272 (W.D. Wash. 2010) (finding institution had created a designated open forum for a privately contracted campaign event when institutional administrators extended invitations to attend to the campus community and faculty had assigned attendance as a requirement for classes).

[38] 454 U.S. 263 (1981).

the United States Supreme Court rejected a public university's contention that the Establishment Clause of the First Amendment would preclude a registered student religious group from using a public university's campus facilities for worship or religious discussion. The Court held that once the university created a forum by making facilities generally available for use by student groups, it could not deny student religious groups the right to meet based on the content of the group's proposed speech. However, Justice Powell, writing for the majority, noted a qualification:

> [A] university's mission is education, and decisions of this Court have never denied a university's authority to impose reasonable regulations compatible with that mission upon the use of its campus and facilities. We have not held, for example, that a campus must make all of its facilities equally available to students and nonstudents alike, or that a university must grant free access to all of its grounds or buildings.[39]

As the Court in *Widmar* acknowledged, a public college or university campus, at least for its students, "possesses many of the characteristics of a public forum."[40] Yet, the campus of a public higher education institution is not a traditional public forum, like a street or a park. Consequently, the public institution may designate some areas of the campus as closed, even to students. Of course, the institution's restrictions must be reasonable in time, place, and manner to ensure students have access to other forums for expressive activity. As a side point, Justice Powell's comments suggest that universities may have greater ability to limit access of their facilities to nonstudents.

Smith v. Tarrant County College District[41] illustrates differences between closed and limited open forums at a public institution. In the closed forum of a classroom and in adjacent hallways, students could be prevented from leafleting to express their views because the protesting students failed to show how preventing leafleting in classes and adjacent hallways imposed any greater restriction on speech than was necessary to ensure the appropriate educational use of the facilities.[42] But when imposing leafleting restrictions on open spaces on the campus, a different judicial standard was imposed. Restrictions must support a compelling state interest and be narrowly tailored to achieve that interest in these contexts.

Student-Initiated Speakers and Protests

Restrictions regarding student protests on campus must also support a compelling state interest and be narrowly tailored to achieve that interest.

---

[39] *Id.* at 268, n.5.
[40] *Id.*
[41] 694 F.Supp.2d 610, (N.D. Tex. 2010).
[42] However, the college's prohibition on the symbolic wearing of empty holsters violated the First Amendment, as there was no evidence that the restriction was warranted by a reasonable forecast of substantial disruption. *Id.* at 618.

Understanding of this standard has been rigorously tested over the past few years as student protests have received a great deal of media attention. Many of the highlighted instances involve a controversial outside speaker invited on campus by a student group or organization. A campus policy prohibiting cosponsorship of student speech by an off-campus person or organization was ruled unconstitutionally overbroad. While the institution's policy was to preserve campus space for the use of students and faculty, the court reasoned the regulation was not narrowly tailored to achieve the intended purpose because its literal reading broadly prohibited any speech by students that involved an off-campus organization in almost any conceivable way, whether in planning, managing, or funding the activity.[43]

Outdoor areas of a public institution's campus are often regarded as limited open forums.[44] Decisions in this area of the law have not always been uniform, however, particularly regarding student protest on the campus.[45] Crafting regulations to govern student free speech in open areas of a public institution's campus requires sensitivity to judicial demands for content-neutral standards and careful, "narrow tailoring" of institutional policies.[46] For example, a policy requiring students to refrain from religious speech violated the constitutional rights of students protesting abortion because the prohibition was content-based and not narrowly tailored to serve a compelling state interest.[47]

To satisfy the narrow tailoring prong, the public institution must set explicit criteria for permit denials in limited open forums. For example, in *Rock for Life - UMBC v. Harbowski*,[48] an anti-abortion student group that proposed to exhibit a graphic display on campus was denied an opportunity to exhibit in a high student-traffic area because administrators were concerned students viewing the display would feel "emotionally harassed" by its graphic anti-abortion content. The group challenged institutional policy on facility use, claiming terms like "emotional harassment" in the policies were overbroad, content-based restrictions on free speech. A federal district court agreed, emphasizing that the institution's policy appeared to grant administrators unconstitutionally

---

[43] Smith v. Tarrant Cty. College Dist., 694 F.Supp.2d 610, 637 (N.D. Tex. 2010).

[44] *See* Gilles v. Farland, 281 Fed. App'x. 501, 511 (6th Cir. 2008) (finding that the open areas on a public university campus are limited public fora).

[45] *Compare* Univ. of Utah Students Against Apartheid v. Peterson, 649 F. Supp. 1200 (D. Utah 1986) (reasoning that student "shanties" erected to protest institutional investments in apartheid South Africa could not be removed from the campus lawns solely on the basis of administrative discretion to determine the institution's best interest), *with* Students Against Apartheid Coalition v. O'Neil, 838 F. 2d 735 (4th Cir. 1988) (holding student "shanties" could be restricted from an area of the campus which was a historic landmark because the institution's revised regulation was a content-neutral time, place and manner restriction and provided the student protestors with alternative areas of the campus for the conduct of the protest).

[46] *See, e.g.,* OSU Student Alliance v. Ray 699 F.3d 1053 (9th Cir. 2012) (questioning the validity of a university unwritten policy governing the distribution of off-campus materials where policy appeared, apparently in relation to this specific incident, out of the blue "like a bolt").

[47] Orin v. Barclay, 272 F.3d 1207, 1215 (9th Cir. 2001).

[48] 594 F. Supp. 2d 598 (D. Mass. 2009).

broad power to restrict the content of student speech.[49] While the institution might impose reasonable time, place, and manner restrictions on student free speech, the restrictions could not confine a student protest to a remote area of the campus.

Designating the entire campus as a "free speech zone" and restricting student speech to issues "intended to serve or benefit the entire university community" was regarded as unconstitutional in *Roberts v. Haragan.*[50] The federal district court reasoned that "to the extent the campus has park areas, sidewalks, streets, or other similar common areas, these areas are public forums, at least for the university's students, irrespective of whether the university has so designated them or not."[51] While the court acknowledged that the institution could designate limited open forums for students, it held the institution could not restrict those already in existence:

> [A]ny restriction of the content of student speech in these areas is subject to the strict scrutiny of the "compelling state interest" standard, and content-neutral restrictions are permissible only if they are reasonable time, place, and manner regulations that are narrowly tailored to serve a significant government interest and leave open ample alternative channels of communication.[52]

Yet, some institutions have effectively crafted regulations for limited open forums that identify outdoor "speech" zones on campus. For instance, in *ASU Students for Life v. Crow,*[53] outdoor zones on the university's campus could be used by recognized student organizations, but student groups were limited to a one-zone reservation per organization. Written policies stipulated that a student organization could invite the participation of an external group in an approved zone if the external group provided a certificate of insurance and paid a fee consistent with insurance indemnification and vendor status. The federal district court, in ruling on the constitutionality of the policies, found that the institution's outdoor zones were limited public forums. Specifically, the one-zone limit and the insurance and vendor payment requirements were sufficiently content-neutral and reasonable in light of the purposes of the forum, placing no more than an incidental burden on speech.[54]

---

[49] *See also* Coleman v. Gettysburg Coll., 335 F. Supp.2d 586 (M.D. Pa. 2004) ("[T]he Constitution precludes government from imposing limitations on expression based on viewpoint when the only injury alleged is personal affront."). *Id.* at 606.

[50] 346 F. Supp. 2d 853 (N.D. Tex. 2004).

[51] *Id.* at 861. *See also* Univ. of Cincinnati Chapter of Young Americans for Liberty v. Williams, 2012 WL 2160969 (S.D. Ohio June 12, 2012).

[52] *Roberts* at 862.

[53] 2008 U.S. Dist. LEXIS 18698 (D. Ariz. 2008), *affirmed in part*, 2009 U.S. App. LEXIS 27047 (9th Cir. 2009).

[54] *But see* Burbridge v. Sampson, 74 F. Supp. 2d 940, 950 (C.D. Cal. 1999) (granting injunctive relief because the policy implicated a content-based restriction and failed to demonstrate that its provisions were necessary and narrowly drawn to further a compelling interest).

Figure 2: Typical Types of Forums on Public Campuses

Non-public Forum	•Classrooms (including online class discussions) •Libraries •Laboratories •Residence Halls
Limited Public Forum	•Outdoor areas on a public campus (sometimes) •Campus cafeterias and student activity centers •Any area/room that could be closed, but is made available for student or public use
Traditional Public Forum	•Public sidewalk on the periphery of campus (for both public and private institutions) •Outdoor areas on a public campus (sometimes)

Disruptive Speech

Along with the place (or forum) of the speech, the nature of the speech can be considered. Importantly, an evaluation of the nature of the speech should not consider the content of the speech (unless it is in one of the five categories of unprotected speech described above), but rather the disruption the speech causes or may cause. The expansion of First Amendment free speech rights to public college and university students began with a controversy involving the application of a ban on wearing armbands at a public high school. The Supreme Court's decision in *Tinker v. Des Moines Independent Community School District*[55] involved a high school principal's decision to suspend students whose silent protest of the Vietnam War violated a recently developed policy prohibiting the wearing of such armbands. Although the students had been wearing the armbands for a part of the school day without incident, they were subject to short-term suspensions for refusal to remove the armbands once they were discovered. The Court found that the wearing of an armband to protest the Vietnam War was a constitutionally protected form of symbolic free speech and noted that no disturbance had occurred during the period in which the students were in school. The Court admonished the school administrator, emphasizing that a desire to avoid unpopular or controversial viewpoints would not justify punishing students for expressing their views.

In one of the most oft-quoted lines in the history of First Amendment jurisprudence, the majority opinion in *Tinker* observed, "it can hardly be argued that either students or teachers shed their constitutional rights to freedom of speech or expression at the schoolhouse gate."[56] Administrators may limit students' expressive conduct only if it "materially and substantially

---

[55] 393 U.S. 503 (1969).

[56] *Id.* at 506.

interferes with the requirements of appropriate discipline in the operation of the school," or it is foreseeable that the speech would cause this result.[57] Put another way, absent evidence of substantial disruption or material interference, the First Amendment protects a student's protest related to religious, political, or philosophical expression.

The Supreme Court addressed disruptive speech in higher education in *Healy v. James.*[58] The controversy in *Healy* focused on institutional recognition of a local chapter of Students for a Democratic Society (SDS). Students in the local SDS chapter disavowed affiliation with the national group that had a reputation for initiating protests that had resulted in violent disruption on college campuses. Although a student/faculty committee recommended recognition for the local chapter, the college president denied recognition out of concern over the student group's affiliation with the controversial national organization and disagreement with the national organization's philosophy.[59] The Court held that the denial of recognition restricted the student organization's ability to communicate by denying them access to meeting rooms, bulletin boards, the student newspaper, and other campus venues, and thus was a form of prior restraint of speech that would violate the First Amendment. The college's decision would have been constitutionally permissible only if officials could have shown that the group's activities were directed at inciting or producing "lawless action" that substantially disrupted or materially interfered with the institution's environment.[60]

Together, *Tinker* and *Healy* affirm that institutional officials may justify the suppression of student speech on the basis of material interference or substantial disruption in the operations of the institution. Institutional authorities, however, need not await an instance of substantial disruption or material interference before acting to protect health and safety. While "undifferentiated fear or apprehension of disturbance"[61] would not justify the suppression of free expression, the institution may establish a reasonable forecast of substantial disruption or material interference.

Demonstrating that there is a "reasonable forecast" is a burden the institution must shoulder. For example, in *Orin v. Barclay,*[62] community college officials allowed a demonstration to proceed for approximately four hours before campus security officers saw evidence of threatening behavior from an increasingly hostile crowd and called local police for support. On arrival, local police determined that the confrontation had escalated, observed that violence was imminent, and directed the protesters to disperse. When protesters refused to disperse, arrests were made. The federal appeals court determined

---

[57] *Id.* at 513. Note that some legal scholars read a second prong to the *Tinker* test – whether the speech "collides" with or "invades" the rights of others. Typically, in the educational setting, this would mean disrupting a student's ability to learn.

[58] 408 U.S. 169 (1972).

[59] *Id.* at 185-187.

[60] *Id.* at 189.

[61] *Tinker*, 393 U.S. at 508.

[62] 272 F.3d 1207 (9th Cir. 2001).

that the imminent threat of violent disruption justified the order to disperse, and the court held that there was no constitutional violation of free speech by law enforcement officials at the scene.[63]

On the other hand, a college will not satisfy this burden when its forecast of disruption is based on "undifferentiated apprehension of a disturbance."[64] In *Smith v. Tarrant County College District*, students challenged a policy that prohibited them from wearing empty holsters to class.[65] They had intended to wear empty holsters as part of a national statement on gun policy. The court found that the college's attempts to prevent students from wearing empty holsters did not satisfy the *Tinker* standard. In other words, speech—symbolic or uttered—that simply makes administrators uncomfortable cannot be restricted for that reason alone.

Similarly, disruptions must constitute a material interference and/or a substantial disruption, rather than just an inconvenience to administrators. In *Shamloo v. Mississippi State Board of Trustees*,[66] for instance, a federal court found that a college violated students' First Amendment rights when they were disciplined for failure to conform to university regulations that required advance scheduling of meetings or gatherings on campus. Here, the university failed to meet its burden under *Tinker*; the evidentiary basis for disruption was a university official's belief that the proximity of classrooms to the plaza in which the demonstrators rallied would have interfered with class activities.[67]

Issues concerning student speech rights in the context of electronic communications are growing. Like the cases involving on-campus speech, however, courts often turn to the *Tinker* test to assess the constitutional question. For instance, in *Murkowski v. University of Delaware*,[68] a student filed suit for being disciplined under the university's "disruptive conduct" policy for posting allegedly threatening and offensive comments on a website he created that was maintained through the public university's server. The website comments ranged from misogynistic fantasies involving rape to a "Relationship Advice Pamphlet" that advised punching a pregnant student in the stomach as a means to abort a fetus. A federal district court found that the student's postings were a sophomoric attempt at humor and shock, but held the comments were constitutionally protected free speech. Although the institution's administrators were motivated by genuine concern for the safety of students, the university could not substantiate that the postings on the site rose to the level of threatening speech, or caused material interference or substantial disruption in the

---

[63] *Id.* at 1216-1217.

[64] Smith v. Tarrant Cty. College Dist. 694 F.Supp.2d 610 (N.D. Tex. 2010).

[65] *Id., supra* note 37.

[66] 620 F.2d 516 (5th Cir. 1980).

[67] *Id.* at 522. *See also* Pro-Life Cougars v. Univ. of Houston, 259 F. Supp. 2d 575 (S.D. Texas 2003) (ruling that university policy offered no guidance on how to determine "potentially disruptive" and left too much discretion in the hands of a lower-level official to restrict rights of students).

[68] 575 F. Supp. 2d 571 (D. Del. 2008).

operations of the university.[69] Importantly, *Tinker* requires something more than the suspicions of individual school officials. The forecasted or actual disruption must be "material" and/or "substantial," not simply uncomfortable.

Civility Codes

Since the late 1980s, colleges and universities have initiated policies to regulate speech on campus in an effort to create an environment free from harassment based on race, ethnicity, gender, religion, national origin, age, and sexual orientation. These "civility codes" evolved out of a desire on the part of institutional officials to ensure a welcoming environment for a diverse range of students.

However, courts have expressed constitutional skepticism with respect to these codes. Many have been struck down because vague language could have a chilling effect on the exercise of student speech.[70] To be sure, courts are sympathetic to colleges' intentions to promote respect among their student bodies. But, noble goals alone will not ensure constitutionality. Moreover, the Constitution does not affirmatively require a university to adopt a civility code.[71]

Bair v. Shippensburg University[72] represents a good example of a code that did not pass constitutional muster because its restrictions were overly broad and, the court noted, could have a chilling effect on speech. Enjoining the institution from enforcing code provisions, the court noted that the discrimination policies had the effect of prohibiting protected forms of expression and "[s] imply utilizing buzzwords applicable to anti-discrimination legislation does not cure this deficiency."[73]

A federal court adopted similar reasoning in *College Republicans at San Francisco State University v. Reed*.[74] At issue were civility code sanctions against students participating in a campus antiterrorism rally who stomped on the flags of Hamas and Hezbola, with the word "Allah" written in Arabic on each flag. In rejecting any institutional sanction based on the university's requirement that students be civil to one another in the interests of good citizenship, a federal district court emphasized:

> The First Amendment difficulty with this kind of mandate should be obvious: the requirement "to be civil to one another" and the directive to eschew behaviors that are not consistent with "good citizenship" reasonably can be understood as prohibiting the kind

---

[69] *Id*. at 592-93.

[70] *See, e.g.*, Dambrot v. Cent. Mich. Univ., 55 F.3d 1177, 1182 (6th Cir. 1995); UMW Post, Inc. v. Bd. of Regents of Univ. of Wis., 774 F. Supp. 1163, 1180 (E.D. Wis. 1991); Doe v. Univ. of Mich., 721 F. Supp. 852, 867 (E.D. Mich. 1989).

[71] *See, e.g.*, College Republicans at San Francisco State v. Reed, 523 F.Supp.2d 1005 (N.D.Cal.2007).

[72] 280 F. Supp. 2d 357 (M.D. Pa. 2003).

[73] *Id. at* 371-72.

[74] *College Republicans, supra* note 64.

of communication that it is necessary to use to convey the full emotional power with which a speaker embraces her ideas or the intensity and richness of the feelings that attach her to her cause. Similarly, mandating civility could deprive speakers of the tools they most need to connect emotionally with their audience, to move their audience to share their passion.[75]

In granting the injunction to prevent the institution from applying the institutional policy, the court rejected the elements of the code that required civility, but affirmed as constitutional the university's policy prohibiting conduct that "threatened or endangered the health and safety of members of the community."[76]

In another case involving a civility code, *Roberts v. Haragan,*[77] a law student successfully challenged a university's speech code that prohibited "physical, verbal, written or electronically transmitted threats, insults, epithets, ridicule or personal attacks" that [a]re "sufficiently severe or pervasive to create an objectively hostile environment for that individual by interfering with or diminishing his or her ability to participate" in university programs and activities.[78] Balancing the speech code's restrictions on freedom of expression against the interests of the institution, a federal district court acknowledged that the code might be enforced in classrooms and similar closed academic venues,[79] but insisted that "application of the Speech Code to the public forum areas on campus would suppress substantially more than threats, 'fighting words,' or libelous statements that may be considered constitutionally unprotected speech, to include much speech that no matter how offensive, is not proscribed by the First Amendment."[80] The interests of the university must, at some point, give way to the First Amendment interests of the individual.[81] *Roberts* suggests that the constitutional strength of those policies weakens in proportion with the distance from more traditional educational settings (e.g., the classroom).[82]

In *McCauley v. University of the Virgin Islands,*[83] a student challenged a public university's code as vague and overbroad. The student had been charged with violations based on his attempts to intervene with the alleged victim of a sexual assault on behalf of a friend who was accused of the assault. Two provisions of the code were found to be unconstitutional. The portion of the code that permitted punishment of students for displaying any unauthorized

---

[75] *Id.* at 1019.

[76] *Id.*

[77] 346 F. Supp. 2d 853 (N.D. Tex. 2004).

[78] *Id.* at 867.

[79] But see DeJohn v. Temple Univ., 537 F.3d 301 (3d Cir 2008), in which a student prevailed on a claim that the university's policy on sexual harassment violated his free speech right, in the context of a classroom, to argue against a policy permitting women to serve in combat.

[80] *Id.* at 872.

[81] *Id* at 873. ("At some point, the University's interests must attenuate and the students' interests in having a true public forum open to their free-expression interests must predominate.").

[82] *Id.*

[83] 618 F.3d 232 (3rd Cir. 2010).

or offensive sign at sports events, concerts, and social-cultural events was overbroad because, the court found, it could be used to arbitrarily silence protected speech. Also deemed overbroad by the court was the prohibition banning speech that could cause emotional distress, since it could be used to punish any protected speech, without forewarning, based on the subjective reaction of the listener. Finally, the court found a provision prohibiting lewd, indecent, or obscene conduct was not overbroad. It could be interpreted to prohibit only speech that was unprotected by the First Amendment under applicable constitutional tests for obscenity.

Still, civility codes can survive constitutional scrutiny. For example, in *Esfeller v. O'Keefe*,[84] a student was charged with repeatedly harassing his former girlfriend through email and the social networking sites, MySpace and Facebook. He had also physically confronted her. The student was charged with conduct code violations that included extreme, outrageous, or persistent acts or communications that are intended or reasonably likely to harass, intimidate, harm, or humiliate another. The Fifth Circuit Court of Appeals rejected overbreadth and vagueness claims, unlike several cases noted above. Significantly, the code's qualifying language—requiring that the conduct be persistent, extreme, or outrageous, and reasonably likely to cause harassment or intimidation—allowed the court to conclude that the code was narrowly tailored.[85]

As noted earlier in the chapter, the pressure for college administrators to address offensive and hateful language on campus is great. However, administrators must understand the limits of the law and consider means other than suppressing protected speech to address campus climate.

Student Organizations

Recognition and funding of student organizations by public higher education institutions raises freedom of speech, freedom of association, and religious liberty issues. Withholding official recognition to a student organization has consistently been subject to constitutional challenge. Litigation has resulted when institutions have denied recognition to gay, lesbian, and bisexual organizations;[86] student organizations viewed as potentially disruptive to the educational environment;[87] or student religious organizations requesting access to campus facilities.[88]

---

[84] 2010 WL 3035144 (5th Cir. 2010).

[85] *See also* O'Neal v. Alamo Cmty. Coll. Dist. 2010 WL 376602 (W.D. Tex. 2010) (holding that an institution may proscribe "true threats," which are not constitutionally protected speech).

[86] *See* Gay Student Org. of the Univ. of N.H. v. Bonner, 376 F. Supp. 1088 (D.N.H. 1974); Gay Alliance of Students v. Mathews, 544 F.2d 162 (4th Cir. 1976); Gay Lib. v. Univ. of Mo., 588 F.2d 848 (8th Cir 1977), *cert. denied*, 434 U.S. 1080, *reh'g. denied*, 435 U.S. 981 (1978); Gay Student Servs. v. Texas A. & M. Univ., 737 F.2d 1317 (5th Cir. 1984), *cert. denied*, 471 U.S.1120 (1985); Gay & Lesbian Student Ass'n v. Gohn, 656 F. Supp. 1045 (W.D. Ark. 1987), *rev'd.*, 850 F.2d 361 (8th Cir. 1988).

[87] *See* Healy v. James, 408 U.S. 169 (1972).

[88] *See* Widmar v. Vincent, 454 U.S. 263 (1981).

Higher education institutions often assess student activity fees used to fund student access to athletic events, student health services, and campus events such as speakers and concerts. Typically, a portion of student activity fees is placed under the control of student government or a student/administrator committee to be allocated to promote an array of student organizations and activities fostering an enhanced educational environment on campus.

Two United States Supreme Court decisions have clarified student First Amendment rights based on challenges to institutional practices in allocating fees among recognized student organizations. In *Rosenberger v. Rector and Visitors of the University of Virginia,* [89] students sued the institution, alleging First Amendment violations for its refusal to approve payment for the cost of a religiously oriented student publication that had been developed by a recognized student organization. In *Rosenberger*, the Supreme Court concluded that a public university could not discriminate between viewpoints of student organizations, including those with religious viewpoints, in allocation of the financial resources available to recognized student organizations.

The Court rejected the institution's claim that the religious viewpoint espoused by the student organization justified the denial of funding. Having arranged to pay third-party outside contractors for the costs of a variety of publications prepared by recognized "contracted independent organizations," the university was prohibited from relying on funding guidelines that restricted financial support for student groups that promoted "a particular belief in or about a deity or an ultimate reality."[90] Recognizing that the public university had designated a limited open forum when it established its system for student organizations, the Court's majority concluded the university could not engage in viewpoint discrimination based on the views of the student groups it had recognized and chosen to subsidize. Under this reasoning, funding decisions must be made through a method that would "allocate the scarce resources on some acceptable neutral principle."[91]

Following *Rosenberger*, the evolution of controversies involving student freedom of speech moved to the question of whether a public university— through its student government association, and with the ratification of the university governing board—could compel students to pay a mandatory activity fee intended to fund recognized student organizations. Some students objected to the allocation of mandatory fees to student organizations that advocated viewpoints with which they disagreed. In *Regents of the University of Wisconsin v. Southworth*,[92] the United States Supreme Court gave prominence to the university's "important and substantial purposes"[93] in facilitating a wide range of student free speech. Aligning student speech to the mission of a public university, the Court majority emphasized that these institutions must be free

---

[89] 515 U.S. 819 (1995).

[90] *Id.* at 825.

[91] *Id.* at 835.

[92] 529 U.S. 217 (2000).

[93] *Id.* at 231.

to adopt policies designed to ensure that "students have the means to engage in dynamic discussions of philosophical, religious, scientific, social and political subjects in their extracurricular campus life outside the lecture hall."[94]

Returning to the reasoning in *Rosenberger,* the majority in *Southworth* imposed a standard of viewpoint neutrality on institutions that collect and allocate mandatory student fees in support of extracurricular student organizations. Given the range of organizations in such a forum, it is certainly probable that some students will find the views of some student organizations objectionable or offensive. Since the creation of such a forum is justified by the institution's objectives in facilitating the open exchange of ideas and enhancing education, the integrity of the institution's practice must be judged by the extent to which it adheres to the principle of neutrality in providing access and allocating funds to recognized student groups.

In *Southworth*, an issue related to whether student government could hold a campus referendum on whether to fund a particular student organization was remanded for further consideration by the lower court. The majority questioned whether appropriating funds to a particular student organization based on a decision of the majority was consistent with viewpoint neutrality. Reasoning that the "whole theory of viewpoint neutrality is that minority views are treated with the same respect as are majority views,"[95] the Court emphasized that majority rule is not viewpoint-neutral because all viewpoints are not treated the same. The Supreme Court remanded the case for a determination of whether the institution's student government had "unbridled discretion" to determine which student organization should receive funding.[96]

A federal appeals court issued what has become known as "Southworth II."[97] In this case, the federal appeals court reviewed institutional guidelines established to allocate student government funding in light of a dual requirement: The institution's allocation guidelines must meet a standard of viewpoint neutrality and, as a corollary to this test, the guidelines must prohibit unfettered discretion on the part of those institutional administrators who apply the guidelines. The appeals court reasoned:

> Just as speakers may self-censor their speech to obtain access to a physical forum, so too may students self-censor their activities and speech to avoid being denied access to the forum of money. Moreover, if the student government lacks specific and concrete standards to guide its funding decisions, it could use its unbridled discretion to discriminate on the basis of viewpoint. Yet that viewpoint discrimination would go unnoticed because without standards there is no way of proving that the decision was unconstitutionally motivated.[98]

---

[94] *Id.* at 233.

[95] *Id.* at 235.

[96] *Id.* at 236.

[97] 307 F.3d 566 (7th Cir. 2002).

[98] *Southworth* at 580.

In holding that the university's standards met the two tests of constitutionality, the court noted that the institution's policies required university officials and student government leaders to take an oath to uphold the principle of viewpoint neutrality and funding policies. Furthermore, the policies set forth clear criteria to guide the student government in allocating funds by restricting the degree of discretion available to officials in making allocations and requiring a clear and timely statement of the basis for funding.[99] The court reasoned that by adopting specific deadlines for funding decisions, institutional agents could not delay a decision until the recognized student organization decided to self-censor itself, or until the proposed activity was no longer viable. Furthermore, the use of an administrative appeals process would check the student government's discretion by requiring that funding decisions be transparent and supported by a reasonable rationale, thus thwarting "any attempt at closed-door stealth viewpoint discrimination."[100] One aspect of the review process was particularly noteworthy in ensuring viewpoint neutrality because it required institutional agencies allocating funds to compare awards. By comparing funding decisions, the court reasoned the institution can assess whether funding agencies, "while purporting to apply the Funding Standards in a viewpoint-neutral way, nonetheless treated similar [student groups] with varying viewpoints differently."[101]

The court did strike down two criteria, one putting limits on a minimum number of years as a recognized organization before it could receive funds and another that took a group's history of receiving funding into account in funding decisions. The court found that both criteria would discriminate against less-traditional organizations, and also might give advantage to student organizations that had benefited from institutional recognition and funding during the period in which the allocation system was in violation of federal constitutional standards.

Other federal courts have applied a similar standard requiring viewpoint neutrality. In *Amidon v. Student Association of SUNY Albany*,[102] a federal appeals court held that the student government association (SA) must use viewpoint-neutral objective criteria in determining the level of funding for recognized student organizations (RSOs), but reasoned that such a policy would not prohibit an institution from allocating scarce resources unevenly among RSOs:

> The SA may therefore consider the varying costs RSOs will face in communicating their messages and providing their services, such as the size of space needed or the costs of distributing programs

---

[99] *See also* Collegians for a Constructive Tomorrow-Madison v. Regents of Univ. of Wisconsin Sys., 820 F. Supp. 2d 932 (W.D. Wis. 2011) (holding that a funding criteria does not have to completely eliminate any chance a decision maker may not apply it fairly, so long as there are appropriate procedural safeguards to appeal decisions).

[100] *Southworth* at 588.

[101] *Id.*

[102] 508 F.3d 94 (2d Cir. 2007).

to attendees. If an RSO demands an amount of funding that does not genuinely reflect its costs and needs, the SA is free to provide less. But the university must ensure that the allocation decision is based upon an RSO's objective financial needs.[103]

Amidon also considered whether a student referendum could be used to advise on whether funding would be provided to a specific RSO. The court noted the university had created a limited open forum by recognizing student organizations and providing a funding mechanism to support them through the student government association. *Amidon* followed the logic in *Southworth* and reasoned that denial of recognition or funding would amount to denial of access to the forum. It further noted that even the use of an advisory referendum in the allocation of the fee was unconstitutional, as it compromised a decision-making process that must be viewpoint-neutral. The court clarified as follows:

> Consistent with public forum principles, our decision does not foreclose the use of advisory referenda that are reasonable in light of the forum's purpose and viewpoint neutral. For example, we see no impediment to using an advisory referendum (or, perhaps more aptly labeled, a survey) to ascertain how many students anticipate attending a specific event for which an RSO seeks funding as a means of assessing that RSO's prospective costs. The referendum at issue here, which asks simply whether an RSO should receive a certain amount of funding, plainly crosses the line and fails to provide the protection of viewpoint neutrality the Constitution requires.[104]

A better understanding of the viewpoint neutrality requirement could solve many disputes. For example, in 2019 the student government of Texas State University voted to ban a conservative student group from campus. Campus administrators quickly clarified that the student government had no authority to ban any official student organization from campus because of their viewpoint and that "Texas State supports the constitutional rights of all ... students, faculty, staff, and visitors."[105]

The recognition and funding of religiously affiliated student organizations has been a particular concern for public institutions in recent litigation. For example, in *Badger Catholic v. Walsh*,[106] the denial of funding for a religious speaker sponsored by a religious student organization was challenged. The Seventh Circuit Court of Appeals found constitutional the university's practice of reimbursing the expenses of religious speakers through a program equally available to secular speakers. In this case, because the university established

---

[103] *Id.* at 105.

[104] *Id.*

[105] Katherine Mangan, *Students' Ban of Conservative Group Prompts Outrage. But It's Unenforceable, University Says*, THE CHRONICLE OF HIGHER EDUCATION (Apr. 10, 2019), *available at* https://www.chronicle.com/article/Students-Ban-of/246097.

[106] 620 F.3d 775 (7th Cir. 2010).

a public forum, it could not exclude religious speakers. Reimbursement for a religious group's activities must be made on the same basis as reimbursement for other student groups.

In *Christian Legal Society v. Martinez*,[107] the United States Supreme Court considered the question of whether a public law school could condition official recognition and funding on a student group's agreement to open membership and leadership to all students. The law school had developed a nondiscrimination policy that required all recognized student organizations to unconditionally accept any student who wished to participate, become a member, or seek leadership positions. A law student religious group required a statement of faith that excluded anyone who engaged in unrepentant homosexual conduct or held beliefs different from those in the statement of faith. Because the student group's policy barred students based on religion and sexual orientation, the law school denied recognition to the group for failure to comply with the institution's "all comers" policy.

The Court's majority limited analysis to whether the law school's all-comers policy, as applied to the student religious group, violated the First Amendment. It ruled the policy to be a reasonable, viewpoint-neutral condition on access to the registered student organizations forum, emphasizing that the policy promoted educational opportunities beyond the classroom, complied with state law prohibiting discrimination, and avoided undue administrative interference with student groups. Justice Ginsburg, writing for the majority, noted the student religious group, despite being denied recognition under the policy, continued to host events on campus and used electronic means of communication accessible through the institution's servers and email. Thus, the institution provided adequate channels for the student group's communication to take place. The policy was found content-neutral in application; it applied to all recognized student organizations and did not single out the student religious group because of their point of view.

In dissent, Justice Samuel Alito argued the policy as written should be analyzed to determine if it actually targeted religious groups. He observed that the "adoption of a facially neutral policy for the purpose of suppressing the expression of a particular viewpoint is viewpoint discrimination"[108] and contended that the majority ignored strong evidence that the institution's policy was not viewpoint-neutral and merely a pretext for viewpoint discrimination (e.g., promoting sexually and religiously inclusive policies). Justice Alito disagreed with the majority's view that the restrictions placed on the student religious group by the policy were insubstantial and, instead, asserted that the group's alternatives to exercise speech were severely curtailed. He concluded a "forced inclusion" policy unduly burdened a student group's right to expressive association.[109]

---

[107] 561 U.S. 661 (2010).

[108] *Id.* at 3017.

[109] *Id.* at 3010, *quoting* Boy Scouts of Am. v. Dale, 530 U.S. 640, 648 (2000).

The *Martinez* decision, when taken together with other Supreme Court decisions involving student free speech and association rights in higher education, makes it clear that free speech issues remain prominent and subject to judicial scrutiny. Justice Alito's dissent signals that even those policies that may appear to be neutral may be vulnerable if used by an institution as a subterfuge to deny recognition to selected student groups. In fact, an institution's all-comers policy could be vulnerable if it results in "hostile takeovers" in which large numbers of students sign up to participate in a student group with whose precepts they fundamentally disagree.[110]

There are other viewpoints that can cause confusion for campus administrators. In *Gerlich v. Leath*,[113] the Eighth Circuit Court of Appeals found that Iowa State University engaged in viewpoint discrimination upon prohibiting an officially recognized student group to use ISU's trademarked symbols on the group's shirts. The student group, NORML (National Organization for the Reform of Marijuana Laws) ISU, had several of its trademark licensing designs denied by ISU because the designs included a cannabis leaf. NORML ISU followed all protocols for a recognized student group to request trademark licensing and was initially approved by the school. However, when word leaked through the press, Iowa politicians put pressure on ISU administrators to rescind the approval. ISU hastily passed another trademark licensing policy that would allow denial of NORML ISU's request. The court found that NORML ISU's First Amendment rights were violated because ISU administrators, having created a limited public forum through their trademark licensing program, discriminated against their speech on the basis of viewpoint. "The state engages in viewpoint discrimination when the rationale for its regulation of speech is 'the specific motivating ideology or the opinion or perspective of the speaker'"[111]. In this case, the administration of the trademark licensing program was not narrowly tailored to achieve a compelling state interest in order to justify the viewpoint discrimination.

Student Publications

Disputes centered on student publications implicate free speech and freedom of the press under the First Amendment. In addition, they involve a range of issues, including funding, censorship and distribution of student publications. The general rule applicable to student publications is that public colleges and universities may place restrictions on expression in student publications only if the restrictions are content-neutral and are not predicated on disagreement with the message of a particular publication.

---

[110] *Id.* at 2923.
[111] *Id.* at 705.

Funding

The United States Supreme Court addressed a public university's refusal to fund a student group's publication as noted previously in our discussion of *Rosenberger v. Rector & Visitors of the University of Virginia.*[112]

Other courts have addressed reductions or terminations in funding for student publications, finding them impermissible when based on the content of the publication. In *Stanley v. Magrath*,[113] state legislators attacked a controversial humor edition of a student newspaper, and state regents instituted a refund system allowing students to regain student fees allocated to the paper. When the editors of the paper argued that the regents' policy adversely affected the paper and was a direct result of the content of the humor edition, a federal appeals court agreed, reasoning that disagreement with the content of the paper's humor edition was a substantial and motivating factor in the funding change. The court concluded that "[a] public university may not constitutionally take adverse action against a student newspaper, such as withdrawing or reducing the paper's funding, because it disapproves of the content of the paper."[114] The court noted that enormous political pressure had been placed on the regents because of the controversial edition and emphasized that refund systems were not put into place on any of the other campuses in the state university system, a fact that suggested intent to punish the student newspaper for its humor edition.

Although courts confirm constitutional violations when institutional funding is withdrawn based on a student publication's content,[115] funding decisions regarding a campus newspaper may be justified when unrelated to First Amendment issues. For example, in *Olson v. State Board for Community Colleges*,[116] a state college instituted a new budget process requiring a line-item request, with which the editors of the student newspaper failed to comply. When the student senate offered the paper a significantly reduced budget allocation, the student editors filed suit, asserting that the reduced funding was a First Amendment violation. A state appeals court affirmed a trial court decision that the motivation for the funding reduction was the result of the paper's lack of cooperation with regard to the budget process, as well as an attempt to reasonably control the escalating costs relative to production of the newspaper. The appeals court held that there was substantial evidence on the record that the editorial content of the paper was not a motivating factor in the decision to reduce the paper's funding.

---

[112] 515 U.S. 819 (1995).

[113] 719 F.2d 279 (8th Cir. 1983).

[114] *Id.* at 282. *See also* Student Gov't Ass'n v. Bd. of Trustees of Univ. of Massachusetts, 868 F.2d 473 (1st Cir. 1989) (noting that once a state has created a forum, it cannot close that forum on the sole basis that it disagrees with the speech).

[115] *See, e.g.*, Joyner v. Whiting, 477 F.2d 456 (4th Cir. 1973) (finding that college is under no obligation to establish a paper, but if it does it may discontinue support only for reasons other than dissatisfaction with the editorial content).

[116] 759 P.2d 829 (Colo. Ct. App. 1988).

Censorship and Prior Review

Papish v. Board of Curators of the University of Missouri[117] is one of several decisions in which student editors were vindicated when institutional officials sought to punish them for an exercise of free speech reflected in the content of a student newspaper.[118] Similarly, bans on student publications have been regarded with suspicion by judges. One of the earliest cases involving a ban on distribution of a student-produced newspaper was *Channing Club v. Board of Regents*.[119] A federal district court found that the university had no substantial justification to ban the paper in that case —no university functions had been disrupted and no hostile remarks or threats of violence had been made. Noting that other publications, with similar language and content, were sold at the same campus location as the banned publication, the court reasoned the ban violated the First Amendment because "the State does not become privileged to ban a publication merely because it is edited and published by students."[120]

Student publications that receive financial support from the public institution and produced under agreement with, and oversight from, university personnel may be regarded as "sponsored" by the institution. An emerging issue is whether these sponsored publications may be subject to greater oversight and potential censorship based on the institution's legitimate educational objectives. The landmark K-12 student newspaper case, *Hazelwood Independent School District v. Kuhlmeier,* provides judicial guidance with respect to many of these cases.[121]

In *Hazelwood*, high school students filed suit after their principal removed two articles from the school-sponsored newspaper based on concern that the topics (teen pregnancy and parental divorce) were inappropriate for the age and maturity of some high school students, and might compromise privacy rights. The United States Supreme Court reasoned the high school's sponsored newspaper was a nonpublic forum and held that school administrators may exercise editorial control over the content of school-sponsored student newspapers, as long as their actions are based on legitimate pedagogical concerns.

Some courts reluctantly apply the *Hazelwood* analysis to student publications in the higher education setting, emphasizing that college students are less impressionable than secondary students and a college or university student newspaper is a limited open forum. In *Kincaid v. Gibson*,[122] the editor of the institution's sponsored student yearbook at a public university published a

---

[117] 410 U.S. 667 (1973).

[118] *See* Trujillo v. Love, 322 F. Supp. 1266 (D. Colo. 1971) (student editor reinstated after her removal for articles critical of the college president and campus police); Schiff v. Williams, 519 F.2d 257 (5th Cir. 1975) (president's decision to fire student editors for poor quality of work failed to substantiate any evidence and therefore violated students' freedom of speech); Thonen v. Jenkins, 491 F.2d 722 (4th Cir. 1975) (president sought to punish two student editors for using a "four-letter word" in an editorial critical of the institution's dormitory policies).

[119] 317 F. Supp. 688 (N.D. Tex. 1970).

[120] *Id.* at 8-9.

[121] 484 U.S. 260 (1988).

[122] 236 F.3d 342 (en banc) (6th Cir. 2001).

smaller-than-expected publication without the supervision of university officials. When the yearbook returned from the printer, the institutional administrator contended that the publication was of poor quality and was "inappropriate." These objections included criticism about the yearbook's purple cover, its "destinations unknown" theme, the lack of captions under many photos, and the inclusion of current events unrelated to the institution. Administrators decided to confiscate the yearbooks and withhold them to prevent distribution to the university community. The editor and another student sued, claiming a violation of their First Amendment rights.

A federal appeals court evaluated the policies and practices that applied to the publication of the yearbook at the institution, the nature and compatibility of the yearbook with expressive activity, and the context in which the yearbook was published. Several findings of fact were dispositive. First, the institution's express policy characterized the yearbook as a student expressive activity and placed editorial control of the yearbook in the hands of student editors, without mention of standards for quality control. Second, this "hands-off" policy had been the continuing practice of institutional administrators and a campus review board. Third, the yearbook was produced for students in the university community; thus, there could be no reason to suppress the yearbook on the grounds that it might not be suitable for the intended audience. The court reasoned that the actions of university officials reflected disagreement with the philosophic position taken by the editors of the yearbook in violation of rights to free speech and press under the First Amendment.

In another student press case, *Hosty v. Carter*,[123] three students at a public university sued after the dean of student affairs and services at the institution implemented a prior-review policy for the student newspaper once the newspaper started printing articles about university employees. Although the newspaper's policy was to have a faculty adviser read stories intended for publication at the request of the student editors, the adviser customarily gave advice but did not make content decisions. The dean changed this policy when she informed the newspaper's printing company that a school official was required to review and approve the newspaper's content before printing. The appeals court affirmed that the student newspaper operated in a limited public forum and was not subject to censorship when the institutional sponsor decided that the particular speech might be offensive or unsuitable for a particular audience.[124]

Several courts have acknowledged that even the commercial advertising space of a student newspaper falls within the sphere of an open public forum, particularly when student editors are directed by institutional officials to remove

---

[123] 325 F. 3d 945 (7th Cir 2003).

[124] 412 F.3d 731 (7th Cir. 2005) (holding that qualified immunity protected the dean from liability because the law on the issue was unsettled and the dean had no reason to know that her actions were unconstitutional).

previously approved advertisements,[125] or the institution's policy restricting advertisements varies with the viewpoint of the advertisement.[126] Yet, courts have split on the issue of whether prohibitions on alcohol advertisements in newspapers violate the First Amendment. In some instances, however, student newspapers have been restricted in placing certain advertisements that violate state laws.[127] In these cases, courts have applied the test used to assess restrictions placed on commercial speech.[128]

Courts have permitted student editorial control over content in papers, provided that institutional officials do not interfere.[129] For example, in *Sinn v. The Daily Nebraskan,*[130] a federal district court ascribed significant authority to student editorial control of advertising. The newspaper was operating under a policy that prohibited ads indicating the sexual preference of the advertiser. The federal appeals court concluded that the student editors of the newspaper retained substantial control of the publication and its advertising pages could not be construed to be a public forum. In affirming editorial discretion, the court concluded that the advertisers had no constitutional right that would compel the newspaper to open its columns to all who are willing to pay to publish their sexual orientation in a roommate advertisement.

Distribution

Controversies involving restrictions on literature distribution on campus often fail the narrow-tailoring requirements imposed by judges. A representative case addressing the requirement for narrow tailoring is *Justice for All v.*

---

[125] *See, e.g.,* Lueth v. St. Clair Cmty. Coll., 732 F. Supp. 1410 (E.D. Mich. 1990) (holding that a demand that a student editor refuse a commercial advertisement for a nude dancing club violated the requirement for narrowly tailored regulations designed to achieve a compelling state interest).

[126] *See* Portland Women's Health Ctr. v. Portland Cmty. Coll., 1981 U.S. Dist. LEXIS 17072 (D. Or. 1981) (prohibiting institutional publishers from making selective exclusions from the advertising section based solely on the content of an advertisement promoting a women's health center); Rutgers 1000 Alumni Council v. Rutgers, The State Univ. of N.J., 803 A.2d 679 (N.J. Super. Ct. 2002) (ruling that an alumni magazine's rejection of an advertisement opposing intercollegiate sports because it was "issue-oriented" or "advocacy" was not consistent with previous instances of the publication having accepted such ads).

[127] *Compare* Educ. Media Co. at Va. Tech. v. Swecker, 602 F.3d 583 (4th Cir. 2010) (upholding government ban on alcohol advertisement in student papers as supporting a compelling interest and being narrowly tailored) *with* The Pitt News v. Pappert, 379 F.3d 96 (3d Cir. 2004) (applying the same test as in *Swecker* but reaching an opposite result).

[128] *Id.* That test asks the following: (1) Is the commercial speech protected?; (2) Is the government-asserted interest substantial?; and (3) Are the means narrowly tailored? Central Hudson Gas & Electric Corp. v. Public Service Commission of New York, 447 U.S. 557, 566, 100 S.Ct. 2343, 65 L.Ed.2d 341 (1980).

[129] *See, e.g.,* Miss. Gay Alliance v. Goudelock, 536 F.2d 1073 (5th Cir. 1976), *cert. denied,* 430 U.S. 982 (1978), in which the Fifth Circuit concluded that it could not intervene in an editorial decision because there was no evidence of state action, given the lack of administrative or faculty participation in the decision to reject an advertisement.

[130] 829 F.2d 662 (8th Cir. 1987).

Faulkner.[131] During a photographic exhibit on the main plaza of the public university, a student anti-abortion group attempted to hand out leaflets that read, "Life is Beautiful – Choose Life." University officials attempted to stop the distribution and the student group filed suit to challenge the university's restriction of literature distribution, which required that all printed materials distributed on campus bear the name of a university-affiliated person or organization responsible for their distribution. The student group contended that the policy was an unconstitutional restriction on free speech in a designated public forum, while the university argued that the policy was a reasonable, viewpoint-neutral regulation of speech within a limited public forum. The Fifth Circuit found the institution's policy invalid under the First Amendment.

The federal appeals court reasoned that the university had created a designated public forum and, though it was "inevitable" that some sacrifice of anonymity would be required of anyone seeking to distribute materials in the forum, it concluded that the "requirement that speakers identify themselves to every person who receives their message . . . sacrifices far more anonymity than is necessary to effectively preserve the campus forum for its intended beneficiaries."[132] Finding that the institution's policy was not narrowly tailored to realize a significant government interest, the court ruled that it was not valid under the First Amendment.

A California community college's speech code regulating materials was challenged in *Burbridge v. Sampson.*[133] The college's policy held that posting or distributing materials required obtaining prior approval from the president or a designee. Officials suggested the policy was intended to promote an educational rather than commercial environment, preventing commercial exploitation, fraud, or harassment of students and employees. A federal district court reasoned that the policy was content-based because a designated college official must read the content and approve its posting or distribution; the court insisted the policy must serve a compelling government interest and be narrowly tailored to achieve that interest. The court concluded that while the college's stated interests may be substantial or even compelling, its argument did not establish how the content-based restriction on speech furthered these interests or how the regulations were narrowly tailored to achieve them, thus invalidating the policy. Prior restraint policies, as the one in *Burbridge*, will attract particular scrutiny from courts.[134]

An unwritten distribution policy regarding student group publications did not pass constitutional scrutiny when one case reached a federal court of

---

[131] 410 F.3d 760 (5th Cir. 2005).

[132] *Id*. at 771-772. *See also* Bowman v. White, 444 F.3d 967 (8th Cir. 2006).

[133] 74 F. Supp. 2d 940 (C.D. Cal. 1999).

[134] Khademi v. S. Orange Cnty. Cmty. Coll. Dist., 194 F. Supp. 2d 1011, 1023 (C.D. Cal. 2002) ("Although prior restraints are not unconstitutional per se, the Supreme Court has repeatedly stated that any system of prior restraint bears a heavy presumption against its constitutional validity.") (internal quotations and citations omitted).

appeals. In *OSU Students Alliance v. Ray,*[135] a group of students who operated a newspaper filed suit against the public university and administrators in their official and individual capacities, arguing that their First Amendment rights had been violated when the university removed the plastic bins in which they distributed the paper. The university had removed the group's newspaper bins pursuant to an unwritten policy regulating the location of distribution bins for off-campus papers, purportedly in an effort to keep the campus clean and to prevent interference with maintenance crews or ADA requirements.

The court of appeals ruled in favor of the students, finding several of the university's actions problematic. To begin with, enforcement of the policy was *ad hoc*, leaving too much discretion to officials. In this particular case, it found the enforcement was unannounced and came about like a "bolt out of the blue" aimed in particular at the students' paper.[136] To be sure, the university's failure to codify the policy was not fatal; the court would have tolerated an unwritten policy that was evenly applied.[137] Yet, on these facts, the administration appeared to selectively direct enforcement of the policy at this group.

Practicums and Internships

Practicums and internships are at the core of many higher education programs. For instance, most teacher training programs require that pre-service teachers commit to some time in a classroom before receiving a diploma or state certification. Similarly, medical programs for nurses and doctors require pre-profession practicums as a condition of their diploma. These settings raise interesting legal questions related to the First Amendment rights of students when a public university attempts to regulate their speech made in such contexts. Indeed, students may be part of a university program, but fulfilling the program requirements "off-campus." Under these circumstances, what constitutional rules apply?

A recent case decided by the Sixth Circuit Court of Appeals addresses how a school's honor code may play an important role in these claims. In *Yoder v. University of Louisville,* a nursing student was dismissed from her program because of disparaging comments regarding patients that she made on social media. The student claimed this violated her First Amendment rights.[138] At the outset, it should be noted that comments were made as part of a course observation (and not a practicum). However, the case may be instructive for those cases that directly stem from an internship, *per se,* because fact patterns would be quite similar.

The federal district court held and the Circuit Court of Appeals affirmed that the student did not have First Amendment protection. Importantly, the student, as a condition of her becoming part of the program, signed a confidentiality agreement and honor code that prohibited her from disseminating

---

[135] OSU Student Alliance v. Ray, 699 F.3d 1053 (9th Cir. 2012).
[136] *Id.* at 1063.
[137] *Id.* at 1063-64.
[138] 526 Fed. Appx. 537 (6th Cir. 2013).

patient information. Because of this agreement, the student could not raise a First Amendment claim arising out of her failure to abide by that code. To the extent the First Amendment was implicated by the code or confidentiality agreement, the court found that the limits imposed by the school were based on "legitimate pedagogical concern."[139]

Courts have also decided internship cases by analyzing the case under the jurisprudence governing public employees.[140] The case of *Snyder v. Millersville* is representative.[141] In *Snyder*, a student completing her "practice teaching" posted negative comments about her students and staff at her placement school. She was removed from the placement and, consequently, did not complete the program and obtain the necessary teaching credential. In this case, the court applied the First Amendment jurisprudence related to public employee free speech rights. Under this analysis, the court found that the speech was not a matter of public concern, as required under the applicable test, and determined the speech was not protected.[142]

Summary

The scope of First Amendment rights applied to students in public higher education institutions is broad, and the exceptions to free speech and association are narrowly restricted. Decisions of state and federal courts reflect a clear protocol in evaluating First Amendment free speech claims by students. Once a controversy arises, the initial judicial inquiry will address whether the particular speech or conduct is constitutionally protected within the sphere of the First Amendment. If the speech falls within the range of First Amendment protection, a judge will consider both the context and content of the speech. Assessing the context of the speech means a determination must be made as to the nature of the forum created by the institution. In assessing the content, the reviewing court must balance the interests of the student or students in exercising freedom of speech against the interests of the institution in restricting or prohibiting that speech.

The nature of the forum may influence the extent to which an institution must extend free speech protections. If the forum is exclusively dedicated to

---

[139] *Id.* at *7. *But cf.* Tatro v. Univ. of Minn., 816 N.W.2d 509 (Minn. 2012) (cautioning that schools should not treat student agreement to codes of conduct related to professional behavior as a waiver of student First Amendment rights).

[140] Broadly speaking, a number of tests are available to courts in assessing First Amendment claims by public employees. Under the *Pickering* test, courts ask whether the speech was a matter of public concern and, if so, they then balance the individual's rights against the needs of the government. *Pickering v. Bd. of Educ.*, 391 U.S. 563 (1968). Under, *Garcetti*, courts must determine if the speech was made "pursuant to official duties." If so, then it is not protected speech and they do not even apply the *Pickering* test. *Garcetti v. Ceballos*, 547 U.S. 410 (2006).

[141] Snyder v. Millersville Univ., 2008 WL 5093140 (E.D. Pa. Dec. 3, 2008).

[142] *See also* Miller v. Houston County Bd. of Educ., 2008 WL 696874 (M.D. Ala. Mar. 13, 2008) (upholding dismissal from preparation program where student used her substitute teaching employment in fulfillment of her internship requirements; therefore, her speech was made pursuant to "official duties" and not protected).

the institution's specific educational objectives and regarded as nonpublic, then the institution may promulgate reasonable rules that restrict speech in order to preserve the setting for its primary educational purpose. If the forum is open, either by the institution's express designation or as a function of custom and practice, then the institution must justify its regulations restricting the forum under a significantly more demanding constitutional test. Institutions can ameliorate the impact of restrictions to a particular forum if they ensure the availability of alternative venues for expression.

If a student's speech occurs within an open forum, a judge will weigh the extent to which the institution's regulation of that speech is content-neutral. Judges are particularly concerned with content-based policies or practices that serve as a pretext to suppress speech because of disagreement with the speaker's viewpoint. Consequently, institutional regulations should emphasize restrictions that are content-neutral and focus on reasonable time, place, and manner restrictions on student speech.

Some content-based restrictions on free speech are of sufficient importance that the regulation will outweigh the free speech right, provided that the institution has narrowly tailored and carefully applied the regulation to achieve that interest. Public colleges and universities have substantial interests in promoting an educational environment, providing safety and security, and avoiding substantial disruption or material interference with their primary educational missions. They also have important interests in assuring the free flow of pedestrian traffic, avoiding interference with access to facilities, maintaining the aesthetic character of the campus, ensuring the effective operation of essential services, and preserving an educational rather than a commercial atmosphere.

In addition, regulations must be narrowly tailored to avoid a challenge that they are overbroad or vague. If a regulation might serve a legitimate purpose in proscribing unprotected speech, it could be applied in such a way as to circumscribe a substantial amount of protected expression, resulting in the invalidation of the entire policy. Narrowly tailoring also requires that institutions avoid granting unbridled authority to administrators charged with making decisions about whether to approve or disapprove expressive activities.

Our higher education institutions occupy a special place in our society. Courts recognize this point and, accordingly, they frequently defer to the decision-making authority of academics within the realm of the academy's educational expertise. However, that judicial deference will fade when the fundamental principles of free speech—a paramount concern of our constitutional democracy—are the focus of a controversy. Administrators in public colleges and universities must show heightened sensitivity to the importance of student free speech on campus, while honoring the fundamental mission of the institution.

Discussion Questions

1. The nature of the forum (e.g., closed, limited, etc.) plays a significant role in many of these cases. Take two or three cases to discuss how the courts applied a particular forum analysis to reach their respective conclusions.

2. Find a news report involving the discipline of a university student for speech. Be sure that the case has not yet been tried. Use the legal principles and cases set forth above to determine if you think the university's actions complied with the Constitution.

3. Find a policy from a university or college that attempts to govern the speech of its students. Using the cases and principles from this chapter, determine if it passes constitutional muster.

4. Assume you are an administrator at a public university. You want to develop a policy that regulates solicitation at student dormitories. What constitutional principles are relevant for your consideration?

5. Say that the U.S. Supreme Court decides to hear a case concerning the legality of hate speech on campus. Would you recommend that the Supreme Court change the existing legal standards on hate speech? Why or why not? What are the potential negative implications of your choice?

14 Student Residential Privacy Rights

Richard Fossey, J.D., Ed.D.
University of Louisiana at Lafayette

Do students who reside in college dormitories enjoy Fourth Amendment protections against unreasonable searches in their dorm rooms, protections that put constitutional constraints on university officials and law enforcement officers who conduct dormitory-room searches? The short answer is yes. Students who reside in college dormitories do not have a diminished expectation of privacy; they enjoy the same constitutional protections against unreasonable searches as students who reside in private dwellings.[1] As one court put it, university students are adults, and dorm rooms are homes. "To suggest that a student who lives off campus in a boarding house is protected but that one who occupies a dormitory room waives his constitutional liberties is at war with reason, logic, and law."[2]

Nevertheless, case law reveals the constitutionality of a dormitory-room search may depend on the answer to a variety of questions. For example, if college officials search a dormitory room independently of police, do their institution's regulations or the language in a student housing contract grant them this authority? What was the motivation of the searchers? Did they enter a student's room in furtherance of their institution's legitimate interest in preserving health, safety, and an educational atmosphere, or were they pursuing a criminal investigation? Were college officials acting independently of law enforcement authorities when they conducted their search, or were they acting in concert with them? Did the affected student consent to the search? If so, was the consent voluntary or coerced?

The Fourth Amendment's Prohibition against Unreasonable Searches: An Introduction

The Fourth Amendment to the United States Constitution states: "The right of the people to be secure in their persons, houses, papers, and effects, against unreasonable searches and seizures shall not be violated; and no War-

---

[1] Piazolla v. Watkins, 442 F.2d 284, 289 (5th Cir. 1971).
[2] People v. Cohen, 292 N.Y.S.2d 706, 713 (N.Y. Dist. Ct. 1968).

rants shall issue but upon probable cause, supported by Oath or affirmation, and particularly describing the place to be searched, and the persons or things to be seized."[3] Under the Fourth Amendment, the police may not search homes without a warrant issued by a magistrate or judge, who must issue it only if law enforcement authorities can show they have a high level of suspicion the search will turn up specific evidence of criminal wrongdoing. Under the exclusionary rule articulated by the Supreme Court, evidence obtained by police in violation of an individual's Fourth Amendment rights must be excluded from admission in that person's criminal trial.[4]

Courts have recognized some exceptions to the warrant requirement. For example, the police are not required to obtain a warrant if they are in a place where they lawfully have the right to be and seize evidence that is in "plain view."[5] Likewise, law enforcement authorities can conduct searches at the nation's international borders without a warrant.[6] Police are not required to obtain a warrant if an individual with lawful authority over the property being searched voluntarily consents to a warrantless search.[7] Likewise, the police are not required to obtain a warrant in certain emergency situations in which it would not be practical to obtain a warrant prior to conducting a search.[8]

The *Chrisman* Decision: The Supreme Court Upholds Dormitory Search by Campus Police

Although the U.S. Supreme Court has interpreted the Fourth Amendment on numerous occasions, the Court has only interpreted the Fourth Amendment once in a case involving a college student. In *State of Washington v. Chrisman*, the Supreme Court upheld a dormitory room search conducted by a Washington State University police officer after the officer arrested Carl Overdahl, an underage student, for illegal possession of alcohol.[9] The officer accompanied Overdahl—then under arrest—to his dormitory room so Overdahl could obtain his identification. Overdahl's roommate, Neil Chrisman, was in the room. While standing in the doorway of the students' room, the officer noticed a pipe and what appeared to be marijuana seeds lying "in plain view" on a desk. The officer entered the room and, after determining that the seeds were marijuana seeds, he informed both students of their *Miranda* rights.

The officer then called a second officer, and Overdahl and Chrisman were told that it would be necessary to search their dormitory room. The officers told the two students they had "an absolute right" to insist the officers obtain a search warrant before conducting the search, but that they could waive that

---

[3]   U.S. Const. amend. IV.

[4]   Mapp v. Ohio, 367 U.S. 643 (1961).

[5]   State of Washington v. Chrisman, 455 U.S. 1, 7 (1982).

[6]   United States v. Montoya de Hernandez, 473 U.S. 531, 537 (1985).

[7]   Godette v. Stanley, 490 F. Supp. 2d 72 (D. Mass. 2007).

[8]   Brigham City v. Stuart, 547 U.S. 398 (2006).

[9]   State of Washington v. Chrisman, 455 U.S. 1, 7 (1982).

right.[10] Overdahl and Chrisman conferred, and then both gave consent to the search, signing a written search consent form.

The officers' search turned up more marijuana and a quantity of LSD. Chrisman was charged with possession of more than 40 grams of marijuana and possession of LSD, both felonies under Washington law. He was convicted of both offenses, but the Washington Supreme Court reversed the decision, holding that the warrantless search of Chrisman's dormitory room violated his Fourth Amendment rights.

The State of Washington appealed the Washington Supreme Court's opinion to the U.S. Supreme Court. The Court, applying well-established precedents, reversed the Washington Supreme Court's decision, ruling that the police officers had no constitutional obligation to obtain a warrant before entering Chrisman's dormitory room. The first officer had the right to accompany Overdahl, who was under arrest, to the dormitory room that Overdahl and Chrisman shared and to remain with Overdahl while he obtained his identification. Moreover, the marijuana the first officer observed from the dormitory-room doorway was in "plain view."

Impact of College Policies and Housing Contracts on Lawfulness of Dormitory Searches

In addition to the Supreme Court's *Chrisman* decision, several lower courts have ruled on the legality of dormitory-room searches under the Fourth Amendment. In many of these cases, university student housing policies or student housing contracts have been important factors in the courts' decisions.

In *State v. Hunter*,[11] a student at Utah State University was prosecuted for theft after university officials searched his dormitory room and discovered a stolen university sign and university banner. The university's housing director conducted the search in an effort to determine the source of repeated incidents of vandalism and disruption in a dormitory inhabited mostly by varsity athletes. A football coach, custodian, and university police officer accompanied the housing director during the search.

After waiving his *Miranda* rights and confessing to the theft, Hunter was charged with a criminal misdemeanor. In the criminal proceedings, Hunter sought to suppress his confession and the evidence taken from his dormitory room on the grounds that university officials searched his room without a warrant in violation of the Fourth Amendment. A trial court agreed with Hunter and suppressed both Hunter's confession and the stolen sign and banner.

On appeal, a Utah appellate court reversed the trial court, ruling that Hunter's confession and the seized sign and banner could be admitted into evidence. The court noted that Hunter had signed a housing contract in which the university reserved "the right to enter and inspect residence hall rooms

---

[10] *Id.* at 4.
[11] 831 P.2d 1033 (Utah Ct. App. 1992).

at any time."[12] Searches would be conducted, the contract stated, whenever necessary "to protect and maintain the property of the University, the health and safety of its students, or whenever necessary to aid the basic responsibility of the University regarding discipline and the maintenance of an educational atmosphere."[13]

In the appellate court's view, the university had a responsibility to maintain "a safe and proper educational environment" and that the search of Hunter's room was reasonable; therefore, the search of Hunter's residence hall room did not violate the Fourth Amendment.[14] In ruling against Hunter, the court emphasized that university officials had not entered Hunter's room at the behest of the police or as part of a joint criminal investigation. Although a university police officer participated in the search, the court concluded his presence was solely "to provide assistance in the event that [the housing director] confronted problems he was not able to handle on his own."[15] In the court's view, the search did not circumvent the Fourth Amendment's restrictions on police actions.

Hunter indicates public university officials may conduct warrantless searches of students' dormitory rooms without a warrant if university policies or housing contracts give the university the right to inspect student rooms, and searches are conducted pursuant to the university's responsibility to maintain a safe and orderly educational environment. On the other hand, university officials clearly violate the Fourth Amendment if they search student rooms without warrants for the purpose of assisting the police to pursue a criminal investigation.

Piazzola v. Watkins,[16] an important Fifth Circuit decision, illustrates this point. Acting on information provided by two student informers, university officials and state law enforcement officers searched six or seven dormitory rooms at Troy State University, including rooms occupied by Frank Piazzola and Terrance Marinshaw. The searchers found marijuana. Piazzola and Marinshaw were both convicted of drug possession and remanded to an Alabama prison. After appeals in the Alabama state courts proved fruitless, the prisoners applied for a writ of habeas corpus in federal court. A federal trial judge granted habeas corpus and ordered the students to be released from prison.

On appeal, the Fifth Circuit affirmed. The Fifth Circuit acknowledged that Troy State University enjoyed "broad supervisory powers" to adopt a regulation allowing university officials to inspect student dormitory rooms so long as the regulation "is reasonably construed and limited in its application to further the University's function as an educational institution."[17] Nevertheless, the Fifth Circuit emphasized, "[A] student who occupies a college dormitory

---

[12] *Id.* at 1037.

[13] *Id.*

[14] *Id.* at 1036.

[15] *Id.* at 1038.

[16] 442 F.2d 284 (5th Cir. 1971).

[17] *Id.* at 289.

room enjoys the protection of the Fourth Amendment."[18] Therefore, universities cannot construe a housing regulation to mean that students living in dormitories have consented to warrantless searches of their dormitory rooms by the police. "Otherwise," the court said, "the regulation itself would constitute an unconstitutional attempt to require a student to waive his protection from unreasonable searches and seizures as a condition to his occupancy of a college dormitory room. Clearly the university had no authority to consent to or join in a police search for evidence of crime."[19]

In short, the Fifth Circuit concluded law enforcement officers and university officials violated the Fourth Amendment when they searched students' dormitory rooms in a quest to find drugs without first having obtained warrants. The Fifth Circuit upheld the trial court's decision granting habeas corpus for both imprisoned former university students, thus springing the young men from prison. *Piazzola* is a stern reminder that colleges and universities should not assume broad language in their student housing policies justifies dormitory-room searches by college officials acting in concert with law enforcement officers.

This point was also emphasized in *Devers v. Southern University*,[20] a Louisiana case, wherein university officials expelled student Patrick Devers after they conducted a "dormitory sweep" that turned up twelve bags of marijuana in Devers's dormitory room. The university justified its search through language in its student housing policy, which stated "[t]he university reserves all rights in connection with assignments of rooms, inspection of rooms with police, and termination of room occupancy."[21]

Devers sued, arguing the university's housing policy was unconstitutional on its face, and a trial court agreed. On appeal, the university argued it had an interest in keeping drugs and weapons out of its dormitories that justified its search policy, citing *State v. Hunter* to support its position.

A Louisiana appellate court rejected the university's argument and ruled its broad housing policy was unconstitutional. The Louisiana court distinguished the case before it from *State v. Hunter*, pointing out that Utah State University's housing policy authorized authorities to inspect dormitory rooms for health and safety reasons and to maintain discipline. Southern University's policy was much broader and allowed university officials and police officers to search students' dormitory rooms for any reason.

Officials' Motivation for Searching a Dorm Room May Determine the Search's Constitutionality

A critical question in many of the dormitory-search cases concerns the motivation of university officials when they conduct a search. Did they enter the dormitory room pursuant to the institution's legitimate interest in maintain-

---

[18] *Id.*

[19] *Id.* at 289-290.

[20] 712 So.2d 1991 (La. Ct. App. 1998).

[21] *Id.* at 204.

ing health and safety or the institution's educational atmosphere, or were they aiding the police in a criminal investigation?

This distinction clearly is illustrated in *State v. Kappes*,[22] one of the few dormitory-search cases involving a female student. In that case, two student resident advisors used a master key to conduct a routine inspection of a dormitory room occupied by Gretchen Kappes, a freshman at Northern Arizona University. They discovered a pipe and two marijuana butts in plain sight on a desk in the room. One of the student resident advisors called her supervisor, and the supervisor called the campus security office.

Three law enforcement officers arrived, but two left to get an administrative search authorization from the dean of students. Before the authorization was obtained, Kappes returned to her room, where an officer advised her of her Miranda rights and put her under arrest. Kappes became upset, pulled a bag of marijuana out of a nearby closet and gave it to the arresting officer. She was later convicted of possession of marijuana.

Kappes appealed her conviction on the grounds the search of her dormitory room violated the Fourth Amendment, but an Arizona appellate court upheld the legality of the police officers' actions. The court acknowledged other courts had held that when a police officer initiates a criminal investigation and enters a student's dormitory room without a warrant, evidence from the search must be excluded. Likewise, if a school official enters a student's room at the request of or in cooperation with the police and act without a warrant, the evidence obtained must be suppressed. "But," the court reasoned, "where the entry is made by a student advisor conducting a routine dormitory inspection announced in advance, we cannot say that the intrusion is the result of government action which will invoke the fourth amendment, and consequently, the exclusionary rule." [23]

The court pointed out the purpose of the room inspection was not to collect evidence for criminal proceedings against Kappes, but to make sure dormitory rooms were being used in accordance with university regulations. In fact, in the court's view, the student advisors were not governmental actors but private persons who were lawfully in Kappes's room and, therefore, not constrained by the Fourth Amendment. The student advisors were justified in allowing law enforcement officers to enter the room, where they found the marijuana butts in plain view.

Even if the student resident advisors were considered to be governmental actors, the court continued, their entry into Kappes's room was reasonable. "The right of privacy protected by the fourth amendment does not include freedom from reasonable inspection of a school-operated dormitory room by school officials," the court articulated. Indeed, the court continued, "It is entirely appropriate that [the university] routinely inspect its dormitory rooms

---

[22] 550 P.2d 121 (Ariz. Ct. App. 1976).

[23] *Id.* at 124.

for orderliness and safety, and its authority to do this does not compromise a student's right to the protection of the fourth amendment."[24]

Privacy Rights of Nonstudents in Dormitory Rooms

Although it is now well established that college students have privacy rights in their dormitory rooms that are protected by the Fourth Amendment, non-students do not have such rights. This principle is illustrated by a 2014 decision by the Massachusetts Supreme Judicial Court.

In *Commonwealth v. Copney*,[25] Massachusetts' highest court ruled that a nonstudent has no privacy expectation in a dormitory room. In that case, Brittany Smith, a Harvard student, allowed Jabrai Jordan Copney, a non-student, to reside in Smith's Harvard dorm room over a period of several months. In May 2009, Copney was involved in a robbery that went awry, and Copney allegedly shot and killed a drug dealer, who was the intended victim of the robbery, as the dealer attempted to flee. Spectators saw three men fleeing from the site where the attempted robbery occurred, including one man wearing a black and orange varsity jacket.

Police quickly connected Smith to the robbery because the drug dealer's cell phone showed he had called Smith's number shortly before the robbery. Fearing Smith might be in danger (so they said), state and local police officers entered Smith's dorm room without a warrant and found a black and orange varsity jacket. The police posted a guard at Smith's room and returned with a warrant authorizing them to seize the jacket. At Copney's murder trial, the black and orange jacket was admitted into evidence over Copney's objection. Copney was convicted of murder and he appealed, arguing that he had a privacy interest in Smith's dorm room and that police had entered it without a warrant in violation of the Fourth Amendment.

Massachusetts' highest court rejected Copney's arguments and affirmed his conviction. Smith's right to allow Copney to reside in Smith's dorm room depended upon getting Harvard's permission, which she did not obtain. "Where the owner of the premises, Harvard, expressly forbade the type of use and occupancy involved, [Copney] may not claim that his subjective expectation of privacy was objectively reasonable."[26]

Moreover, Copney's argument failed on two additional grounds. Even if Copney had an expectation of privacy over Smith's dorm room, he abandoned that right when he fled Massachusetts for New York after the robbery. "[Copney's] departure from Massachusetts was abrupt," the court noted, "and he manifested no intent to return to Massachusetts."[27] In addition, the court

---

[24] *Id.*

[25] 11 N.E.3d 77 (Mass. 2014). The discussion of *Copney* previously appeared as an online essay in *Teachers College Record*. Richard Fossey, Commonwealth v. Copney: *Does a murder suspect have a constitutional right to privacy in his Harvard girlfriend's dormitory room*, TEACHERS COLL. REC., ID Number 17797 (2015), *tcrecord.org*.

[26] *Id.* at 82.

[27] *Id.*

ruled the warrantless entry into Smith's room was justified under the "emergency aid" exception because police reasonably may have believed that Smith could be in danger.

A University's "Special Needs" May Justify a Warrantless Search

In addition to the authority to search that comes from university regulations or student-housing contracts, a university may justify a dormitory search based on "special needs" that do not pertain to law enforcement. *United States v. Heckenkamp*,[28] a Ninth Circuit opinion, suggests as much, although the main focus in that case pertained to a remote search of a student's computer by a university official, not a dormitory search.

In *Heckenkamp*, Jeffrey Savoy, a computer network investigator at the University of Wisconsin, learned that someone had hacked into the university's computer network. Savoy investigated and determined the culprit might be Jerome Heckenkamp, a graduate student who had been terminated from his job at the university's computer help desk for unauthorized activity.[29] Savoy was concerned especially because the intruder had gained access to a server that maintained email accounts for 60,000 individuals at the University of Wisconsin. Students were preparing for final exams at the time, and Savoy believed destruction of email during this critical time particularly would be disruptive to the university.

At some point, Savoy notified FBI Special Agent Terry Rankhorn of what he had found, and Rankhorn told Savoy that he intended to get a warrant to seize Heckenkamp's computer. Savoy later determined university security interests required him to take Heckenkamp's computer offline immediately. Although Agent Rankhorn advised Savoy not to take action because the FBI was in the process of obtaining a warrant, Savoy acted anyway. Accompanied by a university detective named Scheller and other university police officers, Savoy entered Heckenkamp's dormitory room and disconnected the network cord that attached Heckenkamp's computer to the university's network. While Savoy and the police were still on the premises, Detective Scheller found Heckenkamp, who gave Savoy the password to his computer, waived his Miranda rights, and authorized Savoy to make a copy of Heckenkamp's hard drive. On the following day, FBI agents, acting under the authority of a warrant, searched Heckenkamp's computer and his dormitory room.

Federal authorities later prosecuted Heckenkamp for intentionally accessing a protected computer without authorization. Heckenkamp sought to suppress evidence obtained from Savoy's remote search of his computer, the copy of Heckenkamp's hard drive that Savoy had obtained, and the search of his room and computer by the FBI. The trial court denied the motion, and Heckenkamp appealed.

---

[28] 482 F.3d 1142 (9th Cir. 2007).

[29] *Id.* at 1144.

On appeal, the Ninth Circuit ruled that the University of Wisconsin had "special needs" to ensure the integrity of its computer system that justified Savoy's search—even though Savoy had not obtained a warrant. "Under the special needs exception," the Ninth Circuit instructed, "a warrant is not required when special needs, beyond the normal need for law enforcement, make the warrant and probable-cause requirement impracticable." There was no evidence Savoy was acting at the behest of law enforcement authorities when he conducted his independent investigation of Heckenkamp's activities; indeed, he apparently proceeded against the FBI's advice. "Under these circumstances," the court concluded, "a search warrant was not necessary because Savoy was acting purely within the scope of his role as a system administrator."[30] Therefore, Savoy's remote search of Heckenkamp's computer did not violate the Fourth Amendment.

Medlock v. Trustees of Indiana University: A Regulatory Dorm Search by University Employees Does Not Require a Warrant

Medlock v. Trustees of Indiana University,[31] decided in 2013 by the Seventh Circuit Court of Appeals, promises to become one of the leading cases on the constitutionality of dorm searches at public universities. Written by the Seventh Circuit's esteemed Judge Richard Posner, the decision approved actions by Indiana University (IU) employees (graduate students) who conducted a routine inspection of Zachary Medlock's dormitory room after providing ample notice that an inspection would take place.

As noted in the Seventh Circuit's opinion, IU's student housing officials gave students one week's notice that their dormitory rooms would be inspected, and students were reminded of the inspection via intercom on the day the inspection took place. While inspecting Medlock's dorm room, two graduate students spied a clear plastic tube containing a substance one inspector believed to be marijuana. An inspector called campus police, and an officer arrived, confiscated the tube and departed. Continuing their inspection of Medlock's room, the graduate students found a rolled-up blanket at the bottom of Medlock's door, "presumably intended to keep smoke from wafting into the bathroom...while [Medlock] smoked marijuana in his bedroom."[32] Medlock had left his closet door slightly ajar; and the inspectors, looking in, found a six-foot-high marijuana plant in Medlock's closet. The students again called campus police, who obtained a search warrant. A police search turned up various items associated with smoking marijuana, including pipes and a fluorescent light (commonly called a "grow light"), which could be used to

---

[30] *Id*. at 1147.

[31] 738 F.3d 867 (7th Cir. 2013). The discussion of *Medlock* previously appeared a an online essay in *Teachers College Record*. Richard Fossey, Medlock v. Indiana University: *A university is sued after suspending a student who was caught growing marijuana in his dorm room*, TEACHERS COLL. REC. ID Number 17457 (2014), tcrecord.org.

[32] *Id*. at 870.

grow marijuana indoors. They also found 89 grams of marijuana, not including the marijuana plant.[33]

Police arrested Medlock for felony possession of marijuana, but officials later dropped the charges. The university's dean of students suspended Medlock for one year, and a university administrative hearing upheld this decision. Medlock returned to IU after his one-year suspension, and the university gave him a part-time job while he resumed his studies. Nevertheless, he sued the university, claiming a violation of his right to due process and his right to privacy under the Fourth Amendment; he asked a federal court to expunge the university's disciplinary record pertaining to the marijuana incident. A federal trial judge dismissed his case, and Medlock appealed.

Judge Posner, writing for a Seventh Circuit panel, affirmed the trial court's decision. In Judge Posner's opinion, Medlock's lawsuit was "near frivolous."[34] In particular, there was no merit to Medlock's due process claim. "The in-your-face flagrancy of Medlock's violation of university rules ... and of Indiana's criminal law, required the university to take immediate remedial action if its commitment to its rules, and to legality, was not to be questioned," Posner observed. Rejecting Medlock's argument that he was entitled to a pre-deprivation hearing prior to being suspended, Posner wrote the court was "reluctant to encourage further bureaucratization by judicializing university disciplinary proceedings,"[35]

Posner denied Medlock's Fourth Amendment claim as well. Medlock had argued evidence seized in the dorm-room search should have been excluded at his IU suspension hearing because it had been obtained without a warrant in violation of the Fourth Amendment. Posner rejected Medlock's arguments. First, the judge pointed out, the exclusionary rule only applies to criminal proceedings. Even if the evidence had been obtained in violation of the Fourth Amendment, that violation would not bar the university from considering the evidence at a campus administrative proceeding. In any event, Posner wrote, Medlock's Fourth Amendment rights were not violated. Medlock consented to have his room searched for contraband and health or safety violations. "He could have lived off campus and thus have avoided being governed by the code. He chose to trade some of his privacy for a dorm room." [36]

Moreover, the student inspectors who visited Medlock's dormitory room were engaged in a "lawful regulatory search" that did not require a warrant.[37] Warrants are not required, Posner ruled, when governmental actors are advancing "special needs" beyond the needs of law enforcement. Requiring a warrant in a school setting "would unduly interfere with the maintenance of the swift and informal disciplinary procedures needed [in such a setting]."[38]

---

[33] *Id.*
[34] *Id.* at 873.
[35] *Id.* at 871.
[36] *Id.* at 872.
[37] *Id.*
[38] *Id.*

Posner acknowledged IU campus police were engaged in a criminal investigation when they searched his dorm room, and Medlock had not consented to such a search. Nevertheless, in Posner's view, the intrusion on Medlock's privacy by campus inspectors was already complete before a police officer arrived on the scene and any further intrusion into his privacy by the police presence was minimal.

The *Medlock* decision is in harmony with earlier judicial decisions about routine dorm-room inspections, but it is likely to be particularly persuasive because a highly respected federal appellate court judge wrote it with great clarity. For higher education officials, *Medlock* is most significant for its ruling that routine dorm-room inspections by university officials are regulatory searches that do not require a warrant so long as the searches are not conducted for law enforcement purposes.

Dormitory Searches by Private Colleges and Universities

Of course, private colleges and universities are not governmental entities, and they do not operate under Fourth Amendment constraints unless they conduct searches in concert with the police or at the behest of law enforcement authorities. *State v. Burroughs*,[39] decided by the Tennessee Supreme Court, illustrates this principle. In this case, police arrested Derron Burroughs, a student at Knoxville College, a private educational institution, after a search of his dormitory room turned up cocaine.

Burroughs occupied the room pursuant to a policy in the student handbook that authorized campus personnel to conduct "unannounced, unscheduled" entries into dormitory rooms for the purpose of maintaining "law and order."[40] In addition, Burroughs's housing contract allowed college authorities to enter dormitory rooms unannounced. Acting on information that Burroughs's room might contain drugs, Chester Petty, the director of housing and director of Burroughs's dormitory, searched Burroughs's room and found a white, powdery substance that turned out to be cocaine. Petty reported what he found to a senior college administrator, who called the Knoxville Police Department. After his arrest for criminal possession of illegal drugs, Burroughs sought a court order excluding the evidence seized by Petty when he searched Burroughs's room. Burroughs argued Petty had acted as an agent of the police when he conducted the search; thus, the search, which Petty conducted without a warrant, violated the Fourth Amendment.

The Tennessee Supreme Court upheld the search. The court acknowledged private actors may subject themselves to Fourth Amendment constraints when they operate as agents of the police, but Petty had not searched Burroughs's room at the request of law enforcement authorities. Petty was authorized under

---

[39] 926 S.W.2d 243 (Tenn. 1996).
[40] *Id.* at 244-45.

Burroughs's housing contract to enter Burroughs's room unannounced, and he searched Burroughs's room before the college contacted the police. "Thus," said the Tennessee Supreme Court, "Petty conducted the warrantless search not as an agent of the state, but as a college official whose purpose and actions were in furtherance of college policy, not state policy." [41]

Duarte v. Commonwealth,[42] a Virginia case, involved facts somewhat similar to the *Burroughs* decision. William Duarte, a student at Averett College, a private entity, was convicted of marijuana possession after college officials searched his room, found marijuana, and turned it over to the police. Duarte appealed his conviction, arguing that the trial court should have suppressed the evidence obtained in the dormitory search, which was obtained without a warrant.

A Virginia appellate court reviewed the facts surrounding the search and upheld Duarte's conviction. As the court explained, T. A. Smith, a municipal police detective, telephoned Pat Morgan, dean of students at Averett College, seeking information about Duarte in connection with a criminal investigation. Morgan told Smith that she probably would search Duarte's room, but Smith, fearing Morgan's intervention might hamper his investigation, urged her not to do so. Morgan and Smith communicated again about Duarte, but Smith never mentioned a search of Duarte's room. Morgan then directed two college employees to conduct an "inventory search" of Duarte's room and confiscate any contraband or stolen items. The officials did as Morgan directed and found several bags of marijuana and drug paraphernalia, which they gave to Morgan. Morgan then called Detective Smith, who went to Morgan's office and took custody of the contraband. Duarte later confessed to Morgan that he bought the marijuana intending to sell some of it to cover his costs.[43]

Reviewing these facts, a Virginia appellate court found no grounds for voiding Duarte's conviction. The Fourth Amendment does not apply, the court stated, to searches conducted by private parties acting on their own initiative. Although Morgan communicated with Detective Smith about Duarte and told him she might search Duarte's room, Smith did not encourage her to do so. On the contrary, Smith asked her not to search Duarte's room. Since Morgan acted as a private party and not as an agent of the police when she ordered a search of Duarte's room, the evidence obtained from the search properly was admitted into evidence.

A Student's Consent to a Dormitory Search

Although it is well established that students have a reasonable expectation of privacy within their dormitory rooms that protects them from warrantless searches by the police, students can waive their Fourth Amendment rights by voluntarily consenting to a police search. Such consent must be clear and

---

[41] *Id.* at 246.

[42] 407 S.E.2d 41 (Va. Ct. App. 1991).

[43] *Id.* at 42.

unambiguous, however; it may not be simply implied. For example, in *Commonwealth v. Carr*,[44] a 2010 decision, the Massachusetts Supreme Judicial Court ruled that two students at Boston College had not consented voluntarily to a search of their dormitory room by campus police, and thus the evidence the officers seized during a warrantless search could not be used to prosecute the students for possession of illegal drugs. In that case, three Boston College police officers and two campus housing administrators went to a dormitory room occupied by Daniel Carr and John Sherman, prompted by a tip from other students that Carr might have a weapon in his room. One officer entered the room, while the other two officers stood just outside the door. The officer ordered a student visitor to leave the room and then questioned Carr and Sherman. In response to the officer's questions about a possible weapon, Carr produced a "fake" gun (a realistic copy of a .45 caliber handgun) from under a bed, and Sherman turned over a folding knife. Police later found a smaller knife in the room and a kubotan, a martial arts weapon.

Based on concerns that other weapons might be in the room, the officer asked for permission to search the room. Police gave both students a printed form containing two parts: a *Miranda* waiver and a written consent to search. Carr and Sherman signed the *Miranda* waiver, but neither signed the consent-to-search portion of the form. Police then searched the room and found a bag of psilocybin mushrooms, a bag of marijuana, ten marijuana cigarettes, and two bags of white powder later identified as cocaine.

Carr and Sherman were prosecuted for trafficking in cocaine and possession of marijuana and psilocybin with intent to distribute, and they sought to suppress the evidence that officers seized during the warrantless search of their dormitory room. A trial court ruled the students had not voluntarily consented to the search and suppressed the evidence. An intermediate trial court reversed, but the Massachusetts Supreme Judicial Court agreed with the trial court, ruling that Carr and Sherman had not consented voluntarily to the search.

"When the police rely on consent to justify a warrantless [search]…the prosecution has the burden of proving that the consent was, in fact, freely and voluntarily given," the Massachusetts Supreme Judicial Court ruled. "If either the officer's request or the occupant's response is so ambiguous that we are unable to discern whether the occupant voluntarily consented to [the search], our inquiry will be over and the entry must be deemed unlawful."[45]

In the court's opinion, the conversation between police and the students did not clearly show Carr and Sherman had consented to the search, and they had not given written permission to search their room when they were offered the opportunity to do so. Furthermore, even if they had consented, there was ample evidence that their consent was not truly voluntary. Armed police officers blocked the dormitory room's only exit, the court pointed out, while college

---

[44] 936 N.E.2d 883 (Mass. 2010). The discussion of *Carr* previously appeared as an online essay in *Teachers College Record*. Richard Fossey, Commonwealth v. Carr: *Cocaine, a dorm room, and the Fourth Amendment*, TEACHERS COLL. REC. ID Number 16286 (2011), tcrecord.org.

[45] *Id.* at 888.

administrators stood outside the door. One officer's statement, "'I would like to search the room,' sounded more like an order than a request," in the court's view. The state's highest appellate court agreed with the trial court's conclusion that "an objective person would not have felt able to refuse the officer's request or leave the room."[46]

Conclusion

In summary, college students who reside in campus dormitories at public universities have a reasonable expectation of privacy in their dorm rooms that is protected by the Fourth Amendment; officials cannot search these rooms for law enforcement purposes without a valid warrant. Nonstudents, however, have no such reasonable expectation of privacy in dormitory rooms that they have vacated or live in as guests in violation of college housing rules.

A line of cases indicates that college and university officials may search students' dormitory rooms for non-law-enforcement purposes without offending the Fourth Amendment if the search is authorized by language in a housing contract or a reasonable regulation adopted to maintain safety, security, and an educational environment conducive to learning. In addition, the Ninth Circuit has ruled that campus authorities may conduct searches in areas where students have objectively reasonable expectations of privacy without obtaining a warrant if officials are motivated by a "special need" to protect the university's security that is separate and apart from law enforcement concerns. Furthermore, the Seventh Circuit has ruled that university student inspectors may conduct a "lawful regulatory search" of a dormitory room to advance "special needs" beyond the needs of law enforcement without the necessity of obtaining a warrant. However, campus officials cannot rely on language in their regulations or student housing contracts to justify warrantless searches that are conducted pursuant to a criminal investigation.

In their treatise on higher education law, Kaplin and Lee advise campus administrators to notify students and seek their consent before entering dormitory rooms based on health and safety concerns when it is feasible to do so. Giving students advance notice before searching dormitory rooms is an expression of courtesy, Kaplin and Lee point out, and an indication that college officials respect students' privacy. In addition, college and university officials may be more likely to prevail in court when the legality of a dormitory search is disputed if they gave students advance notice before entering dormitory rooms without students' permission.[47]

Finally, although college students may waive their Fourth Amendment rights and consent to a police search of their dormitory rooms, campus police would be wise to obtain a warrant and not rely on a student's consent to justify a warrantless search. The presence of armed police officers in the cramped

---

[46] *Id.* at 890.

[47] WILLIAM A. KAPLIN & BARBARA A. LEE, THE LAW OF HIGHER EDUC. 1000 (2013).

confines of a dormitory room almost always has a coercive quality, and a court might well be sympathetic to a student's argument that whatever consent the student gave under those circumstances was coerced and not voluntary.

15 Campus Safety

Robert C. Cloud, Ed.D.
Baylor University

In the early morning hours of April 5, 1986, Jeanne Clery, a freshman at Lehigh University in Pennsylvania, was raped and murdered in her dormitory room by another student who entered the dormitory intent on theft. Jeanne had left the door to her room unlocked for her roommate who had lost her key. Ironically, Jeanne's parents, Howard and Connie Clery, were relieved when she chose to attend Lehigh University instead of Tulane University in New Orleans because they believed their daughter would be safer at Lehigh, a smaller, private institution located in rural Pennsylvania.[1] Unfortunately, Mr. and Mrs. Clery did not know that Lehigh University and the surrounding area had an accelerating crime rate that exceeded what one might expect at an institution of its size.[2]

This chapter focuses on two seemingly disparate issues: campus safety and student privacy. Unfortunately, the two issues overlap most glaringly when students commit violent acts on campus, and university administrators can find themselves pulled in opposite directions when they attempt to find a proper balance between the two. On the one hand, administrators are obligated to protect the privacy rights of students, but they are also responsible for compiling and disclosing information about students who may pose a threat to themselves or others and intervening when necessary to ensure campus safety and secure property. Over time, the pendulum swings back and forth between maintaining student privacy and monitoring inappropriate student behavior, with pressure to compile and disclose information about aberrant behavior increasing in recent years in the wake of rising levels of campus violence. Federal laws and regulations now require colleges and universities to inform students about local crime rates and protect them as much as possible from related dangers. The Crime Awareness and Campus Security Act of 1990[3] was the first in a series of federal statutes intended to achieve that goal.

---

[1] Beverly Beyette, *Campus Crime Crusade: Howard and Connie Clery Lost Their Daughter to a Crazed Thief: Now They're Angry and Fighting Back*, LOS ANGELES TIMES, Aug.10, 1989, http://articles.latimes.com print/1989-08-10/news/vw-301_1_campus-crime-statistics.

[2] *Id.*

[3] The Crime Awareness and Campus Security Act; The Jeanne Clery Disclosure of Campus Security Policy and Campus Crime Statistics Act, a part of the Higher Education Act of 1965, 20 U.S.C. § 1092(f) (2006).

Campus Safety

The Crime Awareness and Campus Security Act of 1990 (The Clery Act)

After the investigation of Jeanne Clery's murder, her parents concluded that inadequate campus security was the cause of her death and testified that they would not have permitted her to attend Lehigh in the first place if they had known about the crime rate on and around the campus prior to her enrollment. Maintaining that students and their parents have a right to know about crime rates on a given campus before enrolling, the Clerys founded Security on Campus (SOC) with funds they received in the legal settlement with Lehigh and began lobbying tirelessly for federal legislation that required the reporting and dissemination of campus crime statistics by all postsecondary institutions in the nation.[4] The Clerys' efforts through SOC prompted a thorough congressional review of the campus crime issue, and the findings were sobering. Congress discovered that there was no national clearing house for the compilation, analysis, and dissemination of campus crime statistics. Students and their parents did not have access to general information about postsecondary crime statistics, much less the crime rates on specific campuses where they were applying for admission. Indeed, no one had easy access to the information, including state and federal governments, law enforcement agencies, and higher education leaders. The entire structure for compiling and reporting campus crime was primitive when compared with other services provided to students by the federal government and educational organizations. In response to the information void and obvious need, Congress passed the Crime Awareness and Campus Security Act of 1990, which is also now known as The Clery Act in honor of Jeanne and her parents. The Clery Act is the principal federal law addressing safety and security in American higher education, mandating the annual compilation and distribution of crime rates and safety policies by all postsecondary institutions participating in the federal student financial aid program.[5]

Since September 1, 1992, all postsecondary institutions have published annual campus crime reports for constituents and the Department of Education.[6] Reporting requirements are amended periodically to meet changing needs of institutions, law enforcement agencies, and the federal government. For example, the Campus Sexual Assault Victim's Bill of Rights in 1992 required institutions to develop policies and procedures to deal with and report sexual assaults.[7] Campus Safety Reports must now include crime statistics from the previous three years and safety policies and procedures in place to control

---

[4] *Id.*

[5] Robert C. Cloud, *Safety and Security on Campus: Priority Number One in Higher Education,* 295 Educ. L. Rep. 457 (Sept. 26, 2013) [hereinafter, Cloud, *Safety and Security on Campus*].

[6] The Crime Awareness and Campus Security Act of 1990, § 204 (f)(1).

[7] Cloud, *Safety and Security on Campus, supra* note 5, at 466.

crime. Crime statistics must document exactly where and when crimes occurred to assist in future crime-prevention initiatives. Institutions must report the following crimes separately: homicides; sexual assaults; armed robbery and aggravated assault; burglary; motor vehicle theft; arson; and violations of alcohol, drug, and firearms laws. Victims of sexual assault must be informed about their right to notify police and the duty of college personnel to assist them in reporting the attack.[8] Colleges and universities are also required to disclose which crimes, if any, were hate crimes that targeted victims because of their race, gender, sex, religion, ethnicity, or disability.[9]

Campus Safety Reports must also include the institution's procedures for reporting crimes, the institution's relationships with law enforcement agencies, drug and alcohol policies and laws that apply to the campus, and the institution's policy on timely warnings to all campus constituencies in emergency situations. Finally, colleges and universities are required to name and describe educational programs on substance abuse and sexual assault that are available to students and employees. In addition, reports must now include emergency response and campus evacuation procedures and missing student notification procedures (effective in 2008).[10] In accordance with previous practice, the Higher Education Opportunity Act of 2008 amended the Clery Act to require institutions to notify next-of-kin persons and law enforcement agencies when a student has been missing from on-campus housing for twenty-four hours.[11]

In addition to the annual report of crime statistics, the Clery Act also requires institutions to maintain a campus crime log open to the public.[12] A log for the previous sixty-day period must be kept available for immediate inspection, and the log for the earlier period must be made available within two days. The log must contain the nature, date, time, and location of every crime reported during the specific time period.[13]

Primarily because of the April 16, 2007 tragedy at Virginia Polytechnic University (Virginia Tech), the Clery Act now requires postsecondary institutions to issue "timely warnings" that notify the entire campus community when a dangerous situation or significant emergency poses an immediate threat to the health and safety of students and employees.[14] Institutions are required to notify all constituencies quickly through a variety of means including emails, texting, telephone networks, and a public address system, unless the administration determines that a warning could place individuals at even greater risk of harm. After its review of the Virginia Tech disaster, however, the Department of Education (DOE) recommended that institutions issue timely warnings if there is any possible threat to the safety of students and staff—evidence that

---

[8] 20 U.S.C.A. § 1092 (f)(1)(F)(i).

[9] 34 C.F.R. § 668. 46 (c)(3).

[10] 20 U.S.C.A. § 1092 (f).

[11] 20 U.S.C.A. § 1092 (j).

[12] 20 U.S.C.A. § 1092 (f)(4).

[13] *Id.*

[14] 20 U.S.C.A. § 1092 (f)(I)(J)(i). *See* Commonwealth of Virginia v. Peterson, 749 S.E 2d 307 (Va. 2013).

the DOE considers personal safety and campus security to be top priorities on college and university campuses.[15] In other words, postsecondary administrators dealing with potentially dangerous situations should opt on the side of personal safety and apologize later if a warning proves to be unnecessary and disruptive to campus operations. Clearly, the DOE has sent a message to administrators that it is better to be safe than sorry when personal safety is at risk.

In summary, current provisions in the Clery Act meet the goals first articulated by Howard and Connie Clery and then addressed by Congress in 1990. There is now a national clearing house on campus crime statistics that serves two essential functions: It permits parents and students to review the crime statistics and safety records of specific postsecondary institutions prior to matriculation; and it informs current students and employees about relative crime rates on their campuses and the related risks of harm to them and their associates.[16]

The Annual Fire Safety Report

The Annual Fire Safety Report is another federal law aimed at protecting students on postsecondary campuses. Mandated in the Higher Education Opportunity Act, the Fire Safety Report must be submitted annually by all institutions with on-campus student housing.[17] Like the annual Campus Safety Report, the Fire Safety Report requires colleges and universities to report both statistics and policies. Respondents must list the number of fires in campus housing (if any), the number of fire-related injuries and deaths, and the value of all fire-related damage during the previous three years.[18] Institutions are obligated to report only those fires that occurred in on-campus housing units, because the law focuses on whether dormitories comply with all fire and safety codes. Fires in administration and classroom buildings do not have to be reported, regardless of the costs and injuries or deaths.[19] In addition to statistics, Fire Safety Reports must include institutional policies on the following: a description of the fire alarm and sprinkler systems in every building, the number of fire drills conducted in each unit, fire safety rules, evacuation procedures, fire safety education programs, a list of individuals to whom fires are reported, and strategic plans for maintaining and improving fire safety systems.[20]

Just as The Clery Act requires postsecondary institutions to maintain daily crime logs, the Higher Education Opportunity Act requires institutions to maintain fire safety logs that are open to public inspection. Fire safety logs,

---

[15] Final Program Review Determination, from the U.S. Dep't of Educ. to Charles Steeger, President, Virginia Tech, OPE ID: 00375400 (Dec. 10, 2010).

[16] Donna L. Gurley, *Student Privacy and Campus Safety,* in CONTEMPORARY ISSUES IN HIGHER EDUCATION LAW 365-66 (Richard Fossey, Kerry Brian Melear, & Joseph C. Beckham eds., 2011) [hereinafter Gurley].

[17] 20 U.S.C.A. § 1092 (i).

[18] 20 U.S.C.A. § 1092 (i)(I)(A).

[19] 34 C.F.R. § 668.49.

[20] 20 U.S.C.A. § 1092 (i).

like the Annual Fire Safety Reports, include only fires in on-campus student housing along with the nature, date, time, and location of each fire.[21]

Institutional Liability for Violent Acts on Campus

A postsecondary institution can be found liable for a violent act committed against a student by a third party if the institution had a duty to protect the injured student. While colleges and universities do not have a general duty to protect their students from the violent acts of others,[22] a duty may arise under certain circumstances. Dall identified six factors that courts use to determine whether a duty to protect exists: the foreseeability of the injury; the risk involved; whether the institution had insurance; the degree of relationship between the institution's act(s) and the injury; the burden that would result from placing liability on the institution; and other policy considerations.[23] Many of these factors come into play when a special relationship exists between the institution and the injured student. Three circumstances often create special relationships between students and institutions: (1) when the institution has knowledge of foreseeable harm, (2) when the institution is the landlord, and (3) when the campus police are responsible for campus security.[24] For example, if a student poses an obvious and foreseeable threat to himself or others, the institution may have a duty to protect other members in the campus community from harm. Likewise, if a student has threatened other individuals on the campus and administrators are aware of the threats, the institution should assume a duty to protect those who have been threatened, or at the very least to warn them of the threat.[25]

Furthermore, institutions can create a special relationship with students when they provide campus housing, particularly if undergraduate students are required to live on campus for a specified period of time (e.g., the freshman and sophomore years). In this circumstance, the institution has a legal duty to ensure safety and security by providing adequate lighting, maintaining all door locks properly, and monitoring traffic into and out of the housing facili-

---

[21] 20 U.S.C.A. § 1092 (i)(3)(A).

[22] Bradshaw v. Rawlings, 612 F.2d 135, 138 (3rd Cir. 1979)("Our beginning point is a recognition that the modern American college is not an insurer of the safety of its students.").

[23] Jane A. Dall, *Determining Duty in Collegiate Tort Litigation: Shifting Paradigms of the College-Student Relationship*, 29 J.C. & U.L. 485, 493 (2003).

[24] Brett A. Sokolow, W. Scott Lewis, James A. Keller, & Audrey Daly, *College and University Liability for Violent Campus Attacks*, 34 J.C. & U.L. 319, 322 (2008). [hereinafter Sokolow, Lewis, Keller, & Daly; *College and University Liability*].

[25] Tarasoff v. Regents of Univ. of Cal., 17 Cal. 3d 425, 551 P. 2d 334, 131 Cal. Rptr. 14 (Cal. 1976) [hereinafter *Tarasoff*] (Awareness that a student poses a foreseeable threat to himself or others can create a special relationship and a duty to protect the individuals in danger, or to warn them at the very least. Failure to protect or warn students and/oremployees who are injured in such a foreseeable assault can result in a successful liability claim against the institution.). *See also* Stanton v. Univ. of Maine Sys., 773 A. 2d 1045 (Me. 2001) (A business invitee is one who is invited to the premises (campus) for transacting business between inviter (college) and invitee (student) and who is owed a duty of care by the inviter).

ties at all hours.[26] Institutions are expected to maintain dormitories and other housing facilities in a reasonably safe manner to protect residents from all types of crime, from petty theft and burglary to rape and murder.[27] In addition, postsecondary institutions accept a duty to protect students and employees when they create campus police forces.[28] Where campus police departments exist, members of the campus community assume (and expect) that all officers are adequately trained and competent enough to deal with all types of crime and criminals, thereby creating a special relationship between the institution and its constituencies.

Regardless of whether a college or university has a legal duty to protect its students and employees, best practice requires governing boards and administrators to protect everyone from foreseeable dangers. Ethical and prudent educational leaders practice preventive law through proactive policies and procedures intended to protect the entire campus community. Then, in instances where an injured student or employee sues the institution for negligence and failure to protect, the institution can document its good faith and continuing efforts to prevent foreseeable injuries and protect the community, thereby escaping or mitigating damages.

Liability for Negligent Hiring or Retention of Institutional Employees

Carelessness in hiring and retention practices can result in successful liability claims against postsecondary institutions. Students who are assaulted by college employees can win damages if the court determines that the institution hired and retained a person that the institution knew or should have known posed a danger to others on the campus. Consequently, postsecondary institutions should assess the degree to which an employee's position gives him or her access to students and then decide whether a background check on the person for previous criminal activity is necessary. Failure to conduct a background check on custodial employees who work inside student residence halls could be considered negligence if a custodian enters a student's room and assaults or murders the student. On the other hand, an institution might not be deemed negligent in failing to conduct a background check on an employee who washes dishes in a campus cafeteria even if that employee enters a residence hall without authorization and commits a violent act against a student. Under the circumstances, the institution might claim successfully that there was no reason to anticipate that the dishwasher would ever enter a dormitory with intent to commit a crime. Students who are injured by college

---

[26] Sokolow, Lewis, Keller, & Daly; *College and University Liability, supra* note 24, at 328.

[27] Mullins v. Pine Manor Coll., 449 N.E.2d 331 (Mass. 1983). Colleges generally undertake voluntarily to protect their students from danger. Pine Manor undertook the duty, and the undertaking was not gratuitous. All students, including Mullins, paid for security services either through their tuition or a dormitory fee. Reasonable security is an indispensable part of the bundle of services which all colleges, including Pine Manor, provide their students.

[28] Sokolow, Lewis, Keller, & Daly; *College and University Liability, supra* note 24, at 328.

employees can and do sue the institution claiming negligent hiring and/or retention of the employee. Such claims, of course, are based on the premise that the college knew or should have known that the employee posed a danger to others on the campus. For example, a student who is sexually assaulted by an employee who is a convicted sex offender can file a negligence claim against the institution, and the institution will likely be held liable for the employee's foreseeable assault.

While a claim for negligent hiring alleges negligence at the time the employee is hired, a claim for negligent retention arises when an institution continues to employ an individual who has demonstrated a pattern of aberrant or dangerous behavior that threatens the safety and well-being of others in the workplace. For example, in *Bloomer v. Becker College*,[29] students complained to the college administration that an instructor in the equestrian program was sexually harassing them. College leaders responded by reprimanding the teacher and warning him of the consequences if the harassment continued. Subsequently, the instructor allegedly provided alcohol for a female student and then fondled her on a college-sponsored trip, and the student sued the college for negligent hiring and failure to supervise the instructor. Based on the facts in the case, the court allowed the student's claim to proceed since college leaders knew that the instructor had sexually harassed the students and yet had failed to take appropriate action to prevent further injury to students. Clearly, college leaders must act quickly and decisively when they learn that an employee is endangering students or other employees; otherwise, the institution can be found liable for negligent retention and required to pay damages.[30]

Liability for Negligent Admission of Students

When a college or university admits a student whose previous behavior indicates that he or she may present a danger to the campus community, the institution can be held liable for negligent admission if that student harms another student or an employee. Negligent admission is a legal doctrine based on the premise that the institution knew or should have known that a particular individual posed a danger to others on the campus, yet admitted him or her despite the apparent risks to others.[31] More than ever before, public colleges and universities are admitting students with criminal records and others who are under indictment for alleged criminal acts and awaiting trial. Obviously, the presence of these individuals on campus poses unprecedented safety issues and ethical dilemmas for postsecondary leaders. Convicted felons who have served their prescribed sentences and paid their debts to society, or have been paroled, have legal rights to attend public institutions and prepare for more productive futures as long as they comply with institutional policies and the law. On the other hand, their presence on campus can raise legitimate concerns

---

[29] No. 09-11342-FDS, 2010 WL 3221969 (D. Mass. 2010).

[30] *Id.*

[31] Gurley, *supra* note 16, at 373.

in the minds of other students who are aware of their presence. Furthermore, current students who are under indictment can pose different challenges for college administrators. By law, the accused are innocent until proven guilty, and they cannot be monitored, suspended, expelled, or otherwise disciplined without cause and due process. These facts notwithstanding, other students may not wish to attend classes or interact with a convicted felon or a person under indictment, particularly if the indictment alleges violent crime(s). College and university administrators are pressed to protect the rights of all concerned in this complex and perplexing arena. The following three court decisions between 1987 and 2003 reflect the challenges faced by postsecondary administrators in balancing an individual student's right to privacy with the campus community's rights to safety and security.

In *Eiseman v. State of New York*,[32] the State University College at Buffalo admitted Larry Campbell, an ex-felon with a history of drug addiction and related criminal activity. Campbell had served his prescribed sentence and was entitled to unconditional release from the state penitentiary under state law. Accordingly, the College at Buffalo admitted him into a special rehabilitation program designed to extend educational opportunities to disadvantaged persons, including convicted felons. Unfortunately, the decision to admit Campbell proved to be a disaster. Soon after beginning classes, Campbell raped and murdered Rhona Eiseman and murdered Thomas Tunney, a fellow student. Eiseman's estate, through her parents, filed a negligence action against the University for failing to warn her about the foreseeable danger posed by Campbell. While acknowledging that the family's desire for recovery from the tragedy was understandable,[33] the Court of Appeals ruled that Campbell's release was required by state law and, therefore, that the University and state could not be found liable. The State of New York and the University were immune from lawsuit because the decision to admit Campbell was a discretionary function, and the University had no duty or authority to restrict Campbell's activities or to warn other students about his presence on the campus.[34] In summarizing its decision, the Court of Appeals stated that "consistent with conditions of parole [in New York at least], an individual returned to freedom can frequent places of public accommodation, secure employment, and if qualified, become a student."[35] Therefore, the State College at Buffalo had no duty or authority to monitor, much less control, Larry Campbell's activities on or off the campus. In the end, the Court of Appeals ruled that New York state law and Campbell's right to privacy trumped the campus community's right to be protected from an obvious danger.

Conversely, in *Nero v. Kansas State University* (KSU),[36] the Kansas Supreme Court ruled that the university did have a duty to warn Shana Nero

---

[32] 70 N.Y.2d 175, 511 N.E.2d 1128, 518 N.Y.S.2d 608 (1987) [hereinafter *Eiseman*].

[33] *Eiseman, id.* at 612.

[34] *Id.* at 608.

[35] *Id.* at 616.

[36] 861 P.2d 768 (Kan. 1993) [hereinafter *Nero*].

about the presence of an indicted sex offender living in her coed dormitory. The Supreme Court held that Nero could sue KSU after she was raped by Ramon Davenport on June 2, 1990 in a dormitory laundry room. KSU officials had allowed Davenport to enroll in a summer intersession course while he was under indictment for the alleged sexual assault of another KSU student in April of the previous spring semester. In their wisdom, KSU administrators assigned Davenport to a room in Goodnow Hall, a coed dormitory where Nero lived and the only campus housing open during that summer intersession. In her pleadings, Nero claimed status as a business invitee with a special relationship to the university, a legal status which entitled her to protection from foreseeable dangers on the campus.[37] Ultimately, the Kansas Supreme Court ruled that KSU had a duty to protect Nero for four reasons. First, KSU was not obligated to assign a dormitory room to Davenport during the intersession, particularly in light of the serious charges pending against him. Second, in light of the circumstances, the decision to assign Davenport to a coed dormitory in close proximity to unsuspecting females did not seem wise. Third, assigning Davenport to Goodnow Hall may have given Nero a false sense of security, making her more vulnerable to assault than she might have been otherwise.[38] Fourth, and finally, the injury to Nero was not only foreseeable, it was predictable to a reasonable person. In an interesting closure to the case, Davenport pled guilty on August 29, 1990 to the April 1990 sexual assault charge after the district attorney agreed to drop the charges in the *Nero* case.[39]

The *Nero* case is an excellent example of the dilemmas facing postsecondary administrators dealing with student privacy and campus safety issues. KSU officials tried to balance Davenport's rights to privacy and due process with Nero's right to personal safety. Balancing the interests of the two parties proved to be very difficult. While extending the benefit of the doubt to Davenport (who was accused but not convicted), KSU leaders failed to warn or protect Nero from an obvious threat to her safety. Administrators can profit from an analysis of the *Nero* case that addresses two questions: (1) How could KSU administrators have handled the situation more effectively? (2) What can be done to prevent comparable incidents in the future?

The facts in *Eiseman* and *Nero* highlight the importance of warning students about dangers on the campus while making good-faith efforts to respect the privacy rights of all. Few would argue that students do not have a right to be informed about dangerous persons on their campuses. Indeed, the United States Supreme Court affirmed that right in its 2003 decision in *Smith v. Doe*.[40] In *Smith*, the Supreme Court upheld an Alaska state law that requires the names of convicted sex offenders to be registered on the Internet, thereby eliminating any reasonable argument supporting the privacy rights of sex offenders. Consequently, it seems clear that colleges and universities can

---

[37] *Tarasoff, supra* note 25, at 14.

[38] *Nero, supra* note 36, at 780.

[39] *Id.* at 772.

[40] 538 U.S. 84 (2003).

legally inform students and employees about the presence of convicted sex offenders on their campuses.

Background Checks for Students: A Growing Trend

Driven by concerns about campus safety, an increasing number of postsecondary institutions are requiring student applicants to self-disclose their criminal backgrounds. Although most application forms state that failure to disclose previous felony convictions is grounds for dismissal, some students who have committed felonies in the past do not disclose, hoping that their lies will not be uncovered. Consequently, many institutions are now requiring background checks on all applicants. Because of the costs involved, institutions often require students to pay for the background checks. Furthermore, many institutions contract with outside agencies to conduct the background checks to mitigate any allegations that the process is unfair or prejudicial.

Behavioral Intervention Teams

Background checks on all student applicants are helpful in identifying potentially disruptive or dangerous students during the admissions process. However, background checks are not fail-safe, because some students do not engage in dangerous behavior until after they are admitted to the institution. After being admitted, a student may become disruptive in class, make violent threats, stalk or bully other students or employees, or submit writing assignments that indicate a propensity toward violence or suicide. To complicate the situation, he or she may behave strangely in only one environment while appearing to be quite normal in other settings. Consequently, faculty and staff who interact with the student may have different perspectives about his or her personality and psychological stability. It is imperative that institutions collect and triangulate as much information as possible about troubled students, and behavioral intervention teams (BITs) are an effective means to that end.[41] Many postsecondary institutions are now using BITs to identify and triangulate information from a variety of sources about the disruptive, antisocial, and/or threatening behavior of currently enrolled students. BITs serve as clearing houses for troubled and potentially dangerous students, providing college officials with information they must have before referring the student for appropriate treatment or removing him or her from the institution, either voluntarily or involuntarily.

---

[41] Wileen Weisenback Keller & Stephenie Hughes, *A Model for Assessment and Mitigation of Threats on the College Campus*, 49 J. EDUC. ADMIN., 76, 78 (2011).

Student Safety and the Evolving Special Relationship Doctrine

Special relationships between colleges and their students have existed for a long time. Originally based on the *in loco parentis*[42] responsibilities of college officials, special relationships created a duty on administrators, as surrogate parents, to control student behavior and reciprocally gave to students an expectation that the institution would protect them from harm.[43] Consequently, early special relationships were paternalistic and tended to favor institutional authority over students' rights to privacy and due process, but the relationships between colleges and their students changed significantly after World War II and with the introduction of constitutional theory into higher education campuses in 1961.[44] The special relationship doctrine has been evolving in higher education since that time, and the following cases are benchmarks in that evolutionary process.

Tarasoff v. Regents of the University of California

The California Supreme Court's decision in *Tarasoff v. Regents of the University of California*[45] set a precedent in the evolution of the special relationship doctrine in colleges and universities. On August 20, 1969, Prosenjit Poddar informed a University of California (UC) psychotherapist that he intended to kill an unnamed but identifiable person, Tatiana Tarasoff, when she returned from a vacation. The psychotherapist notified UC police, and Poddar was detained briefly, but released when he appeared to be rational and promised to stay away from Tatiana. Neither the UC psychotherapists nor the police warned Tatiana or her parents. On October 27, 1969, Poddar murdered Tatiana, prompting her parents to file suit claiming that the UC defendants were liable for her death because of their failure to warn about the threats of an obviously dangerous person. The defendants responded that they had no legal duty to warn because the confidentiality required in the doctor-patient relationship superseded any duty to warn.[46]

After considering the facts in the case, the court, *en banc*, ruled that although there is ordinarily no duty to warn under the common law of torts, an exception does exist when the defendant stands in a special relationship with either the dangerous person or the aggressor's *foreseeable victim*. Citing

---

[42] Black's Law Dictionary 803 (8th ed. 2004) (*In loco parentis* is the supervision of a young adult by an administrative body such as a university). *See also* Gott v. Berea Coll., 161 S.W. 204, 206 (Ky. 1913)(College officials stand *in loco parentis* concerning the physical and moral welfare and mental training of students.).

[43] Restatement (Second) of Torts, § 15 (Am. Law Inst. 1977) (duty of care may arise from either (a) a special relationship which imposes a duty on the actor to control a third party's conduct or (b) a special relationship between the actor and the other party which gives to the other an expectation of protection).

[44] *See, e.g.,* Dixon v. Alabama State Bd. of Educ., 294 F.2d 150, *cert. denied*, 368 U.S. 930 (5th Cir. 1961).(a public university must afford students procedural due process before expelling them for alleged misbehavior).

[45] *Tarasoff, supra* note 25.

[46] *Id.*

foreseeability as the most important factor in any departure from the common law of torts, the court held that the relationship between a psychotherapist and his/her patient does indeed constitute such a special relationship.[47] The court concluded that the UC psychotherapists were liable because they were obligated to protect an endangered, identifiable person and that their responsibility in that regard superseded privacy rights in the doctor-patient relationship. As the court said in its summation, "We conclude that the public policy favoring protection of the confidential character of patient-psychotherapist communications must yield to the extent to which disclosure is essential to avert danger to others. The protective privilege ends where the public peril begins."[48] In the end, the California Supreme Court's ruling in *Tarasoff* set forth three conditions in which a duty to warn and protect arises: (1) There is a special relationship between the defendant and either the dangerous person or the potential victim; (2) The risk of harm is readily foreseeable; and (3) The potential victim is readily identifiable.[49]

Commonwealth of Virginia v. Peterson

April 16, 2007 was perhaps the darkest day in the history of American higher education. At approximately 7:00 a.m., Seung Hui Cho, a senior at Virginia Tech (VT) University, shot and killed two persons in a campus dormitory. After changing clothes, he joined the flow of students going to and from classes. University and city police secured the crime scene, incorrectly concluding that the killer was no longer on campus.[50] Perhaps to avoid alarming the entire campus community, police and the university administration chose not to warn all campus constituencies immediately about a very dangerous situation. The warning that was finally issued about 9:00 a.m. was not timely and did not state explicitly that two persons had been murdered on campus and that the killer was at large.[51] Tragically, Cho entered Norris Hall on campus soon after 9:00 a.m. classes began, carrying two semiautomatic handguns. He chained the exterior doors shut and began entering classrooms and shooting anyone he saw. Responding to 911 calls for help, police were on the scene in three minutes and inside the building within 10 minutes, but by then Cho had shot and killed 30 more people, 25 students and five faculty, and then killed himself. In two hours, 32 innocent people were dead, and 17 more were wounded on a public university campus where safety and security had always been priorities.[52]

In the aftermath of the horror, investigators determined that Cho had a history of serious emotional and psychiatric problems and that VT faculty,

---

[47] *Id.* at 343

[48] *Id.* at 347.

[49] *Id.* at 334.

[50] Gordon K. Davies, *Connecting the Dots: Lessons from the Virginia Tech Shootings*, CHANGE, Jan.-Feb. 2008, at 10.

[51] *Id.* at 12.

[52] *Id.* at 10.

counselors, and police were aware of his erratic behavior long before his unspeakable acts of April 16. Faculty members and dormitory directors had expressed their concerns about Cho to the VT behavioral intervention team and Cook Counseling Center (CCC) on numerous occasions. Indeed, the CCC collected information on Cho's mental state three times during the fall semester 2006 and on December 12, a clinical social worker recommended that Cho be detained for a complete psychological assessment. On December 14, a probate judge ruled that Cho was mentally unstable and directed him to seek outpatient treatment at the CCC.[53] Incredibly, the CCC never provided any services to Cho because he did not keep the one appointment that was scheduled. Notwithstanding the judge's order, no one notified the court, VT police, or the administration that Cho had not received the court-mandated assessment and treatment—an inexcusable failure that placed students and faculty in mortal danger four months later.[54] Cho was permitted to enroll in January 2007 for the spring semester without receiving any treatment, and the rest is history.

Soon after the April 16 disaster, the parents of two students who were murdered in Norris Hall filed suit against VT for negligence and failure to protect their children. In 2012, a jury ruled for the families, awarding $4 million to each family. The awards were later reduced to $100,000 in accordance with state law.[55] In October 2013, the Virginia Supreme Court reversed the jury's verdict and ruled unanimously that VT officials could not have foreseen the second set of shootings in Norris Hall. Based on information available at the time, VT officials believed that the assailant had fled the area and posed no further danger to anyone else on the campus. Therefore, they had no duty to warn or protect others because Cho's murderous acts were not reasonably foreseeable.[56]

The tragedy at VT has prompted spirited discussion and reflection about the special relationships that exist between universities and their students and the related duty of institutions to warn and protect students and staff from foreseeable danger. Ensuring safety on accessible campuses where thousands of students and staff come and go at all hours is very difficult, if not impossible. As Gordon Davies said in summarizing his article on the Virginia Tech disaster, "There may not be a way to ensure that a mass killing like the one at Tech never happens again, but we can lessen the chance that one will."[57] Higher education leaders can and must do no less.

Regents of University of California v. Superior Court

On October 8, 2009, Damon Thompson, a student at the University of California, Los Angeles (UCLA) attacked Katherine Rosen, a classmate in

---

[53] *Id* at 12.

[54] *Id.*

[55] Sara Lipka *Virginia Tech Was Not Negligent, State Supreme Court Rules*, CHRON. HIGHER EDUC. (Nov. 15, 2013), at A21.

[56] Commonwealth of Va. v. Peterson, *supra* note 14.

[57] Gordon K. Davies, *supra* note 50, at 19.

a chemistry lab. Wielding a kitchen knife, Thompson stabbed Rosen repeatedly, inflicting life-threatening wounds. Rosen survived, and Thompson was charged with attempted murder. Rosen sued UCLA for negligence, arguing that UCLA has a duty to protect students from foreseeable harm while they are in the classroom.

In its 2018 decision, the California Supreme Court ruled that UCLA has a special relationship with its students and a legal duty to protect them from foreseeable dangers in classrooms and other curricular settings, including a duty to protect them from other students the university knows to be dangerous.[58] *Regents of University of California v. Superior Court* is an important decision because the Court held that colleges and universities have a duty of care to warn and protect enrolled students from foreseeable harm because of the special relationships that exist between those institutions and their students. In the court's view, the college-student relationship "fits within the paradigm of a special relationship," although the relationship is not a perfect fit. The special relationship between colleges and students extends only to activities over which the institution has a reasonable measure of control.[59] Consequently, postsecondary institutions owe a duty of care to protect students from foreseeable threats to their safety in classrooms and during "other curricular activities."[60] The duty of care does not extend to behavior outside the classroom over which the university has little or no control.[61]

The decision in *Regents of University of California* is important because the case involved a student who was brutally attacked by another student in a chemistry laboratory, and university officials were aware that the attacker suffered from mental illness.[62] In light of current concerns about safety on university campuses, interest in the special relationship between institutions and their students and the related duty of care will increase, and future litigation activity may increase accordingly.

Nguyen v. Massachusetts Institute of Technology

In May 2018, the Massachusetts Supreme Judicial Court ruled in *Nguyen v. Massachusetts Institute of Technology*[63] that universities within its jurisdiction have a limited duty to prevent their students from committing suicide. On June 2, 2009, Han Duy Nguyen, a graduate student at Massachusetts Institute of Technology (MIT) committed suicide immediately after a telephone conversation with his faculty advisor during which Nguyen was admonished for sending an unprofessional email to one of his faculty mentors. Nguyen had struggled academically and emotionally since beginning doctoral studies at MIT, and the conference call was the culmination of a series of discussions with faculty

---

[58] Regents of Univ. of Cal. v. Sup. Ct., 413 P.3d 656 (Cal. 2018).

[59] *Id.* at 668.

[60] *Id.* at 673-74.

[61] *Id.* at 669.

[62] *Id.* at 656.

[63] 96 N.E. 2d 128 (Mass. 2018).

on a variety of issues including poor study habits, learning disabilities, and chronic depression. Although program faculty supported Nguyen in dealing with his problems, he never performed at an acceptable level. When Nguyen performed poorly on his general examinations in 2009, faculty mentors actually recommended passing him anyway with the understanding that he would withdraw from the doctoral program and enroll in a related master's degree program.[64] Nguyen adamantly rejected the faculty's proposal and took his own life shortly after the June 2 telephone conversation.

Nguyen's father sued MIT, the faculty advisors, and other MIT employees alleging that they negligently breached a duty to prevent Nguyen from harming himself. The trial court dismissed the case, ruling that there was no breach of duty. On appeal, the Massachusetts Supreme Court affirmed the trial court's decision, but it ruled that universities do have a limited duty to prevent students from committing suicide under three conditions. "We conclude that a university has a special relationship with a student and a corresponding duty to...prevent his or her suicide in the following circumstances. Where a university has actual knowledge of a student's suicide attempt that occurred while enrolled at the university or recently before matriculation, or of a student's stated plans... to commit suicide, the university has a duty to take reasonable measures...to protect the student from self-harm."[65] The court described the following measures as "reasonable:" development of a suicide prevention protocol, providing clinical care for vulnerable students, and notifying the student's emergency contacts.[66] In the end, the court ruled that MIT and its employees had breached no duty to Nguyen and were not responsible for his death. [67]

Thomas v. Board of Trustees of Nebraska State Colleges

In the fall of 2010, Tyler Thomas, a 19-year-old female freshman, lived in a dormitory at Peru State College (PSC) in Nebraska. Joshua Keadle, a 29-year-old male, lived in an adjacent room. Thomas disappeared on December 3, 2010 and was never seen again. Keadle was questioned by the police and admitted being alone with Thomas near the Missouri River on the morning of her disappearance, but invoked his constitutional privilege against self-incrimination when pressed and refused to answer any more questions. Subsequently, Thomas was declared dead by a Nebraska state court, but her body was never recovered.

In the wake of this tragedy, LaTanya Thomas, Tyler's mother, filed two lawsuits against the Board of Trustees of the Nebraska State Colleges, seeking to hold the Board liable for her daughter's death. Both cases were dismissed on the Board's motion for summary dismissal, and both dismissals were upheld on

---

[64] *Id.* at 136
[65] *Id.* at 142-43.
[66] *Id.* at 146.
[67] *Id.* at 128.

appeal (*Thomas v. Nebraska State Colleges*, 2016[68] and *Thomas v. Nebraska State Colleges*, 2017[69]). She filed one suit, claiming that the Board was liable for damages under Title IX of the Education Amendments of 1972. Then, Thomas filed a second suit in Nebraska state court alleging negligence by the Board. Testimony in the case documented that Keadle had been charged with "forcible fondling" of an 18-year-old female and convicted of a misdemeanor theft conviction.[70] In September 2010, two coeds accused Keadle of sexually harassing them. Keadle acknowledged responsibility regarding the first claim, but denied responsibility for the second. College officials directed Keadle to obtain online training and complete ten hours of community service, prompting the housing director to recommend that he be removed from the dormitory.[71] A federal district court dismissed LaTanya Thomas's Title IX claim, and the Eighth Circuit Court of Appeals upheld the lower court's opinion, ruling that there was "no genuine issue of material fact as to whether the Board had actual knowledge that Keadle posed a substantial risk of…harm to students based on his previous known conduct, or whether the Board acted with deliberate indifference, both of which are required for a [successful] Title IX claim based on a student's action against the plaintiff."[72] Citing the Supreme Court's 1998 decision in *Gebser v. Lago Vista Independent School District*,[73] the Eighth Circuit concluded that a single complaint against a teacher (or student) for making inappropriate sexual remarks to others was insufficient to establish actual knowledge of an inappropriate sexual relationship.

In a second suit, a Nebraska trial court dismissed Tanya Thomas's negligence action, ruling that the Board of Trustees owed no duty of care to Thomas for Keadle's acts. On appeal, the Nebraska Supreme Court disagreed with the trial court, concluding that the Board did, in fact, owe Thomas a duty of care.[74] Nevertheless, the Supreme Court affirmed the trial court's ruling in favor of the Board, finding that Keadle's actions were not foreseeable: "[N]o reasonable fact finder could find that the harm that occurred was a reasonably foreseeable risk based upon the circumstances present in the case."[75]

The courts' decisions in the *Thomas* cases were consistent with established Title IX jurisprudence and negligence law. In retrospect, however, it is reasonable to ask whether Peru State officials erred by not removing Keadle from his room in a mixed-gender dormitory since he had a criminal record and had been accused of sexual harassment by two PSC students. In October 2017,

[68] Thomas v. Bd. of Trs. of Nebraska State Colleges, 667 Fed. Appx. 560 (8th Cir. 2016) (unpublished decision).
[69] Thomas v. Bd. of Trs. of Nebraska State Colleges, 895 N.W. 2d 692 (Neb. 2017).
[70] *Id.* at 697.
[71] Thomas v. Bd. of Trs. (2016), *supra* note 68, at 561.
[72] *Id.* at 562.
[73] Gebser v. Lago Vista Indep. Sch. Dist., 524 U.S. 274 (1998).
[74] Thomas v. Bd. of Trs. (2017), *supra* note 69, at 699.
[75] *Id.* at 700-701.

almost seven years after Tyler Thomas disappeared from the PSC campus, Joshua Keadle was charged with her murder.[76]

In summary, the courts' decisions in *Tarasoff*, *Commonwealth of Virginia*, *Regents of University of California*, *Nguyen*, and *Thomas* reflect the evolving nature of special relationships between postsecondary institutions and their students. In general, courts now agree that the college-student relationship does meet the legal criteria for a special relationship, "although the relationship is not [always] a perfect fit."[77] Consequently, the special relationship between colleges and their students normally extends only to dormitories, classrooms and curricular activities over which institutions have reasonable control. Foreseeability is a primary factor considered by the courts in determining whether an institution has a legal duty to warn and/or protect students from harm under the special relationship doctrine.

Student Privacy

The Family Educational Rights and Privacy Act (FERPA)

The Family Educational Rights and Privacy Act, or FERPA, is the most comprehensive federal law protecting student privacy.[78] Enacted in 1974 and also known as the Buckley Amendment, FERPA protects the privacy of a student's education records in primary and secondary schools as well as post-secondary institutions and prohibits their disclosure to third parties, including parents, without the written permission of the student. Before the passage of FERPA, institutions could retain "secret files" on students, including an individual teacher's negative comments, to which the student had no access. Such biased and negative comments could follow the unknowing student throughout his or her career and cause future teachers to view him or her in a negative and unfair light. Under FERPA, "education records" are defined broadly to include any documents that contain information directly related to a student, including academic, financial, and disciplinary records.[79] Other types of records on a student are excluded from the law including sole possession notes, law enforcement records, and treatment records. Sole possession notes are those created by an employee of the institution for personal use and that are not shared with anyone else, including a professor's personal notes about a student's performance or behavior.[80] Law enforcement records are records created, maintained, and used by campus police for law enforcement purposes. FERPA excludes law enforcement records from the definition of education records because their disclosure could interfere with the investigation of a

---

[76] Paul Hammel,"Joshua Keadle charged with murder in disappearance of Tyler Thomas, a Peru State Student from Omaha." *Omaha World-Herald*, Oct. 19, 2017.

[77] Regents of Univ. of Cal., *supra* note 58, at 668.

[78] 20 U.S.C.A. § 1232g.

[79] 20 U.S.C.A. § 1232g(a)(4)(A)(i).

[80] 0 U.S.C.A. § 1232(g)(a)(4)(B).

crime or endanger a potential witness or informant.[81] Treatment records are records created and maintained by medical and psychological professionals on campus and used only for treatment purposes; their confidentiality is protected under the doctor-patient relationship.[82]

FERPA ensures that students have access to their educational records. Students who request to see their records must be allowed to do so within a reasonable period of time, but in no case later than 45 days after the request is made.[83] If a student maintains that information in his or her record is inaccurate or misleading, he or she is entitled to a hearing to request that the material in question be deleted or amended. If institutional officials refuse to make the requested changes, the student has a legal right to place a written statement in his or her record rebutting the accuracy of the contested statements.[84] The right of a student to review his or her educational records is not absolute. A student is not entitled to see his or her parents' personal financial records or letters of recommendation that he or she has previously agreed are confidential.[85]

Most postsecondary institutions publish a student directory containing a list of students and their academic major, grade classification, and local address. This is possible because FERPA permits institutions to designate certain types of information as "directory information" which may include a student's name, address, telephone number, major, participation in extracurricular activities, height and weight of a student athlete, previous degrees received, and most recent institution attended.[86] Institutions must decide which directory information will be released, then inform students what information will be disclosed, and give students the opportunity to opt out of such disclosures.[87]

The most important consequence of FERPA in postsecondary institutions is that it prohibits disclosure of a student's education records without his or her written consent. Such consent must identify the person to whom the record may be disclosed, the specific information to be released, and the reason for the disclosure.[88] While at the K-12 level, FERPA rights belong to the parents of a student under the age of 18; those rights transfer to the student when he or she enrolls in a college or university, regardless of whether the student has reached the age of 18 or not. The transfer of FERPA rights from parents to student is difficult for some parents to accept, and college officials are often confronted by irate parents requesting information about their child's academic performance, class attendance, and/or behavior. Many postsecondary institutions try to avoid such unpleasant meetings by encouraging students to sign a release giving their parents continuing access to their education records.

---

[81] 20 U.S.C.A. § 1232g(a)(4)(B0(ii).
[82] 20 U.S.C.A. § 1232g(a)(4)(B)(iv).
[83] 20 U.S.C.A. § 1232g(a)(1)(B).
[84] 20 U.S.C.A. § 1232g(a)(1)(D).
[85] 20 U.S.C.A. § 1232g(a)(1)(C).
[86] 20 U.S.C.A. § 1232g(a)(5)(A).
[87] 20 U.S.C.A. § 1232g(a)(5)(B).
[88] 20 U.S.C.A. § 1232g(b)(2)(A).

Recognizing that a total ban on the disclosure of education records would paralyze educational processes, FERPA specifies a limited number of exceptions in which record disclosure is legal. By far, the most important of these exceptions is the right of institutional employees to share student records with other employees who have a legitimate interest in the information. In other words, a university employee may access a student's records to the extent necessary to perform his or her job.[89] Examples of necessary access to student records include the following: transfer of grades by professors to the registrar's office, the transfer of financial information from the financial aid office to the bursar, and the transfer of academic information from the registrar to scholarship committees. FERPA does not give college employees unlimited access to students' records, and virtually all institutions prevent employees from accessing records beyond the scope of their assigned job duties through policy and practice. Under FERPA, postsecondary institutions may disclose information to another institution where a student intends to enroll, to outside agencies processing a student's request for financial aid, to accrediting agencies, to government agencies in response to a subpoena, to educational research organizations, and to others during a health or safety emergency.[90] In light of the current concern about campus violence, the health and safety exception is of special interest.

Until recently, university administrators were reluctant to release information in student records to law enforcement agencies even when they believed that a student was dangerous and posed a threat to the community. Administrators were concerned about reactions of the Department of Education (DOE) when institutions disclosed information necessary to protect the health and safety of students and others. Subsequently, the Code of Regulations was amended and now states that if university officials can articulate a significant threat and a rational basis for their decision, the DOE "will not substitute its judgment for that of the ... institution."[91] If the institution's decision to disclose a student record to protect the health and safety of the student or others was reasonable in any way, the DOE will not second-guess the decision.

The outcome of disciplinary procedures is usually protected, but federal law mandates that the victim of a violent crime or a non-forcible sex offense has the right to know the results of a student disciplinary proceeding against the alleged attacker, including whether the defendant violated the student code of conduct and any sanctions levied by a disciplinary committee.[92] Furthermore, if a student is found to have committed a crime of violence or a non-forcible sexual offense, that information may be released to individuals other than the victim(s).[93] Institutions may respond to valid subpoenas for student records, but only after giving the student notice and an opportunity to move to quash

---

[89] 20 U.S.C.A. § 1232g(b)(1)(A).

[90] 20 U.S.C.A. § 1232g(b)(1).

[91] 34 C.F.R. § 99.36.

[92] 20 U.S.C.A. § 1232g(b)(6)(A).

[93] 20 U.S.C.A. § 1232g(b)(6)(B).

the subpoena. Conversely, if a subpoena in a criminal matter states that the student should not be notified, then the institution should release the records without informing the student. In all cases, FERPA requires institutions to maintain records documenting the date of any information disclosure, as well as to whom the disclosure was made.[94]

Postsecondary institutions are required to inform students of their FERPA rights in writing on an annual basis. Most institutions now provide the written notice electronically. The Family Policy Compliance Office of DOE enforces FERPA.[95] The ultimate sanction for a systematic failure to comply with FERPA is the cessation of federal funding, although there are no recorded instances of that happening to date.[96] FERPA applies to both public and private colleges and universities because virtually all private institutions receive federal funding through federal financial aid programs.[97]

In summary, FERPA's coverage is broad, but it should be remembered that the law protects only student education records from disclosure. FERPA does not prevent the disclosure of information that a university employee may know without consulting the records. If parents ask a faculty member whether their son or daughter has been attending class regularly, the teacher may respond based on personal knowledge. If the student has been absent from class an excessive number of times, the teacher is not violating the student's FERPA rights by disclosing that the student has not been attending class regularly. Furthermore, university personnel who are aware that a student has been involved in an accident can inform parents about the accident without fearing that FERPA is being violated.

The Health Insurance Portability and Accountability Act

The Health Insurance Portability and Accountability Act (HIPAA)[98] is another federal law protecting individual privacy. Enacted in 1996, HIPAA was designed to extend health insurance coverage for workers changing or leaving jobs and to reduce fraud in the healthcare system.[99] "Covered entities" under HIPAA are those that provide medical care and transmit information electronically related to that care. University and college clinics that provide healthcare and transmit or receive information related to that care must comply with HIPAA's provisions which mandate how diagnoses, treatment protocols, and charges are to be coded for electronic transmission.[100]

An important component of HIPAA is the Privacy Rule, which is intended to protect individually identifiable health information which is defined in the

---

[94] 20 U.S.C.A. § 1232g(b)(4)(A).

[95] 24 C.F.R. § 99.60.

[96] 20 U.S.C.A. § 1232g(b)(1).

[97] FERPA applies to all postsecondary institutions, but it rarely applies to private primary and secondary schools because most do not receive federal funding.

[98] Pub. L. No. 104-191, 100 Stat. 1936.

[99] *Id.*

[100] 45 C.F.R. § 162. *See* Administrative Simplification Provisions.

law as Protected Health Information (PHI). PHI includes the individual's health history, medical treatments, and the medical bills related to those treatments. Unless an individual authorizes the release of his or her PHI, healthcare providers may disclose that information only under very limited circumstances, such as when multiple healthcare providers are partnering in the treatment of a patient. The Security Rule in HIPAA requires medical providers to implement security measures that prevent third parties from accessing PHI.[101]

All university clinics that provide medical care and transmit related information electronically must comply with the Administrative Simplification provisions of HIPAA, although HIPAA explicitly excludes "education records" and "treatment records"[102] as defined by FERPA from the definition of PHI. Consequently, the Privacy Rule and the Security Rule in HIPAA do not apply to student health records at university health clinics. Conversely, if a covered university clinic provides care to faculty and staff, the Privacy and Security Rules do apply. When an on-campus clinic serves both students and nonstudents, the university may administer the records separately or opt to apply the privacy rule to student records as well as nonstudent records.[103]

The Gramm Leach Bliley Act (GLBA)

The Gramm Leach Bliley Act (GLBA) governs organizations engaged in certain financial activities and requires covered entities to protect the privacy of customer information.[104] Colleges and universities are covered under GLBA because they retain large collections of nonpublic information about their customers (i.e., students and their parents). Institutions must inform their customers each year of their policies regarding the types of information they collect, whether they disclose information to third parties, and if so, what information is disclosed and to whom.[105] If customer information is disclosed, then customers must be given an opportunity to opt out of the disclosure.[106] Institutions covered under GLBA must implement an information security system that details how it will access, collect, process, distribute, protect, store, use, transmit, and dispose of customer information.[107] While tiresome and onerous to develop and implement, the aforementioned regulations secure customer information, protect against external threats to data security, and protect confidential information from unauthorized access.[108]

---

[101] *Supra* note 98

[102] 45 C.F.R. § 160.103

[103] *Supra* note 98.

[104] 16 C.F.R. § 313.3(n).

[105] 15 U.S.C.A. § 6803.

[106] 15 U.S.C.A. § 6802.

[107] 16 C.F.R. § 314.2.

[108] 15 U.S.C.A. § 6801.

State Common Law Tort Claims Protecting Privacy

In addition to federal laws protecting student privacy, state laws also often protect student privacy rights. While state laws may provide even greater privacy protection than federal law, they cannot reduce the level of protection guaranteed under federal law. There are a number of torts based upon an invasion of privacy. Although they may differ from state to state, each cause of action will have the same elements and will protect the same interest. If the institution is public, the viability of a student's claim will depend on whether the state has given up sovereign immunity for the particular cause of action. In some situations, a student will not be able to sue the institution but could file a claim against individual employees.

The tort of "intrusion upon seclusion" arises when someone meddles in another's personal affairs or physically intrudes on someone at a time when privacy was reasonably expected.[109] The intrusion must be an act that would be highly offensive to a reasonable person. For example, a university employee who removes a student's medical records from the clinic files without proper authorization has "intruded upon the student's seclusion." Placing hidden cameras in areas where students have an expectation of (and right to) privacy, such as dormitory rooms and/or bathrooms, is another example of "intrusion upon seclusion" that provides legal cause for action.

In *Jennings v. University of North Carolina at Chapel Hill*,[110] a soccer coach was accused of sexually harassing his female players. According to the players, he "constantly interrogated members of his team, including Plaintiffs, regarding their personal lives, including but not limited to their sexual activities" and "constantly coerced and intimidated the members of his team, including Plaintiffs, to report to him, the sexual activities of their teammates, and placed unwanted and uninvited telephone calls to [one of the players] for the purpose of monitoring her activities." The district court denied the coach's motion for summary judgment, finding that his behavior could be highly offensive to a reasonable person.[111]

A second invasion of privacy tort occurs when someone makes public a private fact about another person that would be highly offensive to a reasonable person, and the private fact is not of legitimate concern to the public.[112] For example, students often disclose personal information during counseling and advising sessions with college and university employees. If a counselor or academic advisor later violates the student's confidence and repeats the information to others in a manner that a reasonable person would consider extremely offensive, then the student may very well have cause for legal action for "public disclosure of private facts."

---

[109] RESTATEMENT (SECOND) OF TORTS, § 652B (AM. LAW INST. 1977).

[110] 240 F. Supp. 2d 492, 515 (M.D.N.C. 2002).

[111] *Id.*

[112] RESTATEMENT (SECOND) OF TORTS, § 652D (AM. LAW INST. 1977)

Published photographs can constitute a public disclosure of private facts if the photograph reveals private information about an individual. For example, photographs showing students awaiting a disciplinary hearing, taking classes in a remedial program, or entering the office of a counselor could be offensive to a reasonable person under certain circumstances. On the other hand, photographs taken in public places will rarely be actionable because a student has no expectation of privacy while in public places.

Public disclosure of private facts (unlike intrusion upon seclusion) requires that the offending party reveal information to other persons. Videoing a student in his or her dormitory room without the student's knowledge would constitute intrusion upon seclusion. Streaming that video on the Internet would be a public disclosure of private facts, even if the video was produced initially with the student's consent. For example, a student may participate in a study about drug use and abuse and voluntarily provide personally embarrassing information. Even though the student voluntarily provided the information, subsequent disclosures of the information may be highly offensive to a reasonable person.

Public disclosure of private facts differs from defamation in that it involves the release of *true* statements, while defamation involves the publication of *false* statements. Furthermore, while defamation may occur when a false statement is communicated to only one other person, the public disclosure of private facts requires disclosure to enough people that the information has the potential to become common knowledge in the community.

A third cause of action protecting student privacy is "appropriation of name or likeness." This tort arises when someone uses another person's name or likeness for his or her own benefit.[113] While it is usually no problem to photograph students in public places, colleges and universities that wish to use a student's name or photograph in any type of promotional material should request the student's written permission to do so.

Finally, there is a privacy cause of action known as "false light." This claim may arise when an individual is portrayed in a false manner that would be highly offensive to a reasonable person, and the individual or institution acts in reckless disregard regarding the falsity of the matter.[114] For example, an institution conducting a campaign against underage drinking might publish material including photographs of underage students drinking alcohol. A student who appeared in one of the photographs who was not underage and/or not drinking might have a legitimate claim for being portrayed in a false light if a reasonable person would have been highly offended under the circumstances. If a student's privacy is violated, he or she may have more than one option for redress. If an institutional employee discloses private information about a student or portrays the student in a false light, the student may sue under state law for invasion of privacy and also file a complaint with the Family Policy Compliance Office in the Department of Education.

---

[113] RESTATEMENT (SECOND) OF TORTS, § 652C (AM. LAW INST. 1977).
[114] RESTATEMENT (SECOND) OF TORTS, § 652E (AM. LAW INST. 1977).

Conclusion

Federal law requires colleges and universities to inform students about foreseeable dangers on the campus and to protect students from those dangers as much as possible. The Crime Awareness and Campus Security Act of 1990 (The Clery Act) is the most important federal statute intended to ensure student safety. On the other hand, federal law also requires postsecondary institutions to protect the privacy of all students. The Family Educational Rights and Privacy Act (FERPA) of 1974 is the most important federal law mandating the protection of students' privacy rights.

In recent years, the mandate to protect student privacy has collided with the need to protect campus communities from violent acts committed by troubled students. In life-threatening situations, personal safety must trump personal privacy. Escalating campus violence in recent years has made it clear that institutions must collect, analyze, and disclose information about dangerous students when necessary to protect the safety and lives of others on the campus. Behavioral intervention teams appear to be the most efficient and effective administrative procedure to accomplish this purpose. Recent changes to federal regulations have assured postsecondary administrators that they can take preemptive steps to prevent campus violence without violating student privacy laws.

16

Equal Protection Clause

Philip T.K. Daniel, J.D., Ed.D.
The Ohio State University

Christopher C. Thomas, J.D., M.Ed.
Frost Brown Todd, LLC

Origin of the Fourteenth Amendment

The Fourteenth Amendment's legislative history and the drafters' original intent offer little, if any, assistance in modern application. Indeed, in *Brown v. Board of Education*,[1] the United States Supreme Court permitted re-argument to especially consider the circumstances surrounding the adoption of the Fourteenth Amendment in 1868. A unanimous Court ultimately determined that when it came to legislative history, there was simply "not enough to resolve the problem"[2] of one of the most important Supreme Court cases of the day. In the Court's eyes, the Equal Protection Clause's legislative history was, at best, "inconclusive."[3]

The Passage of the Amendment: A Mechanism to Protect Newly Freed Slaves

In the immediate aftermath of the Civil War, former slaves continued to find themselves victims in the South. Southern whites, having built an economy that was largely dependent on involuntary servitude, attempted to preserve their way of life through the use of Black Codes.[4] The Black Code of Mississippi, for example, prohibited freedmen from renting or leasing land. It also required freedmen to have a lawful home or place of employment, and written evidence thereof. Perhaps most abhorrent, the code gave civil officers the power to arrest

---

[1]   347 U.S. 483 (1954).

[2]   *Id.* at 489.

[3]   *Id.*

[4]   The term "Black Codes" refers to those laws passed in the southern United States, mostly after the Civil War, that mandated the segregation of blacks in all public places and conveyances. In particular, the codes intensified a policy that left former slaves without rights to citizenship or gainful employment. BLACK'S LAW DICTIONARY 154 (5th ed. 1979).

any freedman or any "freed negro" who had quit his/her job prematurely, and to "carry back" that freed person to his/her previous employer.[5]

To some extent, the harshness of these Black Codes ultimately backfired on Southern politicians, and in time solidified northern support for civil rights legislation. Radical Republicans—Northern politicians who controlled both houses of Congress—in time passed the Civil Rights Act of 1866 and extended citizenship to freedmen. This Congress also gave blacks the right to purchase and sell real property and the "equal benefit of all laws and proceedings for the security of person and property, as enjoyed by white citizens . . . .[6] Unfortunately, the Radical Republicans quickly learned that even federal laws could not contain the animosity the South felt toward freed blacks. President Andrew Johnson, a Southerner himself, vetoed the 1866 Civil Rights Act, stating that it upset the balance of power between the federal government and the states.[7] Johnson was not alone; a number of other critics of the Civil Rights Act questioned its constitutionality and Congress's power to pass such broad legislation, powers that were traditionally reserved for the states.[8] Although a congressional majority easily overcame the presidential veto, many elected officials were cognizant that a future Congress could change the law. Thus, the best way to preserve the civil rights of blacks was to enshrine these protections in the Constitution itself, thereby making the 1866 Civil Rights Act a constitutional mandate and designating the enforcement of civil rights a federal power. In the minds of the Radical Republicans, only an amendment to the Constitution itself would be capable of permanently protecting the civil rights of the newly freed blacks.

John A. Bingham, author of section one of the Fourteenth Amendment, explained that he sought for all "human beings . . . the precious right of life, liberty, and the pursuit of happiness."[9] Some Radical Republicans thought the Fourteenth Amendment would end racial discrimination altogether in the South[10] and some commentators feel that such a revolutionary purpose is precisely what spurred opposition to the amendment.[11] Moderate Republicans were aware of this political reality and recognized that if the bill was too specific, it could ignite racial prejudice in the North and the West; therefore, the

---

[5] LAWS OF THE STATE OF MISSISSIPPI (Jackson, 1866), 82-84.

[6] GEORGE P. SANGER, ed., THE STATUTES AT LARGE, TREATIES, AND PROCLAMATIONS OF THE UNITED STATES OF AMERICA (Boston, 1868), 14:27.

[7] CHRISTOPHER WALDREP & LYNNE CURRY, THE CONSTITUTION AND THE NATION 156 (2003) [hereinafter Waldrep].

[8] CHARLES REDENIUS, THE AMERICAN IDEAL OF EQUALITY 76 (1981) [hereinafter Redenius].

[9] WALDREP, supra n. 7, at 172.

[10] Derek W. Black, The Contradiction Between Equal Protection's meaning and its Legal Substance: How Deliberate Indifference Can Cure it, 15 WM. & MARY BILL RTS. J. 533, 548 (2006) (citing HOWARD J. GRAHAM, EVERYMAN'S CONSTITUTION 20, 315 (1968)).

[11] Id. (citing WILLIAM E. NELSON, THE FOURTEENTH AMENDMENT: FROM POLITICAL PRINCIPLE TO JUDICIAL DOCTRINE 96-97 (1988)).

Fourteenth Amendment was purposefully crafted vaguely and ambiguously to increase the likelihood that it would be adopted.[12]

These vagaries and ambiguities complicate any attempt to pinpoint the legislative intent of the Amendment's drafters. Evidence is available, however, that speaks to what the drafters and politicians thought the Fourteenth Amendment meant in 1868, to wit: 1) the Amendment would act as an ethical expression of fundamental and natural rights, as captured in the original Bill of Rights, and would extend these rights to freed slaves;[13] 2) the Amendment would prohibit class legislation, or legislation where a group of people is singled out for unfair treatment;[14] and 3) the Amendment would elevate an entire class of former slaves to citizenship status.[15]

Some academics and historians reach back to 1868 in hopes of uncovering the original intent of the Fourteenth Amendment's Equal Protection Clause. They believe that understanding the drafters' original intent would be useful in guiding the Equal Protection Clause's modern application. It need be recognized, however, that the Amendment's language has always been ambiguous, such that the language carries no "true" meaning. Instead, the language is given meaning by persons that interpret it in their day and age. As Justice Oliver Wendell Holmes, Jr. stated, "[E]qual protection of the law must grow in relevance and fulfillment with the felt necessities of the times . . .prevalent moral and political theories, institutions of public policy—ours and our children's, as well as our ancestors."[16] Thus, Congress' actions and the Supreme Court's interpretations of equal protection following its ratification likely provide the best indications as to what the Equal Protection Clause truly means.

In designing the first and fifth sections of the Fourteenth Amendment, Congress attempted to close any loopholes that the South could use to deny civil rights.[17] Section One contained negative language prohibiting states from passing laws that denied newly-freed blacks' rights,[18] and this initial prohibition is punctuated by Section Five, which delegated power to Congress "to enforce, by appropriate legislation, the provisions of this article."[19] But the South continued to struggle under these restrictions, and in response Congress exercised its power by passing the Civil Right Acts of 1870, 1871, and 1875.[20] The Radical Republicans had achieved significant legislative victories in the passage of these acts.

The 1876 election, however, would mark the end of these Republican successes. The Democratic Party candidate, Samuel Tilden, won the popular vote,

---

[12] Redenius, *supra* note 8, at 77.

[13] Black, *supra* note 10, at 551-52.

[14] Melissa L. Saunders, *Equal Protection, Class Legislation, and Colorblindness*, 96 MICH. L. REV. 245 (1997).

[15] *Id.*

[16] Black, *supra* note 10, at 557 (citing OLIVER WENDELL HOLMES, JR., THE COMMON LAW 1 (1881)).

[17] Redenius, *supra* note 8, at 77.

[18] U.S. CONST., amend. XIV, § 1.

[19] U.S. CONST. amend. XIV, § 5.

[20] Redenius, supra note 8, at 77.

albeit not the electoral majority. The parties faced a political standoff. After much negotiating and backroom politicking, the Democrats and Republicans forged a deal whereby the Republican candidate, Rutherford B. Hayes, would become president if, and only if, the Republicans would end their policy of Reconstruction.[21] After this election, Republicans turned their attention to capitalism and industrialization, and left the civil rights of newly freed blacks to essentially dissolve.[22] From 1875 to 1957, Congress did not pass another piece of civil rights or voting rights legislation, and watched idly as Jim Crow laws multiplied throughout the South.[23] This period demonstrates how ineffective paper rights and legal guarantees can be "in the absence of support by the value systems of the people and their elected officials[;] [o]nly when strong ties exist among the ideals held by the people, the written expression of those ideals, and governmental action can a broad social policy be implemented."[24]

The Court's Interpretation (and Circumscription) of the Amendment

With Congress out of the civil rights picture, federal courts were left center stage with the responsibility of determining the meaning and application of the Equal Protection Clause. The U.S. Supreme Court's first test arrived in 1873 as the *Slaughterhouse Cases*.[25] In this famous case, the Louisiana legislature had passed a law, presumably for health reasons, that created a monopoly for butchers within certain parishes in and around the city of New Orleans. Some Louisiana butchers were therefore effectively excluded from their trade because they operated outside of these particular parishes. Not surprisingly, these tradesmen brought a claim against the state of Louisiana and used the Fourteenth Amendment as their primary weapon. The Supreme Court, under the auspices of preserving a federal system, quickly denounced the efficacy of any such challenge based on the new amendment. The Court held that the regulatory power Louisiana had exercised was a traditional police power of the state and thus not a power that could be curtailed by the federal government. After disposing of the butchers' arguments, the Court, composed mostly of Southern judges, decided to move in for the kill. The Court related that, in light of the almost "all too recent to be called history," a "*most casual examination of the language*" of the amendments reveal that their sole purpose was the "freedom of the slave race, the security and firm establishment of that freedom, and the protection of the newly-made freedman and citizen from the oppressions of those who had formerly exercised unlimited dominion over him."[26] In short, the Court held that the Fourteenth Amendment was designed only to protect former slaves, and that Congress could not possibly

---

[21] *Id*. at 87.
[22] *Id*.
[23] *Id*.
[24] *Id*. at 78.
[25] 83 U.S. 36 (1873).
[26] *Id*. at 72.

have intended that the Amendment disturb traditional state's rights beyond the issues of slavery and citizenship for blacks. This powerful and purposeful oversimplification of the Amendment's history essentially eviscerated its most legally-potent language, the Privileges and Immunities Clause. Even today the construction of the Privileges and Immunities clause is controlled by the *Slaughterhouse* Court's vindictive holding. Civil rights scholars and historians have routinely recognized the *Slaughterhouse Cases* as among the worst decisions in Supreme Court history, ranking it alongside the *Dred Scot* decision[27] and *Plessy v. Ferguson*.[28]

The Court reemphasized its federalism argument within the same judicial term in *Bradwell v. State*.[29] In *Bradwell*, a female plaintiff brought an equal protection claim against the State of Illinois for prohibiting her from practicing law because she was a woman. The Court simply held that this law was well within a state's police powers, and although there did exist privileges and immunities that states could not abridge, practicing law was "not one of them."[30]

From these initial interpretations, it became clear that the Court would not endorse the possible remedial uses of the Fourteenth Amendment. Instead, the Court allowed the Southern social and Northern business agendas to commandeer the law's usage. The Court's next two cases, *U.S. v. Cruikshank*[31] and *U.S. v. Harris*,[32] also dealt severe blows to the protections offered by the Amendment. In these cases, African Americans had been murdered by white mobs, and the federal government had prosecuted only after the states had refused to do so. The convicted mob members appealed, arguing that the federal government had no authority to prosecute them. The Court declared that because the Fourteenth Amendment only protected against state actions, the Enforcement Act,[33] and its subsidiary Ku Klux Klan Act, were both unconstitutional, as these acts sought to regulate private behavior. The Court stated that the Fourteenth Amendment "prohibits a State from depriving any person of life, liberty, or property. . . but this adds nothing to the rights of one citizen

---

[27] Dred Scott v. Sandford, 60 U.S. 393 (1856).

[28] 163 U.S. 537 (1896). The late Prof. Charles Black said of *Slaughterhouse*, "This is probably the worst holding, in its effect on human rights, ever uttered by the Supreme Court." CHARLES BLACK, A NEW BIRTH OF FREEDOM, 55 (1999). And according to Prof. Lawrence Tribe, "there is considerable consensus among constitutional thinkers that the Supreme Court made a scandalously wrong decision in this case." RONALD LABBE & JONATHAN LURIE, THE SLAUGHTERHOUSE CASES: REGULATION, RECONSTRUCTION AND THE FOURTEENTH AMENDMENT, 2 (2003).

[29] 83 U.S. 130 (1873).

[30] *Id*. at 139.

[31] 92 U.S. 542 (1876).

[32] 106 U.S. 629 (1882)

[33] The Enforcement Act was designed to protect black voters. Unfortunately, those who witnessed such violations were usually unwilling to testify, so further legislation was soon necessary. There was a Second Enforcement Act in 1871 and a Third Enforcement Act (known as the Ku Klux Klan Act), also in 1871, which served the same basic purposes. This Third Act strengthened sanctions against those who impeded black suffrage: it gave the President the right to use federal forces to enforce the law.

against another."[34] This was reemphasized in the *Civil Rights Cases*[35] where the Court declared that the 1875 Civil Rights Act was unconstitutional. The 1875 Act required hotel operators, restaurants, and theaters not to discriminate on the basis of race, but the Court held that unless "State law has been passed, or some State action through its officers and agents . . . no legislation of the United States under said amendment, nor any proceeding under such legislation, can be called into activity . . ."[36]

The importance of this limitation is clear: it established a theoretical framework for interpreting the language of the Fourteenth Amendment that would make the Court's passivity, even in the face of mob murder, appear legally sound. There is no doubt that, to some extent, the state had created the circumstances that contributed to the murders at issue; the social and racial structures that led to the crimes could be traced directly to state involvement, be it the ancestry of the Black Codes or the emerging Jim Crow laws. But if the Court could remove this state involvement—here by promoting the myth that there exists a pre-political, stateless world—then the blacks would have no recourse under the Fourteenth Amendment for these "private" actions, regardless of how integral the state's involvement had actually been in setting the stage.

Finally, in 1896, the Court decided the seminal case *Plessy v. Ferguson*.[37] In *Plessy*, an African American plaintiff brought an equal protection claim against the state of Louisiana, challenging a law that required railroads to provide separate cars for black passengers and to partition existing cars into black and white sections to "promote the comfort of passengers."[38] The Court held, again, that the law was "within the competency of the state legislature in the exercise of their police power."[39] In fact, the Court pointed to the practice of school segregation in the North, where the civil rights of African Americans had been enforced the longest and most earnestly, as a clear example of the law's legitimacy.[40] The Court concluded that the exercise of state police power must simply be "reasonable . . . in good faith for the promotion of the public good, and not for the annoyance or oppression of a particular class."[41] The Court added that in determining reasonableness, legislatures can act in light of "established usages, customs and traditions of the people, and with a view to the promotion of their comfort, and the preservation of the public peace and

---

[34] *Harris*, 106 U.S. at 609.

[35] United States v. Stanley,109 U.S. 3 (1883).

[36] *Id*. at 22.

[37] 163 U.S. 537 (1896).

[38] *Id*. at 550.

[39] *Id*. at 544.

[40] *Id*. at 544 (referencing Roberts v. City of Boston, 59 Mass. (5 Cush.) 198 (1849)). The Supreme Court of Massachusetts held that state law did not require education for black students [even though] blacks were taxed for education at the same rate as whites. *See* P.T.K. Daniel, *The Not So Strange Path of Desegregation in America's Public Schools*, in THE PROMISE OF JUSTICE (Mac Stewart, ed. 2008).

[41] *Plessy*, 163 U.S. at 550.

other order."[42] There is no doubt that the legally mandated separation of the races in Louisiana was designed for the oppression of blacks. But the Court found that while the state law may not have treated blacks and whites equally in substance, it nonetheless treated them equally in form (blacks were separated from whites and whites from blacks). Thus, the court found that both blacks and whites received equal protection of the laws. Consequently, the doctrine of "separate but equal" was conceived, solemnizing racial segregation until *Brown v. Board of Education* was decided some 58 years later.

Altogether, the Equal Protection Clause of the Fourteenth Amendment as originally enacted by Congress and interpreted by the United States Supreme Court was primarily, if not entirely, an effort to protect former slaves. Though pushback initially frustrated these intentions through *Slaughterhouse, Bradwell, Cruikshank, Harris* and *The Civil Rights Cases*, Justice Holmes' words about the Fourteenth Amendment would prove prophetic, and the Equal Protection Clause would in time expand with society's evolving definitions of morality and equality.

Modern Interpretation and Application of the Equal Protection Clause

A Brief History of the Fourteenth Amendment and Desegregation in Education

Following *Plessy* and leading up to *Brown v. Board of Education*, federal courts exclusively applied the separate but equal doctrine to matters of race in education. Even though these cases do not necessarily demonstrate an evolution in Fourteenth Amendment legal doctrine, they do illustrate the Supreme Court's willingness to enforce African Americans' new right to substantially similar education. The first notable example of this came when the Court struck down a Missouri law that required black students to travel outside the state to a neighboring state's law school instead of attending the University of Missouri.[43] Missouri argued that because it offered to pay the difference in tuition, Missouri in fact offered African Americans a substantially similar education opportunity as the whites who attended Missouri's law school. The Court—not impressed—held that forcing African Americans to leave the state did not provide a substantially equal education and was overly burdensome. The law therefore violated African Americans' right to the equal protection of Missouri law.[44]

Twelve years later in *Sweatt v. Painter*, the Court held that a new law school that the state of Texas had created especially for African Americans, with the specific purpose of providing a separate but equal legal education, was nonetheless not comparable to the facilities that the state offered exclusively

---

[42] *Id.*
[43] Missouri ex rel. Gaines v. Canada, Registrar of the Univ. of Missouri, 305 U.S. 337 (1938).
[44] *Id.* at 351-53; *see also* Pearson v. Murray, 169 Md. 478 (1936).

for whites at the University of Texas Law School.[45] In reaching its conclusion, the Court considered the number of faculty and their qualifications, the schools' respective libraries and law reviews, and course curriculum as well as other objective factors. The Court also considered intangible factors such as the professors' prestige and reputation, the influence of alumni, and the overall esteem of the universities. Most importantly, the Court took into consideration the black students' need to interact with white students, since the majority of people with whom they would be dealing would be white.[46] These arguments illustrate the Supreme Court's slow but sure movement toward substantive equality.[47]

The final step on the Court's path to *Brown* came in *McLaurin v. Oklahoma State Regents for Higher Education*,[48] where the Court held that: 1) once a state admits blacks to a white institution, the state can no longer segregate them from white students to "prohibit the intellectual commingling of students," within classrooms and facilities and 2) the refusal of individuals to commingle where the state presents no such bar is vastly different than an imposition imposed by the state not to interact.[49] Thus, in terms of post-secondary education, the Court in *McLaurin* adjudicated exact equality between the races and used intangible factors to enrich and expand African American educational opportunities where they did not exist two or three decades earlier.

Missouri ex rel. Gaines, Sweatt, and *McLaurin* had paved the doctrinal path for the Court's ultimate rebuke of school segregation: *Brown v. Board of Education of Topeka.*[50] The lower court decisions that led up to *Brown* reveal the truly unique social and legal climates that surrounded the landmark decision. *Brown* was actually a case that combined lawsuits from Kansas, Delaware, Virginia and South Carolina. The South Carolina case was especially dramatic and included future Justice Thurgood Marshall who, as lead attorney for the plaintiffs in *Brown,* endured threats and intimidation as his case moved forward.[51] Marshall's case was first heard in the U.S. district court for the Eastern District of South Carolina. Prior to delivering its decision, the court related how the plaintiffs had requested the court to explicitly

> hold that segregation of races in public schools, as required by the [South Carolina] Constitution and the statutes of South Carolina, is of itself a denial of the equal protection of the laws guaranteed by the Fourteenth Amendment[.][52]

---

[45] 339 U.S. 629 (1950).
[46] *Id.* at 632-35.
[47] *See also* McKissick v. Carmichael, 187 F.2d 949 (1951).
[48] 339 U.S. 637 (1950).
[49] *Id.* at 641.
[50] 347 U.S. 483 (1954).
[51] Richard Kluger, Simple Justice: The History Of Brown v. Bd. Of Education And Black America's Struggle For Equality (1977).
[52] Briggs v. Elliott, 98 F. Supp. 529 (E.D.S.C. 1951).

Though the district court pointed out that the school facilities available to black children were not equal to the school facilities provided to white children, the judge rendering the opinion proceeded to distinguish public secondary education from post-secondary education. He remarked that professional contacts and professional development do not matter in public-secondary education, and that public school was not voluntary. Finally, the court noted that public schools are *in loco parentis* and must bend to the "wishes of the parent as to the upbringing of the child."[53] Ultimately, the court deferred to *stare decisis* and held that if "segregation is no longer wise, that is a matter for the legislatures and not for the courts."[54] District Judge Waring's dissent describes the racism and violence surrounding these segregation decisions. Waring referenced leading politicians and governors—specifically South Carolina's governor—who had declared that desegregation would endanger "white supremacy" and that if this be the case, public states should abandon public education altogether. Waring concluded by noting how courts all over the land had stricken down segregation in upper education and "declared unequivocally that segregation is not equality";[55] Waring, along with many others, was ready to extend desegregation to public schools. The stage was set for *Brown* and the era of desegregation.

The Era of Desegregation in Schools

Following re-argument to consider the circumstances surrounding the adoption of the Fourteenth Amendment, the *Brown* Court determined that it "must consider public education in the light of its full development and its present place in American life throughout the nation" to determine if segregation deprived African Americans of the equal protection of the laws.[56] In holding that it did, the Court cited the "feeling of inferiority" that community segregation had created in black students, a feeling unlikely to ever be undone. The Court referenced compelling psychological evidence that demonstrated how the state law that forced segregation among students not only denotes inferiority, but also affects the ability of black children to learn properly, which in turn retards educational development among black students.[57] Because of these evidence-based negative repercussions of segregation, the Court found that segregated education could never be equal.

Months later, in *Brown v. Bd. of Education II*,[58] the Supreme Court vested power in the federal courts to remedy the effects of segregation. The Court cautioned lower courts to use equitable principles and practical flexibility in shaping its remedies to the consequences of racial segregation and to make

---

[53] *Id.* at 535.
[54] *Id.* at 537.
[55] *Id.* at 547 (Waring, J., dissenting).
[56] Brown v. Bd. of Education, 347 U.S. 483, 492-93 (1954).
[57] *Id.* at 494.
[58] 349 U.S. 294 (1955).

"good faith compliance at the earliest practicable date"[59] with *Brown I*. What followed, however, was widespread evasion, resistance and delay to the Court's mandate. The same district court in South Carolina that denounced segregation leading up to *Brown I* held that schools that were open to all races without discrimination did not offend the Constitution if children of different races voluntarily chose to attend different schools.[60] The court held that the Constitution did not require integration, it merely forbade discrimination.[61]

Resistance to *Brown* was so widespread and persistently defiant that even ten years after the high court's decision, minimal progress had been made toward dismantling the dual education system in states.[62] In 1968, fourteen years after *Brown* was handed down, the United States Supreme Court finally struck down the "voluntary" freedom-of-choice plans articulated by federal courts, such as South Carolina's Eastern District, as a defense against forced integration, and insisted on a true desegregation plan that "promises realistically to work now."[63] In *Green v. County School Board of New Kent*, the Court went on to state that school districts that operated under *de jure* segregation (segregation mandated by law) had an "affirmative duty to take whatever steps might be necessary to convert to a unitary system in which racial discrimination would be eliminated root and branch."[64] Following this proclamation to extinguish all remnants of *de jure* discrimination, federal district courts were afforded expansive powers in order to supervise districts and manage their efforts to remedy desegregation. In *Swann v. Charlotte-Mecklenburg Bd. of Education*,[65] the Supreme Court upheld lower court decisions governing student and teacher assignments, facilities equalization, school location, and transportation, all in the name of desegregation.

Swann may appropriately be considered the high-water mark of the Court's strategy of empowering the lower federal courts,[66] and as the public grew weary of judicial imposition, the Court began to retreat from the stance it had taken in *Green*.[67] After *Swann*, the Court slowly but surely began to recede from the strong anti-subordination declaration it had announced in *Brown*. In 1973, the Court held that a school district's choice to acquire funding for its district through the collection of local property taxes—a method that, not surprisingly, resulted in an unequal distribution of resources between rich and poor districts—did not violate the Equal Protection Clause.[68] The decision only added to the allure of suburban schools and white flight.

---

[59] *Id.* at 299.

[60] Briggs v. Elliott, 132 F. Supp.776 (E.D.S.C. 1955).

[61] *Id.* at 777.

[62] William D. Araiza, et. al, Constitutional Law: Cases, History, and Dialogues 902 (2006).

[63] Green v. County School Bd. of New Kent, 391 U.S. 430, 439 (1968).

[64] *Id.* at 438.

[65] 402 U.S. 1 (1971).

[66] William D. Araiza, *Courts, Congress and Equal Protection: What Brown Teaches US About the Section 5 Power*, 47 Howard L.J. 1999, 206 (2004).

[67] Araiza, *supra* note 63, at 904.

[68] *See* San Antonio Indep. Sch. Dist. v. Rodriguez, 411 U.S. 1 (1973).

The following year the Court held that a district court in Michigan could not force the inclusion of Detroit suburbs in a plan to desegregate inner-city Detroit schools since the suburbs were not guilty of *de jure* segregation, and were thus beyond the remedial powers of the district court.[69] The case, *Milliken v. Bradley*, signaled the end of the Supreme Court's willingness to make *Brown*'s mandate for educational equality "a living truth."[70] Instead, the Court held that the power of federal courts to demand integration could only be used inside those districts that had a proven history of discrimination.[71] Thus the newly created suburbs became safe havens for fleeing whites; new suburban school districts, though created by the state, would effectively be immune from integration efforts. District lines would serve as a fictional stopping point for remedial efforts, and if whites could escape these boundaries of the urban centers, they could also escape the reach of *Brown*. Justice Thurgood Marshall, dissenting in the bitterly divided 5-4 decision, exposed the ideological decision as "a reflection of a perceived public mood that we have gone far enough in enforcing the Constitution's guarantee of equal justice."[72] The Court had once again permitted American metropolitan areas to become "two cities – one white, the other black."[73]

More cases offering the proverbial nail in the coffin for *Brown* arrived in the 1990s. In 1992, the Supreme Court held that lower courts could, piece by piece, give control over school districts back to the local school boards as the school districts came into compliance with select desegregation requirements.[74] The Court stated that "though we cannot escape our history, neither must we overstate its consequences in fixing legal responsibilities"[75] and that "demographic forces causing population change"[76] were not related to *de jure* segregation and thus were not subject to oversight under the Equal Protection Clause. The Court concluded that as the "*de jure* violation becomes more remote in time and these demographic forces intervene, it becomes less likely that a current racial imbalance in a school district is a vestige of the prior *de jure* system."[77] Justice Ruth Bader Ginsburg, in dissent, stressed the inequity of shortchanging the ability of remedial programs to achieve educational equality between races in public schools after only seven years of remedial efforts in the face of more than two centuries of discrimination and slavery

---

[69] Milliken v. Bradley, 418 U.S. 717 (1974).
[70] Cooper v. Aaron, 358 U.S. 1, 20 (1958).
[71] *Milliken*, 418 U.S. at 745.
[72] *Id*. at 814.
[73] *Id*. at 815. Two years later, in Pasadena City Bd. of Educ. v. Spangler, the Court would even prohibit a federal court from exercising its remedial powers *inside* a district with a past history of discrimination, since the district had complied with a desegregation mandate for one year and had achieved unitary status. 427 U.S. 424, 434-36 (1976).
[74] Freeman v. Pitts, 503 U.S. 467 (1992); *see also* Missouri v. Jenkins, 515 U.S. 70 (1995).
[75] *Freeman*, 503 U.S. at 495.
[76] *Id*. at 496.
[77] *Id*.

in America.[78] Despite the Court's minority belief that district courts should have more power to further integrate schools, the majority opinion permits *de facto* segregation and only remedies remnants of *de jure* segregation, which appears to be almost extinct.[79]

For about 25 years, the evils of *de jure* segregation provided federal courts with a special justification for using race-conscious factors in remedying desegregation. Yet today, as remnants of *de jure* segregation have faded into history, schools without remnants of *de jure* discrimination that wish to use racial classifications for benign, remedial purposes are nevertheless subject to the same strict scrutiny analysis that was once used as a means to equality in *Brown*.

Strict Scrutiny and Active Integration

Higher Education

Two U.S. Supreme Court cases decided in 2003, *Grutter v. Bollinger*[80] and *Gratz v. Bollinger*[81], presently shape active racial integration in post-secondary education. Both cases relied almost entirely on *Regents of the University of California. v. Bakke*, wherein the Court held that even if a university's goal of achieving diversity was constitutionally sound, an applicant's race could not be given more weight than other factors.[82] While status as a racial minority could count as a "plus" in an applicant's profile, it must be considered alongside all other variables in an admissions determination.[83] Further, the Court reemphasized that the Fourteenth Amendment applied to every *individual* and is applied equally to all races, despite society's efforts to benefit one disadvantaged race at the expense of others.[84]

In *Gratz*, the University of Michigan College of Literature, Science, and Arts had designed an admissions procedure geared toward increasing minority enrollment and achieving diversity, but the Court held that the admissions process was unconstitutional. The College admissions office used a point system that was favorable to students of color. The College identified African Americans, Hispanics, and Native Americans as underrepresented minorities and awarded them an automatic twenty points, which made the factor of race decisive for "virtually every minimally qualified underrepresented minority

---

[78] Missouri v. Jenkins, 515 U.S. 70 (1995) (Ginsburg, J., dissenting).
[79] Not totally extinct, though. In U.S. v. Mississippi, 505 U.S. 717 (1991), the Court struck down admission requirements to Mississippi's prestigious universities that required ACT scores that were based on vestiges of discrimination. The Court held that the State previously selected the requisite ACT score in order to discriminate against blacks from getting into white schools after *Brown*.
[80] 539 U.S. 306 (2003).
[81] 539 U.S. 244 (2003).
[82] 438 U.S. 265 (1978).
[83] *Id*. at 317.
[84] *Id*. at 289-90.

applicant."[85] The Court held that this minority classification failed to consider each applicant as an individual and to weigh the personal qualities that would contribute to a university setting. Thus, even though the Court deferred to the finding in *Bakke* that diversity may be a compelling state purpose, the admissions process in *Gratz* was not sufficiently narrowly tailored to achieve this purpose, as race was used as a deciding factor in determining whether or not a student would contribute to campus diversity. The Court considered the admissions policy to be equivalent to a racial quota, and therefore unconstitutional.

In *Grutter*, the Court found itself on the other side of the fence, holding that the University of Michigan's Law School admissions process permissibly used race as a plus factor in a calculus of other variables in making admissions decisions.[86] The Court established—while also using *Bakke* as a backdrop—that because diversity at the university level was a compelling state interest, the use of race in admissions was justified.[87] The Court emphasized that not every decision that is based on race is objectionable, and that race-based governmental action must be viewed in context.[88] The Court went on to state that while a quota system or a system that insulates a class of people from competition would not be narrowly tailored to achieving a compelling state interest, a university nonetheless may consider race as a plus factor, as this would not insulate an applicant from competition.[89] The Court even recognized that the use of a mathematical formula in an admissions program in order to achieve a critical mass of persons of color does not necessarily constitute a quota system, so long as such applicants are still competing against all other applicants. The Court concluded that the law school had engaged in a holistic, individual review of each applicant's file in order to achieve diversity, and that race had not singularly determined whether or not an applicant of color would be accepted.

As a parting shot in *Grutter*, the Court cautioned that narrow tailoring requires a "good faith consideration of workable race-neutral alternatives that will achieve the diversity the university seeks."[90] Also, race-based government remedial action must be limited in time, and would be subject to continuing oversight to assure it will do the least harm to affected individuals.[91]

Recently, the Supreme Court again re-emphasized the limits of *Gratz* and *Grutter*, while upholding the state's compelling interest in diversity and stressing the importance of strict scrutiny review. In *Fisher v. University of Texas*,[92] a white female student was denied admission to the University of Texas. Prior to this, the state of Texas had enacted a statute that required state universities

---

[85] *Gratz*, 539 U.S. at 272.

[86] Grutter v. Bollinger, 539 U.S. 306 (2003).

[87] *Id*. at 325, 330.

[88] *Id*. at 327.

[89] *Id*. at 334.

[90] *Id*. at 339.

[91] *Id*. at 341-42.

[92] 570 U.S. 297 (2013) (*Fisher I*).

to admit all students who graduated high school in the top ten-percent of their high school class. The University of Texas, after admitting those students in the top ten percent, allocated the remaining seats in the incoming class amongst the remaining in-state and out-of-state applicants using a holistic review process that considered race, as well as other qualities such as extracurricular hobbies, leadership qualities, and socioeconomic status as factors. The white female student denied admission filed suit, alleging that UT impermissibly considered race in its admission policy in violation of the Equal Protection Clause of the Fourteenth Amendment. Specifically, she argued that there were race-neutral alternatives, like the top ten percent plan, that could have substantially achieved UT's interest in promoting diversity without resort to race-based considerations.

In deciding *Fisher I*, the Supreme Court, in a 7-1 decision, remanded the case back to the Fifth Circuit for reconsideration, finding that the Circuit Court had failed to apply a "strict scrutiny" standard of review. The Court held that, while the university was entitled to deference on its conclusion that diversity was necessary to its academic goals, it was the judiciary's duty to ensure that the university's use of race was narrowly tailored to achieve that compelling state goal.[93] To this end, the lower court was required to conclude that "no workable race-neutral alternatives would produce the educational benefits of diversity."[94] Instead of applying this standard, the Court held that the Fifth Circuit erroneously "presumed that the school had acted in good faith."[95] Because of this, the Court vacated the lower court's decision and re-manded so that the lower court could apply the proper standard. Importantly, the Court in *Fisher I* did not overrule the notion that diversity constituted a compelling state interest. However, in their concurring opinions, Justices Scalia and Thomas both intimated that they would support overruling *Grutter* and its compelling interest in diversity in the future,[96] leaving equal protection in the higher education context on somewhat unsteady ground, until the Court decided *Fisher II* in 2016.[97]

After the lower court decided the case on remand, the Supreme Court again agreed to hear the *Fisher* case, this time upholding UT's race-conscious admission policy in a 4-3 decision. The majority opinion, authored by Justice Kennedy, held that UT's policy was narrowly tailored to the state's compelling interest in promoting the educational benefits that flow from diversity. While the Court affirmed the university's compelling interest in diversity, it did caution that this interest must not be defined so as to be "elusory or amorphous."[98] Coupled with the Court's earlier decisions that racial quotas are impermissible, this decision places universities in an uncomfortable position when articulat-ing their goal. They must persuasively articulate their rationale for pursuing

---

[93] *Id.* at 310.

[94] *Id.* at 312.

[95] *Id.* at 298.

[96] *Id.* at 315.

[97] Fisher v. Univ. of Tex., 136 S. Ct. 2198 (2016).

[98] *Id.* at 2211.

diversity and adequately define the "critical mass" of diversity that they are seeking to achieve without falling back on strictly numerical definitions. The Court did find that UT's policy properly navigated this balance but warned that universities "should remain mindful that diversity takes many forms" and that "formalistic racial classifications may sometimes fail to capture diversity in all of its dimensions."[99]

In regard to whether UT's policy of race-conscious admissions was narrowly tailored, the Court held that it was. Significant to this decision was the university's deliberate decision-making process before instituting race as a factor in admissions and the university's evidence that race-neutral alternatives were less effective and insufficient to meet its goal of diversity. Interestingly, in evaluating this evidence, the Court relied on quantitative evidence provided by the university as well as qualitative evidence in the interviews of former minority students who, prior to the race-conscious admissions policy, "experienced feelings of loneliness and isolation."[100] While it's unclear what weight the Court gave this evidence, this consideration echoes the Court's earlier consideration of the harm caused by segregation in *Brown*. Whether this foreshadows a return to an interpretation of the Equal Protection Clause that lends itself more towards an anti-subordination interpretation remains unclear, but what is clear is that affirmative action in higher education remains constitutionally viable, though with stringent limitations.

K-12 Education

Even though *Fisher II* affirmed the use of race as a factor in admission to institutions of higher education, the Supreme Court has not been as receptive to the use of racial classifications in the context of K-12 public schools. Most recently, this was demonstrated in *Parents Involved in Community Schools v. Seattle School District (PICS)*,[101] where public school districts in Louisville, Kentucky and Seattle, Washington had voluntarily used the concept of diversity to create student assignment plans within their boundaries. A plurality of the Court, joined by Justice Kennedy's concurring opinion, first recognized that neither plan was brought forth in an effort to remedy *de jure* segregation. Therefore, the Fourteenth Amendment would only permit the school districts to use race-based assignments if their plans could survive strict judicial scrutiny. Next, the plurality distinguished *Grutter* from *PICS*'s fact pattern; most importantly, *Grutter* applied to diversity in higher education. As the Court had related in *Grutter*, context matters. As a result, *Grutter* was not controlling in the K-12 context.[102]

The plurality opinion, absent Kennedy, simply held that racial diversity for its own sake was not a compelling governmental purpose and that a racial

---

[99] *Id.* at 2210.
[100] *Id.* at 2212.
[101] 551 U.S. 701 (2007).
[102] *Id.* at 724-25.

balance should not be achieved merely for its own sake.[103] A majority of the Court, which included a concurrence from Justice Kennedy, then held that the districts' means of achieving diversity, without a *de jure* violation, did not meet the test of strict scrutiny. As a result, the student assignment plans were unconstitutional.[104] Moreover, according to the Court, there was no evidence that the districts had made a good faith effort to achieve their goals by using race-neutral alternatives.[105]

In a somewhat surprising turn, Justice Kennedy, who had written a strong dissent in *Grutter*, extended the *Grutter* decision and stated that diversity is a "compelling educational goal [public school] district[s] may pursue."[106] He further stated that race can be a factor taken into account to ensure that all people have equal opportunity. He asserted that school officials are not limited to the strictures of *de jure* discrimination and, further, they may take steps to mitigate the effects of *de facto* discrimination (discrimination created "naturally" and not by law) where appropriate.[107] That is, school officials could use racial classifications, if narrowly tailored to meet the goal of diversity, as a response to *de facto* segregation. He went on to state that even though some justices profess the Constitution to be color-blind, in the real world, such an axiom simply does not work. In the end, Kennedy's opinion is paradoxical: he seeks to have diversity—which requires race-based classifications—be recognized as an honorable compelling interest, and yet he declares, almost in the same breath, that students cannot be defined by any racial classification.

Affirmative Action and States' Rights

More recently, the Court has begun to justify its "hands off" approach to racial equality by transforming the issue into one of federalism. For example, in *Schuette v. Coalition to Defend Affirmative Action, Integration & Immigrant Rights & Fight for Equality by Any Means Necessary (BAMN)*, the Court addressed a state constitutional amendment that prohibited affirmative action in public education, employment, and contracting.[108] Various organizations brought suit against state officials, universities, and other state actors to challenge this anti-affirmative action provision under the Equal Protection Clause of the U.S. Constitution. The Court ultimately found that there was no constitutional authority to set aside the Michigan constitutional amendment. In so doing, the Court emphasized that the issue before it did not concern "how the debate about racial preferences should be resolved"[109] or "the constitutionality, or the merits, of race-conscious admissions policies in higher education."[110]

---

[103] *Id*. at 724-24.
[104] *Id*. at 757.
[105] *Id*. at 735.
[106] *Id.* at 783.
[107] *Id*. at 788.
[108] 572 U.S. 291 (2014).
[109] *Id*. at 314.
[110] *Id*. at 300.

Instead, the Court framed the question as one grounded in notions of democracy, addressing only "whether, and in what manner, voters in the States may choose to prohibit the consideration of such racial preferences."[111]

In its opinion, the Court did acknowledge the well-established principle that "when hurt or injury is inflicted on racial minorities by the encouragement or command of laws or other state action, the Constitution requires redress by the courts."[112] However, the Court found that there was no injury here—instead, it was an issue about whether voters could preclude government officials from favoring one race over another. Thus, the Court largely deflected the issues of race, affirmative action, and the values of diversity, instead resting its decision on democratic concerns and the right of citizens to act through the political process. As such, *Schuette* may signal a change of course in affirmative action and equal protection jurisprudence for the future, tempered somewhat though by the Court's decision in *Fisher II*.

Contemporary Degrees of Judicial Scrutiny under the Fourteenth Amendment

Rational Basis

There exist at least three levels of judicial scrutiny under the Fourteenth Amendment. The Amendment, in practice, protects individuals against laws enacted by legislatures, or policies created by government officials, that seek to classify them—and thus treat them differently—because of their memberships in certain classes. The Supreme Court, on a case-by-case basis, has determined over time which classes need protection under the Fourteenth Amendment, referring to those groups as "protected classes."[113] Yet different protected classes are given different degrees of protection. That is to say that classes such as race, given the severity of race-based discrimination in American history, are given more protection than other classes, e.g. economic status. In effecting such protection, federal courts review or "scrutinize" laws that seek to classify such protected classes at levels of scrutiny that correspond to the level of protection given to a class.

Though it can be said that all legislation affects people differently to some extent, legislation that does not classify individuals on the basis of their membership in a protected or suspect class is subject to the lowest degree of scrutiny. This lowest degree of scrutiny thus pertains to legislative classifications that are not suspect or that do not pertain to a "class of persons characterized by some unpopular trait or affiliation . . . that reflect[s] any special likelihood of bias on the part of the ruling majority."[114] In these cases, such classifications

---

[111] *Id.* at 301.

[112] *Id.* at 313.

[113] *See* Hamilton v. Foti, 372 Fed.Appx. 480, 484 (5th Cir. 2010) (in order to qualify for equal protection an individual must show the protected class to which he/she belongs).

[114] N.Y. City Transit Auth. v. Beazer, 440 U.S. 568, 607 (1979).

are valid "unless they bear no rational relationship to the State's objectives".[115] This degree of rationality has traditionally been granted wide latitude by the Supreme Court. For example, in *New York City Transit Authority v. Beazer*, the New York City Transit Authority had prohibited all persons receiving methadone treatment for heroin addiction from working. The Court held that the policy served "general objectives of safety and inefficiency," was impartial, and had been applied evenhandedly to all persons.[116] The law thus survived the Court's low level of review and was deemed a valid classification.

Rational basis review has also been applied to "state legislation restricting the availability of employment opportunities."[117] For example, the availability of employment opportunities has been restricted on the basis of age. The Supreme Court held that even though the category of "aged persons" is not "wholly free of discrimination,"[118] it has not experienced a "history of purposeful unequal treatment or been subject to unique disabilities on the basis of stereotyped characteristics not truly indicative of their abilities."[119] In *Massachusetts Bd. of Retirement v. Murgia*, the state of Massachusetts required its police officers to retire at age 50 regardless of an officer's perfect health. The Supreme Court held that the policy clearly did not violate the Equal Protection Clause because it was rationally related to the State's purpose of assuring the physical preparedness of its uniformed police.[120] Age-based classifications are, therefore, subject to the lowest level of judicial scrutiny, the rational basis test.[121]

Even though States are afforded broad discretion under the rational basis standard, it is not boundless. In *City of Cleburne v. Cleburne Living Center*, for example, a Texas city denied a permit to a group home for disabled persons pursuant to a city zoning ordinance that prohibited such homes.[122] The Court first noted the general premise that "legislation is presumed to be valid when rationally related to a legitimate state interest."[123] Applied to social and economic issues, this means that states are entitled to wide latitude under the Equal Protection Clause. The Court also recognized that states have good reason to single out disabled persons in order to care for them, and that such legislative activity warrants rational basis review. However, the record revealed that the city had no rational basis for imposing the ordinance other than to harm, not help, a politically unpopular group. Hence, the Court concluded that the ordinance was not rationally related to any legitimate purpose, and because the ordinance could not survive even the lowest level of judicial scrutiny, it was found to be a violation of the Fourteenth Amendment.[124]

---

[115] *Id.*

[116] *Id.* at 593.

[117] Massachusetts Bd. of Retirement v. Murgia, 427 U.S. 307 (1976).

[118] *Id.* at 314.

[119] *Id.*

[120] *Id.* at 315-16.

[121] *Id.* at 314-15.

[122] 473 U.S. 432 (1985).

[123] *Id.* at 440.

[124] *Id.* at 450.

One contemporary issue regarding rational basis is what level of scrutiny applies to discrimination based on sexual orientation. Historically, discrimination based on sexual orientation has been subject to rational basis review.[125] In a trio of more recent cases, however, the Supreme Court has largely skirted the issue, while at the same time striking down different laws that treated same-sex couples differently than opposite-sex couples. First, in *Lawrence v. Texas*,[126] the Court invalidated a Texas law that criminalized same-sex couples who engaged in certain sexual conduct. Relying primarily on Substantive Due Process but also drawing on Equal Protection ideals, the Court held that "[t]he Texas statute furthers no legitimate state interest which can justify its intrusion into the personal and private life of the individual."[127] This holding echoes the language of rational basis, but the Court also invoked fundamental rights of privacy in defending its position, leaving the level of scrutiny applied unclear.[128]

Similarly, the Court in *United States v. Windsor*[129] again struck down a law treating same-sex couples differently without articulating what judicial standard was being applied. This time, the Court struck down the federal Defense of Marriage Act. Again, the Court invoked the language of rational basis, holding that the law furthered "no legitimate purpose,"[130] but did not explicitly articulate what test it was applying. At the same time though, language in the opinion suggested that same-sex couples constituted a protected class that the legislature could not single out for disparate treatment. Ultimately, this issue endures even after the Court's most recent decision in *Obergefell v. Hodges*,[131] which struct down state same-sex marriage bans on both Substantive Due Process and Equal Protection grounds. Writing for the Court, Justice Kennedy, who also authored the majority opinions in *Lawrence* and *Windsor*, held that marriage was a fundamental right and that it would violate Equal Protection to deny that right to same-sex couples. However, like *Lawrence* and *Windsor*, the Court did not clearly articulate what level of scrutiny it was applying in striking down the law. Ultimately, with regards to discrimination based on sexual orientation, while the level of scrutiny applied is currently

---

[125] *See, e.g.*, Romer v. Evan, 517 U.S. 620, 631 (1996) (striking down a Colorado law that discriminated based on sexual orientation as not being rationally related to a legitimate governmental interest).

[126] 539 U.S. 558 (2003).

[127] *Id.* at 578.

[128] For a discussion of this point, see Justice Scalia's dissent. *Id.* at 586 (Scalia, J., dissenting).

[129] 570 U.S. 744 (2013).

[130] *Id.* at 775.

[131] 135 S. Ct. 2584 (2015).

uncertain,[132] the Supreme Court has been highly skeptical of laws that seem to impose "second-class" status on same-sex couples.[133]

Intermediate Scrutiny

Intermediate scrutiny was created largely in response to gender discrimination. To trace the development of women's rights under the Equal Protection Clause is to tell the history of society's perception of women in America. In 1873, the Supreme Court ruled that denying women admission to the practice of law solely because of their gender was within the States' police power, and thus did not constitute a violation of the Fourteenth Amendment. [134] In 1948, the Court held that Michigan could deny awarding liquor licenses to women because the granting of liquor licenses was "one of the oldest and most untrammeled of legislative powers"[135] and Michigan could, beyond question, "forbid all women from working behind a bar."[136] Clearly, legislative classifications based on gender were not seen as harmful forms of discrimination. Often, they were perceived as paternalistic laws passed for a woman's own protection. Yet finally, in 1971, women were recognized as a class of persons that deserved protection under the Equal Protection Clause. In *Reed v. Reed*,[137] a woman challenged an Idaho probate code that gave men mandatory preference over women when it came to appointing an administrator for a decedent's estate. The Court announced that state classifications that categorized women must be "reasonable, not arbitrary,"[138] and bear "substantial relation to the object of the legislature."[139] The Court held that the proposed purpose of administrative convenience was not without legitimacy, but the state's means of discriminating against an entire sex was not substantially related to its interest. Though the Court claimed to be using the rational basis test, the decision's language suggested a more searching level of review.

Before intermediate scrutiny was established as the standard level of judicial scrutiny for gender classifications, the Court temporarily used strict scrutiny in the case of *Frontiero v. Richardson*[140] and compared gender-based classifications to classifications based on race and national origin, which merit

---

[132] In light of these Supreme Court decisions, some lower courts have held that sexual orientation discrimination is a form of sex discrimination and is thus subject to intermediate scrutiny. *See, e.g.*, Hively v. Ivy Tech Cmty. Coll. of Ind., 853 F.3d 339 (7th Cir. 2017) (holding that "discrimination on the basis of sexual orientation is a form of sex discrimination"). Other courts, however, have continued to apply rational basis review to such claims. *See, e.g.*, Ondo v. City of Cleveland, 795 F.3d 597 (6th Cir. 2015) (holding that there was "no basis for reviewing Plaintiffs' equal-protection claim [based on sexual orientation discrimination] on any basis more stringent than rational-basis review").

[133] *Windsor*, 570 U.S. at 771.

[134] Bradwell v. the State, 83 U.S. 130 (1873).

[135] Goesaert v. Cleary, 335 U.S. 464, 465 (1948).

[136] *Id.*

[137] 404 U.S. 71 (1971).

[138] *Id.* at 76.

[139] *Id.*

[140] 411 U.S. 677 (1973).

strict judicial scrutiny.[141] The *Frontiero* Court, after outlining America's unfortunate history of sex discrimination, held that administrative convenience was not enough to save the governmental policy in question. But following *Frontiero*, the Court faced much more difficult legislative classifications based on sex, including statutes that reflected legitimate differences like pregnancy in *Geduldig v. Aiello*.[142] From cases such as *Geduldig*, the Court recognized that the sexes are not fungible between men and women, and developed intermediate scrutiny as a result.

In 1980, the Court held that a Louisiana statute granting a husband the right to unilaterally sell property owned jointly with his wife, without her consent, violated the Equal Protection Clause.[143] Despite the proffered governmental interests that one of the spouses must be designated to manage the property, the Court held that the State's interest did not rise to an "exceedingly persuasive justification"[144] to discriminate on the basis of gender.

The Court extended equal protection to men, as well. The Court held that a Mississippi statute excluding men from enrolling in the Mississippi University for Women—at the time, the nation's oldest all-female, state-sponsored college—solely because of their sex, violated the Equal Protection Clause.[145] The State's primary justification for the exclusion was present-day compensation for historical discrimination against women in post-secondary education.[146] The male applicant sought admission into the School of Nursing; the Court declared that educational affirmative action in favor of women was inappropriate since, historically, women had ample opportunity to receive an education in nursing and the statute perpetuated a stereotype that nursing is exclusively a woman's profession.[147]

More recently, in 1996, the Court held that Virginia's statute excluding women from the Virginia Military Institute (VMI) violated the Equal Protection Clause.[148] VMI's mission, creating citizen soldiers, was accomplished through an adversative method of instruction including physical rigor comparable to the rigors of Marine Corps boot camp, mental stress, absolute equality of treatment, absence of privacy, minute regulation of behavior, and indoctrination of desirable values.[149] Virginia first justified the gender-based discrimination on the grounds that single-sex education affords pedagogical benefits to some students. The Court briskly dismissed this interest because Virginia could not show VMI was established or maintained for the purpose of providing single-

---

[141] *Id.* at 682.
[142] 417 U.S. 484 (1974).
[143] Kirchberg v. Feenstra, 450 U.S. 455, 456 (1981).
[144] *Id.* at 461 (quotations omitted).
[145] Miss. Univ. for Women v. Hogan, 458 U.S. 718, 719 (1982).
[146] *Id.* at 727.
[147] *Id.* at 729.
[148] U.S. v. Virginia, 518 U.S. 515, 524 (1996).
[149] *Id.* at 522.

sex education; rather it was an *ex-post* rationalization inconsistent with VMI's original mission.[150]

Next, Virginia argued that admitting women to VMI would deprive both men and women of the special aspects of a VMI education. The Court found this unpersuasive since it amounted to unfounded sex-based generalizations no different than other "self-fulfilling prophecies" previously used to deny women rights and opportunities in law and medicine.[151] Virginia could not provide an "exceedingly persuasive justification" for its gender-based discrimination and, as a result, was forced to change its laws and admit women to VMI.[152]

Intermediate scrutiny, like all levels of scrutiny, is a two-pronged test. When not applied to gender-based classifications but involving, for example, parentage, intermediate scrutiny typically requires that a state demonstrate its actions are substantially related to the achievement of an important governmental objective.[153] For gender discrimination, however, states must show an "exceedingly persuasive justification" for the classification that is not based in societal stereotypes, a standard that no doubt reflects the discrimination and imbalance of political power women face in America. Oddly, despite the fact that closer scrutiny for gender-based classifications was developed in the context of the Women's Rights Movement, state action that discriminates against men is now reviewed under the same standard of intermediate scrutiny thus requiring the state to demonstrate a "persuasive governmental purpose" for its actions.[154]

As with sexual orientation discrimination under rational basis, there is current uncertainty surrounding whether intermediate scrutiny under the Equal Protection Clause applies to state action that discriminates on the basis of transgender identity. The Supreme Court has not yet addressed the issue, but lower courts have found guidance in the Court's decision interpreting Title VII's prohibition on sex discrimination in employment in *Price Waterhouse v. Hopkins.*[155] In *Price Waterhouse*, the Court held that a plaintiff could make out a sex discrimination claim under Title VII when she was discriminated against for failing to conform to her employer's beliefs, or sex stereotypes, about how individuals of her sex ought to act, look, and behave. Subsequent lower courts have expanded this sex-stereotyping claim and have concluded that discrimination based on transgender identity is inherently discrimination based on sex stereotyping.[156] This has influenced both how lower courts interpret Title IX, which prohibits discrimination based on sex in education, and transgender discrimination under the Equal Protection Clause. In addressing the Equal

---

[150] *Id.* at 535.
[151] *Id.* at 543-43 (citation omitted).
[152] *Id.* at 546.
[153] *Id.* at 533.
[154] *Id.*
[155] 490 U.S. 228 (1989).
[156] *See, e.g.,* Glenn v. Brumby, 663 F.3d 1312, 1316 (11th Cir. 2011) ("[a] person is defined as transgender precisely because of the perception that his or her behavior transgresses gender stereotypes.").

Protection issue, some lower courts have held that transgender identity-based discrimination is subject to intermediate scrutiny under the Equal Protection Clause as a form of sex discrimination.[157]

In much the same way that expanding societal recognition of women's rights led to sex-based discrimination being evaluated under intermediate scrutiny, it seems that something similar is currently happening in regard to discrimination based on sexual orientation and transgender identity. The full arc of this trend, however, including its status before the Supreme Court, has yet to be seen.

Strict Scrutiny

As discussed above, when a state makes distinctions based on race or national origin, the appropriate level of scrutiny is strict scrutiny. This most incisive review is used because the "factors are so seldom relevant to the achievement of any legitimate state interest that laws grounded in such considerations are deemed to reflect prejudice and antipathy . . . ."[158] In order to survive judicial review, racial classifications must be narrowly tailored to serve a compelling state interest, regardless of which race is burdened or benefitted by a particular classification. In other words, a court would evaluate a policy that considered being a racial minority a "negative" or "undesirable" factor under the same heightened standard of review as one that considered it a "plus." Utilizing strict scrutiny in this manner makes it difficult for policy makers to undertake any race-conscious measures, as it effectively shifts the burden to the states, or educational institutions, to prove both that "its goal of diversity is consistent with strict scrutiny" and that "the admissions process meets strict scrutiny in its implementation."[159]

This use of strict scrutiny as the test for remedial race-based discrimination is a relatively novel concept, arguably designed by conservative Supreme Court justices in reflection of society's waning support for black-white social equality. However, the prevalence of racial inequality has stepped to the forefront again with societal movements like Black Lives Matter, spawned by outrage over the shooting of Trayvon Martin and several other tragedies involving police shootings of young black men. How the Court will respond to this increase in racial tension and awareness remains to be seen.

Conclusion

The substantive potency of the Equal Protection Clause has always been a reflection of the social and political circumstances of the day. In the Recon-

---

[157] Whitaker v. Kenosha Unif. Sch. Dist. No. 1 Bd. of Educ., 858 F.3d 1034, 1051 (7th Cir. 2017) (holding that intermediate scrutiny applied when a school district's policy could not be stated without reference to sex and the policy treated students "who fail to conform to the sex-based stereotypes associated with their assigned sex at birth" differently).

[158] City of Cleburne v. Cleburne Living Center, 473 U.S. 432, 440 (1985).

[159] *Fisher I*, 570 U.S. at 311.

struction era it was a means for reconciling two cultural ideologies that had divided the nation. It had served as a radical tool for political equalization. Soon after its inception, an evolution of national ideology would distort its objectives, and the *Slaughterhouse* cases would render it as powerless as the paper upon which it was written.

Yet decades later it would emerge as the foundation for a new road to equality. *Brown v. Board of Education* was the result of a generation of Supreme Court precedent interpreting the Amendment's words, and the authors of *Brown* successfully breathed new life into the meaning of "equal protection of the laws". Though the high-water mark of the Supreme Court's push for racial equality would come soon after in *Swann*, and ultimately begin to recede in *Milliken v. Bradley*, the Amendment's potential as a means to equality would remain intact. Generations of citizens have drawn on its ideals to combat a variety of societal discrimination, including race- and sex-based discrimination to contemporary challenges against discrimination based on sexual orientation and transgender identity.

Ultimately, the Fourteenth Amendment's capacity to remedy disparities between different groups has fluctuated greatly. But one truth endures: The Fourteenth Amendment's ultimate power remains vested in the collective conscience of its creators, the American people.

Discussion Questions

1. The way in which law and society intersect is a theme that underlies this entire chapter. Based on the cases herein, and your life experiences in general, do you think society dictates the law or the law dictates society? Which should it be? Should courts be leaders or followers?

2. This chapter outlines several "classifications," i.e., race, gender, age, and the respective levels of review they are afforded. Do you think these classifications and levels of review should evolve over time, to reflect ever-changing societal norms, or do you think they should remain consistent? If you advocate for evolution, how are policy makers expected to draft policies with constantly changing guidelines? If you advocate for consistency, isn't there some danger in perpetuating inequality, archaic stereotypes, and the status quo… even when not in society's best interest?

3. Do you believe diversity, in and of itself, is a compelling state interest? If so, how and why? And at what level? College? High School? Elementary School? Is judicially ordered desegregation the answer? If students want to attend a certain school to be among peers with similar ethnic backgrounds, does the government have the right to deny them that desire?

4. Although the Supreme Court continues to denounce the derisive slogan often associated with strict scrutiny—i.e. that it is "strict in theory, but fatal in fact"—the Court nonetheless continues to bolster strict scrutiny review. To survive strict scrutiny, a policy must be narrowly tailored to

further a compelling government interest. Moreover, government and university officials are afforded little to no deference in their decision-making capacities. In light of these requirements, is there some credence to the accusation that strict scrutiny is fatal in fact? Or is this heightened review necessary to protect against the dangers of race-based policies? Do you think there should be different standards of review based on whether the policy at issue benefits or burdens the target population?

5. Consider the following two scenarios:

    (1) A black female student is denied admission into a predominantly white Ivy League university, despite meeting all admissions criteria. She sues the university alleging discrimination.

    (2) A white male student is denied admission into a traditionally black college, despite meeting all admissions criteria. He sues the university alleging discrimination.

    What is your gut reaction to those situations? Were you more sympathetic towards Student A? If so, why? Is there a meaningful difference between these two scenarios? Should there be? In your mind, what was the main distinction between the two hypotheticals: the type of college, the race of the student, or the gender of the student?

17

Legal Issues in Business Management

R. Craig Wood, Ed.D.
University of Florida

John Dayton, J.D., Ed.D.
University of Georgia

Introduction

Contemporary institutions of higher education are complex organizations with a multitude of tasks beyond educating students. Institutions of higher education differ greatly in the types of functions they perform, as they have different missions and different educational purposes. While the core mission of colleges and universities is education, the business management of colleges and universities is an essential and complex undertaking, often overlooked by both faculty and students. This chapter provides an overview of selected topics and issues that influence the business management of institutions of higher education.

Institutions of higher education operate under myriad constraints, rules, regulations, charters, statutes, and court decisions, all impacting the business management of the organization. These constraints vary depending upon the classification of the institution. A state legislature may have a variety of statutes, rules, and regulations applicable to public community colleges that are expressly inapplicable to four-year institutions. A state legislature may create state governing agencies with highly specific rules and regulations applicable to public colleges and universities, and yet leave selected universities outside the control of those governing agencies.

A state's governance structure often yields a wide range of structural controls, and these structural controls influence the financial practices of institutions of higher education within that state. Public institutions of higher education may have different controls, financial and otherwise. Private institutions are incorporated within the state and governed by the provisions of the articles of incorporation.[1] Public institutions may also operate under a

---

[1] Trs. of Dartmouth Coll. v. Woodward, 17 U.S. 518 (1819). For a more detailed discussion of the *Dartmouth* case and its foundational role in defining the lawful boundaries between private institutions and government authority, *see*, John Dayton, Higher Education Law: Principles, Policies, and Practice 42 (2015).

corporate charter, but most public institutions of higher education are created by statute or state constitutional mandate, and are thus considered to be agents of the state.[2] While some states refer to higher education within the state constitution, and a few states grant constitutional autonomy to selected institutions of higher education,[3] it remains a state legislative responsibility to appropriate and account for the funds provided to public institutions.

Institutions of higher learning may also be subject to a variety of local rules and regulations. Such rules and regulations include fire and safety codes, building codes, health codes, traffic control, water and utility usage policies, and a host of other local rules and regulations intended to protect public safety and welfare. Local governmental agencies generally possess this regulatory authority based on delegation of express powers by the state legislature.

Private and public institutions may exist within the same local community, but be regulated quite differently. For example, specific state statutes, rules, and regulations generally regulate public institutions through an administering agency; for example, a board of regents. A private institution would not be regulated by such rules and regulations, but still likely falls under the general health and safety regulations of the local government.

In some states, a public institution may be considered an agency of the state and thus immune from regulation by a local agency. Where immunity from local regulation is asserted, it must be clear that the public institution is engaged in an activity that is purely governmental or discretionary in nature and not in some way a proprietary function.[4] While the interpretation of what is a governmental function, as opposed to a proprietary function, will vary from state to state, an illustration of immunity from local building code regulation based on exercise of a discretionary function is provided in *Board of Regents v. City of Tempe,*[5] where the court observed:

> The essential point is that the powers, duties, and responsibilities assigned and delegated to a state agency performing a governmental function must be exercised free of control and supervision by a municipality within whose corporate limits the state agency must act. The ultimate responsibility for higher education is reposed by our constitution in the state. The legislature has empowered the board of regents to fulfill that responsibility subject only to the supervision of the legislature and the governor. It is inconsistent with this manifest constitutional and legislative purpose to permit a municipality to exercise its own control over the board's performance of these functions. A central, unified agency, responsible to state officials rather than to the officials of each municipality

---

[2] *See, e.g.,* Henn v. State Univ. of Iowa, 22 Iowa 185 (1867); Weary v. State Univ., 42 Iowa 335 (1876); Neil v. Ohio A&M Coll., 31 Ohio St. 15 (1876).

[3] *E.g.,* California, Michigan, and Minnesota.

[4] *See, e.g.,* Bd. of Trs. v. City of Los Angeles, 122 Cal. Rptr. 361 (Cal. Ct. App. 1975).

[5] 356 P.2d 399 (Ariz. 1960).

in which a university or college is located, is essential to the efficient and orderly administration of a system of higher education responsive to the needs of all the people of the state.[6]

On the other hand, where an institution is engaged in an activity that may be judged as a proprietary function, local ordinances may take control. In the illustrative case of *Board of Trustees v. City of Los Angeles*,[7] a state university leased certain facilities to a circus. The local municipality had ordinances regulating the operations of such entertainment activities. The court supported the municipality and ruled against the university. The court distinguished between proprietary and discretionary functions, and then noted:

> The general statutory grant of authority to promulgate regulations for the governing of the state colleges and the general regulations promulgated pursuant to that authority contain no comprehensive state scheme for regulating the conduct of circuses or similar exhibitions with specific references to the safety, health, and sanitary problems attendant on such activities. Nor can the board point to any attempt by it to control the activities of its lessees for the purposes of protecting the public, the animals, or the neighboring community. In the absence of the enforcement of the city's ordinance, there would be a void in regulating circuses and similar exhibitions when those activities were conducted on university property, hereby creating a status for tenants of the university which would be preferential to tenants of other landowners. This preferential status, under the circumstances, serves no governmental purpose. The subject matter of the Los Angeles Municipal Code has not been preempted by the state.[8]

Revenue Sources

Public institutions of higher education generally receive revenues from student tuition, state aid or appropriations, sponsored research, donations, and endowment income. Private institutions are dependent on the same resources, although state appropriations are not as prominent a factor in operating revenues. Many state legislatures fund scholarships and loan programs that permit students to use the funding at either a public or private institution within the state. Several state legislatures provide direct grants to private institutions based on the number of students served by a private school who are residents of the state. Some universities also benefit from land-grants under the Morrill Act.[9]

---

[6]   *Id.* at 406-407.
[7]   122 Cal. Rptr. 361 (Cal. Ct. App. 1975).
[8]   *Id.* at 365.
[9]   7 U.S.C. § 321 (1862).

Most institutions of higher education also receive revenues from a variety of other sources such as student fees, student fiscal assessments, athletic sources, and cash flow investments. Many institutions of higher education may enhance revenues by the sale of utilities, the sale of excess equipment, and a host of miscellaneous sources that vary from institution to institution.[10] Often these revenues are unique and may derive from such diverse sources as licensing agreements and patent royalties.

Because student tuition generally is a large portion of the revenue stream, litigation challenging an institution's discretionary authority to increase tuition can threaten university finances. Courts are reluctant to limit the authority of institutions to impose tuition increases, and generally sustain the authority of institutions to increase tuition provided there is an adequate basis in law for the institution's exercise of such authority.

In 1998, students sued the City University of New York (CUNY) regarding tuition increases imposed on CUNY's community colleges. The lawsuit initially prevented CUNY from imposing tuition increases, but only until the City of New York met its funding obligation to CUNY. The appellate court ruled that CUNY was not an agency of the state for purposes of the students' claim for prevailing party attorney fees, but also reasoned that even if CUNY were regarded as an agency of the state, the students were not the prevailing parties under the statute in that CUNY prevailed on the main issue in the case, its ability to raise tuition.[11] In 2004, students sued the University of Maryland System over a mid-year tuition increase.[12] Among a variety of claims, the students claimed that the Consumer Protection Act was violated. The court of appeals ruled that the Board of Regents were protected by state sovereign immunity, the Consumer Protection Act did not apply to the state, and that no evidence was presented of a signed, written contract between the parties that waived such immunity. Thus, no breach of contract concept could be broached in that no such contract existed to begin with.

If, however, tuition costs continue to rise, and incomes remain flat, calls for federal action on college affordability are likely to increase.[13]

Besides appropriations and tuition, charitable giving is also an important revenue source. A central factor supporting charitable giving is the concept of tax-exempt status, for without the incentive of lowering one's tax liability, many benefactors might be less motivated to give. Nearly every institution

---

[10] For a limitation of leasing arrangements, *see, e.g.,* Rocky Mtn. Nat. Gas v. Colorado Mtn. Jr. Coll., 385 P.3d 848 (Colo. App. 2014; regarding ground leases, *see,* Howard Town Ctr. Developer v. Howard Univ., 278 F. Supp. 3d 333 (D.D.C. 2017): ASA Coll. v. Dezer Intracoastal Mall, 250 So. 3d 731 (Fla. App. 3 Dist. 2018).

[11] Apollon v. Giuliani, 675 N.Y.S.2d 38 (App. Div. 1998).

[12] Stern v. Bd. of Regents, 846 A.2d 996 (Md. 2004).

[13] *See* Timothy Chessher, *Keeping Up with the American Dream,* 41 SETON HALL LEGIS. J. 387 (2017); Omari Scott Simmons, *Class Dismissed: Rethinking Socio-economic Status and Higher Education Attainment,* 46 ARIZ. ST. L.J. 231 (2014); Julie Margetta Morgan, *Consumer-Driven Reform of Higher Education: A Critical Look at New Amendments to the Higher Education Act,* 17 J.L. & POL'Y 531 (2009).

receives gifts, pledges, and estates that are donated to the college or university for educational purposes.[14] Assuming that the institution is legally qualified under tax law as a nonprofit institution, such gifts are generally tax deductible and may qualify for certain federal and state tax benefits.[15]

Justice Marshall wrote in *McCulloch v. Maryland* in 1819 that "the power to tax involves the power to destroy."[16] Generally, institutions of higher education are exempt from most forms of taxation because they are engaged in public purposes. Education and tax exemption have a concurrent history in which the courts have looked favorably on granting a variety of educational institutions some form of tax exemption.[17] This is particularly true for public institutions for, as a Wisconsin court stated in 1950: "When public property is involved, exemption is the rule and taxation is the exception."[18]

The U.S. Supreme Court's 1983 decision in *Bob Jones University v. United States*[19] established a legal landmark on tax exemptions for charitable giving to institutions of higher education. The principal question before the Court was whether the university, located in Greenville, South Carolina, qualified for tax-exempt status under the Internal Revenue Code. Supporting a national policy discouraging racial discrimination in education, the Internal Revenue Service had denied the university tax-exempt status due to its practice of racial discrimination on the basis that "a [private] school not having a racially nondiscriminatory policy as to students is not 'charitable' within the common law concepts reflected in sections 170 and 501(c) (3) of the Code"[20]

The Court described Bob Jones University as a private corporation, operating a school with 5,000 students, from kindergarten through college and graduate school. The university was dedicated to the teaching and propagation of fundamentalist Christian religious beliefs that included espousal of the view that the Bible forbids interracial dating and marriage. To effectuate this belief, African Americans were completely excluded from attendance until 1971. From 1971 to May 1975, the University accepted no applications from unmarried African Americans, but did accept applications from those already married to others of the same race. Beginning in 1975, the University permitted unmarried African American students to enroll, but a disciplinary rule prohibited interracial dating and marriage.

In this case the U.S. Supreme Court had to balance the interests of a sincerely held religious belief and the resultant noninterference with religious

[14] *See, e.g.,* Mark J. Cowan, *Taxing and Regulating College and University Endowment Income: The Literature's Perspective,* 34 J.C. & U.L. 507 (2008).

[15] *See, e.g.,* Gina M. Lavarda, *Nonprofits: Are you at Risk of Losing your Tax-exempt Status?,* 94 Iowa L. Rev. 1473 (2009).

[16] 17 U.S. 316 (1819).

[17] *See, e.g.,* Lawrence Bus. Coll. v. Bussing, 231 P. 1039 (Kan. 1925); Birmingham Bus. Coll. v. Whetstone, 82 So. 2d 539 (Ala. 1955); Simpson v. Jones Bus. Coll. 118 So. 779 (Fla. 1960).

[18] State *ex rel.* Wis. Univ. Bldg. Corp. v. Breis, 44 N.W.2d 259 (1950).

[19] 461 U.S. 574 (1983).

[20] *Id.* at 579.

practice, with the public policy of nondiscrimination against minority racial groups. In a lengthy opinion delineating the relationship between charitable giving and the receipt of tax-exempt status, the Justices emphasized the century-old case of *Perin v. Carey*, and observed: "[I]t has now become an established principle of American law, that courts of chancery will sustain and protect . . . a gift . . . to public charitable uses, *provided the same is consistent with local laws and public policy.*[21]

The Court went to great lengths to explain its denial of the university's claim. The Court examined the concept of charitable trusts over the years and noted the consistency of the courts, emphasizing that "the purpose of a charitable trust may not be illegal or violate established public policy."[22] The Justices reinforced the concept that institutions of higher education that practice any form of racial discrimination for any reason should not receive tax-exempt status:

> Few social or political issues in our history have been more vigorously debated and more extensively ventilated than the issue of racial discrimination, particularly in education. Given the stress and anguish of the history of efforts to escape from the shackles of the "separate but equal" doctrine of *Plessy v. Ferguson*, it cannot be said that educational institutions that, for whatever reasons, practice racial discrimination, are institutions exercising "beneficial and stabilizing influences in community life," or should be encouraged by having all taxpayers share in their support by way of special tax status.

> There can thus be no question that the interpretation of §170 and §501 (c)(3) announced by the IRS in 1970 was correct. That it may be seen as belated does not undermine its soundness. It would be wholly incompatible with the concepts underlying tax exemption to grant the benefit of tax-exempt status to racially discriminatory educational entities, which "exer[t] a pervasive influence on the entire educational process." Whatever may be the rationale for such private schools' policies, and however sincere the rationale may be, racial discrimination in education is contrary to public policy.[23]

Institutions of higher education accept gifts in order to further the mission and goals of the organization. Although lawful restrictions on the use of the gift may sometimes limit the discretion of the institution's agents in applying the funds generated from a gift to the financial needs of the institution, these gifts generally contribute to the operating revenues of the institution. A gift is a transfer of something of value from one party to another without compensation. Thus, the donor who gives the gift will no longer

---

[21] *Id.* at 588, quoting Perin v. Carey, 65 U.S. 465, 501 (1860) (emphasis added by the Court).

[22] *Id.* at 591.

[23] *Id.* at 595.

have direct control of the gift; it now belongs to the new owner who, subject to any lawful conditions, may otherwise do with the property as he or she wishes. However, if property were contractually given to a university, with specific deed stipulations, and where the contract had clear and unambiguous terms that the parties accepted, the property could be viewed as a fee simple determinable estate under state statutes. For example, if such a situation were to exist, and where the terms could be enforced, with the clause that the property would be returned, if it were not used for an educational purpose, the heirs would have potential claim to the property in question.[24] A trust, on the other hand, is the transfer of an item having value, in which the person bestowing the trust will preserve some form of regulation over the item in question from the beneficial owner. While trusts take many forms, the most common in the higher education environment is that of a charitable trust.[25]

An early dispute illustrates the nature of such a trust. In 1867, a Massachusetts court in *Jackson v. Phillips*[26] noted the distinct differences between a charitable trust and other forms of trusts. The court stated:

> The most important distinction between charities and other trusts is in the time of duration allowed and the degree of definiteness required. The law does not allow property to be inalienable, by means of a private trust, beyond the period prescribed by the rule against perpetuities, being a life or lives in being and twenty-one years afterwards; and if the persons to be benefited are uncertain and cannot be ascertained within that period, the gift will be adjudged void, and a resulting trust declared for the heirs at law or distributees. But a public or charitable trust may be perpetual in its duration, and may leave the mode of application and the selection of particular objects to the discretion of the trustees.[27]

In a 2003 case, the University of Nebraska sought to have the intent of certain charitable trusts changed. The university argued that the original trusts were designed for student loans and, each year, fewer and fewer students applied for these loans. Thus, the university sought to have these funds utilized for student scholarships. The appellate court noted that the legal doctrine of *cy pres*, as well as the doctrine of deviation, did not apply, in that no evidence was presented at trial regarding the inability of the university foundation to loan the moneys. *Cy pres* only applies in that the effect would not be an adjustment to the trust, but a change as to the intent of the trust. Thus, the substitution of the effect of the *cy pres* doctrine can only be admitted if it were within the scope of the donor's dominant purpose. Therefore, the court upheld the trust and ruled against the university.[28] Generally, when

---

[24] Atlanta Develop. Auth. v. Clark Univ., 784 S.E.2d 353 (Ga. 2016).

[25] *See generally* Carolyn M. Osteen, *Miscellaneous Charitable Gift Rules,* SN078 ALI-ABA 23 (2008).

[26] Jackson v. Phillips, 14 Allen 539 (Mass. 1867).

[27] *Id.*

[28] *In re* R.H. Plummer Mem'l Loan Fund Trust, 661 N.W.2d 307 (Neb. 2003).

circumstances change, making the trust no longer operable, the trustees must petition the appropriate court to modify the purposes of the trust. Trustees are generally bound by a fiduciary duty to act in a manner that is consistent with the perceived desires of the original donors and the purpose of the trust. When the literal construction of the trust is no longer legal or practicable, the trustees may petition a court to invoke the doctrine of *cy pres*. [29] This doctrine provides for judicial interpretation and modification of the trust instrument so as to conform to the general intention of the testator while modifying the literal terms of the trust in order to avoid an illegal or impracticable result.[30]

Construction Contracts

Controversies regarding bidding, awarding, and managing construction contracts have always been a highly litigious area within higher education law. As Piele stated:

> [C]ontroversies over construction bids and contracts continue to represent the largest number of property cases reported . . . With few exceptions, these cases are routine disputes between colleges or universities and contractors over such issues as the return of bid bonds, recovery of additional costs for construction delays, payment for extra work, reimbursement for increased costs of building materials . . . and recovery of damages for defective construction.[31]

Cases reflect conflicts between building contractors and higher education institutions at every phase of the contracting process. For example, one contractor sued regarding the rejection of the firm's construction bid with a community college in Ohio.[32] The community college had rejected the bid because the contractor failed to satisfy a minority business enterprise requirement included in a minority set-aside program adopted by the community college and required in the bid specifications. The community college asked the trial court to grant summary judgment based on qualified immunity. The court determined that if the community college sought to implement a race-conscious affirmative action plan, it must present evidence of an institutional history of past discriminatory practice in order to justify such a plan. Finding that the stated purpose of the minority set-aside policy failed to mention past discrimination and appeared directed at societal

---

[29] *See, e.g., In re* Mary Holbrook Russell Mem'l Scholarship Fund, 730 N.Y.S.2d 702 (N.Y. Sur. 2001).

[30] *See* Susan N. Gary, *The Problems with Donor Intent: Interpretation, Enforcement, and Doing the Right Thing*, 85 CHI.-KENT L. REV. 977 (2010).

[31] P. Piele, *Chapter 2: Property* in YEARBOOK OF HIGHER EDUCATION LAW 23 (D. Young, ed. 1979). Forty years later this statement continues to be true, *see e.g.,* Framan Mech. Inc. v. State Univ. Const. Fund, 58 N.Y.S. 3d 676 (A.D. 3 Dept. 2017); Berkeley Cement v. Regents of the Univ. of Calif., 242 Cal. Rptr. 3d 252 (Cal. App. 5 Dist. 2019); New York Univ. v. Turner Const. Co., 81 N.Y.S. 3d 16 (A.D. 1 Dept. 2018).

[32] Buddie Contracting v. Cuyahoga Cmty. Coll., 31 F. Supp. 2d 584 (N.D. Ohio 1998).

discrimination, rather than a previous history of institutional discrimination, the court rejected the qualified immunity defense, holding that the community college administrators knew or should have known that their actions in rejecting the firm's construction bid violated the construction company's equal protection rights.[33]

Generally, cases involving suits between contractors and colleges and universities are contingent upon applicable state statutes, the actual bidding process, and the wording of the contract. A survey of reported cases includes issues related to the return of bid bonds,[34] recovery of additional costs,[35] payments for extra work,[36] and reimbursement for increased costs of building materials, as well as a host of additional issues.[37] Further, public institutions of higher education may be subject to prevailing wage statutes that apply to state agencies. Thus, the institution may have to pay wages on projects via contractors' services that are equal to the private sector. Generally, prevailing wage laws apply to all public projects, and public institutions fall within the scope of these laws.[38]

Goods and Services

Institutions of higher learning purchase a wide variety and large amount of goods and services every academic year. Applicable state statutes, contract law, and the uniform commercial code largely govern such purchases.[39]

While a contract usually incorporates the basic elements of an offer, acceptance, compensation, and other consideration, issues of performance and additional state statutory requirements may also be involved. State statutes on procurement codes, bid procedures, and qualified bidders govern purchasing by public institutions of higher learning, and each state has controlling statutes. Most states have highly specific statutory guidelines in terms of procedures, awards, method of payments, and manner of proof in terms of qualifications, workers compensation, and insurance. Similar to the area of construction contracts, this area generates numerous lawsuits involving institutions of higher education concerning disagreements over the elements of a contract and, when a public institution is involved, compliance with state statutes. In some instances, implied contracts can be enforced.

For example, a food service provider successfully sued Texas Southern University for a variety of claims when the university failed to pay for

---

[33] *See also* Katherine M. Planer, *The Death of Diversity? Affirmative Action in the Workplace after Parents Involved,* 39 SETON HALL L. REV. 1333 (2009).

[34] *See, e.g.,* Balliet Bros. Constr. v. Regents of Univ. of Cal. 145 Cal. Rptr. 498 (Ct. App. 1978).

[35] *See, e.g.,* R & R. Constr. Co. v. Junior Coll., 370 N.E.2d 599 (Ill. App. Ct. 1977).

[36] John Grace & Co. v. State Univ. Constr. Fund, 390 N.Y.S.2d 243 (App. Div. 1976).

[37] *See, e.g.,* Christiansen Bros. v. State of Wash, 586 P.2d 840 (Wash. 1978); ABL Mgmt., Inc. v. Bd. of Supervisors of Southern Univ., 773 So. 2d 131 (La. 2000).

[38] *See, e.g.,* W. Dudley McCarter, *Prevailing Wages Must be Paid on Public Works Construction Projects,* 67 J. Mo. B. 144 (2011).

[39] *See, e.g.,* Daniel D. Kopka, *Uniform Commercial Code Resources,* 88 MICH. B.J. 50 (2009).

contracted services. The appellate court ruled that the university waived any sovereign immunity status when the plaintiff provided evidence that the university ordered, accepted, utilized, and failed to pay for the contracted services. The court did note that in this case the university was immune from suit on tort and constitutional issues, but was subject to contract claims.[40]

In another example, Eastern Connecticut State University was successful in defending its actions regarding the bidding of a fire alarm system. The initial winning bid was disallowed due to a bid irregularity, and the university admitted that the bid specifications needed to be refined and the project rebid. The next lowest bidder, who had met the terms of the initial bid, sued to compel the university to accept its bid under the initial bid specifications. The Supreme Court of Connecticut ruled on behalf of the university, stating that the losing bidder could show no statutory authority for its position. Thus, the university was free to start over the entire project in terms of revising the bid specifications and awarding the contract.[41]

The selling of goods and services by institutions is generally an auxiliary activity that, depending upon applicable state statutes, may or may not be taxed. Generally, if the goods or services were provided by a nonprofit agency and purely educational in nature, then most jurisdictions allow tax-exempt status. Even if the university were to engage in activities in the nature of entertainment, e.g., football, these activities may not necessarily be taxable.[42]

In purchasing professional services, the case of *Board of Trustees v. Coopers & Lybrand* illustrates the responsibilities of both the service provider and the service purchaser.[43] The Board of Trustees of Cook County Community College sued the firms of Arthur Anderson and Coopers & Lybrand alleging professional negligence and breach of contract resulting from audits that did not detect illegal, inappropriate, and high-risk investments made by the college treasurer. The Supreme Court of Illinois ruled that the audit interference doctrine applied. This doctrine holds that an auditor may assert a client's negligence as a defense against a claim of professional malpractice where that client's negligence interfered with the auditor's performance of the audit. The Supreme Court of Illinois ruled that there was sufficient evidence for the jury to conclude that the accounting firms' audit led to financial harm to the college, but the evidence also supported a finding that the college was comparatively negligent, and the auditors were entitled to a setoff of the total damages.[44]

---

[40] Tex. S. Univ. v. Araserve Campus Dining Serv., 981 S.W.2d 929 (Tex. Ct. App. 1998).
[41] Blesso Fire Systems v. Eastern Conn. State Univ., 713 A.2d 1283 (Conn. 1998).
[42] *See, e.g.*, City of Boulder v. Regents of the Univ. of Colo., 501 P.2d 123 (Colo. 1972); City of Morgantown v. W. Va. Bd. of Regents, 354 S.E.2d 616 (W. Va. 1987).
[43] Bd. of Trs. v. Coopers & Lybrand, 803 N.E.2d 460 (Ill. 2003).
[44] *Id.* at 474.

Private Sector Competition

Contemporary institutions of higher education offer a variety of auxiliary services, ranging from housing and food service to travel agencies and beauty salons. In some cases, these services are contracted out to the private sector while the university or student government organizations provide oversight. Some universities and colleges also own and operate service facilities, such as a hotel and conference center for the school of restaurant and/or hospitality management programs, or even an airport for flight training and airline services-related programs. Given the ever-expanding role of universities, the examples and instances of universities engaged in such activities are perhaps endless. Additionally, many institutions sell lucrative rights to do business on campus to certain vendors. For example, it is not uncommon for one soft-drink distributor to have a license to operate soft-drink machines on campus. In most universities, private for-profit franchises lease spaces in order to do business. An example of this is the growing popularity of food courts, in which restaurant chains lease space from the university to offer food services to students.

Many state legislatures have statutes that prohibit public institutions of higher education from selling goods and services that might compete with the private sector, although some state statutes may allow limited competition by particular exception. The exceptions may include educational programs and related activities, and it is not uncommon for the appropriate state board to review and authorize all such activities in order to minimize potential conflicts.

The authority for universities to engage in such operations depends upon whether constitutional and statutory provisions allow them. The question typically posed is this: "Can the public college or university engage in a commercial enterprise when the enterprise is reasonably incidental to or closely connected with a legitimate function of the state?" A case addressing this question is *Long v. Board of Trustees,*[45] in which an Ohio Court of Appeals upheld Ohio State University's decision to purchase the stock of a defunct private bookstore and operate the bookstore for students. The court noted that this service was "reasonably incidental" to the university's mission. Another early and oft-cited case is *Batcheller v. Commonwealth ex rel. Rector and Visitors of the University of Virginia.*[46] In this case, the issue was whether the university could own and operate an airport. The university argued that it had a program in aeronautical engineering, and thus the airport was necessary to offer clinical experiences to the students. The permit issued by the State Corporation Commission gave permission to the university to operate an airport for civil airplanes involved in commercial aviation. Plaintiffs argued that the commission had no authority to issue the permit, as the university

---

[45] 157 N.E. 395 (Ohio Ct. App. 1926).
[46] 10 S.E.2d 529 (Va. 1940).

had no authority to operate such an airport. The court quoted the commission in upholding the legal authority of the University of Virginia to operate the airport in question:

> The University in making application for the permit in question was not asking for the right to engage in commercial aviation, but only for the right to operate and conduct an airport for the landing and departure of civil aircraft engaged in commercial aviation, upon which there could be instruction in student flying so necessary and essential to its course in aeronautics . . . [T]he University will be authorized by the permit to own and operate an airport upon which aircraft engaged in commercial aviation may land or take off, but this would not involve it in a purely commercial or industrial enterprise, but, as has been shown, in an enterprise necessary to and incidental to the full and complete instruction in the course in aeronautics which it has established.[47]

Competing with private, for-profit enterprises continues to be litigated in state forums. For example, a for-profit firm brought suit against Montana State University regarding the university's plan to rent and offer catering services to nonstudents.[48] The firm argued that the statutes that permitted such activities were an improper delegation of authority and violated the policy against utilizing taxes for nonpublic purposes. The Montana State Supreme Court upheld the statutory authority of the university, finding that the revenues from these activities were earmarked for capital outlay, which was clearly a public purpose.

Competition with the private sector can take many forms and circumstances. In a somewhat unusual case, the University of Pennsylvania had made known for quite some time that it viewed a coin-operated laundry and arcade that bordered its campus to be a public nuisance. While it is axiomatic that a university can raise public health and safety concerns about the operation of a private, for-profit business adjacent to its campus, going beyond this right of petition may lead to a tort claim for interference with a private, for-profit firm's right to engage in a lawful business activity. In this case, the question before the appellate court was whether the university had gone too far in its actions against the for-profit firm operating the businesses. The opinion of the court stated:

> [T]he crux of the plaintiffs' complaint is that the University went beyond merely complaining or petitioning the government; plaintiffs claim that defendants were integrally involved in not only initiating (or publicizing or vocalizing or rallying public support around) a complaint, by in, among other things, carrying out the Cease Operations order that L & I [License and Inspections] issued to plaintiffs' business. . . . University police officers were present

---

[47] *Id. at* 535.

[48] Duck Inn v. Mont. State Univ., 949 P.2d 1179 (Mont. 1997).

at the time the L & I representative executed the Cease Operations Order, and they directed patrons to leave because the businesses were being shut down. There is no petitioning element to this activity. As plaintiffs put it, "Here the University defendants went far beyond 'making their wishes known to the government.'". . . The official presence of a University police officer at the posting and execution of the Cease Operations Order went beyond mere petitioning, and thus there is a genuine issue of material fact as to whether the University's course of conduct as a whole went beyond First Amendment protected activity.[49]

Another area related to competition with the private sector is the authority of public institutions to exercise eminent domain. Public higher education institutions may have the statutory authority to acquire property by eminent domain for public purposes appropriate to their mission. A taking by eminent domain may involve a range of legal issues, including whether the purpose of the condemnation is necessary to achieve a public purpose or what constitutes a fair price in order to compensate the owner of the property.[50] For example, the University of Minnesota was denied the right to take property by eminent domain when it failed to establish that the taking was necessary to realize its educational purposes.[51] The appeals court ruled against the taking by eminent domain because the university had failed to identify a specific purpose for the property in its master plan, had suggested several different but mutually exclusive uses to which the property might be put, and had not developed a plan to deal with soil contamination on the site.

Property Management

Individuals commonly bequeath money or items of value to higher education institutions for future use. Often, such items of value are included as gifts in estates. These gifts are generally converted to trust funds in order to implement the purposes of the gift. Universities may accept or reject a gift, depending upon the nature of the gift and whether the gift is restricted or unrestricted. Assuming the university accepts a gift for a restricted purpose, a public institution must do so only if the gift meets a public or educational purpose.

The difficulty within this arena is that once a university accepts such a gift and implements the purposes of the gift, the purposes for which the gift was originally accepted may no longer be needed for the educational

---

[49] We, Inc. v. City of Phila. Dept. of Lic. & Inspec. 983 F. Supp. 637 (E.D. Pa. 1997).

[50] *See, e.g.,* Bd. of Regents v. Comanche Apts., 568 S.W.2d 449 (Tex. 1978); Lin v. Houston Cmty. Coll. Sys., 948 S.W.2d 328 (Tex. Ct. App. 1997); Cook v. Cleveland State Univ., 122 S. Ct. 2648 (2001); Bd. of Sup'rs LSU v. 1732 Canal St., 159 So. 3d 470 (La. App.4 Cir. 2013).

[51] U.S. CONST. amend. V ("nor shall private property be taken for public use, without just compensation"). *See also,* William A. Kaplin & Barbara A. Lee, THE LAW OF HIGHER EDUCATION 606 (2007).

operations of the university in the future. Plaintiffs must, however, establish that they have legal authority to challenge university decisions on the use of gifts. A case in point occurred in 1999, in which the heirs of a trust given to Yale University (as well as alumni donors and students) sued the university.[52] Yale University planned to demolish the divinity school quadrangle, which had been constructed with the trust fund. A Connecticut Court of Appeals dismissed the suit, noting that the gift was an unrestricted gift and that the trust in question did not give control of the property to the trust. Further, the court ruled that the heir did not have standing to sue because the control was not in the name of the trust. The donors and the students also lacked standing in that they collectively and individually failed to allege an actual injury or have a legal interest in the dispute.

In a similar instance involving a challenge to a college's decision regarding property management, an individual plaintiff sued a college for liquidating real property that was part of its campus. The appellate court ruled on behalf of the college, holding the plaintiff lacked standing in that he was not a trustee, director, or officer of the college, and that the college was engaged in actions that were reasonable and that promoted its educational interests by allowing for the payment for the sale of the property to be used to pay the college's debts.[53]

In many instances there is a tension between a university and local planning agencies. Often, local planning agencies attempt to control a university's actions via rules and regulations that may or may not be within the agency's purview. Such was the case in *President and Directors v. Board of Zoning Adjustment*.[54] In this case, the District of Columbia Court of Appeals noted that the local planning agency had gone beyond its authority in directing Georgetown University to engage in a host of actions involving student activities and the placement of buildings on the campus and in the community. This tension is also illustrated in *City of Marina v. The Trustees*, in which the local municipality attempted to have the Trustees of the California State University pay for environmental impact costs related to traffic and other safety issues associated with the development of a new campus on a closed military base.[55] The Court of Appeals noted that the municipality had no authority to direct the California State University system to pay such moneys, and the university system had no authority to pay the moneys even if it fully desired to do so, as the outlay was outside the university's mission and scope.

---

[52] Russell v. Yale Univ., 737 A.2d 941 (Conn. App. Ct. 1999).

[53] Friends World Coll. v. Nicklin, 671 N.Y.S.2d 489 (App. Div. 1998).

[54] 837 A.2d 58 (D.C. 2003).

[55] 135 Cal. Rptr.2d 815 (Cal Ct. App. 2003); *but see*, Montclair State Univ. v. Cnty. of Passaic, 191 A.3d 614 (N.J. 2018).

Intellectual Property Management

While a more complete discussion of intellectual property issues in higher education can be found elsewhere in this text, a range of issues involving intellectual property, patent and trademark protection, and licensure agreements relate to the business operations of colleges and universities. Generally, the intellectual property rights of faculty and the contractual rights of parties participating in patent and royalty contracts are detailed in individual agreements, university policies, or state rules and regulations. However, this does not necessarily mean that the institution can unilaterally change the terms of those contracts to which it had previously agreed.[56]

An ongoing issue in most research universities is the ownership of intellectual property. While intellectual property could be widely construed as lectures, textbooks, and other such activities, the most lucrative and visible application is research that may be patented, and thus sold or licensed for significant sums of money.[57]

For example, Yeshiva University was successful in suing a former research assistant for the ownership rights in a cell line and antibodies related to the treatment of Alzheimer's disease. The appellate court upheld the trial court, noting that the university directed the work and its intended result, and thus the university was entitled to the ownership of the research.[58]

Another issue related to intellectual property management is the management of royalty payments. An illustrative case occurred in 1999, when the Internal Revenue Service sought back taxes from Oregon State University and the University of Oregon after the institutions conducted an affinity credit card program.[59] Both universities had received income of over a half million dollars each in exchange for allowing their names to be used on bank credit cards. The IRS position was that these moneys constituted business income. The tax court and the Ninth Circuit Court of Appeals rejected the IRS complaint and held that the funds generated from the credit card programs were royalties to the universities.

In an age when universities are dependent on funds from patents and royalties to augment operating revenues, universities are inclined to aggressively pursue these funds. The University of Minnesota sued a private business with which it had a licensing agreement over the amount of royalties due the university.[60] Columbia University prevailed on one element of a patent infringement claim in the area of genetic engineering when the

---

[56] See, e.g., Kucharczyk v. Regents of Univ. of Cal, 946 F. Supp. 1419 (N.D. Ca. 1996); Shaw v. Regents of the Univ. of Cal., 67 Cal. Rptr.2d 850 (Cal. Ct. App. 1997); Bd. of Trs. of the Univ. of Ill. v. Micron Technology Inc., 245 F. Supp.3d 1036 (C.D.Ill. 2017).

[57] See e.g., New York Univ. v. Pfizer Inc., 53 N.Y.S. 3d 284 (A.D. 1 Dept. 2017); Univ. of S. Fla. v. Comentis Inc., 861 F.3d 1234 (11th Cir. 2017).

[58] Yeshiva Univ. v. Greenberg, 681 N.Y.S.2d 71 (App. Div. 1998).

[59] Or. State Univ. Alumni Ass'n v. Comm'r of Internal Revenue Serv., 193 F.3d 1098 (9th Cir. 1999).

[60] Regents of Univ. of Minn. v. Glaxo, 44 F. Supp. 2d 998 (D. Minn. 1999).

federal district court ruled that federal courts had jurisdiction to determine the amount of royalties within the United States, as well as beyond its borders. [61]

However, claims of a violation of licensing agreements also may be brought against the college or university. A federal trial court rejected the University of California's defense of Eleventh Amendment immunity when a firm sued the university over a patent marketing agreement. New Star Laser sued the university over what it asserted was a binding licensing and marketing agreement after the university had awarded the licensing agreement to another firm. The court reasoned that a receipt of a patent was evidence that the university had waived its immunity. [62]

Often, universities are subject to suit in holding and exercising patents that could possibly produce substantial revenues. Texas A&M University successfully defended itself regarding a patent process by which it utilized federal moneys as a subcontractor and subsequently filed and was awarded a patent for highway safety barriers. The plaintiffs fell short in their obligation to produce clear and irrefutable evidence that the university failed to disclose that the federal government financially assisted in the research, failed to demonstrate that this information was material, and failed to demonstrate that the university acted with the intent to deceive the Patent Office. [63]

A related area, one that has sparked great concern among universities over the years, is trademark infringement. Universities are generally concerned with the inappropriate uses of university names and symbols, such as athletic mascots, as well as the potential loss of revenue from such unauthorized usage. Generally, if the university can show that such usage is without the permission of the university, is unlicensed, or is harmful to the image of the university, then courts will uphold trademark infringement claims by the university. [64] In at least one instance, trademark infringement has involved the names of the University itself in which it was alleged to cause confusion to the public. [65]

Land Use and Zoning

Decisions in higher education institutions can be influenced by the decisions of local community zoning boards. Constraints on a university's strategic plan, and the ability of a university to be flexible in land and property use, can create unanticipated financial costs. In terms of sovereignty, a state institution that is constitutionally chartered would have a superior position as

---

[61] Trs. of Columbia Univ. v. Roche Diagnostics, 126 F. Supp. 2d 16 (Mass. 2000).

[62] New Star Laser v. Regents of Univ. of Cal., 63 F. Supp. 2d 1240 (E.D. Cal. 1999); *see also* Genentech v. Regents of Univ. of Cal., 939 F. Supp. 639 (S.D. Ind. 1996).

[63] Trinity Industries Inc. v. Road Sys., Inc., 235 F. Supp. 2d 536 (E.D. Tex. 2002); *see*, Transcardiac Therapeutics v. Yoganathan, 85 F. Supp. 3d 1451 (N.D. Ga 2014); Adaptix v. Alcatel-Lucent USA, 137 F. Supp.3d 955 (Ed. Tex. 2015).

[64] *See, e.g.,* Villanova Univ. v. Villanova Alumni Educ. Found., 123 F. Supp. 2d 293 (E.D. Pa. 2000).

[65] *See* Florida Int'l Univ. Bd. v. Florida National Univ., 830 F.3d 1242 (11th Cir. 2016).

compared to local community colleges.[66]

There is a lengthy case history of private institutions seeking to overturn zoning regulations in the courts. These cases involved highly specific fact scenarios and reached mixed results.[67] Several of the cases challenged the constitutional authority of the local governmental agency to apply zoning ordinances to higher education institutions.[68] In some instances, an institution may have operated under special exceptions to local ordinances and then, often due to a change in mission, clientele, or status, the special exception is challenged and the zoning agency rescinds the special exception previously granted.[69] In other cases, the higher education institution may request variances regarding applicable zoning regulations. As one court explained:

> A variance is an exercise of the power of the governmental authority to grant relief, in a proper case, from the liberal application of the terms of an ordinance. It is to be used where strict application of the ordinance would cause unnecessary and substantial hardship to the property holder peculiar to the property in question, without serv-ing a warranted and corresponding benefit to the public interest.[70]

There is an abundance of case law in which individual or collective neighboring property owners have sued institutions of higher learning regarding property issues.[71] For example, in *Bidwell v. Zoning Board*,[72] local residents of a municipality challenged the local zoning board's decision to grant a change in a residential area to allow a private college to construct a library adjacent to its campus. When the validity of these changes is in question, the institution may be required to intervene in order to support the zoning board's decision and demonstrate that there was no abuse of discretion on the part of the board.

A discussion of the applicability of land usage and zoning requirements between institutions of higher education and local agencies also raises the fundamental issue of the applicability of relevant statutes, rules, and

---

[66] *See, e.g.,* Appeal of Cmty. Coll. of Del. County, 254 A.2d 641 (Pa. 1969); Regents of the Univ. of Cal. v. City of Santa Monica, 143 Cal. Rptr. 276 (Cal. Ct. App. 1978).

[67] *See, e.g.,* Regents of Univ. of Cal. v. City of Santa Monica, 143 Cal. Rptr. 276 (Cal. Ct. App. 1978); Anderson v. Assoc. Professors of Loyola, 385 A.2d 1203 (Md. Ct. Spec. App. 1978); Northwestern Univ. v. City of Evanston, 370 N.E.2d 1073 (Ill. App. Ct. 1977); York v. Athens Coll. of Ministry, 821 S.E.2d 120 (Ga App. 2018).

[68] *See, e.g.,* Prentiss v. American Univ., 214 F.2d 282 (D.C. Cir. 1954); Nw. Coll. v. City of Arden Hills, 281 N.W.2d 865 (Minn. 1979); Yanow v. Seven Oaks Park, 94 A.2d 482 (N.J. 1953); Long Island Univ. v. Tappan, 113 N.Y.S. 2d 795 (N.Y. App. Div., 1952), *affirmed* 114 N.E. 2d 432 (N.Y. 1953); Application of LaPorte, 152 N.Y.S. 2d 916 (N.Y. App. Div. 1956), *affirmed*, 141 N.E.2d 917 (N.Y. 1957).

[69] *See, e.g.,* Marjorie Webster Jr. Coll. v. Dist. of Columbia, 309 A.2d 314 (D.C. 1973); New York Inst. of Tech. v. LeBoutillier, 305 N.E.2d 754 (N.Y. 1973); Lafayette Coll. v. Zoning Hearing Bd., 588 A.2d 1323 (Pa. Commw. Ct. 1991).

[70] Arcadia Develop. Corp. v. Bloomington, 125 N.W.2d at 851 (Minn. 1964).

[71] *See, e.g.,* Pierce Jr. Coll. v. Schumaker, 333 A.2d 510 (Pa. Commw. Ct. 1975); Citizens Assn of Georgetown v. Dist. of Columbia, 365 A.2d 372 (D.C. 1976).

[72] 286 A.2d 471 (Pa. Commw. Ct. 1972).

regulations.[73] The case of *Rutgers v. Piluso*[74] illustrates the use of a general balancing test, where the interests of the local community are balanced against the interests of the state. In that case, the court observed:

> The rationale which runs through our cases and which we are convinced should furnish the true test of immunity in the first instance, albeit a somewhat nebulous one, is the legislative intent in this regard with respect to the particular agency or function involved. That intent, rarely specifically expressed, is to be divined from a consideration of many factors, with a value judgment reached on an overall evaluation. All possible factors cannot be abstractly catalogued. The most obvious and common ones include the nature and scope of the instrumentality seeking immunity, the kind of function or land use involved, the extent of the public interest to be served thereby, the effect local land use regulation would have upon the enterprise concerned, and the impact upon legitimate local interests . . . In some instances one factor will be more influential than another or may be so significant as to completely overshadow all others. No one factor, such as the granting or withholding of the power of eminent domain, is to be thought of as ritualistically required or controlling. And there will undoubtedly be cases, as there have been in the past, where the broader public interest is so important that immunity must be granted even though the local interest may be great. The point is that there is no precise formula or set of criteria which will determine every case mechanically or automatically.[75]

The court went on to state:

> With regard to a state university . . . there can be little doubt, that as an instrumentality of the state performing an essential governmental function for the benefit of all the people of the state, the legislature would not intend that its growth and development should be subject to restriction or control by local land use regulation. Indeed, such will generally be true in the case of all state functions and agencies.[76]

---

[73] *See, e.g.,* State *ex rel.* County of Hamblen v. Knoxville Coll., 60 S.W.3d 93 (Tenn. Ct. App. 2001) In this instance, the college forfeited its right to claim exempt property tax status in that it did not appeal twice during applicable periods as allowed by statute. *See,* Turner v. County of Erie, 24 N.Y.S.3D 812 (A.D. 4 DEPT. 2016); applicability of state environment laws, *see,* Friends of the Coll. of San Mateo v. County Comm., 378 P.3d 687 (Cal. 2016); Haleakala v. Univ. of Hawaii, 382 P.3d 176 (Haw. 2016). *See also,* Flores v. Board of Land and Natural Resources, 424 F.3d 469 (Haw. 2018). For applicability of landmark preservation laws *see,* Univ. of Washington v. City of Seattle, 399 P.3d 519 (Wash. 2017).

[74] 286 A.2d 697 (N.J. 1972).

[75] *Id.* at 702-703.

[76] *Id.* at 703.

Taxation

Public and private colleges and universities typically enjoy exemption from state and federal taxes because of the public purposes served by their educational mission. When these institutions become involved in enterprises that are unrelated to that primary mission, however, they may be vulnerable to taxation. By way of illustration, this section focuses on exemption from property taxes imposed by state and local government, while another chapter surveys the range of taxation issues that can arise between town and gown. For example, the Michigan Department of Treasury sued the University of Michigan in order to compel the university to charge sales taxes on activities ranging from photocopying in the library to food service and lodging for continuing education students, but a state appeals court ruled that the university did not have to charge sales taxes on these particular services.[77] In another case, the City of Chicago sued the University of Illinois Board of Trustees to force the board "to collect parking, amusement, and telecommunications taxes and remit those funds to the City."[78] In a complex holding, the state appeals court ruled that the city did not have the statutory authority to collect amusement and parking taxes from the university, but state a statute specifically allowed the city to require the Board of Trustees to collect and remit all municipal telecommunications taxes.

While the general rule is that public and private colleges do not pay property taxes on land and its improvements when these resources are being utilized for an educational purpose, the question often arises as to whether a given piece of property or a facility on the property meets the test for an educational purpose. These cases depend on the exact wording of the controlling statutes, the charter of the institution, and a determination of how the property is actually utilized by the institution.[79]

In a case illustrating the complexity of land use and taxation, a private, for-profit company challenged a determination that it must pay a privilege tax on buildings it constructed in a university research park. While the land itself was owned by the university and not subject to a property tax, the state imposed a privilege tax on the use of the property if the property were used in connection with a for-profit business. In determining whether the privilege tax applied, the state supreme court carefully scrutinized the statutory exemptions to the privilege tax and ruled that the tax was not applicable to the for-profit business because it paid rental fees to the university.[80]

---

[77] Univ. of Mich. Bd. of Regents v. Dep't of Treasury, 553 N.W.2d 349 (Mich. Ct. App. 1996).

[78] Chicago v. Bd. of Trs. of Univ., 258 Ill. Dec. 253, 689 N.E.2d 125 (Ill App. Ct. 1997).

[79] See, e.g., City of Wash. v. Bd. of Assess., 704 A.2d 120 (Pa. 1997); Case Western Reserve Univ. v. Tracy, 703 N.E.2d 1240 (Ohio 1999); Hays County Appraisal Dist. v. Southwest. Tex. State Univ., 973 S.W.2d 419 (Tex. Ct. App. 1998).

[80] See, e.g., County Bd. of Equalization of Salt Lake County v. Utah State Tax Comm'n, 927 P.2d 176 (Utah 1996).

State-owned institutions are usually exempt from paying *ad valorem* taxes, as such property is expressly exempt under state statutes regarding property taxation. Private institutions of higher education that are chartered or statutorily authorized under state procedures generally enjoy tax-exempt status based on state statutory language exempting charitable, religious, and educational organizations from *ad valorem* taxes. This is assuming that these private institutions are genuinely educational, nonprofit, eleemosynary organizations pursuant to state statutes. It is important to note, however, that university-related organizations may seek property tax exemptions for a variety of reasons. Generally, the activity must be educational in nature and be nonprofit in order to qualify for a tax exemption.[81]

Relying on the *Dartmouth* Doctrine,[82] the Indiana Court of Appeals held that all property owned by Butler University was tax-exempt. The university was founded in 1850 with a charter from the state that expressly exempted all property "held" by the university. While the state's Board of Tax Commissioners argued that the university had to use property for its educational function in order to receive tax-exempt status, the university argued the term "held" embraced all property whether or not it was used for strictly educational purposes. The state appeals court ruled on behalf of the university in that the charter was intended to embrace all property held by the institution whether it was used for educational purposes or not.[83]

Private institutions of higher education receive tax exemption generally because of the educational, religious, or charitable mission in which they engage. It is important to note that the institution, depending upon applicable state statutes, must be engaged in its educational, religious, or charitable mission in order to receive the exemption for each piece of property or activity. This generally includes college dormitories and related properties. Thus, the home of the president of an institution of higher education may be exempt from property tax if it were indeed utilized for the educational institution's purposes and activities. However, the president's home could lose its tax-exempt status when state law doesn't allow the exemption, or when the usage of the property varies from a legitimate educational purpose.[84]

Institutions of higher learning engage in a variety of functions. Many of these functions are clearly educational in nature and no legal question generally arises concerning taxes. However, when the institution engages in activities that are not clearly educational, the question of tax exemption may require judicial resolution. In *Southern Illinois University v. Booker*,[85] the

---

[81] *See, e.g.*, Illini Media Co. v. Dep't of Revenue, 216 Ill. 69 (Ill. App. Ct. 1996); Student Housing Auth. v. Brazos County, 460 S.W.3d 137 (Tex. 2013).

[82] Trs. of Dartmouth Coll. v. Woodward, 17 U.S. 518 (1819).

[83] Butler Univ. v. State Bd. of Tax Comm'rs, 408 N.E.2d 1286 (Ind. Ct. App. 1980).

[84] *See, e.g.*, Appeal of the Univ. of Pittsburgh, 180 A.2d 760 (Pa. 1962); *In re* Albright Coll., 249 A.2d 833 (Pa. Super. Ct. 1968); Cook Cnty. Collector v. Nat'l Coll. of Educ., 354 N.E.2d 507 (Ill. App. Ct. 1976); Bexar Appraisal v. Incarnate Word Coll., 824 S.W.2d 295 (Tex. Ct. App. 1992).

[85] 425 N.E.2d 465 (Ill. App. Ct. 1981).

issue was whether Southern Illinois University should receive tax-exempt status regarding married student housing operated by a foundation created by the university. The university chartered the foundation for the purposes of buying and selling property and maintaining property for the purposes specified by the trustees of the university. The university argued that the married student housing was property of the state, and thus exempt. The county argued that the legal ownership was the foundation and not the university. The court upheld the university's position, finding that the university, not the foundation, controlled the property and enjoyed the benefits of the property. Noting that the foundation created by the university was a convenience in aid of long-term financing, the court emphasized the use and benefit derived from the property in holding that it was tax-exempt:

> The property is used to house students of the university. The facilities are controlled, operated, and maintained by the university. From funds derived from the operation of the property, the university pays annually as rent the amount of the foundation's mortgage payments, as agent of the foundation, transmits the sum to the Federal National Mortgage Association. Furthermore, when the mortgage is eventually retired, the university will receive title to the improved property with no further payments whatsoever required as consideration for the transfer. The foundation holds but naked legal title to property plainly controlled and enjoyed by the university and hence the state.[86]

It is important to note that states treat the taxation of institutional assets in a variety of ways. Some states examine the actual usage of the property, while others simply examine if the university owns the property. In some instances, a partial tax assessment is made depending upon its usage.[87] Judicial scrutiny of tax exemption often involves careful analysis of the history and intent of the applicable state statute. For example, the North Carolina Supreme Court heard an appeal as to whether property owned by the University of North Carolina was tax-exempt regardless of its usage. The cities of Chapel Hill and Carrboro attempted to place on the tax rolls several properties owned by the university, most notably an historic inn owned and operated by the university. The state supreme court examined the Royal Proprietary Grant of 1665, in which the government was granted tax-exempt property, and upheld the exemption of all university property, regardless of its usage.[88]

---

[86] *Id.* at 471.

[87] *See, e.g.*, Tusculum Coll. v. State Bd. of Equalization, 600 S.W.2d 739 (Tenn. Ct. App. 1980).

[88] *In re* Univ. of N.C., 268 S.E.2d 472 (N.C. 1980).

Student dormitories are, with rare exceptions, nontaxable.[89] Sorority and fraternity houses may or may not qualify for tax-exempt status.[90] The nature of the university property and how it is utilized has a major influence on the determination of the property's tax-exempt status. For example, in *Princeton University Press v. Borough of Princeton*[91] a university press was denied an exemption, as the court reasoned:

> There is no question that the petitioner has been organized exclusively for the mental and moral improvement of men, women, and children. The press's publication of outstanding scholarly works, which the trade houses would not be apt to publish because of insufficient financial returns, carries out not only the purposes for which it was organized but also performs a valuable public service. It cannot be likewise concluded, however, that the property is *exclusively used* for the mental and moral improvement of men, women, and children as required by the statute. A substantial portion of the Press's activity consists of printing work taken in for the purpose of offsetting the losses incurred in the publication of scholarly books. Such printing, which includes work done for educational and nonprofit organizations other than Princeton University, is undertaken for the purpose of making a profit. Hence, in this sense the printing takes on the nature of a commercial enterprise and, therefore, it cannot be said that the property is exclusively used for the statutory purpose.[92]

However, despite a similar factual context, another court ruled on behalf of the university in *District of Columbia v. Catholic Education Press*.[93] The court stated:

> The Catholic Education Press does not stand alone. It is a publishing arm of the University. It is an integral part of it. It has no separate life except bare technical corporate existence. It is not a private independent corporation, but to all intents and purposes it is a facility of the university . . . If the Catholic University of America, in its own name, should engage in activities identical with those of its subsidiary, the Catholic Education press, we suppose its right to exemption from taxation on the personal property used in such activities would not be questioned. We see no reason for denying

---

[89] *See, e.g.*, Southern Ill. Univ. v. Booker, 425 N.E.2d 465 (Ill. App. Ct. 1981).

[90] *See, e.g.*, Alford v. Emory Univ., 116 S.E.2d 596 (Ga. 1960); Johnson v. S. Greek Housing Corp., 307 S.E.2d 491 (Ga. 1983); Cornell Univ. v. Bd. of Assessors, 260 N.Y.S.2d 197 (N.Y. App. Div. 1965); Univ. of Rochester v. Wagner, 408 N.Y.S.2d 157 (N.Y. App. Div. 1978), *affirmed*, 392 N.E.2d 569 (N.Y. 1979); City of Memphis v. Alpha Beta Welfare Assn., 126 S.W.2d 323 (Tenn. 1939).

[91] 172 A.2d 420 (N.J. 1961).

[92] *Id.* at 424. *See also* City of Ann Arbor v. Univ. Cellar, 258 N.W.2d 1 (Mich. 1977) in which the affiliated corporation was found not to be tax-exempt.

[93] 199 F.2d 176 (D.C. Cir. 1952).

the exemption to the university merely because it chooses to do the work through a separate nonprofit corporation.[94]

In summary, courts consider a number of factors in granting higher education institutions and affiliated associations and enterprises tax-exempt status. First, the court will consider whether the educational institution owns the buildings and land associated with the enterprise. Second, there must be an absence of profit motive, and no agent or employee receives a pecuniary benefit from the operation of the enterprise other than reasonable compensation for services. Third, the enterprise must be one that is reasonable and natural for an educational institution to operate or maintain. Finally, the court must determine that the use of the property is wholly in support of an educational purpose consistent with the mission of the higher education institution.[95]

This chapter introduces a wide range of higher education financial issues that are highly dependent upon federal, state, and local applicability. Given that a university engages in a wide range of activities, the applicability of these regulations varies among institutions of higher education as well as the controlling state statutes. Generally, state institutions, as long as they are within the education mission, are afforded great flexibility as to sources of revenue, manner of expenditures, and applicability of taxes and local ordinances. However, as discussed herein, there are numerous exceptions, fact-specific guidelines, and controlling statutes as to make broad generalizations less useful for any introduction. As higher education institutions continue to serve populations in a variety of ways and means, such legal issues will remain for the future.

Discussion Questions

1. Higher education institutions generally receive revenues from student tuition, state aid or appropriations, sponsored research, donations, and endowment income. How are these streams of income changing over time? How are these changes affecting institutional resources, faculty salaries and benefits, and the costs of tuition? What can be done to reduce the costs of higher education and student debt burdens?

2. Controversies regarding bidding, awarding, and managing construction contracts, and goods and services contracts, have always been highly controversial and litigious areas for higher education institutions. Compliance with state laws and institutional policies in these areas is essential. Review your state's laws governing bidding on state contracts. Are your institutional policies and practices consistent with state laws? What can be done to assure legal compliance? What can be done to assure that the processes are fair and equally open to all parties?

---

[94] *Id.* at 178-79.
[95] *See* In re Atl. Coast Conference, 434 S.E.2d at 944 (N.C. Ct. App. 1993).

3.   Generally the intellectual property rights of faculty are detailed in individual agreements, university policies, or state rules and regulations. Higher education institutions generally claim rights to lucrative patents and royalties in the sciences, engineering, agriculture, etc., but not the usually more modest royalties faculty members may earn on their artistic performances, lectures, books, etc. Is the only basis for this differential treatment of intellectual property that claiming rights to the latter isn't as fiscally viable as the former for the university? Should the university have a right to claim ownership over all intellectual property produced while in university employment? Why or why not?

4.   There is an abundance of case law in which individual or collective neighboring property owners have sued institutions of higher learning regarding property issues, e.g., land use and zoning. What laws govern these disputes in your state? What can university officials do to reduce conflicts and litigation over property disputes with local residents and city governments?

5.   The general rule is that public and private colleges do not pay property taxes on land and its improvements when these resources are being utilized for an educational purpose. What impact does this have on cities and communities where substantial tracts of land and property are not on local tax rolls because of educational exemptions? Educational institutions still impact local infrastructure and services costs. Who pays for this? Does the presence of the educational institution contribute to the local economy in other ways sufficient to offset the loss of tax revenue resulting from educational purpose exemptions?

18 Intellectual Property

Philip T. K. Daniel, J.D., Ed.D.
The Ohio State University

Patrick Pauken, J.D., Ph.D.
Bowling Green State University

"Intellectual property" is a product of the human intellect—literary or artistic works, inventions, business methods, or industrial processes—distinct from personal property and real property. Intellectual property law is covered in the law of copyrights, patents, and trademarks. From the words of this definition alone, it can be argued quite easily that nearly every activity engaged in by students, staff, and faculty at colleges and universities is to further the production or protection of "intellectual property."

While the practice of intellectual property (IP) in higher education finds most of its energy in intellectual property policies drafted and enforced by colleges and universities, the inspiration for the law of copyrights and patents comes from the U.S. Constitution:

> The Congress shall have Power ... To promote the Progress of Science and useful Arts, by securing for limited Times to Authors and Inventors the exclusive Right to their respective Writings and Discoveries.[1]

Central to most constitutional analyses is a balance of rights. With respect to intellectual property in higher education, the balances are twofold. First, the law of intellectual property attempts to strike a balance between an individual's rights to ownership and profit and the public's right to make use of discovered knowledge and inventions. Second, and directly related to IP policies at colleges and universities, there must also be a balance between the ownership rights of the individual author or inventor, generally a faculty member or student, and the ownership rights of the college or university. The legal issues affecting intellectual property in higher education involve both creation and use of intellectual works. Examples include copyright protection for the teaching and scholarship products; copyright infringement for improper use of protected works; patent ownership and profit for researchers and universities; and trademark licensing and protection of names, logos, symbols, and pictures

---

[1] U.S. CONST. art. I, § 8.

445

associated with colleges and universities. There are particular applications and legal developments of intellectual property law in cyberspace.

Copyright

Copyrights are intangible rights granted by federal statute to an author or originator of an artistic or literary work.[2] They are called "copyrights" because many rights are protected within one copyrightable work. These rights, discussed in more detail below, include the right to perform, display, and reproduce the work publicly.

Under 17 U.S.C. Section 102(a), copyright protection exists in "original works of authorship fixed in any tangible medium of expression." In copyright law, originality is not difficult to establish; any modicum of originality will suffice.[3] The Supreme Court stated that the term original, as used in copyright, "means only that the work was independently created by the author . . . and that it possesses at least some degree of creativity."[4] For example, question items on exams are original works of authorship for copyright law purposes.[5] To be fixed, a work must be sufficiently embodied in a copy or a phonorecord—by or under the author's authority—to allow its perception, reproduction, or communication.[6] Important to the concept of "fixed," the statute defines "medium of expression" broadly to include expression made with the aid of a machine or device. Any work prepared by students, staff, or faculty on computers or word processors is not protected until it is saved as a file (on computer or disk) or printed in hard copy. In educational settings, speeches and lectures given by instructors are not generally protected under copyright law, as they are not typically fixed in a tangible medium. The speaker's notes, though (either in hard copy or saved on computer), are copyrightable as items in their own rights. Of course, the speeches and lectures themselves become copyrightable and protected by law if they are original and recorded verbatim under the speaker's authority. These recordings may be more plentiful and regular today with the growing prevalence of teaching by distance education, either on the Internet or via broadcast to off-campus sites.

The Copyright Act lists eight categories of protected works:

1. Literary works
2. Musical works, including any accompanying words
3. Dramatic works, including any accompanying music

---

[2] 17 U.S.C. §§ 101, et seq.

[3] Bleistein v. Donaldson Lithographing Co., 188 U.S. 239 (1903); Gross v. Seligman, 212 F. 930 (2d Cir. 1914).

[4] Feist Publ'ns, Inc. v. Rural Telephone Service Company, 499 U.S. 340, 345 (1991) (authority for originality should come from *Feist* or cases following it because *Feist* clarified the meaning of originality and corrected other circuits' erroneous application).

[5] *See, e.g.,* Educ. Testing Services v. Katzman, 793 F.2d 533 (3d Cir. 1986).

[6] Under 17 U.S.C. § 101, a "phonorecord" is a material object in which sounds (other than those accompanying an audiovisual work) are fixed and from which sounds can be perceived, reproduced, or communicated. Examples are LPs, cassettes, and compact discs.

4. Pantomimes and choreographic works
5. Pictorial, graphic, and sculptural works
6. Motion pictures and other audiovisual works
7. Sound recordings
8. Architectural works[7]

In addition, the subject matter of copyright also includes compilations (collective works) and derivative works, but protection for a work employing preexisting copyrighted material does not extend to any part of the work in which such material has been used unlawfully.[8] The copyright in a compilation or derivative work extends only to the material contributed by the author of such work, as distinguished from the preexisting material employed in the work. Examples of collective works include periodical issues, anthologies, and encyclopedias, in which each contribution is a separate and independent work compiled into a collective whole. A derivative work is a work based on one or more preexisting works, such as a translation; musical arrangement; dramatization; fictionalization; motion picture version; sound recording; art reproduction; abridgment; condensation; or any other form in which a work may be recast, transformed, or adapted.

Copyright does not extend to any idea, procedure, process, system, method of operation, concept, principle, or discovery.[9] But, while ideas are not copyrightable, the expression of them is protected as long as the requirements described above are met. The idea-expression dichotomy is critical to the work of universities and university personnel. A few examples may suffice. First, computer programs are protected under copyright law, but only the expressive elements of them.[10] Second, data from psychological experiments are copyrightable expressions of facts or processes.[11] Similarly, nonfiction works, often produced by faculty researchers, are protected by copyright as well; such works require creativity and originality, even if the factual elements of the work are not themselves copyrightable.

Of particular importance in the idea-expression debate within copyright law are the roles of free speech and academic freedom. When does free speech (e.g., on or about the works of other authors) cross the line and infringe copyright? Melville Nimmer, one of the foremost writers on copyright law, spoke on this debate and offered the following as a balance:

> In some degree, [the idea-expression line] encroaches upon freedom of speech in that it abridges the right to reproduce the 'expression' of others, but this is justified by the greater public good in the copyright encouragement of creative works. In some

---

[7] 17 U.S.C. § 102.

[8] 17 U.S.C. § 103.

[9] 17 U.S.C. § 102(b). *See also* Mazer v. Stein, 347 U.S. 201, 217 (1954).

[10] 17 U.S.C. § 117. *See also* Autoskill, Inc. v. Nat'l Educ. Support Sys., Inc., 994 F.2d 1476 (10th Cir.), *cert. denied*, 510 U.S. 916 (1993).

[11] Applied Innovations, Inc. v. Regents of the Univ. of Minnesota, 786 F.2d 626 (8th Cir. 1989).

degree it encroaches upon the author's right to control his work in that it renders his 'ideas' per se unprotectable, but this is justified by the greater public need for free access to ideas as part of the democratic dialogue.[12]

First Amendment defenses to copyright infringement claims rarely succeed, and when they do, the rationale favoring the defendants in infringement lawsuits generally tips in favor of "fair use" (discussed below) instead of free speech.

Exclusive Rights

As any faculty or student researcher/teacher knows, a central feature to academic and professional success is public recognition and acceptance of his or her original work. Copyright law helps to acknowledge authorship by protecting against unauthorized copies, performances, or derivative works. Under the Copyright Act, a copyright owner has the exclusive rights to do and to authorize any of the following:

1. To reproduce the work in copies or phonorecords
2. To prepare derivative works
3. To distribute copies or phonorecords to the public by sale or other transfer of ownership, or by rental, lease, or lending
4. To perform the work publicly (literary, musical, dramatic, and choreographic works, pantomimes, and motion pictures and other audiovisual works)
5. To display the work publicly (literary, musical, dramatic, and choreographic works, pantomimes, and pictorial, graphic, or sculptural works, including the individual images of a motion picture or other audiovisual work)
6. To perform the work publicly by means of a digital audio transmission (sound recordings)[13]

Initially, all of these rights are held in their entirety by the author(s) of the work,[14] but one or more of the exclusive rights may be transferred or licensed to others. Transfer of copyrights is a common occurrence in higher education, as institutions draft and enforce IP policies, and as journals and book publishers often require an author to assign reproduction and distribution rights in return for publication. An interesting recent application of section 106 came when the National Council of Teachers Quality (NCTQ) filed a public records request with a university, requesting disclosure of course syllabi. The

---

[12] Melville Nimmer, *Does Copyright Abridge the First Amendment Guarantees of Free Speech and Press?*, 17 U.C.L.A. L. Rev. 1180, 1192-93 (1970).

[13] 17 U.S.C. § 106. The Copyright Act examines the scope of particular exclusive rights according to the nature of the work: pictorial, graphic, and sculptural works (17 U.S.C. § 113); sound recordings (§ 114); distribution and performance of nondramatic musical works (§§ 115, 116); and noncommercial broadcasting (§ 118).

[14] 17 U.S.C. § 201. *See also* the discussion below on ownership and duration of copyright.

court held for the university, finding that the university properly asserted the Copyright Act's protection against unauthorized copying and distribution of copyrighted works of faculty.[15]

Limitations on Exclusive Rights

The Copyright Act includes several express limitations on exclusive rights, giving students, staff, and faculty the opportunity to make use of copyrighted works, usually for teaching and research purposes.[16] Three of these statutory limitations are particularly applicable to higher education settings: fair use, reproduction by libraries and archives, and certain performances and displays (including those in classrooms and in distance education programs).

Fair Use

Fair use of a copyrighted work, including reproduction in copies or phonorecords, "for purposes such as criticism, comment, news reporting, teaching (including multiple copies for classroom use), scholarship, or research, is not an infringement of copyright."[17] The spirit of fair use serves to balance the rights between owners and users of copyrighted works—a balance between the creation and discovery of information, as well as the dissemination and use of it—and thereby serves the greater purposes of the copyright laws.[18]

If the use of a copyrighted work is fair, then the user does not need to obtain advance consent of the copyright holder. However, the fair use doctrine is an affirmative defense for alleged copyright infringers. In such cases, the defendants have the burden of proof to show that their use was fair.[19] In determining whether the use made of a work in any particular case is a fair use, the following four factors are applied:

1) the purpose and character of the use, including whether such use is of a commercial nature or is for nonprofit educational purposes;

2) the nature of the copyrighted work;

3) the amount and substantiality of the portion used in relation to the copyrighted work as a whole; and

4) the effect of the use upon the potential market for or value of the copyrighted work.[20]

---

[15] Nat'l Council of Teachers Quality, Inc. v. Curators of the Univ. of Missouri, 446 S.W.3d 723 (Mo. Ct. App. 2014).

[16] 17 U.S.C. §§ 107-112, 117, 119.

[17] 17 U.S.C. § 107.

[18] U.S. Copyright Office, *Circular 21: Reproduction of Copyrighted Works by Educators and Librarians* (2009).

[19] Coll. Entrance Examination Bd. v. Pataki, 889 F. Supp. 554, *modified on recons.*, 893 F. Supp. 152 (N.D.N.Y. 1995); Robinson v. Random House, Inc., 877 F. Supp. 830 (S.D.N.Y. 1995); Rubin v. Brooks/Cole Publ'g Co., 836 F. Supp. 909 (D. Mass. 1993); Ass'n of Am. Medical Colleges v. Mikaelian, 571 F. Supp. 144 (D. Pa. 1983).

[20] 17 U.S.C. § 107.

Note that a court's analysis and application of these factors is engaged on a case-by-case basis; the factors are not necessarily given equal weight.[21] For example, in a case where a university provided scanned, digital copies of copyrighted works without paying permissions fees to the publishers, the court held that the fourth factor (the effect on the market) weighed more in this case's analysis than the first factor (the educational use).

Three landmark Supreme Court cases help to outline the fair use doctrine and offer guidance on the proper balance between the rights of copyright holders and users of their works, particularly with respect to the public interest served by the dissemination of information. In *Sony Corporation of America v. Universal Studios*,[22] the Supreme Court held that the sale of VCRs to the general public did not violate the copyrights held on the television programs that are broadcast on public airwaves. The material at issue in the case was broadcast for free to the public at large. The purpose of the use (recording a television program for later viewing) served the public interest in "increasing access to television programming, an interest that is consistent with the First Amendment policy of providing the fullest possible access to information."[23]

A more complete application of the four fair use factors came in the Court's decision in *Harper & Row, Publishers, Inc. v. Nation Enterprises*.[24] In 1977, former President Gerald Ford contracted with Harper & Row to publish his memoirs. Two years later, as the memoirs were nearing completion, Harper & Row (as copyright holders) negotiated a pre-publication agreement with *Time* magazine to publish a 7,500-word excerpt of the memoirs in advance of the book's publication. *Nation Magazine* obtained an unauthorized copy of the memoirs and published an excerpt before *Time*'s scheduled release date. As a result, *Time* canceled its article and refused to pay the remaining fees it owed to Harper & Row. Harper & Row filed suit against the publishers of *Nation Magazine*, alleging a violation of copyright. The Supreme Court held that the use was not fair, ruling that the right of first publication is one of the exclusive rights under section 106 of the Copyright Act. Under each of the fair use factors, the Court favored Harper & Row. On the first and second factors, despite *Nation*'s claim of "news reporting" as the nature of the use, the Court found that the defendant had, in fact, intended to supplant the plaintiff's right of first publication. Fair use presupposes "good faith and fair dealing."[25] On the third factor, the Court held that while the amount of the taking was not so high quantitatively, the qualitative amount was substantial. Finally, Harper & Row's loss of $12,500 from *Time*'s contract cancellation was enough for the Court to find damage to the market.

---

[21] *See, e.g.,* Cambridge Univ. Press v. Albert, 906 F.3d 1290 (11th Cir. 2018). The factors should not be treated as a simple mathematical formula.

[22] 464 U.S. 417 (1984).

[23] *Id.* at 425.

[24] 471 U.S. 539 (1985).

[25] *Id.* at 562.

In the third Supreme Court decision, *Campbell v. Acuff-Rose Music, Inc.*,[26] Acuff-Rose, the holder of the copyright in Roy Orbison's rock ballad, "Oh, Pretty Woman," filed suit against the rap group 2 Live Crew after the rap group parodied the classic rock song. In a unanimous opinion, the Supreme Court reversed in favor of the defendant, emphasizing that commercial use of a copyrighted work is only one of the factors in the fair use analysis. The Court noted that the more transformative the new work is, the less significant the other fair use factors become. Here, the heart of any parodist lies in the ability of the listener to recognize enough of the original to know it is a parody; to be declared a fair use, the parody must also be viewed as a new composition that is, in effect, a comment on the original. The Court finally held that the markets for the two songs were different enough not to damage Orbison's (Acuff-Rose's) market in the original. Fifteen years following *Acuff-Rose*, the Fourth Circuit Court of Appeals considered the alleged transformative use of student papers in an online plagiarism detection database and determined that the use was, indeed, transformative (and, therefore, "fair") because the papers were not being used for their original purpose.[27] Similarly, the Second Circuit Court of Appeals held that the creation of digital copies of copyrighted works for a nonprofit library's database was transformative and fair in order to provide superior search capabilities and to facilitate access for patrons with visual disabilities.[28]

When examining the purpose and character of the use, courts will look at whether the use by the alleged infringer is commercial or noncommercial and public or private.[29] Generally, a primarily commercial use will evidence an unfair use[30] while a primarily noncommercial use will evidence a fair use, though the use determinations are not automatic. For example, direct economic benefit or profit motive is not required for a finding of commercial use. In *American Geophysical Union v. Texaco, Inc.*,[31] the defendant disseminated scientific and technical information to its many researchers by copying the contents of the plaintiff's journals instead of purchasing them. The defendant's stated goal was to disseminate information to researchers rapidly, but the court found that the decision to copy the journals was primarily for business purposes and, hence, an unfair use. Similarly, Napster's provision of the opportunity for computer users to download copyrighted music for free was not a transformative use, but a primarily commercial one.[32] More directly related to the work of colleges and universities, the Court of Appeals for the Third Circuit, in *American*

---

[26] 510 U.S. 569 (1994).

[27] A. V. v. iParadigms, LLC, 562 F.3d 630 (4th Cir. 2009).

[28] Authors Guild, Inc. v. Hathitrust, 755 F.3d 87 (2d Cir. 2014).

[29] Private uses are more often deemed fair uses than public uses are. *See, e.g.*, Sony Corp. of Am. v. Universal Studios, 464 U.S. 417 (1984) (use of VCRs to record television programs for home viewing is a fair use).

[30] *See, e.g.*, Henry Holt & Co. v. Liggett & Myers Tobacco Co. (1938); and Loew's Inc. v. Columbia Broadcasting System (1955).

[31] 60 F.3d 913 (2d Cir. 1994).

[32] A & M Records, Inc. v. Napster, 239 F.3d 1004 (9th Cir. 2001).

Medical Colleges v. Mikaelian, held that the use of exact copies of questions from MCAT medical college tests in the business of preparing students to take the test was an unfair use.[33]

Despite the holding in *Mikaelian,* educational purposes generally lean toward a finding of fair use.[34] The express language of section 107 makes the distinction, though, between nonprofit and for-profit educational uses. In order to make the distinction, the plaintiff (copyright holder) must present evidence of present or future harm to the market for the copyrighted work. Consequently, the fact that students are the ultimate users of copyrighted works does not automatically dictate a finding of fair use.[35] In higher education, one controversy arises in cases of course packet copies of multiple works for students to purchase. Largely, the courts are in agreement that commercial copying services must obtain the copyright holders' permission before including copies of protected works in compiled course packets.[36] The same may be said for the production and compilation of digital copies of copyrighted works for students to access online, particularly in light of the significant threat of market substitution.[37] Although the commercial nature of producing and selling such course packets generally outweighs the educational purposes involved and protects the intellectual property of the copyright holders, there is some sympathy for the creativity of the faculty member in compiling the course packet and the flexibility for the students' access to ideas.[38]

On the second fair use factor, the nature of the copyrighted work, courts will generally weigh two considerations: 1) whether the copyrighted work is published or unpublished; and 2) whether the work is fiction or fantasy, or whether it is nonfiction, factual, or scientific. If the copyrighted work used by the alleged infringer is fantasy or fiction (generally considered high in creativity and originality), then the court will weigh the second factor against a finding of fair use. Some of the determinations seem rather easy. Although certainly worthy of copyright protection, some works are produced and disseminated for informational purposes and designed with fair use in mind.[39] The use of copyrighted informational works leans toward a finding of fair use, but the determination is not so easy when courts must consider the always controversial line between ideas (not protected) and the expression of them

---

[33] 571 F. Supp. 144 (D. Pa. 1983), *aff'd without op.,* 734 F.2d 3 (3d Cir. 1984).

[34] A national school tournament of academic games for students is a fair use of the games acquired from the plaintiff copyright holder. Allen v. Academic Games League of Am., 89 F.3d 614 (9th Cir. 1996).

[35] MacMillan v. King, 223 F. 862 (1914) (the court rejected the fair use defense from a teacher who copied substantial portions of an economics text for student use).

[36] Princeton Univ. Press v. Mich. Document Services, Inc., 99 F.3d 1381 (6th Cir. 1996); and Basic Books, Inc. v. Kinko's Graphics Corp., 758 F. Supp. 1522 (S.D.N.Y. 1991).

[37] Cambridge Univ. Press v. Albert, 906 F.3d 1290 (11th Cir. 2018).

[38] The district court judge in the *Kinko's* case, *supra* note 37, found a copyright violation, but noted that the determination in such circumstances should remain case-by-case.

[39] Examples include form books and books of quotations. Copying is actually expected. *See, e.g.,* Am. Inst *of* Architects v. Fenichel, 41 F. Supp. 146 (D.C.N.Y. 1941) (copying a form from a form book and delivering copies to six clients is a fair use).

(protected). In nonfiction writing, scientific writing, and even in history[40] and biography,[41] multiple authors may interpret the same sets of facts and will often engage similar treatment of them. This does not dictate that a later work is an infringement of all those that came before. There are exceptions, however. Nonfiction, fact-based, and/or scientific works may have creativity, originality, and marketability, rendering many uses of them unfair. In *Iowa State University Research Foundation, Inc. v. American Broadcasting Company*, the Second Circuit held that the unauthorized copying and broadcasting of a student-produced film on a wrestler was an infringement on the marketability of the film.[42] If the copyrighted work is unpublished, courts will weigh this factor against a finding of fair use.[43] As discussed above, the author has the right to control first publication of his or her work.[44] For example, if a teacher provides her students with an unpublished writing produced by that teacher, future publication rights still belong with the teacher.[45]

The determination for the third fair use factor, the amount and substantiality of the work used, is generally guided by the principle that the more material taken from the copyrighted work, the more likely a court will be to determine that the use is unfair. However, the measure of "more material taken" is made both quantitatively and qualitatively.[46] For example, the same number of words taken from a novel as from a short poem could certainly give way to different fair use determinations. On the quantitative end of the principle, fair use has been found where the alleged infringer took only twenty-nine words of a 2,100-word magazine article[47] and 4.3% (7000 words) of the words in a book.[48] But, unfair use has been found in a case where eleven pages of thirty-five were copied,[49] 10% of unpublished letters were either closely paraphrased or directly copied,[50] and where an entire dissertation was distributed via a university library.[51] If the quantitative use is high, the fourth fair use factor, effect on the market, may play a role and dictate a finding concerning unfair use. In *Quinto v. Legal Times of Washington, Inc.*, a federal district court held

---

[40] Eisenschiml v. Fawcett Publ'ns, Inc., 246 F.2d 598 (7th Cir. 1957); and Holdredge v. Knight Publ'g Corp., 214 F. Supp. 921 (S.D. Cal. 1963).

[41] Rosemont Enters., Inc. v. Random House, Inc., 366 F.2d 303 (2d Cir. 1966), *cert. denied*, 385 U.S. 1009 (1967).

[42] 621 F.2d 57 (2d Cir. 1980).

[43] Salinger v. Random House, Inc., 811 F.2d 90 (2d Cir. 1987).

[44] Harper & Row, Publishers, Inc. v. Nation Enters., 471 U.S. 539 (1985).

[45] Lish v. Harper's Magazine Found., 807 F. Supp. 1090 (S.D.N.Y. 1993).

[46] Campbell v. Acuff-Rose Music, 510 U.S. 569 (1994). See also Cambridge Univ. Press v. Albert, 906 F. 3d 1290 (11th Cir. 2018).

[47] Consumers Union of U.S., Inc. v. Gen. Signal Corp., 724 F.2d 1044 (2d Cir. 1983), *cert. denied*, 469 U.S. 823 (1984).

[48] Maxtone-Graham v. Burtchaell, 803 F.2d 1253 (2d Cir. 1986), *cert. denied*, 481 U.S. 1059 (1987).

[49] Marcus v. Rowley, 695 F.2d 1171 (9th Cir. 1983).

[50] Salinger v. Random House, 811 F.2d 90 (2d Cir.), *cert. denied*, 484 U.S. 890 (1987).

[51] Diversey v. Schmidly, 738 F.3d 1196 (10th Cir. 2013).

that the publishing in a legal newspaper of 92% of a student's law review article constituted an unfair use in that it preempted the only market for the article.[52]

On the qualitative end of the principle, the key determinant is whether the "heart" of the original work has been taken. Quoting only the factually explanatory material from the copyrighted source may not amount to an unfair use,[53] but when the part taken is the essence of the original work,[54] or the portion with the most popular appeal,[55] the use will likely be unfair. Parodies raise interesting discussions on the third fair use factor. On one hand, too much taking could be considered an unfair use. But, in order for the parody to work, the parodist must use enough of the original material for the audience to recognize the source.[56] Following *Acuff-Rose*, the Court of Appeals for the Eleventh Circuit held that Alice Randall's "The Wind Done Gone," a parody of Margaret Mitchell's "Gone With the Wind," was not an infringement of copyright.[57] Randall wrote "The Wind Done Gone" as a critique (through parody) of Mitchell's original story's treatment of African Americans. The court relied on traditional fair use principles and allowed the publication of the parody. The purpose and character of the use, while ultimately in the form of a commercial product, were those of critique. The court noted that the second factor, the nature of the copyrighted work, is given little weight in parody cases because parodies almost always target well-known expressive works. On factor three, the court ruled the amount and substantiality of the portion used as inconclusive, in that a parody must use enough of the original work in order to be effective, but the parody itself must also build on the original work. Finally, the court held that "The Wind Done Gone" is unlikely to displace sales of Mitchell's original work.

In *Harper & Row*, discussed above, the Supreme Court held that the final fair use factor, the effect of the allegedly infringing use on the market for the original work, was the most important element.[58] The Court presented a burden-shifting test for this element. First, the copyright holder must show, with reasonable probability, the causal connection between the infringement and loss of revenue.[59] Then the alleged infringer must show that the damage would have occurred even without this use. Finally, the plaintiff-copyright holder must show that with continued use by the defendant, the future market will be damaged. Important to the inquiry is the effect not only on the cur-

---

[52] 506 F. Supp. 554 (D.D.C. 1981).

[53] Diamond v. American-Law Pub. Corp., 745 F.2d 142 (2d Cir. 1984).

[54] H.C. Wainwright & Co. v. Wall Street Transcript Corp., 558 F.2d 91 (2d Cir. 1977); Marcus v. Rowley, 695 F.2d 1171 (9th Cir. 1983); Harper & Row, Publishers, Inc. v. Nation Ents., 471 U.S. 539 (1987).

[55] Robertson v. Batten, Barton, Durstine, and Osborn, Inc., 146 F. Supp. 795 (D. Cal. 1956).

[56] *See, e.g.*, Campbell v. Acuff-Rose Music, 510 U.S. 569 (1994); and Fisher v. Dees, 794 F.2d 432 (9th Cir. 1986).

[57] Suntrust Bank v. Houghton Mifflin Co., 268 F.3d 1257 (11th Cir. 2001).

[58] 471 U.S. 539 (1985).

[59] Lack of monetary damages from defendant's use does not validate the fair use defense. Marcus v. Rowley, 695 F.2d 1171 (9th Cir. 1983).

rent market for the original work, but also the markets for derivative works.[60] Moreover, if the markets for the two "competing" works are different, then the use by the later work is more likely to be a fair use.[61] With respect to the teaching, scholarship, and research uses of copyrighted works, litigation reveals that fair use will generally be recognized as long as the use does not adversely affect the copyright holder's market.

The use of brief quotes and passages from earlier works in a biography of the author of those works is considered a fair use, since the use does not affect the market for the biography subject's preexisting writings.[62] On the other hand, when suitable copies of works are available from the copyright holders for purchase or license, then wholesale copying will not be considered fair, as in cases involving the copying and archiving of scientific research articles,[63] the recording of audio visual works from educational television broadcasts when suitable copies are available for sale,[64] the copying of a plaintiff's secure SAT test questions,[65] and the copying of course packet materials for student study purposes without paying permission fees.[66]

An interesting development in the modern technological age is the effect on multiple markets for copyrighted works. In the newsworthy case of *A & M Records, Inc. v. Napster, Inc.*,[67] the plaintiffs (engaged in the business of recording and distributing copyrighted musical compositions and sound recordings) alleged that Napster was liable for contributory and vicarious copyright infringement when it provided for transmission and retention of sound recordings through the use of digital technology. The court held that these uses were unfair under copyright law. The purpose here was commercial (to avoid the hassle of purchasing music), not transformative (downloading is not transformative; it is just a new medium), and wholesale in the amount taken. Finally, two markets were harmed by Napster, the established traditional sales market and the relatively new online market, both belonging to the authors/creators of the work.

---

[60] Campbell v. Acuff-Rose Music, 510 U.S. 569 (1994).

[61] In *Acuff-Rose*, the challenged parody was a piece of rap music with a different market from the source work, a classic rock ballad.

[62] New Era Publ'ns Int'l v. Carol Publ'g Group, 904 F.2d 152 (2d Cir.); *stay denied*, 497 U.S. 1054, *cert. denied*, 498 U.S. 921 (1990) (critical biography of L. Ron Hubbard). *See also* Higgins v. Detroit Educ. TV Found., 4 F. Supp. 2d 701 (E.D. Mich. 1998) (use of short excerpts of plaintiff's music in anti-violence videos was fair and not damaging to plaintiff's market). *But see* Craft v. Kobler, 667 F. Supp. 2d 120 (S.D.N.Y. 1987) (court held that defendant's use of quotations from earlier works was too extensive).

[63] Am. Geophysical Union v. Texaco, Inc., 60 F.3d 913 (2d Cir. 1994) (archiving is not a transformative use; copying deprives the publisher of revenue).

[64] Ency. Britannica Educ. Corp. v. Crooks, 542 F. Supp. 1156 (W.D.N.Y. 1982).

[65] Educ. Testing Servs. v. Katzman, 793 F.2d 533 (3d Cir. 1986).

[66] Princeton Univ. Press v. Mich. Document Servs., 99 F.3d 1381 (6th Cir. 1996).

[67] 239 F.3d 1004 (9th Cir. 2001).

Library Reproduction

The next limitation on a copyright holder's exclusive rights is a library or archives' right to reproduction of certain works.[68] Under section 108 of the Copyright Act, a library or archives may reproduce only one copy or phonorecord of a work or distribute such copy or phonorecord, as long as the reproduction or distribution contains a notice of copyright and is not made for commercial advantage.[69] In order to take advantage of this limitation, the collections of the library or archives must be open to the public or available not only to researchers affiliated with the library or archives, but also to other persons doing research. Higher education libraries will almost certainly qualify here.

Section 108 also allows for additional copies to be made. In the case of unpublished works, three copies or phonorecords may be made for purposes of preservation and security or for research use in another library or archives. In the case of published works, three copies or phonorecords may be made for the purpose of replacement of a copy or phonorecord that is damaged, deteriorating, lost, or stolen, or if the existing format in which the work is stored has become obsolete, as long as the library has determined that an unused replacement cannot be obtained at a fair price. Regardless of whether the work is published or unpublished, any reproduction made in digital format may not otherwise be distributed in that format and may not be made available to the public in that format outside the premises of the library or archives.[70]

One case is illustrative and offers some reprieve to the libraries and archives. In *Williams & Wilkins Company v. United States*, the Supreme Court held that extensive photocopying by government libraries of medical journal articles at the request of individuals and other libraries was not an infringement of copyright where the copyright holders failed to show harm.[71] Additionally, the Court noted that such copying accommodates the interests of science, medicine, and medical research.

A final, relatively new provision of section 108 grants an additional right to libraries and archives. During the last twenty years of any term of copyright of a published work, a library or archives (including a nonprofit educational institution that functions as a library or archive) may reproduce, distribute, display (including in facsimile or digital form) a copy or phonorecord of such work, or portions thereof, for purposes of preservation, scholarship, or research. However, this right does not apply if the work is still subject to normal commercial exploitation, if a copy or phonorecord of the work can be obtained at

---

[68] 17 U.S.C. § 108.

[69] The rights of reproduction and distribution under section 108 do not apply to a musical work, a pictorial, graphic or sculptural work, or a motion picture or other audiovisual work other than an audiovisual work dealing with news.

[70] Note that section 108 does not foreclose an analysis under the fair use doctrine. In other words, libraries may still assert a fair use defense in cases where such a defense is applicable, along with the protections of section 108. Authors Guild v. HathiTrust, 755 F.3d 87 (2d Cir. 2014).

[71] 420 U.S. 376 (1975).

a reasonable price, or if the copyright owner provides notice that the work is commercially available.

Classroom Use

An extremely important limitation on the exclusive rights of copyright holders is the allowance of certain performances and displays of copyrighted works in classroom activities.[72] Today, with distance and online education, the definition of "classroom" is broadened in scope—one defined in relatively recent copyright legislation developments.

Section 110(1) speaks to the traditional classroom. This section permits the performance or display of a copyrighted work by instructors or students "in the course of face-to-face teaching activities" of a nonprofit educational institution in a classroom or similar place devoted to instruction. In the case of a motion picture or other audio visual work, the performance, or the display of individual images, the copy used must be lawfully made and the person responsible for the performance copy must not know or have reason to know that it is not lawful. Aside from this limitation, there is no other intellectual property constraint on the types of works covered by this provision. As long as other legal requirements are met, teachers and students are free to read aloud from texts, act in plays, sing or play a musical instrument, show movies, or display texts or pictures by way of audio-visual equipment. The definitions of "teachers" and "students" may not be broad enough to include people outside of the professors of record and those students actually enrolled in the course, with the exception of guest lecturers and instructors. As a result, the definition of "teaching activities" is likely not broad enough to include larger educational assemblies and presentations outside the traditional classroom.

The Technology, Education, and Copyright Harmonization Act of 2002 (the TEACH Act) significantly broadens the definition of the classroom. The TEACH Act, codified in section 110(2), permits the following educational activities in distance education and/or online settings:

1. Performance of a nondramatic literary or musical work
2. Performance of reasonable and limited portions of dramatic literary works
3. Display of any work in an amount comparable to that which is typically displayed in the course of a live classroom session, by or in the course of a transmission

The TEACH Act permits (in distance education or online environments) the same activities as would be permitted in traditional classroom environments. Students may now receive classroom materials at home, from another educational institution, or in school or college computer labs. There are, however, several institutional requirements. First, the performance or display must be made at the direction of, or under the actual supervision of, an instructor. Second, it must be an integral part of a class session offered as a regular part

---

[72] 17 U.S.C. § 110.

of the "systematic mediated instructional activities" of an accredited nonprofit educational institution.[73] Third, the performance or display must be directly related and of material assistance to the teaching content of the transmission. Fourth, and particularly important, the transmission must be made solely for (and to the extent technologically feasible) students officially enrolled in the course and officers or employees of the educational institution as part of their official duties. Fifth, the college or university must institute policies regarding copyright; provide informational materials to faculty, students, and relevant staff members that accurately describe and promote compliance with copyright law; and provide notice to students that materials used may be subject to copyright law. Finally, the college or university must apply technological measures that reasonably prevent the retention and accessibility of the copyrighted work for longer than the class session, reasonably prevent the unauthorized further dissemination of the copyrighted to others, and not engage in conduct that could reasonably be expected to interfere with technological measures used by copyright owners to prevent such retention or unauthorized further dissemination.[74] Importantly, the exemptions permitted under section 110(2) do not apply to copyrighted works produced or marketed primarily for distance education. These materials (e.g., distance education courses for sale) have their own market and must be legally acquired. Similarly, course reserves are not applicable to these exemptions; their use must be approved elsewhere in copyright law.

Copyright Ownership, Duration, and Registration

College and university personnel—including students, faculty, staff, and administrators—create countless copyrightable works every day, such as books, articles, computer programs, lesson plans, exams, class handouts, outlines, lecture notes, term papers, musical compositions, art works, and institutional policies and reports. This section of the chapter discusses the ownership, duration, and registration of these and other copyrightable works.

Ownership

Under section 201 of the Copyright Act, unless otherwise agreed by parties to a contract, copyright protection vests initially in the author or authors of the work.[75] The authors of a *joint work* are co-owners of copyright in the entire work. Copyright in each separate contribution to a *collective work*, such as a book with individually authored chapters, is distinct from copyright in

---

[73] Mediated instructional activities are defined as "activities that use copyrighted materials … integral to the class experience, controlled by or under the actual supervision of the instructor and analogous to the type of performance and display that would take place in a live classroom."

[74] Examples of protections universities can implement are passwords, PINs, and time-sensitive access.

[75] The ownership of a copyright may be transferred in whole or in part, and may be bequeathed by will. Similarly, any of the exclusive rights comprised in a copyright may be transferred and owned separately.

the collective work as a whole, and vests initially in the author or authors of each contribution.

In educational and many other professional settings, however, the ownership discussion does not stop there. The work-for-hire doctrine is widely applicable in colleges and universities. Section 101 of the Copyright Act defines a "work made for hire" as:

1. A work prepared by an employee within the scope of his or her employment; or

2. A work specifically ordered or commissioned for use as a contribution to a collective work, as a part of a motion picture or other audiovisual work, as a translation, as a supplementary work, as a compilation, as an instructional text, as a test, as answer material for a test, or as an atlas, if the parties expressly agree in a written instrument signed by them that the work shall be considered a work made for hire.

In the case of a *work made for hire*, the employer is considered the author and owner of all the rights in the work, unless the parties have expressly agreed otherwise in a written instrument signed by them. The work-for-hire doctrine is often codified in the university's faculty handbook or charter.

A central issue in work-for-hire cases is whether the employer-employee relationship exists in the first place. If it does, then strict application of the Copyright Act dictates that the employer is the owner of the work made for hire. If the relationship does not exist, then ownership vests in the author of the work. To answer the relationship question, several factors need to be weighed. In *Community for Creative Non-Violence v. Reid*, the Supreme Court addressed more than a dozen factors (Reid factors) to determine whether the creator of a work is an employee (with ownership vesting in the employer) or an independent contractor (with ownership vesting in the creator):

1. The hiring party's right to control the manner and means by which the product is accomplished

2. The skill required

3. The source of instrumentalities and tools

4. The location of the work

5. The duration of the relationship between the parties

6. Whether the hiring party has the right to assign additional projects to the hired party

7. The extent of the hiring party's discretion over when and how long to work

8. The method of payment

9. The hiring party's role in hiring and paying assistants

10. Whether the work is part of the regular business of the hiring party

11. Whether the hiring party is in the business

12. The provision of tax benefits

13. The tax treatment of the hired party[76]

---

[76] 490 U.S. 730, 751-752 (1989).

Unless the parties agree otherwise, the *Reid* factors tend to dictate that faculty, staff, and administrators are subject to the work-for-hire doctrine.[77] There is some support for a "teacher exception" to the work-for-hire doctrine, however, meaning that faculty members would retain ownership in their creations even if they were completed with university resources. In *Hays v. Sony Corporation of America*,[78] two public high school teachers wrote a manual to explain how to use the school's word processors. The teachers distributed the manuals to students and faculty. Later, when the school purchased new word processors from Sony, the school asked Sony to write a similar manual. Sony proceeded to incorporate much of the teachers' previous work verbatim in the new manual. The teachers sued. A federal district court held that the original manual was a work for hire and was owned by the school. The Court of Appeals for the Seventh Circuit dismissed the case on procedural grounds, but wrote a lengthy opinion on the ownership of teacher-created materials and advocated a teacher exception to the work-for-hire doctrine. Judge Posner, a former law school professor writing for the Seventh Circuit, noted three justifications for the teacher exception: 1) the tradition in the education field is virtually no one questions that the academic author is entitled to his writings; 2) the lack of congressional action in the Copyright Act to defeat the teacher exception already endorsed by previous courts; and 3) the disruption that would be caused in academic settings with the elimination of the teacher exception. Judge Posner concluded that without any "indication that Congress meant to abolish the teacher exception, we might, if forced to decide the issue, conclude that the exception had survived the enactment of the 1976 Act."[79]

Under this exception, it can be argued that college and university administrative officials do not directly supervise their faculty in the preparation of academic books and articles and teaching materials. Other courts have endorsed the teacher exception. In *Williams v. Weisser*, a professor (Williams) sued a businessman (Weisser) who employed a student to take notes in Williams' classes.[80] Weisser then reproduced and sold the notes to other students. Weisser defended the lawsuit by arguing that Williams did not own the course materials and, as such, lacked standing. The court supported Williams and held that he owned the copyrights to his course materials. Similarly, the court in *Sherrill v. Grieves* held that a teacher of military science courses who had reduced his lectures to writing in the form of a book owned the copyrights to the book.[81]

The teacher exception to the work-for-hire doctrine is technically in direct opposition to statutory language, as well as many university IP policies. Yet, it retains strong arguments. First, the spirit of copyright law, stemming from

---

[77] Of course, students and their works can be subjected to the *Reid* balancing test, as well, with much of the work completed by students as teaching, research, and administrative assistants also constituting works for hire.

[78] 847 F.2d 412 (7th Cir. 1988); *see also* Weinstein v. Univ. of Ill., 811 F.2d 1091 (7th Cir. 1987).

[79] *Id.* at 416-17.

[80] 273 Cal.App.2d 726, 78 Cal.Rptr. 542 (1969).

[81] 57 Wash. L. Rep. 286 (1929).

the constitutional provision, grants authorship rights to those who engage in the production and promotion of science and the useful arts—the "sweat of the brow." Second, it is the teacher's initiative and creativity that bring these works to life. Without authorship protection, productive energy and incentive might be lost. Third, the creators are the ones who make the decisions and direct their own work. In effect, it is the faculty members who set their research agendas, write syllabi, and teach courses. Fourth, faculty members are mobile. They often work at more than one college or university over their careers and take their work products with them, a prospect made much more feasible if the faculty members themselves own work products. Fifth, endorsement of the teacher exception is a form of "soft compensation" for the work of faculty members and a good retention tool for universities.[82] Finally, the teacher exception to the work-for-hire doctrine is also supportive of faculty academic freedom. Academic freedom, traditionally, is the "right to pursue scholarship wherever it may lead, the freedom to inquire, to study and to evaluate without the deadening limits of orthodoxy or the corrosive atmosphere of suspicion and distrust."[83] Many universities make policy statements similar to this one in favor of the academic freedom rights of individual faculty members. These policies would seemingly support a teacher exception to the work-for-hire doctrine, with the university deferring to the substantive contributions made by the individual authors and creators.[84]

An evenhanded analysis of copyright ownership also supports a work-product argument in favor of the university. Along with the express language of copyright legislation, on the side of the university's claim for ownership, one can contend that if the institution owns the work product of its faculty, then the free flow of and access to information throughout the university community is maintained. Under such a setup, colleges and universities would not have to worry about technical contracts and payment of royalties every time they wanted to use materials created at their own places of business. Institutional ownership also allows colleges and universities to retain the academic benefits of those creations and the prestige that comes with them. Maintaining institutional ownership prevents conflicts of interest among faculty members who may use their positions as stepping-stones for private consulting. Finally, colleges and universities argue that faculty creations are developed on university time with university resources and, as a result, belong to the university.

---

[82] *See* Sunil Kulkarni, *All Professors Create Equally: Why Faculty Should Have Complete Control over the Intellectual Property Rights in their Creations*, 47 HASTINGS L. J. 221 (1995).

[83] Levin v. Harleston, 770 F. Supp. 895, 925 (S.D.N.Y. 1991), *aff'd in relevant part*, 966 F.2d 85 (2d Cir. 1992).

[84] Note that while there are strong arguments in favor of academic freedom as an individual right, there are also parallel arguments in favor of academic freedom as an institutional right. *See, e.g.,* Urofsky v. Gilmore, 216 F.3d 401, 410 (4th Cir. 2000). In *Urofsky*, six professors challenged the constitutionality of a Virginia law restricting state employees from accessing sexually explicit material on computers that are owned or leased by the state. The Court of Appeals for the Fourth Circuit upheld the statute, in part, on the argument that academic freedom for professors was a professional norm rather than a constitutionally protected individual right.

Duration

The length of a copyright term depends largely on when the work was created and/or published. Copyright Act amendments over the years have changed the terms of copyright protection. The most recent legislation, the Sonny Bono Copyright Term Extension Act of 1998 (CTEA), extended copyright protection by twenty years for both new works and preexisting works not yet in the public domain.[85] Works in the public domain are those works that are not protected by copyright law and may be used freely by everyone. The reasons a work may not be protected include that the term of copyright has expired, that the author failed to satisfy statutory formalities to perfect the copyright, or that it is a work of the United States government. The following table outlines copyright durations:[86]

DATE	PROTECTED FROM	TERM
Created 1-1-1978 or after	When work is fixed in tangible medium of expression	Life of author + 70 years (or if work is corporate authorship, the shorter of 95 years from publication, or 120 years from creation)
Published before 1923	In public domain	None
Published from 1923–1963	When published with notice	28 years + could be renewed for 47 years, now extended by 20 years for a total of 67 years. If not so renewed, now in public domain
Published from 1964–1977	When published with notice	28 years from first term; now an automatic extension of 67 years for second term
Created before 1-1-1978 but not published	1-1-1978, the effective date of the Copyright Act of 1976 which eliminated common law copyright	Life of author + 70 years or 12-31-2002, whichever is greater
Created before 1-1-1978 but published between then and 12-31-2002	1-1-1978, the effective date of the Copyright Act of 1976 which eliminated common law copyright	Life of author + 70 years or 12-31-2047, whichever is greater

---

[85] 17 U.S.C. §§ 301-304.

[86] Lolly Gasaway, *When U.S. Works Pass into the Public Domain*, http://www.unc.edu/~unclng/ public-d.htm. Per Gasaway, the chart may be freely duplicated or linked to for nonprofit purposes. No permission needed. Please include web address on all reproductions of chart so recipients know where to find any updates.

Registration

Formal registration is not necessary to gain copyright protection for newly created works.[87] Nor is it necessary to attach the traditional copyright symbol—the letter "c" inside a circle—to the work. As mentioned above, once an original work is fixed in a tangible medium of expression, the work is protected by copyright law. Copyright registration and placement of a copyright notice on the work are encouraged, however, to provide proper notice to users as to the copyright status and date. If a copyright notice appears on the work, then a defendant in an infringement action will have some difficulty claiming innocent infringement.[88] Registration is required if the copyright holder wishes to recover statutory damages and attorney fees in an infringement lawsuit.[89]

Copyright Infringement and Remedies

Copyright infringement occurs whenever someone other than a copyright holder exercises one of the exclusive rights of a copyright owner without permission, or without a recognized statutory exception to exclusive rights such as fair use.[90] Courts attempt to navigate what is and is not permissible. In a recent example, the U.S. Supreme Court examined whether copyrighted materials that were legitimately purchased overseas and then sold in the U.S. for a profit was permissible. The Court held that the Copyright Act was not intended to place any geographic restrictions on the resale of materials that were lawfully purchased.[91]

Infringement need not be intentional for the copyright owner to recover. Aside from the intentional/innocent infringement dichotomy, there are three types of infringement: direct infringement, contributory infringement, and vicarious infringement. Direct infringement is conducted by a person or service that actually engages in the infringement of the protected copyright. It requires not only imposition, but also volition and involvement.[92] Contributory infringement occurs where one, "with the knowledge of the infringing activity, induces, causes, or materially contributes to the infringing conduct of another" even though "he [or she] has not committed or participated in the infringing acts." This activity often involves copying devices and involves either personal conduct that encourages or assists the infringement, or provision of machinery or goods that facilitate the infringement. To be liable, the alleged infringer must have actual or constructive knowledge of, and must have participated in, the infringing conduct.[93] The negligence law standard of "knew or should have

---

[87] 17 U.S.C. §§ 408, 409.

[88] 17 U.S.C. §§ 401, 402.

[89] 17 U.S.C. § 412.

[90] 17 U.S.C. § 501.

[91] Kirtsaeng v. John Wiley & Sons, Inc., 133 S. Ct. 1351 (U.S. 2013).

[92] *See, e.g.,* Playboy Enters., Inc. v. Frena, 839 F. Supp. 1552 (M.D. Fla. 1993); Sega Enters., Ltd. v. Maphia, 857 F. Supp. 679 (N.D. Cal. 1994); and ALS Scan, Inc. v. RemarQ Communities, Inc., 239 F.3d 619 (4th Cir. 2001).

[93] *See, e.g.,* A & M Records, Inc. v. Napster, Inc., 239 F.3d 1004 (9th Cir. 2001); and In re Aimster, 334 F.3d 643 (7th Cir. 2003).

known" does not apply in contributory infringement cases.[94] Finally, vicarious infringement may be imposed on a person or entity that has the right and ability to supervise the infringing activity and has a direct financial interest in the exploitation of the copyright, even though he or she does not have the intent to infringe or the knowledge of the infringement.[95]

The Copyright Act provides several remedies for those whose copyrights have been infringed. First, a successful plaintiff can acquire a temporary or final injunction to stop the infringing action.[96] Second, a court may order the impounding and disposition of infringing articles.[97] These may include copies or phonorecords of copyrighted works, as well as plates, molds, matrices, masters, tapes, film negatives, or other articles by means of which such copies or phonorecords may be reproduced. Impounding is an available remedy during the pendency of any infringement action, and destruction or other reasonable disposition is an available remedy as part of a final judgment or decree.

Moreover, a copyright owner is entitled to recover any actual damages suffered as a result of the infringing action, plus any additional profits attributable to the infringement that are not taken into account in computing the actual damages.[98] Instead of actual damages and profits, though, the copyright owner may elect, at any time before final judgment is rendered, to recover an award of statutory damages for all infringements involved in the action.[99] Statutory damages are required in cases involving an infringer who is an employee or agent of a nonprofit educational institution, library, or archives acting within the scope of his or her employment who reasonably believed that the infringing use was a fair use. Finally, the court may allow the recovery of full costs by or against any party other than the United States or an officer thereof. Generally, the court may also award reasonable attorney fees to the prevailing party.[100]

The Copyright Act also provides for criminal action to be taken against anyone who infringes a copyright willfully, either for purposes of commercial or financial gain, or by the reproduction or distribution of copies or phonorecords of copyrighted works that have a total retail value of more than $1,000.[101] Punishments have varying ranges of imprisonment and fines, depending on the number of copies made, the financial value of the copyrighted work, and whether the infringer is a repeat offender. When any person is convicted of any criminal violation, the infringer must also forfeit, destroy, or otherwise

---

[94] BMG Rights Mgmt., LLC v. Cox Communications, Inc., 881 F.3d 293 (4th Cir. 2018).

[95] *See, e.g.*, In re Aimster, 334 F.3d 643 (7th Cir. 2003); and Lowry's Reports, Inc. v. Legg Mason, Inc., 271 F. Supp. 2d 737 (D. Md. 2003).

[96] 17 U.S.C. § 502.

[97] 17 U.S.C. § 503.

[98] 17 U.S.C. § 504.

[99] Statutory damages must not be less than $750 or more that $30,000 with respect to the infringement of any one work. Courts also have the power to increase statutory damages in cases where the infringement was willful or to decrease the damages in cases of "innocent" infringement, where the infringer had no reason to believe that his/her action was infringing.

[100] 17 U.S.C. § 505.

[101] 17 U.S.C. § 106.

dispose of the infringing articles and all equipment used in the manufacture of the articles.

Copyright Law in the Digital Age: The Digital Millennium Copyright Act

Even with the passage of laws like the Digital Millennium Copyright Act, copyright law does not fit neatly in the digital age. The challenge is to see how traditional, long-standing law can apply to new media. With the Internet, publication and distribution are made even easier, with less time and expense required. Higher education research can be conducted more efficiently with online libraries and databases. Recall that the requirements for copyright protection are minimal: originality and fixation in any tangible means of expression.[102] Publications in cyberspace vary widely, from quick ideas and email messages to professionally produced corporate newsletters, academic blogs, and scholarly articles in online journals.

Internet publishers may be able to restrict their audiences, at least initially. They may make their publications available only to a select group of people such as subscribers to an online journal, students enrolled in a course, or direct one-to-one communication such as e-mail. But, with or without these early restrictions, the subsequent distribution (and perhaps alteration) of these publications cannot always be controlled or monitored by the copyright holder. In other words, publication, distribution, and infringement are easy, while detection and enforcement are difficult. Nevertheless, the exclusive rights granted to authors under section 106 of the Copyright Act and each of the limitations on exclusive rights, including fair use, apply in cyberspace.[103]

Perhaps the stickiest application of copyright law in cyberspace, as it relates to authorship and ownership of web-created and web-maintained materials, is the work-for-hire doctrine. As discussed above, the teacher exception to the work-for-hire doctrine, accepted by some courts and several commentators, is not recognized in legislation. Without the teacher exception, it is difficult enough to balance the *Reid* factors in favor of faculty members and their creations in the hard-copy world. But, when these copyrightable documents are created and maintained on university-provided systems (including works created for web-based teaching), the connection to the employer as owner becomes stronger, and the distance from the employee-creator becomes greater. Indeed, "institutions have begun to reconsider their policies in light of the potential licensing revenues that faculty-developed software and digital distance learning materials can provide."[104] It is strongly encouraged that colleges and universities revisit their intellectual property policies to strike the proper balance between

---

[102] Computer programs and the hypertext used to create and maintain websites are copyrightable publications.

[103] *See, e.g.*, A & M Records, Inc. v. Napster, Inc., 239 F.3d 1004 (9th Cir. 2001).

[104] JULIE E. COHEN, LYDIA P.LOREN, RUTH L. OKEDIJI & MAUREEN A. O'ROURKE, COPYRIGHT IN A GLOBAL INFORMATION ECONOMY 138 (3rd ed. 2010).

the authorship, ownership, and incentive for the creators and the distribution, use, and promotion of science and useful arts for the consumers. Examples of policy provisions include the following:

1. Joint ownership of teacher-created works for both the faculty member and the university
2. A "shop right" for the host university, where the faculty member owns the work, but the university has a nonexclusive, nontransferable, royalty-free right to use the work for nonprofit educational purposes
3. A "publicity clause" that requires the faculty member to give the hiring institution credit whenever he or she publishes an article, book, or other educational work
4. A contractual or policy-based recognition of the teacher exception to the work-for-hire doctrine
5. A contractual or policy provision that grants creators the ownership and the hiring university a percentage of the income

The Digital Millennium Copyright Act (DMCA) updated United States copyright law to meet the demands of the digital age, combat copyright infringement on the Internet, and conform United States law to the requirements of the World Intellectual Property Organization (WIPO). The DMCA contains within it two central pieces of legislation. The WIPO Copyright and Performances and Phonograms Treaties Implementation Act prohibits the circumvention of technologies that have been installed to prevent online infringement.[105] With some exceptions, the act also prohibits the manufacture and distribution of circumvention devices. The Online Copyright Infringement Liability Limitation Act primarily creates a safe harbor for online service providers against infringement liability of the provider's subscribers.[106] The Act includes a special provision for libraries, archives, and nonprofit educational institutions.[107]

Each of the WIPO treaties obligates the United States to prevent circumvention of technological measures used to protect copyrighted works. As such, the DMCA prohibits the circumvention of any effective "technological protection measure" (e.g., a password or form of encryption) used by a copyright holder to restrict access to its material. Section 1201 divides technological measures into two categories: those for the *restriction of access* to copyrighted works, and those for the *restriction of copying* of those works. This categorization was done to ensure that fair use continues. In some cases, copying a copyrighted work will be considered fair use. Therefore, circumvention of a technological measure that prevents copying may not be an infringement. Gaining unauthorized access to a work, however, will not be supported by a fair use defense.

The DMCA targets computer programs that are commercially limited and primarily designed and marketed for circumvention. There are exceptions,

---

[105] 17 U.S.C. §§ 1201-1204.
[106] 17 U.S.C. § 512.
[107] 17 U.S.C. § 512(e).

however. The following circumvention activities are not prohibited by the DMCA and are, therefore, fair uses of copyrighted works:

1. Circumvention by nonprofit library, archive, and educational institutions solely for the purpose of determining, in good faith, whether they wish to obtain *authorized* access to the work
2. Law enforcement, intelligence, or other governmental activities
3. Encryption research
4. Testing technological devices that are designed to prevent access by minors to certain material on the Internet
5. The collection or dissemination of personally identifying information about the online activities of a natural person
6. Testing the security of a computer, computer system, or computer network with the permission of its owner or operator[108]

A person injured by a violation of section 1201 may bring a civil action for equitable and monetary damages.[109] Special protection is given to non-profit libraries, archives, and educational institutions, which may be entitled to complete remission of damages in circumstances where the violator proves that he or she was unaware and had no reason to believe the alleged acts were infringing.

The statutory limitations on liability relating to online copyright infringement apply only to Internet service providers (ISP).[110] Most colleges and universities offer Internet access to their students, staff, faculty, and sometimes library visitors; therefore, colleges or universities qualify for these limitations. In most circumstances, the ISP will not be liable for the infringing acts of its subscribers—acts that include transitory network communication of infringing conduct, intermediate or temporary storage of infringing text or images, and long-term storage of infringing text or images stored at the direction of the user and not the service provider. As long as the Internet service provider plays no substantive roles in the content, direction, or communication of the infringing material, liability will be limited. The provider must establish that it did not have actual knowledge or awareness that the infringing activity was occurring.[111] The college or university must continue to provide access to sites that are pay-per-access or password protected. But, it also must act to remove or disable copyright-infringing conduct upon notification of claimed infringements. The limitations on liability apply to a service provider only if the ISP has adopted and reasonably implemented, with proper notice to subscribers and account holders, a policy that provides for the termination of subscriptions and accounts of repeat infringers.

---

[108] 17 U.S.C. § 1201(d)-(j).

[109] 17 U.S.C. §§ 1203-1204. Criminal liability exists, as well. But nonprofit libraries, archives, and educational institutions are exempt from criminal liability under the DMCA.

[110] 17 U.S.C. § 512.

[111] Hendrickson v. eBay, Inc., 165 F. Supp. 2d 1082 (C.D. Cal. 2001).

The special provision limiting the liability of nonprofit educational institutions contains a few significant points necessary for elaboration.[112] The provision makes a distinction between faculty and graduate students and the institution itself. In order to limit the liability of the institution for the infringing activities of its faculty and graduate student employees,[113] the Act holds that when such faculty and graduate students are performing a teaching or research function, they are considered to be persons other than the institution. In such circumstances, knowledge or awareness of the infringing activities is not to be attributed to the institution if each of the following factors is met:

1. Such faculty member's or graduate student's infringing activities do not involve the provision of online access to instructional materials that are or were required or recommended, within the preceding three-year period, for a course taught at the institution by such faculty member or graduate student.

2. The institution has not, within the preceding three-year period, received more than two notifications described of claimed infringement by such faculty member or graduate student, and such notifications of claimed infringement were not actionable as knowing material misrepresentations of copyright infringement.

3. The institution provides to all users of its system or network informational materials that accurately describe, and promote compliance with, the laws of the United States relating to copyright.

Litigation under the DMCA, to date, rarely involves colleges or universities directly. Some coverage of the recent developments is instructive, however. The case law involves First Amendment challenges to the DMCA, particularly the anti-circumvention provisions; infringement lawsuits challenging the service provider's knowledge of the users' infringing conduct; fair use defenses; and the safe harbor limitations on liability for service providers. The free speech defenses from the alleged circumventers have failed, by and large. While the courts have generally agreed that the circumvention software developed, used, and distributed by the defendants constituted speech, they have held that the DMCA is a valid content-neutral restriction on that speech. For example, in *Universal City Studios, Inc. v. Corley*, the movie industry sued a number of individuals and organizations that distributed a computer program (DeCSS) designed to circumvent the content scramble system (CSS), an encryption system that prevents copying DVDs.[114] The Court of Appeals for the Second Circuit upheld the district court's grant of a permanent injunction prohibiting defendants from posting the DeCSS program on their website and from posting hyperlinks to other websites containing DeCSS. The court held that

---

[112] 17 U.S.C. § 512(e).

[113] Note that the Act is explicit with respect to its mention of *graduate* students instead of students in general. While undergraduate students may perform teaching and/or research functions as employees of a college or university, there is no mention of undergraduate students in the Act.

[114] 273 F.3d 429 (2d Cir. 2001).

the DMCA was designed to target the program's functional attributes, not its expressive ones. The DMCA does not prohibit making lawful copies of DVDs; it simply prohibits the decryption method of copying.[115] According to the court in *DVD Copy Control Association v. Bunner*, a case with facts similar to those in *Corley*, such an injunction against the distribution of DeCSS "burdens no more speech than is necessary to serve the government's important interest in maintaining commercial ethics."[116]

Online copyright infringement is most certainly a concern for colleges and universities as Internet service providers, whether or not they are aware of the infringing conduct. The Internet access provisions of a college, the popularity and prevalence of Internet music downloads among the college student population, and the noteworthy and newsworthy decisions in *Recording Industry Association of America (RIAA) v. Verizon Internet Servs.*,[117] *A & M Records, Inc. v. Napster, Inc.*,[118] and *In re Aimster Copyright Litigation*[119] have put higher education administrators and students on notice. With a significant exception, the DMCA allows a copyright owner to subpoena an Internet service provider (perhaps a college or university) in order to get the name of a user who has allegedly infringed the copyright owner's rights. In the *Verizon* case, the defendant ISP refused to give the name of an alleged infringer who downloaded 600 copyrighted songs in one day.[120] Verizon argued that the DMCA only applied when the infringing materials are stored on the provider's space, not when the service provider's space is used as a mere conduit for the alleged infringing material. A federal district court rejected Verizon's claim and held that the DMCA offers liability protections to Internet service providers in exchange for their cooperation in copyright enforcement. The Court of Appeals reversed, however, agreeing with Verizon that it is impossible for an Internet service provider to take advantage of the limits on liability (e.g., the removal of infringing materials or the disabling of access to such materials) when the materials are not stored online. When infringing materials merely travel through the provider's space without storage, the provider has no way of identifying the material or the user and, therefore, cannot notify the user of the infringing conduct.

In the *Aimster Copyright Litigation* case, similar to the peer-to-peer file sharing case in *Napster*, the Court of Appeals for the Seventh Circuit upheld an injunction against Aimster, a file sharing service that facilitates the transfer of files between users. Record companies and composers sought preliminary injunctions to shut down Aimster and argued that Aimster's operation constituted contributory and vicarious infringement. Instead of adopting an "actual

---

[115] *See also* United States v. Elcom Ltd., 203 F. Supp. 2d 1111 (N.D. Cal. 2002).

[116] 31 Cal. 4th 864, 878, 75 P.3d 1, 11 (2003).

[117] Nos. 03-7015, 03-7053, 2003 U.S. App. LEXIS 25735 (D.C. Cir. Dec. 19, 2003).

[118] 239 F.3d 1004 (9th Cir. 2001).

[119] 334 F.3d 643 (7th Cir. 2003).

[120] The alleged infringement occurred through peer-to-peer software (KaZaA).

knowledge of infringement" test as the Ninth Circuit did in *Napster*, the Seventh Circuit adopted an "economic balancing test":

> [I]f the infringing uses are substantial, then to avoid liability as a contributory infringer, the provider of the service must show that it would have been disproportionately costly for him to eliminate or at least reduce substantially the infringing uses.[121]

The Seventh Circuit likened Aimster's response to the infringing uses to "willful blindness." Clearly, colleges and universities cannot afford this kind of visual acuity. In order to be eligible for the safe harbor limitations on liability afforded to Internet service providers and, in particular, educational institutions, colleges and universities must actively enforce policies that promote compliance with copyright laws.

Patents

Inspired by the same constitutional clause that gives Congress the power to protect copyrights, patent law grants an inventor rights to exclude others from producing or using the inventor's discoveries, for a limited time, in furtherance of science and the useful arts. Under Title 35 of the United States Code, patents for "novel, useful, and nonobvious" inventions are granted for twenty years, measured from the date of application.[122] In an application for a patent, the applicant must provide a "specification" describing how the invention works and offer "claims" stating what is new, useful, and nonobvious (i.e., patentable) about the invention. Applications for patents are public documents.[123] In the past, universities have provided innovations in many areas, including the MRI, CAT scan, and vaccines.

Unlike copyright law, which takes effect the moment an original work is fixed in a tangible medium of expression, there is no monopoly right in a patented invention until the United States Patent Office issues the patent. The patent office will search through past patents and all relevant literature to ascertain whether the claims are new, useful, and nonobvious. Patents are often granted to some, but not all, claims in an application. A potential patentee may submit an application more than once.

When multiple applications (including recently granted patents) make identical or nearly identical claims, the Patent Office will conduct an "interference proceeding" to determine which application first conceived and reduced the patent to practice. A successful applicant for a patent has the exclusive right to make, use, or sell the invention to the absolute exclusion of others for the twenty-year period of the patent.[124] These rights may be licensed or assigned to others. The Bayh-Dole Act of 1980 allows universities to license

---

[121] 334 F.3d at 653.
[122] 35 U.S.C. § 154(a)(2).
[123] 35 U.S.C. § 111.
[124] 35 U.S.C. § 154.

their patents to the private sector.[125] During the term of the patent, the patent owner has the right to determine who has the right to make, use, or sell the invention.[126] Such licenses may also be made on geographic bases. The law does not require the inventor to put the patent to use, although the exclusive rights act has incentives to make, use, and sell the patent for societal benefits. Exclusivity of rights is important and does not belong to the inventor until application is made. Putting the invention to use is called "working the patent." Allowing others to use it is called "compulsory licensing." It should be noted that patents cannot be renewed. At term expiration, the invention enters the public domain for others to make, use, or sell.

Infringement lawsuits may be filed for alleged unauthorized use of a patent. In such cases, the defendants may argue that the patent was unwarranted (e.g., failure to meet the novelty, utility, and/or nonobviousness requirements). The defendant may also argue that the patentee engaged in inequitable conduct. In addition, any person may ask the Patent Office to reexamine the patent, and any person may seek a declaratory judgment to determine the validity of the patent.

Types of Inventions and Discoveries

Just as in copyright law, ideas are not patentable. In patent law, only the applications of those ideas are protected.[127] These applications come in the form of products and processes, both of which can be patented.[128] Products are physical entities—specifically, machines, manufactures, and compositions of matter. As long as the product fits into one or more of these three categories and meets the other requirements for patentability, it will be patented. Basically, a machine is an inventive thing that does something. A manufacture is a non-natural, human-made product. The most typical composition of matter is a new chemical compound. With these products, the components may be natural, but the composition is human-made.

Processes, contrary to products, are more intangible means to an end. For example, a chemical process that produces a compound through a series of steps may be patentable. Sometimes, the product that comes from the process will not be patented, while the process is. In other words, the patentability of the product is not relevant to the patentability of the process designed to produce it. Consider an experimental drug for the treatment of a disease. In one case, the drug itself may be patented. In another case, perhaps the process of producing the drug will be. Sometimes, both the process and the product

---

[125] 35 U.S.C. § 200-212.

[126] 35 U.S.C. § 261.

[127] Note that applications of ideas must meet the novelty, utility, and nonobviousness requirements of the Act. While the subjects of patents can be very technical and difficult to grasp, mere theoretical abstractions are not patentable. See Alice Corp. Pty Ltd. v. CLS Bank Int'l, 134 S. Ct. 2347 (2014).

[128] There are some exceptions. To be patentable, an invention must be human-made: no naturally occurring substances are patentable. The products of them may be, however. In addition, printed matter is not patentable. The mere making or improving of a form does not warrant a patent. Finally, business methods are not patentable, no matter how "inventive" they may be.

will be patentable. The products and processes defined above are generally known as "utility" patents. There are two other types of patents, however, that are not dependent on utility. The first are plant patents.[129] Plant patentability requires novelty, distinctiveness, and nonobviousness. The second are design patents, obtained to protect a new, original, ornamental design for a manufactured article.[130] The three requirements for patentability of designs are novelty, ornamentality, and nonobviousness.

Novelty, Utility, and Nonobviousness: Issues of Patents and Priority

Section 102 of the Patent Act defines the conditions for novelty of an invention. In layperson's terms, perhaps novelty can be thought of as belonging to the winner of a "race" to invention and patent. Certainly, there are simultaneous projects at colleges and universities around the world where researchers are, for example, searching for cures for diseases. The processes and products that result from these projects are patentable, first, if they are novel—that is, the patent will belong to the winner of the race, the one who first brings the invention from conception to patent application, and then to practice.[131]

Within the novelty conditions are the concepts of anticipation and statutory bar. Anticipation, either domestic or foreign, refers to certain events that occur anytime prior to invention and, if they do occur, prohibit patentability. Statutory bar, on the other hand, refers to domestic or foreign events that occur more than twelve months prior to patent application. Just like anticipation events, statutory bar events also prevent patentability. The following table outlines section 102 of the act and the concepts of anticipation and statutory bar. The entries in the table are those that will *prevent* patentability.

	ANTICIPATION EVENTS Will defeat an applicant's claim for patent if they occur at any time prior to invention	STATUTORY BAR EVENTS Will defeat an applicant's claim for patent if they occur more than 12 months prior to application
DOMESTIC	Prior patent by anyone	Prior patent by anyone
	Description in a printed publication	Description in a printed publication
	Invention known or used by others	Public use or sale

---

[129] 35 U.S.C. § 161.

[130] 35 U.S.C. § 171.

[131] *See, e.g.,* Johns Hopkins Univ. v. 454 Life Scis. Corp., 230 F. Supp. 3d 357 (D. Del. 2017) (the defendant showed by a preponderance of the evidence that it had the definite and permanent idea and that it reduced the invention to practice first).

	Description in another's previously filed and eventually granted application	
	Abandonment of the invention by the applicant him or herself	
	Unabandoned, unsuppressed, and unconcealed invention by others	
FOREIGN	Prior patent by anyone	Prior patent by anyone
	Description in a printed publication	Description in a printed publication
		Prior patent application by the applicant (if a patent is granted prior to domestic application)

Note that the events listed in the table are limited by the "principle of substantial identity." In other words, to defeat an application for a patent, the prior knowledge, use, or other event must be substantially similar to the applicant's invention so as to qualify as a "disclosure" of the process or product. The test for "substantial identity" (substantial similarity) and "disclosure" is whether enough of the invention has already been disclosed so that a person skilled in the applicable art can duplicate the product or process. The one exception to this test is public use of the invention. Public use need not disclose the invention's secrets, but only the benefits of the invention itself. Such public use need not be extensive.

Adding another wrinkle to this discussion is the requirement that the anticipation events raise not only substantial identity to the invention, but also realization of the anticipating events themselves. In other words, the anticipation must be so intentional or noticed that it can be duplicated. For example, if prior knowledge or use of an invention goes unnoticed, then it cannot be considered anticipatory to bar patentability upon later application. On the other hand, if a person is conscious of the existence of a process or a product, an anticipation has occurred, regardless of whether he or she has realized the novelty or utility. This turn of events may occur quite often in a university lab, where students discover new and useful products without realizing it. Imagine a case where a graduate student or postdoctoral student in one of the sciences creates or discovers a new, useful, and nonobvious composition of matter but assumes that the discovery has been made by much more experienced researchers in the past and that, as a new student, they would certainly not be "first in line" if a patent race were to start. Even so, realization of the product itself would be an anticipation event that may later bar a patent application by someone else, while chance discoveries without realization of their existence are not anticipation events.[132]

Some discussion of what it means for a process or product to be "described in a printed publication" is necessary here. The basic principle behind the statutory bar of a patent for information described in a printed publication is that such printed information may already be in the public domain (for patent purposes, not for copyright purposes), even against the claims of the true inventor. In other words, if the invention is described in a printed publication at any time prior to *invention*, or more than twelve months prior to a patent *application*, the patent application will be rejected. *In re Marshall W. Cronyn* provides an example.[133] In *Cronyn*, the Court of Appeals for the Federal Circuit held that senior theses written by undergraduates at Reed College as a graduation requirement did not constitute "printed publications" for patent purposes and, therefore, did not bar the application for patent more than one year after the thesis at issue was written.[134] In order for a publication to be considered "printed" for patent purposes, it must be "sufficiently accessible to the public interested in the art."[135] Dissemination and public accessibility are crucial to this determination. In *Cronyn*, the papers were informally catalogued in the college's library and in each student's department. This administrative setup did not qualify as "accessibility."[136] Furthermore, an oral defense of a thesis in front of three faculty committee members was not sufficient for dissemination.[137]

In the race to patent an invention, priority claims are common. Patent law, at its core, promotes the progress of science and the useful arts and will grant patents to those who claim first and rightful invention to useful, novel, and nonobvious processes and products. The law will not reward slow movement in such matters, as a delay in application may be evidence of an inventor's attempt to extend the patent period or delay the introduction of a useful product to the public. As a result, the law requires reasonable diligence on the part of an inventor.

But what about the case where the delay in application is not due to an attempt to extend the twenty-year exclusive rights, but where the university or faculty member is merely attempting to strike the most lucrative financial deal in advance of application? Delays in patent application are sometimes due to faculty researcher workload with other projects. These issues were discussed

---

[132] *See* Standard Oil Co. (Indiana) v. Montedison, S.p.A., 664 F.2d 356 (3d Cir. 1981).

[133] 890 F.2d 1158 (Fed. Cir. 1989).

[134] Note that the professor/advisor to the student was the applicant for the patent. There was no discussion in the case about the potential ethical issues related to a faculty member applying for a patent on the basis of work produced by a student. Readers, however, are encouraged to consult university policies on the ethics of research and authorship. *See, e.g., Ethical Standards of the American Educational Research Association*, Educ. Researcher 23-26 (Oct. 1992).

[135] 890 F.2d at 1160.

[136] *See also* In re Hall, 781 F.2d 897 (Fed. Cir. 1986) (dissertations were sufficiently and timely catalogued and shelved so as to be accessible).

[137] *See* In re Bayer, 568 F.2d 1357 (C.C.P.A. 1978). C.C.P.A. stands for the Court of Customs and Patent Appeals.

in *Griffith v. Kanamaru*.[138] Griffith was a professor of biochemistry at Cornell University, where he invented a compound useful in the treatment of diabetes. He conceived the invention in June 1981 and reduced it to practice in January 1984. Meanwhile, Kanamaru, a chemist employed at Takeda Chemical Industries, applied in November 1982 for a patent for the same invention. In response to Griffith's application for a patent, the Board of Patent Appeals and Interferences asked Griffith to show priority (i.e., reason) for the delay in application.[139] Griffith cited two reasons, that he was attempting to acquire external funding for the patent work and he was waiting for a particular graduate student to enroll at Cornell.[140] The court rejected both arguments. In effect, holding onto a patent application until the best funding and/or the best graduate research assistants are available will rarely constitute reasonable diligence. "The reasonable diligence standard balances the interest in rewarding and encouraging invention with the public's interest in the earliest possible disclosure of innovation."[141] The court stated that Cornell University had "consciously chosen to assume the risk that priority in the invention might be lost to an outside inventor."[142]

The requirements for nonobviousness of subject matter are codified in section 103 of the Act. Nonobviousness requires that the differences between the current invention and the prior art be significant enough that they would not have been obvious to a person with ordinary skill in the art to which the subject matter pertains.[143]

Ownership and Patentees' Rights

Under section 154 of the Patent Act, patentees have "the right to exclude others from making, using, offering for sale, or selling the invention throughout the United States or importing the invention into the United States, and, if the invention is a process, ... the right to exclude others from using, offering for sale or selling throughout the United States, or importing into the United States, products made by the process."[144] The grant of a patent is not the right to use the invention—the inventor already has that right—but is the right to

---

[138] 816 F.2d 624 (Fed. Cir. 1987).

[139] Pursuant to 35 U.S.C. § 135, priority questions go to the Board of Patent Appeals and Interferences for resolution. If a final decision from the Board is adverse to an applicant for a patent, then the decision shall constitute final refusal of the application. If the decision is adverse to a current patentee, then the decision shall constitute cancellation of the claims involved in the patent.

[140] The graduate student was not scheduled to enroll until Fall 1983.

[141] 816 F.2d at 626.

[142] *Id.* at 628.

[143] 35 U.S.C. § 103. To prevent a patent rejection on the basis of no nonobviousness, the law also requires certain biotechnological processes and their resultant compositions of matter to be patented either simultaneously in the same application or in separate applications with the same effective filing date.

[144] 35 U.S.C. § 135.

exclude others from using it. Furthermore, the patentee is not obligated to put the invention to practice during the period of his or her monopoly.[145]

Upon the expiration of the twenty-year patent term, the patented article becomes public property. While royalties and other assignment contracts are popular between patentees and licensees, patentees are not permitted to extend the term of patent through the use of such agreements, as doing so would be against the public policy and the constitutional inspiration of patent law.[146] Commercial success cannot revive a patent monopoly.[147]

Under section 116, when two or more persons make an invention, they must apply for the patent jointly. Joint inventors are not required to work together physically or at the same time, nor must they make the same type or size contributions, and each joint inventor need not have contributed to each claim on the application. If a joint inventor refuses to join in an application for a patent, or cannot be reached after diligent effort, the remaining inventor(s) may attach that colleague's name on the application on his or her behalf. Similarly, if an inventor is either named or not named on an application as the result of an unintentional error, the Director of the United States Patent Office may amend the application as needed. Regarding the rights of joint owners of a patent, each joint owner "may make, use, offer for sale, or sell the patented invention within the United States, or import the patented invention into the United States, without the consent of and without accounting to the other owners."[148]

University of Colorado v. American Cyanamid [149] provides useful information to college and university personnel involved in collaborative research work. Two medical school professors won a claim against American Cyanamid after another doctor in Cyanamid clandestinely obtained a confidential paper written by the professors and submitted the results in a patent application. In the application, the doctor from Cyanamid claimed sole inventorship, but in fact, the applicant was not one of the inventors at all. By his request, the university professors had conducted research studies on one of the company's products. A federal district court held for the plaintiffs on a claim of unjust enrichment under state law. The court of appeals affirmed.[150]

Policymaking and Institutional Ownership Rights

Patentees have the right, just as they would with any personal property, to assign property rights to other persons or entities, including the rights to make, sell, and use patented articles.[151] It is common in university settings for the universities themselves to be the owners of patents that stem from the work of

---

[145] Bement v. Nat'l Harrow Co., 186 U.S. 70 (1902).

[146] Brulotte v. Thys Co., 379 U.S. 29 (1964).

[147] H.D. Hudson Mfg. Co. v. Standard Oil Co., 60 F.2d 377 (8th Cir. 1932).

[148] 35 U.S.C. § 262.

[149] 342 F.3d 1298 (Fed. Cir. 2003).

[150] Note that unjust enrichment is not based in patent ownership or infringement, and is not preempted by patent law.

[151] 35 U.S.C. § 261.

faculty members and other inventors.[152] Assignment of rights is also popular in colleges and universities, as educational institutions draft and enforce intellectual property policies. These rights may be assigned or licensed in whole or in part.[153] For example, a university policy may require the taking of half of the net income from the invention of a faculty researcher,[154] or it may adopt a sliding scale where the university takes various percentages of the income, depending on the dollar amount. Universities have to be clear in their policy-making, for the income that is derived from a patent does not emanate merely from its initial grant—there are marketing and licensing agreements and future research work with the invention (e.g., new tests, amendments, improvements, etc.). Similarly, faculty and student inventors must be aware of the policies. Even policies that grant percentage of "net income" may be limited if the full ownership of the patent remains with the university.[155]

Patent litigation in higher education often involves the relationships between faculty and student researchers and their institutions. What may seem like harmless and quietly effective patent policies could become loud and harsh when money and business (and ego, perhaps) take over. An important lesson to be learned here is that all faculty members and student employees who engage in the production of intellectual property as part of their employment sign on to their university's intellectual property policies when they sign their contracts. No special contract needs to be signed for the intellectual property policies to take effect.[156] Particularly instructive is the policy from West Virginia University (WVU), at issue in *University of West Virginia v. Vanvoorhies.*[157] Under the policy:

> [T]he University owns worldwide right, title and interest in any invention made at least in part by University personnel, or with substantial use of University resources, and unless otherwise agreed, this Policy applies to any invention conceived or first reduced to practice under terms of contracts, grants or other agreements.[158]

The WVU Policy defines "university personnel" as "all full-time and part-time members of the faculty and staff, and all other employees of the

---

[152] Bd. of Trs. of the Univ. of Ill. v. Micron Tech., Inc., 245 F. Supp. 3d 1036 (C.D. Ill. 2017); Curators of the Univ. of Mo. v. Suppes, no. WD81278, 2019 WL 121983 (Mo. Ct. App. Jan. 8, 2019).

[153] Zenith Radio Corp. v. Hazeltine Research, 395 U.S. 100 (1969).

[154] *See, e.g.,* Senkan v. Ill. Inst. of Tech., No. 93-2044, 1994 U.S. App. LEXIS 7201 (7th Cir., April 12, 1994).

[155] *See, e.g.,* Senkan v. Ill. Inst. of Tech., No. 93-2044, 1994 U.S. App. LEXIS 7201 (7th Cir. April 12, 1994) (policy and practice of awarding the faculty inventor 50 % of the invention's "net income" applied only to "patenting, marketing, licensing, protection or administering the invention," and not to future research grants that used the invention).

[156] *See, e.g.,* Chou v. Univ. of Chi., 254 F.3d 1347 (Fed. Cir. 2001) (under Illinois law, a graduate student was obligated to assign her inventions to the university under the university's patent policy, even though no formal contract was signed requiring such assignment).

[157] 278 F.3d 1288 (Fed. Cir. 2002).

[158] *Id.* at 1292. Under the policy, 30% of the patent's net royalty income goes to the inventor.

University including graduate and undergraduate students and fellows of the University." In *Vanvoorhies*, a WVU graduate student who became a postdoctorate instructor, also at WVU, refused to assign the rights to two inventions to the University. WVU sued and won. Similar breaches of contract claims occur when faculty members refuse to assign their rights under intellectual property policies,[159] when the researchers feel they have been inadequately served by their universities,[160] or when a researcher applies for numerous patents and fails to properly notify the university and fails to acknowledge assignment of ownership to the university.[161]

In a recent case involving another student-professor relationship, a student filed suit against his faculty advisor and a corporation that the faculty advisor founded, arguing that the advisor stole and patented the student's idea.[162] The court held in favor of the defendants, finding that the student failed to show that he contributed to the joint arrival of the idea.

In a case involving alleged violations of university patent policy, a professor filed suit against Yale University for conversion, theft, tortious interference with business relationships, and violation of Connecticut unfair trade laws.[163] Yale counterclaimed with an action for breach of contract. The lawsuit stemmed from an invention developed while the professor was working at Yale.[164] Under Yale policy, all researchers were required to notify Yale first of any invention. Yale then works with the Research Corporation to carry out the patent and commercialization processes.[165] Unless otherwise agreed between the parties, Yale gets ownership of the inventions, the Research Corporation gets the titles to the patents, and the inventors get to share in the licensing royalties. The professor had a longstanding disagreement with Yale's policies (as the percentage of royalties granted to professors decreased over the years with policy amendments) and made this fact known. When the professor developed his invention in mass spectrometry, he did not give the university first notice; instead, he presented it in a paper at a national convention. Furthermore, the professor discouraged Yale from pursuing the patent and significantly downplayed the commercial value of the invention. All the

---

[159] *See, e.g.,* Regents of the Univ. of N.M. v. Knight, 321 F.3d 1111 (Fed. Cir. 2003) (professors refused to assign ownership rights to the university for inventions resulting from cancer research; the university succeeded in a breach of contract claim against the professors).

[160] *See, e.g.,* Kucharczyk v. Regents of the Univ. of Cal., 48 F. Supp. 2d 964 (N.D. Cal. 1999) (professors filed unsuccessful breach of contract claim against their university to recover financial rewards of the patented medical device they developed; but the court held that licensing agreement between the university and a private corporation was not arbitrary and capricious).

[161] Curators of the Univ. of Mo. v. Suppes, no. WD81278, 2019 WL 121983 (Mo. Ct. App. Jan. 8, 2019).

[162] Daneshvar v. Kipke, 266 F. Supp. 3d 1031 (E.D. Mich. 2017).

[163] Fenn v. Yale Univ., 283 F. Supp. 2d 615 (D. Conn. 2003).

[164] The invention ultimately earned Fenn the 2002 Nobel Prize in Chemistry.

[165] It appears relatively common for universities to form affiliate companies to handle patenting, marketing, and licensing of patentable products and processes. *See also* ARCH Development Corp. v. Biomet, Inc., No. 02-C-9013, No. 03-C-2185, 2003 U.S. Dist. LEXIS 13118 (N.D. Ill. July 30, 2003) (ARCH is an affiliate of the University of Chicago).

while, the professor applied for and received the patent, with the support of private companies with whom the professor was to license the invention. A federal district court rejected the professor's claims and found in favor of Yale on its breach of contract counterclaim.

Researchers and universities are not the only plaintiffs in higher education patent cases. In another case with disputed patent ownership, the DuPont Company filed suit against a faculty researcher to enforce a contract it had with Washington State University (WSU), where the professor worked and helped to discover a gene important to fat metabolism.[166] Under WSU's patent policy, the university is the owner of patents developed by employees as a result of their employment. Although the professor notified both his home university and DuPont of his discovery, he claimed that he was the rightful owner since the discovery occurred while he was working in a lab at another university. The court disagreed and found that the two central contracts at issue (the university policy and the license agreement between Washington State University and DuPont) declared DuPont the owner of the patent and licensing opportunities. As intelligent as higher education personnel are, there are many who are unfamiliar with the policies that affect their most outstanding creations and discoveries. This is not to say that colleges and universities do not have legitimate interests in their faculty members' creations. But, it is to say that balances must be struck and education must be offered so that the parties are fully aware of their responsibilities.[167]

More recently, the United States Supreme Court heard a case involving faculty researchers, a university, and a private research company. In *Board of Trustees of Stanford University v. Roche Molecular Systems, Inc.*, the Court had an opportunity to interpret provisions of the Bayh-Dole Act of 1980, which allocates rights in federally funded inventions between the federal government and federal contractors.[168] Pursuant to contract and policy at Stanford, researchers employed by the university agree to assign right, title, and interest in inventions resulting from employment at Stanford. Meanwhile, however, Stanford arranged for researchers to conduct research at Cetus (later Roche) on techniques that assist in the treatment of HIV and AIDS. Cetus obligated the researchers to assign rights in inventions to Cetus, setting up a conflict—to whom do these inventions belong, Cetus or the University? The Court rejected Stanford's infringement claim and held that Bayh-Dole did not automatically vest title in the employing university.

Patent Infringement and Remedies

Patent infringement can be direct, indirect, or contributory. Anyone who, without permission, makes, uses, or sells the patented invention is a direct patent infringer.[169] Direct infringement can be committed innocently. If a person

---

[166] E.I. DuPont de Nemours & Co. v. Okuley, 344 F.3d 578 (6th Cir. 2003).

[167] Inservices and workshops, perhaps at faculty orientations, are encouraged.

[168] 131 S. Ct. 2188 (2011).

[169] 35 U.S.C. § 271(a).

actively encourages another to infringe the patent, then he or she is an indirect patent infringer.[170] Contributory infringement occurs when a person sells or supplies a component of a patented product or an apparatus for use in practicing a patented process, knowing that the component constitutes a material part of the invention and/or is especially adapted for use in an infringement.[171] In most cases of direct or indirect infringement, there is no defense for good faith or ignorance of the patent. However, a patent owner is required to mark a product with a notice of patent or to provide actual notice of the patent to an infringer.[172] In *TC Heartland, LLC v. Kraft Food Brands Group, LLC*, the U.S. Supreme Court held that patent infringement lawsuits may only be filed where the defendant is incorporated or where the defendant committed acts of infringement and has a regular and established place of business.[173]

There are only a few statutory defenses to infringement. In infringement cases, the patent and each of its claims independently are presumed to be valid. These presumptions are rebuttable, nonetheless, with evidence of invalidity (e.g., lack of novelty, utility, or nonobviousness). The defendant also may produce evidence of noninfringement, absence of liability, or unenforceability of the patent. The final statutory defense is a relatively recent enactment. Under section 273, adopted in 1999, a defendant may argue that he or she, acting in good faith, actually reduced the subject matter of the patent to practice at least one year before the effective filing date of the patent at issue and commercially used the subject matter before the effective filing date.

Section 281 of the Act gives patentees the right to enforce intellectual property rights in a civil action. A court, for example, may grant an injunction to halt the infringement.[174] Furthermore, monetary damages in an amount adequate to compensate for the infringement may be awarded.[175] Damages must be in an amount at least as much as a reasonable royalty fee for the use made of the invention by the infringer. The court may hear expert testimony to determine damages and/or what the reasonable royalty would be and has the power to grant treble damages when it is shown that the plaintiff was damaged beyond the reasonable royalty rate.[176] Finally, a court may award attorney fees in exceptional cases.[177] Despite the statutory requirement of "exceptionality" in attorney fees awards, two relatively recent Supreme Court opinions may

---

[170] 35 U.S.C. § 271(b).

[171] 35 U.S.C. § 271(c).

[172] 35 U.S.C. § 287. The notice requirement has one important exception. The patent owner is not expected to provide notice on patented articles that have been reproduced by *other* infringers. As a result, the owner may recover damages even in cases where an infringement occurs through the use of an unmarked item.

[173] 137 S. Ct. 1514 (2017). Formerly, patent lawsuits could also be filed where the defendant had sales.

[174] 35 U.S.C. § 283. See, e.g., Apple, Inc. v. Samsung Electronics Co., 735 F.3d 1352 (Fed. Cir. 2013); and Trebro Mfg. v. Firefly Equipment, LLC, 748 F.3d 1159 (Fed. Cir. 2014).

[175] 35 U.S.C. § 284. For a special provision on additional remedies for infringements of design patents, *see* 35 U.S.C. § 289.

[176] The court may also award reasonable interest and related costs.

[177] 35 U.S.C. § 285.

make it easier to recover. First, the Court, in *Octane Fitness, LLC v. ICON Health & Fitness*, held that entitlement to attorney fees is based on a preponderance of the evidence standard.[178] Second, in *Highmark, Inc. v. Allcare Health Management System, Inc.*, the Court held that appellate courts review "exceptionality" only on an abuse-of-discretion standard and not de novo.[179] The impact here is that attorney fees will be easier to get and may discourage frivolous infringement lawsuits.

Trademarks

In a typical college trademark infringement case, the Court of Appeals for the Eleventh Circuit upheld the University of Georgia's injunctive relief with this vivid replay of the facts:

> In the fall of 1982, when the fancy of Georgia sports fans turned to thoughts of college football, Bill Laite Distributing Co., a Macon, Georgia wholesaler of novelty beers, began marketing "Battlin' Bulldog Beer." The beer was sold in red-and-black cans bearing the portrayal of an English bulldog wearing a red sweater emblazoned with a black "G." The Bulldog had bloodshot eyes, a football tucked under its right "arm," and a frothy beer stein in his left "hand."
>
> Laite hoped that the "Battlin' Bulldog" would pile up yardage and score big points in the always-competitive alcoholic beverage market. Unfortunately, however, the pug-faced pooch was thrown for a loss by the University of Georgia Athletic Association, ... which obtained preliminary and permanent injunctive relief in federal district court based on the likelihood of confusion between the "Battlin' Bulldog" and the "University of Georgia Bulldog."[180]

Collegiate trademarking and licensing of goods and services is a booming business. Without trademark protection for its words, symbols, and slogans, this business would not be nearly as lucrative for higher education institutions. In other words, "imitation may be the sincerest form of flattery, ... but when the imitation consists of commercial reproduction for profit, all bets are off."[181] With such protection, this business, like any similar competitive arena, remains rather litigious. For example, the University of Alabama reported that it issued 153 cease-and-desist letters to protect its trademark between 2003

---

[178] 134 S. Ct. 1749 (2014).
[179] 134 S. Ct. 1744 (2014).
[180] Univ. of Ga. Athletic Ass'n v. Laite, 756 F.2d 1535, 1536-1537 (11th Cir. 1985).
[181] Savannah Coll. of Art & Design, Inc. v. Sportswear, Inc., 872 F.3d 1256 (11th Cir. 2017).

and 2013.[182] The protection asserted for trademark usage may be articulated in university policy, as well, particularly in policies and procedures allowing faculty, staff, and students to use the institution's trademarks in their work. By and large, those policies will be applied consistently and appropriately. However, if a university grants permission for individuals or organizations (e.g., student organizations) to use its trademarks, it must comply with First Amendment free speech.[183]

Unlike patents and copyrights, there is no parallel constitutional provision referring to the promotion or protection of trademarks. The closest constitutional guideline is the Commerce Clause, which permits Congress to regulate interstate commerce. The legal protection of trademarks protects the public from confusion and protects the trademark owner from losing his or her market. Specifically, the intent of the Lanham Act,[184] a current trademark act, is to make "actionable the deceptive and misleading use of marks" in commerce, "to protect persons engaged in such commerce against unfair competition; [and] to prevent fraud and deception in such commerce by the use of reproductions, copies, counterfeits, or colorable imitations of registered marks."[185]

While the commonplace term used is "trademark," the use of the word "mark," protected by the federal Lanham Act and individual state statutes, refers to trademarks, service marks, certification marks, and collective marks. A "trademark" includes "any word, name, symbol, or device, or any combination thereof used ... to identify and distinguish [a person's] goods ... from those manufactured or sold by others and to indicate the source of the goods."[186] Service marks are similar to trademarks but identify and distinguish services instead of goods. Certification marks allow an organization to indicate that goods or services meet certain quality standards or regional standards and exclude all others from making the same claim with the same or similar marks that might cause confusion. Finally, collective marks are trademarks or service marks used by groups to identify membership in those groups. A fine example of a collective mark in higher education is a university's alumni association.[187]

---

[182] Jon Solomon. *University of Alabama Aggressively Defends Trademarks. How Far is Too Far?* AL.Com, http://www.al.com/sports/index.ssf/2013/11/university_of_alabama_aggressi.html (Nov. 17, 2013); *see also*, Diaz v. Glen Plaid, LLC, 2013 U.S. Dist. LEXIS 147266 (N.D. Ala. Oct. 10, 2013) (case involving University of Alabama policing its trademark); Ohio State Univ. v. Thomas, 738 F. Supp. 2d 743 (S.D. Ohio 2010) (university sued over web publications that utilized university's trademarked name).

[183] Gerlich v. Leath, 861 F.3d 697 (8th Cir. 2017) (student organization's use of a cannabis leaf did not violate the university's trademark policies because the organization was not advocating illegal activity, but rather reform of marijuana use laws).

[184] 15 U.S.C. §§ 1051, *et seq.*

[185] 15 U.S.C. § 1127.

[186] *Id.*

[187] Villanova Univ. v. Villanova Alumni Educ. Found., 123 F. Supp.2d 293 (E.D. Pa. 2000).

Distinctiveness, Priority, and Trademark Registration

The primary requirement for trademark protection is distinctiveness—to serve the function of identifying the goods and avoiding confusion, deception, or mistake. Distinctiveness allows the trademark registrant to object to a later user of the same or similar mark.[188] There is a significant exception, though. The rule of "priority" that often favors the first user over others does not apply when the second use is established in good faith in a different geographical market. If a distant second user has no notice of the first mark and acts in good faith, and there is no confusion or other deception, then the second user may prevail in an infringement claim.[189] Priority is codified in section 1052 of the Lanham Act. An applicant for a trademark will not obtain the rights if the use of the mark by the applicant is likely to cause confusion, mistake, or deceit with another existing mark. Actual evidence of confusion, mistake, or deceit is not required; evidence of likelihood, however, is required. In determining likelihood of confusion, the similarity of the marks, similarity of the goods and/or services, the area and manner of concurrent use of the competing marks, and wrongful intent are important factors.

Also significant to this discussion is the effect federal registration has on priority claims. Under section 1072 of the Act, the owner of a federally registered trademark can claim a nationwide constructive notice. With this claim, everyone is presumed to have notice of the mark; in other words, there is no good faith defense in such circumstances. "If the mark at issue is federally registered and has become incontestable, the validity, legal protection, and ownership are proved."[190] In addition to the bar on registration for marks similar to those of others, there is also a bar against geographic marks,[191] immoral marks,[192] and surnames.[193] Of these three, the most applicable to this chapter is the bar on geographic marks. Geographic marks are typically the proper names for geographic entities like nations, states, counties, cities, rivers, and lakes, and are often found in college and university names.

Generally, the four types of marks are generic, descriptive, suggestive, and arbitrary or fanciful.[194] Suggestive and arbitrary marks are the easiest to register and protect because they are typically the most distinctive. For a higher education example, in *Board of Trustees of the University of Arkansas v. Razorback Sports and Physical Therapy Clinic*, the University of Arkansas

---

[188] Bd. of Regents of the Univ. of Houston Sys. v. Houston Coll. of Law, 214 F. Supp. 3d 573 (S.D. Tex. 2016).

[189] *See* Trs. of Columbia Univ. v. Columbia/HCA Healthcare Corp., 964 F. Supp. 733 (S.D.N.Y. 1997) (Columbia Health Care had its primary place of business in Nashville, Tennessee, but had an operation in New York City, where it was alleged to infringe on the name of Columbia University).

[190] *Villanova Univ.*, 123 F. Supp. 2d at 301-302.

[191] 15 U.S.C. § 1052(e).

[192] 15 U.S.C. § 1052(a).

[193] 15 U.S.C. § 1052(e).

[194] *See* Bd. of Regents of the Univ. Sys. of Ga. v. Buzas Baseball, Inc., 176 F. Supp. 2d 1338 (N.D. Ga. 2001).

filed suit against the Razorback Sports and Physical Therapy Clinic, alleging trademark infringement, unfair competition, and dilution of trademark.[195] In finding for the university, the court held, in part, that the term "Razorback" was not a geographic term. In fact, the court found the term "Razorback" to be "arbitrary" for trademark purposes (i.e., not directly descriptive of the goods and services provided), giving the term more strength as a trademark. According to the court, "the resultant identification of a geographic region with a collegiate mark never becomes so strong that it negates the primary identification of the mark with the University, at least not here in Arkansas."[196] Similar arguments can be made for colleges and collegiate mascots that bear the popular nickname of the state, such as Ohio State Buckeyes, Wisconsin Badgers, and Nebraska Cornhuskers.[197]

Registration is easier for "arbitrary" words and pictures than it is for descriptive words and pictures; arbitrary marks can be more easily identified with the one good or service and, as a result, less confused with other goods and services bearing similar or identical marks. For a geographic mark or other descriptive mark to be registrable, it must be established that consumers associate the mark with a single source for the product. Essentially, such a mark would have to acquire what the law terms "secondary meaning," where the public comes to associate the mark with the product synonymously, or by "second nature." One court stated:

> Secondary meaning converts a word originally incapable of serving as a mark into a full fledged trademark. ... An arbitrary, fanciful, or otherwise distinctive word qualifies as a trademark immediately, because in the particular industry it has no primary meaning to overcome.[198]

Generally, for a trademark to withstand competition from an allegedly infringing mark, proof of secondary meaning is not required for arbitrary and fanciful marks, but must be shown for descriptive marks.[199] Secondary meaning is typically shown through long exclusive use of a mark in the relevant market, size or public prominence of the institution, and success of the institution's promotional efforts. The decision in *President and Trustees of Colby College v. Colby College-New Hampshire* provides an example.[200] In this case, the court held that the defendant's name change from "Colby Junior College for Women" to "Colby College-New Hampshire" infringed the trademark held by Colby College, a four-year institution in Waterville, Maine, that had been

---

[195] 873 F. Supp. 1280.

[196] *Id.* at 1287-1288.

[197] In *Univ. of Ark.*, the defendant offered an argument that the state was known as "The Razorback State," and, therefore, the term took on geographic significance. The plaintiffs' Internet search for verifying evidence revealed, however, that most "hits" referred to the University and its athletic teams.

[198] Univ. of Ga. Athletic Ass'n v. Laite, 756 F.2d 1535, 1540-1541 (11th Cir. 1985).

[199] *Id.* at 1540.

[200] 508 F.2d 804 (1st Cir. 1975).

conducting business under that name since 1899. Essentially, the vast majority of the public exclusively identified the name "Colby College" with the one in Maine and not the one in New Hampshire.[201] According to the court, "[t] here is sufficient secondary meaning as long as a significant quantity of the consuming public understand a name as referring exclusively to the appropriate party, for it is undesirable that such a quantity be deceived even if some, relatively small, number is not."[202]

Before moving to more formal discussions of unfair competition and trademark infringement, three additional factors for trademark registration are relevant here. For a mark to be registrable, it must actually be used to identify the goods or services; in other words, identification and distinctiveness must be the primary purposes for the mark. Sometimes, the "trade dress"—a device, name, or design that accompanies the goods—is also registrable, if it serves those primary purposes. In addition, a device that is solely functional or utilitarian cannot be registered as a mark. Goods having such a device could not be identified and distinguished from other goods performing that function because those other goods would have that same device. Finally, and nicely applicable to the identity (and sometimes distinctiveness) of colleges and universities, is color. Color alone will not normally earn trademark protection. Most often, the color will have to combine with some device or design for which color is an integral part in order to gain protection.[203] But if the design is not that complex and the colors are few, then trademark protection will be denied.[204]

Trademark Infringement and Unfair Competition

Lanham Act claims generally fall into two categories. First is a claim for infringement of the plaintiff's service marks or trademarks.[205] There are three elements of a cause of action for infringement: 1) the mark is valid and legally protectable, 2) the mark is owned by the plaintiff, and 3) the defendant's use of the mark to identify its goods or services is likely to cause confusion regarding the source or sponsorship of its goods and services.[206] Second is a claim for unfair competition.[207] The elements of a cause of action for unfair competition are identical to those for infringement, except that they apply to unregistered

---

[201] The plaintiffs offered survey data to confirm this point.

[202] *President and Trs. of Colby Coll.,* 508 F.2d at 807.

[203] *See, e.g.,* President and Fellows of Harvard Coll. v. Harvard Bioscience, Inc., 204 F. Supp.2d 134 (D. Mass. 2002) (the defendant's use of its company name, Harvard Apparatus, is not infringing of the University's trademark, but its use of the same font and crimson color is).

[204] *See, e.g.,* Life Saver Corp. v. Curtiss Candy Co., 182 F.2d 4 (7th Cir. 1950).

[205] Section 32 of the Lanham Act, 15 U.S.C. § 1051.

[206] *See* Villanova Univ. v. Villanova Alumni Educ. Found., Inc., 123 F. Supp. 2d 293 (E.D. Pa. 2000).

[207] Section 43(a) of the Lanham Act, 15 U.S.C. § 1125.

marks, which are protectable if they are found to be distinctive. Unfair competition claims may also take the form of claims for false advertising.[208]

The primary standard in trademark infringement is whether there is a likelihood of confusion. Several factors are analyzed in a determination of likely confusion, and courts differ as to the number of factors and the specific wording of them. However, the following list is representative and comprehensive:[209]

1. The degree of similarity between the owner's mark and the alleged infringer's mark (e.g., with respect to appearance, sound, connotation, and impression)
2. The strength of the owner's mark
3. The price of the goods and other factors indicative of the care and attention expected of consumers when making a purchase[210]
4. The length of time the defendant has used the alleged similar mark without evidence of actual confusion
5. Evidence of actual confusion[211]
6. Intent, or lack thereof, of alleged infringer to pass off the trademark owner as the source or sponsor of the goods[212]
7. The degree to which the products are in competition with one another (the similarity of "trade channels" and "competitive proximity")
8. The extent to which the targets of the parties' sales efforts are the same.
9. Similarity of the goods or services in the minds of the public.
10. Variety of goods with which the mark is used.

All other things being equal, the more similar the marks, the more likely a finding of confusion.[213] Likewise, the more distinctive a mark, the higher

---

[208] In a false advertising claim, if a plaintiff shows false statements and the likelihood of injury, then the plaintiff is entitled to injunctive relief. If the defendant has profited unfairly by these false statements, then the plaintiff may be entitled to damages, as well as injunctive relief.

[209] *See, e.g.,* Fla. Int'l Univ. Bd. of Trs. v. Fla. Nat'l Univ., Inc., 830 F.3d 1242 (11th Cir. 2016); Villanova Univ. v. Villanova Alumni Educ. Found., 123 F. Supp. 2d 293 (E.D. Pa. 2000). Note that fame or popularity of the plaintiff's mark is not enough for confusion. *See* University of Notre Dame v. Gourmet Food Imports Co., 703 F.2d 1372 (Fed. Cir. 1983) (the defendant's use of the mark "Notre Dame" did not infringe the marks owned by the well-known university).

[210] When dealing with a market where the competing goods are stocked close to each other, the marks are similar, and the purchaser spends less time deliberating over purchase (e.g., on an inexpensive item in a supermarket), courts are more likely to find confusion. For bigger ticket items where the consumer is a little more discriminating and deliberative, similar marks are less likely to result in confusion.

[211] *See* Corp. of Gonzaga Univ. v. Pendleton Enters., LLC, 55 F. Supp. 3d 1319 (E.D. Wash. 2014) (Gonzaga University won a trademark infringement suit against a local bar that was using the Gonzaga mascot and other trademarks to promote bar business).

[212] For examples of intent to confuse, *see* Univ. of Ga. Athletic Ass'n v. Laite, 756 F.2d 1535 (11th Cir. 1985); and Bd. of Trs. of the Univ. of Ark. v. Prof'l Therapy Servs., 873 F. Supp. 1280 (W.D. Ark. 1995).

[213] Bd. of Regents of the Univ. of Houston Sys. v. Houston Coll. of Law, 214 F. Supp. 3d 573 (S.D. Tex. 2016) (the University of Houston prevailed in a trademark infringement claim against Houston College of Law, formerly South Texas College of Law, by showing that it was the senior user of the mark and that the likelihood of confusion and threat of irreparable harm were high).

its "strength" and less likely a finding of confusion. Similarity of a mark can come from a variety of directions: physical design; sounds; psychological, commercial, or social connotations and significance; color scheme; or linguistic characteristics. When similar-sounding marks are involved, for example, the inquiry is whether purchases are made under circumstances in which sound is more important than design, appearance, or spelling. This includes whether advertising is regularly done on radio and/or whether orders are typically offered by telephone.

Recall also that the law will provide trademark protection more often for a "fanciful or arbitrary" word or phrase (one that, in words alone, is rather distinctive) than it will for a word or phrase common to everyday language. In *Florida International University (FIU) Board of Trustees v. Florida National University (FNU)*, the Eleventh Circuit Court of Appeals rejected FIU's trademark infringement claim against FNU, which had recently changed its name from Florida National College. The court held that the words "Florida" and "University" were common words in many postsecondary institutions in the state.[214] Furthermore, "international" and "national" have different definitions. Sometimes, those common every day words are found both in and out of universities' names. In *Trustees of Columbia University v. Columbia/HCA Healthcare Corporation*, the court rejected Columbia University's infringement claim against a major healthcare and hospital system, in part because the defendant presented substantial evidence of "third-party use" of the name "Columbia."[215] In other words, the word "Columbia" is used in connection with a variety of businesses, including but not limited to healthcare and education, and has been for years. Such evidence of third-party use will detract from the "strength" of the trademark and lean the case away from a finding of infringement. According to one court, "the use of collegiate marks by local businesses as part of their trade names is an old and venerable tradition."[216] But according to another, "[t]he strength of a mark is a measure of its tendency to identify the goods or services sold under the mark as emanating from a particular … source."[217] Strength depends ultimately on the mark's distinctiveness or its "origin-indicating quality." In addition to the arbitrary nature of the mark and the evidence of third-party use, other indicia for strength of a mark include the presumptive validity of federal registrations; long-term use of the marks; extensive public exposure through advertising, promotion, and

---

[214] 830 F.3d 1242 (11th Cir. 2016).

[215] 964 F. Supp. 733 (S.D.N.Y. 1997).

[216] Bd. of Trs. of the Univ. of Ark. v. Prof'l Therapy Servs., 873 F. Supp. 1280, 1289 (W.D. Ark. 1995).

[217] *Columbia University*, 964 F. Supp. at 744 (internal citations omitted).

unsolicited publicity; and the owner's actions to prevent infringement with cease-and-desist letters.[218]

Actual confusion, as a factor to weigh in a trademark infringement claim, is not required for a plaintiff's success;[219] however, it naturally does not hurt a claim.[220] Similarly, evidence of intentional infringement of a trademark is a near guarantee for injunction and/or damages. But intentional infringement may not occur in an effort to take over the market of a trademark or service mark owner. Instead, an innocent infringer who is notified of a competing mark may continue to infringe, even with the notice, not to damage the investments of the mark's owner, but rather to protect his or her own investments.

On the similarity of the markets, trade channels, and competitive proximity, if the plaintiff and the defendant actually do provide the same services and compete for the same customers, then the trademark owner deserves protection "so that it does not lose confused customers ... and so that people do not think they are receiving goods and services from the owner, when they are in fact receiving them from the infringer."[221] Today, the Internet is of particular importance as a trade channel. Seemingly different products and services from two different providers in vastly different geographic markets could still result in a finding of similar trade channels if the parties depend, at least in part, on the Internet for advertising and sales. In *Board of Regents of the University of Georgia v. Buzas Baseball, Inc.*, the court denied summary judgment motions and found a dispute of fact on whether the defendant's Salt Lake City minor league baseball mascot, "Buzzy," is confusingly similar to the Georgia Tech Yellow Jacket's mascot, "Buzz."[222]

Of course, similar marks (in sound, design, appearance, or impression) may not be infringing when the goods and/or services offered are not at all similar. The real test is whether the marks will confuse relevant consumers. Goods and services are considered similar if they serve the same purposes or fulfill the same needs. Additionally, what may be particularly important to the discussion of similarity and confusion of marks in higher education is not only the similarity or the marks or the goods themselves, but also the similarity of the markets for these goods. Despite differences in goods and services and their markets, consumers may tend to associate different goods if there is a public expectation that the goods came from the same source, say, a university.[223]

---

[218] *See* Bd. of Trs. of the Univ. of Ark. v. Prof'l Therapy Servs., 873 F. Supp. 1280 (W.D. Ark. 1995). *See also* Theta Chi Fraternity, Inc. v. Leland Stanford Junior Univ., 212 F. Supp. 3d 816 (N.D. Calif. 2016) (the court held, in part, that Theta Chi's marks are not famous enough to show that they were diluted by defendants' use of "Chi Theta Chi", despite the fact that "Chi Theta Chi" was an offshoot of a disbanded chapter of Theta Chi at the university).

[219] *Id.* at 1291.

[220] *See* Villanova Univ. v. Villanova Alumni Educ. Found., 123 F. Supp. 2d 293 (E.D. Pa. 2000) (both the plaintiff and the defendant, operating under similar-sounding names, raised money for student scholarships).

[221] *Univ. of Ark.*, 873 F. Supp. at 1290.

[222] 176 F. Supp. 2d 1338 (N.D. Ga. 2001).

[223] *See* Harvard Coll. v. Harvard Bioscience, Inc., 204 F. Supp. 2d 134 (D. Mass. 2002).

But this is a balancing act. On one hand, the "related goods" doctrine should favor the owner of the mark if there is a likelihood that the owner's business will be harmed by the "relationship" it has with the infringing mark. On the other hand, the law does not usually tolerate such monopolies.

Defenses are available in trademark infringement cases, but they come with significant challenges. Recall that formal registration of a trademark carries with it the presumption of validity, meaning that infringement cases begin in favor of the registrant.[224] Even with this presumption, though, the equitable doctrines of laches, estoppel, and unclean hands are applicable. Laches consists of two essential elements, inexcusable delay in instituting the suit and prejudice resulting to the defendant from such delay. In the noteworthy case, *University of Pittsburgh v. Champion Products*, the University of Pittsburgh (Pitt) filed suit against Champion Products for trademark infringement.[225] Champion had sold "Pitt" merchandise—clothing with university words, pictures, and slogans—for decades. For much of that time, Champion produced the merchandise and sold it in off-campus locations. In 1980, however, at the height of Pitt's national football notoriety, the university realized its national market and registered its trade and service marks. Pitt then asked Champion to execute a licensing agreement, but the company refused. In 1981, Pitt filed suit. On the first element of the laches defense, the court held that the university's delay in filing the suit was not inexcusable. Until it became a national power in athletics, Pitt was unaware that Champion's market for such merchandise went well beyond the Pittsburgh area. On the second element, the court found that Champion had not relied to its detriment on Pitt's delay and rejected the laches defense. According to the court, this was not a typical infringement case where both parties are competitors in similar markets, selling similar goods, and confusion is the issue; there was no real consumer confusion here. "With negligible exception, a consumer does not desire a 'Champion' T-shirt, he (or she) desires a 'Pitt' T-shirt. The entire impetus for the sale is the consumer's desire to identify with Pitt ... From this point of view, then, it is Champion which seeks to profit from Pitt's investment."[226] Estoppel is related to laches in that it depends on the defendant's reliance on the plaintiff's implied or active acceptance of the infringing conduct.[227] The doctrine of unclean hands means that "he who comes into equity must come with clean hands;" that is, the plaintiff must act fairly in order to enjoin the defendant's conduct. Importantly, implied license in-fact can defeat equitable defenses, where the parties' conduct is as though they had executed a license for the defendant to use the applicable marks. In *Villanova University v. Villanova Alumni Educational Foundation*,[228] Villanova University and the Villanova Educational Foundation, later the Villanova Alumni Educational Foundation, conducted similar fundraising businesses for

---

[224] 15 U.S.C. § 1057(b).

[225] 686 F.2d 1040 (3d Cir. 1982).

[226] *Id*. at 1047.

[227] *See* Bd. of Regents of the Univ. Sys. of Ga., 176 F. Supp. 1338 (N.D. Ga. 2001).

[228] 123 F. Supp. 293 (E.D. Pa. 2000).

several years with a verbal agreement, later a written agreement, and with full knowledge of each other's activities. When negotiations on a new agreement stalled, the university delivered cease-and-desist letters and filed suit.

In addition, fair and collateral use defenses are available. Fair use permits the utilization of a mark for a purpose other than that which the mark is normally used. In *Villanova*, the defendant offered a fair use defense, that it was using the term "Villanova Alumni" to *describe* its group, not to *mark its trade*. The court held that the use was not merely to describe, but also to acquire and maintain attention. The court held that fair use doctrine applies when the public is not deceived and the mark is used "to tell the truth."[229] Collateral use permits an entity to make use of a trademark as a component of a larger item or project, as long as the entity identifies the mark as protected by trademark. There is a caution, though. The entity making use of the mark must not give the impression the trademark's owner is the sponsor of the larger item or project.

The remedies available for trademark infringement include injunctive relief, an accounting for profits, damages, attorney fees in "exceptional cases," and costs.[230] Injunction is common in trademark infringement cases, but it is necessary to enjoin only illegitimate infringement and still permit legitimate competition. Accounting for profits allows a successful plaintiff to recover lost profits that resulted from the infringement, but the plaintiff need not show that the defendant's profits directly competed with the plaintiff's sales. This remedy supports the public interest in preventing unfair competition. Damages are in addition to the accounting for profits. Court are permitted to award up to three times the amount of any demonstrated actual damages, pursuant to the statutory language, which states that damages must act as compensation for loss to the plaintiff and not as penalty to the defendant.

Domain Names and Protection of Trademarks in Cyberspace

Protection of trademarks and service marks used by colleges and universities has moved into cyberspace. In 1999, Congress passed the Anti-Cybersquatting Consumer Protection Act (ACPA).[231] The ACPA amended the Lanham Act to protect registered "domain names"; "alphanumeric designation[s] which [are] registered with or assigned by any domain name registrar, domain name registry, or other domain name registration authority as part of an electronic address on the Internet."[232] Under the ACPA, any person who registers a domain name that is identical or substantially and confusingly similar to the name of another living person, without that person's consent and with the specific intent to profit from such name, is liable in a civil action.[233] There is an exception

---

[229] *Id*. at 304.

[230] 15 U.S.C. § 1117.

[231] *See* 15 U.S.C. § 1129.

[232] 15 U.S.C. § 1127.

[233] The profit referred to in the ACPA could be from the defendant holding the plaintiff's name "hostage" until selling it back to the plaintiff. *See, e.g.*, March Madness Athletic Ass'n v. Netfire, Inc., No. 3:00-CV-398-R, 2003 U.S. Dist. LEXIS 14941 (N.D. Tex. Aug. 28, 2003).

for the person who registers the name as part of a copyrighted work protected under copyright law. In an action under the ACPA, a court may award injunctive relief, requiring the defendant to shut down the site or to transfer the domain name to the plaintiff. Attorney fees are also available.[234]

Conclusion

Considering the constant advancements in technology, knowledge discovery, and knowledge dissemination, the statutory law of intellectual property – copyrights, patents, and trademarks – is remarkably steady. The TEACH Act, Digital Millennium Copyright Act, and the Copyright Term Extension Act have modernized copyright law fairly well, particularly for the delivery of online curriculum and programs in higher education. Speed of communication and readily accessible sounds, words, and images allow intellectual property to find markets and audiences that were, perhaps at one time, thought impossible. With this speed and technology also come increased possibilities for "patent races" and additional trademark violations. As a result of these new forums and opportunities, inventors and authors and inventors may benefit greatly. And while these benefits may come to institutions of higher education, as well, it is strongly recommended that college and universities regularly review policies, practices, and contracts so that the application of intellectual property law, however steady the statutory language is, can remain at the cutting edge. The "Progress of Science and useful Arts" depends on it.

Discussion Questions

1.   Article I, Section 8, Clause 8 of the U.S. Constitution states: "The Congress shall have the Power ... To promote the Progress of Science and the useful Arts, by securing for limited Times to Authors and Inventors the exclusive Right to their respective Writings and Discoveries." How do the provisions of this clause and the related provisions of intellectual property statutes for copyrights, patents, and trademarks work to balance the rights of individual inventors and authors and the overall interests of society?

2.   What is the purpose of intellectual property law?

3.   What is fair use under the Copyright Act? What's the purpose of fair use? Why and how is fair use important to the work of higher education? What are the four factors courts use to determine fair use in copyright infringement cases? How are each of these factors defined and applied? Which factor, if any, do you believe is the most important one in the balance?

4.   Explain the classroom use exception to exclusive rights under copyright? How does this exception change when the classroom is electronic (e.g.,

---

[234] For a discussion of domain name protection in higher education, *see* Alayne E. Manas, Note, *Harvard as a Model in Trademark and Domain Name Protection,* 29 RUTGERS COMPUTER & TECH. L. J. 475 (2003).

in an online class, either synchronous or asynchronous)? What are the institutional and instructional requirements to maintain the classroom use exception under the TEACH Act? How are these statutory obligations monitored and enforced in colleges and universities?

5. What is a "work-for-hire" in copyright law? How does (or should) this doctrine apply in higher education? Give some examples. Give me arguments for and against its application in educational settings (i.e., the "teacher exception" to work-for-hire)?

6. "Creative Commons" is a nonprofit corporation dedicated to making it easier for people to share and build upon the work of others, consistent with the rules of copyright. It provides free licenses and other legal tools to mark creative work with the freedom the creator wants it to carry, so others can share, remix, use commercially, or any combination thereof. What are the pros and cons to such an operation for the work of higher education?

7. How is patent ownership defined under the law? What are the primary factors courts use to determine patent ownership? How do institutions of higher education general assign patent rights? What are the primary legal issues that arise with patent ownership rights?

8. Distinctiveness, priority, and registration are primary aspects of trademark protection. What impact do you think electronic markets and social media have had on trademark litigation?

9. For quite some time now, there has been much controversy and conversation about the cost of higher education (e.g., tuition, room and board, books, etc.). What about the cost of knowledge? What role does intellectual property law (copyright, patent, and trademark) play in the cost and accessibility of knowledge? Think about the costs of textbooks, journals, and online database licenses. Think also about fair use, its purpose, and its advantages and disadvantages.

19

Intercollegiate Athletics

Joy Blanchard, Ph.D.
Louisiana State University

Though the National Collegiate Athletic Association (NCAA) governs college athletics and promulgates the multitude of regulations by which member institutions, coaches, and student-athletes must abide, state and federal courts have played a significant role in refining and limiting the control and influence the NCAA may have over intercollegiate athletics.[1] Likewise, courts have also defined the legal duties colleges and universities owe their student-athletes. This chapter will provide an overview of the several types of judicial challenges that have been brought forth related to college sports.

Breach of Contract and "Educational Malpractice"

The relationship between student-athletes and institutions is contractual in nature.[2] The letter of intent and scholarship offer constitute a contract. However, courts have granted latitude to coaches and institutions in determining the terms of a scholarship offer, as well as whether it will be renewed.[3] In *Giuliani v. Duke University*,[4] a student-athlete was recruited out of high school and promised "life-time access to the Duke golf facilities." When the head coach suddenly died and a new head coach was appointed, the student-athlete was notified that his scholarship would not be renewed.[5] When the coach presented Giuliani

---

[1] Because of the uptick in litigation (particularly concussion-related injuries and antitrust challenges), the NCAA reportedly spent $54 million in third-party legal fees in 2018—more than twice the amount it spent four years ago. Rick Seltzer, *NCAA Lawyers Up,* INSIDE HIGHER ED (July 16, 2019), *available at* https://www.insidehighered.com/news/2019/07/16/ncaa-spending-outside-lawyers-rises-50-percent-two-years.

[2] Even at public institutions, constitutional protections typically do not apply to student-athletes because the rules by which they are governed by stem from a private voluntary association, the NCAA.

[3] NCAA athletic scholarships are renewable one-year contracts, except in the instance of the Power Five (the five largest-revenue producing college athletic conferences), which have been given the option to offer four-year athletic scholarships.

[4] 2010 U.S. Dist. LEXIS 32691 (M.D.N.C. 2010).

[5] The court record states that the coach stipulated if all members of the team wrote a letter supporting Giuliani's continued presence on the team, he would be reinstated. The coach allegedly later instructed players to "back off" and threatened their positions on the roster.

with a document outlining the steps by which he could be reinstated, Giuliani refused to sign and his scholarship was subsequently rescinded without notice. He filed suit, claiming breach of contract, breach of the covenant of good faith and fair dealing, and tortious interference with a contract. The court rejected these claims, finding that previous oral promises by the former head coach were too ambiguous to define and establish definite terms. The court also found that the promises made to the student-athlete did not constitute unlimited and unconditional opportunities—hence showing deference to the new head coach to determine the team's roster.

A state court in Illinois rejected a former student-athlete's breach of contract claim after his athletic scholarship was not renewed, finding that the coaching staff's decision, based on athletic performance and skill, was not arbitrary, capricious, or done in bad faith.[6] Interestingly, the court analogized the case to the deference afforded university professors in deciding course grades, and that such professional judgments were not subject to court review.

Some student-athletes have attempted to assert contractual claims when the educational aspects promised via an athletic scholarship allegedly were not fulfilled. The most notable case of this sort was *Ross v. Creighton University.*[7] Kevin Ross was recruited to play basketball at Creighton University, which he claimed knew of his academic deficiencies and assured that, as condition of his athletic scholarship, he would receive tutoring and support services in order to complete his undergraduate degree.[8] While at Creighton, Ross completed ninety-six of the 128 credits needed to graduate, but many of these credits—including Theory of Basketball and Marksmanship—were inapplicable to any degree program. After leaving Creighton, he had fourth-grade language skills and was reading at a seventh-grade level.

Ross filed suit, alleging "educational malpractice," infliction of emotional distress, and breach of contract. A district court dismissed those claims, noting in particular that the state had not previously recognized claims of educational malpractice and that in other states those claims had not been successful. However, on appeal a court reversed the lower court's dismissal of contract claims and remanded for further review, stating:

> We read Mr. Ross' complaint to allege more than a failure of the University to provide him with an education of a certain quality. Rather, he alleges that the University knew that he was not qualified academically to participate in its curriculum. Nevertheless, it made a specific promise that he would be able to participate in a meaningful way in that program because it would provide certain specific services to him. . . . To adjudicate such a claim, the court would not be required to determine whether Creighton had breached its contract with Mr. Ross by providing deficient academic services.

---

6   Sams v. Bd. of Trs., 65 Ill. Ct. Cl. 127 (Ill. 2013).

7   957 F.2d 410 (7th Cir. 1992).

8   Ross had scored in the bottom five percentile on the American College Test (ACT).

Rather, its inquiry would be limited to whether the University had provided any real access to its academic curriculum at all.[9]

As in similar cases involving academic requirements and promissory estoppel,[10] a college baseball player was unable to prevail in court when he was declared ineligible after receiving erroneous advice from an academic advisor.[11] The student transferred from a junior college to a four-year university, and, per NCAA regulations, the advisor miscalculated the number of electives the student-athlete was allowed to take. The South Carolina Supreme Court declined to recognize the student's argument that the institution assumed a duty of care when it advised him on courses, citing a lack of precedent establishing negligence under that theory.

Most recently—and most notably—the University of North Carolina-Chapel Hill was embroiled in a scandal after records revealed that, from 1993 to 2011, approximately 200 student-athletes were funneled into sham courses with one professor in the African and Afro-American Studies department in order to more easily retain their competitive eligibility. A North Carolina appellate court upheld the dismissal of claims brought by two former University of North Carolina-Chapel Hill student-athletes who sued after they were funneled into these courses, which did not have substantive academic requirements.[12] The plaintiffs alleged breach of contract for not receiving the quality education they were promised when recruited to play at UNC-Chapel Hill. The court found that the plaintiffs failed to demonstrate an actual injury "based on a legally protected interest"[13] and dismissed the case for lack of standing.

Negligent Liability

In order for plaintiffs to successfully bring negligence suits against colleges and universities, they must prove that a duty of care or special relationship existed and that the institution's breach of that duty was the proximate cause of their injuries. Though in most negligence cases the standard of care is construed to be higher in the K-12 setting than in the collegiate setting, college student-athletes prevail in court more often than those in the K-12 setting because of the extensive control institutions exert upon student-athletes and the *de facto* special relationship established vis-à-vis the recruitment process.[14]

This special duty was most notably defined in *Kleinknecht v. Gettysburg College.*[15] Drew Kleinknecht was recruited to play lacrosse at the private

---

[9] 957 F.2d at 417.

[10] Promissory estoppel is the doctrine in which someone relies on the advice of another, usually a person in a position of authority, and that advice is erroneous and following such is to the plaintiff's detriment.

[11] Hendricks v. Clemson Univ., 578 S.E.2d 711 (S.C. 2003).

[12] Arnold v. Univ. of N.C., 798 S.E.2d 442 (N.C. Ct. App. 2017).

[13] *Id.*

[14] Joy Blanchard, *A Comparative Study of K-12 and Higher Education Sport-Related Negligence Litigation*, 6 J. FOR THE STUDY OF SPORTS AND ATHLETES IN EDUC. 201 (2012).

[15] 989 F.2d 1360 (3d Cir. 1993).

college and later died after suffering a heart attack during a practice session. Taking note of the benefit the institution received[16] from his services as a student-athlete, the court stated that the "[c]ollege owed Drew a duty of care in his capacity as an intercollegiate athlete engaged in school-sponsored intercollegiate athletic activity for which he had been recruited."[17] The coaches at Gettysburg College were not trained in CPR, no trainers attended practices, and the nearest telephone was nearly a quarter-mile away. Though the deceased student had no history of cardiac illness, the court found that a duty existed to reasonably prepare for the foreseeable occurrence that a student-athlete may have a medical emergency or become seriously injured.

While student-athletes have had relative success in bringing lawsuits against their institutions for injuries sustained while competing in collegiate sports, institutions also have been able to prevail based on traditionally utilized negligence defenses, particularly no duty or special relationship, sovereign immunity, and assumption of the risk. In *Lanni v. National Collegiate Athletic Association,* a state appellate court affirmed that the NCAA did not owe a student fencer a duty of care related to injuries she sustained at a fencing tournament.[18] Utilizing precedent related to university-fraternity liability cases, the court did not find that the NCAA's role in providing guidance related to student-athlete safety equated to assuming a duty of care.

In other cases, public institutions have successfully garnered summary judgment based on the doctrine of sovereign immunity, such as in *Sorey v. Kellett.*[19] There, a football player at the University of Mississippi died en route to the hospital (transported by a teammate, not athletic trainers or emergency personnel) after complaining of cramping and heat exhaustion. The court ruled that the team physician and trainer were performing discretionary functions at the time of the incident and went so far as to say that "the social costs of litigation against public officials. . . suggest that qualified immunity should be an immunity from suit, not merely a defense to liability."[20] A similar ruling was entered in Florida when a father filed suit after his son died during football practice. The state appellate court reversed a $10 million jury verdict, holding that the athletic association, though a private corporation but significantly entwined with the operations of the public university, should be construed as a state actor and was entitled to immunity.[21]

Additionally, institutions often have been successful by adopting an assumption of the risk defense. In *Rendine v. St. John's University,* a court found that an experienced cheerleader assumed a risk when she voluntarily attempted a partner stunt knowing there was no "spotter" available.[22] A col-

---

[16] *For example,* increased publicity and the hope of attracting more students and student-athletes.
[17] 989 F.2d at 1369.
[18] 42 N.E.3d 542 (Ind. Ct. App. 2015).
[19] 849 F.2d 960 (5th Cir. 1988).
[20] *Id.* at 963.
[21] UCF Athletics Ass'n v. Plancher, 121 So. 3d 616 (Fla Ct. App. 2013).
[22] 735 N.Y.S.2d 173 (N.Y. App. Div. 2001).

lege baseball player did not prevail in his claims against a university when he was hit in the face during a mandatory practice session. The appellate court ruled that the injuries were a result of an accident common in sport, and that the experienced student-athlete knew of the inherent dangers and assumed the risks of participation.[23] Similarly, a California appellate court upheld summary judgment in favor of a university in a case stemming from a swimmer injured during a weightlifting workout.[24]

Though student-athletes do assume a risk by participating in college sports, courts require a reasonable duty of care and, additionally, pay deference to the level of control and influence coaches have over student-athletes—particularly in the awarding and renewal of athletic scholarships. A court in Pennsylvania overturned a ruling for summary judgment in favor of a community college after two football players filed suit for injuries sustained during a tackling drill.[25] Though the institution argued that the student-athletes assumed a risk by participating in football, the court allowed to proceed to trial negligence claims that the college employed two trainers who lacked the education and certification to work with full-contact sports teams. In another case, a court allowed claims to go forward in a case in which a student-athlete was injured while participating in a scrimmage against doctor's orders, out of fear that he would lose his athletic scholarship.[26] Another court ruled similarly when a basketball player suffered permanent injuries because his coach demanded that he continue to play, despite trainers' and physicians' advice that he rest after undergoing several knee surgeries.[27]

The most significant recent test to the student-athlete/institution relationship stems from injuries sustained from repeated head trauma. As of 2014, the NCAA was still attempting to settle a class-action lawsuit related to concussions.[28] As of 2018, 111 lawsuits had been filed against the NCAA related to concussive injuries;[29] that number is only expected to rise,[30] as even a website

---

[23] Bukowski v. Clarkson Univ., 971 N.Y.S.2d 849 (N.Y. 2012).

[24] Cann v. Stefanec, 158 Cal. Rptr. 3d 474 (Cal. Ct. App. 2013).

[25] Feleccia v. Lackawanna College, 156 A.3d 1200 (Pa. Super. Ct. 2017).

[26] Lamorie v. Warner Pacific College, 850 P.2d 401 (Or. Ct. App. 1993).

[27] Searles v. Trustees of St. Joseph's College, 695 A.2d 1206 (Me. 1997).

[28] A $75 million settlement was rejected by a judge, as he expressed concerns that this amount would be enough to effectively carry out the medical monitoring aspect of the settlement during the proposed fifty-year span. Rachel Axon, *Federal Judge Rejects Preliminary NCAA Concussion Settlement*, USA TODAY (Dec. 18, 2014), *available at* http://www.usatoday.com/story/sports/college/2014/12/18/ncaa-concussion-case-settlement-rejected/20574481/.

[29] Jeremy Bauer-Wolf, *A Verdict That Could Have Changed the Tide*, INSIDE HIGHER ED (June 26, 2018), *available at* https://www.insidehighered.com/news/2018/06/26/settlement-highly-anticipated-concussion-lawsuit-against-ncaa.

[30] Steven M. Sellers, *College Concussion Claims Put NCAA at Risk as Tragedies Multiply*, BLOOMBERG LAW (March 5, 2019), *available at* https://news.bloomberglaw.com/product-liability-and-toxics-law/college-concussion-claims-put-ncaa-at-risk-as-tragedies-multiply.

has been established to provide information for the hundreds of potential litigants who would have claims against the NCAA.[31]

As it often takes years (and in some cases, post-mortem) to diagnose sport-related head trauma, courts have not strictly enforced procedural rules related to when claims are filed. The Supreme Court of Ohio reversed a ruling dismissing claims brought by the estate of a deceased former student-athlete who sustained multiple concussive injuries while playing college football in the 1970s.[32] A few years before dying, he was diagnosed with chronic traumatic encephalopathy, dementia, and Alzheimer's disease. The claims, which included failure to notify and educate about the dangers of repeated head injuries, were not time-barred. Similarly, in *Bradley v. NCAA,* a U.S. federal district court did not find that a former student-athlete's claims for negligence related to head injuries was time-barred, as the court looked to when she learned of the lasting injuries suffered because of the head trauma, not when the initial injury occurred.[33]

Racial Discrimination

Title VI of the Civil Rights Act of 1964 prohibits any program or activity receiving federal funding from discriminating on the basis of race.[34] Although this provision applies to both public and private institutions of higher education, its application to NCAA regulations has been unsuccessful. One NCAA provision in particular that has been repeatedly challenged on Title VI grounds is that which requires student-athletes to meet minimum standards on standardized tests. Those who have brought such challenges argued that standardized tests are racially biased and, hence, such minimum requirements have a disparate impact on minority student-athletes.

In *Cureton v. National Collegiate Athletic Association,* the Third Circuit dismissed a suit brought by several African American student-athletes who claimed that using SAT scores to determine preliminary eligibility to Division I sports constituted racial discrimination. These students graduated from high school ranked high among their senior class, but were still unable to compete because of low standardized test scores. The court noted that the NCAA cannot be sued under Title VI as it is not a direct recipient of federal funds. Additionally, though NCAA-member institutions authorize the NCAA to enforce eligibility rules, the NCAA does not exercise control over how institutions utilize federal funds—even those funds which are used to assist with athletic programs.[35]

---

[31] National Collegiate Athletic Association Student-Athlete Concussion Injury Litigation, *available at* http://www.collegeathleteconcussionsettlement.com/.

[32] Schmitz v. NCAA, 122 N.E.3d 80 (Ohio 2018).

[33] 249 F. Supp. 3d 149 (D.C. 2017).

[34] 42 U.S.C. §2000d.

[35] 198 F.3d 107 (3d. Cir. 1999).

A similar challenge was brought before the Third Circuit in *Pryor v. National Collegiate Athletic Association.*[36] The students challenged Proposition 16, a rule passed by the membership of the NCAA in 1992 to tighten academic eligibility standards in an effort to increase graduation rates, claiming that the regulations created a disparate impact on racial minorities. However, the court found that demonstrating disparate impact was insufficient in proving the next prong: that the intent of the NCAA's regulations was to discriminate, a test put forth by the U.S. Supreme Court in *Alexander v. Sandoval.*[37]

Sexual Discrimination and Gender Equity

Title IX of the Education Amendments of 1972 states that "[n]o person in the United States shall, on the basis of sex, be excluded from participation in, be denied the benefits of, or be subjected to discrimination under any education program or activity receiving federal financial assistance."[38] In the context of intercollegiate athletics, the application of Title IX frequently refers to gender equity in participation and opportunity; this includes equality in equipment, practice time, travel accommodations, compensation of coaches, facilities, housing, and publicity.[39]

The U.S. Department of Education developed a three-prong test to measure equity: (1) opportunities must be "substantially proportionate" to male and female students relative to the enrollment of the institution; (2) the institution must continually expand opportunities for female student-athletes; and (3) the interests and abilities of female students have been fully and effectively accommodated.[40] The First Circuit utilized this standard in the landmark case *Cohen v. Brown University.*[41] Members of the women's volleyball and gymnastics teams filed Title IX claims after the university eliminated their teams. Because of budgetary issues, the university had cut two men's and two women's athletic programs. At the time, women comprised nearly 50% of the student body, but less than 37% of student-athletes. Although the cut did not reduce the proportion of athletic opportunities for women, it did reduce the budget for women's athletics. A district court issued a preliminary injunction and it was affirmed on appeal, as the institution had failed to meet the first prong of the compliance test. This was later reaffirmed in *Cohen II,*[42] in which the court mandated that the university submit another plan illustrating how it would become Title IX-compliant.

---

[36] 288 F.3d 548 (3d Cir. 2002).

[37] 532 U.S. 275 (2001) (a case which challenged an Alabama law that required driver's license exams be administered only in English).

[38] 20 U.S.C. §1681 et seq. This applies to both private and public institutions.

[39] William A. Kaplin and Barbara A. Lee, THE LAW OF HIGHER EDUCATION: STUDENT VERSION 5TH ED, 718-9 (2014).

[40] 44 Fed. Reg. 71,413.

[41] 991 F.2d 888 (1st Cir. 1993).

[42] 101 F.3d 155 (1st Cir. 1996).

A more recent challenge was brought when Quinnipiac University attempted to cut women's varsity volleyball, men's golf, and men's outdoor track and field, and in their place establish a women's competitive cheerleading team.[43] A district court granted an injunction blocking the proposed cuts. On appeal that decision was affirmed, holding that the university wrongly attempted to increase the proportion of available opportunities for female student-athletes by eliminating men's teams.[44] Though the difference between female athletic participation and the overall female undergraduate student population was less than 4%, the court still found that the opportunities afforded to women were not equal.

Following that ruling, the institution added women's golf and women's rugby, continued to cultivate the competitive cheerleading squad, and developed a policy that female runners were not required to participate in all three applicable track squads (indoor, outdoor, and cross country), as they previously had been triple-counted in order to skew participation numbers. In order to establish cheerleading/acrobatics as a recognized NCAA sport, Quinnipiac developed the National Competitive Stunt and Tumbling Association, in which only seven other institutions participated.[45] Though Qunnipiac attempted to develop a women's rugby team, only four other institutions across the United States sponsored an intercollegiate team. When the institution filed to lift the previous injunction, the district court pointed out that participants in these new sports—unlike every men's varsity team—were unable to participate in postseason competition and, thus, were not provided a substantive athletic opportunity.[46]

In an exhaustive analysis of athletic offerings at the institution, the court found inequity in relation to opportunity and established a new standard, level of competition. Less than 2% of men's competitive opportunities at Quinnipiac were against teams outside of Division I, while 7.5% of women's competitive contests were against institutions below Division I. (The women's rugby team played the majority of its matches against non-varsity club sport teams.) In the end, although female participants outnumbered male participants at Qunnipiac and were representative of the overall undergraduate population, the court found sixty-two women could not be counted toward Title IX compliance: thirty-six

---

[43] In 2008, the Office of Civil Rights had issued guidelines claiming that cheerleading could not be counted as a sport for purposes of Title IX compliance.

[44] Biediger v. Quinnipiac Univ., 691 F.3d 85 (2nd Cir. 2012). The plaintiffs offered evidence that the men's track and field roster was kept artificially low while the numbers for women's track and field were inflated, as all female participants were required to participate in cross country, outdoor events, and indoor events—and that participation was counted three times in the university's overall count of female athletic participation.

[45] Cheer and acrobatics are not recognized by the Department of Education as a sport for the purposes of Title IX compliance.

[46] Emerging sports are given a 10-year window by the NCAA to become a championship sport, otherwise they are discontinued. Sports with nearly 50 intercollegiate squads have failed to garner official status. Women's rugby, with four intercollegiate teams and nearing the end of the 10-year window, cannot be considered a sport for Title IX purposes. Biediger v. Quinnipiac Univ., 928 F.Supp.2d 414 (D. Conn. 2013).

from cheerleading/acrobatics, twenty-eight from rugby, and three track athletes who were injured and never competed. This new tally no longer made the proportion of female student-athletes equal to the overall undergraduate student population. To remedy this shortfall of twenty-five female athletes, the court ordered that the university restore the women's volleyball team.[47]

Financial hardships are not considered when assessing gender equity in sport. In order to balance the proportion of opportunities available to male and female student-athletes, a number of institutions have attempted to cut men's teams—and have been met with challenges, but with little success. The Seventh Circuit ruled in *Kelley v. Board of Trustees of the University of Illinois*[48] that although the university was eliminating the men's swimming team, the athletic opportunities for male students were still proportionate to the total enrollment. Another challenge, arguing that cutting male teams artificially lowered opportunities for men in an effort to achieve Title IX compliance (i.e., reverse gender discrimination) failed, as the court there deferred to the Department of Education to interpret and enforce Title IX.[49]

Sexual Violence in College Sports

In addition to discrimination based on sex, Title IX governs cases regarding sexual harassment and assault in the educational context. Per the Civil Rights Restoration Act of 1987, which was passed after the U.S. Supreme Court ruled that Title IX applied only to those programs directly receiving federal funds,[50] Congress stated that "if any program within the institution receives federal funds, then the entire institution shall be covered by Title IX and other anti-discrimination laws"[51]—which means Title IX covers interscholastic athletics, as well.

The link between college sports and campus sexual misconduct has been growing stronger. Nearly a third of college sexual assaults are reported to be committed by student-athletes.[52] Not all cases related to sexual assaults and student-athletes have been litigated under Title IX; some plaintiffs have brought suit under a theory of negligence and duty of care, but without much success. In *Tanja H. v. The Regents of the University of California* (1991), a court refused to hold a university responsible for the rape of a female student in her residence hall after a party by four members of the football team, citing

---

[47] *Id.*

[48] 35 F.3d 265 (7th Cir. 1994).

[49] Nat'l Wrestling Coaches Assoc. v. U.S. Dept. of Educ., 263 F.Supp. 2d 82 (D.D.C. 2003), *affirmed* 366 F.3d 930 (D.C. Cir. 2004).

[50] Grove City Coll. v. Bell, 465 U.S. 555 (1984).

[51] Jesse Mendelson, *Sexual Harassment in Intercollegiate Athletics by Male Coaches of Female Athletes: What It Is, What It Means for the Future, and What the NCAA Should Do*, 9 CARDOZO WOMEN'S L. J. 597 (2003).

[52] Judith Siers-Poisson, *Student-Athletes Commit Rape, Sexual Assaults More Often Than Peers*, WI. PUB. RADIO (Jan. 2, 2014), *available at* https://www.wpr.org/student-athletes-commit-rape-sexual-assaults-more-often-peers.

contributory negligence for having willingly consumed alcohol and inviting the men to her residence hall room.[53] The same year of the *Tanja H.* case, Katherine Redmond, a freshman at the University of Nebraska, was twice raped in her residence hall by a member of the football team who had prior arrests for sexual assault, threatening a university employee, disturbing the peace, trespassing, and urinating in public.[54] In 2017, a federal district court failed to dismiss negligence brought by a former student of Baylor University who was sexually assaulted by a student-athlete.[55] The court cited the university's knowledge of the student-athlete's prior sexual assault charges and noted that the university owed a duty of care to the victim.[56]

When cases are brought under Title IX for peer-to-peer assault,[57] courts utilize the two-prong test set forth by the U.S. Supreme Court: Did someone at the institution with the ability to institute corrective measures have actual knowledge of the harassment, and was the institution deliberately indifferent once it learned of the allegations?[58] In *Benefield v. Board of Trustees of the University of Alabama at Birmingham* (2002), a court failed to hold a university liable for the sexual assault of a 15-year-old freshman at the University of Alabama Birmingham (UAB), who was assaulted repeatedly by twenty-six members of the football team.[59] The court rejected the Title IX claims of deliberate indifference; namely, because when Benefield was confronted by campus administrators, she twice denied that she had been sexually assaulted.[60]

In 2006, in *Williams v. Board of Regents of the University System of Georgia,*[61] the Eleventh Circuit allowed a victim to proceed with her Title IX claims against the university and its athletic association, as well as to amend her complaint against the university president and former athletic director. Tiffany Williams, a student at the university, was invited by a basketball player to his residence hall. The two engaged in consensual sex; however, unbeknownst to Williams, the male student-athlete had arranged for his friend, a football

---

[53] 278 Cal. Rptr. 918 (Cal. Ct. App. 1991).

[54] She settled with the University for $50,000; her terms with Peter remain undisclosed. Complaint of Katherine Redmond 19, Redmond v. Univ. of Neb., 1995 WL 928211 (D. Neb. Dec. 5, 1995), *cited in* Timothy Davis & Tonya Parker, *Student-Athlete Sexual Violence Against Women: Defining the Limits of Institutional Responsibility*, 55 WASH & LEE L. REV. 55, 56-7 (1998).

[55] Hernandez v. Baylor Univ., 2017 U.S. Dist. LEXIS 54255 (W. Dist. Tex. 2017).

[56] The notion that institutions could be held liable for sexual assaults committed by student-athletes with known prior records was argued by the author in a previous article. Joy Blanchard, *Ins't Liab. for the Sexual Crimes of Student-Athletes: A Rev. of Case Law and Pol'y Recomm.*, 1 J. FOR THE STUDY OF SPORTS AND ATHLETES IN EDUC. 221 (2007).

[57] The U.S. Supreme Court recognized peer-to-peer harassment as a cognizable claim in Davis v. Monroe County Bd. of Educ., 526 U.S. 629 (1999).

[58] This test was set forth in Gebser v. Lago Vista Independent Sch. Dist., 524 U.S. 274 (1998).

[59] Benefield v. Bd. of Trs. of the Univ. of Ala. at Birmingham, 214 F. Supp.2d 1212, 1213 (D. Ala. 2002).

[60] Regarding negligence claims, the court ruled that although Benefield was not of majority age, the institution did not stand *in loco parentis* nor owe her a duty of care to protect her against the sexual abuse.

[61] 441 F.3d 1287 (11th Cir. 2006).

player, to hide in the closet, and he later raped Williams while the basketball player was in the bathroom. While this occurred, the basketball player called another teammate, who came to the room and also raped Williams. Following the incident, Williams filed a complaint with the campus police department, but a year lapsed after the incident before a campus judicial hearing resulted in no sanction being imposed on the three student-athletes involved.

In her suit, Williams accused the university president and then-athletic director of knowingly recruiting the student-athlete even though he had a record of violent crimes against women. He had been dismissed from one institution for disciplinary issues and dismissed from another after he was accused twice of sexually assaulting two female employees of that college's athletic department.[62] In its decision, the court found sufficient evidence of deliberate indifference because (1) the university recruited the student-athlete despite his criminal past, (2) the university was aware of the assault on Williams, and (3) the university was lax in investigating and adjudicating the case. In fact, by the time the university convened judicial proceedings, two of the accused were no longer students.

Noting that many universities utilized different standards, or even different processes, to investigate sexual assault allegations made against student-athletes, the U.S. Department of Education's Office of Civil Rights stated in its April 2014 "Dear Colleague" letter, "These procedures must apply to all students, including athletes. If a complaint of sexual violence involved a student athlete, the school must follow its standard procedures for resolving sexual violence complaints."[63] The investigation at the University of Montana—in which the settlement with the U.S. Department of Education has become a "blueprint" for institutions to model policy and practice—was first begun after two students claimed that the institution failed to fully investigate their claims that they had been sexually assaulted by members of the football team.[64]

Just as there have been instances in which student-athletes received preferential treatment in the adjudication of sexual assault claims, some student-athletes have argued in court that campus proceedings were biased against

[62] A lawsuit filed by a sophomore at the University Tulsa (Ross v. University of Tulsa, 180 F. Supp. 3d 951 (2016)), stated that basketball player Patrick Swilling, Jr. raped her in January. It outlined three prior alleged incidents involving Swilling: from a woman who reported in 2012 that he raped her while the two were students at the College of Southern Idaho; a woman at Tulsa who reported a sexual assault to campus security; and a woman who said Swilling tried to sexually assault her before friends intervened. See Paula Lavigne & Nicole Noren, *Athletes, Assault, and Inaction*, ESPN Outside the Lines (Aug. 25, 2014), *available at* http:// espn.go.com/espn/otl/story/_/id/11381416/missouri-tulsa-southern-idaho-face-allegations-did-not-investigate-title-ix-cases?src=mobile.

[63] U.S. Department of Education "Dear Colleague," April 2014, *available at* http://www.whitehouse.gov/sites/default/files/dear_colleague_sexual_violence.pdf.

[64] Resolution Agreement (University of Montana) (2013), *available at* http://www.justice.gov/crt/about/edu/documents/montanaagree.pdf.

them.[65] In those lawsuits, student-athletes have claimed that they were unfairly targeted and presumed guilty (a version of reverse gender discrimination, so to speak) or that their constitutional due process rights had been violated.

In *Doe v. University of Southern California* (2016), a male student-athlete was accused of violating the student code of conduct after he engaged in a group sexual encounter with a female student-athlete at an off-campus party.[66] The sexual contact between the accused and the victim was consensual, but not with the third parties. Although the campus hearing board did not find the male student-athlete engaged in rape, the board did find that he violated the student code of conduct by encouraging or allowing other students to slap the victim on the buttocks and by "endangering" her by leaving her alone in a bedroom after the last sexual encounter ended. In examining the student-athlete's due process claims, the trial court found that the university had not provided him information regarding the sections of the student code that ultimately formed the basis of his suspension from the university. An appellate court agreed that he had not been afforded a fair hearing and that the evidence did not support the findings of the preliminary campus adjudication board.

Though the majority of sexual violence Title IX claims in college sports allege that a student-athlete was the perpetrator, sometimes, sadly, the sexual abuse comes at the hands of the coaches. The body of case law related to coach-on-athlete harassment is relatively small—perhaps out of fear of retribution, loss of scholarship, or loss of eligibility—and many of the cases that are brought forth are settled out of court.[67]

Perhaps the most notable of these cases was *Jennings v. University of North Carolina*.[68] Anson Dorrance, long-time coach at the University of North Carolina, was among the most successful coaches in women's collegiate soccer history. He was sued by two former athletes for sexual harassment. In 2004, the university settled with one former student-athlete, paying her $70,000 and ordering that Dorrance participate in sensitivity training. Jennings' lawsuit reached the Fourth Circuit, which ruled that, although college sports often creates a close and even jocular relationship between coach and athlete, Dorrance's actions created a hostile environment.

In *DeCecco v. University of South Carolina*,[69] a collegiate soccer player claimed that the university was deliberately indifferent to her allegations of sexual harassment. The team was coached by a husband-wife duo, and the plaintiff alleged that the female coach would get jealous if her husband paid

---

[65] Since 2011 approximately 50 lawsuits brought by male students who were sanctioned (typically expelled) via campus proceedings were pending across the country. Jake New, *Court Wins for Accused*, INSIDE HIGHER ED (Nov. 5, 2015), *available at* https://www.insidehighered.com/news/2015/11/05/more-students-punished-over-sexual-assault-are-winning-lawsuits-against-colleges.

[66] 200 Cal. Rptr. 3d 851 (Ca. Ct. App. 2016).

[67] *See* Mendelson, *supra* note 46. *E.g.*, Ericson v. Syracuse Univ., 45 F. Supp. 2d 344 (S.D.N.Y. 1999); Klemenic v. Ohio State Univ., 263 F.3d 505 (6th Cir. 2001).

[68] 482 F.3d 686 (4th Cir. 2007), *cert. denied* 552 U.S. 887 (2007).

[69] 918 F.Supp. 2d 471, 487 (D.S.C. 2013).

too much attention to some of the female players—retaliating with reduced playing time, harsh treatment, and threats. Though the plaintiff argued the institution's own procedures made it difficult for her to make her concerns known, the court granted the university summary judgment because it did not have actual knowledge of the harassment.

Disability Discrimination

Students with a physical disability attempting to gain access to participation in college sports have utilized the Americans with Disabilities Act[70] and Section 504 of the Rehabilitation Act[71] to contend that participation in college sports is a "major life activity" as defined by law. Like in the classroom,[72] any accommodations that significantly alter the nature of the sport are not construed to be "reasonable accommodations." The U.S. Supreme Court set forth this standard in *PGA Tour, Inc. v. Martin*,[73] in which a professional player with a degenerative circulatory disorder challenged the PGA's prohibition on the use of carts and its requirement that all participants walk the course unaided. The Court's test regarding "fundamental alteration" focused on whether the accommodation would significantly alter an aspect the game, even if evenly applied, or if it would give a person with a disability an advantage over others. Martin prevailed, as the Court did not find the use of a cart would change the nature of the sport or give him a competitive advantage.

In the college sports context, the most noted case related to student-athletes and physical disability is *Knapp v. Northwestern University*.[74] Knapp was recruited by Northwestern University to play basketball despite the fact that a defibrillator was implanted in his body after he suffered a cardiac arrest while playing basketball. When he was later not medically cleared to play or practice, Knapp filed suit per Section 504 of the Rehabilitation Act. The district court construed playing basketball as falling under the definition of a major life activity[75] and granted Knapp's request for an injunction. On appeal to the Seventh Circuit, the court reversed the ruling, finding that participating in sports was not within the scope of major life activities and that Knapp was not "otherwise qualified" to meet the physical requirements of playing college basketball.

Similarly, a college football player who suffered a severe spinal injury filed for an injunction and protection under Section 504 of the Rehabilitation Act after team physicians ordered that he not play or risk the possibility of

---

[70] 42 U.S.C. §12101 et seq.

[71] 29 U.S.C. §794 (a) (1999).

[72] *E.g.,* Southeastern Cmty. Coll. v. Davis, 442 U.S. 397 (1979).

[73] 532 U.S. 661 (2001).

[74] 101 F.3d 473 (7th Cir. 1996), *cert. denied*, 520 U.S. 1274 (1997).

[75] Under the ADA Amendments Act of 2008, a major life activity includes but not limited to caring for oneself, performing manual tasks, seeing, hearing, eating, sleeping, walking, standing, lifting, bending, speaking, breathing, learning, reading, concentrating, thinking, communicating, and working.

permanent injuries or paralysis.[76] A court found participation in football was a "major life activity," as it was connected to his college education, but that limiting his right to participate did not preclude him from learning and obtaining his degree. His case did not fall under the "otherwise qualified" requirement of the Rehabilitation Act, and his request for an injunction to reinstate him to the team was denied.

In 2015, the Fourth Circuit reversed a lower court ruling that would have challenged institutions' ability to determine whether student-athletes are physically suited for competition. This suit was brought by a football player who collapsed during practice after suffering a heat stroke and liver failure, and who later had to receive a lifesaving liver transplant. After two years of rehabilitation, several outside physicians ruled that the student-athlete would be able to return to football, but the university's team physician refused to clear him for competition. The student-athlete sued, claiming that the university violated Section 504 of the Rehabilitation Act and the Americans with Disabilities Act. The district court granted the student-athlete an injunction against the university, finding that monitoring the Core Temp Monitoring System necessary to ensure that the student-athlete's internal body temperature did not exceed acceptable levels did not place an unnecessary burden on the athletic staff, as the student-athlete was going to pay for it himself.[77]

On appeal, the court instead deferred to the university's policy which stated that the determination for fitness to compete in athletic events rested solely with the university's physician, and reversed the injunction.[78] The court also noted that the student-athlete was still at risk for internal injuries as a result of the liver transplant, and that the tests by which the outside physicians relied to determine the student-athlete's ability to return to competition did not simulate the same heat conditions that would be present on the football field. Citing *Knapp v. Northwestern University,* the court did not equate participation in intercollegiate sports to a major life activity.

In addition to claims related to physical disability, student-athletes with learning disabilities have utilized the law to challenge eligibility requirements. In interpreting what constitutes reasonable accommodations, courts have held steadfast that any accommodation that significantly alters the intent of a regulation is unreasonable. In *Cole v. NCAA,*[79] a student-athlete with a diagnosed learning disability challenged the NCAA's academic eligibility requirements. This student's GPA and standardized test scores were significantly below the minimum standard, and the district court concluded that granting a waiver would have exceeded what could be considered a reasonable accommodation and would have compromised the educational intent of the NCAA's regulation.

---

[76] Pahulu v. Univ. of Kansas, 897 F. Supp. 1387 (D. Kan. 1995).

[77] Class v. Towson Univ., 118 F.Supp.3d 833 (D. Md. 2015).

[78] Class v. Towson Univ., 806 F.3d 236 (4th Cir. 2015).

[79] 120 F. Supp. 2d 1060 (N.D. Ga. 2000).

Conversely, in *Matthews v. Washington State University*,[80] a court recognized that a student-athlete with a learning disability had a claim under ADA and that, as long as the student-athlete made successful progress toward degree completion and maintained a satisfactory GPA, he should be allowed to retain eligibility. The court went on to further state that a waiver to that rule would not be an unreasonable accommodation which would serve to significantly alter the intent of the NCAA's regulation to monitor student-athletes' progress toward degree completion.[81]

Due Process

Under the Fourteenth Amendment, no person shall be deprived of "life, liberty, or property without due process of law." In the context of intercollegiate athletics, however, regardless of whether an institution is private or publicly controlled, due process protection does not apply because of the private, voluntary nature of the NCAA and the regulations promulgated by its member institutions. That rationale was set forth by the U.S. Supreme Court in 1988 in *National Collegiate Athletic Association v. Tarkanian*.[82]

In that case, Jerry "The Shark" Tarkanian, legendary head basketball coach who led the University of Nevada Las Vegas (UNLV) to four Final Four appearances and the 1990 national championship,[83] sought an injunction when an NCAA infractions committee imposed sanctions on UNLV that would have required he not coach while the institution served a four-year suspension for major rules violations related to recruiting practices. Tarkanian filed suit based on Fourteenth Amendment due process protections, claiming that the NCAA's actions were performed under color of state law.[84] In reversing a prior ruling by the Nevada Supreme Court,[85] the U.S. Supreme Court noted that the regulations UNLV followed were not promulgated by the State of Nevada but rather by the member institutions themselves, which voluntarily joined the NCAA. Additionally, it noted that the NCAA had no governmental powers in enforcement, as it possessed no power of subpoena or to impose sanctions[86]—rather, it had been UNLV that imposed a sanction on the coach.

Prior to that ruling, federal courts tended to find enough entanglement between the NCAA's enforcement of regulations and the actions of its member public institutions to consider the NCAA's actions to be that of a state actor.

---

[80] 179 F. Supp. 2d 1209 (E.D. Wash. 2001).

[81] In that case, the student-athlete challenged the NCAA's "75/25 rule" that required 75% of a student-athlete's academic credits be earned during the regular academic year.

[82] 488 U.S. 179 (1988).

[83] Though his case against the NCAA was decided in 1988, he remained head coach after reaching a settlement with the NCAA.

[84] The NCAA had indicated that UNLV could face harsher penalties if it did not act against Tarkanian.

[85] 741 P.2d 1345 (Nev. 1987).

[86] The court was unconvinced that, even if the NCAA had threatened greater penalties on the institution if it did not sanction Tarkanian, it constituted state action, *see* 488 U.S. at 197.

One such example was in *Howard v. NCAA*, in which a college soccer player and his institution sought injunctive relief to block NCAA sanctions against the university that also would have rendered the student-athlete ineligible for competition.[87] There, the court relied on the fact that the majority of the NCAA's member institutions were public institutions, which had a large part in setting regulations and policy for the association. The court said the NCAA's actions were "impregnated with a governmental character"[88] that constituted enough governmental entanglement to trigger constitutional due process rights for its member institutions and student-athletes. In *Parish v. NCAA*,[89] the Fifth Circuit similarly found enough evidence to satisfy the entanglement doctrine when student-athletes at Centenary College challenged sanctions imposed on the institution for not enforcing regulations related to minimum academic eligibility requirements.

In the 1980s, a shift occurred following a string of U.S. Supreme Court rulings that limited the application of the state action doctrine.[90] First, in *Arlosoroff v. NCAA*, the Fourth Circuit recognized some state action on the part of the NCAA, but added that it was not a function "traditionally exclusively reserved to the state."[91] There, a tennis player from Duke University sought an injunction after he was declared ineligible for playing in professional matches as part of the Davis Cup team representing his home country of Israel.

More recently, a former college football player sought relief when he was declared ineligible after NCAA investigators found that he had received what they defined to be improper assistance on a course term paper.[92] An appellate court upheld a ruling stating that any claims for injury (i.e., diminished status in the NFL draft because of inability to finish his college football career) were too speculative and were rendered moot when he signed a $270,000 supplemental draft contract with the NFL. The court declined to decide issues related to the NCAA's role in his dismissal, citing its status as a private voluntary organization not bound to provide due process.

Amateurism and Antitrust[93]

The purpose of antitrust law is to protect consumer interests and eliminate cartels that quash the function of a free market. The NCAA, in many ways, operates as a cartel. For one, its member institutions enter into a "horizontal

---

[87]   510 F.2d 213 (D.C. Cir. 1975).

[88]   *Id.* at 220.

[89]   506 F.2d 1028 (5th Cir. 1975).

[90]   Blum v. Yaretsky, 457 U.S. 991 (1982); Lugar v. Edmondson Oil Company, 457 U.S. 922 (1982); Rendell-Baker v. Kohn, 457 U.S. 830 (1982).

[91]   746 F.2d 1019, 1021 (4th Cir. 1984).

[92]   McAdoo v. Univ. of N.C., 736 S.E.2d 811 (N.C. App. 2013).

[93]   Portions of this section come from Joy Blanchard, *Flag on the Play: A Review of Antitrust Challenges to the NCAA. Could the New College Football Playoff Be Next?*, 15 VA. SPORTS AND ENT. L. J. 1, with permission from the editor.

agreement"[94] that governs how member institutions will compete with and against each other. In order to remain in the organization and be able to compete in intercollegiate competition, institutions must adhere to policies and regulations proscribed by the organization.

The Sherman Antitrust Act of 1890[95] outlawed certain anticompetitive business practices:

> Section 1: Every contract, combination in the form of trust or otherwise, or conspiracy, in restraint of trade or commerce among the several States, or with foreign nations, is declared to be illegal.

> Section 2: Every person who shall monopolize, or attempt to monopolize, or combine or conspire with any other person or persons, to monopolize any part of the trade or commerce among the several States, or with foreign nations, shall be deemed guilty of a felony...

Courts employ one of two tests, per se analysis and rule of reason, in analyzing antitrust challenges. Because per se analysis typically is reserved for practices that have been found roundly to be anticompetitive, courts tend to use the rule of reason test when examining antitrust challenges to NCAA authority—as the educational and nonprofit status of the organization makes such determinations less clear. In applying the rule of reason, a plaintiff has the burden of showing how the challenged restriction has an anticompetitive effect on trade. From there, a defendant must demonstrate how the procompetitive effects of the restraint outweigh the anticompetitive aspect of the rule. Finally, if these prima facie elements have been met, a plaintiff must propose a way in which the procompetitive aspects of the restraint can be achieved in a less-restrictive manner.[96]

Arguably, the antitrust case that has had the most significant effect on intercollegiate athletics was *NCAA v. Board of Regents of the University of Oklahoma* (1984).[97] Before this landmark decision, the NCAA controlled how many times and for how much money college football games could be broadcasted.[98] In defending its practice of limiting the number of games fans could enjoy on television—or provide teams with revenue—the NCAA argued that

---

[94] Stephanie M. Greene, *Regulating the NCAA: Making the Calls under the Sherman Antitrust Act and Title IX,* 52 ME. L. REV. 81, 83 (2000).

[95] Ch. 647, 26 Stat. 209, 15 U.S.C.§§ 1-7.

[96] Greene, *supra* note 94, at 86. An example of a procompetitive argument by the NCAA would be that a particular restraint was aimed at maintaining competitive balance among teams. *See* Gregory M. Krakau, *Monopoly and Other Children's Games: NCAA's Antitrust Suit Woes Threaten Its Existence,* 61 OHIO ST. L.J. 399, 410 (2000).

[97] 468 U.S. 85 (1984).

[98] In the 1950s, the NCAA established guidelines, referred to as the "Notre Dame Rule," which were established to open the television market at a time when Notre Dame "dominated the nascent market." Richard J. Hunter & Ann Mayo, *Issues in Antitrust, the NCAA, and Sports Management,* 10 MARQ. SPORTS L.J. 69, 76 (1999).

too many televised games would dilute the "product" and reduce ticket sales.[99] In 1976, sixty-three of the most successful and potentially profitable college teams broke away from the NCAA and formed the College Football Association (CFA).[100] The CFA collectively began to negotiate its own contracts,[101] for which the NCAA responded by prohibiting CFA teams from participating in any NCAA-sanctioned contests in any sport.

The University of Oklahoma and the University of Georgia filed suit on behalf of the other members of the CFA, claiming that the NCAA restrictions unlawfully restricted the market for televised football games. The NCAA countered that its television plan "enhanced competition through efficiency and protection of ticket sales and live attendance at home games of member institutions."[102] A district court ruled that the NCAA's control over football television contracts violated Section 1 and Section 2 of the Sherman Act by fixing prices, threatening boycotts through exclusive network contracts, and placing artificial limits on the number of televised games.[103] The court likened the actions of the NCAA to a "classic cartel"[104] and found that the NCAA's "'output restriction' had the clear effect of raising the price the networks were forced to pay for television rights and creating a pricing structure that was unresponsive to consumer choice (viewer demand)."[105] That decision was upheld by the Tenth Circuit Court of Appeals,[106] and the U.S. Supreme Court voted 7-2 in favor of the CFA. The Court stated:

> The economic significance of the NCAA's nonprofit character is questionable at best. Since the District Court found that the NCAA and its member institutions are in fact organized to maximize revenues . . . it is unclear why petitioner is less likely to restrict output in order to raise revenues above those that could be realized in a competitive market than would be a for-profit entity.[107]

Justice White (a famed college and professional football player himself) foretold, "Permitting a small number of colleges, even popular ones, to have unlimited television appearances, would inevitably give them an insuperable advantage over all others and in the end defeat any efforts to maintain a system

---

[99] The proliferation of college sports on television after the Regents decision inevitably increased institutions' fan base and ticket sales skyrocketed. See BRIAN L. PORTO, THE SUPREME COURT AND THE NCAA: THE CASE FOR LESS COMMERCIALISM AND MORE DUE PROCESS IN COLLEGE SPORTS 67 (2012).

[100] See Jude D. Schmit, A Fresh Set of Downs? Why Recent Modifications to the Bowl Championship Series Still Draw a Flag Under the Sherman Act, 14 SPORTS LAW J. 219, 226 (2007).

[101] NCAA games up to that point had been broadcast exclusively through ABC and CBS.

[102] Greene, supra note 94, at 87.

[103] Bd. of Regents of Univ. of Okla. v. Nat'l Collegiate Athletic Ass'n, 546 F.Supp. 1276 (W.D. Okla. 1982).

[104] Id. at 1295.

[105] Hunter & Mayo, supra note 98, at 78.

[106] Bd. of Regents of Univ. of Okla. v. Nat'l Collegiate Athletic Ass'n, 707 F.2d 1147 (10th Cir. 1983).

[107] 468 U.S. 85, 100 (1984).

of athletic competition among amateurs who measure up to college scholastic requirements."[108] Unfortunately, much of what Justice White predicted came true. After the *Regents* decision, institutions began an "arms race" in which the most successful teams profit the most from postseason games and, in turn, are able to attract the top coaches[109] and recruits—thus creating a perpetual and seemingly impenetrable cycle of the "haves" and "have nots."[110]

More recently, another commercialized market created by college sports was challenged in court: the market for videogames. In 2010, former UCLA basketball standout Ed O'Bannon took the lead[111] in filing an antitrust lawsuit against the NCAA challenging regulations that barred student-athletes (both current and former) in perpetuity from profiting from the use of their image and likeness in the production of videogames,[112] arguing that such regulation was an unfair restraint on trade.[113] A district court judge found that the "challenged NCAA rules unreasonably restrain trade in the market for certain educational and athletic opportunities offered by NCAA Division I schools. The procompetitive justifications that the NCAA offers do not justify this restraint and could be achieved through less restrictive means."[114]

The plaintiffs proposed three alternatives that would allow the NCAA to "achieve the purposes of its challenged rules in a less restrictive manner"[115]: (1) use revenue from licensing agreements to increase the amount of aid given

---

[108] Porto, *supra* note 99, at 81.

[109] With the open market created by the Regents' decision, one effect was the exponential rise in coaches' compensation, which has grown by 750% since that ruling as compared to a 32% rise in faculty salaries. Taylor Branch, *The Shame of College Sports,* THE ATLANTIC (October 2011), *available at* http://www.theatlantic.com/magazine/archive/2011/10/the-shame-of-college-sports/308643/. However, the NCAA had to pay $54.5 million to a class of 2,000 assistant coaches who sued after the NCAA placed a cap on their salaries. *See,* Law v. NCAA, 134 F.3d 1010 (10th Cir. 1998).

[110] The University of Texas has its own 24-hour television network. Nicholas Fram & T. Ward Frampton, *A Union of Amateurs: A Legal Blueprint to Reshape Big-Time College Athletics,* 60 BUFF. L. REV. 1003, 1018 (2012). The Southeastern Conference negotiated a 15-year, $2.5 billion contract with ESPN. *See* Christian Dennie, *Changing the Game: The Litigation That May Be the Catalyst for Change in Intercollegiate Athletics,* 62 SYRACUSE L. REV. 15, 18 (2012).

[111] He was joined by 19 other current and former FBS football and Division I men's basketball players between 1956 and 2014. O'Bannon v. Nat'l Collegiate Athletic Ass'n, 2010 WL 4451906 at 6 (N.D. Cal. 2014).

[112] Libby Sander, *Ed O'Bannon Takes Aim at the NCAA,* CHRON. OF HIGHER EDUC. (July 26, 2010), *available at* www.chronicle.com. Later Oscar Robertson, a former University of Cincinnati basketball star joined the suit. He stopped playing college ball in the 1960s, yet the university and NCAA still profit from the use of his image on trading cards and other memorabilia. Libby Sander, *Oscar Robertson Joins Federal Lawsuit Against NCAA,* CHRON. OF HIGHER EDUC. (Jan. 27, 2011), *available at* www.chronicle.com. In September 2013, EA Sports settled its lawsuit with the student-athletes for $40 million. Steve Berkowitz, *Proposed Video Game Settlement Could Help Current NCAA Players,* USA TODAY (May 30, 2014), *available at* www.usatoday.com.

[113] O'Bannon v. Nat'l Collegiate Athletic Ass'n, 7 F. Supp. 3d 955 (N.D. Cal. 2014).

[114] *Id.* at 963. Such a submarket currently exists in the professional ranks; in 2010, EA Sports paid the NFL players union more than $35 million in royalties. Branch, *supra* note 109.

[115] *Id.* at 982.

to each student-athlete[116]; (2) deposit revenues from licensing agreements into a trust fund for student-athletes to utilize after leaving school or upon graduation; or (3) permit student-athletes to share in the profits of endorsements brokered by their respective institutions.[117]

The court did not find issue with the first proposed alternative, as a cost-of-attendance grant would not alter the amateur nature of intercollegiate sport. The court held a similar opinion regarding the second proposed alternative, noting that allowing student-athletes to earn money from their likeness after their college careers were over would not hurt "consumer demand,"[118] contrary to the NCAA's assertions that the public would be less interested in watching college athletics if the student-athletes were paid. The court did, however, reject the third proposal, citing such an arrangement would promote "commercial exploitation"[119] and erode the amateur ideals of the NCAA.

The district court ruling enjoined the NCAA from enforcing regulations restricting member institutions from offering recruits a share in the revenues generated from licensing their likenesses in addition to full grant-in-aid. It also allowed for Division I basketball and Football Bowl Subdivision programs to deposit in trust an amount payable to athletes in the future; while the NCAA could cap that amount, it could not be for less than $5,000 for every year of a student-athlete's eligibility.

In 2015, a three-judge panel affirmed in part and reversed in part the district court's ruling.[120] The court found that NCAA regulations prohibiting student-athletes from profiting from their name, image, and likeness in perpetuity equated to a price-fixing agreement and that college sports programs "behave as a cartel—a group of sellers who have colluded to fix the price of

---

[116] The cap on aid has been challenged before, such as in *White v. NCAA* (2006 U.S. Dist. LEXIS 101366, 10 (C.D. Cal. 2006)), in which a class of former football and basketball student-athletes claimed the NCAA created a hardship by capping the amount of financial aid student-athletes could receive. The plaintiffs argued that without such a cap, institutions in the market for top student-athletes would have competed against each other to offer better athletic-based financial aid packages and that collusion among the colleges and universities was attributable to the cap on aid. The NCAA agreed to a $228 million settlement—$218 million of which would be paid out over five years to more than 150,000 athletes whose scholarships did not cover the full price of attendance. The other $10 million will be utilized for career development and educational services for former Division I football and men's basketball players. In *Agnew v. NCAA* (683 F.3d 328 (7th Cir. 2012)), a student-athlete challenged the ban on multiyear scholarships, claiming it violated the Sherman Act and prohibited some students from receiving their "bargained for education". The Seventh Circuit upheld the dismissal of his claims for failing to identify a relevant market on which the regulations had an anticompetitive effect, but in dicta noted "Colleges also engage in veritable arms races to provide top-of-the-line training facilities which, in turn, are supposed to attract collegiate athletes. . . These are all part of the competitive market to attract student-athletes whose athletic labor can result in many benefits for a college, including economic gain." *Id.* at 347.

[117] 7 F. Supp. 3d at 982.

[118] *Id.*

[119] *Id.* at 984.

[120] O'Bannon v. NCAA, 802 F.3d 1049 (9th Cir. 2015).

their product."[121] Though the court agreed that the NCAA's restrictions capping student-athlete benefits up to the full cost of attendance was a violation of Section 1 of the Sherman Antitrust Act, two of the three judges ruled that the district court's injunction allowing FBS football programs and Division I basketball programs to deposit in trust up to $5,000 per year of eligible participation did not serve to promote the NCAA's historic mission of promoting and preserving amateurism.

Another potentially "game-changing" case was decided in 2014 that could have allowed for student-athletes to enter into collective bargaining agreements with their respective institutions. Led by the College Athletes Players Association (CAPA),[122] football players at Northwestern University sought to unionize in order to bargain for scholarships that covered the full cost of attendance, assistance with degree completion,[123] and better medical treatment.[124]

At the crux of the players' complaint was that NCAA regulations restricted student-athletes from receiving aid that covers the true full cost of attendance. In its interpretation of the merits of the case, the district National Labor Relations Board (NLRB) office stated that "[a] party seeking to exclude an otherwise eligible employee from the coverage of the [National Labor Relations] Act bears the burden of establishing a justification for the exclusion."[125] It proceeded with the presumption that under the National Labor Relations Act, student-athletes should be classified as employees.[126]

---

[121] *Id.* at 1058.

[122] CAPA is an advocacy group led by former UCLA student-athlete Ramogi Huma. *See* http://www.collegeathletespa.org/.

[123] Brief for Petitioner at 37, Northwestern Univ. and Coll. Athletes Players Assoc., Case 13-RC-121359 (2014).

[124] Though NCAA regulations allow for full medical coverage, at the time of the decision, the institution did not provide it. *Id.* at 36-7.

[125] Northwestern Univ. v. Coll. Athletes Players Assoc. (Decisions and Orders of the National Labor Relations Board, Case 13-RC-121359), *citing* NLRB v. Ky. River Cmty. Care, Inc., 532 U.S. 706, 711-712 (2001).

[126] The term student-athlete was first introduced in an effort to not have athletes classified as employees for the purposes of receiving workers' compensation. *See* Branch, *supra* note 109. However, for a while students-athletes were able to prevail on such claims. *See e.g.,* Univ. of Denver v. Nemeth, 257 P.2d 423, 426 (Colo. 1953) ("A student employed by the University to discharge certain duties, not a part of his education program, is no different than the employee who is taking no course of instruction so far as the Workmen's Compensation Act is concerned."); Van Horn v. Indus. Accident Comm'n, 33 Cal. Rptr. 169, 172 (Cal. Ct. App. 1963) (holding scholarship athlete was eligible for benefits, as he "participated in the college football program under a contract of employment with the college"). With the Northwestern ruling classifying student-athletes as employees, this could expand litigation to successfully include workers' compensation. *See* Michael J. Mondello & Joseph Beckham, *Workers' Compensation and Collegiate Athletes: The Debate Over the Pay for Play Model: A Counterpoint*, 31 J.L. & Educ. 293, 300 (2002). Classifying student-athletes as employees could also imply Title VII employer liability for sexual assaults committed by student-athletes on campus. *See generally* Joy Blanchard, *Institutional Liability for the Sexual Crimes of Student-Athletes: A Review of Case Law and Policy Recommendations.* 1 J. for the Study of Sports and Athletes in Educ. 221.

In a case from 1970 concerning librarians at Cornell University, the NLRB recognized the increasing commercial nature of higher education and that "nonprofit universities' educational purpose was no longer sufficient to justify treating them any differently than other 'employers' under the Act."[127] In *NLRB v. Town & Country Electric,*[128] the U.S. Supreme Court defined an "employee" as "a person who performs services for another under a contract of hire, subject to the other's control or right of control, and in return for payment."[129] In the instance of student-athletes, the scholarship is linked to performance as an athlete—not as a student, as the scholarship can be revoked if the student withdraws or is dismissed from the team.[130] The university controls the "location, duration and manner in which the players carry out their football duties and all are within the control of the football coaches."[131] The NLRB's opinion cited the institution's immense control over playing and practice conditions, as well as the power it exerted in controlling and monitoring student-athletes' private lives in ways the student body at large was not regulated.[132]

After review, the regional office of the National Labor Relations Board (NLRB) certified a bargaining unit comprising all football players at the university receiving athletic scholarships and called for elections to allow the student-athletes to formally decide whether to form a union. In 2015, on appeal, the NLRB declined to recognize the unionization efforts at Northwestern University—which ultimately halted the progress of the movement.

---

[127] Cornell Univ., 183 N.L.R.B. 329, 336 (1970), *cited in* Fram and Frampton, *supra* note 110, at 1028. The institution made $4890 from selling microfilms and the "Germanic and Romanic Reviews" and $21,150 from radio and television broadcast rights to football games.

[128] 516 U.S. 85, 94 (1995).

[129] Brief for Petitioner, *supra* note 123, at 13. However, Northwestern University took issue with the automatic presumption that the student-athletes should be classified as employees, noting in their request for appeal that "the issue posed in this case has never previously been addressed by the Board." Request for Review at 3, Northwestern Univ. and Coll. Athletes Players Assoc., Case 13-RC-121359 (2014).

[130] Brief for Petitioner, *supra* note 123, at 15.

[131] *Id.* "When Congress uses the term 'employee' in a statute that does not define the term, courts interpreting the statute 'must infer, unless the statute otherwise dictates, that Congress means to incorporate the established meaning of that term.'" *Id.* at 8, *citing* 516 U.S. at 94.

[132] Northwestern Univ. v. Coll. Athletes Players Assoc. (Decisions and Orders for the National Labor Relations Board, Case 13-RC-121359) at 15-16. "[P]layers receiving scholarships to perform football-related services for the Employer under a contract for hire in return for compensation are subject to the Employer's control and are therefore employees within the meaning of the Act." Id. at 14, *citing* National Labor Relations Act 9(c)(1) and Section 2(6) and (7). Students signs a scholarship "tender" that sets forth the conditions and provisions of the scholarship. *Id.* The Big Ten Conference was among the first conferences to recently approve four-year renewable athletic scholarships. In 2011, the NCAA amended its bylaws to allow for an additional $2000 per student, but that was suspended after 160 institutions objected. *See* Jake New, *In Shadow of NCAA Lawsuits, Colleges Create New Policies to Address Athlete Rights*, INSIDE HIGHER ED (July 9, 2014), *available at* www.insidehighered.com. Later the Pac-12 Conference joined in the trend to offer multi-year scholarships. *See* Charles Huckabee, *Trend in Athletes' Benefits Widens as Pac-12 Guarantees 4-Year Scholarships*, CHRON. OF HIGHER EDUC. (Oct. 28, 2014), available at www.chronicle.com.

In its request for appeal, Northwestern University argued, "If football student-athletes are allowed to unionize, the patch-work of labor laws that govern colleges playing Division I Football Bowl Subdivision (FBS) football would have a chaotic impact on the sport and the respective universities' administration of the sport."[133] This is a salient point, as there are more than 100 public institutions in the NCAA Division I Football Bowl Subdivision, governed by their respective state laws regarding collective bargaining, and less than two dozen private institutions subject to the National Labor Relations Act. Recognizing student-athletes as employees also could require that the NCAA and its member institutions pay student-athletes workers' compensation benefits.[134] To date, student-athletes have not been able to succeed in seeking workers' compensation benefits. In *State Compensation Insurance Fund v. Industrial Accident Commission*,[135] the Colorado Supreme Court failed to construe the athlete-institution contract as giving rise to an employment situation, stating that the institution received no direct benefit from his participation on the football team. In *Reusing v. Indiana State University Board of Trustees*[136] the Indiana Supreme Court refused to award workers' compensation benefits to an injured college football player, finding that an athletic scholarship did not equate to an employment relationship. The court noted that for tax purposes, such scholarships were not considered as income.

The debate as to whether student-athletes should be considered employees continues on. In *Berger v. National Collegiate Athletic Association*,[137] a group of then-current and former members of the track and field team at the University of Pennsylvania sought to file a class action lawsuit, alleging that NCAA student-athletes should be considered employees under the Fair Labor Standards Act (FLSA)[138] and should at least earn minimum wage for the work they perform. A federal circuit court dismissed claims against the NCAA and other NCAA member institutions for lack of standing. The Seventh Circuit upheld the circuit court's ruling, also noting that the student-athletes lacked standing to bring claims against other NCAA member institutions. However, regarding the FLSA definition of employee, the court looked at the FLSA definition of employee, which is "any individual employed by an employer."[139] The statute goes on to define employ as "to suffer or permit to work,"[140] yet does not define work. The court then rejected the use of the intern test and

---

[133] Request for Review at 39, Northwestern Univ. and Coll. Athletes Players Assoc., Case 13-RC-121359 (2014).

[134] In his memoir, inaugural NCAA executive director Walter Byers admitted the term "student-athlete" was coined to ward off legal challenges from athletes claiming that they should be considered as employees for the purposes of workers' compensation benefits. Walter Byers, UNSPORTSMANLIKE CONDUCT: EXPLOITING COLLEGE ATHLETES (1997).

[135] 314 P.2d 288 (Colo. 1957).

[136] 444 N.E.2d 1170 (Ind. 1983).

[137] 162 F.Supp.3d 845 (S.D. Ind. 2016).

[138] 29 U.S.C. § 201.

[139] 843 F.3d 285, (7th Cir. 2016), *citing* 29 U.S.C. §203(e)(1).

[140] *Id., citing* 29 U.S.C. §203(g).

instead relied on Supreme Court precedent[141] that characterizes the amateur nature of college sports. The court also utilized the Department of Labor's Field Operations Handbook, which noted that when students are engaged in extracurricular activities, they are not to be characterized as employees, and went on to characterize participation in intercollegiate athletics as such.[142]

Summary

The relationship between the NCAA and its member institutions, and student-athletes and the institutions for which they compete, continues to be a complicated and contentious one legally. From the multitude of legal theories explicated in this chapter, one can forecast that a steady amount of litigation will continue to challenge the nature of those relationships. Whether college sports can continue to operate as the commercial enterprise we have come to know remains to be seen.

Discussion Questions

1. Do you think student-athletes should be considered employees? In addition to the availability of workers' compensation benefits, what other legal issues should be considered if the switch from student-athlete to employee is fully implemented?

2. The most highly resourced conferences (also known as the "Big Five") now have greater autonomy within the governance structure of the NCAA and have passed regulations allowing for full grant-in-aid scholarships and multi-year scholarships. What effect do you think this will have on teams from institutions outside of the Big Five? What effect do you think this will have on non-revenue-producing teams at Big Five institutions?

3. A group of faculty and intercollegiate athletics reformers known as the Drake Group have proposed that Congress intercede in regulating some aspects of the NCAA.[143] In what aspects of intercollegiate sport, if any, do you think Congress should get involved? Besides an antitrust exemption, do you think there should be other concessions as part of the tradeoff?

4. A disproportionate amount of sexual assault cases reported on campuses are committed by student-athletes. What policy modifications should institutions enact to address this issue? Athletic conferences? What would you recommend the Office for Civil Rights do to aid in implementing these needed changes?

---

[141] *E.g.*, Nat'l Collegiate Athletic Ass'n v. Bd. of Regents of Univ. of Okla., 468 U.S. 85 (1984).

[142] 843 F.3d, *supra* note 139, at 293.

[143] Allie Grasgreen, Antitrust for the NCAA?, INSIDE HIGHER ED (Oct. 11, 2013), *available at* https://www.insidehighered.com/news/2013/10/11/academics-propose-federal-legislation-restructuring-ncaa#ixzz2hhYQfj1O.

20 International and Global Issues

Amelia L. King-Kostelac, M.A.
The University of Texas at San Antonio
David Hòa Khoa Nguyen, J.D., Ph.D.
Indiana University – Purdue University Indianapolis (IUPUI)

Introduction

Globalization has been one of the most powerful change agents at work in the twenty-first century. Within higher education, this has meant numerous important shifts: changes in curriculum to serve new student populations and emerging economic and technological demands; shifts in funding and organizational structures; and new competitive pressures, often paired with a paucity of resources. Laws in other countries and international treaties are important to consider as students, faculty, and staff are more mobile today than ever.

As students and faculty travel, and institutions engage in business transactions and establish educational programs in foreign countries, legal issues arise. For example, potential liability issues may arise in study-abroad or exchange programs. As students, faculty, and staff are traveling, institutions should understand both their home country's laws and foreign laws to take reasonable steps to protect their students and faculty, and conduct due diligence to assess risks and address those concerns. Some concerns with studying abroad may be political unrest, underage consumption of alcohol or other controlled substances, or challenges participating fully as a result of a disability.

This chapter offers an overview of international legal issues that are pertinent to the policies and operation of universities within the United States, first providing a general background for key historical and contemporary social and political issues pertinent to understanding the ways in which globalization has influenced higher education in the United States, and secondly, examining the laws impacting international higher education, domestic students studying abroad, and international students studying in the U.S.

Historical and Social Context

Although the second half of the twentieth century was marked by a trend toward an opening of national borders and an increase in international trade and complex interconnectedness between nations' economies, this trend arguably has its roots in political and economic trends stretching well back into the colonial era, including economic expansion of major colonial powers into other sovereign nations in Africa, North and South America, and Asia (particularly Southeast Asia and the Pacific Islands). The power relationships established in this early period laid the groundwork for further U.S. and European military expansion and economic imperialism in the eighteenth and early nineteenth centuries. Without the economic activities and resources provided to Western and European nations—including the use of slave labor and access to natural and mineral resources from colonized lands—it is hard to imagine how an equivalent amassing of wealth and resources among a finite number of European nations would have occurred. In fact, many historians now accept that what we commonly call "Modernism" is, in reality, an ideology with its origins in Enlightenment Europe, rising alongside capitalism and largely in response to the economic and resource prosperity created by colonization and slavery.

Neither the Industrial Revolution nor modernisms[1] writ large would have come to exist as they did without the earlier impact of colonialism on the borders and economic prosperity (or lack thereof) of modern nation states.[2] As these changes in labor and living conditions caused shifts in populations from rural areas to (increasingly large) urban cities, they also began to precipitate social revolutions throughout the eighteenth and nineteenth centuries, which led to the emergence of democracies as a new system of political governance. By the twentieth century, nations were deeply entangled in one another's economic activities. In Europe, increasingly conservative nationalist and populist political movements led to the rise of socialist and fascist governments, while elsewhere across the globe, current and former colonial nations continued to fight for economic and political independence. After World War II, these trends coalesced into what is more commonly recognized as the beginning of globalization. Globalization in the late twentieth and early twenty-first century has been driven by the reemergence of nineteenth-century laissez-faire, free-market capitalism, which has further encouraged the interdependence of the world's economies, cultures and populations; often in such ways that have privileged the culture and economic might of former colonial nations of Western Europe

---

[1] *See generally* Peter Brooker, Andrzej Gasiorek, Deborah Longworth & Andrew Thacker, THE OXFORD HANDBOOK OF MODERNISMS (2010). Modernisms/modernities are terms which recognize the disparate, variable ways in which this phenomenon has evolved in different spaces across the globe; they offer an alternative to the more monolithic Modernism/Modernity, which centers European modernism, both historically and ideologically. For further reading discussing the general impact of these historical influences on higher education, *see generally* John R. Thelin, A HISTORY OF AMERICAN HIGHER EDUCATION (3rd ed., 2019), and Craig Steven Wilder, EBONY AND IVY (2014), among others.

[2] As an example, consider that boundaries of a majority of African nations were formalized by European colonial powers at the Berlin Conference (1884-85), when major colonial powers met to determine boundaries for African nations so as to limit fighting between themselves over said territories. French, Belgian, German, British, Spanish, Italian and Portuguese colonial powers together determined the names and specific borders for most states. *See* Martin Shanguhyia & Touin Falola, THE PALGRAVE HANDBOOK OF AFRICAN COLONIAL AND POSTCOLONIAL HISTORY (2018); Olufemi Taiwo, HOW COLONIALISM PREEMPTED MODERNITY IN AFRICA (2010).

and North America. While by no means the universal economic force, it has greatly shaped law and policy within the U.S. This, in turn, influenced the identity of higher education.

Alongside these broader trends, the post-WWII era was also marked by social movements aiming to increase social and racial equity. In the U.S., the civil rights, women's liberation and gay rights movements all resulted in changes to the nation's legal structure in order to address aspects of discrimination and marginalization due to racial and ethnic identity, gender and sexual orientation, religion, age and disability status. From the 1960s through the 1990s, new laws emerged that have provided greater legal protections to many of these groups, including but not limited to: the Equal Pay Act (1963),[3] Civil Rights Act (1964, 1991),[4] Age Discrimination in Employment Act (ADEA) (1967),[5] and Americans with Disabilities Act (ADA) (1990).[6] As many of the topics covered in this chapter will demonstrate, such legal actions aimed at social equity are by no means universal, nor immutable; however, the ongoing debate on what protections should be provided for individuals within these protected classes have resulted in key legal and policy developments that are central concerns for understanding the challenges U.S. colleges and universities face, both domestically and in their operations and relationships internationally.

The latter half of the 20th century saw an increase in transnational policy organizations and international trade agreements.[7] As an example, the North American Free Trade Agreement (1994),[8] or NAFTA, aimed to reduce or eliminate a variety of perceived barriers to trade between the U.S., Mexico, and Canada. This included a variety of embedded agreements regarding environmental, educational, trade and employment policies. It also included increased protections for intellectual property, such that many U.S.-based corporations would be able to more easily exercise proprietary control over various types of software and patents on items such as pharmaceuticals and agricultural products throughout the territory. For colleges and universities, this agreement meant numerous shifts in how transnational relationships and partnerships would be conceived. As higher educational institutions within the U.S. had funding, expenditures and infrastructure which largely dwarfed those

---

[3] 29 U.S. Code Chapter 8 § 206(d).

[4] Pub. L. No. 88-352, 78 Stat. 241 (codified as amended in scattered sections of 2 U.S.C., 28 U.S.C., and 42 U.S.C.); Pub. L. 102-166 (1991).

[5] 29 U.S.C. §§ 621-634 (2013).

[6] 42 U.S.C. §§ 12101-12213 (2013) (amended 2008).

[7] *See*, for example, organizations such as the United Nations (1945)—which replaced the earlier League of Nations (1920-1946)—the International Monetary Fund (1945), the North Atlantic Treaty Organization (1949), the European Union (1993), World Trade Organization (1995)—which was preceded by the 1948 General Agreement on Tariffs and Trade (GATT)—and NAFTA (1994).

[8] The North American Free Trade Agreement. Jan. 21, 1994. H.R. Doc. No. 103-159, vol. 1. In September 2019 negotiations between the three nations resulted in the drafting of the United States-Mexico-Canada Agreement (USMCA); pending ratification of the agreement in all three nations, NAFTA remains in effect.

of Canada and Mexico, this created a situation in which institutions within the U.S. were well-positioned to determine the focus and scope of new programs and international relationships that were not as accessible to institutions with less capital, and to do so with guarantees in place that would protect the intellectual property and academic freedom of faculty and students' research.

For the purposes of understanding international legal issues for higher education, these types of agreements are important, as they can shape how issues such as academic freedom[9] are addressed in different nations. As different nations can have radically different constraints on academic freedom, these types of agreements can determine the degree to which institutions based in the U.S. must be cognizant of ways in which foreign and international laws may differ from national laws protecting intellectual property and faculty and students' speech.

To be clear, globalization and internationalization are not synonymous; however, globalization does provide a great deal of context for increasing international activities and focus in higher education, not the least of which is the prevalence of English as a lingua franca for business, research, and technology sectors, as well as the larger shift of the U.S. away from manufacturing and toward a service- and knowledge-based economy.[10] Whereas globalization refers to large-scale—often abstract—economic trends, internationalization refers to the specific policy and governance choices that colleges and universities make in response to these global trends.

For colleges and universities in the U.S., internationalization can be split into two general categories: 1) the expansion of higher education institutions into other countries via satellite campuses and partnerships with institutions in foreign countries; and 2) the movement of students internationally via study-abroad programs. Both of these issues are addressed within this chapter, with the primary focus being common legal interests and concerns for U.S. institutions and students in these international settings. Economic shifts have served to increase pressure for higher education to provide more specific job-based skills and to produce graduates capable of competing in this globally interconnected landscape, which in turn supplies a rationale for the currently robust interest in internationalization within higher education.

---

[9] Academic freedom refers to the belief that the strength/health of academe requires that scholars have the freedom to teach or communicate ideas without fear of retaliation (i.e., being fired, persecuted, imprisoned, etc.) for their work. Needless to say, laws protecting academic freedom vary widely across the globe. Within the U.S., it is the basis for providing tenure to faculty; however, it is not without controversy or limitations. For further reading, see generally Akeel Bilgrami & Jonathan Cole (eds.), WHO'S AFRAID OF ACADEMIC FREEDOM? (2015); Timothy Reese Cain, ESTABLISHING ACADEMIC FREEDOM: POLITICS, PRINCIPLES, AND THE DEVELOPMENT OF CORE VALUES (2012); Richard Hofstadter & Walter P. Metzger, THE DEVELOPMENT OF ACADEMIC FREEDOM IN THE UNITED STATES (1955).

[10] Philip G. Altbach & Jane Knight, *The Internationalization of Higher Education: Motivations and Realities*, 11 J. OF STUDIES IN INT'L ED. 290 (2007).

U.S. Students and Study Abroad

As noted above, one component of the internationalization of higher education is the movement of students outside national boundaries via study-abroad or certain fellowship programs.[11] Whether discussing international students studying within the U.S. or the presence of U.S. students in other countries, the experience is largely framed around the noncitizen or "outsider" status of the student. Students studying abroad face a wide variety of issues, both in and outside the classroom, which can be loosely grouped into issues related to student experience as well as security. The former governs the kinds of activities, lodging, and curriculum that a student may experience; the latter refers to the necessity to protect students' physical, emotional, and psychological well-being while abroad, as well as efforts to minimize legal entanglements that may arise due to differences in culture and law in foreign countries. As one might expect, the two domains are thoroughly intertwined, with student safety and well-being tied closely to the quality of activities, spaces, and programming provided.

Travel has long been a part of the college experience for students in the U.S., going back to colonial times when students from wealthy families commonly traveled abroad to Europe for both advanced studies in specific fields (i.e., medicine or law) as well as for cultural and historical insight. Even so, the popularity of such travel ebbed and flowed based on a variety of national economic and social trends. In the period following the American Revolution, and again from end of nineteenth century and up through World War I, many politicians and educational leaders decried study abroad as a sign of cultural dependence or inferiority, arguing instead that students' education should focus on developing skills required for civic duties and economic success within the nation. As noted by Scott, "before it became an international institution the university had first to become a national institution—just as internationalization presupposes the existence of nation states."[12]

Nonetheless, the numbers of students travelling abroad gradually increased throughout the 19th century. By the early twentieth century, a wide variety of organizations were engaged in supporting international endeavors, included the establishment of the Rhodes Scholarships (1902) and of organizations such as the American Academy in Rome (1905) and the Institute of International Education (1919). Around this same time period, international students coming to study within the U.S. also began to grow, inaugurating an era of higher education where the flow of students across the globe has become increasingly common and the relationships between higher educational institutions increasingly complex.[13]

---

[11] For example, Fulbright or Rhodes Scholar programs.

[12] Peter Scott, THE GLOBALIZATION OF HIGHER EDUCATION, 123 (1998).

[13] Has de Wit & Gilbert Merkx, *The History of the Internationalization of Higher Education*, in THE SAGE HANDBOOK OF HIGHER EDUCATION, 43 (Darla K. Deardorff, Hans de Wit, John D. Heyl & Tony Adams eds., 2012).

In more recent years one can see this trend continuing. From 1996 to 2007, for example, the number of U.S. students studying abroad more than doubled, rising from less than 100,000 to almost a quarter of a million.[14] As of 2017, this number has tripled, with over 300,000 U.S. students participating in study-abroad programs in countries across every continent.[15] Perhaps unsurprisingly, the booming popularity of study abroad has also led to the presence of these programs being viewed as an indicator of institutional quality. The ability of an institution to provide this experience is viewed as a vital way to expose students to opportunities and experiences seen as vital to students' long-term professional success in a globalized world.

Conducting activity abroad may require compliance with licensure and registration with local authorities. Local laws may require the establishment of a separate legal entity, which will have separate tax and business conse-quences. When entering into business partnerships with foreign institutions or companies, choice-of-law issues may arise if there is a dispute. It is important to examine whether the contract specifies under which country's law the contract will be interpreted. Litigation in a foreign country can look very different; not only the laws, but also the procedures. In addition, hiring foreign employees will require compliance with relevant local employment and tax laws. Different countries may have different requirements unfamiliar to one's home country.

For student affairs professionals and administrators, navigating the legal concerns governing such international activities requires detailed understand-ing of risk and crisis management practices, including variable levels of legal liability regarding issues such as personal injury and accidental death, ap-propriate minimum standards, housing, fire safety, unlawful discrimination, sexual harassment and assault, and lack or oversight of medical care.[16] As the number of students and study-abroad programs grow, the need for infrastructure and staffing to meet these needs has also expanded, leading to the creation of positions like Senior International Officers (SIOs), who seek to oversee both risk management, health and safety support, as well as student affairs and international program administration.

As one might expect, risk management is different from nation to nation, with some locations, such as the U.S., often being described as "risk averse" (aiming to limit or eliminate the potential for certain risks to occur), whereas other nations are known for being more inclined to manage crises as they arise. As noted by Rhodes and Ludeman: "In some countries, such as the United States, legal issues affect important day-to-day activities of campus administrators, and most faculty and staff are aware of their impact. For them, everyday interaction brings the potential for criminal or civil penalties. In

---

[14] *See* Institute of International Education (IIE), Open Doors Report (2008), *available at* http://www.open-doors.iienetwork.org. *Cited in* April H. Stroud, *Who Plans (Not) to Study Abroad? An Examination of U.S. Student Intent*, 14 J. of Studies in Int'l Higher Ed. 491 (2010).

[15] IIE, Open Doors Report (2017), *available at* https://www.iie.org/Research-and-Insights/Open-Doors/Data/US-Study-Abroad.

[16] William P. Hoye, Managing Liability: Business and Academic Operations, 11-16 (2008).

other countries, there may be lesser potential for legal action stemming from an institutional environment. In these settings, liability is less of a concern." [17] That said, U.S. law is now more commonly applied to institutions' activities abroad, particularly in the context of study abroad. This may be at least partially due to the large number of U.S. students enrolling in study-abroad programs, as well as the fact that a large number of international students enroll at U.S. institutions. In any case, the existing predilection toward risk aversion within the U.S. presents student affairs professionals with an exigency to understand the legal risks and liabilities that are commonly faced by their students in international settings, and to have appropriate training/orientation, guidelines, and protocols set forth in advance of any such activities. In fact, legal experts often remind institutions of their duty to provide students participating in study-abroad programs with a reasonable standard of care.[18]

Determining institutional duty of care and legal responsibility can be challenging when colleges and universities contract with third-party vendors as program sponsors. For example, in *Paneno v. Centres for Academic Programmes Abroad, Ltd.,*[19] a Pasadena Community College student enrolled in a study-abroad program through Centres for Academic Programmes Abroad – USA (CAPA-USA). CAPA-USA, a California corporation, contracted with individual colleges and universities and individual students to provide study abroad services. Paneno entered into a contract with CAPA-USA to participate in a Florence, Italy, study-abroad program and lived in an apartment that was procured by CAPA-USA's parent company CAPA-UK. While in Italy, the student fell six stories after his apartment's balcony railing gave way as he leaned on it. Paneno suffered serious injury resulting from the fall, including paralysis. He initially filed suit against CAPA-USA and Pasadena Community College based on premises liability and negligence. Later, he added CAPA-UK as a defendant in the case after learning of its parent-company relationship. While the trial court dismissed CAPA-UK for lack of personal jurisdiction, an appeals court found there was a sufficiently close relationship between the two companies that it availed itself to the general jurisdiction of California courts, given that its marketing materials attempted to disguise CAPA-UK's responsibility of the program and indicated it could only be sued overseas. This case provides an example how challenging it may be to determine legal responsibility when multiple international parties are involved.

Some of the leading causes of court cases and claims against colleges and universities sponsoring international programs fall into several overarching categories: (1) physical and sexual assault and/or injury (sexual harassment/ assault, personal injury and accidental death, motor vehicle and pedestrian ac-

---

[17] Gary Rhodes and Roger Ludeman, *Legal, Health, and Safety Issues: Crisis Management and Student Services in International Higher Education,* in THE SAGE HANDBOOK OF HIGHER EDUCATION, 223, 6 (Darla K. Deardorff, Hans de Wit, John D. Heyl & Tony Adams eds., 2012).

[18] Richard B. Evans. *A Stranger in a Strange Land: Responsibility and Liability for Students Enrolled in Foreign-Study Programs,* 18 J. COLL. & UNIV. LAW 299 (1991).

[19] 13 Cal.Rptr.3d 759 (Cal. Ct. App. 2004).

cidents); (2) unlawful discrimination; (3) oversight or lack of medical treatment; and (4) lack of due process or unfair dismissal claims.[20] Since the mid-1990s, instances of colleges being sued for injury or death have increased. Although colleges in these cases have not been treated as the sole insurer of student safety, institutions have been held to a certain degree of duty of "reasonable" care imposed, meaning that they must take steps to protect faculty, students and/or staff from any kind of reasonably foreseeable harm. When the study-abroad program is in a location known to be unsafe (due to political instability, high rates of criminal activity, etc.), this duty increases as the risk increases.

The legal perspective on student experience is largely governed by issues of access and equity; that is, what are the home institution's legal responsibilities to provide access to different kinds of activities while abroad? If, for example, a student with disabilities wishes to participate in a study-abroad program, what obligations does the home institution have to that student? This can be a fairly complex question when one considers the variability of countries that students may visit as a part of a study-abroad program. The following sections tackle some of the most common legal issues faced by U.S. students studying abroad, with a brief overview of the topic and an outline of key cases provided for each.

Assault, Injury and Accidental Death

Legally speaking, the physical and emotional harm that can be inflicted by incidents of injury or assault comes down to determining whether there has been demonstrable negligence on the part of the university or college in taking steps to mitigate or prevent readily foreseeable risks. Kaplin and Lee offer examples of two cases with differing outcomes to illustrate the boundaries of duty of care for colleges.[21] In one case a small public college, St. Mary's College of Maryland, settled with three students who, along with two other female students, had been raped after their bus was robbed by armed bandits while studying abroad in Guatemala.[22] The plaintiffs claimed that the robbery and subsequent rape could have been prevented if the school had provided better security (including providing security services and traveling in a convoy) and had chosen a safer route for travel. Although the college argued that sufficient safety precautions had been taken, and that the events could not have been reasonably foreseen, in light of there having been no prior incidents, they nonetheless settled with the students. In the second case, a student unsuccessfully sued the University of Minnesota after having been assaulted by a taxi driver during a study-abroad program in Cuernavaca, Mexico. The student claimed the university had been negligent in not providing housing closer to classes or providing students with safe transportation; however, the university was not

---

[20] Hoye, *supra* note 16; Rhodes & Ludeman, *supra* note 17.

[21] William A. Kaplin & Barbara A. Lee, THE LAW OF HIGHER EDUCATION, 111-112 (5th ed. 2014).

[22] Beth McMurrie, *College Settles Suit by 3 Students Over '98 Attack in Guatemala*, CHRON. HIGHER ED. (July 5, 2002), *available at* http://chronicle.com/daily/2002/07/2002070502n.html; *see also* Kaplin & Lee, *id.*

held liable because of a long history of the program operating in the location with no prior assaults (in other words, it could be viewed as an isolated event). [23]

Together, the two cases highlight the unique challenges posed by the student-institution relationship in study-abroad programs.[24] For many institutions, the logistics challenges of knowing the study-abroad site well enough to provide adequate diligence of care for students outstrips the resources they want to or are able to provide. Thus, many institutions contract with third parties, such as the Institute of International Education (IIE), to provide programming.

While institutions are not currently required to report crime numbers for study-abroad programs as they are for incidents on campus, there has been some pressure over the past several years to bring the on- and off-campus requirements for crime reporting in line.[25]

Medical Access and Care

While traveling and studying abroad, injuries and accidents are bound to occur. However, in order to receive medical care and treatment, fluency in the local language can be important. Institutional travel and medical assistance coverage that provides faculty, students, and staff with 24/7 access to medical professionals and/or interpreters to talk in the students' native language can help with limiting and preventing liability. In *McNeil v. Wagner College,*[26] Eileen McNeil visited a town in Austria as part of her overseas study program arranged by her college. During her visit, she fell on ice and broke her ankle. While receiving treatment at the hospital, the study-abroad program's administrator served as her interpreter. After treatment of her ankle, she suffered permanent nerve injuries. McNeil sued the college based on the claim that its agent, the program's administrator, did not inform her that the local physician recommended immediate surgery and thus was negligent in the supervision of her medical care. The trial court granted the college summary judgment, and McNeil appealed. On appeal, the court affirmed the lower court's ruling, finding that the college had no legal responsibility to supervise McNeil's medical care following her accident since New York had rejected the *in loco parentis* doctrine and thus, owed her no duty. Also, evidence did not show that the program administrator was aware of the physician's recommendation.

In another case involving medical care and access to a student, Amy Fay was participating in a three-week international study-abroad trip in Peru sponsored by Thiel College when she became ill.[27] She received care from a medical clinic in Cuzco, but was left in the care of a Lutheran missionary not

[23] Bloss v. Univ. of Minnesota, 590 N.W.2d 661 (Min. Ct. App., 1999).

[24] Evans, *supra* note 18.

[25] Rishabh R. Jain, "When Study Abroad Ends in Death, US Parents Find Few Answers," Wash Post, July, 7, 2017. https://beta.washingtonpost.com/world/the_americas/when-study-abroad-ends-in-death-us-parents-find-few-answers/2017/07/06/8f435116-62b1-11e7-80a2-8c226031ac3f_story.html?outputType=amp

[26] 667 N.Y.S.2d. 397 (N.Y. App. Div. 1998).

[27] Fay v. Thiel Coll., 2001 WL 1910037 (Pa.Com.Pl. 2001).

affiliated with the college. The three faculty members continued on their trip with the other students, while Ms. Fay underwent an unnecessary appendectomy. The plaintiff had asked before the surgery whether it was absolutely necessary, to be transferred to a hospital in Lima, and to call her parents. All of these requests were denied. After the surgery, the surgeon and anesthesiologist sexually assaulted her while she was conscious but under local anesthetic. Ms. Fay sued the college alleging faculty negligence, claiming that if they had not left her alone, she would not have suffered her injuries.

The college claimed that the plaintiff had signed a liability waiver before the trip and asserted that they had no legal duty to her. However, the trial court denied the college summary judgment and found that the liability waiver constituted a contract of adhesion—in other words, it was drafted by the college, the party with power, and both parties agreed that the waiver was presented on a "take it or leave it basis," meaning that the plaintiff did not have any choice but to sign the waiver. As a result, the consent form that the student signed created a "special relationship" between the student and the college, which created a duty. Faculty supervisors had a duty to secure whatever treatment was necessary. Although the college tried to argue that the surgeon's and anesthesiologist's actions were a superseding cause, and even if the faculty were present, they would have been unable to prevent the sexual assault, the court rejected this claim and sent the case to a jury trial. The jury found that the college breached the duty of care owed to the student and that the faculty should have secured and overseen her medical treatment.

Discrimination in International Settings

Differences in infrastructure and transportation can make movement and access challenging for students with physical disabilities, but the lengths to which an institution is legally obligated to go in order to facilitate study abroad is not entirely settled. The Office of Civil Rights (OCR) has indicated that Title II of the Americans with Disabilities Act (1990)[28] and Section 504 of the Rehabilitation Act (1973)[29] do not apply in international settings; however, there are a variety of other federal and state laws which create some legal liability for institutions, particularly if the student can prove that the program failed to provide accommodations that were promised. Although case law is not robust in this area, there is some indication that a student may be able to pursue legal recourse if they can demonstrate a breach of contract or fiduciary duty. Thus, it is important for U.S.-based higher education institutions operating abroad to consider variability in interpretations of the "duty of care" required at that location, and to be aware that claims of breach to such duty are being taken as serious claims in an increasing number of countries.[30]

---

[28] 42 U.S.C. §§ 12101-12213 (2013) (amended 2008).

[29] 29 USC §701, Pub. L. No. 93-112, 87 Stat. 394 (1973).

[30] Rhodes & Ludeman, *supra* note 17

For example, in *Bird v. Lewis & Clark College*,[31] a wheelchair-bound student sued the college and was awarded $5,000 in damages after participating in a study-abroad program in Australia where she had been unable to participate in several activities and experienced difficulties accessing lodging and bathroom facilities without the assistance of others. When the college learned of Bird's disability, the Australian company that made arrangements indicated that the program could be revised to accommodate her disability. The on-site faculty host even met one-on-one with Bird to discuss her needs for living accommodations and medication needs. Bird was informed at that time that while she would not be able to participate in several activities of the program, adequate accommodations would be available, alternative activities would be provided, or adequate facilities would be available. However, upon arrival there was inadequate wheelchair access at approximately twenty-two locations, including steep ramps and curbs, improper shower and toilet access, and no elevators. As far as field activities, she was not able to participate in a number of them due to ground elevation and improper accommodations and facilities. The college asserted that it appropriately accommodated Bird's disability because it paid for taxis, booked a flight while classmates took a train, arranged for a transport van, paid two students to be her helpers, and purchased a special sleeping cot, among other actions.

At the trial court, Bird alleged violations of Title III of the ADA,[32] the Rehabilitation Act,[33] breach of contract, breach of fiduciary duty, defamation, negligence, fraud, negligent misrepresentation, and intentional infliction of emotional distress. Bird also asked that the college should be prevented from releasing her grades, and be required to change its overseas program to prevent the repetition of her experience in the future. The trial ruled against Bird on summary judgment of her claims of defamation and intentional infliction of emotional distress. The remaining claims were tried in court. The jury found that the institution had provided reasonable accommodations, but that the college had breached its fiduciary duty based upon specific reassurances the program had made to the student. On appeal, the case offered illustration of the importance of careful planning and accurate assessment of whether the institution can provide reasonable accommodations, as well as clear articulation of such accommodations for students with disabilities, since it found there was a "special relationship" between Bird and the college.

In a case involving Title IX of the Educational Amendments,[34] six female students from Eastern Michigan University (EMU) claimed gender discrimination and sexual harassment against the university. The plaintiffs were forced to leave a five-week summer study-abroad program sponsored by EMU in South Africa because of the actions of three male students, two of whom were participating in the program and the third was the faculty supervisor's assistant. The

---

[31] 303 F.3d 1015 (2002), *cert. denied,* 538 U.S. 923 (2003).

[32] 42 USCS § 12181 et seq.

[33] 29 USC § 794 et seq.

[34] 20 USC § 1681 et seq.

female students left the program early after repeated incidents of harassment by the three male students that involved a violent altercation. After repeated attempt to involve the faculty supervisor to no avail, the female students left.[35]

The question was whether Title IX could be applied to incidents outside of the United States and if the court had subject matter jurisdiction over these claims. The court found in the affirmative—Title IX has extraterritorial application outside the U.S.—citing that Congress intended for Title IX to apply to every single program of a university or college, including study abroad. EMU argued that under Title IX, it states "[n]o person in the United States ..." shall be discriminated on the basis of sex. The court cited *Gebser v. Lago Vista Independent School District,*[36] stating that Title IX's purpose is "to avoid the use of federal resources to support discriminatory practices and to provide individual citizens effective protection against those practices."[37] As a result, the court found that to limit Title IX jurisdiction over study-abroad programs would be limiting a female's opportunity to participate in these programs and would allow for discrimination abroad when it would be illegal in the U.S.

Enrollment of International Students in the U.S.

With the gradual decline of state financial support for public higher education, many institutions have turned to the enrollment of international students to meet the financial needs of the institution and to diversify its student body.[38] While the number of international students in the U.S. has increased every year, both the amount of that increase and the number of enrolled students have fallen every year since the 2016 elections.[39] Recruitment and enrollment of international students remains a high priority and important to the mission of U.S. higher education, but there are potential legal concerns for institutions to consider. A common theme of allegations from international students against institutions is discrimination based on national origin. Their complaints have also included breach of contract; due process violations; negligence; and discrimination, generally based on race, sex, or age.

---

[35] King, et al. v. Eastern Michigan University, 221 F. Supp. 2d. 783 (E.D. Mich. 2002).

[36] 524 U.S. 274 (1998).

[37] *Id.* at 286-290.

[38] *See generally* Jane Knight, *A Shared Vision? Stakeholders' Perspectives on the Internationalization of Higher Education in Canada,* 1 J. STUDIES INT'L EDUC. 1 (1997), *and* Altbach and Knight, *supra* note 10.

[39] *Open Doors 2018,* INSTITUTE OF INT'L EDUC. (Nov. 13, 2018), *available at* https://www.iie.org/en/Research-and-Insights/Open-Doors/Data.

Discrimination Based on National Origin

The U.S. Supreme Court has focused on the rights of foreign students,[40] and it has found that resident aliens—nonimmigrant persons—are a suspect class.[41] While most lawsuits from international students claimed discrimination based on national origin, student-plaintiffs often failed to meet the legal definition of discrimination. The following cases illustrate the legal definition needed to meet the standard of discrimination, even if some of the plaintiffs in the following cases are not necessarily international students on an F-1, J-I, or similar visa. In *Ikekwere v. Governing Board of Foothill-deAnza Community College District,*[42] the court granted the defendant's motion for summary judgment. Ikekwere began taking classes at the community college in January 2004 in hopes of being admitted to the college's respiratory therapy program. After taking and passing prerequisite classes, Ikekwere was admitted into the program, which consisted of both classroom and clinical evaluations. In order to remain in good standing in the program, students may not receive a grade lower than "C" in core respiratory courses, an "F" in any required program course, nor have three "marginal evaluations." A marginal evaluation is considered to be similar to a failing grade that can arise from failure of performance in the didactic classroom or behaviors in the clinical environment. In May 2006, Ikekwere received a marginal evaluation from a clinical assignment, his third since he had failed the same course twice previously. After being notified of his dismissal, he grieved unsuccessfully with the college and exhausted his administrative remedies. In 2008, Ikekewere filed complaints alleging discrimination based on his race, national origin, and disability. Unfortunately, he was unable to show that a similarly situated non-Black Nigerian was treated differently. While Ikekwere did compare his situation to another Caucasian student, that student only received two marginal evaluations and not three.

Similarly, in *Senu-Oke v. Jackson State University, et al.,*[43] Senu-Oke was dismissed from his Executive Ph.D. program in August 2004. Shortly thereafter, he filed suit against the university alleging violations of his civil rights under

---

[40] *See generally* Nyquist v. Mauclet, 432 U.S. 1 (1977) (Justices found that a New York state law that prohibited resident aliens from receiving state-sponsored scholarships was unconstitutional), *and* Toll v. Moreno, 458 U.S. 1 (1982) (Supreme Court ruled in favor of domiciled nonresident aliens on G-4 visas – those issued to employees and family members of those employed by an international organization. Policy prohibiting in-state resident tuition from these domiciled nonresident aliens was unconstitutional). It is important to note that while these U.S. Supreme Court decisions examined and afforded rights to resident aliens, Section 505 of the Illegal Immigration Reform and Immigration Responsibility Act of 1996 (IIRIRA) no longer permits this practice.

[41] *See generally* Graham v. Richardson, 403 U.S. 365 (1971) (Justices finding that new York law barring resident aliens public benefits unconstitutional), *and* Tayyari v. New Mexico State Univ., 495 F.Supp. 1365 (D.N.M. 1980) (Iranian students argued violation of the Equal Protection Clause of the 14th Amendment for not enrolling students due to the U.S. hostage crisis in Iran; the court ruled in favor of the students).

[42] 2010 U.S. Dist. LEXIS 47288 (N.D. Cal. 2010).

[43] No. 3:06-cv-468, 2008 U.S. Dist. LEXIS 13264 (D. Miss. 2008).

42 U.S.C. §1983 based on discrimination due to his national origin, Nigeria, and not being afforded due process. The Executive Ph.D. program required him to attend an in-person orientation. While Senu-Oke booked a flight and checked into his hotel, he had to return to his home state of Illinois before his Executive Ph.D. orientation took place in Mississippi. He left without notifying the program or faculty; because he failed to attend the orientation program and failed to register, the university claimed he breached his partnership agreement with the institution. The federal district court found in favor of the defendants and granted summary judgment to dismiss the plaintiff's federal claims. The matter was remanded to the state court to litigate state laws. Pertinent to this topic is that the court found there was no intentional discrimination against Senu-Oke based on his national origin and, given the early dismissal, he had very little or no property interests, which would only require minimal due process.

It is important to note that in order to succeed on a claim of discrimination, plaintiffs must meet the legal definition of discrimination;[44] however, trying to find a similarly situated person to show discrimination can be a real challenge. In *Amir v. Marquette University*,[45] an Iranian native claimed that he was unfairly dismissed due to poor academic performance. He appealed his case twice, but he was unsuccessful because he could not provide sufficient evidence that the Caucasian classmate to whom he compared himself was similarly situated.

Issues of Academic Integrity

Issues of academic integrity can be complex for international students since views on plagiarism and cheating in the United States can differ from those in other countries and cultures. For example, in *Alkahadra v. Harvard*,[46] the Saudi native was dismissed for plagiarism when she memorized a journal article and reproduced it nearly verbatim on an exam question. She stated that it was an honest mistake and that in Saudi Arabia, memorization was valued.

Issues of plagiarism among international students have been debated on college campuses. How much latitude should students be given to adjust to the new culture? In 2007, thirty-four business students at Duke University were punished for cheating. A lawyer for sixteen Asian students claimed that their punishment was too harsh compared to penalties for non-Asian students, and that cultural bias played a role.[47] During an appeal to the Duke judiciary committee, the lawyer argued that the Asian students did not understand the

---

[44] *See also* Nguyen v. University of Massachusetts, 72 Mass. App. Ct. 1107; 889 N.E.2d 981; 2008 Mass. App. LEXIS 741 (July 11, 2008) (discrimination based on political beliefs is not a protected class).

[45] 2009 Wisc. App. LEXIS 806; 2009 WI App 174; 322 Wis 2d 572; 776 N.W. 2d 287.

[46] No. 1:10-cv-11083-NG (D. Mass. filed June 25, 2010; dismissed Oct. 25, 2010). *See also* Adam Gaffin, *Saudi dentist alleges discrimination in lawsuit against Harvard,* Universal Hub (Jun. 29, 2010), *available at* https://www.universalhub.com/2010/saudi-dentist-alleges-discrimination-lawsuit-again.

[47] *See generally* Associated Press, *Lawyer: Cheating case hits Asians hardest,* DIVERSEEDUCATION. COM (May 22, 2007), available at https://diverseeducation.com/article/7363/.

honor code and were pressured into confessing without understanding the consequences or their U.S. Fifth Amendment right not to incriminate themselves. The penalties were upheld.

A 2006 investigation at Ohio University discovered extensive plagiarism among international students' theses in the mechanical engineering department and placed blame on the faculty for not enforcing academic integrity. Another student discovered that multiple masters' theses over many years carried the same language, and most if not all of these theses were submitted by international students.[48] The theses were either revoked or removed from the library until revisions were made. This scandal resulted in the demotion of one professor and the termination of another. Both sued the university for defamation, among other charges, claiming that the students had committed the lesser of two kinds of plagiarism—failing to include quotation marks around quotes. The students did cite the author in endnotes. A more serious offense would have been to use the information without citing the author. On appeal, the Ohio Court of Appeals held that generally the professor did not have actionable claims for defamation.[49]

Miscellaneous Issues

A variety of other legal issues relate to the prejudice and stereotype that some have for international students. In *Delacroix v. Santa Clara University,* two Chinese students complained about a business professor for singling them out for being late seven minutes to class, speaking too fast, and making them read the *National Enquirer.* The professor sued the university after learning about the investigation against him, claiming that the institution did not do a proper investigation because it did not want to stifle its pipeline of Chinese students.[50] Similarly, in *Shakir v. Rend Lake College,* the plaintiff sued for retaliation and discrimination when passed over for a promotion in favor of a Caucasian man. Pointing to correspondence referring to his English-language skills, unethical behavior for practicing his Muslim religion, speaking Arabic during school hours, and hiring a non-English-speaking colleague, the plaintiff cited a "hostile and discriminatory atmosphere" at the college.[51] Given these few examples, it is critically important that institutions train and educate faculty and staff on the growing legal and educational implications of having international students on campus.

---

[48] Robert Tomsho, *Student Plagiarism Stirs Controversy at Ohio University,* WALL STREET J. (Aug. 15, 2006), *available at* https://www.wsj.com/articles/SB115560632839035809.

[49] Mehta v. Ohio Univ., 194 Ohio App.3d 844, 958 N.E.2d 598, 274 Educ. L. Rep. 670 (July 14, 2011).

[50] 2008 WL 616289 (filed in Santa Clara Cty. Super. Ct. June 8, 2005; settled Sept. 5, 2006).

[51] 2010 WL 432262, 3:08-cv-00768-DRH (S.D. Ill. Feb. 8, 2010).

International Treaties and Agreements

International agreements and treaties can have legal implications for institutions in a variety of areas. For example, the World Trade Organization's Agreement on Trade-Related Aspects of Intellectual Property Rights (TRIPS) prohibits the unauthorized copying of copyrighted works, such as textbooks. Other copyright agreements include the Berne Convention and the Universal Copyright Convention. In addition to textbooks, these agreements may apply to faculty research, patents, trademarks, and copyrights. It is critical for institutions to understand and determine how work created abroad or with foreign faculty is owned and credited.

The Bologna Agreement, also known as the Convention on the Recognition of Qualifications Concerning Higher Education in the European Region—signed by fifty countries, including the U.S.—created a unified system for evaluating and recognizing foreign degrees and credentials. Beside the Bologna Agreement, other EU regulations also impact international higher education; for example, the European Union's (EU) General Data Protection Regulation (GDPR) has implications for foreign institutions serving those in EU member states, whether it is a physical or online presence. The GDPR protects personal information of EU residents and provides certain rights to access and delete personal data acquired by organizations. The General Agreement on Trade and Services (GATS), signed in 1995, helped to make it easier to offer services across borders, including education. Given the variety of these international legal issues, institutional leaders are challenged to be aware, create a plan, and communicate.

Conclusion

As internationalization and globalization of higher education continue, it is ever more important for higher education and student affairs professionals, faculty, and leaders to understand the vast breadth of legal issues that arise. International students add diversity and vibrancy to our campuses, and our institutions must continue to do a better job of inclusion and engagement.

Discussion Questions

1. How have internationalization and globalization of higher education evolved?

2. What are top legal issues for institutions to consider in study-abroad programs?

3. Given the legal issues brought by international students studying in the U.S., what should U.S. higher education institutions do to respond?

21

History, Race, and Law

LaWanda W. M. Ward, J.D., Ph.D.
The Pennsylvania State University

Delia B. Allen, Ph.D.
The Riley Institute, Furman University

Introduction

The U.S. legal system's foundation has an inextricable relationship with history and race.[1] Thus, some scholars argue history, race, and law combined are salient in defining and addressing current societal issues, especially ones related to higher education.[2] In this chapter, early U.S. Supreme Court cases that defined race are reviewed. Next, three contemporary issues in higher education—finance, race-conscious admissions, and free speech—are discussed to illuminate the ways in which history, race, and law can add new or unacknowledged perspectives. Finally, the role of history, race, and law in higher education is summarized with a focus on how engaging the three together can inform higher education policy formation and praxis.

A discussion of law's role in the historical development of race offers a background for identifying and assessing complexities in contemporary issues in higher education law. Specifically, exploring early legal precedent concerning race and U.S. racial relations can inform perspectives that provide insight into persisting issues in higher education. At its inception in 1789, the U.S.

---

[1] *See* IAN HANEY LOPEZ, WHITE BY LAW: THE LEGAL CONSTRUCTION OF RACE (1996); RICHARD ROTHSTEIN, THE COLOR OF LAW: A FORGOTTEN HISTORY OF HOW OUR GOVERNMENT SEGREGATED AMERICA (2017), KIMBERLÉ W. CRENSHAW, NEIL GOTANDA, GARY PELLER, & KENDALL THOMAS, CRITICAL RACE THEORY: THE KEY WRITINGS THAT FORMED MOVEMENT (1995).

[2] *Id. See also* Shaun R. Harper, Lori D. Patton & Ontario S. Wooden, *Access and Equity for African American Students in Higher Education: A Critical Race Historical Analysis of Policy Efforts*, 80 J. HIGHER EDUC. 389 (2009); Tara Yosso, Lawrence Parker, Daniel Solórzano & Marvin Lynn, *From Jim Crow to Affirmative Action and Back Again: A Critical Race Discussion of Racialized Rationales and Access to Higher Education*, 28 REV. RES. EDUC. 1 (2004).

Supreme Court (Supreme Court), an all-white[3]-men entity, explicitly determined that U.S. citizenship was the right of whites only, establishing a legally
sanctioned racial hierarchy.[4] The use of common knowledge and purported
scientific evidence guided Supreme Court decisions regarding citizenship
eligibility and societal relationships. Several cases demonstrate rationales used
by Justices to render explanations for justifying inequitable treatment under
the law based on race.[5] This chapter is limited to four Supreme Court cases:
Scott v. Sandford (1857), *Plessy v. Ferguson* (1896), *United States v. Ozawa*
(1922) and *United States v. Thind* (1923).

The Legal Construction of Race

Scott v. Sandford

Racial subordination was rationalized and reinforced by the Supreme Court
in two landmark cases using historical accounts of the U.S.'s early formation.
First, in *Scott v. Sandford*,[6] the majority ruled that a formerly enslaved man of
African descent, Dred Scott, could not be granted freedom from slave owner,
John Sandford, because African Americans, free or enslaved, were not citizens
according to the U.S. Constitution.[7] Scott argued that because he lived as a free
person in Illinois and Louisiana, Sandford, had no legal right to own him in
Missouri, and the Missouri Compromise[8] supported that assertion. The majority rejected Scott's arguments and ruled in Sandford's favor. Several justices
in the majority wrote separate concurring opinions with U.S. history as their
primary source to assert the unconstitutionality of the Missouri Compromise,
as well as the non-U.S. citizen status of people of African descent.[9] Justices
McLean and Curtis presented dissenting views, also grounded in history,[10] that
no legal basis existed for the claim that African Americans could not be citizens.
Specifically, Justice McLean pointed out that at the time of the Constitution's
ratification, African American men could vote in five of the 13 states and this
practice made them citizens not only in their states, but in the United States.[11]

---

[3] To reject grammatical support that suggests purported equality among racial and ethnic
groups, the letter "w" appears in lowercase in the word "white" and first letters of historically
marginalized groups are capitalized. *See* Lindsay Pérez Huber, *Using Latina/o Critical Race
Theory (LatCrit) and Race Nativism to Explore Intersectionality in the Educational Experiences
of Undocumented Chicana College Students,* 24 EDUC. FOUND. 77 (2004).

[4] LOPEZ, *supra* note 1.

[5] *See, e.g.,* People v. Hall, 4 Cal. 399 (1854); Hudgins v. Wrights, 11 Va. (1 Hen.& M.) 134
(1806).

[6] 60 U.S. 393 (1857).

[7] *Id.*

[8] Federal law that designated territories west of Missouri as slave-free states. Supreme Court ruled
this law unconstitutional in the *Scott* case. *Missouri Compromise,* Encyclopaedia Brittanica
(July 31, 2019), *available at* https://www.britannica.com/event/Missouri-Compromise

[9] *Scott,* 60 U.S. at 395.

[10] *Id.* at 529.

[11] *Id.* at 533.

Overall, the majority was not persuaded to rule in Scott's favor. One legal scholar asserts that while the majority claimed to be following the Founders' purpose of citizenship in the Constitution, their opinion actually "flouted the written Constitution's letter and spirit".[12] However, given the historical background of normalized human enslavement and servitude, the *Dred Scott* decision aligned with rationalizing a racial hierarchy. To overturn *Dred Scott*, the Fourteenth Amendment was adopted by Congress in 1866 and ratified by the states in 1868.[13] It is important to recognize that the language of the Fourteenth Amendment has not changed since its inception, only the judiciary's interpretation of its purpose and applicability.[14]

Plessy v. Ferguson

In *Plessy v. Ferguson*,[15] the Supreme Court established the "separate but equal" principle that legally supported a racial hierarchy until *Brown v. Board of Education*.[16] Homer Plessy filed a lawsuit alleging the state of Louisiana's law of separate but equal accommodations for African Americans and whites on its intrastate railroads was a violation of the Fourteenth Amendment.[17] Plessy, a biracial man who looked white but was legally identified as African American, used his legal racial label as an important strategy to support the argument that the racial classification was arbitrary and contributed to the law's senselessness.[18]

The Supreme Court's majority did not find merit in the argument that racial classifications were a societal barrier to a civilized society.[19] Instead, scholars argue that the Supreme Court legally sanctioned an institutionalized racial order that normalized being white as a preferred race while simultaneously endorsing subpar treatment of African Americans in all major societal

---

[12] *See* AKHIL REED AMAR, AMERICA'S UNWRITTEN CONSTITUTION: THE PRECEDENTS AND PRINCIPLES WE LIVE BY 273 (2012).

[13] *See* Eric Schnapper, *Affirmative Action and the Legislative History of the Fourteenth Amendment*, 71 VA. L. REV. 753 (1985).

[14] In *Butchers' Benevolent Ass'n v. Crescent City Live-Stock & Slaughter-House Co. (The Slaughter-House Cases)*, 83 U.S. 36, 71, 81 (1873), the Supreme Court's opinion discussed the 14th Amendment's Equal Protection Clause and it recognized the purpose of the Reconstruction Amendments by specifically stating "the one pervading purpose of the Fourteenth Amendment is to be the protection of 'the freedom of the slave race,'" and more specifically expressed that the Equal Protection Clause was intended to protect Blacks only from discrimination. Additionally, the Court stated, "We doubt very much whether any action of a State not directed by way of discrimination against the Negros as a class, or on account of their race, will ever be held to come within the purview of this provision. It is so clearly a provision for that race and that emergency, that a strong case would be necessary for its application to any other."

[15] 163 U.S. 537 (1896).

[16] 347 U.S. 483 (1954).

[17] *Plessy*, 163 U.S. at 541.

[18] *Id.; see also* BROOK THOMAS, PLESSY V. FERGUSON: A BRIEF HISTORY WITH DOCUMENTS (1997).

[19] *Id.* at 551.

entities, including education.[20] An excerpt from the lone dissent of Justice John Harlan would become famous for his appeal to a "color-blind"[21] Constitution.[22] His words would later be used by whites in higher education reverse discrimination cases.[23]

It was almost 60 years before the Supreme Court recognized that "separate but equal" was a mythical phrase.[24] African Americans by far did not have access to resources or opportunities comparable to their white counterparts.[25] The Supreme Court's unanimous decision in *Brown* rendered state-mandated racial segregation of public schools a violation of the Fourteenth Amendment's Equal Protection Clause and eradicated the legal support for the separate but equal doctrine.[26] However, the momentum of racial equality and equitable education resources was short lived. Scholars argue that the Supreme Court's rulings in the K-12 setting during the 1990s[27] thwarted desegregation measures and the Court's subsequent focus has not been on the great racial divide in schools.[28]

United States v. Ozawa

Two cases involving persons of Asian and Indian Sikh heritage, respectively, not only illuminate ways in which the legal sanctioning of white as the default and privileged race impacted efforts to become a U.S. citizen, but also established norms and privileges associated with being recognized as white.[29]

---

[20] *See* Kimberlé W. Crenshaw, *Framing Affirmative Action*, 105 Mich. L. Rev. First Impressions 123 (2007); Neil Gotanda, *A Critique of "Our Constitution is Color-Blind,"* 44 Stan. L. Rev. 1 (1991); Kenneth B. Nunn, *Law as a Eurocentric Enterprise*, 15 Law & Ineq. 323 (1997); Kenneth B. Nunn, *Diversity is a Dead-End*, 35 Pepp. L. Rev. 705 (2008).

[21] We are persuaded by dis/ability critical race scholars to no longer use colorblindness as a metaphor to describe the choice not to render race relevant. The scholars convincingly argue that using colorblind and other physical disability descriptors (e.g., deaf) as metaphors is problematic and does not accurately describe the issue yet renders people with disabilities to be functioning in a deficit state. "Color-evasiveness, as an expansive racial ideology, resists positioning people with disabilities as problematic as it does not partake in a dis/ability as a metaphor for undesired." Subini Ancy Annamma, Darrell D. Jackson & Deb Morrison, *Conceptualizing Color-Evasiveness: Using Dis/Ability Critical Race Theory to Expand a Color-Blind Racial Ideology in Education and Society*, 20 Race, Ethnicity & Educ. 147, 153 (2017).

[22] *Plessy*, 163 U.S. at 552 (Harlan, J., dissenting).

[23] *See, e.g.,* DeFunis v. Odegaard, 416 U.S. 312 (1974); Regents of the Univ. of Cal. v. Bakke, 438 U.S. 265 (1978); Gratz v. Bollinger, 539 U.S. 244 (2003); Grutter v. Bollinger, 539 U.S. 244 (2003); Fisher v. University of Texas (*Fisher I*), 570 U.S. ___ (2013); Fisher v. University of Texas (*Fisher II*), 579 U.S. ___ (2016).

[24] Brown v. Board of Education, 347 U.S. 483, 494 (1954).

[25] *Id.*

[26] *Id.* at 495.

[27] Freeman v. Pitts, 503 U.S. 467 (1992); *Missouri v. Jenkins*, 495 U.S. 33 (1995).

[28] Suzanne E. Eckes, *The 50th anniversary of* Brown: *Is there any reason to celebrate?*, 37 Equity & Excellence in Educ. 219 (2004); Joe R. Feagin & Bernice McNair Barnett, *Success and Failure: How Systemic Racism Trumped the* Brown v. Board of Education *Decision*, 2004 U. Ill. L. Rev. 1099 (2004); Cedric Merlin Powell, *Schools, Rhetorical Neutrality and the Failure of the Colorblind Equal Protection Clause*, 10 Rutgers Race & L. Rev. 362 (2008).

[29] Lopez, *supra* note 1.

Japanese-born Takao Ozawa sought U.S. citizenship by presenting a personal narrative that reflected how he was a "true American."[30] Ozawa blatantly rejected his Japanese ancestry in lieu of recognized American social markers.[31] In court, Ozawa presented evidence that included non-Japanese cultural characteristics such as education and language.[32] Specifically, he testified that he sent his children to an American school in lieu of a Japanese one, and only spoke English in his home.[33] An Asian American woman legal scholar observed that Ozawa's vigorous claims to be an American "reinforce[s] the positive social meanings attached to whiteness."[34] Additionally, she argues that the claims affirm the notion that, to deserve recognition as a full member of society as a full socio-political being, one must be white."[35] Despite his showings of an "American identity," Ozawa was denied U.S. citizenship.[36] Writing for a unanimous Supreme Court, Justice Sutherland reasoned that the lower federal court decisions denying Ozawa U.S. citizenship were constitutional because he was not white or of African descent.[37] The majority also rebuked Ozawa's argument that the Supreme Court should expand the concept of aliens[38] to include people of Asian descent. The majority responded,

On behalf of the appellant it is urged that we should give to this phrase the meaning which it had in the minds of its original framers in 1790 and that it was employed by them for the sole purpose of excluding the black or African race and the Indians then inhabiting this country. It may be true that those two races were alone thought of as being excluded, but to say that they were the only ones within the intent of the statute would be to ignore the affirmative form of the legislation. The provision is not that Negroes and Indians shall be excluded, but it is, in effect, that only free white persons shall be included.[39]

United States v. Thind

The final case in this section about the U.S. historical legal development of race involves an Indian heritage man, Bhagat Singh Thind, who filed a lawsuit after being denied citizenship because he did not meet the criteria for being a "white person."[40] Initially, a federal court granted Thind a certificate of

---

[30] Ozawa v. United States, 260 U.S. 178 (1922).

[31] Yuji Ichioka, *The Early Japanese Immigrant Quest for Citizenship: The Background of the 1922 Ozawa Case*, 4 AMERASIA 1 (1977).

[32] 260 U.S. at 189.

[33] *Id.*

[34] Suzanne A. Kim, *Yellow Skin, White Masks: Asian Americans Impersonations of Whiteness and the Feminist Critique of Liberal Equality*, 8 Asian Am. L.J. 89 (2001).

[35] *Id.* at 100.

[36] 260 U.S. at 199.

[37] *Id.*

[38] "In the United States, an alien is a person who was born outside the jurisdiction of the United States, who is subject to some foreign government, and who has not been naturalized under U.S. law." *Alien*, BLACK'S LAW DICTIONARY (11th ed. 2019).

[39] 260 U.S. at 195.

[40] United States v. Thind, 261 U.S. 204 (1923).

citizenship. However, the U.S. government appealed the decision to a circuit court which, in lieu of deciding the case, requested that the Supreme Court provide instruction on how to resolve the matter. The Supreme Court ruled that Thind was not a white person within the applicable federal statute.[41] Writing again for a unanimous Supreme Court, Justice Sutherland reasoned that white persons can only include those of European descent and if the statute authors desired an expansive category, they would have stated such.[42] Like Ozawa, Thind attempted to demonstrate being eligible for U.S. citizenship by providing white cultural behaviors or connections to Europe, but in both cases they were unable to convince the Supreme Court to rule in their favor.

Centering History, Race and Law in Contemporary Higher Education Issues

A legal scholar asserts that a *Plessy* legacy continues to inform legal interpretations of modern-day race relations and access to societal resources.[43] Specifically, the author posits that because the Supreme Court developed a color-evasive formal equality approach to legitimate segregation within the purposes of the Fourteenth Amendment,[44] a racial hierarchy was normalized and remains intact, mainly characterized by covert discriminatory acts. In other words, formal equality is treating everyone the same which renders race as an inoperable social construct. So, assertions of race's relevance must be substantiated to the satisfaction of those in disbelief of its significance. For example, in order to explain the separate but equal doctrine in *Plessy*, the Supreme Court was able to promote a symmetrical treatment of African Americans and whites based on both groups not being able to access each other's train cars.[45] This logic rendered race innocuous, ignored the conditions of the cars, and relegated race relations to a private matter that African Americans and whites had to work out without government intervention.[46]

In a contemporary context, legal scholars assert that the Supreme Court employs a color-evasive jurisprudence[47] when it defines and decides current

---

[41] *Id.* at 207.

[42] *Id.* at 260-61.

[43] Kimberlé W. Crenshaw, *Comments of an Outsider on the First Amendment, in* THE PRICE WE PAY: THE CASE AGAINST RACIST SPEECH, HATE PROPAGANDA, AND PORNOGRAPHY 169 (Laura J. Lederer & Richard Delgado eds., 1995).

[44] Kimberlé W.Crenshaw, *Colorblindness, History, and the Law, in* THE HOUSE THAT RACE BUILT: ORIGINAL ESSAYS BY TONI MORRISON, ANGELA Y. DAVIS, CORNEL WEST, AND OTHERS ON BLACK AMERICANS AND POLITICS IN AMERICA TODAY 280, 282 (Wahneema Lubiano ed., 1998).

[45] *See Plessy,* 163 U.S. at 544.

[46] Crenshaw, *supra* note 43.

[47] *See* Kimberlé W. Crenshaw, *The Court's Denial of Racial Societal Debt*, 40 HUM. RTS. 12 (2013); Neil Gotanda, *A Critique of "Our Constitution is Color-Blind,"* 44 STAN. L. REV. 1 (1991); David H. K. Nguyen & LaWanda W. Ward, *A Colorblind Discourse Analysis of Higher Education Race-Conscious Admissions in a "Post-Racial" Society*, 92 N.D. L. REV. 551 (2016).

"societal debt," "a racial despair structured and facilitated by law."[48] This purported line of analysis erases historical, racial, and legal realities that can provide more nuanced interpretations of modern-day allegations of racial bias. Affirmative action for whites, initially unnamed yet in effect since the nation's inception and well into the twentieth century, thrived. An exemplar is the Servicemen's Readjustment Act of 1944 (the GI Bill)[49] that provided federal funding for soldiers to attend college, acquire land, and start businesses. However, the law's administration primarily benefitted white soldiers.[50] Consequently, white soldiers were key in creating the U.S. middle class as recipients of over $95 billion dollars in federal funding between 1944-1971.[51] In contrast, affirmative action as a tool of racial equality was introduced during the Civil Rights Movement in the mid-1960s through Executive Order 11246 and required "all government contracts and subcontractors to take affirmative action to expand job opportunities for minorities".[52]

Congress enacted the Civil Rights Act of 1964, which includes Title VI prohibiting federal financial assistance to institutions that discriminated on the grounds of race, color, and national origin.[53] Title VI motivated higher education institutions (HEIs) to adopt affirmative action programs with race as a consideration in the early 1970s as an effort to increase enrollment and provide financial support to students of color, specifically African Americans.[54] Civil rights leaders wanted colleges and universities to admit students of color in much higher numbers to ensure increased educational opportunities and professions for them; however, being denied access to higher education resulted in low numbers of professionals of color. For example, in the 1960s the total number of U.S. doctors, attorneys, and engineers was less than 3% and of that number, approximately 6% were African American professionals.[55] Despite affirmative action programs, issues of access and opportunity remained minimal. In 2019, African Americans represent 5% of the legal profession,[56]

---

[48] Crenshaw, *supra* note 47 at 12.

[49] Pub. L. No. 78-346.

[50] *See* IRA KATZNELSON, WHEN AFFIRMATIVE ACTION WAS WHITE: AN UNTOLD HISTORY OF RACIAL INEQUALITY IN TWENTIETH-CENTURY AMERICA (2005).

[51] *Id*. at 113. *See also* KATZELNELSON, *White Veterans Only, in* WHEN AFFIRMATIVE ACTION WAS WHITE: AN UNTOLD HISTORY OF RACIAL INEQUALITY IN TWENTIETH-CENTURY AMERICA 113 (2005).

[52] Exec. Order No. 11246, 3 C.F.R. § 202 (1964-1965).

[53] Civil Rights Act of 1964 § 6, 42 U.S.C. § 2000 et seq (1964).

[54] Janell Byrd-Chichester, *The Federal Courts and Claims of Racial Discrimination in Higher Education*, 69 J. NEGRO EDUC. 1, 2 (2000).

[55] WILLIAM G. BOWEN & DEREK BOK, THE SHAPE OF THE RIVER: LONG-TERM CONSEQUENCES OF CONSIDERING RACE IN COLLEGE AND UNIVERSITY ADMISSIONS (1998).

[56] American Bar Association, *Legal Profession Statistics* (August 5, 2019), *available at* https://www.americanbar.org/about_the_aba/profession_statistics/ (last visited August 21, 2019).

in 2017 5.8% of doctors, [57] and 4.3% of engineers in 2016.[58] The number of African Americans has significantly increased from the 1960s, yet in each separate profession, the percentages are dismal. Legal analysis developed through color-evasive rationales continue to enable racial inequities despite federal laws and policies implemented to bring about racial inclusion in HEIs.[59] Admissions policies and programs implemented to provide equal opportunity and access to historically disadvantaged racial groups have become contentious and controversial. White applicants denied acceptance to selective HEIs have filed lawsuits alleging reverse discrimination and, since the late 1970s, such claims have found merit with society and the courts.[60]

Race-Conscious Admissions

Within the race-conscious admissions debate, arguments given on both sides shed light on the ongoing relevance of how history, race, and law shape understandings. "Conservatives argue that affirmative action violates the principle of equal treatment and is unfair to innocent whites" while "Liberals reply that it is a reasonable response to past injustice and necessary to assure future broad democratic participation."[61] Ultimately, both sides use the same constitutional provisions to assert their cause. The legal debate is ongoing with more cases being filed about the use of race admissions decisions.[62] Considering the history of access to higher education can be informative in thinking about ways to address the current tensions.

Although HEIs have been a part of the U.S. landscape as early as the seventeenth century,[63] it was not until 1785 that the first public HEI was established. While chartered in 1785, the University of Georgia did not begin admitting

---

[57] *Physicians & Surgeons*, DATA USA, *available at* https://datausa.io/profile/soc/physicians-surgeons#demographics (last visited August 9, 2019).

[58] *Field of degree: Women, men, and racial and ethnic groups*, NAT'L SCI. FOUND., *available at* https://ncses.nsf.gov/pubs/nsf19304/digest/field-of-degree-women-men-and-racial-and-ethnic-groups (last visited August 21, 2019).

[59] Cedric M. Powell, *Harvesting New Conceptions of Equality: Opportunity, Results, and Neutrality*, 31 ST. LOUIS. U. PUB. L. REV. 255 (2011); Angela Onwuachi-Willig, *Reconceptualizing the Harms of Discrimination: How* Brown v. Board of Education *Helped to Further White Supremacy*, 105 VA. L. REV. 343 (2019).

[60] *See, e.g., Fisher II, supra* note 23; Vance R. Newkirk, II, *The Myth of Reverse Discrimination*, ATLANTIC, August 5, 2017, *available at* https://www.theatlantic.com/education/archive/2017/08/myth-of-reverse-racism/535689/

[61] Richard Delgado, *Norms and Normal Science: Towards a Critique of Normativity in Legal Thought*, 139 U. PA. L. REV. 933, 937 (1991).

[62] Students for Fair Admissions, Inc. v. President & Fellows of Harvard Coll., (D. Mass. filed Nov. 2017); Students for Fair Admissions, Inc. v. Univ. of N.C. (M.D.N.C. filed Nov. 2017) (cases filed by Asian heritage students alleging several claims including the use of race disproportionately effects their ability to be admitted)

[63] *See* Wilder *infra* note 116 (Harvard, 1632; College of William & Mary, 1693; Yale, 1701).

white male[64] students until 1801.[65] However, it was not until 1961, 160 years later, that the first African American students were admitted to the University of Georgia.[66] Although some African American students were granted admission into HEIs and received degrees as early as 1823,[67] this occurrence was primarily in the northern states, at private institutions, and nearly two centuries after the first HEI was established. Based on the historical exclusion of African Americans from public white HEIs, it is not implausible to believe that they would continue to have limited access to post-secondary opportunities in the 21st century without federal laws and strategic litigation efforts. Consequently, reports describe barriers to access that exist for people of color seeking admission to public white HEIs.[68] The next three sections provide a brief historical account of African Americans' journey into public white HEIs, an exploration of a dual system created in higher education grounded in race, and a truncated review of early legal history of higher education desegregation. The discussion will conclude with implications of law, specifically its effects, at the intersection of funding, student body composition, and race within HEIs.

Legal Race-based Dual Higher Education Systems

Familiarity with the terms Historically Black Colleges and Universities (HBCU) and Predominantly White Institution (PWI) are essential to understanding discussion nuances about institutional types. Although HBCU has been in use since 1965,[69] PWI is relatively neoteric in its existence within higher education terminology. The need for two categories and what distinctions exist between them are explained by exploring the historical nexus between the creation of U.S. PWIs and race. As previously stated, although HEIs have existed since the seventeenth century, African Americans were not granted access at the same time as their white counterparts. Although states such as Georgia, North Carolina, and South Carolina chartered HEIs to provide public education to

---

[64] In 1918, the first group of white women undergraduates was admitted to the University of Georgia.

[65] The delay was due to challenges with the land. The University of North Carolina at Chapel Hill was chartered in 1789, four years after UGA, and was the first state-chartered university to admit students in 1795. F. N. BONEY, A PICTORIAL HISTORY OF THE UNIVERSITY OF GEORGIA (2000).

[66] Charlene Hunter and Hamilton Holmes were the first Black students admitted to the University of Georgia. *Black History Month: UGA Timeline, available at* https://online.uga.edu/node/5346

[67] Alexander Lucius Twilight (Middlebury College in Vermont, 1823), Edward Jones (Amherst College in Massachusetts, 1826), and John Brown Russwurm (Bowdoin College in Main, 1826) are the first, second, and third known Black men to graduate from a college in the U.S. Mary Jane Patterson was the first Black woman to earn a bachelor's degree in 1862 from Oberlin College. Journal of African Americans in Higher Education Research Department, *Key Events in Black Higher Education: JBHE Chronology of Major Landmarks in the Progress of African Americans in Higher Education, available at* https://www.jbhe.com/chronology/.

[68] LORELLE L. ESPINOSA, JONATHAN M. TURK, MORGAN TAYLOR & HOLLIE M. CHESSMAN, RACE AND ETHNICITY IN HIGHER EDUCATION: A STATUS REPORT (2019).

[69] Higher Education Act of 1965, Pub. L. No. 89-329, 79 Stat. 1219.

its white residents, African Americans were excluded, especially in the U.S. southern states. Except for the University of South Carolina,[70] many large state universities did not admit African Americans until the late 1950s and 1960s. Although racial discrimination and segregation in PWIs were prevalent in all regions of the U.S., these issues were less prevalent in the West.[71]

If race, history, and law are jointly considered a relevant background to higher education's racial composition trajectory, then it becomes noteworthy that when the Civil War ended in 1865 only 40 African Americans had been awarded college degrees throughout the U.S.[72] Prior to the Civil War, there was no structured higher education system for African Americans. In the 1850s the first degree-granting institutions specifically for African Americans were established.[73] From the end of the Civil War until the mid-twentieth century, most African Americans attended HEIs specifically established for them. These institutions were either private and funded by white religious organizations,[74] or public and financially supported by states and the federal government. Although African Americans were not legally prohibited from applying to the state universities, it was rare for them to seek admission because of harsh societal repercussions for attempts to cross the color line barrier that existed prior to and after the Civil War. Consequently, a dual system of public higher education systems was destined to be created.

Morrill Act of 1862

Harvard University, a private institution founded in 1632, is recognized as the first continental U.S. HEI. However, since the Philippines was a U.S. territory, the University of Santo Tomas, established in 1611, is technically the oldest university under the U.S. flag.[75] Early state-chartered and -funded public HEIs are in southern states.[76] During the late eighteenth and early nineteenth centuries, most HEIs in the eastern and northeastern states were private, while

---

[70] Robert Bruce Slater, *The First Black Graduates of the Nation's 50 Flagship State Universities*, 13 J. BLACKS IN HIGHER EDUC. 72 (1996).

[71] *Id.* Black students earned a degree at public white universities in Idaho before any graduated from flagship universities in the Northeast (i.e., Connecticut, Maine, Mass, New Hampshire, Pennsylvania).

[72] *Id.*

[73] Journal of Blacks in Higher Education Research Department, *supra* note 67. (The Institute for Colored Youth 1837 (now Cheyney University in Cheyney Pennsylvania), Lincoln University (1854) in Oxford, Pennsylvania, and Wilberforce University (1856) in Xenia, Ohio).

[74] B. Denise Hawkins, *Echoes of Faith: Church Roots Run Deep Among HBCUs*, DIVERSE ISSUES IN HIGHER EDUC., July 31, 2012, *available at* https://diverseeducation.com/article/17259/

[75] Quentin McSweeney, *Santo Tomas de Manila: The First University of the Philippines*, DOMINICANA 22 (1942).

[76] University of Georgia 1785, University of North Carolina 1789, University of South Carolina 1801, and University of Tennessee 1807.

the newly established ones in the South and Northwest Territory[77] regions were public and state-funded. However, many public institutions founded during the mid-nineteenth century and beyond were funded by both the state and federal government and designated as land-grant universities. Federal funding provided to establish land-grant colleges and universities was made available through the Morrill Act of 1862, also known as the Morrill Land-Grant Colleges Act of 1862 (Morrill Act I).

The Morrill Act I established U.S. land-grant HEIs using federal land sale proceeds.[78] In short, it gave land to states to build HEIs. Being the first federal aid to support higher education, the Morrill Act I was passed to educate farmers and the working class in practical skills for agriculture, mechanics/engineering, and military science.[79] However, many African Americans did not benefit from the Morrill Act I because it was enacted during the Civil War while African Americans were still enslaved. It was not until the expansion of the Morrill Act in 1890, that educational opportunities would be made available to African Americans previously excluded from PWIs. The second legislation known as the Morrill Act of 1890, established land-grant schools explicitly meant to serve African Americans.

Morrill Act of 1890

The Morrill Act of 1890 (Morrill Act II), also known as the Second Morrill Act, was aimed at the former Confederate states to provide African Americans access to public HEIs. In many states, it was not until the enactment of the Morrill Act II that African Americans were able to attend land-grant institutions. Unlike its predecessor, the Morrill Act II provided funds in lieu of land to establish land-grant institutions that were explicitly meant to educate African Americans. In addition, the Morrill Act II prohibited funding distribution to states that discriminated in admitting students based on race unless at least one land-grant college was established in the state for African Americans.[80] Thus, the Morrill Act II required states with racially segregated public higher education systems to provide a land-grant institution for African Americans

---

[77] The Northwest Ordinance of 1787 was written for an orderly expansion of the new nation into the territories north and west of the Ohio River. The first HEI established during the westward expansion of the United States was Ohio University in 1804. R. W. Apple, *Ohio, in* THE AMERICAN MIDWEST: AN INTERPRETIVE ENCYCLOPEDIA 42 (Andrew R. L. Clayton, Richard Sisson & Chris Zacher eds. 2006).

[78] Act of July 2, 1862 (Morrill Act), Pub. L. No. 37-108. (The act committed the federal government to grant each state 30,000 acres of public land for each of its representatives and senators in Congress to be used for the support of public institutions of higher learning. Most states did not build on the designated land but instead sold it and used the proceeds to support existing state institutions or to establish new ones.)

[79] Its official title was "An Act Donating public lands to the several States and Territories which may provide colleges for the benefit of Agriculture and the Mechanic arts." Pub. L. No. 37-108.

[80] The Morrill Act of 1890 stipulated that "no money shall be paid for the support of a college where a distinction of race or color is made in the admission of students...the establishment and maintenance of such colleges separately for white and colored students shall be held in compliance with the provision of this act." Pub. L. No. 51-841.

whenever a land-grant institution was established and restricted for whites only. This provision initiated the establishment of 19 public institutions exclusively designated for African Americans.[81]

The 1890 land-grant institutions were established predominately in Southern and border states[82] (see figure 1). Although the Morrill Act II provided the opportunity to establish several public land-grant institutions for African Americans, the law also provided the opportunity for states to legally engage in racial segregation within PWIs—consequently creating a segregated, dual system of higher education in most Southern states. This legal endorsement of exclusion to all levels of public education existed well into the 1950s and 1960s. Inferences can be made that the Morrill Act II's effect, coupled with the Supreme Court's 1896 decision in *Plessy v. Ferguson*, which established a *separate but equal* doctrine in K-12 public education, have created a racial hierarchy in education that has yet to be dismantled.

Higher Education Act of 1965

Because Morrill Acts I and II expanded PWIs by providing funds solely to establish land-grant institutions, their scope was limited. In 1965, the Higher Education Act (HEA) was established to expand federal funding for non-land grant HEIs.[83] More relevant to this chapter, the HEA also coined and defined the term Historically Black Colleges and Universities (HBCU). The designation of HBCU was given to any institution established prior to 1964 to exclusively educate African Americans. After the Civil War, given the institutionalization of racial segregation prior to the 1960s, it was difficult for African Americans to attend HEIs anywhere other than HBCUs[84]. Ultimately, African Americans were denied admission to PWIs until mid-twentieth century higher education desegregation litigation efforts.

Desegregation Efforts in PWIs

Dismantling the segregated dual higher education system was and remains a complicated, yet strategic endeavor. Several Supreme Court decisions aided in the process, starting with rulings for African Americans to be admitted for graduate studies and ultimately to earn bachelor's degrees. Desegregation

---

[81] JOHN MICHAEL LEE, JR. & SAMAAD WES KEYS, LAND-GRANT BUT UNEQUAL: STATE ONE-TO-ONE MATCH FUNDING FOR 1890 LAND-GRANT UNIVERSITIES 3 (2013).

[82] *Id*. at 2. (Although there is at least one land-grant institution in every state and territory in the United States and the District of Columbia, the 1890 institutions were in the southern and border states the original land grant institutions continued to be racially segregated).

[83] Higher Education Act of 1965, Pub. L. No. 89-329, 79 Stat. 1219. (In addition to increasing federal funding for colleges and universities, the law also aided in the development of scholarship programs and provided low-interest loans to students.)

[84] Matt Stefon, *Historically black colleges and universities*, Encyclopaedia Brittanica, *available at* https://www.britannica.com/topic/historically-black-colleges-and-universities. (In the early twenty-first century there were more than 100 HBCUs in America, but predominately located in the South.)

in PWIs began at the graduate and professional education levels.[85] Supreme Court decisions for these early higher education cases applied the "separate but equal" doctrine from *Plessy*, which either allowed the plaintiff to attend the PWI or motivated states to establish graduate programs at the public HB-CUs. Four key Supreme Court cases demonstrate the admission challenges for African Americans.

Gaines v. Canada

The first lawsuit in the legal strategy to dismantle segregation in education began in 1935 when Lloyd Gaines, an African American man, graduated from Lincoln University, one of the first public institutions established specifically for African Americans. Gaines applied to the University of Missouri Law School, but was refused admission. He sued the university claiming a violation of the Fourteenth Amendment's Equal Protection Clause. The Supreme Court ruled in Gaines' favor and held that since the state of Missouri provided equal opportunity in higher education for both African Americans and white students, denial of access to legal education was unlawful discrimination against Gaines.[86] A decade later, three additional cases were added to the plight for racial justice in education, *Sipuel v. Board of Regents of the University of Oklahoma* (1948), *Sweatt v. Painter* (1950); and *McLaurin v. Oklahoma State Regents* (1950).

Sipuel v. Oklahoma

In 1946, Ada Lois Sipuel Fisher,[87] an African American woman, was denied admission to the University of Oklahoma Law School. Sipuel Fisher sued the university claiming that, under the doctrine of "separate but equal" and because the state of Oklahoma did not provide a comparable facility for African American students, she had the right to be admitted to the law school. The Supreme Court decided in Sipuel Fisher's favor and ruled that the Oklahoma Board of Regents must provide instruction for African Americans that was equal to that of whites. In response, the state of Oklahoma created the Langston University School of Law for African Americans instead of admitting Sipuel Fisher. In short, the Supreme Court found the Langston University accommodations subpar and unequal to those of whites; hence, the Court ordered that Sipuel Fisher be admitted to the law school. After Sipuel Fisher's almost three-year legal battle and a Supreme Court ruling in her favor, she was not

---

[85] Jacqueline A. Stefkovich & Terrence Leas, *A Legal History of Desegregation in Higher Education*, 63 J. NEGRO EDUC. 406 (1994).

[86] Although the University of Missouri would not admit Gaines, it did agree to subsidize his tuition to attend an out-of-state institution. The Supreme Court's majority opinion concluded that the state was obligated to provide Gaines "within its borders facilities for legal education substantially equal to those which the State there offered for persons of the white race, whether or not other negroes sought the same opportunity." Gaines v. Canada, 305 U.S. 337, 351 (1938).

[87] Ada Lois Sipuel Fisher was married at the time of her lawsuit; however, because she submitted her Langston University transcript which only listed her maiden name, the court records do not reflect her marital status.

permitted to enter law school until the summer of 1949. Sipuel Fisher was the only African American, as well as the only woman, in a class of 300 white men. In her autobiography, Sipuel Fisher recalled,

> [I] had to climb the stairs in the large, theatre-style classroom and head to a single wooden chair designated for [me] alone. The chair was set apart from the rest of the class on a back row, marked by a large printed sign that said 'colored.' All the white students had been directed to sit in the first rows of the classroom, making [my] chair, the one with the 'colored' sign nailed to it, isolated and behind the others.[88]

Sweatt v. Painter

Following *Sipuel, Sweatt v. Painter* and *McLaurin v. Oklahoma State Regents* were argued and decided in the same year. In *Sweatt*, Heman Sweatt, an African American man, was offered admittance to a state-sponsored law school newly established for African Americans, but denied admission to the University of Texas Law School based solely on race. The Supreme Court held that although Texas established a law school for African Americans, the legal education provided there was not substantially equal to that which the plaintiff would receive if admitted to the University of Texas Law School.[89] Thus, citing a violation of the Equal Protection Clause of the Fourteenth Amendment, the Supreme Court ordered that Sweatt be admitted to the University of Texas Law School.

McLaurin v. Oklahoma State Regents

The last higher education case pre-*Brown* is slightly different than the previous three cases of denied admissions. In *McLaurin v. Oklahoma State Regents*, plaintiff George McLaurin applied for admission to a doctoral program at the University of Oklahoma and was ultimately admitted under a provision of an amended Oklahoma state law.[90] This legislation allowed African Americans to be admitted to PWIs if instruction was segregated. Accordingly, once McLaurin was admitted, he received segregated accommodations.[91] Although the university modified its exclusionary treatment of McLaurin, the Supreme

---

[88] ADA LOIS SIPUEL FISHER, A MATTER OF BLACK AND WHITE: THE AUTOBIOGRAPHY OF ADA LOIS SIPUEL FISHER 45 (1996).

[89] Sweatt v. Painter, 339 U.S. 629 (1950).

[90] Oklahoma statutes, 70 Okla.Stat. §§ 455, 456, 457, made it a misdemeanor to maintain or operate, teach or attend a school at which both whites and Negroes are enrolled or taught. The Oklahoma legislature amended these statutes to permit the admission of Negroes to institutions of higher learning attended by white students in cases where such institutions offered courses not available in the Negro schools. The amendment provided, however, that, in such cases, the program of instruction "shall be given at such colleges or institutions of higher education upon a segregated basis".

[91] McLaurin was assigned to sit in a row of classroom seats reserved for Black students, he sat at an assigned table in the library, and, while he could eat in the cafeteria, he had a designated table.

Court decided McLaurin's experiences to be in violation of the Fourteenth Amendment's Equal Protection Clause. The Supreme Court ruled that state officials had the legal duty to treat the plaintiff in the same manner as university students of other races because the Fourteenth Amendment precluded the enforcement of the Oklahoma state law that endorsed segregated Oklahoma HEIs.

PWIs were forced to desegregate due to litigation efforts by the National Association for the Advancement of the Colored People (NAACP) Legal Defense and Educational Fund.[92] In summary, the Supreme Court decisions required: (1) a state must offer law school education for African Americans at the same institution as whites (*Gaines v. Canada* (1935) and *Sipuel v. Board of Regents of University of Oklahoma*, 1948); (2) Black students must receive the same treatment in PWI graduate schools as white peers (*McLaurin v. Oklahoma State Regents*, 1950); and (3) a state must provide educational facilities of comparable quality for Black and white students (*Sweatt v. Painter*, 1950).[93] While these cases are over 70 years old, they provide not only a historical framework in higher education law, but also for the understanding of contemporary issues in higher education through a lens of racial awareness.

Legal Race-based, Dual Higher Education System Implications

Inequity at the Intersections of Race and Finance

If one only reads a few media reports about HBCUs' financial status, it is not unreasonable to conclude that a lack of financial resources is a major challenge for those institutional leaders. Although finances are also a challenge for both private and public PWIs, public HBCUs are in lengthy litigation battles to obtain their fair share of state funding.[94] It is argued that this financial struggle has been greatly compromised by inaction and resistance of state legislatures.[95] Previous research reveals that since the establishment of the 1890 institutions, funding has been poor and inequitable compared to PWIs.[96] States often meet the federal requirements for one-to-one matching of land-grant universities for their PWIs, but not HBCUs. In other words, states pay the amount required to receive full federal funding for their designated land-grant PWIs, but not their

---

[92] CONSTANCE BAKER MOTLEY, EQUAL JUSTICE UNDER THE LAW: AN AUTOBIOGRAPHY BY CONSTANCE BAKER MOTLEY (1998).

[93] STEFKOVICH & LEAS, *supra* note 85; Gail M. Epstein, *Desegregation of Public Institutions of Higher Education: Merger as a Remedy*, 56 CHI.-KENT L. REV. 701 (1980).

[94] Coal. for Equity & Excellence in MD Higher Educ., Inc., et al. v. MD Higher Educ. Comm'n et al. (D. Md. filed 2006).

[95] Levirn Hill, *Profiles of Two-Year, Four-Year, & Professional Schools. Black American Colleges and Universities* (1994), *available at* https://aaregistry.org/story/hbcus-in-america-a-short-history/

[96] Walter R. Allen, & Joseph O. Jewell, *A Backward Glance Forward: Past, Present, and Future Perspectives on Historically Black Colleges and Universities* 25 REV. HIGHER EDUC. 241 (2005); K. E. Redd, Historically Black Colleges and Universities: Making a Comeback 26 NEW DIRECTIONS FOR HIGHER EDUC. 33 (1998).

HBCUs in the same category.[97] Thus, it is imperative to note that the inequity in the one-to-one matching between the 1862 and 1890 land-grant institutions is not caused by the federal government, but by state government.

The U.S. Department of Agriculture requires 1890 land-grant institutions to put forth at least 50% of the match; when the minimum match is not provided, HBCUs either apply for a waiver of the one-to-one matching requirement or forfeit the funding altogether.[98] In 2012, only six of the eighteen states with 1890 land-grant HBCUs provided 100% of the required one-to-one match.[99] According to the Association of Public and Land-grant Universities, from 2010-2012, 61.2% (11 out of 18) of the 1890 land-grant institutions did not receive 100% of the one-to-one-matching funds from their respective states for extension or research funding, totaling a net loss of $56,627,199 in funding.[100] Interestingly, in 2017 the Trump administration signed an executive order[101] moving the federal program that supports HBCUs from the Department of Education back to the White House. Whether this change results in HBCUs receiving additional non-matching required federal funds remains unknown. Increased state funding remains questionable as well.

In the meantime, twenty-two U.S. House of Representative members co-sponsored the HBCU Parity Act of 2018 (HR 5122),[102] a bill that will ensure funding for facility improvements at the 1890 land-grant institutions. Government funding disparities between PWIs and HBCUs can be traced to past laws that have yet to be adequately addressed.

Higher Education Institutions Remain Segregated

Even though efforts to desegregate PWIs began as early as the mid-1900s,[103] it has been a slow process, with litigation yielding some results. For example, in *Adams v. Richardson*, a federal court declared that states should not fund dual systems of higher education.[104] The case involved requests for declaratory and injunctive relief against the Secretary of Health, Education

---

[97] LEE & KEYS, *supra* note 81.

[98] *Id.*

[99] *Id.*

[100] *Id.*

[101] Executive Order No. 13779, C.F.R. 12499 (2017), *Presidential Executive Order on The White House Initiative to Promote Excellence and Innovation at Historically Black Colleges and Universities,"* available at https://www.whitehouse.gov/presidential-actions/presidential-executive-order-white-house-initiative-promote-excellence-innovation-historically-black-colleges-universities/

[102] U.S. Representative Al Lawson (D-FL-05) introduced the HBCU Parity Act of 2018 (HR 5122), a bill that will ensure funding for facility improvements at historically black universities that were established under the Second Morrill Act of 1890 and Tuskegee University. Additional information regarding this bill is available at https://www.congress.gov/bill/115th-congress/house-bill/5122/text.

[103] Gaines v. Canada, 305 U.S. 337 (1938); Sipuel v. Board of Regents of the University of Oklahoma, 332 U.S. 631 (1948); Sweatt v. Painter, 339 U.S. 629 (1950); McLaurin v. Oklahoma State Regents, 339 U.S. 637 (1950).

[104] 351 F. Supp. 636 (D.D.C. 1973).

and Welfare and the Department of Health, Education and Welfare (HEW)'s Director of the Office for Civil Rights (OCR).[105] The plaintiffs claimed the government defendants defaulted on their administrative responsibilities under Title VI of the Civil Rights Act of 1964 by continuing to provide federal funds to states that operate segregated systems of higher education.[106] In addition, it was less than thirty years prior that the Supreme Court ruled in *United States v. Fordice* (1992) that patterns of racial segregation remained prevalent in Mississippi's public university system. The Supreme Court found that Mississippi public universities continued to be virtually all African American or all white, thus the state of Mississippi failed at its affirmative duty to dismantle a prior de jure racially segregated public university system.

More recently, lawsuits have been filed in Maryland[107] on behalf of HBCUs claiming that their institutions have historically received less funding and experience inequitable program offerings compared to the states' PWIs. Exploring these lawsuits with race and history at the center of analysis can illuminate contemporary legal challenges due to a current segregated system of higher education. The ongoing funding disparity lawsuit between Maryland HBCUs and PWIs has been in and out of court for twelve years.[108] In 2019, the parties were ordered to enter a settlement mediation.[109]

Effects of the Morrill Act II are still evident in the 21st century. For instance, in 2015 approximately 5% of students attending flagship state universities across the U.S. were African American[110] and in 2017, only 24% of enrollment at intuitions historically established to educate African Americans were other

---

[105] The Department of Health, Education, and Welfare (HEW) is now known as the Department of Education (DOE).

[106] The U.S. District Court of D.C. found that between January 1969 and February 1970, Department of Health, Education, and Welfare (HEW) concluded that the states of Louisiana, Mississippi, Oklahoma, North Carolina, Florida, Arkansas, Pennsylvania, Georgia, Maryland, and Virginia were operating segregated systems of higher education in violation of Title VI. As of the writing of the opinion, HEW had not commenced an administrative enforcement action against any of these ten states nor had these matters been referred to the Justice Department for the filing of suits against any of the ten states. The Court also found that HEW had advanced and continued to advance federal funds in substantial amounts for the benefit of institutions of higher education in the ten states. Adams v. Richardson, 356 F. Supp. 92 (D.D.C. 1973).

[107] In 2006, a coalition for the state's four historically black institutions (Bowie State University, Coppin State University, Morgan State University and University of Maryland, Eastern Shore) sued the Maryland Higher Education Commission, arguing that the state put the institutions at a disadvantage by duplicating similar programs at PWIs. Coal. for Equity & Excellence in MD Higher Educ. v. MD Higher Educ. Comm'n, 295 F. Supp. 3d 540 (2017).

[108] *See* Hawkins, *supra* note 74.

[109] In 2013, the 4th Circuit Court of Appeals held that unnecessary program duplication within Maryland's system of higher education continues to have segregative effects for which the State has no sound educational justification. Holding under *Fordice* (1992), this violates the Civil Rights Act of 1964 and the Equal Protection Clause of the Fourteenth Amendment. By allowing similar programs at better-funded schools, Maryland had created a "separate and unequal" system of public higher education.

[110] Meredith Kolodner, *Black Students are Drastically Underrepresented at Top Public Colleges*, The Hechinger Report, December 18, 2015, *available at* https://hechingerreport.org/black-students-are-drastically-underrepresented-at-top-public-colleges-data-show/

races.[111] Hence, the historical and current relevance of race in higher education render the use of the terms HBCU and PWI significant when describing U.S. HEIs. Even given the legal history and ongoing implications of operating a segregated system of higher education, in 2018, the Trump administration chose to rescind federal guidelines which encouraged HEIs to racially diversify their campuses. This decision jeopardizes racial equity and inclusion within campus communities.

History, Race, and Law in Campus Artifact and Speech Debates

A resurgence in dialogues about hate speech within college campus communities provides an opportunity to rethink the formation of transformative racial equity-oriented higher education policies.[112] Legal scholars who center race in their analysis advocate for a reframing of harmful occurrences, especially assaultive speech[113] in campus communities. When history, race and law are explored in conjunction with one another regarding polarizing issues, debates over controversial campus speech and artifacts may result in revisiting institutional values and relying on somewhat imprecise legal precedent.[114] The relevance of race, history, and law in discussions about racially divisive symbols on campus, academic building names, and campus speech, are discussed in the next section.

Monument Removals and Renaming Buildings

Members of U.S. college campus communities are demanding that Confederate monuments be removed and have either acted themselves or waited for

---

[111] National Center for Education Statistics, *Historical Black Colleges and Universities. Institute of Education Sciences* (2019), *available at* https://nces.ed.gov/fastfacts/display.asp?id=667.

[112] Liliana M. Garces & Cynthia Gordon da Cruz, *A Strategic Racial Equity Framework,* 92 Peabody J. Educ. 322, (2018); Sherry K. Watt, Designing Transformative Multicultural Initiatives: Theoretical Foundations, Practical Applications, and Facilitator Considerations (2015); *see also* Jeremy Bauer-Wolf, *Hate Incidents on Campus Still Rising,* Inside Higher Ed, February 25, 2019, *available at* https://www.insidehighered.com/news/2019/02/25/hate-incidents-still-rise-college-campuses.

[113] Mari M. Matsuda, Charles R. Lawrence, III, Richard Delgado, & Kimberlé Crenshaw, Words That Wound: Critical Race Theory, Assaultive Speech, and the First Amendment 1 (1993). These scholars use the term *assaultive speech* to specifically identify hate speech that requires regulation in campus communities. Assaultive speech is defined as "words that are used as weapons to ambush, terrorize, wound, humiliate, and degrade"; *see also* Cheryl Harris, *More than What Is: What Ought To Be,* Huffington Post, Oct. 24, 2016, *available at* https://www.huffpost.com/entry/more-than-what-is-what-ou_b_8377726.

[114] Nick Hazelrigg, *UC Santa Cruz Removes Catholic Mission Bell,* Inside Higher Ed, June 24, 2019, *available at* https://www.insidehighered.com/quicktakes/2019/06/24/uc-santa-cruz-removes-catholic-mission-bell; *see also* Jeremy Bauer-Wolf, *Legal Grounds to Turn Away White Supremacist Speakers,* Inside Higher Ed, August 17, 2017, *available at* https://www.insidehighered.com/news/2017/08/17/public-universities-are-solid-ground-cancel-richard-spencer-events-legal-experts-say.

administrative authorizations. Some argue that for too long, many HEIs have ignored the role of race in their histories. From the building of early facilities to the maintenance of daily operational duties, African Americans both during slavery and post- Civil War built PWIs with no compensation nor opportunities for them or their families to attend the institutions.[115] In addition, many PWIs have named buildings and erected monuments on their campuses in honor of or to commemorate people who are known to have advocated white supremacy and racial segregation. Due to blatant refusal and failure of these institutions to acknowledge the significance of African Americans within their historical narrative, as well as these institutions' recognition of racially divisive individuals and other symbols linked to the antebellum South, campuses are now grappling with how to address protests, petitions, and contentious discussions regarding the removal or relocation of monuments and renaming buildings. From public institutions such as University of North Carolina at Chapel Hill,[116] Clemson University,[117] and University of Mississippi[118] to private institutions

---

[115] CRAIG S. WILDER, EBONY & IVY: RACE, SLAVERY, AND THE TROUBLED HISTORY OF AMERICAN UNIVERSITIES (Bloomsbury Press, 2013).

[116] The Confederate monument known as Silent Sam was toppled by students and activists in 2018. The monument memorialized UNC students who fought for the Confederacy and were killed during the Civil War. Students took down the monument because the administration would not. Leoneda Inge, *How 2 North Carolina Universities Handled the Removal of Confederate Statues on Campus*, NPR, August 24, 2018, *available at* https://www.npr.org/2018/08/24/641706017/how-2-north-carolina-universities-handled-the-removal-of-confederate-statues-on.

[117] Past efforts failed in 2015 to rename Tillman Hall, recognized as one of the most famous building on the Clemson campus. During spring 2019 the student government passed a resolution for the administration to take immediate action and the necessary steps to rename Tillman Hall and to respond to a student petition calling for the renaming of Calhoun Honors College. Tillman Hall was named after a former South Carolina Governor, Benjamin Tillman, who was a known white supremacist. Calhoun Honors College was named after South Carolina statesman and slave-owner John C. Calhoun, who in the decades leading up to the Civil War vigorously defended slavery in the South. Mollie R. Simon, *Clemson Students and Faculty Want to Rename Calhoun Honors College and Tillman Hall*, GREENVILLE NEWS, March 6, 2019, *available at* https://www.greenvilleonline.com/story/news/2019/03/06/clemson-university-students-want-rename-calhoun-honors-college-tillman-hall/3019258002/.

[118] In 2015, students successfully lobbied the administration to remove the Mississippi state flag, which incorporates the Confederate battle emblem in its design, from campus. In 2017, administrators agreed to the renaming of Vardaman Hall, which was named after James K. Vardaman, a segregationist and former governor. During spring 2019, the University of Mississippi student government voted unanimously in favor of a resolution to remove a Confederate soldier statue from its campus. The fate of the resolution now lies with the administrators. Phil McCausland, *Ole Miss Students Vote Unanimously to Remove Confederate Statue from Campus Center*, NBC NEWS, March 6, 2019, *available at* https://www.nbcnews.com/news/us-news/ole-miss-students-vote-unanimously-remove-confederate-statue-campus-center-n980241.

like Duke University,[119] Furman University, [120] and Georgetown University,[121] higher education administrators have both proactively and reactively began to address their institutions' participation in slavery and segregation.

There are public opinion implications for these reconciliatory actions, because not everyone believes that monuments need to be removed nor buildings renamed.[122] A 2017 Reuter poll[123] found that of its approximately 2000 responses, 54% of Americans wanted Confederate memorials to remain in public spaces, 27% preferred removal, and 19% said they did not know. The poll responses were split along racial and party lines, with whites and Republicans largely supportive of preservation, while Democrats and people of color being more likely to prefer removal.[124] An argument can be made that renaming buildings is nothing more meaningful than a politically symbolic gesture. There is also a gray area or thin line between remembering versus honoring someone with a controversial past. Regardless of the public opinion, discourse, and institutions' administrative decisions, there are legal considerations when renaming and removing relics of the antebellum South from college campus communities.

Race and Law in Historical Memory

Within the past twenty years, several state governments have adopted measures that are designed to prevent Confederate monuments from being

---

[119] At the entrance of Duke Chapel there was a statue of Confederate General Robert E. Lee. In 2017, the administration at Duke quietly took the statue down in the middle of the night—no students, no protests, no state laws to challenge their decision. *See* Inge, *supra* note 117.

[120] In 2017 Furman established a task force to explore its historical connections to slavery. In 2019 the task force recommended ways to recognize the contribution of slaves to the institution's early history. One of several recommendations approved by the administration was the renaming of James C. Furman Hall. James C. Furman who actively defended slavery was the son of the university's namesake, Richard Furman. *See also* Brennan McDavid, *Furman University Cuts Ties to Slavery; Makes Changes in Response to Report*, May 23, 2019, WYFF4 News, *available at* https://www.wyff4.com/article/furman-university-makes-changes-in-response-to-task-force-report-on-slavery/27559935; Furman University's Task Force on Slavery and Justice, Seeking Abraham (2018), *available at* https://www.furman.edu/wpcontent/uploads/2018/07/Seeking_Abraham_Furman_Task_Force_on_Slavery_and_Justice_Report.pdf.

[121] In 2015, students protested for the removal of names from two buildings on campus. The administration agreed to remove the names of two past college presidents, Rev. Thomas F. Mulledy and Rev. William McSherry, who were both involved in the sale of slaves to help secure the future of Georgetown University. *Georgetown University, Georgetown Apologizes for 1838 Sale of 272 Slaves, Dedicates Buildings*, April 18, 2017, *available at* https://www.georgetown.edu/news/liturgy-remembrance-contrition-hope-slavery.

[122] Chris Kahn, *A Majority of Americans Want to Preserve Confederate Monuments: Reuters/Ipsos Poll*, Reuters, August 21, 2017, *available at* https://www.reuters.com/article/us-usa-protests-poll-idUSKCN1B12EG.

[123] *Id.* The Reuters/Ipsos poll was conducted online in English throughout the United States, gathering responses from 2,149 people, including 874 Democrats and 763 Republicans. It has a credibility interval, a measure of accuracy, of 2 percentage points for the entire group and 4 percentage points for the Democrats and Republicans.

[124] *Id.*

removed, as well as other antebellum South memorials.[125] Depending on which side of the debate one finds merit, laws governing historic monuments and buildings in public campus communities can be seen as a convenience or an inconvenience for students, administrators, and alumni. Providing an overview of all state laws about this issue is beyond this chapter's scope, but three exemplars of legal obstacles that all stakeholders encounter are provided. What follows next is a brief account of how state laws affect HEIs and controversial racial symbols.

Imperative to note is that given the private status of institutions like Duke University and Furman University, they do not have to seek permission from state bureaucracies to remove monuments and change building names. For instance, in North Carolina, a state law, the Cultural History Artifact Management and Patriotism Act of 2015, forbids the removal of monuments on public property without permission from a historical board.[126] In South Carolina, the state legislature is responsible for renaming buildings. The South Carolina Heritage Act details the process which requires a two-thirds vote of the General Assembly to alter, remove, or rename historical monuments.[127] *In Mississippi, state law does not allow for any structure related to the Civil War to be relocated, removed, disturbed, altered, renamed or rededicated.[128] Thus, removal of a monument from a public institution would have to be approved by the Mississippi State Institutions of Higher Learning, a twelve-member body appointed by the governor; additionally, due to the landmark status of the monument, a consultation with the Mississippi Department of Archives and History would also be in order. Because legislative bodies and higher education commissions have yet to diversify racially, controversial artifacts can serve as reminders to people of color that they are unwelcomed and not fully respected individuals.

Campus Speech

In Chapter 5, current legal approaches and precedent for understanding campus speech issues are explained. The following discussion is one way hate speech can be analyzed when history, race, and law are considered as relevant for policy formation. Hate speech does not have a subjective definition, rather it is an imprecise catchall term that generally includes verbal and written words and symbolic acts that convey a grossly negative assessment of particular persons or groups based on their race, gender, ethnicity, religion, sexual orientation, or disability. Hate speech is thus highly derogatory and degrading, and the language is typically coarse. The purpose of the speech is more

---

[125] Aneil Kovvali, *Confederate Statute Removal*, 70 STAN. L. REV. ONLINE 82 (2017).
[126] Cultural History Artifact Management and Patriotism Act of 2015 § 3(c), 2015 N.C. Sess. Laws 170.
[127] 2000 S.C. Acts 292 §§ 1, 3.
[128] Miss. Code § 55-15-81 (2013).

to humiliate or wound than to communicate ideas or information. Common vehicles for such speech include epithets, slurs, insults, taunts, and threats.[129]

Arguments have been advanced that hateful speech and hate speech are different, with the former concept being described as offensive, harm-inducing, and declared outside the bounds of decency. Yet, the distinction has not garnered enough support to change legal analysis.[130] In the meantime, people of color are told that everyone bears the burden of this type of speech so that when someone wants to express unpopular ideas or says something labeled offensive, their words are protected.[131] An argument supporting hate speech regulations in campus communities is that the hate versus hateful distinction lacks intellectual merit. For instance, Merriam-Webster defines hate as a noun that is "an intense hostility and aversion usually deriving from fear, anger, or sense of injury" and the derivative, hateful, is an adjective meaning "full of hate: malicious". Hence, what is the difference between hate and hateful? This definition debate can be a distraction and infers either a lack of knowledge about what the terms mean or indifference to their meanings. Ultimately, both choices stymie efforts to address hate speech.

Legal scholars have advocated for race-centered perspectives in discussions about assaultive speech with a focus on historical legal precedent that continues to affect people of color's realities in campus communities, work environments, and broader society.[132] For example, one argument asserts that *Brown* is an assaultive speech case because "the Supreme Court identified the defamatory symbolism of segregation as central to its unconstitutionality and showed that racism achieves its purpose by the construction of meaning."[133] Another scholar insists that *Plessy*'s legal rationale continues in hate speech debates because speech is treated as any other "product" in our societal competitive market. This line of reasoning does not account for the separate but equal doctrine's role in normalizing the power of certain words to not only offend, but potentially create educational experiences overshadowed by fear and stigma.[134] Despite being able to claim academic freedom in classroom settings when inflammatory words are used, some professors have opted not to use such language, especially when students of all races raise concerns.[135]

---

[129] WILLIAM A. KAPLIN & BARBARA A. LEE, THE LAW OF HIGHER EDUCATION 624 (5th ed. 2014).

[130] Foundation for Individual Rights in Education, *Hate Speech*, March 28, 2019, *available at* https://www.thefire.org/issues/hate-speech/.

[131] *See* RICHARD DELGADO & JEAN STEFANCIC, MUST WE DEFEND THE NAZIS? HATE SPEECH, PORNOGRAPHY, AND THE NEW FIRST AMENDMENT (1997); LOPEZ, *supra* note 1.

[132] *See* Crenshaw, *supra* note 43 at 169-75; Lawrence, *supra* note 114 at 53-88; Robin D. Barnes, *The Reality and Ideology of First Amendment Jurisprudence: Giving Aid and Comfort to Racial Terrorists, in* FREEING THE FIRST AMENDMENT: CRITICAL PERSPECTIVES ON FREEDOM OF EXPRESSION 253 (David S. Allen & Robert Jensen eds. 1995).

[133] *See* Lawrence, *supra* note 114, at 53-88.

[134] *See* MARI J. MATSUDA, WHERE IS YOUR BODY?: AND OTHER ESSAYS ON RACE, GENDER, AND THE LAW (1996).

[135] Colleen Flaherty, *A Free Speech Purist Opts Not to Use the N-Word*, INSIDE HIGHER ED, March 8, 2019, *available at* https://www.insidehighered.com/news/2019/03/08/first-amendment-scholar-geoffrey-stone-whos-previously-defended-use-n-word-classroom.

Notwithstanding the rising number of assaultive speech incidents on college campuses, demands for legal protection against them have been met with vehement opposition and critique.[136] As elaborated on in Chapter 5, this resistance is not new, because federal court rulings from the late 1980s and early 1990s invalidated attempts by universities to regulate assaultive speech through campus civility codes. [137] *Doe* involved a campus civility policy that a federal court ruled unconstitutionally vague because, in the court's perspective, there was a lack of clarity about how offensive speech could be differentiated from protected speech. The critiques included that the Michigan policy needed a narrower focus because it restricted classroom discourse; however, when considering the contentious campus climate conditions at the time of the policy, some type of redress was warranted. The court's opinion described incidents that occurred over a three-year period, including anonymous fliers posted advocating violence against African American students and describing them as "saucer lips, porch monkeys, and jigaboos," and a Ku Klux Klan outfit displayed in a residence hall room window.[138] Similar polarizing incidents continue to plague campuses and require administrators to think about ways to address them. [139]

Two years after *Doe*, a Wisconsin federal district court decided the same fate for the University of Wisconsin's policy. While it was more concise and definitive than the one in *Doe* to meet constitutional muster, it also failed.[140] The decisions in *Doe* and *UWM Post* established precedents that have been interpreted as a foreclosure on addressing assaultive speech incidents in campus communities. Additionally, a non-higher education Supreme Court case, *R.A.V. v. City of St. Paul*[141] placed a proverbial seal on the door to racial justice in free speech jurisprudence. A Supreme Court majority ruled that cross burning by a white man in an African American family's yard does not meet the constitutional standard for fighting words,[142] and therefore is not punishable under a racial bias-motivated speech law.

Justice Scalia, writing for a unanimous Supreme Court, reasoned that content-targeted laws are unconstitutional because the government cannot censor unfavorable speech, especially if it can have multiple meanings.[143]

---

[136] Eugene Volokh, *Free Speech and Civility in Universities*, Wash. Post, Sept. 9, 2014, https://www.washingtonpost.com/news/volokh-conspiracy/wp/2014/09/09/free-speech-and-civility-at-universities/?utm_term=.3ba6e0df2855.

[137] Doe v. University of Michigan, 721 F. Supp. 852 (1989); UVM Post et al. v. Board of Regents of the University of Wisconsin, 774 F. Supp. 1163 (1991).

[138] *Id*. at 854.

[139] Anti-Defamation League, *White Supremacist Propaganda Nearly Doubles on Campus in 2017-18 Academic Year, available at* https://www.adl.org/resources/reports/white-supremacist-propaganda-nearly-doubles-on-campus-in-2017-18-academic-year.

[140] Samuel Walker, Hate Speech: The History of an American Controversy (1994).

[141] 505 U.S. 377 (1992).

[142] In Chaplinsky v. New Hampshire, 315 U.S. 568 (1942), a unanimous Supreme Court ruled fighting words cause direct harm to their targets and can be construed to incite immediate breach of the peace.

[143] *See R.A.V.*, 505 U.S. at 391-396.

Critiques of the Supreme Court's reasoning include the rationale was guided by nonhistorical and noncontextual interpretations that burning crosses in the yards of African American families is not always a hate symbol, but can occur for other reasons.[144] Further, the *RAV* decision restricts HEIs from drafting policies that address speech considered beyond First Amendment protection. If one believes that we now live in a race-evasive society, a line of reasoning that hate speech only comes from social misfits and the best way to address their speech is by countering it or accepting its legitimate place in society will be logical. However, this type of legal analysis, grounded in color-evasiveness and an absence of history, continues to be an obstacle for race-centered analyses that could bring about the racial equity that HEIs espouse as their goals.

Summary

History, race, and law are deemed inextricable in the definition and understanding of legal issues that campus leaders grapple with to inform the creation of equitable solutions within higher education.[145] Debates that occur in campus communities represent various perspectives. Ones that are shaped by acknowledging the role of history, race, and law can result in policies and practices that reflect and maintain inclusive educational environments. Campus administrators, faculty, students, and staff benefit from discussions that acknowledge and include the roles of history, race, and law in higher education.

Figure 1

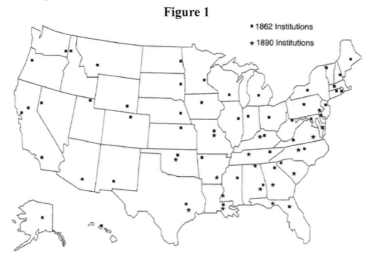

Source: National Research Council. (1995). *Colleges of Agriculture at the Land Grant Universities: A Profile.* Washington, DC: The National Academies Press. https://doi.org/10.17226/4980. *Available at* https://www.nap.edu/read/4980/chapter/2

---

[144] Jeannine Bell, *There Are No Racists Here: The Rise of Racial Extremism, When No One Is Racist,* 20 Mich. J. Race & L. 349 (2015).

[145] Dafina-Lazarus Stewart, *Minding the Gap between Diversity and Institutional Transformation: Eight Proposals for Enacting Institutional Change,* 120 Tchrs. Coll. Rec. 1 (2018).

Discussion Questions

1. Segregation and inequitable funding in HEIs were legalized through U.S. Supreme Court decisions and state and federal laws. HBCUs and PWIs are currently dealing with implications of historical legal decisions, coupled with contemporary issues such as affirmative action bans. Is having racially segregated public institutions in the twenty-first century an issue that needs to be address, why or why not? Regardless of your response to the previous question, what legal actions can be taken to address issues of admissions at racially segregated institutions? What are non-legal actions to consider?

2. Regarding allegations that relics of pre-Civil War and post-Reconstruction are racially divisive, how would you advise campus administrators to approach addressing demands for monument removals and/or building renaming? How would history, race, and law influence your advice?

3. Speech regulation codes are highly controversial in campus communities. If the roles of history, race, and law are collectively considered in discussions, how might legal interpretations and higher education policy formation be affected?

4. In the current debate about race-conscious admissions, the plaintiffs are of Asian descent. They claim they were denied access to Harvard and UNC-Chapel Hill because race is a factor in admissions processes and that there is a discriminatory cap on the number of Asian Americans admitted to both institutions due to diversity efforts. How might the claims be evaluated through a historical, racial, and legal lens?

Constitutional, Legislation & Case Index by Chapter

Chapter 4

First Amendment / 63

Chapter 5

Chapter 8

Chapter 9

Chapter 10

Chapter 11

Chapter 12

Chapter 13

Chapter 14

Chapter 15

Chapter 16

Chapter 17

Chapter 18

Chapter 19

Chapter 20

Chapter 21

U.S. Constitution Overview

Text of U.S. Constitution Articles and Amendments Cited

Bill of Rights: First Ten Amendments to the Constitution [1791]

- First Amendment [Religion, Speech, Press, Assembly, Petition]
- Second Amendment [Right to Bear Arms
- Third Amendment [Quartering of Troops]
- Fourth Amendment [Search and Seizure]
- Fifth Amendment [Grand Jury, Double Jeopardy, Self-Incrimination, Due Process]
- Sixth Amendment [Criminal Prosecutions - Jury Trial, Right to Confront and to Counsel]
- Seventh Amendment [Common Law Suits - Jury Trial]
- Eighth Amendment [Excess Bail or Fines, Cruel and Unusual Punishment]
- Ninth Amendment [Non-Enumerated Rights]
- Tenth Amendment [Rights Reserved to States or People]

Amendment 1 [1791]

Congress shall make no law respecting an establishment of religion, or prohibiting the free exercise thereof; or abridging the freedom of speech, or of the press; or the right of the people peaceably to assemble, and to petition the Government for a redress of grievances.

Amendment IV [1791]

The right of the people to be secure in their persons, houses, papers, and effects, against unreasonable searches and seizures, shall not be violated, and no Warrants shall issue, but upon probable cause, supported by Oath or affirmation, and particularly describing the place to be searched, and the persons or things to be seized.

Amendment V [1791]

No person shall be held to answer for a capital, or otherwise infamous crime, unless on a presentment or indictment of a Grand Jury, except in cases arising in the land or naval forces, or in the Militia, when in actual service in time of War or public danger; nor shall any person be subject for the same offence to be twice put in jeopardy of life or limb; nor shall be compelled in any criminal case to be a witness against himself, nor be deprived of life, liberty, or property, without due process of law; nor shall private property be taken for public use, without just compensation.

Amendment X [1791]

The powers not delegated to the United States by the Constitution, nor prohibited by it to the States, are reserved to the States respectively, or to the people.

Amendment XI [1798]

The Judicial power of the United States shall not be construed to extend to any suit in law or equity, commenced or prosecuted against one of the United States by Citizens of another State, or by Citizens or Subjects of any Foreign State.

Amendment XIV [1868]

Section. 1. All persons born or naturalized in the United States and subject to the jurisdiction thereof, are citizens of the United States and of the State wherein they reside. No State shall make or enforce any law which shall abridge the privileges or immunities of citizens of the United States; nor shall any State deprive any person of life, liberty, or property, without due process of law; nor deny to any person within its jurisdiction the equal protection of the laws.

Overview of Select Clauses of the United States Constitution

Due Process Clause

The Fifth and Fourteenth Amendments to the United States Constitution each contain a Due Process Clause. Due process deals with the administration of justice and thus the due process clause acts as a safeguard from arbitrary denial of life, liberty, or property by the government outside the sanction of law.

Equal Protection Clause

The Equal Protection Clause is a clause within the text of the Fourteenth Amendment to the United States Constitution. The clause, which took effect in 1868, provides "nor shall any State [...] deny to any person within its jurisdiction the equal protection of the laws".

Establishment Clause and Free Exercise Clause

In United States law, the Establishment Clause of the First Amendment to the United States Constitution, together with that Amendment's Free Exercise Clause, form the constitutional right of freedom of religion.

Index